THE WRITINGS OF THE
NEW TESTAMENT

LUKE TIMOTHY JOHNSON

THE WRITINGS OF THE
NEW TESTAMENT
An Interpretation

Fortress Press   Philadelphia

Library of Congress Cataloging-in-Publication Data

Johnson, Luke Timothy.
  The writings of the New Testament.

  Bibliography: p.
  Includes indexes.
  1. Bible. N.T.—Introductions. I. Title.
  BS2330.2.J64 1986   225.6′1   85–16202
  ISBN 0–8006–0886–0
  ISBN 0–8006–1886–6 (pbk.)

1824G85   Printed in the United States of America   1–886 (C)   1–1886 (P)

To Joy

Contents

Preface

I HAVE WRITTEN THIS BOOK FOR THOSE WHO WANT TO UNDERSTAND THE origin and shape of the New Testament writings but are unable to find a comprehensive introduction that is neither repellingly technical nor appallingly trivial. I have called it an interpretation rather than an introduction for the simple reason that most volumes going by the name of introduction are either handbooks devoted to the communication of information concerning a narrow range of scholarly issues or popularized versions of conventional scholarly wisdom for college students. In contrast to both, I have tried to provide a genuine interpretation of Christianity's earliest writings. By so doing I draw the reader into the most important critical questions concerning their understanding. In this sense, every interpretation is also an introduction. By no means is every introduction an interpretation.

The organization of this book, its argument, and the choice of topics have all been dictated by the desire to make these writings intelligible and alive for the contemporary reader who wants to meet and understand them more than scholarly discussions of them. I have considered all the critical issues pertinent to the understanding of the writings, but I have gone beyond presenting a consensus of scholarly opinion. The reader will find in these pages a single "reading" of the evidence from beginning to end—my own. My approach to the writings and the critical issues is independent. It is not, I think, idiosyncratic. I have learned more than I can ever credit to my teachers and to the reading of other scholars. But in this book I advance my own understanding of the New Testament in its origin, in each of its parts, and as a collection. Sometimes I agree with the majority of scholars; sometimes I disagree. I have tried to indicate the reasons for both. As in every attempt to deal with the whole of a subject within a reasonable space, much has been eliminated or abbreviated. More advanced readers should recognize in my sometimes elliptical remarks a thoughtful response to critical scholarship.

In order to keep my argument and presentation clean I have not used footnotes, nor do I refer to other scholars by name in the text. The reader will, I hope, forgive the inevitable air of omniscience that results. It seemed better to restrict references to primary sources, above all to the texts of the New Testament itself. Occasionally even these are so numerous as to make the detection of decent prose a problem. At the end of each chapter I have provided an annotated bibliography. Some entries support my presentation, others provide alternative points of view, still others give the reader additional resources for study. With very few exceptions I have included only literature in English, since the notes are meant to be an aid to the reader rather than a demonstration of learning. Given the rate of translation, not that much of great value is missing. I have also tried to refer to literature that is reasonably available. Translations of primary sources are acknowledged at the head of each bibliographical section.

In everything I write, I discover again and in an ever more humbling degree how much I owe to my teachers. The bibliographical entries do not reveal how much I have taken from Nils Dahl, Wayne Meeks, Abraham Malherbe, as well as Rowan Greer, Brevard Childs, Judah Goldin, Henry Fischel, and Frederick Wisse. For the constant encouragement to stay immersed in the text, my contemporaries William Kurz, Dennis Hamm, Halvor Moxnes, and Jerome Neyrey are owed particular thanks. This book began as lectures at Yale Divinity School. The first stages were worked out together with my good friend and colleague Carl R. Holladay. Our endless debates and our shared passion for the chase mean more to me than I can adequately state. Carl deserves credit for much that might be good in this book. Among my teaching assistants at Yale who went on to become excellent scholars and who offered me much criticism of this point or another are Jouette Bassler, John Fitzgerald, Michael White, David Worley, Tim Polk, Jacqueline Williams, Alan Mitchell, Stan Stowers, Ann McGuire, Tony Lewis, and David Rensberger. Of my students at Yale whose responses to my ideas made a real difference, I must single out Kenneth Frazier, Sam Candler, Mark Burton-Schantz, Jan Fuller, Bill Shepherd, Julie Galambush, and most of all, Nancy Heslin.

My colleagues in the Department of Religious Studies at Indiana University have been outstandingly supportive of this project. To them I owe additional time for writing, as well as support for an Indiana University Summer Faculty Fellowship, which enabled me to complete the first draft of the manuscript. I must thank in particular Sam Preus, David Smith, and Jim Ackerman.

Norman A. Hjelm of Fortress Press was willing to take a chance on supporting this project when it was just a sheaf of lecture outlines. Since then my editor, John A. Hollar, has provided me and the manuscript with unfailingly kind and critical attention. Dr. Barry Blose at Fortress Press gave careful attention to the entire manuscript and greatly improved its prose. My wife Joy and my daughter Tiffany make all things possible and almost everything a pleasure.

Bloomington, Indiana   LUKE TIMOTHY JOHNSON
June 26, 1985

Abbreviations

AB	Analecta Biblica
AGJU	Arbeiten zur Geschichte des antiken Judentums und des Urchristentums
ANRW	*Aufstieg und Niedergang der Römischen Welt*, ed. J. Temporini and W. Haase (Berlin: Walter de Gruyter)
ATR	*Anglican Theological Review*
Bib	*Biblica*
BJRL	*Bulletin of the John Rylands University Library of Manchester*
BZNW	Beihefte zur *ZNW*
CBQ	*Catholic Biblical Quarterly*
CBQMS	Catholic Biblical Quarterly—Monograph Series
CGTC	Cambridge Greek Testament Commentaries
ConBNT	Coniectanea biblica, New Testament
CRINT	Compendia rerum iudaicarum ad novum testamentum
ExpTim	*Expository Times*
GBS	Guides to Biblical Scholarship
HDR	Harvard Dissertations in Religion
HNTC	Harper's NT Commentaries
HTR	*Harvard Theological Review*
HTS	Harvard Theological Studies
ICC	International Critical Commentary
IDBSup	Supplementary volume to *Interpreter's Dictionary of the Bible*, ed. G. A. Buttrick
Int	*Interpretation*
IRT	Issues in Religion and Theology
JAAR	*Journal of the American Academy of Religion*
JBL	*Journal of Biblical Literature*
JCS-D	*Jewish and Christian Self-Definition*, ed. E. P. Sanders, A. I. Baumgarten, A. Mendelson, and B. F. Meyer (Philadelphia: Fortress Press)
JJS	*Journal of Jewish Studies*

JR	*Journal of Religion*
JRS	*Journal of Roman Studies*
JSJ	*Journal for the Study of Judaism in the Persian, Hellenistic, and Roman Period*
JSNT	*Journal for the Study of the New Testament*
JSS	*Journal of Semitic Studies*
JTC	*Journal for Theology and the Church*
JTS	*Journal of Theological Studies*
NCB	New Century Bible
NICNT	New International Commentary on the New Testament
NovT	*Novum Testamentum*
NovTSup	Novum Testamentum, Supplements
NTS	*New Testament Studies*
SBLDS	SBL Dissertation Series
SBLMS	SBL Masoretic Studies
SBS	Stuttgarter Bibelstudien
SE	*Studia Evangelica*
SJT	*Scottish Journal of Theology*
SNTSMS	Society for New Testament Studies Monograph Series
SPB	Studia postbiblica
SR	*Studies in Religion*
TDNT	*Theological Dictionary of the New Testament*, ed. G. Kittel and G. Friedrich
TorSTh	Toronto Studies in Theology
TS	*Theological Studies*
TU	Texte und Untersuchungen
VC	*Vigiliae christianae*
ZNW	*Zeitschrift für die neutestamentliche Wissenschaft*

Introduction

THE READER SHOULD BE AWARE OF THE PURPOSE AND PLAN OF THIS BOOK
from the outset. We seek, as far as possible, to observe the emergence of
the individual writings of the New Testament and the beginnings of the
collection as a whole. We focus on a set of documents usually found with
another collection in the large anthology called the Bible. We place ourselves in attendance at the birth of the New Testament. It seems odd to
speak of the birth of writings, but the word reminds us that the phenomenon we study began as a living expression of a living reality, that it entered
the world in a particular time and place, with a definite and still visible
parentage. To say that we are studying the birth of the New Testament
(NT) only gains specific meaning, however, when we distinguish this task
from three others.

First of all, we are not describing the history of primitive Christianity,
though aspects of that history are inevitably involved in the study. So
important is this distinction that it must be elaborated further. Second, we
are not cataloguing or analyzing all of early Christian literature. The
Christian movement was amazingly prolific in its literary production, and
the NT represents only a portion of what was written. Finally, we are not
specifically delineating the process by which the originally discrete writings became the canon of the NT, though some implications of that process
are examined.

We give attention to the twenty-seven writings of the NT. They are not,
at first sight, terribly impressive: four narratives about Jesus (Gospels) and
one about a few of his followers (Acts); some occasional correspondence by
an apostle (Paul); a handful of letters by other more or less anonymous
leaders; and an apocalyptic vision. They claim no great literary merit.
None directly claims inspiration for itself. But their impact has been
disproportionate to their size or claims. For two thousand years they have
been regarded by much of the western world as inspired by God and God's
very Word, part of a revelation that was recognized as the definitive norm
by which life's meaning is measured. Such disparity between cause and

effect justifies the study of these specific writings and demands that fundamental questions be put to them. It is surprising they are so seldom explicitly asked.

Why do these writings exist at all? This is the question of poets and philosophers, the question of existence. It is not sufficient to recite the properties of an anteater; one must first be stunned by the sheer fact that there is such a creature. The existential question pertains to the NT in a fairly obvious way. It is not at all necessary that religious movements produce writings, still less that they in a short period of time certify them as sacred texts. Not every failed messianic figure generates a literature that insists that he is still alive, and apparently makes this absurd claim plausible to others. Not all communities expecting the imminent end of the world produce documents remarkably unconcerned with timetables for demolition and more concerned with interpreting the past than predicting the future. The production of these writings should be a shock. The poet or philosopher would conclude from such an effect a commensurate cause, whether natural or magical. Something happened that gave birth to these writings.

A second question concerns the type of writings we find in the collection. Why four Gospels? They have unceasingly raised problems because of their perverse combination of agreement and dissonance, because of their refusal to be either simply biographies or simply legends, because of their uncanny verisimilitude and realism, even when their hero is doing patently impossible things. And why these particular letters? Romans, we might understand, and even the Corinthian correspondence. But why *three* pastoral letters, so alike yet so subtly different from each other; so Pauline yet seemingly so unlike Paul? Why both 2 Peter and Jude? Why, above all, Philemon? When we look closely at the writings, we are impressed most of all by their variety, in outlook, form, and symbol. We sense the diversity of the movement that gave them birth, and wonder at the perceived coherence within them that made the community choose these as normative and not others.

Why do these writings look the way they do? This question has two parts, which require equal stress. The first part asks, Why does the NT look so much like the Old Testament (OT)? Of all the obvious and important observations that are seldom expressed, this is the most significant: without any explanation or theoretical justification, these writings continue with the same characters and symbols as the Hebrew Scriptures (OT). The NT writings must be seen as Hellenistic literature, it is true. But their immediate parentage is unmistakable. Little in these documents would be intelligible if not read against the backdrop of Torah, Prophets, and Writings. It was neither accident nor violence that made the NT part of the Bible. The second part of the question, though, is equally important: Why does the NT look so different from the Old? The differences are not minor. Taking the NT seriously demands understanding the OT in an entirely different way. The symbols are the same, yet are radically reworked. The combination of continuity and contrast is expressed in the Pauline phrase "Grace to you and peace from God our Father and the Lord Jesus Christ." An adequate analysis of that phrase would lead to the enigmatic heart of the NT. By taking seriously the dialectic of similarity and difference between the NT and OT, we gain our surest entry into the distinctive character of these writings. But further distinctions must first be made.

WAYS NOT TAKEN

The basic questions concerning the origin and appearance of the NT writings have been answered in ways that, in their inadequacy, help sharpen the focus of this book.

Some have answered the questions by appeal to direct divine inspiration. According to them, the NT looks like the OT because it has the same author, God. The human writers were passive recipients of the divine impulse, secretaries taking down dictation. God simply shifted from Hebrew to Greek. In this explanation, human causality is eliminated. There is, therefore, nothing to explain, for there is no problem. While attempting to take seriously the religious conviction that these writings are authoritative, this position, however, distorts the equally important Christian conviction that God works through human freedom, not by eliminating it. One can, moreover, assert that these writings are authoritative, or even inspired, without using such a crude model of inspiration.

At the other extreme are conspiracy theories for the origin of Christianity and therefore of the NT. According to these theories, the writings serve to cover up what really happened. There are, naturally, several versions of what really happened. Some theories suggest that Jesus did not die on the cross but survived to continue teaching; others, that he died but that his disciples stole his body to spread the word that he had been raised. A further refinement (a more plausible one) has it that Jesus was in fact a revolutionary but that the Gospels portray him, for politically expedient reasons, as simply a religious teacher. The conspiracy theories agree that the disciples manipulated the events of Jesus' life and death, as well as the messianic prophecies from the OT, in order to convince others that he was the expected messiah. Like all conspiracy theories, they tend to attribute at once too much and too little cleverness to the conspirators. Lucian of Samosata's parody *Alexander the False Prophet* shows us how a really successful religious scam could be pulled off in that time. It is unlikely that the disciples would have invented a messiah who fulfilled the prophecies so inadequately: most of the important texts traditionally thought to refer to the messiah, Jesus did not match, nor was it suggested he did. It is hard to conceive that the disciples would have conjured up traditions that treated them as harshly as they are treated in the Gospels. And it goes beyond comprehension why they would have invented a movement that offered them nothing but the fate of their master, rejection and death. Still, conspiracy theories all have germs of truth that give them plausibility. It *is* difficult to discern the "real" Jesus beneath the layers of interpretation in the Gospels. And there was a very real human process involved in the rereading of OT prophecies and the applying of them to Jesus. Indeed, this process is one of the keys to understanding the character of the writings. The process, however, had nothing to do with fraud or deception. It arose from the human impulse to interpret transforming experiences in the light of available symbols.

Other explanations are less radical than the supernaturalistic or paranoid options. They share a tendency to reduce Christianity to some cause other than religious. One makes Christianity begin in the hallucinations of the disciples. This credits the disciples with sincerity but not with rationality. The writings of the NT are thereby seen as rather elaborate rationalizations of delusion. A classic expression of this view says that Jesus did not rise on Easter, faith did. There is, of course, a sense in which this can be asserted. I concentrate in this book on the pivotal importance of Easter faith as the catalyst *both* of the movement *and* of its interpretation. Psychological reduction, however, fails to deal with genuine religious experience and tends to read the texts themselves rather casually.

Another sort of explanation regards Christianity as the distillate of first-century political, social, and economic forces. According to this explanation, the NT writings are the propaganda and ideology of a proletarian movement that, because of its success, had to reinvent itself not as the critic but as the support of society. Or the explanation holds that the Christian movement succeeded because it matched the social needs of the age better than its rivals, such as Judaism and Mithraism. There is, again, truth here: the social world of early Christianity is undoubtedly of great importance, especially for the explanation of its growth and eventual dominance. The attempt to locate the *cause* of the movement in specific economic or social factors, however, is less successful. The writings of the NT do not work particularly well as either propaganda or ideology.

In each of these approaches the attempt to explain results in the loss of richness and complexity. When the religious element of the writings is asserted, the social dimension is lost; when the psychological dimension is emphasized, the religious disappears. Each explanation has merit, but each is too partial to allow for an adequate grasp of the writings. The narrowness of each approach reduces and distorts the writings themselves.

THE SEARCH FOR A MODEL

If the writings of the NT are adequately to be grasped, they must be approached as much as possible on their own terms. Readers must take seriously their self-presentation and adjust their questions to them, rather than force the writings to methodological preconceptions. What is needed above all is an adequate *model* for understanding these texts; one flexible enough to respect the variety of the individual writings, yet sufficiently definite to deal with them as parts of a coherent whole.

What do I mean by a model? A model is a paradigm within which the data appropriate to a discipline make sense. The adequacy of the paradigm can be measured both by the way it covers the data, and by the way it enables further investigation. A model in this sense differs from a method, insofar as it represents a sort of imaginative construal of the materials being studied, a structured picture of both process and product, within which the parts are seen not only to fit but also to function. A model can employ a variety of methods. But methods can themselves easily become unwitting models if we employ our methods without critical self-awareness. That is, a particular way of questioning data can unintentionally become an implicit but comprehensive understanding of what the material is about. When this happens, both data and method can become distorted.

Models and methods can be variously appropriate to the tasks they are asked to perform. A given subject can be fit to several different models, but this is not to say that every model is equally adaptable. Likewise, a subject can be questioned using the tools of different methods, but not every method is appropriate to every purpose. Moreover, a specific model may be asked to do what it cannot, or a particular method of studying texts may fail to raise or respond to the questions deemed significant. When this happens, it is possible that a shift in models or methods is required.

An adequate model for the NT considered as canon would provide an explanatory framework for the birth and development of the writings in the first place (why do they exist?) and for their specific shape (why do they look the way they do?). It would enable us to deal with the documents as writings (that is, as literary productions) and not simply as sources of information. It would account for the process of their development as well as their final literary shape. The model would allow for the an-thropological, historical, literary, and religious dimensions of the texts to be maintained in their integrity and to survive analysis.

Anthropological

At the simplest level, I mean that the writings must be taken seriously as fully *human* productions. Divine inspiration is not excluded, but inspiration is not a fact available for study. Second, the term "anthropological" asserts that these are *fully* human writings, and that intrinsic to being human are religious experiences and ideas. Indeed, much of what anthropologists have traditionally studied has involved the way religions structure the lives of people. Third, the term "anthropological" has a more specific application: in the production of these writings, we find operative the universal dynamics of the human search for meaning. In particular, we find in them the interplay of myth and experience in the shaping of symbolic worlds (see pp. 14–18 below).

Historical

For the moment, I merely note that the NT writings must be understood first of all within their first-century Mediterranean setting, and in particular within the matrix of first-century Judaism. The NT came to birth among social structures and symbols different from our own. The writings are conditioned linguistically by that historical setting. Their linguistic code is not only alien but also only partially available to us. Precisely the "things that go without saying" are not available to us. Every responsible reading therefore demands historical adjustment. The writings are very much conditioned by the times and places of their origin, by the settings and intentions of their authors. The more we can reconstruct those settings and intentions, the better readers we are. If the anthropological pattern of myth and experience provides the broad framework for the model I am proposing, then the specific application of it is found within the historical setting of first-century Judaism.

Literary

An adequate model for the interpretation of the NT must deal with the documents *as writings*. First, however important the prehistory of texts may be, and however helpful distinctions between tradition and redaction may be for exegesis, the complete and finished literary form of a writing is that which demands interpretation within the canon. Second, attention must be given to the literary conventions of the age of composition. The reader must take into account the implications of genre and the uses of rhetoric. Third, the writings must be read in terms of their self-presentation rather than reduced to the status of sources for another body of information. Finally, the model must seek for a fit between the form of a writing and its function, between literary structure and substance. What the term "literary" does *not* mean is a concern only for surface technique or aesthetic effect.

Religious

The writings of the NT are first and foremost religious writings. They were generated by a specifically religious movement, and were written by and for adherents of that movement. These assertions should not meet dispute, but some further distinctions are important. I do not mean to equate "religious" with "theological." There is theology in the NT, but it is no more true that the theology is scholastic or self-conscious than that the literature of the NT is aesthetically motivated. There were philosophers and theologians in that age doing what we do not find being done in the NT: writing systematic treatises on virtues, for example, and composing extended commentaries on authoritative texts. The theology found in the NT is closer to what we would call *pastoral* theology. It works out the implications of religious experience and conviction for life in the community and world. It does not resemble what we call *systematic* theology, which correlates the propositions of belief with more comprehensive philosophical world views. The history of religions school, which flourished in the early years of this century, rightly protested against the tendency to regard the writings of the NT as theological treatises and asserted that they more strongly resembled the writings of popular religion in Hellenistic culture.

The program and promise of the history of religions school has never been fulfilled. This is partly because scholarship was diverted by the renewal of theology and the resurgence of literary-critical analysis in each postwar period. It may also be partly due to the problems of the program itself. Its understanding of religion tended to be somewhat narrow, at times almost seeming to equate religion with cult. Consequently, more of the NT was explained in terms of cultic activity than appeared plausible. There was also a tendency to *separate* "religion" from theology, ethics, and conscious literary expression, a separation that increasingly appears to be artificial. Finally, the approach tended to be over-rationalistic in its understanding of religious phenomena such as myth and ritual, while showing a reluctance to deal with the actual religious claims of the texts.

I use the term "religious" here to refer to experiences, convictions, and interpretations having to do with what is perceived as ultimate reality. The term points to a way of being human, a way both individual and social that asserts by word and deed that human existence is bound by, and defined in reference to, realities transcending everyday categories. To use the language of the Bible, the religious has to do with the totally other and powerful reality called the Holy One. To call these writings religious, therefore, does not prejudge their social setting, literary form, or intellectual sobriety. But it does recognize that they claim to be speaking about life before God. Their subject matter concerns what it means to be human in the light of faith, specifically in light of the experience of the Holy that the first Christians claimed to have had in Jesus.

The NT writings approach us as witnesses to and interpretations of specifically religious claims having to do with the experience of God as mediated through Jesus. They never claim, we notice, to mediate that

experience themselves. They only witness and interpret. It should go
without saying, therefore, that the contemporary reader cannot reach that
experience by using the tools of anthropology, history, and literary criticism. But the contemporary reader can claim to come in contact with the
witness and interpretation.

HISTORICAL METHOD BUT NOT
HISTORICAL MODEL

At this point, a delicate distinction must be drawn. I have already
asserted the importance of recognizing the historical dimension of the NT
texts. Because of the linguistic conditioning of the texts, because of the
peculiar claims of the creed, with its specifically historical elements, and
because of the nature of the Christian community, which claims continuity
with a people of the past, this historical appreciation will continue to be
desirable, necessary, and inevitable. The use of historical-critical methods
therefore is entirely appropriate. Among the tasks necessary to the study
of the NT are the attempts to hear the text in its first voice, to distinguish
between levels of tradition, to evaluate sources, to determine the time,
provenience, and authorship of writings, and to describe their social
settings. On the other hand, these tasks can be carried out within the
framework of different models. I am suggesting here that it is not history
as method that requires qualification, but history as the overarching model
for understanding the NT.

Despite many minor disaffections, the historical model remains dominant in NT scholarship. The historical model provides a distinctive imaginative construal of the writings and the task of studying them. First, the
task: in answer to the question, What are these writings about? this model
responds, They are about the history of the primitive Christian movement.
The goal set by this model is the description, or possibly even the reconstruction, of that historical development. At least ideally it is a goal that is
detachable from the writings themselves. If we could ever achieve a
definitive picture of that development, the writings could be consigned to
the archives, and we could move to the next historical period. The writings
themselves, we see, play a secondary role: they are nothing more or less
than *sources* for the reconstruction. The historian evaluates the writings as
historical sources (are they first- or secondhand, authentic or inauthentic?), and asks of them questions that yield specifically historical information. Indeed, this model can use only such information. Whether the topic
is ideas, rituals, literature, or institutions, the end result is the same: a
picture of historical development. This model is neither unsophisticated
nor without virtue.

Even taken on its own terms, however, the historical model has a difficult time with the texts of the NT. The problems stem from the paucity of genuine historical data in the writings, and the artificiality of the canonical frame for the historical enterprise. The two problems influence each other. The historical model has traditionally worked within the canon. It was obvious, of course, that as historical sources, the canonical writings were greatly deficient: they were fragmentary and biased. But the need to do history, with the stakes being regarded as theologically significant, led generations of investigators to proceed as though these pieces of the puzzle were the only ones. They were like people hunched over a hundred-piece jigsaw puzzle with only twenty-seven pieces in hand, and constrained to fit the pieces into some pattern of dependence and development. Not surprisingly, the resulting pictures were sometimes grotesque.

The interplay between dating and development was especially problematic. History lives off chronology but is never content with chronology. It seeks causality, which is to say, development. The historical model is not satisfied with a rich but disjointed collection of vignettes of the NT period. It reaches insatiably for sequence, for the possibility of a narrative. In fact, however, the NT canon offers, and will always offer, only scattered vignettes of the earliest Christian period. Worse, Christianity was at first so unnoticed by outsiders that there is little external framework for dating the writings so that they could be securely used as sources for a developmental picture.

Faced with the irreducible deficiency of their sources and the aim of doing history, investigators did the best they could. But the lack of data and controls led them inevitably to a focus on data that were assumed to be traceable, namely ideas. Even this, however, was made possible only by the employment of developmental models that helped fill in the gaps between documents. The process was circular, of course. The circularity was only occasionally broken by scholars who time and again allowed the stubbornly fragmentary data to upset the symmetry of developmental schemes.

These observations on the historical model are not novel. It has been more vigorously and acutely criticized by its practitioners than by its detractors. The critics have deplored the overemphasis on theology and the neglect of data from outside the canon. They have recognized the narrowness of the imaginative portrayal of first-century Christianity as something like a university, in which professors read and respond to one another's papers. They have questioned the tendency to stress only the temporal side of the space-time continuum, so that ideas and institutions appear to develop everywhere together in neat patterns through time.

As a result of these criticisms and the rich archaeological finds of this age, historians of early Christianity are making greater use of resources outside the canon: not only extra-canonical writings from within Christianity and literary sources both Jewish and Greek, but also archaeological evidence that makes more concrete our sense of those times and places. Second, historians are giving greater recognition to the importance of place. They are less attached to overarching theories of development for the whole and are patiently studying the particular characteristics of regional development. Now, not the Church but the church at Corinth and the church at Antioch are the subjects of investigation. Third, historians of early Christianity are giving greater attention to the social realities of the first-century world, recognizing that not only ideas but the structures that support those ideas are the stuff of history. These investigations have yielded a more complete picture of the NT texts themselves. For example, conflicts that formerly were thought to reflect specific and competing Christian theologies are now recognized as variations on disputes within Hellenistic culture, in specific social settings. The sociological analysis of the NT is not a fad; it is a better way of doing history.

An unfortunate aspect of this otherwise encouraging development is that many conclusions concerning the NT writings themselves (on matters of dating, dependencies, perspectives, etc.) have been left untouched, even though the methods for reaching them are now seen to be deficient. Nor has this broader conception of the historical model moved much beyond the programmatic stage. But it does indicate the direction in which the historical model is now being developed, and it is one in which the frame of the canon appears even more artificial than it did in the past.

If the model of history has as its goal the description of early Christianity, then it should use all available sources, without giving any priority as historical sources to the canonical writings. The NT writings can legitimately be placed in lines of development with gnostic and other apocryphal documents, as well as with those of the patristic period, without considering which are scriptural or which are orthodox. From the perspective of the historical model, the refusal of a historian to move outside the canon of the NT would appear to be motivated by other than genuinely historical convictions. The critical historian may with some legitimacy question the good faith and self-awareness of those who protest they are doing the history of early Christianity when in fact all they know or care about are the canonical writings.

The refinement of the historical model, therefore, has made even more acute the question of its adequacy as a model for understanding the canonical writings of the NT. The deficiencies that were there from the beginning are now becoming clearer. There are three major inadequacies of this model. First, it can give no special consideration to the writings of the canon and it certainly cannot justify giving exclusive attention to them. In the logic of the model, the canon becomes a significant historical factor not at the earliest period but only later.

The second inadequacy of the historical model is literary. It treats the writings of the canon only incidentally *as writings;* its primary interest in them is *as historical sources.* This is not to deny the effort expended on specifically literary analysis within historical scholarship but to recognize that it was always carried out in the service of historical reconstruction. Historical analysis of NT literary forms is highly developed; genuine literary analysis of the NT writings in their integrity is still in its infancy.

The third inadequacy in the historical model has been its inability to deal with the *religious* content of the writings except in a comparative, developmental, or theological fashion. And although form criticism tried to align religious settings and literary forms, it did so by abstracting the forms of the smaller literary units from the larger literary setting. The connections between the logic of literary works and the logic of the religious experiences or convictions they express still require examination. Historians, moreover, have shied away from asking the question of origination in the strictest sense—from asking what sort of religious experience gave rise to the Christian movement and motivated the writings that now interpret it. In short, the historical model, which is now being refined as it abandons the confinement of the canonical frame, is of little help for interpreting the canonical writings of the NT as *religious* literature.

There is need for a model that, if it does not demand that exclusive attention be given to the documents of the canon, at least allows the legitimacy of such exclusive study. This model would recognize the value of studying the normative collection of a religious tradition on its own terms, as the classic expression of that tradition and an expression that engenders further understandings. It would respect the anthropological, historical, literary, and religious dimensions of the writings. It would allow the study of their individual production, without forgetting their eventual anthological status. It would be able to ask the question of origination in specifically religious terms. It would be able to recognize the specific and distinct voice of each writing. It would recognize that those who canonized the NT writings found an implied harmony that distinguished these voices from others.

AN EXPERIENCE-INTERPRETATION MODEL

To argue the need for some other model is not to insist that the other model is better in every respect but only to insist that it enables an appreciation of the NT writings in their literary and religious dimensions better than the historical model does. The model I am using owes something to sociological and anthropological models but more to the reading of Jewish midrashim and the NT writings themselves. It applies the analysis of social responses to religious experience, within the specific situation of the first-century Jews who claimed to have experienced the ultimate in Jesus of Nazareth. The tag "experience-interpretation" points both to the component elements of the writings and to the dynamics of their production. The appropriateness of the model will become clearer if we work into it indirectly by considering its premises.

The Making of Symbolic Worlds

A symbolic world is not an alternative ideal world removed from everyday life. To the contrary, it is the system of meanings that anchors the activities of individuals and communities in the real world. Nothing is more down to earth and ordinary than a symbolic world. Like the grammar and syntax of a language, a symbolic world looks odd only when isolated from its task. The task of a symbolic world is that of making our lives work.

One of the great benefits of sociological analysis to the study of the NT has been its reminder that humans are not simply individuals but always parts of social systems. Even rebels and hermits play roles within larger social organisms. The Christian reality, likewise, is first of all a social reality. The first writings of the movement are addressed not to individuals but to gatherings (*ekklesiai;* see, e.g., 1 Thess. 1:1; 2:14).

The development that has come to be called the sociology of knowledge, moreover, reminds us that social systems are more than mechanical arrangements in which human intentionality plays no role beyond the filling of specific roles and functions. That the social system of which we are a part works (or even exists) at all is not only because of what we *do* but above all because of what we *think.* Social arrangements are constructions of human knowledge and commitment. The way humans organize themselves in the world depends little on biology and less on instinct but a great deal on human beings' ideas about themselves and the world. Because of this, social groups are both fragile and conservative. Fragile, because they depend for their existence on the deep consensus and commitment of their members; conservative, for the same reason: the world is frightening without a home.

These abstract propositions can be illustrated by an analysis of a universally recognized social entity within the symbolic world of academia, the group called the class. Notice first how it is *within* the academic world that the term "class" has a specific meaning that requires no further definition—to distinguish it from, for example, the homonymic term referring to economic-social rank.

A class is a social group. It gathers periodically and engages in certain joint activities. It is not imaginary, but "real"; both insiders and outsiders can know it as the class in room 201. Closer analysis, however, shows that the class exists only because its members agree that it is real and continue to be committed to that perception. Whenever individuals miss class sessions or whenever individuals disrupt the ritual class activities, its fragile existence is threatened. If enough people miss a lecture or if everyone starts giggling in the middle of a lecture, chaos results: the social world collapses. And if all the students should suddenly decide to drop the course, the class would no longer exist as a social reality. It may continue to be listed in the school catalogue and the teacher may show up every day, but there will be no class.

We notice as well, however, that as long as the group continues in its perception that the class is real and continues in its commitment to it, there is no need to debate what it means and what it is for, at every session. The ground rules for classes do not need to be debated within the symbolic world of academia. They are understood. There are definite rituals: the teacher stands there, we sit here; she lectures, we listen; we take exams, she grades them. If these rituals are radically or persistently questioned, the delicate social structure is once more threatened.

As this example of the class shows, the connections between the way we think and the way we structure our lives are deep. In the normal way of things, the way we think (our ideology) and the way we arrange ourselves (our social structure) will reinforce each other. We tend to interpret our social arrangements by reference to the sort of people we think we are; and our self-understanding tends to make our social arrangements appear natural and even inevitable.

A symbolic world, then, is a system of shared meaning that enables us to live together as a group. It includes more than specialized concepts; it involves in particular the fundamental perceptions that ground the community's existence and that therefore do not need debate or justification. The symbols pervade every level of the group's life. They affect spatial and temporal arrangements and the rituals that mark them. They are built into that special language the group shares, its argot: the symbolic world shared by a group can be discerned from the things that go without saying, the references implied by phrases such as "and so forth," or even by gestures. A NT phrase like "do you not know," for example, points to such a shared range of understanding and bears within it an implied rebuke: those so reminded *should* know (see 1 Cor. 3:16; 5:6; 6:2).

The symbolic world shapes, and is shaped by, the customary actions of the group, from simple signs of greeting and farewell to the complex systems of exchange involved in mating. That such symbols of interaction work at all, of course, is precisely because they do not need to be reinvented by every individual. It is because an American boy and girl think it natural to date and go steady that these rituals function as stages of the mating process in our symbolic system. Only in the light of alternative practices does the relativity of our own become apparent. It was once thought natural for a man to stand, take off his hat, and offer a chair when a woman entered a room. Only because of an altered ideology do we now see such rituals as embodying a specific and socially structured ideology concerning men and women.

Symbolic World and Religious Myth

A symbolic world involves more than linguistic shorthand and a web of customs. It includes the broadest, most inclusive self-understanding of the group. Why do we exist at all? Why do we look the way we do? Questions of origin and of distinction are ultimate questions. In societies that are life societies, that is, organized in a more intensive and inclusive fashion than clubs and schools, such ultimate questions tend to be answered with reference to transcendent powers. Correlative to a profound human sense of contingency is the awareness of dependence on an "other" (whether singular or plural in name or manifestation) to which must be credited not only the start but the continuation and peculiar configuration of this people. Reference to transcendent powers implies a "religious" response to the ultimate questions of origin and destiny. The sense of contingency and dependence imply being bound by a power beyond the control of the individual but perhaps not beyond the community's reach.

These implicit understandings are given narrative shape by myth. As an anthropological category, myth does not refer to false stories but to narratives that seek to clothe the transcendent in the immanent structures of language and by so doing express the meaning inherent in the structures of shared life. In a society's myths, we find the linguistic expression of its deepest self-understanding: how it has come to be, why it is different from others, what its future is. The recital of these myths renews the rituals of the society, and the rituals make self-evident the "truth" of the myths. The myths and the rituals make each other work, and because they do, they enable the life of the group to continue.

The terms "symbolic world" and "myth" can be used interchangeably but can also be distinguished. The term "symbolic world" is best used of the whole complex system of actions and words that constitute the self-understanding of a group, including physical as well as linguistic products. The term "myth" is best taken as referring to the narratives or parts of narratives that give linguistic expression to this self-understanding by asserting its ultimate origin. Both the symbolic world and the myth obviously serve to interpret social life. There are other forms of interpretation, such as philosophy and hermeneutics, that depend on these more fundamental symbolic structures. The tolerance of symbolic worlds for divergent interpretations varies; at times the interpretation of a myth may be so fundamentally new that it constitutes a different myth. Then the foundations of the symbolic world will shift.

These remarks have not had the aim of establishing a technical vocabulary, but of asserting a fairly simple but important point, which is of the first importance for grasping the character of the NT writings: humans are unstable and instinctually deprived creatures with an insatiable thirst for stability and meaning; the creation of meaning is essential to both stability and survival; meaning is found in the world of symbols shared by a society, from its manner of greeting to its myth of divine creation; inherent in this world of symbols is a process of interpretation.

The description I have been giving is obviously idealized. There is seldom so close a fit between the various factors involved in the making of human society. Three tensions in particular deserve attention. The first is the tension that can exist between the symbolic world of a specific group and the symbolic structures of the wider, pluralistic world. So long as a people is totally isolated from others, its own symbols will function rather well to stabilize its common life. But when a group confronts alternative symbolic worlds, other ways of structuring life, with perhaps equally plausible appeals to divine origination expressed by an equally impressive battery of myths, then the stabilizing force of the first group's symbolic structure is inevitably weakened. Myths are relativized by the mere existence of other "ultimate" explanations. The confrontation with pluralism is threatening to a group's identity, and the group can respond in different ways: it can close up, communicate, or convert. Each response will have some effect on the group's previous symbols.

Another tension is that between the group and the individual. There are degrees to which individuals of a society fit within, or even accept, its self-understanding. All are born into some sort of symbolic world, and most simply accept it as the world (the ways things naturally are) and pass this understanding on to the next generation. They therefore help make that world even more "real" by adding the density of age to the symbols. But others in the group will be less wholehearted in their participation. Even in the most credulous societies, skeptics and heretics are not lacking. Such marginal participation also threatens the symbolic structure of the group, for it depends on total commitment to exist. Every community must therefore learn to deal with deviance. Sometimes it must resort to excommunication. The ritual of excommunication reveals the fragility of social life and how it depends on a concerted commitment to a certain way of knowing the world. The individual may be in tension with the group's knowledge and commitment in another way than by skepticism, of course, for there are also charismatic figures, prophets who seek to renew or reinterpret the group's commitment to its primordial symbols. One of a group's hardest tasks is distinguishing between types of marginal activity. Some threaten the group's identity by erosion; some by renewal.

Experience and Interpretation

A third tension is one intrinsic to the life of individuals and communities alike. It is the dialectic between experience and interpretation. This dialectic is of such fundamental importance for the model I am proposing that some attention must be given it. The basic point, however, is simple: myths and symbols serve to interpret human experience, but sometimes they fail; when this happens, they must be abandoned or reshaped.

First of all, my symbolic world not only interprets my experience after the fact or in an extrinsic way; it actually gives me the capacity to perceive, to have my experience in the first place. Symbols shape my experience. I perceive the rotation of the earth on its axis in relation to the sun as the sun rising, because of my symbolic world. I do not perceive the same phenomenon as god rising from the death of night, though someone in another symbolic world might well perceive it that way. The same point can be illustrated by an indefinite series of examples. I extend my hand to greet a stranger, and smile. The stranger approaches me the same way. Because of our shared symbolic world, we both perceive the interchange and gesture as friendly. In the ordinary course of things, it is, and the experience confirms the perception. When it does, the symbolic world is strengthened, and the mythic structure legitimating handshakes is renewed.

But the process can go the other way. What if the stranger should grasp my hand violently and slap me in handcuffs? What if he seizes my hand and cuts it off at the wrist? Then my experience radically disconfirms my symbolic world, which says that handshakes are friendly and signs of peace. This experience shakes my view of the world, and the symbolic structure is threatened. In light of this experience, I must now struggle to find meaning where it appears to be absent. The quest for meaning is relentless; life cannot continue without it. We try first to stretch our symbols to cover the experience. Perhaps the stranger was an enemy in disguise, and his handshake a camouflage. His act of violence was anomalous, and the exception proves the rule: our myth is saved, our world secure.

Myths stretch to cover experience, and sometimes stretch exceedingly far. Remote islanders, with only a simple set of stories to norm their simple existence of wood and water, were visited by anthropologists who descended in helicopters, waving candy bars and cameras. Then the anthropologists departed. And the islanders stretched their simple stories to include such a totally other experience, so that now they had sky visitors and gift bearers in their symbolic world.

The elastic capacity of myths and symbols is, however, finite. Some experiences are so powerful and radical they threaten to collapse the very structure of the world, that is, the very structure of meaning. In our time, there is no better example than the Holocaust. The absurd death of six million Jews at the hands of the Nazis, the systematic murder of a people guilty only of being Jewish, tore to shreds the symbolic world of Judaism as it existed before that event. This social experience—and it was one experience, though lived in millions of agonizing ways—created a massive displacement in a symbolic structure two thousand years and more in the making, and so decisively that the basic symbols of Torah and messiah became, in a decade, empty of their previous content for millions of people. We can go further and state without paradox that the Holocaust was a religious experience in the proper and qualified sense of that word. Evil, too, is a religious category. And this was an experience of the "otherness" of evil so powerful that it shattered the capacity to explain or even intelligently to perceive it.

Yet, the search for meaning continues. Even in the face of apparently limitless and meaningless evil, there is the human struggle to understand. But what can be used, once the myths have been destroyed? Some have responded to the Holocaust with silence, insisting that any words will distort the event by diminishing it. But a time will come when the experience of the Holocaust will be interpreted with words. When it is, it must be with the bits and pieces of the myths that now lie scattered about. Torah will eventually encompass even the Holocaust. The myth, of course, will no longer look the same as it did before. The old symbols will be there, but they will be read in an entirely new way because of the event that forced the process of reinterpretation in the first place. And it will take time for the new interpretation itself to take on the force of myth, that is, have the power to shape new experiences in a way that seems natural and even inevitable.

This dialectic of experience and interpretation is the basic model I am proposing for the understanding of the writings of the NT. It allows us to answer the fundamental questions of origin and shape: why the documents were written and why they look the way they do. It places the birth of the NT within the symbolic world of first-century Judaism. It allows us to ask about the experience that generated, indeed, necessitated, the process of interpretation. And it enables us to read each of the writings of the NT as specific *modes* of interpretation: the reshaping of the symbols of Judaism in the light of the experience of a crucified and raised Messiah.

The model also gives us the framework for our investigation. We need to ask first about the shape of the symbolic world of first-century Judaism within Hellenistic culture. Then, we need to look at the experience of the first Christians that forced the reshaping of that symbolic world. Next, we need to look in detail at each of the writings as specific ways of interpreting those new religious convictions and experiences. Finally, we need to explore the implications of the fact that those writings were gathered into a normative canon.

BIBLIOGRAPHICAL NOTE

Among standard scholarly introductions to the NT, that of T. Zahn, *Introduction to the New Testament*, 3 vols. (New York: Charles Scribner's Sons, 1909 [1905]), is still unmatched for the depth and vigor of its textual analysis. The most useful one-volume compendium is W. G. Kümmel, *Introduction to the New Testament*, trans. H. C. Kee (Nashville: Abingdon Press, 1975). Although uneven in quality, H. Koester's *Introduction to the New Testament*, 2 vols. (Philadelphia: Fortress Press, 1980), contains much useful information, particularly in its first volume, *History, Culture, and Religion of the Hellenistic Age*. Among textbook introductions, that of H. C. Kee, *Understanding the New Testament*, 4th ed. (Englewood Cliffs, N.J.: Prentice-Hall, 1982), is solid if unexciting, while that of N. Perrin, *The New Testament: An Introduction* (New York: Harcourt Brace Jovanovich, 1974; 2d ed., with D. C. Duling, 1982), remains exciting though idiosyncratic. For treatments of the development of the NT, see Hans von Campenhausen, *The Formation of the Christian Bible*, trans. J. A. Baker (Philadelphia: Fortress Press, 1972); A. von Harnack, *The Origin of the New Testament*, trans. J. R. Wilkinson (New York: Macmillan Co., 1925); C. F. D. Moule, *The Birth of the New Testament*, 3d rev. ed. (San Francisco: Harper & Row, 1982); and E. Lohse, *The Formation of the New Testament*, trans. M. E. Boring (Nashville: Abingdon Press, 1981).

The basic pattern of conspiracy explanations of early Christianity has remained rather constant. One can compare H. S. Reimarus, *The Goal of Jesus and His Disciples*, trans. G. W. Buchanan (Leiden: E. J. Brill, 1970 [written before 1768]), and H. Schonfeld, *The Passover Plot* (New York: Bantam Books, 1966). The options are laid out with customary verve by D. Strauss, *The Life of Jesus Critically Examined*, ed. P. Hodgson (Philadelphia: Fortress Press, 1973 [1835]), 735–44). Strauss himself developed a mythological approach to the NT that is very close to the one I use, but with significant differences. Strauss was hampered by rigid presuppositions and relatively undeveloped critical tools, but his insight was nevertheless great.

For examples of psychological reductionism, see E. Fromm, *The Dogma of Christ* (New York: Holt, Rinehart & Winston, 1955), and R. L. Rubenstein, *Paul My Brother* (New York: Harper & Row, 1972). For a reading of earliest Christian history from the perspective of a Marxist reduction, see K. Kautsky, *Foundations of Christianity*, trans. H. F. Mins (New York: S. A. Russell, 1953).

On the development of the historical-critical model, see W. G. Kümmel, *The New Testament: The History of the Investigation of Its Problems*, trans. S. MacL. Gilmour and H. C. Kee (Nashville: Abingdon Press, 1972), and S. Neill, *The Interpretation of the New Testament 1861–1961* (London: Oxford Univ. Press, 1964). A shorter treatment is that by E. Krentz, *The Historical-Critical Method* (Philadelphia: Fortress Press, 1975). Criticism of the method by scholars taking it very seriously is exemplified by J. A. T. Robinson, *Redating the New Testament* (Philadelphia: Westminster Press, 1976), and M. Hengel, *Acts and the History of Earliest Christianity*, trans. J. Bowden (Philadelphia: Fortress Press, 1979).

The classic expressions of the history of religions approach to the NT are W. Bousset's *Kyrios Christos: A History of the Belief in Christ from the Beginnings of Christianity to Irenaeus*, trans. J. Steely (Nashville: Abingdon Press, 1970), and R. Bultmann, *Theology of the New Testament*, 2 vols., trans. K. Grobel (New York: Charles Scribner's Sons, 1951–55). On this approach see C. Colpe, *Die Religionsgeschichtlicheschule* (Göttingen: Vandenhoeck & Ruprecht, 1961).

The movement to treat the history of earliest Christianity without regard to considerations of canon was given great impetus by W. Bauer's *Orthodoxy and Heresy in Earliest Christianity*, ed. R. A. Kraft and G. Krodel; trans. P. J. Achtemeier et al. from the Philadelphia Seminar on Christian Origins (Philadelphia: Fortress Press, 1971), and given programmatic expression by J. M. Robinson and H. Koester in *Trajectories Through Early Christianity* (Philadelphia: Fortress Press, 1971). See also H. Koester, "New Testament Introduction: A Critique of a Discipline," in *Christianity, Judaism, and Other Greco-Roman Cults: I. New Testament*, ed. J. Neusner, Studies in Judaism in Late Antiquity 12 (Leiden: E. J. Brill, 1975), 1–20.

The so-called sociological approach to early Christianity is not entirely novel (see Kautsky, *Foundations*, and S. J. Case, *The Social Origins of Christianity* [Chicago: Univ. of Chicago Press, 1923]), but it has come into its own. For a popular treatment, see H. C. Kee, *Christian Origins in Sociological Perspective* (Philadelphia: Westminster Press, 1980), and for a review of the options, H. E. Remus, "Sociology of Knowledge and the Study of Early Christianity," *SR* 11 (1982): 45–56. To date, the theoretically oriented approaches of J. G. Gager, *Kingdom and Community: The Social World of Early Christianity* (Englewood Cliffs, N.J.: Prentice-Hall, 1975), and G. Theissen, *Sociology of Early Palestinian Christianity*, trans. J. Bowden (Philadelphia: Fortress Press, 1977), have received more attention than the carefully crafted studies of E. A. Judge, *The Social Pattern of Christian Groups in the First Century* (London: Tyndale Press, 1960); A. J. Malherbe, *Social Aspects of Early Christianity*, 2d enl. ed. (Philadelphia: Fortress Press, 1983); W. A. Meeks, *The First Urban Christians: The Social World of the Apostle Paul* (New Haven: Yale Univ. Press, 1982); and G. Theissen, *The Social Setting of Pauline Christianity: Essays on Corinth*, trans. and ed. J. Schutz (Philadelphia: Fortress Press, 1981). As for the now burgeoning literary approach to the NT, a taste can be got from R. A. Spencer, ed., *Orientation by Disorientation: Studies in Literary Criticism and Biblical Literary Criticism* (Pittsburgh: Pickwick Press, 1980). An introduction to the impact of interdisciplinary methods on NT study generally within the context of the university is P. Henry, *New Directions in New Testament Study* (Philadelphia: Westminster Press, 1979).

The model I use in this book borrows eclectically from the older studies of myth by scholars such as M. Eliade, *Myth and Reality*, trans. W. Trask (New York: Harper & Row [Torchbooks], 1963); B. Malinowski, *Myth, Magic, and Religion* (Garden City, N.Y.: Doubleday & Co., 1948); and E. Cassirer, *An Essay on Man* (New Haven: Yale Univ. Press, 1944). It also lifts indiscriminately from the theoretical musings of R. Merton, *On Theoretical Sociology* (New York: Free Press, 1967); P. Berger and T. Luckmann, *The Social Construction of Reality* (Garden City, N.Y.: Doubleday Anchor Books, 1967); P. Berger, *The Sacred Canopy: Elements of a Sociology of Religion* (Garden City, N.Y.: Doubleday Anchor Books, 1969); and C. Geertz, *The Interpretation of Cultures* (New York: Basic Books, 1973). Studies of the use of symbols in specific intentional communities have also been helpful, such as R. Kantor, *Community and Commitment* (Cambridge: Harvard Univ. Press, 1972); B. Zablocki, *The Joyful Community* (Baltimore: Penguin Books, 1979); and W. Kephart, *Extraordinary Groups: The Sociology of Unconventional Life-Styles* (New York: St. Martin's Press, 1976).

PART ONE

THE SYMBOLIC WORLD OF
THE NEW TESTAMENT

THE SYMBOLIC WORLD OF THE NT IS SO COMPLEX THAT IT IS MORE ACCURATE TO speak of symbolic worlds, in order to acknowledge the pluralism of that setting. The pluralism was constituted by the diverse combinations of three major elements: Roman rule, Hellenistic culture, and the religious symbols of Judaism. A carefully calibrated description of each is beyond the scope of this, or any single, book. There is scarcely an observation on this world that cannot be countered by another bit of evidence. Beneath the welter of specific phenomena, however, some recognizable patterns can be described.

The reader will do well to recognize the selectivity of the present description and investigate further the matters so inadequately touched on here. The better one's grasp of this symbolic world, the more intelligent will be one's reading of the NT. My focus here is on those aspects of the symbolic world that illustrate the dynamics of experience and interpretation I described in the Introduction. I consider it of the first importance to grasp that the writers of the NT were doing exactly what others were doing in that first-century world: seeking to interpret their religious experience with the available symbols.

Further cautionary remarks are appropriate. The symbolic world of the NT is more than a background, as though the influence went only in one direction, or stopped once Christianity began. Judaism and Hellenism continued to live after the writing of the NT. Judaism, of course, looked different because of its negative response to the messianic claims of the Christians. And Hellenism received back its symbols reshaped, so that in the course of centuries Hellenism itself became a Christian culture. The interactions between the symbols of Hellenism, Judaism, and Christianity were complex and continuing.

Despite a wealth of information available to us about this world, we should not overestimate our ability to understand it. Our sources are fragmentary; we do not have everything that was written. The sources, furthermore, are sometimes difficult to date, as are the traditions they contain; we are not sure how old the ideas in some newer writings are. We do better, therefore, at impressionistic, composite sketches than at precise delineations. Our sources are partial in another sense: they represent the perspectives of the more literate and therefore more sophisticated adherents of religious or philosophical movements and, since they were moved to write, also the more wholeheartedly committed to their ideals. Our notions of that symbolic world are inevitably affected by the accidents of historical preservation. We don't always know what the simple folk were doing, but we might suspect they did not always meet the idealized pictures given us by their spokesmen.

For that matter, it is good to remember that the construction of symbolic worlds— especially of religious symbols—did not occupy all or even the best efforts of those committed to the task. Their symbolic world involved politics, economics, and warfare as much as magic and mystery cults. However much religious symbols legitimated and expressed those other activities, it was probably true then, as now, that greater effort went into making a living than into the interpretation of living. The rabbis complain of the difficulties of manual labor and the troubles caused by gossiping wives. Paul's letters suggest he spent more time journeying and at his workbench than in evangelization. And people of that age continued for the most part to have the good sense to mate and procreate, so that energy given to symbolic structuring had to be taken from those more engrossing occupations.

1

Roman Rule and
Hellenistic Culture

WE CAN BEGIN TO DESCRIBE THE WORLD OF THE NT BY INDICATING SOME
of its limits. Geographically, it was the world of the Mediterranean, those
territories embracing the inland sea that for the ancients made up the
known and civilized world, the *oikoumenē*. What lay outside this world was
both fascinating and frightening, and all the more for being so little
known. Those responsible for the security of the *oikoumenē* worried about
the threat of invasion from the Parthians to the east and various tribes to
the north, but the NT reveals nothing of such awareness or concern.
Temporally, this world began with the conquests of Alexander the Great
(356–323 B.C.E.) and continued at least until the mid-second century of
the Common Era. Although Hellenism is given a new frame by the Roman
Empire, beginning with the accession of Augustus in 31 B.C.E., Hellenistic
culture continues well through the time of the early empire, so that we can
accurately designate the most encompassing symbolic world of the NT as
Greco-Roman culture.

Politically, it was a world shaped by empire. By his conquests, Alexander had already created an empire but died before it could be stabilized.
His successors fought for control of the pieces, and for two hundred years
Antigonids (rulers of Achaia and Macedonia), Seleucids (masters of Asia
and Syria), and Ptolemies (rulers of Egypt) battled for supremacy. The
critical land bridge formed by Palestine made it, as always, a prime
battleground. These internecine battles reflected disagreement not over
the virtues of Hellenism or empire, only about who should rule the
oikoumenē. During their conflicts, however, another power slowly but
steadily came to dominate the Mediterranean. Rome had begun its ter-
ritorial conquests during the time of the late republic and accelerated them
by the competition between Caesar and Pompey. From the middle of the
second century B.C.E., Rome commanded the *oikoumenē*, and the explicit
assumption of imperial prerogatives by Augustus only ratified that fact.
Rome gave political stability to the ideals of Hellenization that had already
been diffused by the conquests of Alexander.

HELLENISTIC IDEALS AND REALITIES

When the twenty-two-year-old Alexander crossed the Dardanelles to conquer the Persian East in 334 B.C.E., he intended more than revenge; he was beginning a mission of cultural hegemony. To that end, he brought with him poets, philosophers, and historians. He had been a student of Aristotle and, considering the Greek way best for all, desired to create one Panhellenic world. He encouraged his soldiers to intermarry with native women to create one race. He set a good example by his marriage to Roxanne. Conquered cities he turned into Greek city-states, and in strategic locations he established new cities. Greek he made the universal language, and he actively encouraged religious syncretism whereby local deities might be identified and then merged with the gods of the Greek pantheon. His successors, and particularly the Seleucids, continued to cultivate his dream of a Hellenized world.

The city-state, the *polis*, was itself the first tool of Hellenization. It was the symbol of Greek culture and its best expression: a place where citizens could meet, market, debate, and vote. The city was the center for culture (*paideia*) and its communication through education. The *gymnasium* offered an opportunity for the learning of both physical and intellectual virtue. For young men destined for military careers, there was the *ephebeion*. In classical Greece, the *polis* was the center around which religious activity was organized. The rituals and liturgies of the city gave to its citizens a sense of personal and communal identity. One was not Greek so much as one was Athenian or Spartan.

Alexander used the *polis* as a means of disseminating Greek culture. Old cities, such as Jerusalem under the Seleucid Antiochus IV, were made Hellenistic by a change of constitution. New cities, such as Alexandria in Egypt, founded by Alexander himself, were Hellenistic from the start. The Hellenistic world, then, was conceived of as an *urban* world. Culture and the city were conterminous. That was the ideal, but the reality was somewhat harsher. In the first century, the major cities were not small; Rome had a million in population, Alexandria probably half that many. They were so big that the ideal of citizen participation was impossible to achieve. Worse, the cities were not really independent. They existed within an empire with complex bureaucracies, military installations, and sometimes oppressive taxation. The sense of local identity given by the ancient *polis* declined, together with the sense of protection offered by local deities and the sense of responsibility demanded of citizens.

For some, the fact of worldwide empire created the possibility of a new kind of identity, one more cosmopolitan. Now one could be a citizen of the world. For others, the picture was bleaker; the loss of local roots meant alienation and despair. If one is equally at home everywhere, does one really have a home anywhere? Both reactions colored the religious symbols of the age.

A second tool of Hellenization was language. This was the most powerful tool, for a language bears with it all the symbols of a culture. Greek became the common language (*koinē*) of the *oikoumenē* and remained so even under Rome, with Latin only much later becoming the official imperial language. Greek was the language of trade and government, of philosophy and religion. Even the Hebrew Scriptures were translated into Greek by the mid–second century B.C.E. in Alexandria, and this Septuagint translation (LXX) was simply Scripture for Hellenistic Jews. It was so, too, for the first Christians. The use of a single language was of obvious importance for communication; it enabled the rapid diffusion of new ideas and old. In such transmission, however, symbols both gained and lost resonances by being clothed in Greek. Still, from the time of Alexander, even the refutation of Greek ways usually demanded the use of the Greek tongue. Not always, however, and not by everyone. Local languages such as Aramaic and Coptic continued to be spoken. The preservation of sacred writings in these tongues enabled local identities to perdure, and sometimes became the focal point for resistance to the empire.

The third tool of Hellenization was religious syncretism. Local gods, such as Baal ha Shemaim, the high god of ancient Canaanite mythology, were systematically identified with their Greek counterparts, such as Zeus Olympus. The idea was to reduce local allegiances in favor of more universal ones. Here we recognize a classic case of using religion as a societal glue. The results were various and multiple. The old Greek pantheon was not strengthened by being so violently stretched, and the Greek myths seemed to lose rather than gain credibility by being universalized. On the one hand, this possibly, in some circles, hastened a movement toward monotheism. It is not a big step from equating divine powers to deciding there is one divine power diversely manifested. So philosophers could use the language of polytheism, but also speak of a single divine providence. Less happily, the loss of prestige suffered by the traditional gods together with the alienation fostered by the empire helped create a perception of the world as governed alternatively by fickle change (*tychē*) or inexorable fate (*heimarmenē*). Such perception gave impetus to the search for religious experiences more profound and personal than were available in the official cults.

The goal of Hellenization was somewhat self-contradictory from the first. The genius of classical Greece lay in the vibrancy of its local traditions. Trying to universalize that genius meant inevitably to distort it. The results of Hellenization were therefore mixed and ambiguous. Certainly, something new came into being. Whether the East had been made Greek, or whether Greece had been orientalized, Hellenistic culture was very different from that of classical Greece. The ideals may have been the same, but they were diffused and subtly altered by the new realities of life. Chief among these realities was the fact of empire. It changed everything. Above all, it established a world in which the individual person had little direct control over his or her life. As a consequence, both religion and philosophy in the Hellenistic period gave increased attention to the individual.

ROMAN RULE

Rome was preoccupied with power and used it with unprecedented efficiency. The Roman version of empire provided both security and the frame of legal legitimation for the force it required. Emperors after Augustus may have been bizarre in their behavior and increasingly desirous of accolades due the divine, but through a complex system of governance, they maintained a remarkably long-lasting peace. The empire ruled relatively safe areas, like Africa and Asia, as senatorial provinces—run, at least ostensibly, by the senate through its governors. Populations that were refractory or threatened with invasion, however—and Palestine was both—were under the explicitly military governance of prefects or procurators. There were, in fact, military colonies and installations throughout the empire, and their manpower was used to quell local disturbances. Rome did not, however, rely entirely on violence to enhance its power. It extended the right of citizenship ever more widely, so that by the middle of the first century, members of military colonies, former soldiers, and even local personages like the Jews of the provincial city Tarsus could enjoy citizenship.

The empire grew by conquest, however, and two significant aspects of life within it were shaped by that fact. First, an already stratified society was swelled at its lower levels by large numbers of slaves and other persons displaced by wars. They congregated in the cities and dangerously distended their populations. Such deracinated peoples were often ready for rebellion or religion or both, and tested the toleration of the empire for deviance. They also placed extreme pressure on the empire's ability to feed them. The dole was a fact of life. Rome was fed at the expense of the provinces, especially of Egypt, the breadbasket of the empire. Rome experienced periodic crises caused by the delay of shipments or the failure of crops. The second fact, therefore, was the constant pressure of taxation on the provinces. Taxes levied on subject peoples were especially severe. In Galilee under Julius Caesar, as much as a quarter of a year's harvest could go as taxes to Rome. Add to that the amount skimmed by local chieftains like Herod and the tax farmers hired to do the collecting—the publicans—

and the amount gouged from local populations was even greater. Small wonder the agents of Rome were hated.

Governance and trade required efficient transportation and communication. The Roman roads were extensive—about fifty thousand miles paved by the year 100 C.E.—and well maintained. Between May and October, after which weather made passage perilous, the Mediterranean could quickly and easily be crossed. The travels of Paul and his companions show that frequent and relatively safe travel was common, though still arduous and very expensive. Hostels were often also brothels, so a mobile and separatist group such as the first Christians needed to make hospitality a prime virtue. The availability and security of travel also encouraged communication. An efficient postal system made letter writing commonplace for commerce, for friendship, and for literary exercise, as we can see in the correspondence of Cicero, Seneca, and Pliny the Younger. Letters were also written for mutual encouragement and support between philosophical communities.

Everyday life in the empire could be harsh. Away from the wide public spaces—and for those not enjoying aristocratic privileges—life even in the capital was hard (see Juvenal *Satires* III.190–320). Streets were narrow, crowded, and dirty; food was simple when not scarce, with meat considered a luxury item. The security offered by the totalitarian state, moreover, exacted a price in freedom.

But on balance, the Roman Empire was of particular and positive importance for the spread of the Christian movement. One universally used language enabled the preaching and acceptance of the message. Great urban centers, filled with mobile and often disaffected populations, encouraged the rapid diffusion of new cults and teachings. Rapid, safe, and frequent travel and letter writing were available. All of these were enabled by the freedom from war and internal danger that marked the *Pax Romana*.

THE PAGAN WORLD

The NT cannot be trusted to give a fair picture either of Jews or of pagans. It was written by converts seeking to demonstrate the superiority of their new life by contrast to both groups. The NT is preoccupied with the concerns of the community and speaks of the outside only as it has impact on the movement. We find in it no interest in the threat of Parthian invasion that so affected Roman policy in Palestine, demanding the settlement of disturbance at any cost. We discover no sensitivity to the threat the movement itself posed to a hierarchical and patriarchal society by its offer of communal egalitarianism to slaves and women.

The NT treatment of pagan society is overwhelmingly negative. In this, it shows its kinship with Judaism. For both, the gentile world is morally degenerate and spiritually benighted. The Gospels (see Matt. 6:7, 32; 15:26) and the letters (see Rom. 1:18–32; 1 Pet 1:14–18) agree that pagan life was "lived in the passions of our flesh," a matter of "following the desires of body and mind" and being "by nature children of wrath" (Eph. 2:3). If anything, the descriptions of vice that come from pagan satirists and moralists are even more condemning. The reality, however, was probably not so dismal. A. D. Nock notes,

> It is . . . a grave error to think of the ordinary man in the Roman empire as a depraved and cruel fiend, dividing his hours between the brothel and intoxication, torturing a slave from time to time when he felt bored, and indifferent to the suffering and poverty of others.

The picture of total depravity, after all, comes to us not only from Christians interested in distancing themselves from their former life but from moralists who themselves embody the highest standards within "pagan" society. Like all moralists, they delighted in exaggerating vices in order to make their appeal to virtue more dramatic, and they found their most vivid examples in those classes of society that could afford the more colorful sins. In fact, Roman law imposed a rather somber standard of morality at least in public, and Hellenistic culture in general was profoundly if unevenly religious in its outlook.

Of course, not every religious expression was of the highest order. Rootlessness and resentment, the loss of a personal sense of worth, the lack of community, the sense of passivity before overarching and impersonal forces—these arouse powerful and often primitive religious responses. Magic and astrology were enormously popular even among the educated; they offered a direct control, or at least foreknowledge, of the future. Wearing protective amulets was common, as was the casting of curses. Credulity and superstition could be found among both the simple and the sophisticated (see Lucian of Samosata *The Lover of Lies*). There was abroad a religiosity easily exploited by spiritual frauds and flimflammers. The Hellenistic world was well acquainted with the charlatan *(goēs),* who might appear in the guise of a sophist or rhetorician or philosopher or thaumaturge or priest but in every costume was the first-century equivalent of the snake-oil salesman, seducing the fearful crowd for personal profit and prestige. The satirist Lucian of Samosata gives us two sharply drawn portraits of such charlatans and the way they fed on the crowd's credulity (see *Alexander the False Prophet* and *The Passing of Peregrinus*). On the other hand, Philostratus's completely admiring account of another wandering preacher, Apollonius of Tyana, indicates what a fine line separated the fake from the sincere in the realm of popular religion and philosophy.

All was not superstition and magic, however; no small part of the preparation for the gospel in the Hellenistic world was played by the development of moral and religious sensitivity in religion and philosophy.

HELLENISTIC RELIGION

Little attention will be given here to traditional Greek or Roman religion, either in their more official forms of public liturgies and the taking of auspices in temples or in their domestic manifestations such as the burning of incense before household gods or the decorating of country shrines. Neither does the imperial cult require much consideration, for although the NT may contain some implicit polemic against it, as in the title Lord of Lords used of Jesus, it remained a minor irritant during the period when the NT was being written. From the first genuflection before Alexander the Great to the deification of Claudius, the imperial cult was a specifically political form of religious manipulation, never pretending to express the longing of human hearts. It first became important to Christianity as the test case for the choice between monotheism and idolatry.

Of far greater importance to the NT are the popular developments within Hellenistic religion that, each in its way, responded to the grimmer religious mood created by empire, a mood in which the classical sense of order, which saw the world as cosmos, turned chaotic. Sometimes by renewing older elements of the tradition and sometimes by fusing them with other traditions, these developments shared an emphasis on personal religious experience and the esoteric rather than exoteric. The religious spirit of Hellenism in the early Roman Empire was one hungry for revelation, for transformation, and for a personal allegiance that would give a sense of identity in an alienating world.

Prophecy was held in high honor; not only the official variety, which involved the discernment of entrails, but especially the kind called mantic. It could be found at ancient sites of oracles such as Delphi and Dodonna, and among the priests of foreign mystery cults. It was characterized by ecstasy and speaking in tongues. Frequently it was accompanied by physical rapture and even self-mutilation. Mantic prophecy was held in reverence from ancient times, since it was regarded as a literal possession of the human psyche by the divine spirit (*pneuma*), an indwelling of the god (*enthusiasmos*; see Plato *Phaedrus* 244A). The revelations uttered may have been difficult to interpret but they were received as divine oracles (Plutarch *The E at Delphi* 387B).

Transcendent power (*dynamis*) was also manifested in miracles such as healings and exorcisms. Wandering charismatics such as Apollonius of

Tyana performed wonders and were sometimes regarded as divine men (*theioi andres*; see, e.g., Philostratus *Life of Apollonius of Tyana* IV.45). Healings were regularly accomplished by the savior gods Serapis and Asklepios. At the shrine of Asklepios, petitioners received the visitation of the god in their sleep and were healed of their illness. Like a first-century Lourdes, the shrine had walls adorned with the relics of the limbs and organs that had been restored, as well as plaques attesting the powers (*arētai*) of the god. Devotion to Asklepios could be both deep and personal, and the ritual meals held at the shrines of gods like Serapis offered a sense of community to their devotees.

Mystery cults had been a feature of Greek religion for centuries, but their appeal had remained limited because they had been restricted to a particular locality or clientele. In the early Roman Empire, the mystery cults gained a far wider appeal. This was partly due to the influx of new deities from the East such as Isis and her consort Osiris, from Egypt, and the mother goddess Cybele, from Phrygia in Asia Minor, who offered the double attraction of being exotic and ancient. The wider appeal of the mysteries may have owed as much, though, to the needs of the age, for these cults offered divine revelation, transformation, and a sense of community. We know little about the actual rituals involved, but we know the initiates saw themselves as saved from the inimical powers at work in the structures of the world, and bound to the god or goddess who accomplished their transformation (Plutarch *Isis and Osiris* 382 E).

A similar attraction was at work in that pervasive but indefinable religious response that is called gnosis. We find elements of this response in the hermetic literature of paganism, the Merkabah mysticism of Judaism, and the gnostic writings of Christianity. At the birth of the NT, gnosis lacked a fully structured form and appears to have become a fully identifiable phenomenon only as the Christian heresy called Gnosticism. In the NT period, though, it was definitely present as a mood and as a variety of inchoate responses to a perception of the world. Beneath all the variations, some elements are consistent: The world is viewed in a profoundly pessimistic way. Human life is alienated from its true source and is imprisoned in materiality. Worldly existence is captive to cosmic forces inimical to God and to humans (see *Poimandres* 15). The religious response is to seek escape through esoteric knowledge and ritual, escape from the power of materiality and the force of fate at work in the social and political structures of the world. Such an escape cannot be complete till death, when the soul can shed its garments of flesh in its ascent to a heavenly, spiritual home (see *Poimandres* 22–25). But even now, ecstatic visions can send the soul on a heavenly journey to discover the mysteries of transcendence.

A sense both of the lowest and of the highest in Hellenistic religious responses can be found in the *Golden Ass* by Apuleius. On the surface, this is a dazzling romance, filled with fantastic and sometimes bawdy tales. At a deeper level, it is a story of a spiritual journey from alienation to restoration. The protagonist, Lucius, is a curious and cunning young man, fascinated by the possibility of controlling Chance (*fortuna*) by magic. He drinks a magic potion, thinking thereby to trick Chance, but of course finds himself tricked by her: he drinks the wrong potion and turns into an ass.

As an animal, in a condition symbolizing his spiritual alienation, Lucius is harried by Chance from one stage of degradation to another. At one point, he is sold as a pack animal to an old eunuch priest, "one of the scum that turns the Great Goddess of Syria into a beggar woman, hawking her along the road from town to town to the accompaniment of cymbals and castanets" (*Golden Ass* VIII.24). These priests include a form of mantic prophecy in their show (VIII.27):

> They would throw their heads forward so that their long hair fell down over their faces, then rotate them so rapidly that it wheeled about in a circle . . . they would bite themselves savagely, and as a climax cut their arms with the sharp knives they carried. One of them let himself go more ecstatically than the rest. Heaving deep sighs . . . as if filled with the spirit of the goddess, he pretended to go stark mad.

Chance seems bent on keeping Lucius imprisoned as an animal. His lowest point is reached when he becomes a performer in a sexual sideshow. Then, while at the port of Cenchrae (near Corinth), he has a sudden vision of the goddess Isis: " . . . fortune seemed at last to have made up her mind that I had suffered enough and to be offering me a hope of release."

Lucius prays to the goddess, and she responds with a long recitation of her names and attributes. We see in this scene how syncretism moved toward monotheism and how a mystery could demand an exclusive allegiance. Isis tells him (XI.5):

> You see me here, Lucius, in answer to your prayer. I am nature, the universal mother, mistress of all the elements. . . . [T]hough I am worshipped in many aspects, known by countless names, and propitiated with all manner of different rites, yet the whole world venerates me. The primeval Phrygians call me . . . the Athenians call me . . . the Egyptians, who excel in ancient learning . . . call me by my true name, namely Queen Isis. I have come in pity of your plight, I have come to favor and aid you. Weep no more, lament no longer; the hour of deliverance, shone over by my watchful light, is at hand. Listen attentively to my orders. . . .

She demands from Lucius faith and complete devotion (XI.6–7):

> [F]rom now on until the very last day of your life, you are dedicated to my service. It is only right that you should devote your whole life to the goddess

who made you a man again. . . . I alone have the power to prolong your life beyond the limits appointed by destiny.

Isis saves him from captivity to Chance, and even from inexorable Fate. She restores him by her help to full humanity and promises him immortality. Lucius finds himself transformed again into his human form; he is initiated into her mystery and that of her consort, Osiris; he enjoys the company of fellow initiates; and he proudly wears the distinctive garb and hairdress of the initiate as he pursues his now worthwhile life as a lawyer and priest of Osiris (XI.20–30).

The *Golden Ass* reveals the craving of ordinary people for some power over their life and some sense of identity in an alienating world. Those desires could be met only imperfectly by magic and astrology. The mysteries offered much more. The case of Lucius indicates that we can add conversion to the list of Hellenistic religious experiences. The commitment of Lucius to Isis did not preclude his honoring other gods, but it did reverse the direction of his life in a fundamental way, and in return for his lifelong commitment to her, he could expect to receive eternal life.

HELLENISTIC PHILOSOPHY

Philosophy had changed since the days of Plato and Aristotle. The philosophical schools continued to compete for adherents and attacked each other polemically. But the "love of wisdom" *(philosophia)* was now equated less with metaphysics and politics and more with the art of living; there was a definite shift from theory to therapy. Philosophy was a way of life. For some, it was a religious calling.

Among the great schools, Stoicism had the most obvious influence. This was surely due in part to the way its concentration on the virtues and duties of the individual fit the societal situation. Fate, Chance, the power of the state—these things are beyond our control. Then what can we do? We can focus on things in our control: our mind, our desires. Stoicism had an officially positive view of reality: the universe was rational, and divine providence *(pronoia)* governed events (see Epictetus *Discourses* I.6). The person who sought to live according to nature, that is, reasonably, would be virtuous and therefore happy. One could be at home anywhere; the ideal was to be a citizen of the world. Nothing could prevent a person from being a fully realized human being, reasonable, self-controlled, and content—not even slavery or exile. Even death was not to be feared, for it too was natural (Epictetus *Discourses* III.5.8–11). Stoics like Musonius Rufus and Epictetus taught an athletic and severe form of virtue, with an extraordinarily strict sexual code and inner-directed morality. The tightness of the Stoic focus, however, was itself an indication that much of life could not be controlled; and the ethics of self-control was a desperate accommodation to a world in which the structures of state and family were many times not according to reason.

No less than religion was philosophy syncretistic in the Hellenistic period. All philosophers agreed that theoretical differences were less significant than practical results. And no tradition was more practical and nontheoretical than Cynicism, which especially infected Stoicism during the early empire. Cynicism represented a totally individualistic approach. It eschewed doctrine in favor of freedom and free speech. Freedom meant living just as one pleased, even when—as often—this meant contravening society's standards. Free speech meant the willingness to revile those who conformed to those same standards. The Cynic responded to an alienating social structure by glorying in an untrammeled individualism. The Cynic hero was Diogenes, and many were the stories that told of his snubs of the great and that demonstrated the excellence of "the free, the open-air, life" (see Lucian *Dialogues of the Dead* and Dio Chrysostom *Oration* 6). The Stoicism of Epictetus was particularly influenced by this Cynic tendency, so much so that his description of the ideal philosopher is really one of the ideal Cynic and Diogenes is for him as important a model as Socrates (Epictetus *Discourses* III.22). Although Stoicism domesticated Cynicism, there remained tensions between the traditions. For the Stoics, perfection was difficult, even impossible, to attain; but for the Cynics, it was simply defined and easily accomplished: freedom and free speech summed it up.

Small wonder, then, that the Cynics, in particular, attracted people who wanted to be called philosophers but did not want to work at it. Satirists have left us wonderful portraits of these would-be philosophers who had all the right equipment (rough cloak, bag, staff, long hair and beard) and right speech (reviling the hypocrisy of others) but all the while sought to fulfill their own appetites, thus enjoying the reputation for virtue without paying its price (Lucian *Timon* 54). Many times these charlatans hit the road; from town to town they would go, reviling passers-by at street corners, preaching in the marketplace. Apollonius of Tyana was one such wandering wise man (see Philostratus *Life of Apollonius* IV.2); an even nobler one was Dio of Prusa, called Chrysostom. He began as a traveling rhetorician but after a conversion experience (Dio *Oration* 13) became a philosopher. Now, though he continued to travel and speak, it was "to aid all men" (Dio *Oration* 77–78).

Not all philosophers were so mobile. Some, like Seneca, were court counselors. Others, like Musonius and Epictetus, were schoolteachers whose "diatribes" were lively pedagogical exercises. Whatever their social setting, philosophers agreed that the good life was the virtuous life. Much of their energy went into the description and dissection of vice and virtue. Sometimes this was by way of acute psychological analysis: a saying attributed to Socrates ran, "Envy is the ulcer of the soul" (Stobaeus, *Greek*

Anthology III.38.48). Sometimes social obligations were systematically displayed as in the tables of household ethics (see Plutarch *Conjugal Precepts* 142E). And at times the sheer listing of vices made the point that all vice is illness and all virtue is health. Few vice lists were as extravagant as that of Philo Judaeus, who declared that the pleasure lover would also be "unscrupulous, impudent, cross-tempered, unsociable, intractable, lawless, troublesome, passionate, headstrong, coarse, impatient of rebuke, reckless, evil planning," and, some 130 vices later, "a scoffer, a glutton, a simpleton, a mass of misery and misfortune without relief" (Philo *Sacrifice of Cain and Abel* 32).

Vice as illness, virtue as health: medicine was one of the governing metaphors for philosophy in this age. The philosopher was a physician, able to diagnose spiritual illness and prescribe the appropriate remedy (Dio *Oration* 32.14–30). The philosophical school, in turn, was a hospital, and the first step toward getting better was recognizing that one was sick: "Men, the lecture room of the philosopher is a hospital; you ought not to walk out of it in pleasure but in pain" (Epictetus *Discourses* III.23.30).

From healing to salvation is not a large leap, and some philosophers had a deeply religious perception of their calling. Epictetus is the most obvious, though not the only, example (see also Dio *Oration* 32.12). Epictetus, who frequently quotes the *Hymn of Cleanthes*, "Lead me thou on, O Zeus and Destiny" (*Discourses* II.23.42), sees his own life as one of service to God (I.16.21) and uses explicitly religious terminology in his description of the ideal Cynic: he is called by God and "has been sent by Zeus to men, partly as a messenger . . . partly as a scout" (III.22.2, and 23). Not all were as pious as Epictetus, but all philosophers conceived of philosophy as more than a course of study; it was a way of life. Philosophers dressed and acted differently from most people. Becoming a philosopher meant turning from one way of life to another; the term "conversion" is an appropriate one. Even the satirist Lucian was aware of this convention. At the end of the *Wisdom of Nigrinus,* a description of one of the few philosophers he admired, Lucian portrays a young man, transformed by Nigrinus's words, telling them to a friend, and then both of them concluding that they would have to return to join with the one who had first wounded them so that he might also heal them (*Nigrinus* 38).

The religious dimensions of philosophy are even more evident in those schools that brought their students into a full community life, like the Pythagoreans and Epicureans. Both based their communal life on the ideal of spiritual friendship. The Pythagoreans made literal application of the ancient proverb "Friends hold all things in common" and pooled their material goods (Iamblichus *Life of Pythagoras* 18). The Epicureans had no organized sharing of possessions but were generous in their expressions of friendship (Epicurus *Fragments* 23, 34, 39, 42). Both schools regarded their founders as virtually divine. Epicurus even had homage paid him during his lifetime (Plutarch *Against Colotes* 1117 A–D). Both groups saw doctrine as a means of ensuring the soul's bliss and were profoundly conservative; the maxims of Pythagoras and Epicurus were memorized by members of the school (Diogenes Laertius *Life of Epicurus* X.12). The Epicureans also used letter writing as a means of maintaining support among communities. These schools offered a sense of identity and a real experience of community that was deeper than any offered by the clubs and associations so common in the Roman Empire. The Epicureans, in fact, concentrated so exclusively on the inner life of the group, advocating the quiet life removed from political activity, that they were sometimes attacked for being misanthropic (Plutarch *Against Colotes* 1225 C–F).

Misunderstanding was not the worst philosophers had to suffer. Though often admired by common folk, they were held in suspicion by authorities (Dio Cassius *Roman History* 52.36.4). Exile was a common fate for philosophers in the empire (Philostratus *Life of Apollonius* IV.35). Rome had a complex attitude toward voluntary groups. It was amazingly tolerant of cults and allowed many other forms of association, from funerary societies to trade guilds. But it was deeply suspicious of any gathering that might foment rebellion. Since philosophers were notorious for challenging the social order, they were possible sources of subversion. Hence, they were more generally suspected and treated more harshly.

THE REINTERPRETATION OF SYMBOLS

The Hellenistic period was one of ferment in both religion and philosophy. Religion took many forms, and philosophy was as various as its adherents. The causes of change were multiple as well. But if one cause were to be isolated as most pivotal, it would unquestionably have to be the fact of empire. It fundamentally altered traditional Greek values by changing the social context for their expression. The manifold developments in religion and philosophy were attempts to respond to the collapse of traditional norms and symbols caused by an alienating societal structure.

It is imperative to recognize, however, that these developments did not invent new symbols; rather, they used and reinterpreted the traditional symbols that were still available. This new use of the traditional past is of the most interest to our investigation. The religious leaders and philosophers of first-century Hellenism did not conceive of themselves as creating new and better ways. To the contrary, they never questioned the notion held by all that antiquity was far superior to novelty. Their job, therefore, was to establish and demonstrate continuity with the traditions of the past as they met these new challenges. In their native mystery cults, they only continued to practice rituals as ancient as their people. When they accepted gods from abroad, it was because they were advertised as being even more ancient than their own, and therefore all the more powerful and worthy of veneration. In fact, openness to barbarian wisdom generally during this time was rationalized as receptivity to a knowledge older than that available to the Greeks. Philosophers, in turn, saw their own concentration on virtue and self-control as continuing precisely the approach of Socrates. This search for ancient precedent and the reinterpretation of symbols can be demonstrated by two features of Hellenistic philosophy: the employment and rereading of authoritative texts, and the use of models from the past.

The Hellenistic world had its sacred texts. Greek culture in fact was one that was shaped throughout its long history by the constant reading and rereading of texts from its remote past. It found the ideal of culture (*paideia*) as the noble expression of virtue (*aretē*) first and best expressed in the heroic poems of Homer. In the *Iliad* and *Odyssey*, and to some extent also in Hesiod and the classical dramatists, the Greeks found tales of great deeds and, as well, the involvement of gods in human affairs. The reading and appropriate use of these texts were basic to the education of rhetors and philosophers alike. The moral philosophy of Hellenism makes frequent citation of these texts. The texts carry with them self-evident and weighty authority.

Since the writing of the Homeric poems, however, much had changed in society and in the understanding of nobility. No longer was virtue of the rustic sort that is illustrated by warriors. The myths of the gods found in Homer and Hesiod were regarded as offensive in light of greater moral sensitivity and scientific knowledge. Tales that spoke of gods' being moved by lust or mating with humans or fighting each other were scandalous. They attributed to gods qualities unacceptable even in humans (see Josephus *Against Apion* II.37.242–249). The classical texts that had provided Hellenism with its fundamental symbolic framework threatened, in other words, to become dysfunctional because of new experiences.

The reaction of some was to abandon the texts. Plato admired the poetry of Homer but mistrusted the tales (*Republic* 378 B–E, 595 B–C) and finally denied poetry a place in his ideal state (*Republic* 398A). The Epicureans, who denied the existence of gods anyway, saw all myths as blinding people to a scientific view of the world (Philodemus *On Piety* 18). But those more committed to the ethical and religious values implicit in possessing such normative texts—their antiquity, their divine inspiration—found it important to save the texts by reinterpreting them. How? Precisely in the light of the new scientific and ethical developments that had caused them to be questioned in the first place.

Antisthenes may have been the first to claim that Homer said "some things in accord with fancy and some in accord with truth" (Dio *Oration*

53.5), but it is with the Stoics that we find systematic use of allegory as a way of saving sacred texts. Simply stated, allegorical interpretation claims that the surface (literal) meaning of the text is only a cipher pointing to another meaning. The text says one thing but means another, and the "real" truth can be reached by knowing the system of meaning (scientific or ethical) that will unlock the text. One such system was etymology; Plutarch passes on a common way of using it: "Cronos is but a figurative name for Chronos (time), Hera for air, and . . . the birth of Hephaestus symbolizes the change of air into fire" (*Isis and Osiris* 363D).

In allegorical interpretation, gods were not really fornicating or fighting; rather, the myths were expressing cosmological, psychological, or ethical truths. Thus, in the *Odyssey*, we read of "the loves of Ares and Aphrodite and how they first began their affair in the house of Hephaestus" (VIII.266–366). It is manifestly a tale of adultery. But in the *Homeric Questions* of Heraclitus (no. 69), we see that the union of Ares and Aphrodite is really the combination of strife and love in harmony. The explanation of Cornutus is very similar (*Compendium of Greek Theology* 19). The texts, in short, are still "true" and still authoritative, but only if understood in the proper way.

Allegorical interpretation was not practiced by all who cited these texts, but the principles involved won wide approval. We even see other myths interpreted allegorically, as when Plutarch says of the Egyptian myths (*Isis and Osiris* 355 B–D), "You must not think that any of these tales happened in the manner in which they are related," and goes on to advise,

> If, then, you listen to the stories about the gods in this way, accepting them from those who interpret the story reverently and philosophically [*hosiōs kai philosophikōs*], and if you always perform and observe the established rites of worship . . . you may avoid superstition which is no less an evil than atheism.

This way of rereading sacred texts provided a precedent that was eagerly followed by Hellenistic Jews. They also had ancient, venerable, and sometimes troublesome Scriptures, which were in need of reverent and philosophical interpretation. Allegory came into its own in the scriptural exegesis of Hellenistic Judaism.

One reason classical texts needed to be maintained in the first place was that they provided models for life. To an extent we can scarcely appreciate, Greek culture was built on the imitation of models from the past. The arts of writing and speaking were based on explicit imitation of examples (*paradeigmata*) found in classical sources. The style of the present so far as possible copied that of the past. Novelty was not a value.

Imitating models was essential to the learning of virtue as well. The Greeks were convinced that virtue could not be learned simply from commands, but had to be learned from observation of its living expression in parent or teacher. The teacher was to be a living textbook of the virtuous life. That is why charlatans who professed virtue but did not live it were so dangerous: they presented false examples to others.

The classical texts needed to be reinterpreted so that the models might continue to function positively. The ideals of virtue were no longer those of the archaic nobleman who fought for honor. Allegory helped the Hellenistic reader discover contemporary virtues beneath those simpler, ruddier ones. And in moral discourse, figures from the myths, like Odysseus, took on new dimensions in line with contemporary perceptions. The figure of Heracles, in particular, was developed in a manner the simple recitals in Hesiod's *Theogony* (450–470) would not lead one to suspect. His labors now were seen as acts of great virtue, and Heracles was the model of the philosopher. The myth had it that Heracles abandoned his children. Epictetus, however, makes this act of neglect a positive virtue. It showed how Heracles saw Zeus as the father of all men and how the philosopher could be happy in any place, even apart from his children (Epictetus *Discourses* III.24.13). As the philosopher was a physician and king, so Heracles (III.26.31; see also Dio *Oration* 1.84)

> was ruler and leader of all the land and sea, purging them of injustice and lawlessness, and introducing justice and righteousness, and all this naked and by himself.

Heracles became a "son of God" (II.16.44) and the model of those who achieved immortality and divine status by their virtue. One who imitated Heracles could hope for the same divine elevation (Pseudo-Heraclitus *Epistle* 4).

Not only mythical figures but also philosophers from the past functioned as models. Socrates and Diogenes were the preeminent examples of the philosophic life. For Epictetus, Socrates was a citizen of the world and kin to the gods (I.9.22); he was free in every respect (I.12.23) and the example that others imitated (I.19.6). He held rank next to Heracles (II.18.22). As for Diogenes, Epictetus measured a potential Cynic this way: "Is he a man worthy to carry the staff of Diogenes?" (III.22.58; cf. Dio *Oration* 4.12–39). Even contemporary philosophers could be models for their students (Lucian *Demonax* and *Nigrinus*). The writing of biographies of philosophical founders, by Diogenes Laertius, for example, enabled students to learn their doctrines and imitate their virtues. The ultimate relationship in which the imitation of a model was demonstrated, of course, was the relationship between father and son (Pseudo-Isocrates *To Demonicus* 9).

These developments were complex and were often colored by religious perceptions. The lines between hero and demigod and immortal and prophet and sage and divine man were often obscure. Precisely the ambiguity and obscurity indicate, however, that both philosophy and religion in that day were open to the transcendent and eager for the experience of transformation

BIBLIOGRAPHICAL NOTE

Unless otherwise noted, all translations from Greek and Latin authors are those found in the Loeb Classical Library (Cambridge: Harvard Univ. Press; London: William Heinemann). The sections of Apuleius in this chapter come from his *The Golden Ass*, trans. R. Graves (New York: Farrar, Strauss & Giroux, 1951), 187, 190, 262, 264–66. The quotation from A. D. Nock occurs in *Conversion* (London: Oxford Univ. Press, 1933), 218.

For introductory surveys of the symbolic world of the NT, see R. Bultmann, *Primitive Christianity in Its Contemporary Setting*, trans. R. Fuller (Philadelphia: Fortress Press, 1956); E. Lohse, *The New Testament Environment*, trans. J. Steely (Nashville: Abingdon Press, 1974); and B. Reicke, *The New Testament Era*, trans. D. Green (Philadelphia: Fortress Press, 1980 [1956]). An engaging introduction to the symbols of the NT world is provided by B. J. Malina, *The New Testament World: Insights from Cultural Anthropology* (Atlanta: John Knox Press, 1981). A selection of primary texts can be found in C. K. Barrett, *The New Testament Background: Selected Documents* (New York: Harper & Row, 1956), and H. C. Kee, *The Origins of Christianity: Sources and Documents* (Englewood Cliffs, N.J.: Prentice-Hall, 1973). Standard treatments of Hellenistic culture include W. W. Tarn, *Alexander the Great* (Cambridge: At the Univ. Press, 1948); idem, *Hellenistic Civilization*, 3d rev. ed., with G. T. Griffith (New York: World Pub. Co., 1952); and M. Hadas, *Hellenistic Culture* (New York: W. W. Norton & Co., 1959).

A classic and stimulating study of the Roman context is found in S. Dill, *Roman Society from Nero to Marcus Aurelius* (New York: World Pub. Co., 1956 [1904]), and in J. Carcopino, *Daily Life in Ancient Rome*, ed. H. T. Rowell, trans. E. O. Lorimer (New Haven: Yale Univ. Press, 1940). A good sense of the imperial atmosphere is given by R. Macmullen, *Enemies of the Roman Order* (Cambridge: Harvard Univ. Press, 1966). Connections to Christianity are explicitly drawn by S. Benko and J. J. O'Rourke in *The Catacombs and the Colosseum: The Roman Empire as the Setting of Primitive Christianity* (Valley Forge, Pa.: Judson Press, 1971). A selection of primary texts is found in N. Lewis and M. Reinhold, *Roman Civilization: Sourcebook II, The Empire* (New York: Harper & Row, 1955).

Aspects of Hellenistic religion are considered by G. Murray in *Five Stages of Greek Religion* (Garden City, N.Y.: Doubleday & Co., 1955); A. D. Nock, *Early Gentile Christianity and Its Hellenistic Background* (New York: Harper & Row, 1964); and M. Nilsson, *Greek Piety*, trans. H. Rose (New York: W. W. Norton & Co., 1969). For the mysteries, an introduction is R. Reitzenstein, *Hellenistic Mystery Religions: Their Basic Ideas and Significance*, trans. J. E. Steely (Pittsburgh: Pickwick Press, 1978). For the pervasive traditions concerning miracles, see H. C. Kee, *Miracle in the Early Christian World: A Study in Sociohistorical Method* (New Haven: Yale Univ. Press, 1983). For the darker side of Hellenistic religiosity, see E. R. Dodds, *The Greeks and the Irrational* (Berkeley and Los

Angeles: Univ. of Calif. Press, 1966 [1951]), and H. Jonas, *The Gnostic Religion: The Message of the Alien God and the Beginnings of Christianity,* 2d enl. ed. (Boston: Beacon Press, 1963). Pertinent primary texts are selected in F. C. Grant, ed., *Ancient Roman Religion* (Indianapolis: Bobbs-Merrill, 1957), and idem, *Hellenistic Religion: The Age of Syncretism* (Indianapolis: Bobbs-Merrill, 1953).

The emphases of philosophy in the Hellenistic period are reviewed in E. Bevan, "Hellenistic Popular Philosophy," in *The Hellenistic Age,* ed. J. B. Bury (Cambridge: At the Univ. Press, 1923); E. Bréhier, *The Hellenistic and Roman Age,* trans. W. Baskin (Chicago: Univ. of Chicago Press, 1965); and Dill, *Roman Society,* 287–440. See also A. J. Malherbe, "Hellenistic Moralists," in *ANRW* (forthcoming). For the importance of imitating models in Hellenistic culture, see W. Jaeger, *Paideia: The Ideals of Greek Culture,* 3 vols., trans. G. Highet (New York: Oxford Univ. Press, 1939–45); H. I. Marrou, *The History of Education in Antiquity,* trans. G. Lamb (New York: Sheed & Ward, 1956); and G. Kennedy, *The Art of Persuasion in Greece* (Princeton: Princeton Univ. Press, 1963).

2

Judaism in Palestine

THE SYMBOLS OF THE NT ARE FUNDAMENTALLY THOSE OF JUDAISM, TO THE extent that the first Christian writings can fairly be considered part of first-century Jewish literature. As the literature—propaganda—of a separatist Jewish group, however, the NT's use of these symbols is complex: it appropriates the riches of Judaism wholesale, but in its need to demonstrate its exclusive claim to these symbols, it shows hostility to those Jews who remain unenthusiastic about the sect or its pillaging. So intricate is the process of identification and separation that a knowledge of first-century Judaism is a necessary condition for the intelligent reading of the NT.

In contrast to the remarkably uniform impression made by the talmudic tradition that dominated Judaism for two millennia and gathered new developments into itself until the contemporary crisis of the Holocaust caused even its great power to be questioned, the Judaism of the first century was anything but uniform. The strain that represented Judaism's future and that after the destruction of the temple in 70 C.E. became normative, namely, the Pharisaic movement, was in NT days only one variety of Judaism among others. Distinctions within Judaism were partially due to geographical and linguistic factors (see chap. 3, on the forms of Judaism in the Diaspora). In Palestine, however, ideological differences were even more significant in shaping many and competing versions of Judaism.

The diversity of first-century Judaism was contained, however, within a consistent framework of self-definition. Pagans could recognize even the most thoroughly Hellenized Jews as members of a "second race." The framework, or symbolic world, shared by all Jews was that found in Torah. In the NT, *torah* is usually translated as "Law," but it is a word infinitely complex in its associations. It refers first to the Sacred Writings of Israel. Besides the five books of Moses (the Law), from which the other uses of the word derive, there were the Prophets and the other Writings. These were the most ancient Scriptures extant; they expressed God's own word, and in them could be found all needful knowledge and wisdom. Everywhere, Jews based their lives on these texts.

Within Torah as text, Jews in every nation and every generation discovered their identity as a people, a sense given to those who share a common story. Because they heard the narratives together, they considered themselves a people in direct continuity with those called by the Lord from Egypt, redeemed from slavery, gifted by covenant in the wilderness, and more: a people awaiting the complete fulfillment of the promise made at the dawn of history to the patriarch Abraham, that in them, all the nations of the earth would be blessed (Gen. 12:3).

Torah also means "commandment," *mitzvah*. When the Lord chose this people out of all the earth, he showed himself as a God of faithfulness and loving kindness (Exod. 34:6). The covenant he made with Israel demanded the same qualities of them. They were to be faithful to the Lord and not turn away to other gods; they were also to show covenantal love to one another (Lev. 19:18). The "love with all their heart" they had toward God (Deut. 6:4) was manifested in their attitudes and actions toward other humans. The commandments spelled out those responses, articulated the demands of covenantal fidelity and love (Deut. 6:1–3). And by observing them, Israel was to show all peoples that God is holy, that is, utterly different from any imaginable powers on earth. Israel was to be a "holy nation" (Exod. 19:6), different from other peoples on the earth: "I am the Lord who brought you up out of the land of Egypt, to be your God; you shall therefore be holy, for I am holy" (Lev. 11:45). This aspect of the commandments, however, became increasingly problematic: what did being holy demand?

Whatever their differences, then, all Jews shared the symbols provided by Torah. They therefore shared a sense of election as God's special people, and a sense of responsibility for manifesting that election by being a people among whom God's rule (God's kingdom) was effective. Precisely because they were so central and interdependent, the symbols of Torah and people became the focus both of the unity and of the diversity among Jews in the NT period.

As we begin to look at the variety of Judaism in Palestine, where both political and religious experiences profoundly altered the shape of these symbols of Torah and people, some caution is required. For the sake of analysis, we will describe traditions and concepts as though they were separate entities. But to speak of apocalyptic thought or rabbinic theology or even Hellenistic Judaism is to name elements that existed not in isolation but in complex combinations. Because there *were* ideologically divided groups in first-century Palestine, it is extremely tempting to distribute ideas and sects in perfect alignment. However attractive, the impulse should be resisted, for experience teaches us that a single mind is capable of holding in fragile equipoise many and logically conflicting ideas. Even more so are communities able to calmly and unself-consciously juggle ideologically self-contradictory notions. In the Qumran community, for instance, we see a group equally devoted to legalism, apocalypticism, mysticism, messianism, zealotry, and liturgy, all at once. And, in the great Rabbi Akiba, we see a patron saint of the legal tradition who was also an adept of mysticism and who proclaimed Bar Kochba (a second-century C.E. revolutionary) the awaited messiah, before Akiba was killed in 130 C.E. as a martyr for Torah with the confession of faith "Hear O Israel" (Deut. 6:4–9) on his lips. Our aim here, then, is to describe some distinguishable features, without pretending that these are all that need to be considered or that they ever existed apart from the living expressions of individuals and communities.

THE POLITICAL CONTEXT

Three factors in particular accounted for the diversity in first-century Palestinian Judaism. First was the pervasive presence and persuasive force of Hellenistic culture. Second was the reality of Greek, then Roman, political hegemony. Third was a traditional interconnection drawn between religious and socio-political realities: both ideology and practice had for a long time tended to identify the fulfillment of the promise to Abraham with the people's secure possession of the land (Gen. 50:24; Exod. 3:16–17; Josh. 1:2–4), had identified God's rule with the Davidic dynasty (2 Sam. 7:11–16), and had sometimes equated the temple with the presence of God in the land (1 Kings 8:22–53).

Palestine was so strategically located that empire builders needed it, and required it secure, if they wished to rule the East. But because it was inhabited by a people with such a peculiar sense of itself—"You shall be my own possession among all peoples; for all the earth is mine, and you shall be to me a kingdom of priests and a holy nation" (Exod. 19:5–6)— Palestine was never a secure imperial possession. From the period of the Maccabee revolt (167 B.C.E.) to the collapse of all messianic hope in the Bar Kochba rebellion (135 C.E.), Palestine was violently torn by political strife. So tense were the years of Jesus' ministry that his proclamation "the Kingdom of God is at hand" (Mark 1:15) could not help being both inflammatory and deeply ambiguous.

The story can be read as one of a brave and united people fighting off foreign culture and despotic rule. That is part of the story, and it is highlighted in the Jewish propaganda of the period. But that is too simple a reading. The story is also one of a people divided within itself over the issues of Hellenism and empire. The struggle for Jewish identity in

Palestine involved opposition to outside forces, and disagreements from within concerning the meaning of being the people of God.

The sad stages of the story are well known and can be quickly noted. Although the Babylonian exile (586 B.C.E.) formed a people whose identity depended exclusively on Torah (Neh. 8:1–8; Ezra 7:10), the return from exile in 538 B.C.E. gave an opportunity to restore the temple (Ezra 3:10–13), and even hope of kingship (Zech. 9:9), to the purified people (Neh. 13:30) who had returned to the land. The years after the restoration are largely silent, broken only by a few sources that indicate that the problems of pluralism continued (Ezra 10:9–44), and those who fought for the rule of Torah in the land did so with increasing rigidity (Mal. 2:10–16). When the sources again allow us sight, we find the land caught between Seleucid and Ptolemy, and the priesthood bought and sold by corrupt Hellenizers (2 Macc. 4:7–16). But when Antiochus IV Epiphanes tried to impose syncretistic worship by placing the statue of Zeus Olympus in the temple and by forbidding observance of Torah (1 Macc. 1:41–57; 2 Macc. 6:1–6), the spark of rebellion was struck by Mattathias and those "zealous for the law" (1 Macc. 2:27).

Surprisingly, the revolt succeeded, aided by Rome's timely but fateful support (1 Maccabees 8). Quite unexpectedly, then, both kingdom and priesthood were restored (1 Macc. 13:41) in the Hasmonean dynasty (143–37 B.C.E.). But it was a kingdom dependent on Roman approval, and a priesthood increasingly in the hands of venal men, so the dream of a restored "inheritance and kingship and priesthood and consecration as he promised through the law" (2 Macc. 2:17–18) was diluted by a harsher reality. Years of squabbling over the priesthood brought at last the decisive Roman intervention by Pompey, in the conquest of Judea (63 B.C.E.), which was followed by steadily increasing subjugation, first under the looser hands of local chieftains, then (in 6 C.E.) under the sterner hands of provincial procurators. Continued resistance to Roman rule led to the Jewish War of 66–70 C.E., which ended in the savage siege of Jerusalem and the destruction of the temple in 70, a date of pivotal importance for the continuing and separate development of Judaism and Christianity. Then, more desperately, sporadic revolts led to the Bar Kochba rebellion, which, once crushed (135 C.E.), ended all hope of identifying the promise of the Lord to Abraham with the temporal rule of Palestine under a Davidic king guided by Torah.

All this history is marked by ambivalence toward Hellenism by Palestinian Jews. Hellenism had made significant inroads well before the time of Antiochus IV; some sixteen cities had been Hellenized, and the first steps toward making Jerusalem a *polis* with a gymnasium were taken, not by the Seleucids but by the leading families of Jerusalem. Many Jews were eager to learn these new and attractive ways: "Let us go and make a covenant with the gentiles round about us, for since we separated from them many evils have come upon us" (1 Macc. 1:12). The use of Greek was pervasive, especially in Galilee. Aristotle is said to have met a Jew from Coelesyria who "not only spoke Greek, but had the soul of a Greek" (Josephus *Against Apion* I.179–181). Indeed, Zeno, the founder of Stoicism, was born in Palestine. Even in the heart of the Pharisaic tradition, Greek culture left its mark. There is a story that Rabbi Gamaliel the Patriarch (early 2d cent. C.E.) had one thousand students, five hundred of whom studied Torah, and five hundred of whom studied Greek wisdom. The seven rules of midrash introduced into the rabbinic tradition by Hillel are borrowed from Greek logic. There are a great many Greek loanwords in the midrashic writings. Even the inscription concerning the building of a synagogue by Theodotus, found in the precincts of the temple, was written in Greek. And as a final irony, the writings that tell of the heroic resistance by the Maccabees were either composed or quickly translated into Greek.

By no means, then, was Greek culture entirely rejected. But even those who welcomed Greek ways sometimes balked at some of the implications. The dividing line for all was syncretism. To be Jewish meant to worship one God only, who admitted no fellows. When it came to the choice between *paideia* and Torah, the Jew had to choose Torah. That some did not, that some thought the choice could be avoided or even regarded syncretism as compatible with claiming Jewish identity, caused those not given to sophisticated rationalizing to recoil and hardened them in their conviction that adherence to Torah demanded resistance to Greek culture in all its forms.

Different responses to Roman rule proved even more divisive. The taste of independence under the Hasmoneans caused many to hope for complete restoration of the Davidic line by an anointed ruler (messiah) who would liberate the land from foreign oppression. But not all Jews were convinced that political rule and the kingdom of God should be so closely identified or that Roman administration of the land was necessarily worse than that of the corrupt Hasmoneans or that promised by the zealots: ". . . it seemed a much lighter thing to be ruined by the Romans than by themselves" (Josephus *The Jewish War* = *JW* IV.3.2). They could argue from Torah that kingship had from the beginning been religiously suspect (1 Sam. 8:4–18; Ezek. 34:1–24). They denied that messianism—particularly a purely political one—represented the totality of religious fervor.

The first major consequence of the Palestinian political context, then, was the division of Jews into mutually antagonistic parties. The well-known "sects" of first-century Judaism represented political as well as theological differences. On the two extremes were the men of action, not thought. On the far right were those who could only be called agents of

Roman oppression, the tax collectors; themselves Jewish, they preyed on the people for Rome and for gain. On the far left were the zealots, whose messianism was concrete and political (Josephus *Antiquities of the Jews* = *Ant* XVIII.1.8) and who worked actively to overthrow by military means the Roman rule, aided by their terrorist wing, the *sicarii*, who carried out assassinations of prominent officials (*JW* II.18; IV.3).

As for those more properly termed sects, the Sadducees, who represented the wealthier and more aristocratic elements including the high priestly families, tended to be cooperative toward Rome and positive toward Hellenism. The Pharisees were largely Judean, urban, and middle-class; they began with definite and active political affiliations (see *Ant* XIII.10.5–6; XVII.2.4), but became increasingly apolitical, not cooperating with Rome (*JW* I.5.2) but not actively opposing it, either. The Essenes were thoroughly separatist in ideology and rejected all things foreign; at least those in the community at Qumran (by the Dead Sea) translated this rejection into an active military resistance to Rome at the end of the sect's life. These sects, however, made up only a fraction of the Palestinian population. The rest of the people, the people of the land (*am-ha-aretz*) have left us no record of their convictions. Of their political and religious proclivities we learn only from the way they are treated by others. The Pharisees, for example, despise the *am-ha-aretz* as sinners for their failure to observe tithes and purity regulations. But for that matter, so could the Essenes have regarded the Pharisees; for them it was not enough to purify the body after possible contact with the heathen, it was necessary to withdraw from every possibility of such contact. These divisions were more serious than disputations over theological niceties. They amounted to opposing claims concerning the nature of God's people.

The second major consequence of the Palestinian political context was the specific transformation of traditional religious symbols. The one most obviously pertinent to the NT is messianism. But one should not think of the hope for an anointed deliverer as either universal in its appeal or uniform in its configuration. The contrast between an earthly, "Davidic" messiah who would lead a political revolution (the desire of the zealots) and a heavenly Son of man who would initiate the reign of God on earth (as suggested by Dan. 7:13–14) is too simple, and inadequately supported by the sources. Such emphases were undoubtedly present (see e.g., *The Psalms of Solomon* 17 and *1 Enoch* 37—71) but were mixed with other elements. At Qumran, for example, there is clearly the expectation of a priestly messiah (see the Qumran *Messianic Rule*, 1QSa.2), a hope reflected in other writings as well (see *Testament of Levi* 8). And at least some versions of messianism appear to have been communal rather than individual. Still, messianism was "in the air" during the first century c.e. in an unprecedentedly pervasive way.

Messianism, however, was only one symbol enlivened by this political context. The fact of religious persecution, first unleashed by Antiochus IV, stimulated the development of other convictions that previously had been, at best, only latent in the tradition: martyrdom, resurrection, and individual judgment. In persecution, people were faced with the choice between the dictates of Torah and of the king (2 Macc. 6:18–30). The consequence of obeying Torah was death. Those who chose to be executed rather than abandon Torah wrote their witness in their blood, and became the prototypes of those later to be called martyrs (2 Macc. 6:31). They could do this, however, only because of the conviction that such a sacrifice would be repaid by resurrection. God would give back life to those who die for his Word (2 Macc. 7:9):

> You dismiss us from this present life, but the king of the universe will raise us up to an everlasting renewal of life, because we have died for his laws.

Resurrection and martyrdom are correlative, and are connected in turn to an increased emphasis on individual judgment (see Ezek. 18:1–32): the people do not rise and fall together, but as they have kept Torah will they be judged by God (2 Macc. 7:23):

> The creator of the world . . . will in his mercy give life and breath back to you again, since you now forget yourselves for the sake of his laws.

These developments indicate as well that the symbols of people and Torah were also in the process of transformation. Now, not all who are born Jewish are really Jews. The people of God is smaller than the historical Israel. Belonging to God's people is a matter of choice, and it hinges on one's allegiance to Torah. But Torah how understood and how strictly observed? How decisive and radical must that allegiance be? These questions led to ever more severe separatism and exclusive claims. The logic ran: those who kept Torah most rigidly must be most perfectly the people of God.

Finally, we can see how the symbol of the temple was revalued. In the popular mind, sanctuary and the land tended to be closely linked (see, e.g., 1 Macc. 3:43, 59). Some calling themselves Jews could apparently live with a statue of Zeus in the temple, but others could not (1 Macc. 1:57). For such as these, the purification and rededication of the temple was of the first importance (1 Macc. 4:36–59). But when the priesthood again became Hellenized, separatists rejected the temple of Jerusalem completely; it was no longer "holy" (cf. the Essene CD 4, 6; IQpHab 12). This did not mean that the symbol of the temple was rejected; for many it was impossible to think of a people without a sanctuary. Some longed for a restored, messianic temple (*Jub.* 1.23–29); others dreamed of heavenly temples that were prototypes for an eschatological sanctuary (*2 Bar.* 4:2–7;

1 Enoch 90.28–29). Still others applied the symbol directly to the purified people itself: the holy remnant was a sanctuary, a temple of God in the land (IQS 7.4–10).

LITERATURE IN PALESTINE

We find the transformation of these symbols in the various kinds of literature written in Palestine after the Maccabean period. We will look briefly at representative apocalyptic writings, as well as some writings from the emerging rabbinic tradition, liturgical materials from Jewish worship, and some writings from Qumran. In each case we seek to discover how their writers' distinctive experiences and convictions reshaped their understanding of traditional symbols found originally in Torah.

Apocalyptic Literature

Apocalyptic literature is the matrix for many of these symbolic transformations. It is an overstatement to call all the NT apocalyptic, but it is accurate to state that much of it is unintelligible apart from apocalyptic categories. The term "apocalyptic" means "revelational." It refers to a distinctive sort of *outlook* found in many forms of literature, and to a particular kind of *writing* produced both by Jews and Jewish Christians. Some of the writing, like the classics Daniel and the NT Book of Revelation, are included in the canon; others, like *1 Enoch* and 4 Ezra, are not and hence are called apocryphal (hidden, noncanonical).

Anticipations of the apocalyptic outlook occur in some later prophets like Zechariah, but the outlook's first full literary expression came in the Book of Daniel (ca. 165 B.C.E.), written in response to the religious persecution under Antiochus IV Epiphanes. In it we already find the major conventions of the literature. Daniel is the hero of the book, a young Jew living in the Babylonian, then Persian, exile. He has visions that astonishingly predict the events of the Maccabean period. The book is pseudonymous and is written at the same time as the events it purports to predict. The conventions indicate the nature of the writing. It is written in an esoteric code, because it is an underground literature aimed at comforting those undergoing persecution and exhorting them to fidelity. Attribution to a prophet of the past was probably a transparent fiction for the readers but served to connect this exhortation to the long prophetic tradition.

The first six chapters of Daniel also have a definite connection to the wisdom tradition. They contain folkloric tales of a pious Jewish youth confounding the sages of a foreign culture. The application to contemporary Hellenism was not difficult to make. The moral of each story is much the same: the true Jew does not commit idolatry even when under threat of death (3:18; 6:5) but remains faithful to Torah (1:8; 3:18; 6:15). The wisdom found in Torah is superior to gentile wisdom (2:28; 4:8; 5:13–17), and shows that God is master of history (2:37, 44; 4:25; 5:18–23). In Daniel 7—12, the same points are made in a dramatically different way. Now, not folk tales but strange nocturnal dreams of the young man carry the message (7:1–4). Here we find the basic literary device of apocalyptic: the vision of things future or things heavenly.

When Daniel interprets each vision, we discover each one tells basically the same story: the history of the recent past and the threatening present. Both the visions and their interpretations tell the reader in a coded way that, despite all evidence to the contrary, God is in control of history. God has, in fact, a divine plan for history: it will seem to go from bad to worse only so that God can intervene to reverse its course, stop the reign of evil, and establish his kingdom among the saints. By what agent will God accomplish this? The visions remain tantalizingly vague. A mysterious figure called Son of man comes on the clouds to receive eternal dominion from the "Ancient of Days" (7:13–14). Who is he? Is he the archangel Michael, who is to arise (12:1–4)? Does the Son of man stand for the people themselves (7:18, 22)? The symbol of the Son of man remains sufficiently impressive yet vague to allow further reinterpretation in light of subsequent experiences and convictions regarding God's intervention to establish a kingdom (cf. 4 Ezra 13; *Ethiopian Enoch;* the Gospels).

The Book of Daniel inaugurated a long tradition of apocalyptic literature. Although the literature's mood was esoteric and mystical, its production owed little to ecstasy. The visionary apparatus is a literary technique, and the complex symbolism of the writing suggests self-conscious literary endeavor. It is essentially a written rather than oral literature: the opening, closing, and sealing of heavenly books play a prominent role. The symbolism requires a shared code between writers and readers for the message to be understood, but although they quickly become standardized in the categories of fabulous beasts, significant numbers, and cosmic catastrophes, the code beneath these symbols is that given by Torah itself. Apocalyptic from the first is anthological; in addition to claiming antiquity by the device of pseudonymity, it exploits references to earlier stages of the tradition (see, e.g., how Zech. 1:18–20 is used by Dan. 7:19–22). It is impossible to allocate the production of this literature to any one of the sects of first-century Judaism, and the literature enjoyed a wide appeal.

Apocalyptic involves more than a distinctive style. It is a specifically religious response to the experience of persecution from without and erosion from within. In literary terms, apocalyptic answers the question posed by the choice between king and Torah. To those suffering for allegiance to Torah, it says, Be comforted; to those tempted to apostasize, it declares, Hold fast. But if the message is so simple, why does it require such an elaborate setting? Because fidelity requires a reason, and comfort demands a support. Here the peculiar apocalyptic interpretation of history comes into play as the support for the religious message.

The apocalyptic view of history is shaped by the tension between conviction and experience. This may require some explanation. We must remember that, despite Job and Qoheleth, the dominant teaching of Torah on human history said that the Lord was not only master of it generally, but in a specific and highly individualized way. The Deuteronomistic principle was plain: if you keep Torah, you will be blessed with long life, posterity, and possession of the land; if you abandon Torah, you will lose possessions and children, and die (Deut. 30:1–20). Before there was religious persecution, however, this conviction could be maintained even when experience disconfirmed it, simply because no experience was so visible and massive that the conviction could be dislodged. People who appeared to be good yet suffered must really have been secret sinners or suffering for their parents' sins.

But persecution is another sort of experience. People are being put to death precisely because they observe Torah. Not because they are impious but because they are pious, their children and possessions are ripped away and their own lives taken. God does not appear to be in charge at all. The forces of evil seem to control history. Those who have abandoned Torah prosper, those who worship idols put the saints to death. The crisis of theodicy created by this conflict between experience—suffering for Torah—and the conviction that Torah brings blessings was real (4 Ezra 6:55–59):

> All this I have spoken before thee, O Lord, because thou hast said that for our sakes thou hast created this world. But as for the other nations, which are descended from Adam, thou hast said that they are nothing, and that they are like unto spittle; and thou hast likened the abundance of them to a drop in a bucket. And now, O Lord, behold these nations which are reputed as nothing, lord it over us and crush us. But we, thy people, whom thou hast called thy first-born, thy only begotten, thy beloved, are given up into their hands. If the world has indeed been created for our sakes, why do we not enter into possession of our world? How long shall this endure?

How then can the meaning of Torah, and its claim that God controls history, be saved? By reinterpreting history itself, and in the process, reinterpreting the symbols of Torah. Though present experience would argue otherwise, history is meaningful; it moves through successive periods to a divinely appointed goal. The nature of that goal and the precise time of its accomplishment are God's own secret, but they are certain to be realized. A classic scenario runs this way: history consists of two great ages (or worlds; *ha olam* and *aiōn* can bear both meanings). This present age (*ha olam ha tzeh)* is dominated by the wicked. Their machinations against the saints are sponsored by cosmic powers inimical to God's reign, frequently represented by the fallen angels (see Gen. 6:1–4). The path of history is like an inverted ellipse; as the power of evil grows more evident, history moves downward toward a situation of absolute evil. But precisely when the nadir of the ellipse is reached, when evil is so overwhelming there is no human hope, God intervenes and begins the age to come *(ha olam ha ba),* when God's rule will definitively be established, the wicked crushed, and the saints rewarded. Apocalyptic is preoccupied with periodization, then (Dan. 9:3, 24–27; 12:5–13; *Jub.* 1.29), because only if history is seen as fulfilling distinct stages can God's control of it be asserted. And only because the end vindicates God's mastery is monotheism saved from the dualistic implications of cosmic conflict between good and evil carried out on apparently equal terms.

Even as it reshaped it, apocalyptic perpetuated the symbolic world of Torah. It explicitly asserted the centrality of the law and the need to keep it, in order to be counted among the elect. It identified Torah as the highest wisdom, based not in human understanding but in divine revelation. In the midst of persecution and apostasy, it spoke the word of prophecy to the people. The visionary apparatus gave even further impetus to the development of other esoteric movements, such as Gnosticism, and resembled the expressions of mysticism found among the masters of the Merkabah (speculation and prayer centered on the throne chariot *(Merkabah)* of Ezekiel). It also provided a coherent symbolic framework for those who claimed to have experienced the radical intervention of God in the world's history, as those claimed who first confessed Jesus to be Son of man.

Rabbinic Tradition

Apocalyptic is plainly shaped by the very historical events it seeks to interpret. The rabbinic tradition, in contrast, rejects analysis of history altogether and is correspondingly hard to locate historically. Three specific reasons make the description of this movement in NT times difficult. First, the Pharisaic movement survived the catastrophe of the Jewish War (66–70 C.E.) and became the dominant form of Judaism for the next two millennia; understandably, it tends to overemphasize its role in the earlier period. Nevertheless, the Gospels confirm that the Pharisees and scribes were indeed important before 70 C.E., and we find them at the center of disputes with Jesus over Torah (see, e.g., Mark 7:1–13). Second, the whole nature of the movement *was* tradition. Its interest was not in constructing new but in passing on ancient teaching. The oral interpretation of Torah that characterizes the movement was regarded as being as old as the written Torah *(Pirke Aboth* 1):

> Moses received Torah from Sinai and delivered it to Joshua, and Joshua to the
> elders, and the elders to the prophets, and the prophets delivered it to the
> men of the great synagogue. These said three things: be deliberate in judging,
> and raise up many disciples, and make a hedge for the Torah.

The third reason is the nature of the sources. The rabbinic movement
began as an oral tradition, and the great compilations of its lore are all
considerably later than the NT. Judah the Prince codified the Mishnah in
200 C.E., and it provided the basis for further interpretations, which were
crystallized in the two versions of the Talmud, the Palestinian (ca. 350
C.E.) and the more authoritative Babylonian (ca. 450 C.E.). Despite their
late composition, the compilations do contain much older material.

The process of defining the movement is made particularly difficult,
however, by the timeless atmosphere of the material, which makes it seem
as though all the world were a classroom. This is not accidental, for the
basic social setting for the development of this tradition was the school,
with a teacher (rabbi) instructing students in Torah and its interpretation.
The Talmud and other rabbinic materials resemble the shorthand notes of
a seminar. Topics are picked up and dropped. Ancient opinions are found
next to the most recent. The point, it quickly becomes clear, is not
systematic thought but the process of discussion itself. This is a tradition
based on the study and the living of Torah. The Talmud shows us the
insatiable, quirky, profound, and sometimes silly questions and answers of
learned men over the connections between Torah and life, in a lively and
sometimes unruly, centuries-long conversation.

The tradition was based on the religious convictions of the Pharisees
concerning Torah and was shaped by the interpretive skills of the scribes
(*sopherim* = men of the book), who appeared already in the time of the
restoration as interpreters of Torah (Neh. 8:4–8). We have already seen
that the Pharisees tried to be apolitical. How then did they understand the
symbols of Torah and the people? Their specific approach can best be
grasped by way of contrast to other groups in the first century.

Little can be said about the vast majority of Jews, the *am-ha-aretz*, for
they left us no records of their convictions. Undoubtedly they were many
times pious in their fashion and devoted to Torah and the cult. So far as the
Pharisees were concerned, however, they were ignorant and untrustworthy
and not fully part of the people (cf. *Mishnah Demai* 2.3; *Gittin* 5.9; *Pirke
Aboth* 2.6; 5.10). The Samaritans, on the other hand, were a significant
part of the Palestinian mix and of the first Christian movement as well,
although their precise importance is harder to weigh. They were of mixed
race and custom (*Tractate Kutim* 1.2):

> The usages of the Samaritans are at times like those of the heathens, at times
> like those of the Israelites, but most of the time like the Israelites.

They were separated from all Jews by their insistence on the priority of

Shechem over Jerusalem (see John 4:20), and they were separated from the Pharisees in particular by their attitude toward Torah, which was profoundly conservative: they accepted only the five books of Moses (Genesis through Deuteronomy) as Torah. On that basis, however, they developed a lively messianic expectation of their own, which centered on a Moses figure, for Deut. 18:15–18 had promised that God would "raise up a prophet like you from among your brethren" (cf., e.g., *Memar Marqah* IV.3). But for the Pharisees, *Tractate Kutim* 1.2 says, "This is the principle: they are not to be trusted in any matter in which they are open to suspicion."

The Jewish historian Josephus describes the Sadducees, Pharisees, and Essenes as philosophical schools (*JW* II.8.2), and given the degree of Hellenization in Palestine, he may not have been far off. He tells us little about the Sadducees, except that they were vaguely Epicurean in their philosophy (*JW* II.8.14; *Ant* XVIII.1.4) and were conservative in their attitude toward Torah. They "say we are to esteem those observances to be obligatory which are in the written word, but are not to observe what are derived from the tradition of our forefathers" (*Ant* XIII.10.6). This worked well for them, for having a close association with priesthood and temple, they could fulfill the purity laws without special applications. A conservative view of Torah led to the rejection of developments owed to the oral tradition, such as belief in the resurrection and angelology.

The Essenes are greatly admired by Josephus. He describes in considerable detail their community of possessions (*JW* II.8.2–4) and their separatist tendencies based in the desire for purity (8.5–9). It is not surprising he sees them as Pythagoreans. He also notes that they are concerned for the prophetic aspects of Torah (8.12), and we will see more of this when we look at the Qumran branch of the Essene movement.

The Pharisees look like Stoics in Josephus's treatment, with a belief in providence and free will (*JW* II.8.14), but he emphasizes above all that they were "skillful in the exact application of the laws" (*JW* II.8.14; *Life* 38) and that they sponsored the oral tradition (*Ant* XIII.10.6). These characteristics, however, do not explain the survival and eventual dominance of the Pharisaic tradition. Partly, of course, attrition played a role. The Sadducees disappeared with the temple; the Essenes and the zealots were wiped out by war with Rome; the Samaritans remained a quaint relic. But the Pharisees had the capacity to adjust to new circumstances. They were not tied to any particular social institution or political program. As urban and middle-class people, they were mobile and adaptable. Above all, their perception of the people and Torah was flexible and progressive, and it was this which enabled them to represent the future of Judaism.

On the one hand, their view of Torah was strict and demanding. To be part of the people, to take the yoke of the kingdom on oneself, was to take on the yoke of Torah, which was binding on all Israel in all its parts. This included the laws of purity and tithing; these did not apply only to the priests of the temple but applied to every Israelite, for the Israelites were a "nation of priests." The Pharisees identified people and Torah, and for this reason above all were able to survive loss of priesthood, temple, king and land.

The genius of the Pharisaic tradition is found above all, though, in its ability to interpret and apply Torah for all Jews. The starting point of the Pharisees can once more be seen as a conflict between conviction and experience. The conviction is that Torah is God's word and therefore eternal and unchanging and, obviously, normative for life. Torah's commandments *(mitzvoth)* make specific demands on every Jew. But the tension is created by the fact that life is *not* changeless; it continually changes. The *mitzvoth* for tithes and purity were addressed to a people living an agricultural existence. Torah demands sharing possessions but spells this out in terms of vines and fields and harvests. But we live in cities, and our circumstances are very different: we must buy food from strangers and engage in trade in order to live. How can we now observe the tithes and keep ritual purity? The options are limited. We could simply abandon Torah or regard it as less than an absolute norm, but that would be to degrade God's word. We could change Torah, but again that would amount to seeing it as a human word. We could keep Torah, by removing ourselves from others and trying to re-establish an agricultural society that we can control. Or we could continue to live in the present world but seek to discover in Torah itself the principles that would allow us to maintain its integrity as an absolute norm, yet deal with the real circumstances of our lives. The Pharisees did not, like the Essenes, leave society for Torah. They stayed in the city and invented midrash.

Midrash (from the verb *darash,* "to search") is a method of contemporizing sacred texts. It is based on the conviction that Torah itself provided the basis for new understanding and contemporary application. Every word and letter of Torah bore the possibility of new meaning; where application was not clear, one had to search the text for ways of resolving the difficulty. Without midrash, the text remains dead; with it, the text is enlivened and speaks to the present with new authority. From the time of Hillel (1st cent. B.C.E.) the Pharisees took over from Greek logic rules for adjudicating textual problems. With an exact and comprehensive knowledge of the details of Torah, these rules helped them to sort out conflicts and establish priorities among, and find appropriate applications of, *mitzvoth.*

So central was this rereading of the text to the tradition, that the synagogue was also called the house of study *(beth ha midrash).* Study, observance, and worship—all articulated Torah in life. It was Torah that gave meaning to life and enabled it to be, in every act, obedience to God's will. Midrash was applied to the strictly legal material of Torah in order to yield a rule of action (*halakah*, from the verb "to walk," therefore, "way of acting"). When midrash was applied to other texts, it was called haggadah (from the verb "to relate," thus, loosely, narratives). Haggadic midrash tended to be freer and more spontaneous, and in it we find much of the spiritual and ethical idealism of Pharisaism. Halachic midrash, though, was more serious, for it had to do with establishing the grounds of righteousness before God.

A short example of halachic midrash will illustrate its religious spirit. One of the *mitzvoth* in Torah was that farmers should not glean all of the wheat in a field but should leave a corner *(peah)* for the poor to glean (Lev. 19:9; 23:22). The intent was to "do justice," by helping the poverty-stricken among the people. But the problems of applying the commandment are immediately evident. Who should qualify as poor, first of all? But then, what constitutes a corner? How big must it be? And how can this principle be translated to other circumstances? These are not trivial questions. Both the needs of the poor and the legitimate needs of the farmer require consideration; the farmer, already heavily taxed, might not be able to feed his family if the corner takes too much of his small field. In the early midrashic tractate *Sifra*, we find the problem dealt with extensively, and the halachic discussion is carried over to the Mishnah, in the tractate *Peah*. Page after page is given to legal discussion; every detail is considered. Is it all senseless? Not at all, once the premises of the tradition are granted. And at the very head of the tractate (*Mishnah Peah* 1.1), we find this fine expression of them:

> These are things whose fruits a man enjoys in this world while the capital is laid up for him in the world to come: honouring father and mother, deeds of loving kindness, making peace between a man and his fellow; and the study of the Law is equal to them all.

Every legalism can, of course, lapse into sheer casuistry and proliferate meaningless regulations at the expense of humanity. This is the charge the Gospels have Jesus bring against the Pharisees especially concerning Sabbath regulations (see Mark 2:23—3:7). And it was around the Sabbath that the most extensive body of rules grew up. This is partly due to the nature of positive commands. It is far easier to set the limits to commands like Don't kill, than it is to commands like Keep holy. It is also due to the fact that the Sabbath was so central to the identity of the people. Already in Torah, it is attached to the practice of God himself (Exod. 20:8–11). It was to be a sign of "differentness," that is, holiness, in the world. And the Sabbath was a unique institution in the ancient world. By it, even pagans recognized the distinctiveness of the Jews and their God who demanded one day a week for himself as holy. But determining the dimensions of the holy is not simple. This day is to be "different" from others; other days are for "work." That is clear enough and is in Torah itself. But what is the meaning of "work"? Midrash located every mention of the term "work" in Torah and came up with a comprehensive list of thirty-nine activities that were named work and must be avoided (*Mishnah Shabbat* 7.2). Now, refusal to light a fire or to tear a thread might seem trivial to the outsider. But such lists "put a hedge around the Torah," so that the central commandment itself would not be broken. The method and its results are disputable, but the severe religious motivation is not.

The religious impulse of the Pharisaic tradition is also found in some of its theological emphases. God was indeed transcendent, "the Holy One," but his presence was made available to humans. A symbol for this was the Divine Presence (*Shekinah*, from *shakan*, "to dwell"), which was with the people in the desert and over Solomon's temple, and was now present in synagogues when Torah was read. Indeed, one's study of Torah placed one in this "shadow of God's presence" (*Pirke Aboth* 3.3):

> If two sit together and words of Torah are between them, the Shekinah rests between them . . . and even if one sits and occupies himself with Torah, the Holy One, blessed be He, fixes for him a reward.

Torah, in fact, is God's eternal blueprint for creation and for righteous human behavior. In it, humans find both joy and freedom. In its study is found wisdom. Yet the emphasis on study does not lead to a neglect of good deeds (*Pirke Aboth* 3.12; cf. *Aboth de Rabbi Nathan* 24):

> Everyone whose deeds are more than his wisdom, his wisdom endures; and everyone whose wisdom is more than his deeds, his wisdom does not endure.

Among these good deeds were the fulfillment of Sabbath and purity regulations, but above all, "deeds of charity," actions by which the covenantal obligations of fidelity and love were expressed toward others, particularly in the help given to the poor and dispossessed (see Babylonian Talmud, *Berakoth* 8a; *Shabbat* 156b).

Torah was a measure that was never perfectly met. Humans were free but subject to drives and impulses that sometimes prevented them from observing Torah in great as well as small things. The remedy for this was not despair but repentance. A saying attributed to Rabbi Eliezer went "Repent one day before your death . . . let him repent today lest he die on the morrow; let him repent on the morrow lest he die the day after; and thus all his days will be spent in repentance" (*Aboth de Rabbi Nathan* 15).

A passage from the Babylonian Talmud, *Makkoth* 24a, illustrates the spirit of this rabbinic tradition both in its apparent frivolity and in its deeper seriousness. The passage begins with the statement "Therefore gave he them Torah and many commandments. . . ." The discussion begins, naturally, with the question, "How many commandments?":

> R. Simlai, when preaching, said, "Six hundred and thirteen precepts were communicated to Moses, three hundred and sixty-five negative precepts, corresponding to the number of solar days, and two hundred and forty-eight positive commands, corresponding to the number of the members of a man's body. . . ."

This sounds a bit silly, especially when it is then supported by texts of Torah. But then other traditions are cited, which systematically reduce and compress the commandments into ever tighter and more religiously focused texts. Now Isaiah and Micah and Amos are quoted, and the intent of Torah is narrowed down, till we reach this conclusion (Babylonian Talmud, *Makkoth* 24a):

> Again came Isaiah and reduced them to two principles, as it is said, "Thus saith the Lord, Keep ye justice and do righteousness. . . ." Amos came and reduced them to one principle, as it is said "For thus saith the Lord unto the house of Israel, seek ye me and live." To this, R. Nachman b. Isaac demurred, saying, "Might it not be taken as 'seek me by observing the whole Torah and live'?" But it is Habbakuk who came and based them all on one principle, as it is said, "but the righteous shall live by his faith."

That is a sentiment we find more strongly expressed only in Paul.

Jewish Worship

One of the most important contexts for the development of Jewish symbols was worship. In worship, after all, the convictions of religion come alive and a community expresses its identity in myth and cult. In the NT period, Jewish worship was performed in the temple, synagogue, and home.

The temple continued to be considered one of the architectural marvels of the world and a center for pilgrimages three times a year, at the feasts of Passover, Booths, and Pentecost, when Jews from all over the world would converge on Jerusalem (see Acts 2:5–11). Sacrifices and prayers continued to be offered in its courts, and both Jesus and the first disciples taught in its precincts (Luke 19:47; Acts 3:11—4:1). By the first century, however, the temple was not the center of piety in the way home and synagogue were.

The origins of the synagogue are obscure. It may have begun in the gatherings of the people to hear Torah while in exile, or it may have started as the local parallel to the worship of the temple, with its three daily prayer times corresponding to the hours of sacrifice (see *Mishnah Taanith* 4.2–4). By the NT period, the synagogue was an institution found in most villages (see Luke 4:15–17), both in Palestine and in the Diaspora (Acts 13:14–15). According to tradition, Jerusalem was filled with synagogues, and there was even one in the precincts of the temple (Babylonian Talmud, *Sukka* 53a).

The synagogue was unique as a place of worship in the ancient world. It had no animal sacrifices, and ritual actions generally were held to a minimum. Its worship centered totally on Torah. In NT times, the synagogue and house of study *(beth ha midrash)* (see Sirach 51:23) seem to have been the same, and its space allowed for a casual but regular rhythm of prayer and study.

Our written sources for the synagogue liturgy are so late (the *Seder Rav Amran Gaon* dates from the ninth cent. c.e.) that we can reconstruct the prayer service only with great caution. The NT writings and the fragmentary discussions of worship in the Mishnah, however, allow us to make some statements (cf. *Mishnah Yoma* 7.1; *Berakoth* 1–2; *Megillah* 4). The entire service was built around Torah: the hearing of God's word in the Scripture readings; the proclamation of it in the midrashic homily; and the prayers and petitions that used the very words of Torah.

The classic form of Jewish prayer is the blessing *(berakah)*. It is the antecedent of prayer forms in the NT and early Christian liturgy (see Eph. 1:3–14; 1 Pet. 1:3–6). Its form is simple though capable of indefinite expansion. It opens with a statement of praise, follows with the reasons for praise, then concludes with renewed praise. The basic form is found already in Psalm 117:

> Praise the Lord all nations!
> Extol him all peoples!
> For great is his steadfast love for us
> and the faithfulness of the Lord endures forever.
> Praise the Lord!

The morning synagogue service had three lengthy blessings *(berakoth)* enclosing the central confession of faith, the *shema:* "Hear O Israel, the Lord your God is One. . . ." One of these is the *Berakah Ahabah:*

> With abounding love hast thou loved us YHWH our God, with great and exceeding pity hast thou pitied us, our Father, our King, for the sake of our fathers who trusted in thee, and whom thou didst teach the statutes of life, be gracious also unto us . . . put it into our hearts to hear, to learn, and to do, all the words of instruction in thy Torah in love . . . and let not thy mercy abandon us forever and ever. Let peace come over us from the four corners of the earth . . . for thou hast chosen us from all peoples and tongues and hast brought us near unto thy great name in love. Blessed be thou YHWH, who hast chosen thy people Israel in love.

The *berakah*, we see, is fundamentally an act of remembrance. God is to be praised for the way he has worked in the past. By remembering his deeds, we are moved again to praise him. Remembrance of this sort acts like myth: it makes the past active in the present.

Another form of synagogue prayer is the *tefillah*. On normal days there were eighteen of these, from which they received the name "the eighteen benedictions," *shemone esre*. They were also called the *amidah* because they were said "standing." The most characteristic of them is the "Blessing of the Name," *Qedushat ha shem:*

> From generation to generation give homage to God, for He alone is high and holy, and thy praise, our God, shall not depart from our mouth forever, for a holy and great king thou art. Blessed be thou, O Lord, thou Holy God.

The *berakah* form of prayer united public worship and private piety. The pious Pharisee would recite up to a hundred smaller *berakoth* privately every day, to "sanctify time."

The synagogue worship included the reading of Torah and a sermon. The readings were from the Law and Prophets, and followed a regular sequence (*Mishnah Megilla* 4.1–10). The most important reading was from the Law. It was read in the original Hebrew. Because the majority of Jews no longer understood Hebrew, however, it was necessary to translate the sacred text into Aramaic. As the text was read, a translator would freely render the text for the people in a paraphrastic fashion, clarifying obscurities and pointing out contemporary relevance. Not a little haggadic midrash found its way into such translations, which, when later written down, were called Targums. They give us one more example of the way worship made a text from the past relevant to newer perceptions. The Hebrew text of Gen. 49:1, for example, reads,

> Then Jacob called his sons and said, "Gather yourselves together that I may tell you what will befall you in days to come."

The Aramaic Targum *Pseudo-Jonathan* rendered Gen. 49:1 this way:

> And Jacob called his sons and said to them: "Purify yourself from uncleanness, and I will show you the mysteries which are hidden, the appointed times which are concealed, what the recompense of reward for the just, the retribution in store for the wicked, and the joys of Eden are." The twelve tribes gathered together around the bed of gold on which he lay. And after the shekinah of the Lord was revealed, the determined time in which the King Messiah is to come was hidden from him.

This is an extraordinary passage; more than an expanded translation, it is a virtual compendium of apocalyptic (hidden secrets, messiah, individual judgment) and rabbinic symbols (*Shekinah*, purification). The truly remarkable part is that this was heard by pious Jews in the synagogue as the

words of Torah. Precisely such reworkings of the text would have been
heard by Jesus and his disciples in the synagogues of Galilee.

After the reading from Law and Prophets, there would be a homily, in
which the speaker would midrashically work out the text and its implications. The earliest description of a synagogue service we possess is found
in the Gospel of Luke (4:16–30). Coming to his home synagogue in
Nazareth, Jesus was asked to read from the prophet Isaiah (61:1–3), and
then to preach. He read the words "The spirit of the Lord is upon me
because he has anointed me to proclaim good news to the poor. . . ." When
he sat down to preach, however, instead of giving a midrashic exposition,
he simply said, "Today this scripture has been fulfilled in your hearing"
(Luke 4:21).

The third place of Jewish worship in the first century was the domestic
liturgy of the meal, such as that celebrated on the Sabbath and at important feasts such as Passover. All meals had a certain sacred character and
were accompanied by blessings (*Mishnah Berakoth* 7–8). Meals, furthermore, symbolized fellowship; to eat together signified spiritual agreement.
The charge against Jesus that he ate with sinners amounted to a charge
that he also was a sinner (Luke 7:34; 15:2). It is possible that the Pharisaic
fellowships (*haburoth*) celebrated at least festival meals together.

The most significant sacred meal in Judaism was the Passover supper.
Though lambs were still slaughtered ritually in the temple, those who
came to Jerusalem for this greatest pilgrimage feast ate the lamb together
with family and friends in lodgings scattered throughout the city. The last
meal of Jesus and his followers was probably such a Passover supper (Mark
14:12, contra John 19:31). Passover celebrated the exodus experience,
when the Lord had taken Israel out of the bondage of Egypt, led them
through the desert, and brought them to the promised land. This was the
paradigmatic experience of redemption, and Passover was a feast of Jewish
freedom. The words and rituals of the meal show us texts from the past
being reinterpreted. In the Passover Haggadah is the classic myth and
ritual of first-century Judaism: "Let each one regard himself as having
come out of Egypt." The words over the bread at once interpret and are
interpreted by Torah:

> This matzah which we eat, what is the reason for it? Because the dough of our
> fathers had not yet been leavened when the king over all kings, the Holy One,
> blessed be He, revealed himself to them and redeemed them. As it is said,
> "And they baked unleavened cakes of the dough which they brought forth out
> of Egypt" (Ex. 12:39).

Likewise with the words said over the cups of wine:

> Therefore we are bound to thank, praise, laud and glorify . . . him who
> performed all these miracles for our fathers and for us. He has brought us

forth from slavery to freedom, from sorrow to joy, from mourning to holiday, from darkness to great light, and from bondage to redemption. Let us then recite before him a new song, Halleluiah.

In the Passover ritual, the myth of the community is renewed and the symbols of Torah once more establish Jewish identity as of a people God has chosen and saved.

Qumran

Despite the warning with which this chapter opened, there still may be the temptation to isolate "apocalyptic," "rabbinic," and "liturgical" aspects of first-century Judaism into airtight compartments. For that reason, one of the greatest contributions made by the Dead Sea Scrolls from Qumran to the study of Judaism and early Christianity has been to show how these various expressions could be united in the experience of a single concrete community.

We will not recount the history of this fascinating and bizarre group of sectarians, doubtless an extreme form of the Essene movement who took the logic of separatism so seriously that they went to the desert "to prepare a way for the Lord" by a life completely devoted to the observance of Torah (IQS 8.13–16) and completely removed from the impure—not only the heathen but all those who remained in contact with the heathen (IQS 5.1–3; 7.24–25; 8.22–24). We know that they gave special allegiance to a teacher of righteousness (CD 20.1; IQpHab 9.9–10) whom they credited with special insight into the meaning of Torah (IQpHab 2.2) and its application to their community. We know too that they had special hostility for the "wicked priests" in Jerusalem whom they regarded as having profaned the temple and polluted the land (IQpHab 8.9; 9.9). We know, finally, that they saw themselves as the replacement for priesthood and temple. The community was a "house of holiness" for the Lord, which offered spiritual sacrifices of praise and study (4QFlor 1.6; IQS 8.6–8; 9.3–11) guided by a leadership of priests and Levites of the order of Zadok (IQS 2.19–20; 5.1–3).

Their application of purity regulations was implacable; because of purity they had a total community of possessions—they could not mingle goods with the impure (IQS 1.11; 6.17–22). Purity demanded an elaborate system of punishments (IQS 6.24—7.23) and the extreme penalty of excommunication when the community's purity was seriously threatened (IQS 5.14–16; 8.22–24). The community was there in the desert as a purified remnant of the people, a realization of what God wanted Israel to be. All other claimants to membership in the people were wrong; only they truly were the people of God. And so they drew to themselves all the symbols of land and Torah and people and temple. More, they were the anticipation of God's eschatological rule. Their community organization would be replicated in the time of the messiah (IQSa 1.19–26), and their sacred meals were a foretaste of those shared with the messiah (IQSa 2.16). And all of this was legitimated by a rigid and comprehensive mythology that based their separation in a cosmic dualism, a battle between children of light, whose origin was God, and children of darkness, whose origin was the prince of darkness (IQS 3.13—4.26).

Immediately after the discovery of these scrolls, elaborate theories abounded as to the dependence of Christianity on the Qumran community. Most of these theories have gone their appointed way. There remains reason to think John the Baptist may have had some contact with the sect and that some ideas and practices may have influenced the earliest Palestinian communities. Hard and direct links, however, have not been established. Qumran is of the first importance not for what it tells us about first-century Christianity but for what it tells us about first-century Palestinian Judaism.

First, in Qumran's library, we find the reading material for a specific group and discover that many tendencies we had formerly thought incompatible or even opposed could comfortably find a home here in one tightly knit group. In addition to the texts of Torah the group diligently studied, there are remains of many apocalyptic works, some of which we knew before (*Jubilees*, 1 *Enoch*), as well as those produced by the community (such as the *War Scroll*, IQm). These we might have suspected. But there are also a number of scriptural commentaries done in several styles: halachic, haggadic, targumic (as in the *Genesis Apocryphon*); liturgical documents (the hymns and the prayers of blessing); and even fragments suggesting the practice of Merkabah mysticism. The Qumran library makes clear to us what we should already have suspected: there is not a one-to-one alignment of texts and communities. Given a coherent ideology of its own, a particular group can read and assimilate—in acccordance with its normative ideology—a variety of apparently divergent traditions.

Second, the Qumran writings have had an impact on scholarly presuppositions concerning cultural influence and doctrinal development in both Judaism and Christianity. There is first the matter of the degree of Hellenism in Palestine. Perhaps Josephus was not far wrong when he saw the Essenes as Jewish Pythagoreans. Certainly their practice of a total "community of goods" for the sake of purity bears far more resemblance to the practice of Greek philosophy than to anything in Torah. Similarly with some of the Qumran symbols: formerly the dualistic language of John's Gospel (truth/falsehood; light/darkness) was thought due to Hellenism, which meant a setting outside Palestine, which then implied a late dating. Since Qumran, such reasoning does not hold. Hellenistic influence there may be. But if so, it was available to the Fourth Gospel, as it was to Qumran, within Palestine during the first century. Similarly also with the question of community structure. Developmental theories of early Christianity were fond of attributing any organization or authority, especially if it was rationalized and self-conscious, to the passage of time and the waning of eschatological fervor and charismatic leadership. Qumran shows us a first-century Jewish community that had an elaborate and highly rationalized organization and authority structure, together with a strict legalism and a penal code, while it maintained an acute eschatological tension far more explicit and time-conscious than anything found in the NT. It should no longer be possible seriously to suggest that charism and order are incompatible, or that eschatology and legalism cannot coexist.

Third, and perhaps most significant, Qumran provides an early and striking analogy to the early Christian community. We find in the writings of the group an example of the same sort of dialectic between experience and interpretation that we find in the NT. Two aspects of this similarity are especially significant: (1) the community's consciousness of being opposed to mainstream Judaism, together with the conviction that it alone represents the authentic and eschatological Israel; and (2) its attempt to find the basis of that consciousness in an idiosyncratic interpretation of Torah.

The community is intensely conscious that it has separated itself from the rest of Judaism. It alone is holy, because it has separated itself from the "sons of the pit" (CD 6.14—7.6), to be part of the remnant God will save (CD 4.9–12). The community's ideology, in turn, appears to be rooted in its foundational experiences. This is of great importance. We find suggestions that in the past a concrete conflict with the "wicked priest" led to the despoiling of the property of the community members (IQpHab 8.8–12; 9.1–6; 12.9–12). There are only hints, but it seems that the historical experience was, in time, elaborated into a comprehensive and cosmic myth of the war between the children of light and the children of darkness.

More fascinating, this kind of experience provides the basis for the community's reading of Torah. We find it especially in the distinctive haggadic midrash called *pesher*, "interpretation." Torah is interpreted as applying directly and explicitly to the existence and calling of *this* group; it is what Torah is all about! It is a prophecy-fulfillment interpretation applied not to Israel as a whole but to this small group that sees itself as the authentic Israel. A good example is the *pesher* on Hab. 2:17. The passage from the prophet reads:

> For the violence done to Lebanon shall overwhelm you and the destruction of beasts shall terrify you because of the blood of men and the violence done to the land, the city, and all its inhabitants.

Then the interpretation (1QpHab 12.2–9):

> This saying concerns the wicked priest inasmuch as he shall be paid for the reward which he himself tendered to the poor. For *Lebanon* is the council of

the community; and the *beasts* are the simple of Judah who keep the law. . . . [I]nterpreted, the *city* is Jerusalem where the wicked priests committed abominable deeds and defiled the temple of God.

Like allegorical interpretation, *pesher* supplies a new code for the reading of the passage. But it is not one derived from ethics or cosmology. It comes from the *experience* of the group itself. Another example is the interpretation of a passage that will be important for Paul (Rom 1:17), namely Hab. 2:4b: "The righteous will live by his faith." How does Qumran understand this? According to 1QpHab 8.1–3,

this concerns all those who observe the Torah in the house of Judah, whom God will deliver from the house of judgment because of their suffering and because of their faith in the Teacher of Righteousness.

The sectarians read their own history in the texts of Torah, employing a method of exegesis that makes the *meaning* of the prophecies to be their fulfillment in the present events. The analogy to the practice of the first Christians is unmistakable and instructive.

In the writings of Qumran, then, as in apocalyptic literature and Rabbinic midrash and the prayers of Jewish worship, we see how particular experiences and convictions lead to specific interpretations of the symbolic world contained in Torah. The symbolic world is shared by all; the process of interpretation is everywhere. The cause for diversity must be sought in the generative nature of the experiences and convictions.

BIBLIOGRAPHICAL NOTE

In this chapter, I have written out the titles of Jewish primary sources whenever possible. For the Qumran writings this is too complex, so I have used the abbreviations found in the Society of Biblical Literature's *Member's Handbook*, 1980.

The translation of 4 Ezra is by G. H. Box in *Apocrypha and Pseudepigrapha of the Old Testament*, vol. 2, ed. R. H. Charles (Oxford: At the Clarendon Press, 1913), 579; that of the Mishnah from *The Mishnah*, trans. H. Danby (London: Oxford Univ. Press, 1933), 10–11, except for *Pirke Aboth*, which comes from R. Travers Herford, *The Ethics of the Talmud: Sayings of the Fathers* (New York: Schocken Books, 1962), 19, 66, 77. The Rabbi Eliezer citation comes from *The Fathers According to Rabbi Nathan*, trans. J. Goldin, Yale Judaica Series 10 (New Haven: Yale Univ. Press, 1955), 82. *Tractate Kutim* is translated by Michael Higger, as found in *Judaism: Postbiblical and Talmudic Period*, ed. S. W. Baron and J. L. Blau (Indianapolis: Bobbs-Merrill, 1954), 68–69. The translation of Babylonian Talmud, *Makkoth*, is by H. M. Lazarus in *The Babylonian Talmud*, ed. I. Epstein (London: Soncino Press, 1935), 30:169–73. The blessings are translated by D. Hedegård, *Seder Rav Amram Gaon*, part 1 (Lund: C. W. K. Gleerup, 1951). The selections from the Passover Haggadah are translated by J. Sloan in *The*

Passover Haggadah, rev. ed., ed. N. Glatzer (New York: Schocken Books, 1953), 49, 51. The selection from Targum *Pseudo-Jonathan* is translated by M. McNamara in *Targum and Testament* (Grand Rapids: Wm. B. Eerdmans, 1972), 140. The Habakkuk Pesher from Qumran is translated by G. Vermes in *The Dead Sea Scrolls in English*, 2d ed. (New York: Penguin Books, 1975), 242, 239.

Standard historical surveys of Judaism in Palestine are available in S. W. Baron, *A Social and Religious History of the Jews*, vols. 1 and 2 (New York: Columbia Univ. Press, 1952–80), and E. Schürer, *A History of the Jewish People in the Time of Jesus*, 2 vols., rev. ed., ed. G. Vermes and F. Millar (Edinburgh: T. & T. Clark, 1973–79). Of particular value is E. M. Smallwood, *The Jews Under Roman Rule from Pompey to Diocletian* (Leiden: E. J. Brill, 1976). The ever-growing scholarship devoted to the subject is indicated by two recent and continuing series, the first being CRINT, sect. 1: *The Jewish People in the First Century*, 2 vols., ed. S. Safrai and M. Stern (Philadelphia: Fortress Press; Assen: Van Gorcum, 1974–76); sect. 2, vol. 2: *Jewish Writings of the Second Temple Period*, ed. M. E. Stone (Philadelphia: Fortress Press; Assen: Van Gorcum, 1984); and the second being the Cambridge History of Judaism, vol. 1: *Introduction: The Persian Period*, ed. W. D. Davies and L. Finkelstein (Cambridge: At the Univ. Press, 1984). A condensed survey of the historical period is found in E. Bickerman, *From Ezra to the Last of the Maccabees* (New York: Schocken Books, 1949).

Special attention is given to the relation of Judaism to Hellenism in M. Hengel, *Judaism and Hellenism*, 2 vols., trans. J. Bowden (Philadelphia: Fortress Press, 1974), and J. Goldstein, "Jewish Acceptance and Rejection of Hellenism," in *Jewish and Christian Self-Definition: Aspects of Judaism in the Greco-Roman Period* (*JCS-D*), ed. E. P. Sanders, A. I. Baumgarten, and A. Mendelson (Philadelphia: Fortress Press, 1981), 2:64–87. See also the classic collection of essays in H. Fischel, ed., *Essays in Greco-Roman and Related Talmudic Literature* (New York: Ktav Pub. House, 1977). On the sects, see M. Simon, *Jewish Sects in the Time of Jesus*, trans. J. Farley (Philadelphia: Fortress Press, 1967); J. Neusner, *From Politics to Piety: The Emergence of Pharisaic Judaism* (Englewood Cliffs, N.J.: Prentice-Hall, 1973); idem, "History and Purity in First-Century Judaism, *History of Religion* 18 (1978–79): 1–17; R. A. Horsley, "The Sicarii: Ancient Jewish 'Terrorists,'" *JR* 59(1979): 435–58.

A great deal has been written in recent years on apocalyptic in every age. For this period, still serviceable is D. S. Russell, *The Method and Message of Jewish Apocalyptic* (Philadelphia: Westminster Press, 1964). More recent studies include P. D. Hanson, ed., *Visionaries and their Apocalypses*, IRT 2 (Philadelphia: Fortress Press; London: SPCK, 1983); M. E. Stone, "Apocalyptic Literature," CRINT 2.2 (1984): 383–441; and J. J. Collins, *The Apocalyptic Imagination* (New York: Crossroad, 1984). See also the collection *Apocalypticism in the Mediterranean World and the Near East*, ed. D. Hellholm (Tübingen: J. C. B. Mohr [Paul Siebeck], 1983). In contrast, little is available on Jewish worship: see, however, A. Z. Idelsohn, *Jewish Liturgy and Its Development* (New York: Schocken Books, 1932), and W. E. O. Oesterley, *Jewish Background of Christian Liturgy* (Gloucester, Mass.: Peter Smith, 1965 [1925]). On the synagogue, see J. Gutmann, *The Synagogue: Studies in Origins, Archeology, and Architecture* (New York: Ktav Pub. House,

1975); A. D. York, "The Targum in the Synagogue and in the School," *JSJ* 10 (1979): 74–86; and J. H. Charlesworth, "A Prolegomenon to a New Study of the Jewish Background of the Hymns and Prayers in the New Testament," *JJS* 33 (1982): 265–85. For messianism, somewhat dated but still available is J. Klausner, *The Messianic Idea in Israel*, 3d ed., trans. W. F. Stinespring (New York: Macmillan Co., 1955).

For an introduction to the rabbinic tradition, three older works are available and helpful: G. F. Moore, *Judaism in the First Centuries of the Christian Era*, 2 vols. (New York: Schocken Books, 1927); S. Schechter, *Aspects of Rabbinic Theology* (New York: Schocken Books, 1961); and H. L. Strack, *Introduction to the Talmud and Midrash* (New York: Atheneum, 1969 [1931]). Similar to Schechter but more recent is E. E. Urbach, *The Sages: Their Concepts and Beliefs*, 2 vols., trans. I. Abrahams (Jerusalem: Magnes Press, 1975). For a portrayal based on more recent scholarship, see J. Neusner, *Judaism in the Beginning of Christianity* (Philadelphia: Fortress Press, 1984), and idem, "The Fellowship (חבורה) in the Second Jewish Commonwealth," *HTR* 53 (1960): 125–42. Very helpful on the development of midrash is G. Vermes, *Scripture and Tradition in Judaism*, 2d rev. ed. (Leiden: E. J. Brill, 1973). For a selection of primary texts, in addition to Baron/Blau (above), there are C. Montefiore and H. Loewe, *A Rabbinic Anthology* (New York: Schocken Books, 1974), and G. W. E. Nickelsburg and M. E. Stone, *Faith and Piety in Early Judaism: Texts and Documents* (Philadelphia: Fortress Press, 1983).

On the Dead Sea scrolls from Qumran, there are the older but still helpful treatment of F. M. Cross, *The Ancient Library at Qumran and Modern Biblical Studies* (Garden City, N.Y.: Doubleday & Co., 1958), and the more recent works by J. A. Fitzmyer, *The Dead Sea Scrolls: Major Publications and Tools for Study*, Sources for Biblical Study 8 (Missoula, Mont.: Scholars Press, 1977); G. Vermes, *The Dead Sea Scrolls: Qumran in Perspective*, rev. ed. (Philadelphia: Fortress Press, 1977); and D. Dimant, "Qumran Sectarian Literature," CRINT 2.2 (1984): 483–550. The real pertinence of the Qumran writings to the understanding of Christian origins is perhaps most succinctly stated by N. A. Dahl, "Eschatology and History in the Light of the Dead Sea Scrolls," in *The Future of Our Religious Past*, ed. J. M. Robinson, trans. C. E. Carlston and R. P. Scharlemann (New York: Harper & Row, 1971), 9–28.

3

Diaspora Judaism

IN THE FIRST CENTURY, FAR MORE JEWS LIVED OUTSIDE PALESTINE THAN within, and the forms Judaism assumed in the Diaspora are of great importance for the understanding of the NT. The term "Diaspora Judaism," however, is not equivalent to "Hellenistic Judaism." In the first place, Hellenization was a significant part of Judaism in Palestine. The forms of Judaism in the Diaspora, moreover, were various and not necessarily "Hellenistic." After 200 C.E., the rabbinic tradition developed in the Diaspora and was centered in the Aramaic-speaking schools of Mesopotamia. The tendency to identify Diaspora and Hellenistic derives from the state of our sources. Most of the information about first-century Diaspora Judaism comes from Alexandria, and it was indeed Hellenistic, not only because it was written in Greek but because it appropriated Greek culture in distinctive ways. Not even this Hellenistic Judaism, however, is completely uniform; in addition to Philo, it produced the *Sibylline Oracles*, with their messianic and apocalyptic overtones.

If Hellenistic and Diaspora are not interchangeable, what value is there to distinguishing Palestinian and Diaspora Judaism? The distinction recognizes that the development of Jewish life and symbols was directly influenced by social and political contexts. Diaspora Judaism was not constantly forced to equate religious and political symbols. The perennial problem facing all Jews, the tension between assimilation and separation, was worked out in a setting less colored by religious persecution and political oppression. No matter how strongly they protested their love for the land, those living away from Palestine could deal with pluralism in a way not granted to those for whom land and religion were much the same.

This sketch of some aspects of Diaspora Judaism, therefore, is deliberately selective. It leaves aside the East, for which we have only later sources, in favor of the West, for which we have extensive contemporary sources. The best reason for this is that Christianity developed westward, encountered first the Greek forms of Diaspora Judaism, and was most deeply and permanently marked by them.

EXTENT AND IMPORTANCE OF
DIASPORA JUDAISM

The Diaspora did not involve small numbers, was not a recent phenomenon, and was not always a result of exile. Already in the days of David
and Solomon, Jews went abroad to serve in military garrisons (2 Sam 8:6)
or for trade (1 Kings 5:14; 9:26–28; 10:15, 22). The great exiles of
722 B.C.E. and 586 B.C.E., of course, involved the deportation of many
Jews to Assyria and Babylon and also caused some to migrate to Egypt
(Jer. 43:6–7). The majority of those who went into exile did not return to
the land. As a consequence, by the first century the Diaspora was the
natural, accepted, and centuries-old context for the transmission of Jewish
identity for the majority of Jews in the world.

In Mesopotamia, the Jewish population was so large and well organized
that it became the new center for Jewish scholarship and remained so into
the medieval period. Syria had very large numbers of Jews especially in the
cities of Damascus and Antioch (JW VII.4.3; cf. also Acts 9:1, 20). Cyrene
in North Africa had been settled with Jews during the time of Ptolemy I
(Ant XIV.7.2), and was cultured enough to produce the multivolumed
history of the Maccabees by Jason (2 Macc. 2:23) and strong enough to be
at least temporarily successful in the revolt of 115–17 C.E. Two thousand
Jewish families were transported from Babylon to Asia Minor at the end of
the third century B.C.E. and formed the basis of an extensive Jewish life
there (Ant XII.3.4; Acts 13:14; 14:1, 6, 24–25; 16:1). Achaia and Macedonia had synagogues in most important urban centers by the first
century (see Philo Embassy to Gaius 281–82; Acts 16:13; 17:1, 10, 17;
18:4), and there was a Jewish community at Rome (Acts 28:17–24).

The Jewish population in Egypt goes back to the sixth century B.C.E.,
and was repeatedly enriched by emigration from Palestine. Philo says there
were a million Jews in Egypt (Against Flaccus 43). During the Maccabean
period, opponents of the Jerusalem priests erected a competing temple at
Hierapolis (Ant XIII.3.1–3), and even earlier, there was an Aramaic-
speaking military colony of Jews at Elephantine. Most Egyptian Jews lived
in Alexandria, from which comes our richest literary evidence. Since
Alexandria was the intellectual capital of the Hellenistic world, with its
great library and museum, it is not surprising that these writings reveal a
lively and positive engagement with Hellenistic thought. In Alexandria,
above all, we find distinctively Greek culture entering into creative
dialogue with Jewish.

Demographic figures for the ancient world are hard to establish, but by
some estimates there were seven million Jews in the first century; of these,
two million were in Palestine, five million in the Diaspora. More important
than the specific number is the proportion. The Jews were visible enough

in the Diaspora to be noticed, for good and ill. In the eastern empire, they may have constituted as much as fifteen percent of the population, and their visibility would have been heightened by their close community life. Josephus quotes the Greek historian Strabo (late 1st cent. B.C.E.):

> The Jewish people had already come into every city, and one cannot readily find any place in the world which has not received this tribe and been taken possession of by it. (*Ant* XIV.7.2; cf. *Embassy* 281–82)

This great overflow of Jews into the wider world was not regarded by its participants as a great tragedy or a circumstance that prevented their singing a song to the Lord in a foreign land (Ps. 137:4). At least since the second century B.C.E., Palestine was overcrowded (*Flaccus* 45–46), and most Jews were glad to be where they were. They filled a variety of social roles. Some were mercenary soldiers (as the Elephantine colony), others farmers, still others craftsmen and traders, ranging from simple peddlers to entrepreneurs. Some Jews enjoyed both wealth and civic importance. Such was the case with the family of Philo. His younger brother Alexander was an Alabarch (*Ant* XVIII.8.1) and he himself led a delegation that was received by the emperor Caligula. Jews in the Diaspora are found at every level of society.

The direct and considerable importance of Diaspora Judaism to Christianity can be summed up in one word: synagogue. In Acts 15:21, James says,

> For from early generations, Moses had in every city those who preach him, for he is read every Sabbath in the synagogues.

Wherever Jews migrated, they took with them the synagogue. In the first century, a vast and intricate network of synagogues, often "houses of prayer" in the Diaspora, covered the Mediterranean world. The synagogues were the center for the maintenance of Jewish identity (*Flaccus* 48), as well as the stepping stone from which Christianity moved into the gentile world. Christianity inherited a long tradition of preaching and teaching and worship carried out in the midst of Greek culture (*Embassy* 312). In the synagogue was read the Septuagint (i.e., Greek) version of Torah. It was the text studied by Jewish scholars (Josephus *Against Apion* II.175). The Septuagint (the Greek OT) was the Bible of the Greek Diaspora, and of the first Christians. It was also the primary symbolic framework for the development of the specifically Christian self-understanding.

The synagogue prepared for Christian evangelization by spreading through the gentile world an awareness of the peculiar and exclusive Jewish monotheism, the high moral code of Torah, and the attractive claim to be God's people. Among those Gentiles first attracted to the synagogue

(*Apion* II.282–86), Christian preachers found their first missionary successes in the Diaspora (Acts 13:42–44, 48, 14:1; 17:4). Most of all, Diaspora Judaism provided an example of the problems and possibilities facing a minority group that sought to maintain its identity in a highly pluralistic environment.

No less than Jews in Palestine did those in the Diaspora look to the texts of Torah for the symbolic expression of their identity. Their understanding of the symbols, however, was shaped by their experience of reading them within a very different sort of world. Jews of the Diaspora were immeasurably freer with regard to Hellenistic culture. They were not so steadily required to choose between God and king. In the first century, there were sporadic and sometimes violent repressive measures taken against the Jews by emperors or local rulers (*Flaccus* 58–95; *Ant* VII.3.2–4), but these seem to have been the exception and a rather recent innovation. Before the first century C.E., Jews of the Diaspora were given the right to be an autonomous group within the city-state (*polis*) of their residence and to live according to their ancestral customs.

The exact legal status of Jews in the empire is difficult to determine. Many individual Jews enjoyed full citizenship (*Flaccus* 53; *Embassy* 349), and Jews as a group seemed to fall into the category of a *politeuma*, that is, a group of aliens of the same ethnic origin who were allowed to follow their own customs and worship their own gods (see *Apion* II.35–47). In Alexandria, Jews were apparently governed by a body of elders (*gerousia*), which functioned as a court for settling disputes (*Ant* XIV.7.2). Since physical proximity made the observance of Torah easier, Jews tended to live close together (*Flaccus* 55), though this was not required; there was no first-century ghetto.

Not only did Jews enjoy freedom, they seem to have been rather significantly privileged. It appears, for example, that Jews were exempt from the obligation to observe syncretistic worship such as would be required of other members of the *polis*. There is no firm documentary evidence for this, but the outrage expressed when the usage was in danger of being suspended suggests that it was a privilege of some consistency and antiquity (*Flaccus* 47; *Embassy* 117, 134; *Apion* II.71–72). The Jews were allowed to meet regularly in their synagogues (*Embassy* 312). They could take a day off work for the Sabbath observance (*Embassy* 156). Jews were exempt from military duty (since it inevitably involved marching under the images of gods), although many of them served voluntarily (*Apion* I.200–204). Most remarkably, the empire recognized the yearly temple tax paid by Jews from around the world to Jerusalem as a sacred fund and protected its transportation to Jerusalem (*Embassy* 216, 313). In short, Diaspora Jews had remarkable freedom to follow Torah and shape their identity by its symbols. The preservation of that identity was complicated, however, by the fact of their being a minority in a pluralistic culture.

THE RELIGIOUS AND CULTURAL
TENSIONS OF DIASPORA LIFE

Like all intentional communities, first-century Judaism in the Diaspora was pulled between opposing attractions. On one side was the powerful appeal of the dominant culture, which invited assimilation. On the other side was the call of the ancestral ways, which demanded that the Jews stay separate. Every community, and every individual Jew, resolved the tension differently, and each resolution involved some conflict.

Assimilation into the dominant cultural context is as natural and understandable as the need for animal warmth. Societies demand a high price from those who would be deviant, either as individuals or groups. It is extraordinarily difficult to be, and to appear to be, different. Assimilation to Greek culture began with the use of a Greek name. Sometimes, this was simply a Greek "public" form of a Hebrew name, such as Paul for Saul (Acts 13:9). Other times, fully Greek names were adopted, as we see with Jason in 2 Macc. 4:7, and with Stephen, Philip, and the other "Hellenists" in Acts 6:5, who had thoroughly Greek names though they were Jewish.

Changing names represented a level of acceptance of the dominant language of the culture. By the first century, most Jews in the Diaspora did not know Hebrew, and had spoken nothing but Greek for generations. For them, Greek was not a foreign tongue, it was their native language. So ancient was this situation that the Septuagint translation (LXX) of Torah was already some two hundred years old by the time of Philo (see *Life of Moses* II.25–40).

Translation of Torah into Greek meant a massive if subtle transformation of symbols. Every translation is an interpretation. Even when the LXX sought to be scrupulously literal in its rendering, something was both lost and gained in the transition from Hebrew forms to Greek ones, for the syntax of the two languages is sufficiently different to give a distinctive structuring even to narratives. Even at the level of individual words, the process of losing some resonances and gaining others is clear. The word "glory" lost some of the sense of "weight" and "presence" that was rooted in the Hebrew, but gained some further sense of "appearance" and "radiance" from other Greek usages. The Greek word *nomos* "law," had a different set of associations and implications than did the Hebrew word *torah*. Losses and gains alike would be imperceptible to Greek-speaking Jews, for they lacked any standard of comparison. The Diaspora Jew who read in the Septuagint of Isa. 7:14 that a *parthenos* would bear a son, would never question whether that was a virgin. The text said it, and the text of the Septuagint was Scripture. In places, moreover, where the LXX itself was much freer in translation, it became something of a Greek Targum, but one unperceived as such by those who heard it in the synagogue.

Another social structure that worked in behalf of assimilation was education. A Jew like Philo, growing up in Alexandria, would regard a fully Greek education as completely normal, certainly not contrary to Torah. In fact, Torah itself expressed Greek wisdom (*sophia*), especially in writings like the Wisdom of Solomon. Study or exercise in the gymnasium did not represent a break with ancestral ways as it did in Palestine (cf. 2 Macc. 4:10–17). The study of Greek poetry and philosophy was not incompatible with the study of Torah, and in Torah itself was found sufficient corrective to the negative side of Greek literature, its associations with idolatry.

In such a context, the synthesis of Jewish and Greek symbols was inevitable and as unconscious and natural as breathing. It would be impossible for Philo, growing up where and when he did (d. ca. 50 c.e.), to look at the heroes of faith in Torah and *not* see them as models of the philosophical life. It was impossible for him, when confronted with the difficulties presented by the literal meaning of Torah, *not* to use for their resolution the allegorical method he had learned in his reading of the Homeric poems and in commentaries on them.

The opposite pole of attraction was separation. However Hellenized Jews became, they remained a distinct and identifiable presence among the pagans. To a remarkable degree, they maintained active contacts with Palestine. They paid the yearly temple tax and went up to Jerusalem when possible for the pilgrimage feasts; the city was filled with Jews from the Diaspora at those times (Acts 2:5–11). They followed the political fortunes of the homeland with lively interest (*Embassy* 188) and were an eager market for Jewish propaganda like the histories of Jason and Josephus.

Their allegiance to Torah as the ultimate and satisfying norm for their lives was what truly separated them from their pagan neighbors, for that allegiance implied certain convictions and demanded certain responses that were alien to Hellenistic culture as a whole. Diaspora Jews might find beauty in Homer, but true wisdom could be found only in Moses; they could read about utopia in Plato but could find the frame for a priestly people only in Torah. Torah they heard read in the synagogue, and Torah provided the words for their prayers. Because of Torah, they kept the Sabbath day holy and observed the other feasts (*Flaccus* 117) even when societal pressure made it difficult. Because of Torah, they observed special dietary practices and practiced circumcision (*Embassy* 361) even when such practices were regarded as barbarous by their neighbors. Because they shared the same symbolic world of Torah, Diaspora Jews maintained close ties with Palestinian Jews, even sending to the temple archives announcements of marriages (*Apion* I.32–36), although such connections might make them suspect at home. Perhaps even more emphatically than Jews in Palestine, those in the Diaspora remained a part of the people because of their intense and exclusive allegiance to Torah (*Apion* II.232–35).

No other cult was so exclusive in its claims; no school of philosophy was so inclusive in its demands. The distinctiveness of Diaspora Jews generated among their gentile neighbors a very mixed response. One side of the response was positive, especially among rulers and the better-educated. Sophisticated Greeks were fascinated by "barbarians" generally, and the Chaldeans ranked with the Egyptians as objects of interest. Philosophers saw Judaism as an ancient and praiseworthy form of wisdom. And the strong community ties of the Jews undoubtedly attracted many proselytes and God fearers from among the pagans (*Apion* II.179–96). Judaism in the first century was an aggressive and growing phenomenon.

Among those threatened by Jewish claims, such as the priests of other cults, and among those less sophisticated in their tastes, the Jews were, however, a constant irritant because of their difference. Popular resentment could easily turn to hostile actions (*Embassy* 120–26; *Apion* II.32). The official privileges enjoyed by the Jews seemed to have been particularly offensive to some. They saw that the Jews took from the *polis* but did not give to it. They were exempt from worshiping the civic gods on whose protection the safety of the city depended (*Apion* II.65). Indeed, the monies that should have been given in support of the public service (*leiturgeia*) of the city were sent to a foreign temple. The Jews had the privileges of Hellenistic culture but not the responsibilities. Even the regular Sabbath observance could prove disruptive for the economy in a world that did not have weekends. The mix of imperial privilege and local resentment was a volatile one, and Jews could be charged with the refusal to mingle with others (*amixia*) and hatred of mankind (*misanthropia*) by those who viewed their separateness as a scandal.

Anti-Semitism as an explicit and articulate response to Judaism seems to have originated in Alexandria, in the time of Ptolemy II. An Egyptian priest named Manetho wrote a history of Egypt, in which the Jews played an inglorious role (*Apion* I.227–250). The account was filled with scurrilous suggestions concerning both Moses and the Jews (I.249), and it began the long and drearily repetitive history of hatred. The charges were already familiar by the first century: Jews were really atheists, for they did not worship the gods, and their own was invisible. Or perhaps it was really the worship of an ass's head (*Apion* II.80); perhaps Gentiles were captured by Jews to be killed and cannibalized (II.92–96). All the customs of the Jews were fair game for mockery and innuendo (*Apion* II.137–42). The most persistent charge, however, reveals the genuine source of irritation: misanthropy (*Apion* II.121–24, 291). In a pluralistic world, a group that kept to itself and claimed exclusive possession of the truth was bound to be resented by some. Similar charges of misanthropy and failure to mix were made, in fact, against the other two groups who most combined dogmatic claims and strong community ties: the Epicureans and the Christians.

THE RESPONSE OF JEWISH APOLOGETIC

A minority group under attack for its distinctiveness can react in three ways. It can intensify the efforts to assimilate and become indistinguishable from its critics; it can intensify its separatist qualities and cultivate an insider-against-outsider mentality; or it can seek to defend and explain its way of life to others. This last is the way of *apologetic*. Of the three, it is surely the noblest: less craven than the panic to assimilate and less defensive than the utter refusal to communicate. In broadest terms, nearly all the flood of writing from Alexandrian Judaism can be called apologetic, in the sense that it attempted to demonstrate the beauty of the distinctive way of Torah to those who shared the same language but worshiped different gods.

Jewish apologetic literature helps us understand early Christian writings by its choice of topics and the marshaling of its arguments, but most of all by the very nature of the enterprise. Apologetic makes a statement about the group's view of outsiders; it presumes a world of good will and openness to rational argument. The writing of apologetic may have been the greatest oblique compliment paid by Jews and Christians to that corrupt pagan world. Something is also said about insiders: they are people open to the wider world, eager to bridge the misunderstandings separating them from others and confident that their shared culture will enable such bridge building.

Ostensibly addressed to outsiders for purposes of persuasion, apologetic is in reality aimed as much at insiders, for purposes of pride. The attempt to make ourselves intelligible to others helps make us intelligible to ourselves. Apologetic strengthens community identity even as it seeks to communicate it. In the process, however, the community's symbols themselves become transformed. To make our position clear to outsiders, we must use language and symbols familiar to them; our aim is greater understanding and tolerance, not less. Inevitably, we color our self-portrait in shades familiar and acceptable. Continuity and commonality are stressed more than dissension and distinction.

To a large extent, then, the categories of the discussion are provided by the outsiders. For Alexandrian Jews, that meant the categories of Greek wisdom. In apologetic literature, therefore, Judaism appears as another, though infinitely superior, form of Greek philosophy. The most obvious example is the description of Palestinian Jewish sects by Josephus (*JW* II.8.2). He calls them schools of philosophy and aligns their teachings with those of the Stoics, Epicureans, and Pythagoreans. By so doing, he not only made them intelligible to Greek readers, but also reinterpreted them for his fellow Jews, causing them to see themselves as philosophers. Torah *was* a form of wisdom, was it not?

In the Wisdom of Solomon (1st cent. B.C.E.), the ancient wisdom tradition of the Jews is cast in a distinctively Hellenistic mold. Not only does language about vice and virtue abound and the concept of immortality assume an important role, but the whole history of Israel from creation to the wilderness (chapters 10—19) is told as the work of a personified Wisdom (*Sophia*), which, according to 7:25–26, is

> a breath of the power of God, and a pure emanation of the glory of the almighty ... a reflection of eternal light, a spotless mirror of the working of God and an image of his goodness.

In the middle of the account of the exodus, the author makes an extended attack on idolatry (chaps. 13—16), saying that "all men who were ignorant of God were foolish by nature" (13:1). Such attacks were of course standard fare in the Prophets (cf. Is. 44:9–20), but in Wisdom, we find a sympathy for the plight of the pagan that the prophets never had (13:5–7):

> ... for from the greatness and beauty of created things comes a corresponding perception of their creator. Yet perhaps these men are little to be blamed, for perhaps they go astray while seeking God and desiring to find him. For as they live among his works, they keep searching, and they trust in what they see, because the things that are seen are beautiful.

In a wonderfully succinct fashion, these few lines show how thoroughly Jewish convictions are wedded to profoundly Hellenistic perceptions.

Certain themes recur frequently in Hellenistic Jewish apologetic literature. In a culture where old was better than new, and East better than West, the antiquity and oriental roots of Judaism were attractive features and were therefore stressed. The purity and beauty of the synagogue worship was favorably contrasted to pagan cults. And to counter the charge of misanthropy, the laws of Torah were shown to be philanthropic.

The theme of antiquity could in its crudest form become a kind of cultural one-upmanship. The claim that one tradition was older than another, if proved, carried considerable weight, especially when combined with a first-century version of cultural diffusion (*Apion* I.7–8). In some texts, it is suggested that Moses was not only older than the Greek gods but was the founder of Greek culture (*Apion* II.168). Josephus claims that Pythagoras learned from Moses (*Apion* I.165) and that all the philosophers borrowed from Hebrew wisdom (*Apion* II.281). Nowhere is this claim

made in more startling fashion than in fragment 3 of the Alexandrian
Artapanus (mid-2d cent. B.C.E.):

> Moreover this Moses became the teacher of Orpheus. On reaching manhood,
> he made many useful contributions to mankind; and in fact he invented
> ships, machines for laying stones, Egyptian weapons, implements for draw-
> ing water, implements for fighting, and the study of Philosophy. He also
> divided the state into thirty-six Nomes, and assigned which god was to be
> worshipped in each. He also assigned the sacred books to the priests.

In addition to the antiquity of Moses and his being the source of Greek
philosophy (not to mention Egyptian idolatry!), the usefulness and philan-
thropy of his inventions are stressed. The theme of antiquity is constantly
stressed by Josephus (his history of the Jews was not accidentally named
Antiquities). In *Ant* I.16, he says of his main source, Moses the author of
the Pentateuch,

> he was born two thousand years ago, to which ancient date the poets never
> ventured to refer even the birth of their gods, much less the actions or laws of
> mortals.

Lest we think such cultural competition was found only in the Diaspora,
there is this fragment from a mid-second-century B.C.E. Palestinian Jew,
Eupolemus (frag. 1):

> Moses became the first wise man and was the first to pass along the alphabet
> to the Jews. And the Phoenicians received it from the Jews, and the Greeks
> received it from the Phoenicians. And Moses was the first to write laws for the
> Jews.

As these passages make clear, Moses is a central figure for Jewish
apologetic. And in the descriptions of Moses, we find the transformation
of the biblical figure into one shaped by Hellenistic perceptions. What
happened to Heracles in Stoic-Cynic philosophy (and in Philo; cf. *Embassy*
81, 90) happens to Moses in Hellenistic Jewish apologetic: the hero of the
past is perceived through the symbols of present experience and conviction. Moses comes to resemble the philosopher-king.

Already in Plato's *Republic* (473D, 540D–E), the ideal ruler was seen as
both philosopher and king. He could rule wisely because he himself was a
wise man (*sophos*), one who personified virtue. In the treatises on kingship
in the Hellenistic period, the same theme is found (Dio *Oration* 1.34–35;
2.26; 4.78–139). And we find it once again in the Hellenistic Jewish *Letter
of Aristeas*. This purports to tell the story of the translation of the Septuagint, but is also a piece of Jewish propaganda. It appropriates the
symposium motif from Plato: the king invites the seventy-two Jewish
translators to a banquet (181) and during its long duration poses questions
to them (187–293) concerning virtue. Their answers, predictably, astound

the king and show the superiority of Jewish wisdom: "They were far superior to them [the Greek philosophers] both in conduct and in argument since they always made God their starting point" (235). Many of the questions posed by the king have to do with the qualities of kingship and good statecraft (211, 222, 265, 271, 279). The scholars respond with typical observations concerning the king's virtues, with this addition: what characterizes the true *sophos* is the fear of God and the keeping of his commandments. In this writing, there is the use of a thoroughly Hellenistic literary genre and philosophical topic (*topos*), and both are put to the service of Jewish ethical teaching. It is within this context that the thought of Moses as the perfect philosopher-king begins to make sense, for he surely was a leader of the people and revealed his wisdom in Torah. Moses was the model of the wise ruler before Plato ever thought of it. Thus, when Josephus describes the death of Moses, he does so in these terms, in *Ant* IV.8.49:

> He lived in all one hundred and twenty years ... having surpassed in understanding all men that ever lived and put to noblest use the fruit of his reflections. In speech and in addresses to a crowd he found favor in every way, but chiefly through his thorough command of his passions, which was such that he seemed to have no place for them at all in his soul, and only knew their names through seeing them in others rather than in himself. As a general he had few to equal him, and as prophet none, insomuch that in all his utterances one seemed to hear the speech of God himself.

Except for the mention of Moses as a prophet, Josephus has described the *sophos* skilled in rhetoric, learned, controlled, virtuous in legislation, a leader in battle. Such a perception was not unique to Josephus. In his *Life of Moses*, Philo shows the ways Moses fills perfectly the office of lawgiver (II.8–65), high priest (II.66–186), and prophet (II.187–291). All of these are biblical categories. But Philo introduces all of them by the consideration of Moses as king (*Moses* I.148):

> The appointed leader of all these was Moses, invested with his office and kingship, not like some of those who thrust themselves into positions of power by means of arms and engines of war and strength of infantry, cavalry and navy, but on account of his goodness and his nobility of conduct and the universal benevolence which he never failed to show. Further, his office was bestowed upon him by God, the lover of virtue and nobility, as the reward due to him.

In Philo, not only Moses but all the patriarchs are transformed into *sophoi* each of whom in his fashion embodies some aspect of virtue and wisdom. Moses, however, was the embodiment of all virtue and a model for others to follow, both in his legislation and in his life (*Moses* I.158):

> For he was called God and King of the whole race. And he is said to have

'entered into the darkness where God was' (Ex 20:21), that is, into the unseen and invisible substance which is the immaterial model of all things, and to have apprehended things never revealed to mortal nature. And he put himself and his life forward into the middle like a well-executed sketch, thus setting forth an extremely beautiful and divinely formed object as a model for those who wish to copy it. And happy are those who have stamped this image upon their own souls, or have even tried to do so.

It would be a mistake to think of Josephus, Philo, and the other Hellenistic Jewish writers as engaging in a deliberate distortion of the biblical witness in order to win friends for the Jews. Nowhere is such a motivation suggested. Indeed, Josephus tells us he is the soberest of historians, neither deleting nor embellishing (*Ant* I.17). What then is at work? Simply the transformation of the symbols of Torah, accomplished in what was in all likelihood an unconscious and intuitive process of translating Torah into terms not only the writers' readers but also they themselves best understood. When Josephus and Philo describe the patriarchs as *sophoi*, they are only telling us what they see in the text. Such descriptions, in fact, show us how far assimilated into Greek culture even these staunch defenders of Judaism were.

PHILO OF ALEXANDRIA

Philo of Alexandria (d. ca 50 C.E.) is, next to Paul, the most visible and ambiguous figure in first-century Diaspora Judaism. The difficulty in assessing his importance is connected to the state of our sources. Philo was well loved by the early Christian writers, and they preserved much of this voluminous writer's work. With the possible exception of Josephus, he remains the only fully rounded figure of his time and faith. Consequently, we do not know whether he should be regarded as a unique case or as a representative figure. There is evidence that much of what we find in Philo is paralleled in other places but that he combined elements in a manner distinctive to himself.

Philo's importance for the understanding of the NT does not lie in the way some of his concepts seem to anticipate those found in the early Christian writings, as striking as those sometimes are: the notion of the *Logos* "Word" as intermediary between God and humans, for example (see, e.g., *Who Is the Heir?* 205–6; cf. John 1:1–2; Heb. 1:1–3), and the idea that the demands of Torah can be embodied even by those who have not received the law of Moses (*On Abraham;* cf. Rom. 2:12–16). Nor is his significance to be found in the way ideas similar to his appear to be presupposed by NT arguments (see 1 Cor. 15:45–50; Heb. 7:4–9). As impressive as those connections sometimes are, they remain isolated threads of similarity in greatly dissimilar fabrics.

The greatest significance of Philo for the study of the NT is analogous to the importance of Qumran. Much as the Qumran community showed us how diverse traditions could coexist in a single setting, Philo shows how the mind and heart of a single Diaspora Jew could bring together many diverse traditions and viewpoints and forge them into a single coherent vision. Knowing how Philo could be so many things at once helps us understand how another multifaceted Diaspora Jew, Saul of Tarsus, could also contain within himself seemingly contradictory elements. And seeing how the communal heritage and personal experience of Philo could issue in a distinctive reinterpretation of Torah helps us grasp how the author of the Letter to the Hebrews could combine a similar heritage and quite a different religious experience, and derive a hauntingly similar yet clearly divergent reinterpretation of Torah.

Philo was totally at home within Greek culture. He knew little if any Hebrew and read Torah in the Septuagint (LXX) translation. He could quote Homer as easily as Torah and sometimes quoted them side by side (*On Dreams* 152–62). He was well acquainted with the sort of allegorical interpretations that had been applied to Homer (*Embassy* 93–113; *On the Decalogue* 54). He was not a systematic thinker, though he was conversant with philosophical opinions and used them in a typically eclectic fashion. He shared with the Pythagoreans a fascination with numbers and was always delighted when Torah provided him the opportunity to expound their deeper sense (*Decalogue* 20–31). Platonism had an obvious influence on him. When in Genesis (1:26–27; 2:7) he confronted two accounts of the creation of man, for example, he suggested that the first creation was of the heavenly prototype, which was androgynous. Only in the material creation do we find division into sexes (see *Allegorical Interpretation* I.31; *Questions on Genesis* I.4). Likewise, the LXX rendering of Exod. 25:40, where God tells Moses to make a tabernacle "according to the image of them" shown on the mountain, is exploited by Philo in thoroughly Platonic fashion, as it also was by the author of Heb. 8:5 (cf. *Questions on Exodus* 82; *Allegorical Interpretation* III.102).

It is in his interpretation of Torah that Philo's Hellenistic culture is most evident. Just as the Stoics used allegory to deal with the difficulties presented by Homeric poems, Philo used allegorical interpretation to show the deeper meaning of Torah. The literal meaning of the text remains important to him but sometimes presents insuperable difficulties: contradictions, impossibilities, scandals. The true meaning of Torah must be found at the level of the Spirit that guided Moses in its composition, that is, in a spiritual interpretation. This means, in effect, by means of an allegorical reading. In *On the Posterity and Exile of Cain* 1–11, Philo in commenting on Gen. 4:6 ("And Cain went out from the face of God. . . .") begins,

> Let us here raise the question whether in the books in which Moses acts as God's interpreter we ought to take his words figuratively, since the impression made by the words in their literal sense is greatly at variance with the truth. For if the Existent Being has a face . . . what ground have we for rejecting the impious doctrines of Epicurus, or the atheism of the Egyptians or the mythical plots of play and poem of which the world is full? . . . [T]he only thing left for us to do is make up our minds that none of the propositions put forward is literally intended and to take the path of figurative interpretation so dear to philosophic souls. . . .

Philo is perfectly capable of a literal interpretation, and in many of his writings (e.g., in the *Life of Moses*) he carefully expounds the literal narrative. But he is never far from the allegorical interpretation. As with his predecessors in this approach, he made much of etymologies; thus, in *On Joseph* 28 he writes:

> After the literal exposition, we can pass to the examination of the figurative sense, for all, or nearly all of the texts of the exposition of the Law, have an allegorical meaning. The Hebrews thus name the character we are here studying "Joseph", and the Greeks "addition of a Lord"; a happy choice, and altogether appropriate to the thing signified, for . . .

Philo does not have a consistent framework for his allegorical interpretations, but one aspect of his interpretive task demands attention, and that is its mystical connotations. Philo suggests that he himself was a mystic. When speaking of the creation of humanity, and the way in which the mind is the true image of God, he moves into a near rhapsodic passage, which seems clearly to be autobiographical. In *On the Creation* 71, he says that the mind at times

> is seized by a sober intoxication, like those filled with Corybantic frenzy, and is inspired, filled with a longing far other than theirs and a nobler desire. Wafted by this to the topnotch ark of the things perceptible to the mind, it seems to be on the way to the great King himself; but amid its longing to see him, pure and untempered rays of concentrated light stream forth like a torrent, so that by its gleams the eye of understanding is dazzled.

There is, furthermore, a connection between his mystical experiences and his reading of Torah. For Philo, it appears that Torah itself contains the possibility of leading the soul into these deeper perceptions of the divine reality. He is capable of speaking of it in terms suggestive of a mystery religion, as in *On the Cherubim* 48:

> I myself was initiated under Moses the God-Beloved into his greater mysteries, yet when I saw the prophet Jeremiah and knew him to be not only himself enlightened but a worthy minister of the holy secrets, I was not slow to become his disciple.

It is extraordinarily difficult to know how to evaluate such statements—

whether they are part of an elaborate literary conceit or whether they point to a form of esoteric Jewish mysticism that read the same Torah as the uninitiated, but read it with different eyes. Certainly, there were mystics in first-century Judaism such as the practitioners of Merkabah mysticism among the Pharisees; and when Philo speaks of being "on the way to the great King himself" he is using language strongly reminiscent of that used of the heavenly throne chariot.

What is clear is that his personal experience did not draw him away from Judaism. He was a leader of the Jewish community in Alexandria, and represented it in a time of crisis before the emperor Caligula (*Embassy* 178–83; cf. Josephus *Ant* XVIII.8.1). When the Alexandrian community was threatened, he responded with the polemical tractate *Against Flaccus*. A great deal of his writing was intended to interpret Judaism for the sympathetic outsider. Philo had no use for those who abandoned the observance of Torah and he abhorred idolatry. He never suggests that the literal fulfillment of the commandments was unnecessary (*Embassy* 211–12; *On the Migration of Abraham* 89–93; cf. Josephus *Apion* I.42–43).

As a mystic, however, the surface meaning of the text could never be enough. For Philo, genuine religion had to do with the contemplative experience. He shows great admiration for the Essenes (*Hypothetica* 11.1–18) and, if he had not been needed by the community in an active role, might well have joined their Egyptian counterparts, the Therapeutae (*On the Contemplative Life* 14–18). Instead, he allegorizes the text of Torah, so that it reveals, beneath its literal stories, a shimmering world of symbols pointing to mystical realities. Indeed, he may well have regarded his interpretation as a religious service. He says, for instance, in *On the Special Laws* III.6:

> Yet it is well for me to give thanks to God even for this, that though submerged I am not sucked down into the depths, but can also open the soul's eyes, which in my despair of comforting hope I thought had now lost their sight, and am irradiated by the light of wisdom, and am not given over to lifelong darkness. So behold me daring, not only to read the sacred messages of Moses, but also in my love of knowledge to peer into each of them and unfold and reveal what is not known to the multitude.

Philo's reading of Torah was shaped by his cultural heritage as a Hellenistic Jew and by his personal experience as a mystic. In his writings, we find as serious attention to the text of Torah as in any Palestinian midrash. His life is as defined by the symbols of Torah as was that of any Pharisee. Yet his understanding of Torah is very different. In Philo we find nothing of the apocalyptic or the casuistic; we find no expectation of a messiah, nothing of martyrdom; we find, instead of resurrection, immortality of the soul;

and righteousness in him looks very much like virtue. One wonders, in fact, if Hillel and Philo would really have understood each other.

CONCLUSION

We have seen how the normative symbols of the first century were being transformed by the experiences and convictions of those to whom they mattered. We have paid special attention to the ways in which Jews who shared the same texts and symbols in Torah, could derive such diverse understandings of them. The same symbolic world, the same process of seeking to understand those texts and thereby to understand their life—yet in each case, the differences have derived from the specific nature of the experience and the convictions to which it gave birth. The same symbolic world of Torah was shared by those who wrote the NT. To understand their distinctive reshaping of those symbols, it is necessary to learn what we can of the experience they had and the convictions to which they committed themselves.

BIBLIOGRAPHICAL NOTE

The translations from Greek sources in this chapter are from the Loeb Classical Library except for the citation from *Aristeas*, by H. T. Andrews in *Apocrypha and Pseudepigrapha of the Old Testament*, ed. R. H. Charles (Oxford: Clarendon Press, 1913) 2:115.

For historical surveys of the Diaspora, see S. Baron, *A Social and Religious History of the Jews*, vols. 1 and 2, 2d rev. ed. (New York: Columbia Univ. Press, 1952–80); E. M. Smallwood, *The Jews Under Roman Rule from Pompey to Diocletian* (Leiden: E. J. Brill, 1976), 121–43, 220–55; and above all, V. Tcherikover, *Hellenistic Civilization and the Jews*, trans. S. Appelbaum (New York: Atheneum, 1970). For the variety of literature produced by so-called Hellenistic Judaism, see the succinct and helpful articles in CRINT 2.2 (1984) by G. W. E. Nickelsburg, "Stories of Biblical and Early Post-Biblical Times," 33–87, and "The Bible Rewritten and Expanded," 89–156. See also in CRINT 2.2, J. J. Collins, "The Sibylline Oracles," 357–82; and M. Gilbert, "Wisdom Literature," 283–324. A good sense of the atmosphere is given by C. H. Dodd, *The Bible and the Greeks* (London: Hodder & Stoughton, 1935), and J. J. Collins, *Between Athens and Jerusalem: Jewish Identity in the Hellenistic Diaspora* (New York: Crossroad, 1983). The difficulty of correlating archaeological evidence with the picture we get of Diaspora Judaism in the Acts of the Apostles is illustrated by A. T. Kraabel, "The Disappearance of the 'God-Fearers,' " *Numen* 22 (1975): 96–130.

On Josephus, see H. St. John Thackeray, *Josephus: The Man and the Historian* (New York: Ktav Pub. House, 1968 [1928]); S. Cohen, *Josephus in Galilee and Rome: His Vita and Development as a Historian* (Leiden: E. J. Brill, 1979); T. Rajak, *Josephus: The Historian and His Society* (Philadelphia: Fortress Press, 1984); and

H. W. Attridge, "Historiography" and "Josephus and His Works," in CRINT 2.2 (1984): 157–84 and 185–232. For a full discussion of figures such as Artapanus and Eupolemus, see C. R. Holladay, *Fragments from Hellenistic Jewish Authors*, vol. 1: *Historians* (Chico, Calif.: Scholars Press, 1983).

A nontechnical introduction to Philo is available in S. Sandmel's *Philo of Alexandria: An Introduction* (New York and London: Oxford Univ. Press, 1979), and in the fine portrayal by E. J. Goodenough, *An Introduction to Philo Judaeus*, 2d rev. ed. (New York: Barnes & Noble, 1963). Also on Philo, but involving as well an interpretation of much of Hellenistic Jewish literature, is E. J. Goodenough, *By Light, Light: The Mystic Gospel of Hellenistic Judaism* (New Haven: Yale Univ. Press, 1935); see also P. Borgen, "Philo of Alexandria," CRINT 2.2 (1984); 233–82. For the way in which the figure of Moses would be interpreted in this tradition, see D. Tiede, *The Charismatic Figure as Miracle Worker* (Missoula, Mont.: Scholars Press, 1972), and C. R. Holladay, *Theios Anēr in Hellenistic Judaism* (Missoula, Mont.: Scholars Press, 1977).

PART TWO

THE CHRISTIAN EXPERIENCE

WE CAN NOW CONSIDER THE PRIMAL CHRISTIAN EXPERIENCE, IN WHAT IS AT ONCE a critical and difficult stage of this study. We have surveyed some symbols by which Jews and Greeks interpreted their lives, symbols that gave shape to and were in turn shaped by their changing experiences. Soon we will attend to diverse literary expressions of the new symbolic world being created by the Christian experience. But if we are to perceive the NT as a fully human production, we cannot move easily and automatically from the "background" to the Christian writings, with scarcely a glance at the questions most demanding an answer: Why were they written in the first place? What made such a prolific and odd literary production necessary? What happened to give both Hellenism and Judaism such new substance and shape? Between the symbolic world of first-century Judaism and the symbolic world of the NT, *something happened*. This is the subject of our investigation.

Our approach is cautious and circumspect, for the subject has many ambiguities. We are searching for the experience that is at best only implicit in the writings themselves. Our method requires us to extrapolate; we must be willing to move behind explicit statements to their implicit presuppositions. Such a quest is obviously perilous. The very term "experience" is not without obscurity. How does one isolate an experience? Science naturally shudders at such elusive and ill-defined subjects. And if the definition of experience is difficult, the search for religious experience is worse. Is there such a thing, and how do we know? What are its distinguishing characteristics? Are religious experiences a distinct category, or should they be "reduced" to clearer concepts less dependent on personal testimony and transcendent references? Finally, our task is made more quixotic still by our quest for the primordial Christian experience, which not even the Christian writings identify as such or explicitly relate.

The reader, therefore, stands warned. What follows claims truth but cannot defend that claim against all challenges. I cannot give exact scientific support for everything I assert. But for that matter, I would have a great deal of trouble convincing someone of my existence, if it were seriously enough questioned. Yet from this text before you, you might suspect that someone is alive and active in its production. With just such a suggestive purpose, I write this section. I do not pretend to answer definitively the questions concerning the primordial Christian experience. But I want to show they are the right sort of questions to ask if we want to understand the first Christian writings.

We are asking, then, about the displacement made by the Christian experience in the symbolic world of the first century. We may be no better able to penetrate to the core of that experience than we can to that of the experience of the Holocaust in the twentieth century, which has also massively displaced the world of Jewish symbols. As with the Holocaust, however, we can at least begin to wonder at what happened to so shake a world.

4

The Claims of
the First Christians

THE QUESTION, WHAT HAPPENED? IS FORCED ON US BY THE REALIZATION OF how remarkable this phenomenon really was. Christianity began in obscurity. Its putative founder was executed and its first adherents scattered in fear and confusion. It was propagandized by provincials whose message appeared as nonsense to the sophisticated. With significant exceptions, its chief appeal was to the outcast and marginal elements of society, finding significant numbers of converts among transients, slaves, and women. From the first, it was violently persecuted. Yet, in the course of four centuries, Christianity became the dominant religious fact of Hellenistic culture. It swept all before it, becoming at last the established cult of the empire that had sought to extirpate it, the very form of wisdom for the sages who had reviled it, a movement with such resilient and catholic embrace that it gathered all the charms of its cultic rivals and philosophy itself into a triumphant procession, securing at last the allegiance of the cultured, the rich, and the powerful.

Whether this development is regarded as good or bad, it happened. How can it be explained? Political, social, and economic factors undoubtedly abetted the movement's success, but they do not account for everything. Nor can the unparalleled growth of the movement be credited to its being a more profound religion than others, or a higher form of ethics, or a unique offer of salvation. Hellenistic moralists taught an ethics just as pure and far more coherent. Judaism was a religion just as profound and far more ancient. The mystery religions offered a revelation just as transcendent and far more esoteric. The key to Christianity's success lies not in its teaching but in its experience of power. What distinguishes the movement is its claim to have actualized the "good news of God" to humans. What accounts for its spread is its ability to make the claim plausible, persuasive, and even present, for others.

The NT is a window through which we can see the movement in the period before it achieved political and cultural acceptance, yet when it had already begun to shape its distinctive self-consciousness. It is instructive, therefore, to locate in these writings the claims being made by the Christians, and contrast them to the perception of the movement by its first outside observers. The disparity is startling. We expect some divergence, for there is always distance between a group's self-appreciation and its reputation. What insiders see as an army of liberation appears to outsiders as a gang of terrorists; a cult regarded by its adherents as the vanguard of eschatological battle is seen by outsiders as a band of self-deluded visionaries.

In the case of the NT however, the disparity is particularly strong. Precisely because of the movement's success and because all contemporary readers are to some extent themselves shaped by a world fundamentally altered by that success, an imaginative leap is required to perceive how surprising and even outrageous the claims of the first Christians were. If it had remained what at first it appeared destined to be, one more odd cult from the East, then we could see with fresh eyes the bizarre nature of its claims, just as the fragments from Qumran seem all the more singular in their self-aggrandizement since the traces of the community disappeared beneath the sand for two thousand years. To place the Christian claims in the proper perspective, we must begin from the outside and look in.

CHRISTIANITY FROM THE OUTSIDE

The insignificance of the Christian movement in the eyes of the world during the NT period is shown most clearly by its being so systematically ignored by both Jewish and Hellenistic writers. Among Jewish writers, there is next to nothing. The historian Josephus thoroughly describes all the Jewish sects in first-century Palestine, but of the Christians he either knew or chose to say very little. He gives favorable notice to John the Baptist and recounts his death under Herod but makes no connection between John and Christianity (*Ant* XVIII.5.2). He barely mentions Jesus in a passage dealing with the interregnum between the procurators Festus and Albinus. Josephus says (*Ant* XX.9.1) the high priest Ananus took the occasion to summon the Sanhedrin, the Jewish governing council:

> and brought before them the brother of Jesus who was called Christ, whose name was James, and some others; and when he had formed an accusation against them as breakers of the law, he delivered them to be stoned. . . .

Another passage mentioning Jesus (*Ant* XVIII.3.3) is so reworked by Christian interpolations that we can say, at most, that Josephus placed Jesus in the time of troubles during the procuratorship of Pontius Pilate.

The Talmud contains only few and obscure references to Jesus and Christians. Later censors may have had a hand in excising other, unflattering notices. In the present Talmudim, only a handful of passages appear to mention Jesus directly (see, e.g., Babylonian Talmud, *Sanhedrin* 43a, b; 103a; 107b), while some others apparently allude to him (e.g., Sanhedrin 106b), but none of them is indisputably about Jesus. Still other rabbinic materials speak unfavorably about the heretics *(minim)* and we can sometimes correlate those descriptions with what we know about the Christians (see e.g., *Koheleth Rabbah* 1.8; Babylonian Talmud, *Sanhedrin* 43a; *Mekilta* par. 66b). For the most part, the rabbinic polemic by silence was operative and effective. Only because we know of Jesus and the Christians from the NT can we even suspect references to them in these materials, they are so veiled. Even the clearest of them, moreover, are late, and do not constitute independent contemporary testimony about the movement. However compelling they may be to the Christian reader, they are but tiny droplets in the great ocean of the Talmud. In sum, we learn next to nothing about Jesus and the first Christians from those we would expect to be most interested in them. The Essenes are given much more attention.

Greco-Roman sources contain slightly more information. In Suetonius's *Life of Claudius* (early 2d cent. C.E.), one line appears in a passage describing the emperor Claudius's handling of various foreign peoples (25.4):

> Since the Jews constantly made disturbances at the instigation of Chrestus, he expelled them from Rome.

This notice corresponds with Acts 18:2, which tells us that Paul met in Corinth a Jew

> called Aquila whose family came from Pontus. He and his wife Priscilla had recently left Italy because an edict of Claudius had expelled all Jews from Rome.

But of the identity of "Chrestus," we know nothing, as apparently neither did Suetonius. Is there a garbled reminiscence of a commotion caused by preaching about Christ? If so, to the Roman historian writing some fifty years later, it was still primarily a matter of Judaism. Christians are not even seen as a separate group.

A fuller account is found in Tacitus's *Annals* (early 2d cent. C.E.). He recounts the great fire in Rome under Nero, and says (XV.44.2–8):

> Nero fastened the guilt and afflicted the most exquisite tortures on a class hated for their abominations, called Christians by the populace. Christus, from whom the name had its origin, suffered the extreme penalty during the reign of Tiberius at the hands of one of our procurators, Pontius Pilate, and a deadly superstition, thus checked for the moment, again broke out, not only in Judaea, the first source of the evil, but also in the city, where all things hideous and shameful from every part of the world meet and become popular.

Tacitus knows of the Christians as an identifiable group, not simply as part of Judaism. They are numerous enough at Rome in the sixties to be noticeable, yet sufficiently a minority to offer no resistance to the violent whim of an emperor. Tacitus gives us valuable information concerning the execution of Jesus, but for this conservative Roman, the sect is simply a noxious superstition, typical of the bizarre cults that flowed to Rome from the East (cf. Juvenal *Satires* III.62 and Suetonius, *Life of Nero*, 16.2).

The earliest firsthand pagan report about Christians was filed by Pliny the Younger, governor of Bithynia (ca. 112 C.E.). Pliny is worried about the great numbers this sect is attracting. He writes to the emperor Trajan for advice. He doesn't know quite how to handle the situation. Should he execute Christians only if they are guilty of other crimes as well, or simply because they bear the name of Christian, or only if they prove to be obstinate when offered the chance to recant? By means of torture, he was able to obtain information, which he passes on to Trajan (*Letter* X.96):

> They maintained, moreover, that the amount of their fault or error had been this, that it was their habit on a fixed day to assemble before daylight and recite by turns a form of words to Christ as to a god; and that they bound themselves with an oath, not for any crime, but not to commit theft or robbery or adultery, not to break their word, and not to deny a deposit when demanded. After this was done, it was their custom to depart, and to meet again to take food, but ordinary and harmless food. . . . I discovered nothing else than a perverse and extravagant superstition.

A final Hellenistic account of the Christian movement before the end of the second century comes from the satirist Lucian of Samosata (120–80). In his *Passing of Peregrinus*, he attacks the charlatan Cynic philosopher Proteus Peregrinus, whom Lucian considers the very type of the false philosopher, striking virtuous poses only out of vainglory. Among those duped by Peregrinus was a group of Christians (*Peregrinus* 11–13):

> It was then he learned the wondrous lore of the Christians by associating with their priests and scribes in Palestine. And—how else could it be—in a trice he made them all look like children; for he was prophet, cult leader, head of the synagogue, and everything, all by himself. He interpreted and explained some of their books, and even composed many, and they revered him as a god, made use of him as a lawgiver, and set him down as a protector, next after that other, to be sure, whom they still worship, the man who was crucified in Palestine because he introduced this new cult into the world.
>
> Then at length Proteus was apprehended for this and thrown into prison, which itself gave him no little reputation as an asset in his future career and the charlatanism and notoriety-seeking that he was enamoured of. Well, when he had been imprisoned, the Christians, regarding the incident as a calamity, left nothing undone in the effort to rescue him. Then, as this was impossible, every other form of attention was shown him, not in any casual way, but with assiduity; . . . people even came from the cities of Asia, sent by the Christians

at their common expense, to succour and defend and encourage the hero. They show incredible speed whenever any such public action is undertaken; for in no time at all, they lavish their all. So it was, then, in the case of Peregrinus; much money came to him from them by reason of his imprisonment, and he procured not a little revenue from it. The poor wretches have convinced themselves, first and foremost, that they are going to be immortal and live for all time, in consequence of which they despise death, and even willingly give themselves into custody, most of them. Furthermore their first lawgiver persuaded them that they are all brothers of one another after they transgressed once for all by denying the Greek gods and by worshipping the crucified sophist himself and living under his laws. Therefore they despise all things indiscriminately and consider them common property, receiving such doctrines traditionally and without any definite evidence. So if any charlatan and trickster able to profit by occasions comes among them, he quickly acquires sudden wealth by imposing on simple folk.

Even though he confuses some aspects of Christian teaching and practice, and even though he regards Christians as simple-minded and easily gulled followers of a superstition, Lucian witnesses, however hazily, to certain aspects of Christianity as they are also found in the NT: community possessions, sacred books, faith, prophets, belief in life after death. He also has a certain grudging respect for these simple folk.

Out of all the writings of the first and second century that have come down to us, then, such are the references to Jesus and Christians: a sentence here, a paragraph there. The picture of Christianity is vague and confused. It is connected to Judaism. It had a crucified founder. Its adherents are stubborn, unenlightened, and perverse. All in all, it is a particularly odious form of superstition. The dominant attitude is one of contempt. Christianity is regarded as insignificant and possibly risible, one among many cults with dubious pasts and no futures. The full impact of this casual dismissal comes only when we realize that all these accounts come from a period after the writing of all, or nearly all, the NT texts. The shock is even greater when we turn at last to the claims being made by those first Christian writings.

CLAIMS OF THE CHRISTIANS

The pagan perception of the first Christians was not totally inaccurate. These Christians did sing hymns to Christ as to a god (see Phil. 2:6–11; Col. 1:15–20; Rev. 5:11–16). Some of them, at least, put their possessions into a community of goods (Acts 4:32–36), or generously contributed to the needs of other communities (Acts 11:27–30; Rom. 15:25–29). They did share common meals (Acts 2:42; 1 Cor. 11:18–34). They were stubborn in their convictions, even when persecuted (1 Thess. 2:14—3:10; 2 Cor. 11:23–29; Heb. 10:32–39). They expected to "live forever" (Rom.

6:23; Gal. 6:8; 1 Tim. 1:16; 1 John 5:11). These characteristics do not, however, by themselves distinguish Christians from other communities in the Hellenistic world. Such activities and attitudes were found among many others.

But if their pagan observers had read the Christian writings, they would have been astonished at the extraordinary claims the movement made about itself. Far from regarding itself as a benighted group of fanatics doomed to disappear, it staked for itself—apparently from the very first—a claim on the fortunes of the whole world. Its message would extend to the ends of the earth (Acts 1:8) and would make followers from among all nations (Matt. 28:19). It saw itself as enjoying a real ascendancy over the world. Paul tells the Corinthians in 1 Cor. 3:22 that

> the world or life or death or the present or the future, all are yours; and you are Christ's; and Christ is God's.

To members of the Corinthian church who were going to court with suits against each other, he says (1 Cor. 6:2–3):

> Do you not know that the saints will judge the world? And if the world is to be judged by you, are you incompetent to try trivial cases? Do you not know that we are to judge angels?

The Christians play a pivotal role in the future of the world. They help reconcile the world to God (2 Cor. 5:19; Rom. 11:15) and anticipate the whole world's rebirth into freedom (Rom. 8:20–22). The Christian community is the place where God's purpose for the world is revealed (Eph. 3:9–10):

> The plan of the mystery hidden for ages in God who created all things; that through the church the manifold wisdom of God might now be made known to the principalities and powers in the heavenly places.

The community participates already in a victory over the world (1 John 5:4–5):

> This is the victory that overcomes the world, our faith. Who is it that overcomes the world but he who believes that Jesus is the Son of God?

This victory will come to complete accomplishment: "The kingdom of this world has become the kingdom of our Lord and of his Christ, and he shall reign for ever and ever" (Rev. 11:15). The seer John has this vision of the end (Rev. 22:4–5):

> The throne of God and of the lamb shall be in it, and his servants shall worship him; they shall see his face, and his name shall be on their foreheads. And night shall be no more; they need no light of lamp or sun, for the Lord God will be their light, and they shall reign for ever and ever.

What can we make of these claims? Were the first Christians megalomaniacal? All these statements antedate by decades the first casual notice of the group by outsiders. It is as though the North American colonies in 1690 declared themselves to be a world political power. Faced with the distance between the worldly circumstances of this group and its cosmic claims, it is necessary to look at the basis for the claims. What did Christians offer in support of such statements?

The claims of the first Christians were based *on their experience.* Their claims expressed realities that they said they currently enjoyed. But what was their experience? It is impossible to cut entirely beneath the variety of literary contexts and symbolic expressions in the NT to isolate, in a physical or psychic sense, a core experience. But we can describe some aspects of that experience by observing a number of its effects.

It led to a fundamental release from the cosmic forces that, in the perceptions of the age, dominated human existence; Christians were no longer subject to those "powers and principalities" (1 Cor. 2:6–10; Rom. 8:38; Eph. 2:1–10; Col. 1:13; 1 Pet. 3:22). It meant as well a release from repressive systems of law, which those "elements of the universe" had used to keep humans in bondage (Gal. 3:23—4:7; Rom. 6:15–23; 2 Cor. 3:6–18; Col. 2:8–23). At a more personal level, it involved an escape from the terror and anxiety before contingency and death, that led to the bondage of compulsion (Rom. 8:14–15; Heb. 2:14–15; 1 John 4:17–21). A central symbol for this experience was, therefore, salvation. When the Christians spoke of salvation, they meant not only something that would happen but something that had in some way already happened to them (Rom. 1:16; 10:10; 1 Cor. 1:18, 21; 15:2; Eph. 2:5–8; Titus 3:5; Jas. 1:21; 1 Pet. 3:21; Phil. 1:28; 2 Pet. 3:15; Jude 3; Rev. 12:10).

Can we get any closer to the nature of this experience? What did salvation mean in terms of concrete human life in this world? We can discern certain qualities ascribed to Christians, such as recur as well in writings of Hellenistic philosophy. Thus, the Christians experience freedom *(eleutheria;* see Rom. 6:18–22; Gal. 5:1, 13; 2 Cor. 3:17; Jas. 1:25; 1 Pet. 2:16; 1 Cor. 9:1, 19) and free speech or boldness *(parrēsia;* Acts 2:29; 4:13, 29, 31; 2 Cor. 3:12; 1 Thess. 2:2; Eph. 3:12; Phlm. 8; Heb. 4:16). The ideas of freedom, release, redemption, liberation, salvation point to a transfer from one, negative, condition, to another, positive, one. The condition is defined partially by those forces describing bondage, but it is also defined positively in terms of certain dispositions and capacities: "For freedom Christ has freed you" (Gal. 5:1). Free speech indicates an empowerment, a capacity to confront opposition without fear, to express one's identity in a variety of circumstances with courage and confidence. These are listed in the texts not as ideals for which to strive but as realities:

Christians "have" freedom and free speech; they exercise those capacities in their lives.

The Christians also spoke of certain states in which they found themselves. One of these was peace (Rom. 5:1; 1 Cor. 7:15; 2 Cor. 13:11; Eph. 2:17; 4:3; Phil. 4:17; Col. 3:15; Jas. 3:18), and another is joy (Rom. 5:3; 1 Pet. 4:13; Acts 13:52; Phil. 2:2; 1 John 1:4). Sometimes, the two states are listed together (Rom. 14:17; Gal. 5:22). Peace is a relationship not only with other humans but also with God—a relationship or state that is not challenged by temporal conflicts. Joy is a state that transcends the conditioned nature of happiness and is found even in the midst of tribulation and suffering (2 Cor. 1:4–7; 1 Thess. 3:6–9; Heb. 12:1–3; Jas. 1:2; 1 Pet. 4:13). Accompanying these states were certain dispositions, such as faith, hope, and love (1 Thess. 1:2–3; 1 Cor. 13:13; 1 Pet. 1:3–9). These were not abstract terms but living qualities, which could be described behaviorally in terms of the attitudes and actions toward which they tended. Thus, hope did not grieve at the death of community members (1 Thess. 4:13); faith resisted temptation and persecution (1 Pet. 5:9), and love was not arrogant or rude (1 Cor. 13:5).

If we try to cut deeper beneath the symbolization, we see that the Christian experience had to do with *power*. The Christians said they had been touched by an awesome force that in turn empowered them—a particularly paradoxical claim, given their circumstances. The terms for this power are various. It can be called an authority (*exousia;* see John 1:12; 1 Cor. 8:9; 9:4; 2 Cor. 10:8; 13:10; 2 Thess. 3:9) or an energy (*energeia;* see Eph. 3:20–21; Col. 1:29; 1 Cor. 12:6, 11; 1 Thess. 2:13; Phlm. 6; Heb. 4:12; Gal. 3:5; 5:6) or a power (*dynamis;* see Rom. 1:16; 15:13, 19; 1 Cor. 1:18; 6:14; 2 Cor. 6:7; 13:4; Gal. 3:5; Eph. 3:20; Col. 1:29; 1 Thess. 1:5; 2 Thess. 1:11; 2 Tim. 1:7; Heb. 2:4; 2 Pet. 1:16). This power manifested itself outwardly in certain "signs and wonders" (Acts 4:30; 5:12; 14:3; Rom. 15:19; 2 Cor. 12:12; Heb. 2:4) such as healings, prophecies, and spiritual utterances, but above all in the proclamation of the "good news" (Rom. 1:16; 1 Cor. 1:18; 2:5; 2 Cor. 4:7; 1 Thess. 1:5; 2 Tim. 1:8; Jas. 1:21). It also manifested itself inwardly by the spiritual transformation of those who received it (Gal. 3:5; Rom. 12:2; 1 Cor. 2:16; 2 Cor. 3:18; Eph. 4:23; Col. 3:10; 1 Pet. 1:22). This power, finally, was not self-generated but was transmitted to them from another to whom it properly belonged (Rom. 1:4; 16:25; 1 Cor. 1:24; 5:4; 12:3; 2 Cor. 1:4; 6:7; 12:9; 13:4; Eph. 3:16, 20; Phil. 3:10, 21; Heb. 5:7; Jas. 4:12; Jude 24; 2 Tim. 1:7; 1 Pet. 1:5; 2 Pet. 1:16). None of the elements I have here listed is found in the NT as a goal to be striven for; rather, each is spoken of as a present and past reality. The relationships, states, dispositions, and transformations are *experienced*, not just desired. The case is succinctly stated by Paul: "The Kingdom of God does not consist in talk but in power" (1 Cor. 4:20).

Because of this new empowerment, Christians said they represented something entirely new in the world. They shared in a new covenant with God (1 Cor. 11:25; 2 Cor. 3:7–18; Heb. 9:15) and in a new life (Rom. 6:4; Eph. 4:24). Indeed, they were part of an entirely new creation: "If anyone is in Christ, there is a new creation; the old has passed away, behold the new has come" (2 Cor. 5:17). Paul continues, "All this is from God." The power with which they had been touched came from God, who always created anew (1 Cor. 1:28–30; Rom. 4:17; 2 Cor. 4:6). The Christian experience anticipated the completion of God's renewal of the world: "According to his promise we wait for new heavens and a new earth, in which righteousness dwells" (2 Pet. 3:13). Or, as the seer John says, "Then I saw a new heaven and a new earth, for the first heaven and the first earth had vanished, and there was no longer any sea . . . then He who sat upon the throne said, 'Behold, I am making all things new' " (Rev. 21:1, 5). The note of newness is distinctive. The Christians meant by it not novelty, but a more fundamental transformation, renewal. Although the quest for novelty was as lively in that world as ours (see Acts 17:19–21), the claim by a philosophy of religion to be new would not automatically have been regarded as a mark of its authenticity. It was an age for which antiquity had a higher value.

The claim to experience sets the first Christians decisively apart in the world they shared with Greeks and Jews. Greek philosophy offered wisdom, but particularly in Stoicism, it was achieved at great cost of time and effort. Even the more direct route followed by Cynics was regarded by them as being only for the elite. The Christians, in contrast, claimed a superior wisdom that came by way of revelation in the present from God and that was available by gift, not by study (see 1 Cor. 1:30; 2:7; Eph. 1:8; 3:10; Col. 1:9; Jas. 3:15–17). The authority of Christian leaders and teachers did not rest, as with the rabbis, on age or education or the unbroken chain of tradition from the past, so that even a Hillel was required, notwithstanding his brilliance, to cite precedents for his opinions. Authority for the Christians came immediately from God (1 Cor. 7:40; Rom. 1:1; Gal. 1:1; Eph. 3:3; 1 Tim. 1:18; 1 Pet. 5:1), and the voice of prophecy was alive in the community (1 Cor. 12–14; Rev. 1–3; 1 Thess. 5:20).

The prayers of blessing shared by Christians with Judaism did not simply recall God's mercies of the distant past, in the hope of their renewal in the future. Christians gave thanks for God's present and continuing work among them, and prayed that what he had begun, God might complete in them (Rom. 1:8–14; 1 Cor. 1:4–9; 2 Cor. 1:3–7; Eph. 1:3–14; Phil. 1:3–11; 1 Thess. 1:3–5; 1 Pet. 1:3–8). Much of the exhortation (*parenesis*) of the NT, consequently, is based not on norms provided by past precedent, whether written or oral, but on the norm provided by the gift given them in the present: "Become in fact what you already are" (cf. 2 Tim. 1:6–8; Heb. 12:18—13:17; 1 Pet. 1:21—2:3; 1 John 3:16–18; Col. 2:20—3:17; Phil. 2:1–13; Eph. 4:1—5:20).

Like the sectarians of Qumran and other apocalypticists, the Christians looked forward to an eschatological climax to history (1 Cor. 15:20–57; 1 Thess. 4:13—5:3; 2 Thess. 2:8–12; Heb. 9:28; Jas. 5:7–11; 1 Pet. 1:7–9; 2 Pet. 3:10–13; Rev. 21:1—22:5). But unlike them, the Christians saw the beginning of that culmination in their present experience; in addition to a "not yet," there was a definite "already." Indeed, the distinctiveness of the experiential basis for the Christian movement can be traced in the usage of the simple word "now" through the texts of the NT. In the single Letter to the Romans, Paul says that *now* God's righteousness is being revealed (3:21, 26), *now* they have been made righteous (5:1), *now* they have been reconciled to God (5:11), *now* they are freed from sin (6:22), *now* they are discharged from the law (7:6), *now* there is no condemnation for God's people (8:1), *now* is the mystery of God being revealed (16:26). Or, as Paul says in another place, "Behold, *now* is the acceptable time, behold *now* is the day of salvation" (2 Cor. 6:2; cf. Gal. 4:9; Eph. 2:2; 3:5; Heb. 9:26; 1 John 3:2; 1 Pet. 1:12; 2:20; 3:21; 2 Tim. 1:10; Col. 1:22, 26).

Finally, in contrast to those Jewish sects who clarified their own claims of being the remnant of God's people by excluding others—whether pagans, or apostates from Torah, or those who associated with either— Christians claimed that their experience of God's favor was available not just to one nation, or to an elite group within it, but to all humans: "All those who call on the name of the Lord shall be saved" (Acts 2:21, 39; Rom. 10:11–13).

It is in the experience of the first believers that the origin of Christianity and of the NT must be sought. *Something happened* in the lives of real women and men; something that caused them to perceive their lives in a new and radically altered fashion and compelled them to interpret it by means of available symbols. The NT is incomprehensible if seen as a collection of theological writings in an abstract or theoretical mode. The NT is the furthest thing from such a scholastic enterprise. There is theology to be found in it, to be sure, but it is a theology that consists not in working out corollaries to propositions but in pursuing reflection on a present and continuing experience of the most fundamental sort—religious experience. It was because men and women of the first-century Mediterranean world, both Jews and Greeks, found their lives suddenly and inexplicably transformed by a new and unsuspected power, from a new and confusing source, that they were forced to reflect on their lives in a new way and infuse the symbols of their world with new content.

If we grant that something happened, however, then we must face the still harder question, What happened? What experience could be profound enough and powerful enough to change timorous followers into bold and prophetic leaders? What power could transform a fanatic persecutor into a fervent apostle? What unseen hand shaped, out of the unpromising materials of Galilean *am-ha-aretz* and Corinthian transients, a community that would eventually change the contours of the known world by its proclamation of "good news from God" (1 Thess. 2:2)? We must turn next to that question, knowing full well that it is impossible to answer it entirely. Something happened, but what?

BIBLIOGRAPHICAL NOTE

Translations from Latin and Greek authors are from the Loeb Classical Library. A review of the evidence concerning Jesus and Christians from Jewish and pagan sources is found in M. Goguel, *Jesus and the Origins of Christianity*, vol. 1, trans. O. Wyon (New York: Harper & Row, 1960 [1933]), and in F. F. Bruce, *Jesus and Christian Origins Outside the New Testament* (Grand Rapids: Wm. B. Eerdmans, 1974). A fuller treatment of the Jewish writings is found in J. Lauterbach, "Jesus in the Talmud," in *Rabbinic Essays* (Cincinnati: Hebrew Union College Press, 1951), 473–570; and R. T. Herford, *Christianity in Talmud and Midrash* (New York: Ktav Pub. House, 1903). For the Roman side, see S. Benko, *Pagan Rome and the Early Christians* (Bloomington: Ind. Univ. Press, 1984). Shorter treatments in the light of recent scholarship are the essays by L. Schiffmann, "At The Crossroads: Tannaitic Perspectives on the Jewish Christian Schism," in *JCS-D* 2:115–56; and R. Wilken, "The Christians as the Romans (and Greeks) Saw Them," in *JCS-D* 1:100–125; see also H. W. Basser, "Allusions to Christian and Gnostic Practices in the Talmudic Tradition," *Journal for the Study of Judaism* 12 (1981): 87–105.

5

The Resurrection Faith

TURNING TO THE QUESTION, WHAT HAPPENED? MEANS FACING THE MOST difficult part of this inquiry. It is one thing to collect statements that make it clear that some sort of powerful experience generated the movement. It is quite another to attempt a description of that experience.

Part of the problem is conceptual. Saying what experience is becomes more difficult the more exact we try to be. Luckily, reality is not totally constricted by our ability neatly to define it. When we hear a report of someone's personal experience, we expect both a pointer to something outside the subject, and an element of interpretation, even if we cannot always distinguish the elements of objectivity and subjectivity in the report itself.

The problems of description and definition are even greater when we deal with religious experience. How is it distinguished from other experiences? Does it have unique components? Can it be reduced to other, non-religious factors, or is it an irreducible, unique sort of human event?

Religious experiences must be placed in the continuum of all of life's experiences. The religious element in life emerges from and responds to other aspects of life. No single kind of event can automatically be designated religious. The religious dimension of life can be as pervasive and protean as the economic.

Personal testimony may here count for more than logical analysis, as it does also in the case of the aesthetic. Most of us work with a rough-and-ready sense of the human experience of beauty. We recognize that when it is real, the response to beauty cannot be collapsed into the appetitive or aggressive drives of the human animal. Yet the more we try to pin down such a response conceptually, the more it recedes. What we all experience, none of us can adequately define.

Recognizing the inevitably subjective and allusive character of the task, then, we can begin to speak of authentic religious experience. The word "authentic" is important, since religious experience can be distorted in many ways. Precisely the variety of the counterfeits, in fact, makes us cautious even with what is genuine. Experience should here be taken to exclude that which is merely momentary or purely sensory, emotive, or irrational. Nor does it refer only to so-called peak experiences. Far from removing a person from "real life," religious experience is about what is perceived to be most real in life. Far from being localized in the emotions or intellect or will, religious experience involves all of the human person— emotions, will, and mind—in a response to what is most real.

The note of response is important, for it distinguishes authentic religious experience from fakery; this is not a matter of projection, fantasy, or autosuggestion. Magic may be rooted in the attempt to control one's environment. But authentic religious experience is rooted in the subject's being reduced to powerlessness and placed in question by a force outside the person's control. That which is experienced is not a puzzle to be solved but a frightening mystery that escapes human manipulation and refuses to be grasped by human knowledge.

Religious experience involves an encounter with the holy, the mystery of the totally other that opens like a chasm before humans in unexpected ways, forcing a halt to the round of busyness and distraction, making impossible the repression of its presence. The human being inexplicably finds himself or herself locked, bound, caught in a tension between attraction and repulsion. The awesome power confronting the person is dangerous yet seductive. It organizes existence around itself. It demands, above all, attention. It carries with itself the weight of an absolutely authoritative presence.

Obviously, my description is culturally conditioned. Not everything called religious has this sense of a response to one "totally other." But I am myself shaped by the symbols I seek to describe and can therefore only affirm that the experiences of Moses before the burning bush (Exod. 3:1–21), Isaiah in the temple (Isa. 6:1–8), and Job before the whirlwind (Job 42:1–6) correspond to something real that reappears in the writings of the NT. In this tradition, the power that intrudes into the realm of the ordinary with threatening force and dangerous charm is always the One Power who, however named, is God—who reduces to insignificance all pretension to glory and establishes humans precisely as creatures.

The human response to such a powerful presence is, of all experiences, the most characterized by intensity and inclusiveness. Although often spectacular and extraordinary, it need not be. A more consistent characteristic is the power's ability to organize life around itself and impress a sense of a "necessity" to act. Genuine religious experience, in other words, is not only felt, it is acted out in a consistent pattern. When I speak about religious experience as being the cause of the Christian movement and therefore of the NT, this is the sort of experience I mean.

But my description is still too idealized. It makes overly consistent a phenomenon often fragmentary and contradictory. It gives the impression that the phenomenon is a matter of pyrotechnics, rather than sometimes a matter of a still small voice (cf. 1 Kings 19:1–19), or that it is invariably positive and beneficent rather than sometimes negative and harmful, or that it is exhaustive and once and for all—whereas no human experience, possibly excepting death, has such finality. To understand the religious experience of the NT in particular, further qualifications are necessary.

Religious experiences are conditioned by the subject's degree of awareness, by the situation in which the experience occurs, and by the experience's degree of intensity. It is possible to speak of a community experience, but the character and quality of that experience will be different for each member. The Holocaust again provides a helpful analogy. Certainly, all Jews since 1933 have "experienced" the Holocaust. Some "went through it" by being gathered into ghettos, forced to emigrate, dispossessed, shot, or by surviving work and extermination camps. Other Jews went through it differently, by having relatives killed or hearing how they survived, or by receiving education in home, school, or synagogue. Even those who went through it physically and therefore experienced it most intensely had widely different experiences. Some suffered the final indignities in an almost subhuman way, the Nazi brutalization process having worked effectively. Others maintained their awareness and sensitivity—and with them the capacity to suffer—to the very end. For some the intensity of religious faith diminished not at all, and Hasidic songs were sung by some marching to the gas chambers. For others that same march brought only the bitter confirmation that faith was illusory.

A similar diversity is found in the religious experiences of the first Christians. Some had experiences more immediate, profound, and intense than others. Some had their experience mediated by others, called witnesses. And the NT testifies to the mixed motives, desires, and conflicts, not to mention levels of awareness, that were present in first-generation communities. Not all Christians had religious experiences of the same intensity and authenticity.

Human experiences are also mediated by the available symbols of a person's world. In the very act of perception, in the experience itself, there is already a form of interpretation. There is no naked experience of the holy. The totally other is mediated by that which is not totally other, our symbols. The more powerful the one encountered, of course, the more those symbols will stretch and even shatter.

Any attempt to isolate a religious experience in the NT at the purely physical or psychic level, or to find an experience that is not already interpreted, is therefore doomed to fail. To be reported at all, experience needs the clothing of language. Whatever the physical or psychic components of the experience of power undergone by the first Christians, the power was already perceived by them as that of the Holy Spirit.

The NT writings show us a variety of religious experiences, but behind them all is the first and fundamental experience, which found expression in this conviction: Jesus is raised. This is the one experience without which there would be no Christian movement and therefore nothing to explain or interpret. It is the necessary cause of the production of the NT.

THE RESURRECTION EXPERIENCE

Christianity is not at base a religion of mystical enlightenment. Jesus is not revered as a sage who reached union with the divine and then showed others the way to that same unity. The primordial Christian experience is not seen as others experiencing *what* Jesus himself experienced; that is regarded as unique and unspeakable. Christianity, rather, begins with Jesus' followers experiencing Jesus after his death in an entirely new way. Like Judaism, Christianity is a religion of personal encounter with the Other. The primitive Christian experience consisted in encountering the Other in the risen Jesus. *The resurrection faith is the birth of Christianity.* It deserves our close and repeated attention.

In the earliest extant Christian writing (ca. 50 c.e.), Paul writes to the young Thessalonian church and reminds its members (1 Thess. 1:9–10) of the terms of their conversion and how they

> turned to God from idols to serve a living and true God, and to wait for his son from heaven, whom he raised from the dead, Jesus, who delivers us from the wrath to come.

Paul goes on to say that this conviction is the basis for their own hope of a future life (1 Thess. 4:14):

> Since we believe that Jesus died and rose again, even so, through Jesus, God will bring with him those who have fallen asleep.

Writing to the Corinthian church some five years later, Paul recalls for them the basic framework of the "good news" that had founded their community (1 Cor. 15:3–8):

> For I delivered to you as of first importance what I also received, that Christ died for our sins in accordance with the scriptures, that he was buried, that he was raised on the third day in accordance with the scriptures, and that he appeared to Cephas, then to the Twelve. Then he appeared to more than five hundred brethren at one time, most of whom are still alive, though some have fallen asleep. Then he appeared to James, then to all the apostles. Last of all, as to one untimely born, he appeared also to me.

This recital bears the marks of a traditional formulation. Paul "received" it himself and "passed it on" to them. Its importance is indicated by his insistence that they are at present being saved by this message if they remain in it (1 Cor. 15:2). The odd phrase "in accordance with the scriptures" will occupy our attention later. For now, we note that Paul is here relating the *experiential base* of the "good news." He has delivered to the Corinthians not only a conviction, "He was raised," but also the report of something experienced by others, "He appeared" (or, "He was seen"). It was something experienced by over five hundred people. Some of them are still available to verify their experience. Nor is this simply an experience Paul heard about from others; he had it himself. Although Paul had not known Jesus when he was alive, he now reports that "he appeared also to me." Here we have a firsthand witness of the resurrection experience.

Paul does not describe his experience in physical or psychological terms, but only with religious symbols. He characteristically associates his experience of the risen Lord with his call to be an apostle: "Am I not free? Am I not an apostle? Have I not *seen* the Lord Jesus?" (1 Cor. 9:1). And in a statement defending his call to be an apostle, he says (Gal. 1:15–16):

> For I would have you know, brethren, that the gospel which was preached by me is not man's gospel. For I did not receive it from a man, nor was I taught it, but it came through a revelation of Jesus Christ. . . . But when He who had set me apart before I was born, and had called me through his grace, was pleased to reveal his son to [in] me, in order that I might preach him among the Gentiles, I did not confer with flesh and blood. . . .

Finally, there is the strange account in 2 Cor. 12:1–5, in which, with language strongly reminiscent of Jewish Merkabah mysticism, Paul speaks of "visions and revelations of the Lord" experienced by a "certain man" fourteen years previously, visions that brought him to the "third heaven" and showed him things "that cannot be told." Again, Paul says nothing about the psychic dimensions of the experience, except the enigmatic, ". . . whether in the body or out of the body I do not know" (12:3). We cannot say for certain that Paul is referring here to his experience of the risen Jesus, though it is certainly possible.

The Acts of the Apostles proves three accounts of Paul's encounter with the risen Jesus, once in direct narrative (9:3–8), and twice as reported by Paul in defense speeches (22:6–11; 26:12–18). The accounts diverge in some of their details (in 9:7, his companions hear the voice but see no one; in 22:9, they see the light but hear nothing), but they agree that it was an encounter with Jesus, which resulted in Paul's being sent to proclaim the "good news" to the Gentiles. In this, they also fundamentally agree with Gal. 1:15–16.

Attempts to explain Paul's turnabout from persecutor to apostle on the basis of psychological categories have the charm of familiarity to contemporary readers. It does not seem implausible to us that Paul could have consciously rejected the messianic movement, yet tortured in his conscience, have been unconsciously drawn to it until at last this internal tension broke within him. Then, in a classic reversal of psychological denial, he embraced fanatically that which he had fanatically detested. Unfortunately, Paul does not appear to have been a tormented soul. When he talks about his former life, he seems untroubled and even smug (Gal. 1:13–14; Phil. 3:4–6). And while Paul's blindness could be called a hysterical reaction (Acts 9:8–17), such a diagnosis does not significantly clarify the nature of his experience.

Moreover, attention to the psychological dynamics of Paul's experience distracts us from the aspect of the event regarded as most significant by both Paul and the author of Acts. Paul *did not* encounter a Jesus who was still living in an ordinary, human way. He encountered a Lord, that is, a transcendent and commanding presence. This is the most consistent feature of all the resurrection accounts: the commanding and empowering word that comes from the risen one. Jesus' presence, furthermore, was not mediated by some objective factuality, but by a personal, spiritual relationship. That is a weak term for a strong reality. We notice that in Gal. 1:16, Paul says that God was pleased "to reveal his son *to* me," but the Greek phrase can also be rendered "*in* me." Paul's experience was that not of an object but of another subject who was exercising personal power over Paul. In the Acts narrative, the voice asks Paul, "Why are you persecuting me?" when in fact Paul was persecuting not the human Jesus but the messianic community. But the voice insists, "I am Jesus, whom you are persecuting" (Acts 9:5). Paul experiences Jesus as one who is alive and powerfully present *in* the messianic community.

Paul reports that his experience of the risen Lord was not unique. Over five hundred people, many of them still alive some twenty years after the event, could say, "I have experienced the risen Jesus; he appeared to me." In the Gospels, we find narratives that recount a handful of these experiences. It should be noted that these narratives are not to be identified with either the number or the nature of the resurrection experiences. They tell us nothing, for example, about an appearance to "five hundred at one time" or an appearance to James. The Gospel narratives are ancient and stem at least in part from eyewitness accounts. But in their present form, they are shaped by the continuing experience of the believing community over a period of some forty years, and in them the resurrection event is given a very definite cast. The point here is simple: the Gospel narratives are selective and are shaped to teach the community; the *claim* to have encountered the risen Lord or to have experienced the power of his presence is not coextensive with these *stories*.

The Gospels contain two basic kinds of resurrection narratives. The first are called empty-tomb accounts (see Mark 16:1–8; Matt. 28:1–8; Luke 24:1–11; John 20:1–10). Followers of Jesus come to the tomb to anoint him after his death and discover that he is not there; they are told by one or more messengers to deliver this news to the disciples: "He is raised." The empty-tomb stories make several points that can be recognized as responding to charges that the resurrection was a hoax perpetrated by the disciples, a charge made explicit in Matt. 28:11–15 (see 27:62–66). Thus, the stone was too heavy to be rolled away by human agency; the emptiness of the tomb is a complete surprise to the visitors; the other disciples need to be informed of the fact; even then they are incredulous. These emphases, however, do not exhaust the significance of the empty-tomb accounts. The main point is that Jesus is absent from the place of death and that he goes "before them" (see Mark 16:7). Like the tomb itself, these narratives lie open for new encounters with Jesus. He is not where he was buried (his old life is closed), but his new life cannot be defined precisely in time and space (he goes before them). The linens left behind bear mute testimony to one freed from the bonds of death (John 20:6–9).

The second sort of resurrection narratives are called appearance accounts (see Mark 16:9–20; Matt. 28:9–20; Luke 24:13–49; John 20:11—21:23). These narratives, too, reveal certain apologetic emphases: some stress the reality of Jesus' body, to make clear that the one who now lives is to be identified with the one who died (Luke 24:39–43; John 20:26–28). But they also show the sudden, surprising, and unmanipulated nature of these encounters. Jesus intrudes into their midst. They do not make him present. They are frightened when he does appear. Furthermore, he is there not as a shadow of his former self but as a more powerful and commanding presence. These stories are dominated by the words spoken by Jesus. He interprets the Scripture and commands them to proclaim the message to others. In these accounts especially, we can detect the characteristics of religious experience: the sudden intrusion of power, the reaction of fascination and fear, and the sense of being commissioned. The experience of the holy leads to action; the experience of the risen Lord leads to proclamation.

It is useless to tease such narratives into saying something other than what they say. They tell us the tale not of a great psychological struggle that issued in conviction but of a surprising and totally unexpected encounter that issued in mission! Great insight into the experience of the first believers is not gained from the cynical romanticism of E. Renan, who, trying to account for the resurrection faith, finally pins most of it on Mary Magdalene:

Let us say, however, that the strong imagination of Mary Magdalene, played an important part in this circumstance. Divine power of love! Sacred moments in which the passion of one possessed gave to the world a resuscitated God!

Less silly, though ultimately no more adequate, is the conclusion of A. Loisy, who said that Jesus did not rise on Easter, but faith did:

> Thus did belief in the resurrection of Jesus come to its birth, and the manner of it may be called spontaneous. The faith of his disciples in his messianic future was too strong to admit of self-contradiction, too strong to give way under the refutation thrown upon it by the ignominy of the cross. Faith raised Jesus into the glory he expected; faith declared him living forever, because faith itself was determined never to die. Quickened by the ordeal, faith produced out of itself visions that brought balm to its anguish and strength to its affirmations. With the fragments of a shattered hope, and building on the death of Jesus, which might have killed their faith outright, the disciples founded the religion of Jesus the Christ. Unconsciously, faith produces for herself all the illusions she needs.

Such explanations place the birth of Christianity in neurosis and illusion. Resurrection is simply the coming to life of a vain hope or an infatuated love. Like conspiracy theories, such explanations appeal to the hermeneutics of suspicion, to the presupposition that religious texts fundamentally function to camouflage other, less noble human appetites. And as with conspiracy theories, there is little in the texts themselves to support such interpretations. We know absolutely nothing of Mary Magdalene's emotional stability, even if she were the only one who had the experience, which the texts emphatically do not say. And the statement that the disciples' faith was too strong to die simply flies in the face of the texts, which agree on little but are unanimous on this: the disciples had little faith in Jesus and abandoned him completely at the end. Furthermore, these explanations show little understanding of the nature of religious experience, and so miss entirely the import of the texts and the real nature of the Christian confession of the resurrection of Jesus.

The experience of the resurrection does not have to do with fugitive visions of a poltergeist. It is not a belief that Jesus was resuscitated and then resumed his former way of living. It does not depend on the individual mystical flights of persons in the past. The Christian witness of the resurrection does not say that Jesus was spotted in passing by a few people before going away. Even the narrative that comes closest to suggesting that (Acts 1:9–11), which has Jesus ascending into heaven, is misread if understood that way. In Acts, the presence of the resurrected Lord is just as strong after the ascension as before it, indeed stronger; but it is a presence in a new mode.

The resurrection experience cannot be confined to the narratives of the Gospels, for the fundamental experience and conviction were available to those who neither saw the tomb nor had a vision of Jesus. The experience of his powerful presence was possible because he was alive and caused it. If we were to compress these observations, we could say that the resurrection experience that gave birth to the Christian movement was the experience of the continuing presence of a personal, transcendent, and transforming power within the community.

This understanding of the resurrection is given expression in the Gospel narratives. In John 20:20–23, the risen Jesus tells the disciples, "As the father has sent me, even so I send you,"

> and when he had said this, he breathed on them and said to them, "Receive the Holy Spirit. If you forgive the sins of any, they are forgiven; if you retain the sins of any, they are retained."

This clearly states that the empowerment of the disciples, which enables them to carry on the mission of Jesus in the world, derives from a Holy Spirit, which comes directly from Jesus himself (see John 14:18–31). The command of the risen Lord in Luke 24:47–49 is similar:

> You are witnesses of these things. And behold, I send the promise of my father upon you; but stay in the city, until you are clothed with power from on high.

Here, the commission to be witnesses finds its empowerment which comes from Jesus. In Acts 2:1–4, Luke provides a narrative symbolization of this empowerment, on the day of Pentecost:

> They were all filled with the Holy Spirit and began to speak in other tongues, as the Spirit gave them utterance.

This is followed by the first proclamation of Jesus as risen Lord, in Peter's speech. What requires interpretation by Peter first of all is the ecstatic condition of the disciples (Acts 2:12–13). It was their experience of power that demanded explanation. Peter says that this experience is a fulfillment of *prophecy* (Joel 2:28–32; Acts 2:17–21):

> In the last days . . . I will pour out my spirit and they shall prophesy . . . before the day of the Lord comes . . . and whoever calls on the name of the Lord shall be saved.

This text, in turn, is itself interpreted through the recital of the death and resurrection of Jesus (2:22–31). The experience and the conviction are brought together in Acts 2:32–33:

> This *Jesus*, God *raised* up, and of that we are all *witnesses*. Being therefore exalted at the right hand of God, and having received from the father the promise of the *Holy Spirit*, he has poured out *this which you hear and see*.

Beginning with the experience, the interpretation involves the understanding of Torah in the light of the death and resurrection, and returns again to the starting point, the experience of power. *The possession of the Holy Spirit is the experiential correlative to the confession that Jesus is Lord.* Peter concludes: "Let all the house of Israel therefore know assuredly that God has made him both Christ and Lord, this Jesus whom you crucified" (Acts 2:36).

When we turn our attention from narrative material to statements found in other NT writings, we find these relationships even more clearly delineated. In chapter 4, I showed how the first Christians claimed freedom, boldness, joy, perseverance in suffering, and newness of life. All of these claims, I suggested, are connected to statements about the experience of power. Now we can observe that the source of this power is said to be, with remarkable consistency, the Holy Spirit. Indeed, for all practical purposes, we can say that the symbol of the Holy Spirit in these writings corresponds to the experiential term "power."

According to Acts 2:38 (cf. Matt. 28:19), the Holy Spirit was bestowed upon entrance into the community:

> Repent, every one of you, in the name of Jesus Christ for the forgiveness of your sins, and you shall receive the gift of the Holy Spirit.

It was the Holy Spirit that worked mighty deeds among believers (Gal. 3:3–5), which empowered them to proclaim (Acts 4:8; 1 Thess. 1:5; 2 Tim. 1:6) and indeed to confess their faith in the first place. Paul says in 1 Cor. 12:3:

> No one speaking by the Spirit can say, "Jesus be cursed," and no one can say, "Jesus is Lord," except by the Holy Spirit.

And it was the Holy Spirit that brought about the transformation of their consciousness (Titus 3:5; 1 Cor. 2:12).

This Holy Spirit is not an impersonal force; it is the life-giving presence of the risen Lord: "Because you are sons, God has sent the Spirit of his son into our hearts, crying, Abba, Father" (Gal. 4:6). This comes across even more clearly in 2 Cor. 3:17–18:

> Now the Lord is the Spirit, and where the Spirit of the Lord is, there is freedom. And we all, with unveiled faces, beholding the glory of the Lord, are being changed into his likeness from one degree of glory into another; for this comes from the Lord, who is the Spirit.

The connection between the Holy Spirit and the presence of Jesus is drawn again by Paul in 1 Cor. 2:12 and 16. He states first the origin of the Spirit, "We have not received the spirit of the world, but the Spirit which is from God," and closes the discussion with the statement, "We have the mind of Christ." And in Rom. 8:11, the connection is made explicitly to the resurrection:

If the Spirit of Him who raised Jesus from the dead dwells in you, He who raised Jesus from the dead will give life to your mortal bodies also through his Spirit which dwells in you.

Finally, in the context of an extended discussion of the resurrection (1 Cor. 15:45), Paul makes this statement, which we can take as summation:

The first man became a living being; the last Adam became a life-giving spirit.

As these references indicate, the explicit correlation between the resurrection confession ("Jesus is Lord") and the experience of the Holy Spirit is a prominent feature of Paul's theology. But it is not exclusively a Pauline preoccupation. In addition to the texts I cited earlier, others where one can observe similar connections include 1 Pet. 1:12; 3:18; 4:6; Heb. 2:4; 4:12; 6:4; Jas. 4:5; 1 John 3:24; 4:13; 5:8; Jude 19, 20; Rev. 2:7; 4:2; 19:10.

The resurrection faith, then, meant more than a conviction that Jesus had resumed his life for a time and appeared to some of his followers. It was a conviction, corroborated by the present experience of his power even years after his death, that he was alive in a new and powerful way; that he shared, indeed, God's life. He was Lord, and his lordship was exercised in the world through his life-giving Spirit.

This confession, we should note, was no less scandalous in that world than in ours. It did not take the development of modern physics to make the resurrection a dubious proposition to sophisticated minds. Paul was mocked by some among his Stoic and Epicurean audience when he tried to preach Jesus' resurrection in Athens (Acts 17:32). The death and resurrection of Jesus was as paradoxical then as now, eluding logic and fleeing any response but faith or incredulity.

For the sake of clarity, we can reduce the proposition to all its frightening simplicity. First, that a man who everyone knew was killed is now alive; that is bad enough. But further, that what happened and is still happening in this singular historical person affects radically and powerfully the existence of every human being, because that man now shares the life of the ultimate, transcendent power of God. That is too much for the mind to grasp without protest!

It was the second part of the proposition that was particularly offensive to the messianists' fellow Jews. The shape of their objection helps us see the distinctive nature of the resurrection faith. At least one important sect of first-century Judaism, the Pharisees, believed fervently in the resurrection of the dead (see Acts 23:8). At least as a proposition, the resurrection would not have bothered them. The resurrection they awaited, however, was one destined for the just, and it was to be the eschatological event, the manifestation of God's kingdom. The confession that Jesus was resurrected was impossible for them, because, by the norm of Torah, he was not a just man; indeed his death was one that Torah declared cursed by God (Deut. 21:23; cf. Gal. 3:13). Even less could his resurrection be considered the eschatological event, for history manifestly continued on its course. Also implicit in the Christian confession was the claim to represent the authentic Israel, on the basis of having received the promise of the Spirit (see Acts 2:33; Gal. 3:14). That was an implication most Jews could not accept. Ultimately, it was not the confession of Jesus as Messiah that divided Christians from other Jews, for it was possible for Jews to make such confessions—as Rabbi Akiba did in the case of Bar Kochba—without apostasizing from Torah. It was the confession of a crucified sinner as resurrected Lord that was divisive. And this points us once more to the centrality of this confession for the birth of the Christian movement.

The conviction that Jesus is alive and powerfully active in the believing community is the implicit, and sometimes explicit, presupposition of all the writings of the NT. The Jesus of the Gospels is not simply a past figure of fond remembrance. He is living Lord confessed and experienced in the community, whose words now address believers not out of past weakness but out of present strength. The Jesus of the NT letters and Book of Revelation is not a static moral teacher or exemplar but a living and active presence, shaping through his spirit the community's identity: speaking through the church's prophets, teaching through its teachers, and healing through the hands of the believers.

It is because of the conviction that Jesus was alive and active that there was the expectation of his coming again to establish the kingdom among people. We have already seen the connection Paul drew between the resurrection and his coming (*parousia*) in 1 Thess. 4:14. It is also in connection with the resurrection that he states in 1 Cor. 15:24–28:

> Then comes the end, when he delivers the kingdom to God the father after destroying every rule and every authority and power. For he must reign until he has put all enemies beneath his feet. . . . When all things are subjected to him, then the son himself will also be subjected to him who puts all things under him, that God may be everything to everyone.

Another writer, for whom the resurrection means precisely that Jesus is alive and making intercession for everyone always, says (Heb. 9:27–28),

> Just as it is appointed for men to die once and after that comes judgment, so Christ, having been offered once to bear the sins of many, will appear a second time, not to deal with sin, but to save those who are eagerly awaiting him.

From the conviction that Jesus is alive and is commanding Lord comes the compulsion to proclaim the "good news," not alone on the basis of past commission but also on the basis of present command (Acts 13:2):

While they were worshiping the Lord and fasting, the Holy Spirit said, "Set apart for me Barnabas and Paul for the work to which I have called them."

And it was the risen Lord's spirit that was active in the words of the Church's prophets (Rev. 10:8–11):

Then the voice which I had heard from heaven spoke to me again, saying, "Go, take the scroll which is open in the hand of the angel who is standing on the sea and on the land" . . . and I took the little scroll from the hand of the angel and ate it; it was sweet as honey in my mouth but when I had eaten it, my stomach was made bitter. And I was told, "You must again prophesy about many peoples and nations and tongues and kings."

From the conviction that the risen Lord was present to them through the Spirit of God which was holy, derives the church's sense of itself as the authentic Israel upon which had come the spiritual fulfillment of the promise to Abraham (see Acts 2:33, 38–39; Gal. 3:14), the faithful remnant of the people of God (Rom. 9:22–33), and the dwelling place of the Spirit—therefore, the temple of God's presence (1 Cor. 3:16–17; Eph. 2:19–22; 1 Pet. 2:4–10).

If we were to ask which came first, the conviction that Jesus was alive or the gift of the Spirit that touched the believers with that life, we would be asking a question impossible to answer. The narratives suggest that the conviction, based on appearances, came first, and the empowerment by the Spirit came after. And this order respects the line of causality: the Spirit is given humans because Jesus is raised. But which occurred first in the experience of the Christians, we cannot say. From the first, experience and conviction, power and confession, were inextricably mixed, and together they formed the primordial experience of Christianity.

THE NEED TO INTERPRET

If the resurrection faith gave birth to the Christian movement, it also created the need for interpretation. This is simply because the resurrection faith is rooted in paradox. That a man everyone knows died is now alive and the source of power for all humans, that a person who died as a sinner is now the source of the forgiveness of sins for all others, is not a garden-variety opinion. It is a conviction and an experience that creates multiple and vexing problems for human understanding, specifically for those touched by this experience and committed to this conviction. I can here only indicate a few of the questions that had to occur very shortly to those who committed themselves to this crucified and raised Messiah.

Was Jesus' death on the cross really the death of a sinner and one cursed by God, as Torah would seem to indicate? If so, how do we reconcile our experience of life through him and our understanding of Torah? Must we choose between the legitimacy of Jesus' messiahship and the ultimacy of Torah? Or if he was not a sinner, then what is sin, and what is the meaning of justice? What was it about the man Jesus that caused God to raise him from the dead and install him as Lord?

If Jesus is Lord as we confess, then what is his relation to the God we call Father? Can there be two powers in heaven? Can God have partners and still be one? And what is Jesus' relation to the world, and to this community? Is the presence of his spirit so final and strong that it cannot be broken? If we in this church share the power of his resurrected life through the gift of his Spirit, why should we have to die? And, more pertinent, how should we live? Since he is present to us in power and his kingdom is somehow actual in his dominion as Lord, what more is there to look for?

How can we reconcile the presence of the Holy Spirit among us and the continuing presence of sin as well? If God is victorious over evil in the resurrection of Jesus, why then are we powerless in a hostile world? And if we are the authentic Israel, what does that mean for the historical people of God? If they have rejected Jesus as Messiah, does that mean they are rejected by God? And if so, does that mean God does not keep his promises? And if he has not kept his word to Israel, how can we be sure of his word to us?

It was not enough for the first Christians to experience the transforming transcendent power of the Spirit and proclaim that Jesus was Lord. They had also to find meaning, to interpret their lives in the light of this overwhelming experience. Out of the struggle of the first believers to find meaning in the paradox of the holy's being mediated to them through the death of a man, and the paradox of that power's being present to them in weakness as well as strength, emerged the interpretation of their existence. The world of symbols toward which they inevitably turned? The symbolic world of Torah, which they shared with their fellow Jews. The interpretive key for their new reading? The paradox of the dead and raised Messiah.

BIBLIOGRAPHICAL NOTE

The citation on pages 104–5 comes from E. Renan, *The Life of Jesus*, trans. J. H. Holmes (New York: Modern Library, 1927 [1863]), 357, and that on page 105 is from A. Loisy, *The Birth of the Christian Religion and the Origins of Christianity*, trans. L. P. Jacks (New York: University Books, 1962 [1933, 1936]), 97–98. The tradition of Loisy lives on in studies that attribute belief in the resurrection to the resolution of cognitive dissonance, finding it in a different place than I do here. Rather than thinking that the dissonance is caused by the disciples' hopes' being shattered by the crucifixion, I locate it in the experience of the resurrection, which shatters their symbolic world. See the very similar treatments of H. Jackson, "The

Resurrection Belief of the Earliest Church: A Response to the Failure of Prophecy?" *JR* 55 (1975): 415–25; and U. Wernick, "Frustrated Beliefs and Early Christianity," *Numen* 22 (1975): 96–130. Even more elaborately, the resurrection of Jesus is a disease of language according to P. E. Devenish, "The So-Called Resurrection of Jesus and Explicit Christian Faith: Wittgenstein's Philosophy and Marxsen's Exegesis as Linguistic Therapy," *JAAR* 51 (1983): 171–90.

For background to the remarks made in this chapter on religious experience, see R. Otto, *The Idea of the Holy*, trans. J. W. Harvey (London: Oxford Univ. Press, 1950); W. James, *The Varieties of Religious Experience* (New York: Macmillan Co., 1961 [1902]); J. Wach, *The Comparative Study of Religions*, ed. J. Kitagawa (New York: Columbia Univ. Press, 1958); M. Eliade, *Myth and Reality*, trans. W. Trask (New York: Harper & Row, 1963); G. Van der Leeuw, *Religion in Essence and Manifestation*, 2 vols. (New York: Harper & Row, 1968); and the phenomenological analyses of experience by G. Marcel, as in *Mystery of Being*, vol. 1: *Reflection and Mystery*, trans. G. S. Fraser (Chicago: Henry Regnery Co., 1969); and idem, *Creative Fidelity*, trans. R. Rosthal (New York: Farrar, Straus & Giroux, 1964).

Among some of the older, classic discussions of the resurrection faith, see D. Strauss, *The Life of Jesus Critically Examined*, ed. P. Hodgson (Philadelphia: Fortress Press, 1973 [1835]), 735–44, for a full range of naturalistic explanations. In contrast, F. C. Baur is terse and circumspect in *The Church History of the First Three Centuries*, ed. A. Menzies (London: Williams & Norgate, 1878 [1853]), 1:42: "The view we take of the resurrection is of minor importance for the History." The discussion by J. Weiss in *Earliest Christianity*, ed. F. C. Grant (New York: Harper & Row, 1959 [1914]), 1: 14–44, is full, critical, but ultimately psychologizing, as is that by M. Goguel in *La Foi à la Resurrection de Jesus dans la Christianisme primitif* (Paris: E. Laroux, 1933).

At least the older discussions took the issue seriously. Many recent histories of Christianity reduce the resurrection to a one-liner or less; see, e.g., W. H. C. Frend, *The Rise of Christianity* (Philadelphia: Fortress Press, 1984), 86; P. Johnson, *A History of Christianity* (New York: Atheneum, 1979), 32; H. Chadwick, *The Early Church* (New York: Penguin Books, 1967); H. Conzelmann, *History of Primitive Christianity*, trans. J. Steely (Nashville: Abingdon Press, 1973), 38–42. In contrast, see the serious treatment by L. Goppelt, *Apostolic and Post-Apostolic Times*, trans. R. A. Guelich (Grand Rapids: Baker Book House, 1970), 8–24.

Recent discussions are influenced by the challenging essay of R. Bultmann, "New Testament and Mythology," in *New Testament and Mythology and Other Basic Writings*, sel., ed., trans. S. M. Ogden (Philadelphia: Fortress Press, 1984 [1941]), 1–43. See for example W. Marxsen, *The Resurrection of Jesus of Nazareth*, trans. M. Kohl (Philadelphia: Fortress Press, 1970); R. Fuller, *The Formation of the Resurrection Narratives* (Philadelphia: Fortress Press, 1971); H. von Campenhausen, "The Events of Easter and the Empty Tomb," in his *Tradition and Life in the Church: Essays and Lectures in Church History*, trans. A. V. Littledale (Philadelphia: Fortress Press, 1968), 42–89. On the form of the resurrection accounts, see C. H. Dodd, "The Appearance of the Risen Christ: An Essay in Form-Criticism of the Gospels," in *Studies in the Gospels*, ed. D. Nineham (Oxford: Basil Blackwell, 1955), 9–35; see also W. O. Walker, "Post-Crucifixion

Appearances and Christian Origins," *JBL* 88 (1969): 157–65; and S. M. Gilmour, "The Christophany to More Than Five Hundred Brethren," *JBL* 80 (1961): 248–52. A generally sympathetic Jewish analysis of the resurrection of Jesus illustrates the final points of this chapter. Although Jesus may have been raised, this would still not signify that he was Messiah, for the world continued as it had always done. See P. Lapide, *The Resurrection of Jesus: A Jewish Perspective* (Minneapolis: Augsburg Pub. House, 1983).

6

Jesus in the Memory of the Church

THE NATURE OF THE CHRISTIAN EXPERIENCE DEMANDED INTERPRETATION as well as proclamation, and this interpretation inevitably centered on the person of Jesus. The reason is simple. The one who appeared to the disciples as risen Lord identified himself as the same Jesus who had died by execution on the cross. The man they had known as one who preached, healed, and suffered, they now knew as the powerful bestower of the Spirit. If the community gathered by that Spirit was to advance its own story, it was necessary for it to come to grips with Jesus' story. The continuing identity of the community and the living memory of Jesus were, therefore, inextricably intertwined. It is to the shaping of that memory that our investigation now turns.

ANAMNESIS

In quite different ways, the letters and Gospels of the NT represent crystallizations of memory, the literary distillation of traditions about Jesus that were transmitted and developed during the years after the event of Jesus' death and resurrection. In the Gospels, the story of Jesus is obviously central and explicit. The instruction of the church and the interpretation of its story is in them only implicit. Our present consideration of the memory of Jesus therefore serves as a natural transition to the reading of those documents. But it should be asserted that the memory of Jesus was no less important for the Book of Revelation and the epistolary writings. In them, the instruction of the church and the interpretation of its story are central and explicit. Still, the memory of Jesus plays an important if implicit role in them as well.

When we speak of the memory of Jesus *in* the Church, we do not mean simply a mechanical recall of information from the past. We mean, rather, the sort of memory expressed by the Greek term *anamnesis* (see Luke 22:19; 1 Cor. 11:24, 25). It is a recollection of the past that enlivens and empowers the present as well. Such memory is not restricted to the mental activity of individuals; it is found above all in the ritual and verbal activity of communities. So we have found in the Jewish Passover Haggadah that the recital of the events of the exodus long ago made the power of these events contemporaneous to the present generation: "Let everyone regard himself as having come out of Egypt." Anamnesis in earliest Christianity had a further complexity, for the one remembered from the past was also being experienced as present here and now. Jesus was not simply called back from the past by mental activity. The present experience of his power threw constant light on the experience of him in the past.

Memory such as this is intimately bound up with the *identity* both of individuals and of communities. The individual's story defines who she is as a person. The myth of a people defines it as a community. Individual or communal amnesia is a terrifying phenomenon precisely because anamnesis *is* identity. Without a past, we have no present and little hope for a future. The early church's identity was bound up with the memory of Jesus. It sought an understanding of its present in his past, just as it was motivated to search out his past by the experience of his presence.

Personal memory is always and inevitably *selective*. Not all of the past is remembered, for not all of the past is pertinent to the present. That much of the past is remembered which is important for the present life of a community. Selectivity, however, is not random: it derives from the continuing experience of those who remember. The present situation stimulates the memory of the past, calls out from shadow to the light of recollection. It is at least partially because the church faces opposition from its fellow Jews that it remembered how Jesus faced such opposition and responded to it. Some things are remembered, of course, simply because they were so important and impressive then and continue to be important and formative now. It did not take the breaking of bread to make Christians remember what Jesus said and did at his last meal with his disciples, though the breaking of bread was an appropriate occasion for perpetuating that memory.

The memory of the past is also *shaped* by the continuing experience of the community. As new experiences place old ones in different perspective, the human story is constantly revised. Former obscurity comes to clarity, former insignificance now looms large, as our present situation shapes our past. The meaning of a past crisis is affected by our present perception of it as preparatory or analogous to the crisis we are now going through. Our grasp of the present moment enables us to perceive in our past a more intelligible and universal shape.

So also was the memory of Jesus selected and shaped by the continuing experience of Christian communities. The process was made more complex by the distinctive nature of its continuing experience: the one they remembered was present to them now in power. Everything the believers remembered about his past words and deeds was colored by their standing on the other side of the resurrection experience. However faithful they intended to be to the past, their memory could not help being marked by their present perception. The one who spoke then in parables, also spoke now through prophets; the one who healed then, now healed through the hands of believers. The interpenetration of past and present experience made the development of Jesus traditions extraordinarily complex.

Nor was the memory of Jesus unaffected by contact with the diverse and changing circumstances of the first Christians. Their need to confront themselves, one another, and the world during a period of turbulent growth and conflict also colored their perceptions of Jesus. A number of these circumstances are located in the social contexts of the early Church. What were these social contexts and how could they help select and shape the memory of Jesus?

THE SOCIAL CONTEXTS OF TRADITION

The specific social settings of earliest Christianity must themselves be placed within the framework of the missionary expansion over the forty-year period preceding the writing of the first Gospel. The Acts of the Apostles provides the only sustained narrative of the spread of the gospel. Its treatment is selective and affected by its theological purposes, but it provides invaluable information that is corroborated by other NT writings.

In Acts 1:8, Jesus tells the apostles, "You shall receive power when the Holy Spirit comes upon you; and you shall be my witnesses in Jerusalem, and in all Judea and Samaria, and to the end of the earth." Luke uses this prophecy as an organizing principle for his narrative. He shows the "word of God" progressing from its center in Jerusalem (chaps. 1—8) to Judea and Samaria (chaps. 8—10), then to Antioch (chap. 11), and from there, through the missionary work of Paul and his companions (chaps. 13—28), to Rome, the "end of the earth" (28:16). Luke's theological concern accounts for two emphases in this picture: he demonstrates the peaceful continuity of the mission from Jerusalem to the gentile world; and, he shows that preaching began in synagogues and, only after its rejection there, moved to the Gentiles (13:46–47; 18:6; 28:25–28).

Acts oversimplifies in other ways. It tells us nothing about missionary activity in some areas of obvious historical interest. Concerning Egyptian or Galilean Christianity, he tells us nothing; of Syrian Christianity (apart from the brief notes on Damascus and Antioch), very little. As a good Hellenistic author, furthermore, Luke is interested mainly in cities; he never mentions rural evangelization. His irenic purpose leads him to downplay conflict and discord in the earliest communities, even though they can be spotted readily between the lines of his narrative (Acts 6:1–7; 9:26; 11:2; 15:1–21, 39; 21:21). And from Acts 13 onward, his focus is so tightly on Paul that all other developments vanish. The reader discovers that when Paul arrives in Rome as a prisoner, there is already a Christian community there (28:16) even though Luke did not trouble to describe the evangelization of the empire's capital city!

Despite its limitations, Acts provides an important framework for understanding the spread of Christianity. First, it makes clear that the movement grew by the establishment of churches. Christianity was a movement of social groups. The social setting for tradition is, therefore, intrinsic to the nature of the movement. Second, Acts shows how rapidly the message sped across vast geographic areas. Within seven or eight years after the death of Jesus, separate communities existed in Jerusalem, Judea, Samaria, and Syria. In twenty years there were communities in Cyprus and Asia Minor; after twenty-five years, communities flourished throughout Macedonia, Achaia, and possibly Dalmatia. Thirty years after Jesus was killed, there was a Christian community in Rome. These are conservative assertions.

The rapidity of Christianity's growth had real implications for the memory of Jesus. It meant that his memory had to be transmitted and preserved through new and changing circumstances. An immediate and fundamental transition was from a predominantly rural setting—presupposed by most of Jesus' words—to the urban settings addressed by Paul and Peter. Some linguistic adjustments were also required. Greek was spoken throughout the empire, and there were Greek-speaking Christians even in the earliest Jerusalem community. But the present Greek form of Jesus' words often suggests the presence of an Aramaic substratum. Insofar as his words required translation, therefore, subtle shadings of meaning would be both gained and lost. The movement's rapid spread into the pluralistic culture of the Diaspora meant as well that the memory of Jesus could be affected by contact with other traditions, such as those of Diaspora Judaism and Hellenistic philosophy and religion.

The point of these observations is simple. The evidence of the NT does *not* suggest that after the resurrection there was a long period of tranquil recollection and interpretation carried out under the tight control of a single stable community that, having forged the memory of Jesus into a coherent and consistent form, transmitted it to other lands, languages, and cultures. The evidence points in the opposite direction: there was no long period of tranquillity; the first community was from the beginning harassed and persecuted; the spread of the movement was carried out by many messengers and required flexible adjustment to new circumstances; the growth of a community's self-understanding and its memory of Jesus were mutually shaping influences. In the light of this evidence, what is surprising is not the diversity found in the memory of Jesus but that there is any consistency at all! Three community contexts were particularly important for both the growth and the stabilization of the Jesus traditions in the early church: preaching, worship, and teaching for the common life.

Preaching

The historical importance of this context is clear, but the determination of how much Christian preaching found its way into the NT writings or how much it transmitted the memory of Jesus is very difficult. Concerning its importance, it suffices to note that early Christianity was a missionary movement, and the proclamation (*kēryssein*) of what God had done in the death and resurrection of Jesus brought communities into existence in the first place (*kerygma* = what is proclaimed). NT letters allude with some frequency to the initial proclamation that founded churches (see Gal. 4:13; Col. 1:3–7; Phil. 1:5; 1 Thess. 1:5; Heb. 2:1–4; Jas. 1:21; 1 Pet. 1:22–25). Because letters were written to churches already in existence, they presuppose and do not contain that earliest proclamation. Even letters like Hebrews and 1 Peter, which may have originated as homilies, move well beyond the first stage of missionary preaching (see Heb. 6:1–3; 1 Pet. 2:2). These sermonic letters do, however, pay relatively explicit attention to the significance of Jesus' earthly life and suffering (see 1 Pet. 2:21–25; Heb. 5:7–10; 12:1–3). Paul also appears to make reference to the narration of Jesus' death in his mention of the initial preaching made to the Galatian churches, "before whose eyes Jesus Christ was publicly displayed as crucified" (Gal. 3:1). Otherwise, we find only fragments of preaching in the letters similar to those I already mentioned in the discussion of the resurrection, that is, 1 Thess. 1:9–10 and 1 Cor. 15:3–8: ". . . the Gospel which you received, in which you stand, by which you are saved" (1 Cor. 15:1–2; see Gal. 4:4–7; Rom. 10:14–17). These texts show that it was preaching that turned hearers from their former lives to belief (Acts 2:37; 10:44; Gal. 3:2–5; 1 Pet. 1:13–22; Heb. 6:1) and commitment to the God who made Jesus both Christ and Lord. It is in this sense that preaching was foundational for early Christianity; faith came by "hearing" (Gal. 3:5; Rom. 10:5–17).

But how important was preaching for the preservation or formation of the memory of Jesus? A decision on this depends to some extent on one's judgment concerning the missionary speeches found in the Acts of the Apostles. Similar speeches are put into the mouth of both Peter (Acts 2:16–36; 3:12–26; 10:34–43) and Paul (Acts 13:16–41; 17:22–31). Paul's sermon to a pagan audience in Athens (17:22–31) is distinctive, but the others are strikingly similar. They maintain with more or less consistency that the age of fulfillment has dawned in Jesus, who is a descendant of David and carried out a ministry; that he was crucified, and raised by God as Messiah; that the Holy Spirit confirmed God's vindication of Jesus; and that Jesus would again return. On the basis of this message, a call is made for repentance. In Peter's speech of Acts 10:34–43, moreover, one can discern an outline resembling the Synoptic account of Jesus' ministry.

The critical question here is the extent to which Acts uses genuinely traditional materials or patterns of preaching. The answer is made difficult by observing Luke's by no means negligible literary methods. That both Paul and Peter follow this pattern would seem to indicate its traditional character. But then we notice that Luke has Peter and Paul work very similar miracles and that, together with all the first leaders of the community, they are described in stereotypical terms for theological purposes of Luke's own. We further observe that Luke uses speeches as a Hellenistic historian, to interpret and advance his narrative; that he systematically reworks any source he uses; and that he is generally fond of archaizing, especially in sayings material (see the canticles of Luke 1—2). On literary terms, the determination becomes nearly impossible.

To challenge the antiquity of the speeches, however, does not deny that their *pattern* may have been traditional. In their focus on the death and resurrection of the Messiah in fulfillment of the Scripture as the basis for repentance, they agree with the summary statements of the kerygma we find in the letters. Further than this, it is not easy to go. While it is more than likely that some account of Jesus' words and deeds was found even in initial preaching, it is not possible to specify more closely what sort of materials would have been used, whether they would have been part of a standard repertoire, or what function they might have performed.

A somewhat surer point of contact between the activity of preaching and the memory of Jesus may be found in the apologetic function of preaching. At least some early Christian preaching was done in Jewish synagogues (Acts 13:13–16; 14:1; 17:1–3; 18:4–5; 19:8; Rom. 1:16). At times, it led to disputation with Jews who opposed this proclamation of a crucified messiah. Acts mentions several public controversies between the messianists and their fellow Jews (6:9–10; 9:22, 29; 18:4, 28). Two of them explicitly state that the argument was over the messianic claims of Jesus and involved a disputation over the proper understanding of Torah (Acts 17:2; 19:8). Messianist preachers would have been required to answer objections from other Jews such as we find answered in the Passion narratives of the Gospels: Was Jesus a sinner and a criminal? Was his death one cursed by God? Was he rightly condemned as a seducer of the people by a legal Jewish court? Was Jesus' body stolen from the tomb by his disciples to perpetrate a fraud? Since the death and resurrection of the Messiah was the focus of the early kerygma, it would also be the obvious point of attack for those not accepting its message, and therefore the first part of Jesus' story requiring interpretation.

Worship

In worship, the convictions and experiences of religion come alive, and this context was important for developing the memory of Jesus in the church. The community's ritual and myth centered on what God had done through the death and resurrection of Jesus; the memory of him could not but have played a significant role in its worship.

Places of Worship

The Christian community remembered that Jesus had cleansed the temple as a prophetic act (Mark 11:15–18; pars.) and had taught in its precincts before his death (Mark 11:27; 12:35, 41; pars.). In the narrative about the earliest Jerusalem church, Acts shows the disciples attending temple services together (2:46; 3:2) and the apostles both preaching and healing in its courts (3:11–12; 5:42). We cannot be sure how long this continued, though it obviously came to an end with the destruction of the temple in 70 C.E. The practice seems to have had little effect on the memory of Jesus or even the use of temple symbolism for the community, which was employed very early (see 1 Cor. 3:16–17; Eph. 2:19–22; Heb. 10:19–25; 1 Pet. 2:4–8; Rev. 21:22).

Both in Jerusalem and in the Diaspora, Jewish Christians shared at least for a time in the worship of the synagogue. Acts shows Christians preaching Jesus in that context. That at least some messianists wished to remain as worshipers in the synagogue is shown by the necessity of nonmessianist Jews' expelling them (Mark 13:9; Matt. 23:34; John 9:22; 12:42; 16:2; Acts 6:11; 18:7–17), a practice that preceded the formal composition of a *birkat ha minim* (sometime after 85 C.E.), which finally forced Christians out of the synagogue worship. The NT writings use "synagogue" only once for the Christian worship assembly (Jas. 2:2; although cf. *proseuchē*, "place of prayer," in Acts 16:13, 16). The usual term used is *ekklesia* (e.g., in 1 Thess. 1:1; 1 Cor. 14:23). The main contribution of the synagogue to Christian worship was supplying the forms of prayer and the practice of reading and interpreting Torah as part of worship.

The dominant place for Christian worship in the NT period was the house (*oikia, oikos*). Even before Pentecost, Acts shows us the Galilean disciples gathering in an "upper room" for prayer (Acts 1:13), and the first believers who attended temple services were also "breaking bread in their houses" (Acts 2:46). People gathered in households to hear preaching (Acts 10:33; 16:32; 18:7), to pray (12:12), and to break bread and hear preaching (20:7–12). As the basic societal unit in the Roman Empire was the household, so we see "whole households" converting at once to the Christian movement (Acts 11:14; 16:15, 31; 18:8; John 4:53; 1 Cor. 1:16), with the heads of such households probably providing the place for worship as well as some leadership functions. We find repeated mention of the church that meets at an individual's house (Rom. 16:5; 1 Cor. 16:15, 19; Col.4:15; Phlm. 2). The house setting probably had some impact on the self-identification of the community as the "household of God" (1 Pet. 4:17; 1 Tim. 3:15; see Gal. 6:10; Eph. 2:19) and on the use of household ethics for exhortation, such as were employed in Hellenistic moral philosophy (see Col. 3:18–4:6; Eph. 5:21—6:9; Titus 2:1–10; 1 Pet. 2:13—3:7), as well as on the use of some terms like "edification," *oikodomein*, for the activity of establishing and maintaining community identity (Matt. 16:18; Rom. 14:19; 15:2, 20; 1 Cor. 3:9; 8:1; 10:23; 14:4, 17; 1 Thess. 5:11; 2 Cor. 10:8; 13:10; Eph. 4:16) and like "steward," *oikonomos*, for leadership within the community (1 Cor. 4:1; 9:17; Col. 1:25; Titus 1:7; 1 Pet. 4:10). It was a context that is reflected in some of Jesus' sayings, where the household, the steward, and the master of the household all figure prominently (Matt. 7:24–27; 12:25–29; 13:27, 52; 16:8; 20:1; Mark 10:29–30; 13:34–35; Luke 12:39–48; John 8:35; 14:2). No more definite connection can be made.

Forms of Worship

Cult. Cultic actions are natural occasions for the transmission of communal memory. The two main cultic activities of the early church were Baptism and the Lord's Supper. Each attracted to itself a body of tradition. Baptism, of course, was the ritual of initiation into the community (Acts 2:38, 41; 8:12, 36; 9:18; 10:48; 16:15, 33; 1 Cor. 1:15–16) that took the place of the Jewish ritual of circumcision (Col. 2:11–12). Aspects of the ritual action may be reflected in symbols of washing (Acts 22:16; 1 Cor. 6:11; Heb. 10:22; Eph. 5:26; Titus 3:5), of light (Eph. 1:18; 5:8–9, 14; 1 Pet. 2:9; 2 Tim. 1:10; Heb. 6:4), the taking off and putting on of garments (Gal. 3:27; Col. 3:8–10; Eph. 4:22–25; Jas. 1:21; 1 Pet. 2:1), and of unification of opposites (1 Cor. 12:13; Gal. 3:28; Col. 3:11). The symbolism of death and rising appears to be connected to Baptism even before Paul (Rom. 6:3–11; Col. 2:12) and is implied by the sayings of Jesus (Mark 10:39) as well as by the accounts of his baptism by John in the Jordan (Mark 1:9; Matt. 3:16; Luke 3:21; John 1:32–33). The Christian experience of Baptism also provided a perspective for the reinterpretation of Torah, as in the typological reading of the exodus story by Paul in 1 Cor. 10:1–5 and of the Noah story by Peter in 1 Pet. 3:20–21.

The second cultic context for the development of the memory of Jesus was the meal. Acts lists "breaking bread in houses" as one of the activities of the first believers (2:42, 46) and describes one occasion of such activity at which Paul also preached (Acts 20:7, 11; cf. 27:35). That meal was celebrated on the first day of the week, which Paul also specifies as a day of assembly (1 Cor. 16:2) and the Book of Revelation calls the Lord's day

(Rev. 1:10). As we have seen, all meals in Judaism had a certain sacrality, being accompanied by blessings. Such was undoubtedly also the case with these special meals, which are called love feasts (*agapai*) in Jude 12 and 2 Pet. 2:13. Some if not all of these meals derived their special character from the remembrance of Jesus' final meal with his disciples. Paul calls such a meal the Lord's Supper (*kyriakon deipnon;* 1 Cor. 11:20), and specifically connects the sharing of bread and wine at it to the actions and words of Jesus the night before his death (1 Cor. 11:23–25):

> I received from the Lord Jesus what I also delivered to you, that the Lord on the night when he was betrayed took bread, and when he had given thanks, he broke it and said, "This is my body. . . ."

As the remembrance of the exodus at the Passover meal made that event real for every Jew, so the remembrance of Jesus' words and gestures at his last meal makes effective the presence of the Lord.

Paul's use of this tradition is obviously close to the accounts of the last supper at which Jesus performed those actions and said those words (Matt. 26:26–29; Mark 14:22–25; Luke 22:19–22). The meal context was also an appropriate setting for the memory of Jesus' miraculous feeding of the multitudes—notice the language of blessing and breaking in those accounts—during his ministry (Matt. 14:15–21; 15:32–39; Mark 6:34–44; 8:1–10; Luke 9:10–17; John 6:1–14, 53–58). The conviction that Jesus was truly present as risen Lord among those who shared these meals (cf. 1 Cor. 11:27–32) also made them a congenial setting for the remembrance of those resurrection accounts in which Jesus eats and drinks with those to whom he appears (Luke 24:28–35, 41–43; John 21:9–14; cf. Acts 10:40–41).

Prayer. Communal worship also involved the use of set prayer forms. In these we find the influence of the synagogal liturgy on early Christianity, as well as the decisive impact of the experience of Jesus. This is seen at once in the blessing formula (*berakah*), which as we saw, was the standard form of Jewish prayer. We find the blessing used in Eph. 1:3–14; 2 Cor. 1:3–7; 1 Pet. 1:3–9ᐧ (cf. Rom 1:25; 9:5). But in them the stereotyped opening "Blessed be the Lord" is fundamentally modified by the Christian conviction that Jesus too is somehow Lord ("Jesus is Lord"; 1 Cor. 12:3; Rom. 10:9; Phil. 2:11), so that these blessings begin, "Blessed be the God and father of our Lord Jesus Christ." The special filial relationship between Jesus and God is locked into this prayer formula (cf. Rom. 15:6; 1 Cor. 8:6; 2 Cor. 11:31; Col. 1:3; 2 John 3).

A similar blessing formula is found in a prayer of Jesus, wherein he addresses God as Father (Luke 10:21; cf. Matt. 11:25–26):

> I thank [*exhomologoumai*] thee Father, Lord of heaven and earth, that thou

hast hidden these things from the wise and understanding and revealed them to babes; yes, Father, for such was thy gracious will.

God is also addressed as Father in the prayer that, according to Luke 11:2–4 and Matt. 6:9–13, Jesus taught his disciples to pray; the two versions of the prayer are different, with Matthew's seven-membered version more closely resembling the form of Jewish prayer. On major feasts, the *amidah* or prayers said while standing consisted of seven rather than eighteen benedictions, and the phrases of the Matthean version (esp. the fifth, sixth, and ninth) resemble parts of those benedictions and especially the doxological *kaddish*, or sanctification of the name: "Magnified and sanctified be his great name in the world which he created according to his will. May he establish his kingdom during your life."

The interpenetration of the prayer forms of the early church and the living memory of Jesus can be seen especially in the perdurance of three Hebrew and Aramaic expressions in early Christian worship. In 1 Cor. 16:22, writing to a Greek-speaking, largely gentile community, Paul says, "If anyone has no love for the Lord, let him be accursed. Our Lord, come!" "Our Lord, come!" is in Aramaic: Paul uses the word *maranatha*. That Paul can employ the Aramaic in this context and presume its intelligibility is fascinating. It indicates first that it was a foreign-language phrase used by the community itself, in all likelihood in its liturgy of the Lord's Supper (cf. 1 Cor. 11:26: ". . . you proclaim the Lord's death until he comes"). Second, it means that Paul, who founded the community, handed on to it a tradition (cf. 1 Cor. 11:23) that had its origin in Aramaic-speaking circles, probably in Palestine. Third, it indicates that Jesus was called Lord *(maran)* in the early Palestinian communities as well as in the Diaspora.

A second Aramaic expression quoted by Paul is "abba." It is a diminutive, affectionate form for "father." Paul cites it in Gal. 4:6 (cf. Rom. 8:15):

Because you are sons, God has sent the spirit of his son into our hearts, crying "Abba, Father."

This is probably also a liturgical expression, as indicated by the context in Galatians (see 3:23–29). What is most striking here is not simply that the Spirit enables the cry, or that it is spoken in Aramaic even by Greek-speaking Christians, but that the cry "Abba" is one most distinctively associated with Jesus in his earthly life. The most significant occurrence is when Jesus prays to God before his death (Mark 14:36):

Abba, Father, all things are possible to thee; remove this cup from me. Yet, not what I will, but what thou wilt.

The third expression is in Hebrew, and in it the interrelationship of the church's prayer and the memory of Jesus is particularly complicated. It is the simple word "Amen." As used in Jewish prayer, it expressed an affirmative response to a statement or wish made by others, "So be it" (see, e.g., 1 Cor. 14:16), or even to a prayer said by oneself. It typically came at the end of a statement and in this form is used through the epistolary writings of the NT (Rom. 1:25; 11:36; 15:35; 1 Cor. 16:24; Gal. 1:5; Eph. 3:21; Phil. 4:20; 1 Thess. 3:13; 1 Tim. 1:17; Heb. 13:21; 1 Pet. 4:11; 2 Pet. 3:18; Jude 25; Rev. 1:6–7). On the other hand, one of the most distinctive aspects of Jesus' own speech, as reported in all four Gospels, is his use of Amen. Jesus, however, used it to affirm the truth not of another's statement but always of his own, and he never said it at the end of a statement but always in the beginning: "Amen, I say to you" (see, e.g., Matt. 5:18; 16:28; Mark 8:12; 11:23; Luke 4:24; 21:32; John 1:51; 5:19). In the light of this, one can only wonder at the characterization found in Rev. 3:14. The risen Lord, seen in a vision, employs the phrase "The words of the Amen, the faithful and true witness, the beginning of God's creation." And in 2 Cor. 1:18–20, again with specific reference to Jesus, Paul says,

> As surely as God is faithful, our word to you has not been yes and no. For the son of God, Jesus Christ, whom we preached among you, Silvanus and Timothy and I, was not yes and no; but in him it is always yes. For all the promises of God find their yes in him. That is why we utter the Amen through him, to the glory of God.

Finally, as reported by Pliny the Younger, the Christians also sang "hymns" to Christ. The worship services undoubtedly included the singing of songs, psalms, and hymns (Eph. 5:19; Col. 3:16; 1 Cor. 14:26; Rev. 5:9; 14:3; 15:3). Through certain formal features—use of an introductory relative pronoun, rhythmic strophes—it is possible to detect at least fragments of such hymns in the NT epistolary literature, where they are used as the basis for exhortation (Col. 1:15–20; 1 Tim 3:16; 1 Pet. 1:22–25; 3:18, 22; Phil. 2:6–11). Of these, the hymns in 1 Peter and Philippians show the clearest interest in and resemblance to the memory of Jesus as described in the Gospels. The several numinous hymns of the Book of Revelation (e.g., 4:11; 5:9) are addressed both to God and to "the Lamb," and are almost purely songs of praise.

Spiritual Utterances. The pervasiveness and importance of this aspect of early Christian worship is difficult to assess. There is scattered evidence of speaking in tongues and prophecy in several writings (see Acts 2:4; 11:27; 21:9–10; Mark 16:17; 1 Thess. 5:20; 1 Tim. 4:14; Rev. 19:10; Rom. 12:6). We also hear of prophets as persons with gifts sufficiently regular in their manifestation to be recognized together with apostles and teachers (1 Cor.

12:28; Eph. 2:20; Rev. 10:7; Acts 13:1). We find a detailed account of these activities, however, only in 1 Cor. 12:1—14:40, which is devoted to the problems generated by a too unstructured expression of these gifts. We cannot even say whether the manifestation of these gifts took place in conjunction with or separate from other forms of worship, such as the Lord's Supper. The distinctive feature of these forms of speech is that they are regarded as directly inspired by the Holy Spirit—in effect, by the Spirit of Jesus (1 Cor. 12:4–11). Speaking in tongues was fundamentally an ecstatic mode of prayer (see 1 Cor. 14:2, 14–16). Prophecy, in contrast, although it was equally inspired (1 Cor. 12:10), had a rational element to it (1 Cor. 14:19) and issued in speech intelligible to others (1 Cor. 14:16). Paul therefore sees prophecy as speech which can build up (*oikodomein*) the community in its faith (1 Cor. 14:4–5, 12, 17, 24–25). That much is clear.

More difficult to determine is the content of prophetic "revelations" (1 Cor. 14:26, 30) and the relationship of these sayings to the memory of Jesus. If "prophetic words" (2 Pet. 1:19) were introduced as a "word" (2 Thess. 2:2) or the "word of God" (Rev. 1:2, 9; 19:9) or the "word of the Lord" (1 Thess. 4:15), on the pattern of oracles in Torah (Isa. 1:10; Jer. 2:2; Amos 7:16), then there could easily develop complex relationships between what came from the Lord as life-giving Spirit now present to the community (see 2 Cor. 3:18) and what came from the Lord by way of memory of what Jesus said in his earthly ministry (cf. the ambiguity in 1 Cor. 7:10; 11:23; 14:37; 1 Thess. 4:2; 2 Thess. 3:6).

An example of such complexity is the saying that Jesus would return "like a thief." In Rev. 3:3b, we find it as a statement of the risen Lord, delivered through prophecy to the church:

> If you will not awake, I will come like a thief, and you will not know at what hour I will come upon you.

It appears as a classic case of prophetic revelation. Yet, immediately before it, comes "Remember then what you received and heard; keep that and repent" (Rev. 3:3a). Is the prophet repeating an earlier tradition in his own prophetic utterance? If so, what was its source? Next, we find the tradition in a letter by Paul, who tells the Thessalonians (1 Thess. 5:2 and 2 Pet. 3:10):

> You yourselves well know that the day of the Lord will come like a thief in the night.

Finally, we find it in the Gospels. In an eschatological discourse of Jesus (Matt. 24:43; Luke 12:39), there is this variation in the mouth of the earthly Jesus:

> Watch, therefore, for you do not know on what day your Lord is coming. But

know this, if the householder had known in what part of the night the thief was coming, he would have watched and not let his house be broken into.

The possible relations between these versions are obviously many. The prophetic utterance to the community could have initiated the saying, with its subsequently becoming part of the memory of Jesus reported in the Gospels. Or the prophetic word could have recalled in the power of the Spirit a word said by Jesus during his ministry, and this prophetic utterance then might have affected the way it was reported in the Gospel narrative. These options do not even consider the possibility of current proverbial expressions' affecting the memory at either end. We cannot, it goes without saying, determine the direction of the flow of influence. But we can observe the complexity and learn from it how the memory of Jesus was undoubtedly influenced by what was said by him in the past as teacher and what was perceived to be coming from him in the present as risen Lord.

Another example, of the judge at the door, makes the point even clearer. In Rev. 3:20, there is a prophetic message of the risen Lord:

Behold, I *stand at the door* and knock; if anyone hears my voice and opens the door, I will come in to him and eat with him and him with me.

In the Letter of James 5:8–9, we find the same image in an eschatological warning:

Establish your hearts, for the coming of the Lord is at hand. Do not grumble, brethren, against one another, that you may not be judged. Behold, the *judge is standing at the doors.*

And we find the image in an eschatological saying of Jesus (Matt. 24:33; Mark 13:29):

So also, when you see these things, you know that he is near, *at the very doors.*

The same image, in sum, occurs in a prophetic utterance of the risen Lord, in a parenetic letter, and in the Gospels. A final note: Is there a connection between this saying and the self-characterization of Jesus in John's Gospel as "the one who comes through the doors" (John 10:2)?

Reading and Preaching. Here in all probability is a case of a practice's being so well established that we find little specific evidence for it. The church remembered that Jesus had read in the synagogue and preached there (Luke 4:16–30; cf. Mark 6:1–6; Matt. 13:53–58; John 6:59), as Paul had done also (Acts 13:13–16). And Acts shows us Paul preaching to an assembly gathered for the Lord's Supper (20:7–9). But we have no specific report of the reading of Torah in the assembly for the earliest period, although Paul tells Timothy to "attend to the reading, prayer, and teaching" in the church at Ephesus in his absence (1 Tim. 4:13). The practice was so much a part of synagogal worship that we can assume its continuance in Christian worship with some confidence, particularly since it continued into the period for which we have ample documentation. Furthermore, the reading of Paul's letters out loud to the gathered assembly (2 Cor. 7:8; Col. 4:16; 1 Thess. 5:27; 2 Thess. 3:14) suggests a precedent for such public reading. The two NT letters that have often been thought to have originated as sermons (1 Peter and Hebrews) are marked by a very vigorous use of scriptural interpretation, such as would be appropriate for homiletic midrash. But beyond such suggestive remarks, we cannot go.

Teaching for the Common Life

The memory of Jesus was also selected and shaped by the experience of churches as they tried to live out the implications of their new identity within the structures of the world. The question of how to live in the light of their transcendent and powerful transformation was real. But equally pressing were the questions posed by their mundane circumstances. The first Christians had to deal with critical and obviously spiritual issues such as the discernment of true prophecy from counterfeit (1 Cor. 14:29; 1 Thess. 5:19–21; 1 John 4:1–3), but they were equally required to answer questions about the manifestations of that Spirit in their life together (Gal. 5:13–26), a life that included the realms of political and social structures, work and leisure, diet, and sexual activity. Did their new experience of God in Jesus have any implications for these aspects of their lives?

The necessity of coming to terms with such areas accounts for the development of teaching (*didaskalia, didachē*) in the early church. Teaching is an activity with many functions and settings, and the traditions that can be associated with it are extensive. Teaching could find many occasions. In Acts 19:9–10, Paul is said to have spent two years in Ephesus debating in the lecture hall of Tyrannus. Paul sees himself as a teacher to his communities (1 Cor. 4:17; cf. 1 Tim. 2:7; 2 Tim. 1:11). If he followed the practice of some Cynic philosophers, he may even have taught his close followers while practicing his trade as a leather worker (Acts 18:3; 1 Thess. 2:9; 2 Thess. 3:6–12). Paul also taught his communities through trusted delegates whom he sent to remind communities of his teachings and instructions (1 Cor. 4:17; Phil. 2:19–24; 1 Tim. 4:11; 2 Tim. 2:2; Titus 2:1).

There were also local teachers in Pauline and other churches (Acts 13:1; 1 Cor. 12:28; Eph. 4:11; Rom. 12:7; Gal. 6:6; 1 Thess. 5:12; Jas. 3:1). In 1 Cor. 14:26, a "teaching" is placed among charismatic gifts such as tongues and prophecy, but most teaching was probably carried out in a nonecstatic context. Some communities may have followed the synagogal practice in which study of Torah and prayer flowed one into the other naturally; thus the synagogue was both house of study and place of prayer. If Christian teaching took place in this context, we can locate such communal activities as midrash and diatribe, both of which are reflected in NT writings as products, but both of which presuppose a process that is communal and scholastic. Such a context allows us to make some sense of the Pauline prohibitions against women speaking in the assembly (1 Cor. 14:34–36; 1 Tim. 2:11–15), even though it is clear that they are already praying and prophesying during worship (1 Cor. 11:5). If we take seriously the mention of teaching (1 Cor. 14:26) and learning (1 Tim. 2:11–12) in these passages, we may find Paul (as elsewhere; see, e.g., 1 Cor. 11:2–16) clinging to the residual cultural perception that moral teaching was a distinctively masculine obligation, specifically associated with the transmission of moral precepts from father to son (see 1 Cor. 4:14–15), whereas motherhood was the culturally appropriate mode for women to exercise influence over children's formation (1 Tim. 2:15). Despite this, it is clear that women were in fact also teaching—otherwise there would be no need for correction—and took an active part in the Pauline mission (Rom. 16:1, 3, 6, 12).

The ambiguities of life together and the need to clarify the relationship of that life to the gospel proved to be influential in shaping the memory of Jesus. The questions formed by the church's life stimulated the memory of what Jesus had said and done, and the framing of those questions inevitably had impact on the eventual shape of the memory as it was passed on. At the same time, there was undoubtedly something to remember. The process was not one of untrammeled creative fantasy. The first generation of believers was not so caught up in a charismatic cloud that it could not distinguish between its own handiwork and tradition, or that it thought that such a distinction was unimportant.

The best example is Paul's carefully qualified discussion of virginity and marriage in 1 Corinthians 7. In successive sentences, he distinguishes relative degrees of authority for his statements. In 7:8, he says "To unmarried widows, *I* say . . ."; but in 7:10, he asserts, "To the married I give charge, *not I but the Lord,* that a wife should not separate from her husband. . ." We see here that Paul distinguishes what he offers on his own authority and what is backed by a command of the Lord—and this from one who asserts that he too had the Spirit of God (7:40). And, of course, we find such an absolute prohibition against divorce enunciated by Jesus in the Gospels (Mark 10:11; cf. Matt. 5:31–32; 19:3–9; Luke 16:18). We do not know, unfortunately, whether Paul had that command by oral tradition from the past or by prophetic announcement in the present— or both. But he makes clear he did not invent the saying. This is made even more obvious, when he continues in 7:12, "To the rest *I* say, *not* the

Lord . . .," and in 7:25, "Concerning the unmarried, I have no *command of the Lord*, but I give my opinion."

In response to the questions raised by their worldly circumstances—which were immediately evident and troublesome, not needing many years to become obvious—teachers sought to find precedent for the community's practices (Why do we act this way?), and guidance for the community's decisions (What should we do in this situation?). They sought to find both in the words and deeds of Jesus. That they did so is the clearest sign of the importance of the memory of Jesus for the identity of the Christian community.

The community could, for example, find precedent for its practice of sending out preachers two by two (Acts 13:2; 15:40; 18:5; 1 Cor. 9:6) and for the preachers' practice of shaking the dust off their feet when rejected by their hearers (Acts 13:51), in the practice and commands of Jesus (Mark 6:7–12; Matt. 10:14; Luke 9:5; 10:1, 11). As the preachers exercised gifts of healing within the community (1 Cor 12:9, 28–30), they could find the pattern of their healing by prayer and anointing for forgiveness of sins (Jas. 5:14–15) in the healing deeds of Jesus that led to the forgiveness of sins (Mark 2:9–10; pars). If they did not observe the Sabbath as other Jews did but met together on the resurrection day, they could find precedent for their freedom from the Sabbath law in the deeds and words of Jesus (Mark 2:23–28; pars.; John 5:2–9). Those who chose not to observe days of fasting (Gal. 4:10; Rom. 14:5–6) found an example in the freedom of Jesus from fasting (Mark 2:18–21; pars.). Those who did choose to fast, could also find warrant in the words of Jesus (Mark 9:29; Matt. 6:16–18). Those who enjoyed open fellowship with Jew and Gentile alike (Gal. 2:12–13; Acts 11:1–18) found a precedent in the free fellowship Jesus enjoyed with sinners and tax collectors (Mark 2:15–17; pars.). In cases like these, it is impossible for us to determine whether the practice came from the example or whether the example was at least partially shaped by the practice.

Teaching also sought to give guidance for future practice. The demands of the gospel were not obvious in every circumstance. Paul was able, we have seen, to apply a saying of the Lord to one aspect of sexual behavior, namely, divorce, and he could call on the whole range of Jewish precedent to exclude obvious sexual immorality (see 1 Cor. 5:1–5; 1 Thess. 4:3–8). But for other aspects of sexual behavior, he could offer only advice. We see a similar situation with regard to work. Should Christians who expect the return of the Lord, perhaps imminently, continue their worldly occupations, making a living, earning money for their families? The answer was not obvious (1 Cor. 7:29–31). Paul faced a critical example of the problem in Thessalonica (1 Thess. 4:11; 2 Thess. 3:6–12). Here Paul reminds the

community not only of his own example of working for a living (2 Thess.
3:7–9) but also of the command that he had earlier given for all to work
(3:10), a command he calls part of the *tradition* they had received from him
(3:6). Now he emphatically repeats the command, "in the Lord Jesus
Christ" (3:12). Had Paul handed on to them sayings of the Lord regarding
work? He was certainly aware of specific commands of Jesus concerning
such practical matters as support for the gospel (see 1 Cor. 9:14; 1 Tim.
5:18). And if so, did these commands resemble the sort of sayings we find
in Luke 10:7; 12:37–48; and 17:7–10? We cannot be certain, but it is
possible.

Paul faced the problem of diet in Corinth. Did Christians need to
establish alternative sources for their food to ensure its purity, or could
they purchase and eat their food anywhere without regard for its possible
contact with idolatry before it reached them? In Paul's careful discussion
of this issue (1 Corinthians 8—10), he does not refer to any decision made
by the church as a whole (cf. Acts 15:23–29), nor does he refer to any
sayings of Jesus. In some communities, however, a similar problem must
have activated the memory of a teaching by Jesus on just this point, for in
Jesus' controversy with the Pharisees over purifications, the direction of
Jesus' teaching is succinctly summarized: "Thus he declared all foods
clean" (Mark 7:19).

Other practical questions required answering. How were Christians to
use their material possessions? Were the commandments of Torah binding
for them, and if so, how? Their memory of Jesus made it clear that the love
of God and of neighbor was at the heart of their obligation (Gal. 5:14;
Rom. 13:8–10; Jas. 2:8; Mark 12:28–34; Matt. 22:34–40; Luke 10:25–
28). But what did that mean in specific cases? Who was the neighbor?
These issues are raised in the epistolary literature, and we find teachings
on these issues in the sayings and stories of the gospel tradition (see, e.g.,
Luke 10:25–37; 12:13–34; 16:1–13). The precise connection between the
questions and the answers cannot, however, be firmly established.

Today's critical reader, therefore, faces a very real problem. It is impossible to sort out exactly what came from the earthly Jesus and what
originated in the spirit-filled utterances from the "risen Lord." This was
not, however, a problem for those who lived by these utterances. For them,
the same Holy Spirit was at work in the deeds and words of Jesus in the
past as was at work among them now. Both the present worship of Jesus as
Lord and the memory of Jesus as teacher shaped the identity of the
church. The selecting and shaping of that memory was regarded not as
betrayal or distortion but as a deeper insight and understanding of the past
by those who continued to live in the presence of the beloved, whose
present power opened up new appreciations of his past (see John 2:22;
7:39; 12:16; 20:9–10). The words of Jesus in his last discourse in the

Fourth Gospel (John 14:25–26) give accurate expression to the religious understanding that underlay all this development of tradition concerning Jesus:

These things I have spoken to you, while I am still with you. But the Counselor, the Holy Spirit, whom the father will send in my name, he will teach you all things, and bring to your remembrance all that I have said to you.

THE FORMS OF MEMORY

The memory of Jesus was affected not only by the social contexts of churches, but also by certain persistent habits of human memory, the ways it molds the past into usable portions for the present. An awareness of these patterns, together with the simple observation that in the various canonical Gospels we find individual short segments of material of striking similarity being used in quite different arrangements, leads us to the awareness that the Gospels are written compositions that employ diverse traditions handed down by oral—and perhaps also some written—transmission over a period of some forty years. The traditions were handed on, furthermore, not in ordered or sustained narratives, but in short sayings and stories. Their stereotypical patterns result from the process of telling and retelling in community contexts. As stones grow smooth with regular rubbing, so do stories often repeated. We turn, then, to some consideration of those sayings and stories in which the memory of Jesus was mediated to the Gospel writings. The process of transmission may be grasped in its essential lines by developing a rather extended analogy, one whose anachronistic character and simplicity will remind us that these observations are not a matter of science but of appreciating the art of storytelling.

We can imagine a family remembering its recently deceased matriarch and can observe the process of remembering Grandmother. The family as a social group engages in this sort of memory above all at ritual occasions, such as holiday meals and ceremonies of passage like graduations, weddings, and funerals. The occasion, or some part of the ritual, will trigger the process of remembrance. Someone will begin, "Remember how Grandma used to say . . . ," and then all will chime in. The basic form of remembrance is the short tale or anecdote. Even Grandma's wise sayings or memorable mannerisms are related to tales that set up the significant point.

Many of the stories sound alike. The matriarch quite likely repeated herself in word and action in her long life and was observed by different witnesses. She may have said quite similar things to different grandchildren, just as she undoubtedly baked more than one pie. Her repeated and characteristic behavior in the past, therefore, aids the process of forging the memory of her into set forms. While the stories are being told, there is also mutual correction taking place. Older members with longer memories correct errors of sequence ("No, she said that *after* Grandpa died") and false attribution ("Grandma didn't say that; Aunt Hilda did"). When eyewitnesses are no longer around, the next generation is dependent on the form and sequence of the stories the earlier process of criticism left as established. Then an even more formal shape is given to the memories. There is a collection of Our Grandmother stories capable of being told and retold even by generations who never knew her at all except as mediated by these tales.

Closer analysis of the casual family stories over a Thanksgiving turkey shows that they tend to fall into categories. The largest of the categories are those of Things Said, and Things Done. Repeated settings and patterns provide the basis for further categories: Arguing with Grandpa stories, or Advice to the Grandchildren stories. There might even be a loose collection of Grandma's One-Liners, sayings whose occasion no one can any longer recollect but whose bite and wit are so clearly hers that they are treasured as "typical of Grandma." Do they resemble bits of wisdom available elsewhere? It does not matter; Grandma made them her own and gave them her own personal stamp and style.

No one is in the least disturbed by a lack of exact chronology in these stories or by a certain amount of repetition or by the failure to get all the details straight. This is not a biography that is being researched but a family remembering its beloved founder. The memory of her makes her come alive again, just as the eating of the pumpkin pie prepared according to her secret recipe almost makes her appear in the kitchen door.

An observation of several families thus reminiscing about their grandmothers would yield an even greater stock of remarkably similar stories. Since grandmothers do tend to act alike in certain ways, cultural stereotypes of "typical grandmotherly" behavior develop. Sometimes it is hard to tell how much the shape of our very real memories of our grandmother may be affected by these larger cultural patterns. That our grandmother happened to fit several of these stereotypes, however, in no way diminishes our sense of her as real and singular in her presence to us.

Oral tradition of this sort has certain consistent tendencies. First, the specific details of time and place are rapidly lost, for the simple reason that they are largely irrelevant. What is important is the significant saying or deed, not the occasion; the point of the story is who grandmother was and therefore who we are. Second, and for the same reason, the punch line or decisive gesture is remembered far more clearly than the setup or situation. Indeed, at times the situations almost appear to be interchangeable.

Sometimes only the punch line is remembered and the family debates the appropriate setting. Third, the more often the stories are repeated, the shorter they get. They become more formulaic, tighter in focus, snappier. As a result, the stories also tend to resemble each other more. The first time a story is told, it is filled with extraneous detail and subjective reactions. With frequent repetition it is reduced to the essentials.

The possibility of applying this analogy to the development of the memory of Jesus in the church seems clear. We have seen how ritual occasions and the need for community teaching stimulated the memory of Jesus among those who believed in him as risen Lord. We have also observed that the community's need for precedent and guidance gave this memory a definite shape, even as it shaped the community's identity.

The analogy also helps us see how a large number of stories about Jesus in the Gospels fall into stereotypical *forms;* but first some cautionary remarks concerning the limits of this sort of analysis. There are limits, first, to our analytic precision. It is possible to divide the memories of Jesus into Things Said, and Things Done, of course, as it is possible to describe other subgroupings. It must, however, be recognized not only that there are mixed forms (e.g., an exorcism story and a controversy story joined together into a literary whole, as in Mark 1:21–28) but also that some materials escape classification altogether. Second, care must be taken not to deduce too easily from the *form* of a story its life-setting or function within that setting. The real value in cataloguing these forms is twofold: it enables us to appreciate how the memory of Jesus was carried by means of such short units rather than by complex discourses and narratives; and the description of a formal pattern enables us to detect deviations from it, which may prove helpful for the understanding of a particular story.

Among the sayings of Jesus, we find controversy stories, parables, aphorisms, and other looser discourses. Controversy stories (e.g., Mark 2:15—3:6; 7:1–23; 10:2–9; 12:13–17, 18–27, 28–34; pars.) have a regular sequence of elements: (1) an action by Jesus or his disciples (2) stimulates a challenge from opponents, leading to (3) a pronouncement by Jesus. The pronouncement is often a well-formed statement of more general application than the particular situation that generated the controversy. In his parables, Jesus compares some readily observable natural or human phenomenon to the kingdom of God he is proclaiming. Some parables are used for attack (Mark 3:23–27), others for defense (Luke 15:4–10); some attempt to make clearer (Matt. 13:24–30), others to mystify (Mark 4:3–8). They range from simple analogies (Matt. 13:44–46) to extended allegories (Mark 12:1–11), but all of them give a narrative form to metaphor.

In Jesus' aphorisms, we find single striking statements that can easily be separated from, or are only loosely attached to, their literary setting in the gospel story. Sometimes they are found joined together by the mnemonic device of catch-words (see, e.g., Mark 8:34–37). Other sayings material is less easily categorized. The apocalyptic discourse of Jesus in Mark 13, for example, can be broken down into individual units (aphorisms, parables), but it also holds together as a sustained discourse.

The stories about Jesus also fall into some formal patterns. The most regular patterns are found in the healing and exorcism stories. In healings, we find a set pattern: (1) the notice of the sickness, (2) the action by Jesus, (3) the result, (4) the reaction of bystanders (see, e.g., Mark 1:30–31, 40–45; 2:1–12; 5:21–42; 7:31–37; 8:22–26; pars.). The pattern of the exorcisms tends to be very similar: (1) the notice of the demoniac, (2) the dialogue between spirits and Jesus, (3) the command to depart, (4) the physical sign of departure, (5) the restored state of exorcised person, (6) the reaction of bystanders (see, e.g., Mark 1:23–26; 5:1–13; 7:24–30; 9:17–29; pars.). Other stories about Jesus, such as his nature miracles (e.g., Mark 4:35–41; 6:45–52; pars.) and his feeding of the crowds (Mark 6:34–44; 8:1–10; pars.), are harder to fit to set forms; and some stories, like that of the transfiguration (Mark 9:2–8 pars.), resist categorization completely.

Two further literary remarks can be made about these patterns. First, the formal shape of many of the stories suggests that they were shortened and tightened with repetition, and thus grew to resemble each other; that they preserved the essential deed or saying more accurately than the circumstance; and that they had little concern for geography and chronology. Second, the stories about Jesus also resemble stories found in the broader cultural world of the first century. The form if not the substance of many of Jesus' sayings can be paralleled in parables told by rabbis, in *chreia* (short biographical vignettes with pronouncements) attributed to philosophers, and in controversy stories found in both traditions. The healings and exorcisms of Jesus can be paralleled by similar accounts in Hellenistic religious aretalogies and biographies.

Finally, a historical observation. Nothing in this sort of formal analysis leads to a firm judgment concerning the fidelity of the church's memory of Jesus or its historical basis. That our family has twenty stories about Grandmother baking pies neither proves nor disproves that she baked at least one pie in her long life. That our twenty pie-baking stories could be matched by thousands of others about grandmothers neither confirms nor disconfirms the culinary skills of our particular grandmother. Such stories do, however, say something about the community that preserves that sort of memory. They indicate as well that Grandmother was the sort of person about whom pie-baking stories were appropriate. And if each Thanksgiving our family eats a pie baked according to her secret recipe, that gives an edge to the memory.

THE MEMORY OF JESUS' DEATH

The hardest memory of Jesus and the one most requiring interpretation was his death on the cross. The shape and extent of that interpretation best show us the range of the church's creativity in transmitting Jesus' memory. I begin with some general observations on the Passion narratives of the four Gospels, which recount Jesus' last hours, from his final supper with his disciples to his burial. Then I will raise questions concerning the origination of the accounts, and I will return once more to the texts.

All four canonical Gospels have Passion narratives (Matt. 26:1—27:66; Mark 14:1—15:47; Luke 22:1—23:56; John 13:1—19:42). In each, the narrative is extensive, by far the longest segment in Jesus' story. This length is more impressive because the Passion narratives of each Gospel is a sustained narrative, rather than the sort of loose sequence of smaller units we find in the story of Jesus' ministry. Each is a narrative, moreover, that shows fastidious attention to detail. Notices of time and place elsewhere in the Gospels tend to be casual and vague; here they are specific. Elsewhere, long stretches of time can be indicated by "and then," whereas here we find virtually a minute-by-minute account.

The Passion narratives, furthermore, have a relatively high degree of agreement between them. The agreement is most striking between the Synoptic Gospels and the Gospel of John. The agreement of the Synoptics (Matthew, Mark, Luke) among themselves can to some extent be credited to their literary interdependence. Differences of detail and emphasis persist, to be sure; but by contrast to the rest of the story of Jesus, and in essentials, the Passion accounts show a remarkable unanimity. Finally, each Gospel meticulously prepares for the suffering and death of Jesus ahead of time, so the course of the narrative as a whole points in that direction. In the Synoptics, Jesus formally predicts his death three times (Mark 8:31; 9:31; 10:33–34; pars.). In John, repeated mention of Jesus' "hour," his "being lifted up," and his "being glorified" serve the same function of foreshadowing the cross (John 2:4; 3:14; 7:6, 39; 12:27–32).

These observations tend to support the conclusion that the Passion narratives are the earliest sustained accounts of Jesus' memory, indicating that the part of Jesus' life most requiring interpretation was its last hours. This is further supported by Paul's close agreement with a small segment of that narrative in his report of Jesus' words at the last supper, in 1 Cor. 11:23–25, written some twenty years after the event.

Paul's First Letter to the Corinthians also provides us with some insight into the reason it was necessary to crystallize this memory of Jesus so early in the church's life. When discussing the resurrection experience (p. 101), I cited 1 Cor. 15:3–8, the kerygmatic tradition. Before Paul speaks of the resurrection "according to the Scripture," he says that Jesus "died according to the Scripture and was buried." He also insists that this is the message by which they are being saved—unless they believed in vain (1 Cor. 15:2). Why was this insistence necessary? Because the cross was the difficult part of the message to accept. Everywhere in 1 Corinthians, we meet a congregation that was richly gifted with spiritual powers (1 Cor. 1:5, 7) and that understood this bestowal of power as one that established its members in a position of reigning in God's kingdom (4:8). They were not eager to hear that part of the message that implied the need to suffer. Indeed, when Paul refers to his preaching to them, he says that the cross is foolishness to those who are perishing but the "the power of God" to those being saved (1:18). He says further that the cross is "a stumbling block to the Jews and a folly to Gentiles." Why? "Because Jews demand signs and Gentiles seek wisdom" (1:22), and Paul's preaching did not meet those expectations, "but we preach Christ crucified" (1:23; cf. Gal. 3:1).

Paul here makes it plain that the preaching of the crucified Messiah reversed the expectations of his hearers' symbolic world. Not only the expectations of outsiders were overturned, we hasten to add, but the expectations of insiders as well. The cross was the part of their experience of Jesus that demanded immediate and intense interpretation. The cross was a slippery machine for saving: people could slide from it in several directions (see also Gal. 1:6; 2:17; 3:1–5).

By the standards of Hellenistic heroes, Jesus' end was obviously not impressive. He had faced death not with apathetic calm but with wrenching anguish; he had left his followers not with words of memorable grace but with a cry of utter desolation (Matthew and Mark); he had not embraced a dignified suicide but endured a grisly execution; he did not bypass death in apotheosis or escape it by his sophistry or use it as an opportunity to demonstrate virtue. He was simply executed like a common criminal. To Greeks and Christians who thought like Greeks, the cross was foolishness and weakness; the divine power *(dynamis)* did not work thus.

Jesus' death was even harder to reconcile with the claim to have experienced the Holy Spirit through him, for those who lived within the symbols of Torah. When they looked to Jesus for signs of messiahship, they were disappointed. He failed miserably and palpably by any zealot test of messiahship: he did not restore kingship but only bore its mocking title on his tree. But his death was particularly a "stumbling block" (see Rom. 9:33; 1 Pet. 2:8; Luke 20:17, with reference to Isa. 8:14) to those Jews who hoped for a religious messiah, one who would establish the rule of God's righteousness under Torah. Not only did he not fulfill in any visible or significant fashion recognized messianic texts (e.g., Psalms 45; 89; 2 Sam. 7:11–16; Mic. 5:2–4; Amos 9:11; Mal. 3:1–4; 4:5; Isa. 9:2–7; 11:1–16; 49:8–13; 52:1–12), but he was not even a recognizable martyr like the

Maccabees, who died in defense of Torah. No, he was from his beginning to his end a "sign of contradiction" (Luke 2:34), standing in complete opposition to their understanding of how God manifested his power and righteousness. His life and death alike challenged the status of Torah as the absolute norm for life. In his manner of living, he was a sinner (2 Cor. 5:21), and in his manner of dying, he was cursed by God. Torah could not, on this, be clearer: "Cursed be every man who hangs upon a tree" (Deut. 21:23). In the light of Jesus' death, this text must have been cited in accusation against the first Christians (see Gal. 3:13). Far from being the source of the Holy Spirit, Jesus was cursed by God and his death proved it!

For those who believed in Jesus as risen Lord, the problem was not less severe. How could they ease the tension between their experience of the power of life from Jesus and the conviction they shared as hearers of Torah, that God did not work through sinners? Once more, we find the conflict between experience and symbolic world. And it is here we find the impetus to interpretation; not only to defend their faith from outside attack but also to support it against inner erosion and confusion.

Now we can return to Paul's puzzling statement that Jesus' death was "in accordance with the Scripture." How could it be, if Torah itself called his death a curse? Because of this contradiction, the first Christians turned again to the normative texts of their symbolic world. They read Torah again, for they had to find meaning. This was an instinctive move. The same texts that condemned Jesus were the normative texts by which they understood their experience as well. But now they had to read them in the light both of the resurrection and of the manner of Jesus' death. And this led them to texts they had never before considered messianic, led them to read old texts in new ways. It was as though their eyes were opened. Indeed, two Gospels make this aspect of the resurrection experience quite clear. In John's Gospel, it was when Jesus was raised that the disciples began to understand *both* what he had said and done *and* the Scripture (John 2:22; 12:16; 20:9). In Luke's appearance accounts, the risen Lord "opens the eyes" of the disciples to the real meaning of Torah: "Beginning with Moses and the Prophets, he interpreted to them in all the Scriptures the things concerning himself" (Luke 24:27; cf. 24:44–46).

To which texts were their eyes opened as a result of the experience of the crucified and raised Messiah? In light of the resurrection, they appropriated the text that spoke of a king exalted to dominion but whose rule is not yet fully achieved (Ps. 110:1; cf. Acts 2:34; 1 Cor. 15:25; Heb. 1:3; Mark 12:36; pars.). But in light of the suffering, they discovered texts that spoke not of a dominating king but of a lowly one (Zech. 9:9), and of a stone that was rejected by builders but has become the cornerstone (Ps. 118:22). Above all, they read with fresh eyes passages speaking of a just person who suffered at the hands of others not because of misdeeds but because of an allegiance to the Lord, hoping the while for vindication from God for his fidelity; passages such as these they found in Psalms 69 and 22 (cf. also Wis. 2:12—3:11; 4:7–18). And in the Suffering Servant songs of Isaiah, they found almost the precise pattern of what, in fact, they had experienced in Jesus: a righteous one whose death was in obedience to God and an offering for others (Isa. 42:1–4; 49:1–7; 50:4–11), and for whose shameful death God gave a reward of being "exalted and lifted up" (Isa. 52:13—53:12). In the encounter between Philip and the Ethiopian eunuch (Acts 8:29–40), the God fearer who was reading Isa. 53:7–8 asked Philip of whom the prophet spoke, himself or another: "Philip opened his mouth, and beginning with this Scripture, he told him the good news of Jesus" (Acts 8:35).

Such rereading and reinterpretation of the texts of Torah enabled the Christians to place the experience of Jesus within their symbolic world. The way they read those texts would never find agreement among those Jews who did not share their experience or their conviction. But for them, the interpretive process was effective and convincing. They were not manipulating or distorting the texts; they were simply and truly seeing them in a new way. And these perceptions had to affect both the way they remembered the story of Jesus' last days and the way they told that story. Now, the death of Jesus appeared to them not as accursed, but as a death in which he bore the curse of others (Gal. 3:13). Jesus was not a sinner but a just man (Luke 23:47; Acts 3:14). His death was not a punishment of him but a sacrifice for others (1 Cor. 15:3; Rom. 3:24–25). His death was not an accident but a fulfillment of God's will (Eph. 1:5–10). His death did not appear to be obedience to Torah but it was in fact a radical obedience to the God who revealed Torah (Phil. 2:8; Heb. 5:8), and in light of it, Torah would need to be reevaluated as the ultimate norm of righteousness. These convictions they found confirmed by Torah itself. The categories of interpretation became their categories of perception, and these progressively became the symbols by which they told the story itself.

In Jesus' Passion predictions, we find expressed the conviction not only that Jesus knew of his fate and accepted it but that this fate was part of God's plan: "the son of man must [dei] suffer" (Mark 8:31; Luke 9:22; 17:25; cf. Luke 24:26; Acts 17:3). In the Passion narrative itself, when Jesus comes to the supper, he tells his disciples that "the son of man goes as it is written of him" (Mark 14:21). As he gives them the cup of his blood, he says it is "for many" (Mark 14:24; cf 10:45), words that directly recall the death of the servant "for many" in Isaiah 53:12. After the supper, Jesus himself cites the Scripture concerning his disciples' betrayal (Mark 14:27, citing Zech. 13:7):

You will all fall away, for it is written, "I will strike the shepherd, and the sheep will be scattered." But after I am raised up, I will go before you to Galilee.

The impact of this rereading of Torah shows itself most emphatically in the description of Jesus' death. It is the moment of greatest scandal. It appears meaningless as fact; yet for believers, it is the revelation of "the power of God," and meaningful. In this scene, we find the very words of Torah shaping the story of Jesus' last moments. There is considerable variation between the Synoptics and John here. John also uses the words of Torah to tell the story, but he uses entirely different texts to do so. I take notice only of Mark's account. At the moment of his own death, Jesus cries, "My God, my God, why have you forsaken me?" Mark cites this in Hebrew and has the bystanders, ironically, misunderstand it. The readers hear it translated and understand. They recognize it as the beginning of the psalm of God's servant who suffers and is vindicated (Psalm 22), and they know the end of the story. A closer look at Mark 15:23–37 indicates that the words of Torah have provided more than a citation. Woven into the bare facts of the account are details that are shaped directly and unmistakably from the very words of the Psalms, so that Mark 15:23 = Ps. 69:21; Mark 15:24 = Ps. 22:18; Mark 15:29 = Pss. 22:7, 109:25; Mark 15:31 = Ps. 22:8; Mark 15:34 = Ps. 22:1; Mark 15:36 = Ps. 69:21. In this way, the story of Jesus' death is truly "according to Torah."

How did the continuing experience of Christians affect this memory of Jesus' death? They saw it from the other side of the resurrection and so remembered it in the light of Jesus' power and the conviction that he was the Just One and God's son. They saw it, further, in the light of their experience of conflicts with Jews over messianic claims that involved attacks on Jesus' death as that of a sinner. They remembered it, finally, as interpreted through the reading of Torah.

But did they invent or create this memory of Jesus' death? Of course not. Precisely the need for interpretation, precisely the problematic nature of that event, argues for its historicity. This community would not have invented a crucified messiah, since it showed itself so eager to escape the implications of that fact. When we read the Passion narratives of the Gospels, therefore, we find a memory unquestionably selected and shaped by the experience of the church. But it is equally a memory that itself shaped the church.

What we have discovered here can be applied, one suspects, with a somewhat lesser degree of certainty, to the other memories of Jesus. Something happened, but the search for its meaning must recognize the element of interpretation that is always present. Indeed, only *as* interpreted could it be remembered at all.

CONCLUSION

Here I have tried to give an account of the generative experience that makes intelligible both the need to remember Jesus and the shape those memories took. Such an attempt must always be more suggestive than conclusive; perhaps that is its value. If the reader now turns to the individual writings of the NT with a sense that the process of their composition is somehow intelligible, the exercise is well rewarded.

And as the reader turns to the Gospels and letters and Book of Revelation, it should be with the realization that these diverse writings are crystallizations of traditions that developed in complex and multiform contexts, that they were written as witnesses and interpretations for other believers, and that they continue to engage, in their diverse literary forms, the symbolic world of first-century Judaism and Hellenism, as they translate the story of Jesus for the continuing life of the church.

BIBLIOGRAPHICAL NOTE

This chapter's title is borrowed from the book by N. A. Dahl, *Jesus in the Memory of the Early Church* (Minneapolis: Augsburg Pub. House, 1976) wherein one can find his seminal article on *anamnesis*. Together with the title essay of another Dahl collection, *The Crucified Messiah* (Minneapolis: Augsburg Pub. House, 1974), the article is of fundamental importance for understanding the development of the gospel tradition.

Various aspects of the social dimension of the earliest Christian movement are found in G. Lohfink, *Jesus and Community: The Social Dimension of Christian Faith*, trans. J. P. Galvin (Philadelphia: Fortress Press, 1984); R. Banks, *Paul's Idea of Commmunity: The Early House Churches in Their Historical Setting* (Grand Rapids: Wm. B. Eerdmans, 1980); and E. A. Judge, *The Social Pattern of Christian Groups in the First Century* (London: Tyndale Press, 1960). One of the best attempts to place the development of traditions within the social contexts of worship and controversy is C. F. D. Moule, *The Birth of the New Testament*, 3d rev. ed. (New York: Harper & Row, 1982).

On the speeches of Acts and their relation to the gospel tradition, see C. H. Dodd, *The Apostolic Preaching and Its Development* (New York: Harper & Row, 1964 [1935]); idem, "The Framework of the Gospel Narrative," in his *New Testament Studies* (New York: Charles Scribner's Sons, 1952), 1–11. Less confident of the traditional nature of these speeches is M. Dibelius, "The Speeches of Acts and Ancient Historiography," in his *Studies in the Acts of the Apostles*, trans. M. Ling (New York: Charles Scribner's Sons; London: SCM Press, 1956), 138–85. For the apologetic function of preaching, see B. Lindars, *New Testament Apologetic: The Doctrinal Significance of the Old Testament Quotations* (Philadelphia: Westminster Press, 1961); and with an emphasis on the generative power of the Scripture, C. H. Dodd, *According to the Scriptures: The Substructure of New Testament Theology* (London: Nisbet & Co., 1952). The issue of the exclusion of messianists from the synagogue is treated by R. Kimmelman, *"Birkat ha minim and the Lack of Evidence for an Anti-Christian Jewish Prayer in Late Antiquity,"* in *JCS-D* 2:226–44; see also W. Horbury, "The Benediction of the *Minim* and Early Jewish-Christian Controversy," *JTS* 33 (1982): 19–61. The complicated question of getting from Christian prophets to the traditions about Jesus is thoroughly treated by M. E. Boring, *Sayings of the Risen Jesus: Christian Prophecy in the Synoptic Tradition* (New York and Cambridge: Cambridge Univ. Press, 1982).

The middle section of this chapter represents an attempt to convey the valuable contributions of the discipline called form criticism, without getting caught in its semantic or historical tangles. For introductory treatments, see E. McKnight, *What is Form Criticism?* (Philadelphia: Fortress Press, 1969), and R. Bultmann and K. Kundsin, *Form Criticism,* trans. F. C. Grant, (New York: Harper & Brothers, 1934). For a survey of the literature, see W. G. Doty, "The Discipline and Literature of New Testament Form Criticism," *ATR* 51 (1969): 257–321. The classic early studies available in English are those of M. Dibelius, *From Tradition to Gospel,* trans. B. Woolf (New York: Charles Scribner's Sons, 1934), and R. Bultmann, *The History of the Synoptic Tradition,* rev. ed., trans. J. Marsh (New York: Harper & Row, 1968). The tendency of early form criticism to postulate an excessively creative community was countered from the side of rabbinic practice by H. Riesenfeld, *The Gospel Tradition and Its Beginning: A Study in the Limits of "Formgeschichte"* (London: A. R. Mowbray & Co., 1957); idem, *The Gospel Tradition* (Philadelphia: Fortress Press, 1970); and B.Gerhardssohn, *Memory and Manuscript: Oral Tradition and Written Transmission in Rabbinic Judaism and Early Christianity,* trans. E. J. Sharpe (Lund: C. W. K. Gleerup, 1961). From the side of Greek biographical techniques see G. Kennedy, "Classical and Christian Source Criticism," in *The Relationships Among the Gospels: An Interdisciplinary Dialogue,* ed. W. O. Walker, Jr. (Dallas: Trinity Univ. Press, 1978), 125–55. Sane and helpful comments on the shaping of forms can be found in V. Taylor, *The Formation of the Gospel Tradition* (London: Macmillan & Co., 1957). For an example of the crosscultural form-critical work more recently done, see the essays in R. Tannehill, ed., *Pronouncement Stories, Semeia* 20 (1981).

The impact of form-critical methods in the study of Jesus traditions can be observed by comparing the older study of T. W. Manson, *The Teaching of Jesus: Studies in Its Form and Content* (Cambridge: At the Univ. Press, 1935), to N. Perrin, *Rediscovering the Teaching of Jesus* (New York: Harper & Row, 1967). A systematic attack on the methodological soundness of traditional form-criticism was made by E. Güttgemanns, *Candid Questions Concerning Gospel Form Criticism,* trans. W. G. Doty (Pittsburgh: Pickwick Press, 1979), and more recently by W. Kelber, *The Oral and the Written Gospel: The Hermeneutics of Speaking and Writing in the Synoptic Tradition, Mark, Paul, and Q* (Philadelphia: Fortress Press, 1983), 1–43. In this chapter, I obviously take the position exactly opposite Kelber's (pp. 185–99) with regard to the early development—whether oral or written—of the Passion narratives.

PART THREE

THE SYNOPTIC TRADITION

THE SYNOPTIC GOSPELS (MATTHEW, MARK, AND LUKE) ARE IN SOME RESPECTS THE most distinctive and treasured writings in the NT canon. They are not by any reckoning the first composed. They certainly postdate Paul's letters, even though their traditions were being transmitted and transformed during the period of his ministry. Why, then, do I treat them first in this book? Simply to make the point that I am engaged not in a history of earliest Christianity or of the development of its concepts, but rather in an interpretation of its writings. The point is made emphatically by discussing documents written between the years 60 and 90 C.E. (Gospels) *before* those written between 40 and 60 C.E. (Pauline letters). There is also the literary logic of building on the analysis of the previous chapter, by showing how the memory of Jesus is shaped into sustained narratives.

Why then only the Synoptics and not also the Gospel of John? The decision to treat the Fourth Gospel separately owes nothing to any judgment concerning the supposedly more ancient or reliable traditions found in the Synoptics. The Fourth Gospel is considered later simply because it is quite another sort of narrative about Jesus, best understood by being read with the other writings from the Johannine symbolic world (see "The Johannine Traditions," part 6). I treat the Synoptics together because they share not only the same symbolic universe but even the same narrative framework. Indeed, they also share a complex relationship of literary interdependence.

Determining the exact nature of that literary relationship—the "Synoptic problem"—is not easy. The problem is that the Greek text of these three Gospels is in many places so nearly identical that some form of borrowing from one to another must have taken place at some stage of written rather than oral transmission. Just as striking, however, are the many, often minute, differences between them over those same stretches.

How can both similarity and diversity be accounted for? Most scholars think that Mark was written first and that Matthew and Luke followed Mark in the composition of their narratives, deriving from him the basic order of the story as well as much of their material. Matthew and Luke also used material not derived from Mark. Some of this non-Markan material is again so nearly identical that a written document conventionally called Q (= *Quelle*, i.e., "source") is posited as their additional resource. Finally, Matthew and Luke each have distinctive material gathered from still other hypothetical sources denominated M and L, respectively.

Such is the "two source" solution to the Synoptic tangle. A minority of scholars still resist it, claiming that the ancient tradition—going back to Papias in the second century—of Matthean priority is correct. They insist that the fact that Matthew and Luke share the same order of events as Mark does not entail their use of Mark; it could mean that Mark was the condenser of the other two. At the level of logic, this makes sense. But when one sits down with the Greek text in three columns and patiently sorts through the data, it is difficult to maintain that position. It is far easier to explain rationally the acceptance of the ninety percent of Mark that the other two adopt and adapt to their purposes than it is to explain a Markan rejection of the juiciest parts of Matthew and Luke, together with the stylistic vulgarization of the remainder.

The two-source hypothesis covers most of the data simply, but some anomalies remain, reminding us that we have in our possession only a hypothesis. We need occasional reminding that Q means only what is left out of Mark but shared by Matthew and Luke; it has no existence except as a scholarly abstraction. The possible influences from a continuing oral tradition and liturgical harmonization, furthermore, make the textual relations between these three Gospels even more complex. We must therefore be modest in our literary judgments.

Among such judgments that the reader will simply find bracketed out of the pages to follow are these: the possible prehistory of specific passages; the successive layers of Q, if layers there be; and minute discriminations between an evangelist's traditions and the use he puts them to. I will periodically point out the differences between the three Gospels, based on the study of the synopsis. The point of these observations is not to establish any literary or religious line of dependence but simply to sharpen our perception of each evangelist's method and message.

I consider the hypothesis of Markan priority to be correct and assume it in this book. But my reading of each Gospel *does not depend* on the correctness of that hypothesis. My approach is closer to that of literary criticism. My concern above all is with the final form of the text. The awareness that this final stage of composition resulted from a complex oral and written process, however, makes us sensitive to the peculiar density of these texts, as well as more appreciative of the simplicity and coherence of their finished condition.

Finally, a few preliminary words are in order concerning the nature of these writings and the possible reasons for their composition. The issue of genre does not require an elaborate discussion. The Gospels are obviously narratives about the life, death, and resurrection of Jesus. Despite occasional resemblance to Hellenistic legends and aretalogies, the form of the Gospels most closely resembles that of Hellenistic biographies. In tone they aspire to something more than entertainment or even edification. They retain something of the distinctive historical-mythical character of the church's primitive kerygma.

The reader is aware from the start of each of these narratives that the main character is not simply an admirable figure from the past, a teacher like Socrates or a wonderworker like Apollonius of Tyana. He is rather the one believed to be now alive and powerfully present. The words and deeds of his past are given deep resonance by the sounding board of the readers' present experiences and convictions. Christian readers could not help finding something of their story in his, for with his resurrection, they saw him as caught up in their story.

But why were such narratives written in the first place? This question is not easy to answer. Some have found the motivation for writing in specific problems facing Christian communities. The evangelists are seen as responding to these situations by telling the story of Jesus in such a way as to give guidance to their own generation. Sometimes external problems, such as persecution or the delay of the second coming, the Parousia, are suggested. Other times the problems suggested are those arising from internal divisions created by disagreements over the nature of discipleship or even of Jesus himself. Problems like these existed in early Christian communities. Traces of them can sometimes be discerned in the Gospel stories. But they were not new problems. Paul had already met all of them and had responded by sending delegates or writing letters. Such problems do not themselves explain why these early Christian teachers began to use the form of a written narration for their instruction, or why that narrative took the shape it did.

An older and simpler explanation may be closer to the mark: the human desire to remember Jesus and preserve that memory accurately for the generations to follow. The desire to set it down whole and get it right is sufficiently universal to require no special defense in the case of aging eyewitnesses and ministers of the word, who shaped the story of Jesus for the ages to follow. What is more interesting is that they fixed the tradition not in the form of propositions but in the form of realistic narratives. These lifelike portrayals of Jesus dominate the NT canon and provide the sharpest contrast to the literary productions of Gnosticism. For these believers, the story of the human being Jesus had continuing importance for the community that now confessed him as life-giving Spirit. The line from proclamation to the Gospel is extended by narrative. However realistic, the Gospels were not disinterested histories. They selected and shaped the story of Jesus for readers who already knew that story in some form, in accord with deliberate literary and religious purposes. In their witnessing, therefore, they interpreted, just as by their interpreting, the Gospels bore witness.

7

The Gospel of Mark

IN SOME WAYS, THIS SHORTEST OF THE GOSPELS IS ALSO THE STRANGEST and most difficult to grasp. This may account in part for the benign neglect of it in the history of interpretation. One could call the use of Mark by Matthew and Luke, as well as by Tatian in his second-century harmony of the Gospels—the *Diatesseron*—a sign of success, but in the process Mark was eclipsed by having its substance placed within the more open and easily intelligible narratives of the others.

Mark's Gospel was little read and less studied. This was partly due to the widespread opinion that he had only condensed Matthew's version, and partly due to the fact that his narrative met liturgical and catechetical needs less adequately than his Synoptic successors'. No commentary on Mark appeared until the sixth century and not another until the ninth. Even the patristic writers who know Mark belongs in the canon cannot agree on which of the allegorical beasts he should represent (see Irenaeus *Against Heresies* III.2.8 and Augustine *On the Harmony of the Evangelists* VI.9). What small attention patristic writers paid Mark was due largely to his supposed role as Peter's translator and therefore as connected to the apostolic witness. This tradition went back at least as far as Papias, perhaps based on the association of Mark with Peter in 1 Pet. 5:13. Even Papias felt it necessary to apologize for Mark's apparent lack of narrative order, assuring his readers that Mark had omitted nothing essential of what he had heard from Peter, and had made no error (Eusebius *Ecclesiastical History* III.39.15).

In sharp contrast, Mark has been the most popular of the Synoptics for scholars of the twentieth century. The first reason was the thought that Mark provided the earliest and most reliable historical source for those who quested for the historical Jesus. When the Synoptic problem was solved in favor of Markan priority, Mark's Gospel was regarded as free from the dogmatic accretions found in Matthew and Luke, and therefore as a clean witness. The hypothesis was shaken first by the discovery of the "messianic secret," Mark's peculiar way of at once revealing and hiding the significance of Jesus within the narrative (see 1:25, 34, 44; 3:12; 5:43; 7:36; 8:30; 9:9; cf. 5:19; 16:7). This pattern suggested something more than a guileless chronicle; in fact, it suggested a dogmatically motivated composition. Even more threatening to the perception of Mark as an unstained historical record was the work of the earliest form critics, who dismantled the narrative framework of Mark, saying that he was only an editor who had mechanically stitched together units of oral tradition.

The current favor accorded Mark began with pioneering literary-redactional studies. They showed that Mark's peculiar emphasis on Galilee (esp. 14:28; 15:41; 16:7) was a theological symbol. Likewise, Mark's anachronistic use of the term "gospel," *euaggelion*, revealed a self-conscious awareness of the multilayered nature of his narrative (see 1:1, 14, 15; 8:35; 10:29; 13:10; 14:9). As a result, Mark's Gospel was seen less as a direct witness to the life of Jesus or to the period of oral transmission than as a witness to the Christian communities of Mark's day.

Two main preoccupations characterize the study of Mark's Gospel today. The first takes seriously Mark's ability to reveal something of the historical setting it addressed, and seeks to find within Mark's narrative clues for the deciphering of history. Such readers find in Mark's treatment of the disciples, for example, an allegorical attack on some specific group of heretics or ecclesiastical leaders in the Markan community. The second preoccupation has been generated by the allusive character of Mark's narrative. For many readers, Mark is not the simplest but the most sophisticated of the evangelists, whose compositional techniques appear remarkably contemporary. Mark is therefore the subject of purely literary studies, often carried out in conscious dialogue with contemporary models of literary criticism.

APPROACHING MARK'S NARRATIVE

Calling Mark a literary genius is probably excessive. On the other hand, it is proper to appreciate the decisive turning point his Gospel represented in the shaping of Christian traditions. We do not know who Mark really was or where he wrote. We do not know Mark's readers, although they were certainly already Christian and obviously read Greek. So far as we can tell, however, Mark was the first to connect the notion of "good news," *euaggelion*—first understood as what God had accomplished in the death and resurrection of the Messiah—to a narrative of what Jesus himself had said and done, calling it too, "good news," *euaggelion* (1:1). It was a momentous decision with profound religious implications. By shaping Jesus' ministry so that it led inexorably to the Passion, Mark forced his readers to understand Jesus' words and deeds not as independent modes of revelation but as inextricably linked to that finale. And because Mark set out the traditions about Jesus in narrative form, the term "gospel" would henceforth have the sense of a literary medium as well as a message.

We can no longer reconstruct Mark's motivation for his writing or even determine when he did it. The absence of anachronism in his description of the temple's end (13:5–23) suggests a time before the end of the Roman War (67–70 C.E.); how long before, and whether connected to those hard circumstances, we do not know.

Nor is it easy to find one's way into Mark's narrative itself. Even its beginning and end, as we shall see, have been debated. The more Mark's tale is pondered, the more it resists easy characterization. Apparently artless and straightforward at a first reading, its reticence invites speculation from those who persist in questioning the text. Out of what silence did Mark's story emerge? What sources were available to him, and how did he use them? When his readers first heard Mark's narrative recited, did it challenge, correct, or confirm their previous implicit understanding of Jesus' story? What did Mark himself want the narrative to accomplish? All these questions escape easy answers.

There are clues within the narrative itself that enable the contemporary reader to approach the heart of Mark's message. The first is the literary structure of the Gospel. Mark not only tells a story, he establishes deliberate and meaningful connections between parts of it, signaling those connections to the careful reader. The way a narrative is structured is often one of the most important clues to its significance.

A second sort of clue is the way Mark delineates the characters in his narrative. Most important is the figure of Jesus. Mark had several means of subtly shaping Jesus' literary presentation. He could employ various messianic titles in meaningful combinations, such as Christ, Teacher, Lord, Son of God, and Son of man. Likewise, Mark could describe Jesus' characteristic actions in terms that would suggest to his readers the images of great persons of the Hellenistic world, such as thaumaturges or sages. He could also use the language of Torah in order to connect the story of Jesus to earlier scriptural stories, thus creating deeper resonances to the story of Jesus itself. We have already observed how Mark did this in the Passion narrative (see chap. 5, above). Finally, Mark could delineate characters by the interactions between them. There is the unseen but critical relationship between Jesus and the One whose will dominates the narrative and who speaks only to identify Jesus (1:11; 9:7), and whom Jesus calls Abba (14:36) as obedient son. Next, there is Jesus in conflict with opponents, above all in Mark's narrative, the scribes (see, e.g., 2:6; 3:22; 7:1; 8:31). Then there is the often mute role played by those crowds among whom Jesus acts, whose own responses are variable. Finally, there is the interaction between Jesus and his chosen followers, the "disciples." In Mark's Gospel, it is this relationship that yields the most persuasive indications of Mark's religious purposes in writing. It is with the disciples that Mark's readers would most naturally identify, and through their characterization Mark could most directly instruct his readers.

In the sections that follow, I attempt to pursue some of these clues in Mark's text. First, I consider some of the specifically literary aspects of the narrative. Then, I review Mark's story as a whole, giving particular attention to the relationship between Jesus and the disciples.

DECIPHERING THE LITERARY CLUES

Style and Structure

By the high standards of Greek rhetoric, Mark's prose is unimpressive. Indeed, both Matthew and Luke find his Greek in constant need of correction and improvement. Mark can be prolix and clumsy (see, e.g., 1:35; 9:3). His sentence structure is paratactic (that is, he joins clauses with "and" rather than by using relative pronouns and subordinate conjunctions), and this, together with his frequent use of the adverb "immediately," *euthus*, gives his narrative an immediate, sometimes even frantic, quality. He is also fond of slipping into the historical present in the middle of a story, thereby also giving a sense of immediacy, as storytellers do even today (see, e.g., 5:35–43). Mark helps his readers by translating Aramaic words into Greek (see 3:17; 5:41; 7:11; 15:22, 34) but sees no need to do so with Latin loanwords (see 5:9; 6:37; 12:15; 15:39).

Mark's compositional skills do not, at first glance, inspire much more respect. Like a recent scholar who accused Mark of clumsy construction, early form critics thought of him simply as an editor whose clusters of topically arranged materials, such as seed parables (4:3–32), controversy stories (2:15—3:6), and sayings on discipleship (8:34–37), were already organized in the process of oral transmission. They noted that Mark makes few real transitions, often being content to join vignettes by "and" or "immediately"; his chronological references are vague and unhelpful (see 9:2; 14:1; 15:42). Sometimes, he can follow the actions of Jesus hour by hour (1:21–38; 14:12—15:37); in other places, he can summarize an indeterminate period of ministry with a single line (10:1). For those seeking in the Gospel a clean linear development like that in Luke-Acts, Mark is a disappointment.

But he is far from being a careless editor. He is, in fact, an author of no mean skill. The careful reader can find in his story signs of a very special compositional technique that makes his narrative less linear and more dialectical. Sometimes his narrative arrangement, which first appears to be repetitive and clumsy, actually provides important clues for understanding.

An illustration of Mark's way of making his reader look twice, and therefore more closely, can be found in the series of stories between 4:35 and 8:27. The stories occur in a series of matching sets. A miracle on water in 4:35–41 is mirrored by a second in 6:45–52. The healings of 5:21–42 correspond to that in 7:31–37. A multiplication of bread in 6:34–44 appears a second time in 8:1–10. A saying on the meaning of bread in 6:52 is matched by another in 8:14–21. This whole cycle of doublets helps move the story from the question asked by the disciples in 4:41, Who is this man? to the question put by Jesus to the disciples, "Who do you say that I am?" (8:29). In the paragraphs that follow, I will touch on some other examples of Mark's literary techniques.

Sets of Three

It has long been noted that Mark has a fondness for threefold patterns. He puts together three seed parables (4:3–32), three popular opinions about John (6:14–15), three popular opinions about Jesus (8:27–28), three predictions of the Passion (8:31; 9:31; 10:33–34), three failures of the disciples to stay awake in the garden (14:32–42), three denials of Jesus by Peter (14:66–72). There is more than a simple fascination with a number or a law of folklore at work here: for Mark, the triad becomes an architectonic principle.

This can be seen first of all in his frequent use of literary intercalation. In its smallest form, two fragments of one story frame a third passage in something of a sandwich arrangement. For the contemporary reader, the method closely resembles the cinematic technique of cutting from one scene to another without smooth transition. Mark's reader is forced to see the frame and the middle together, in tension. The central story is illuminated—or darkened—by its placement within the frame, whereas the outer story is given density by being filled in this fashion.

A striking example occurs early in Mark's narrative. In Mark 3:21, we see Jesus' family on its way to seize him since they think he is crazy ("beside himself"). We find them again in 3:31–35, knocking at the door of the house where Jesus is seated with his followers. They ask to see Jesus. He refuses to see them and identifies those in a circle about him as his real family, those who do the will of God. By itself this framing story would be a straightforward if negative account about the mutual rejection found in the family of the Messiah. Notice, however, that Mark inserts within this frame a controversy between Jesus and the scribes from Jerusalem (3:22–30). They accuse him of casting out demons by demonic power. He responds with a parable about a house divided! He also pronounces on the sin against the Holy Spirit that cannot be forgiven, because, Mark tells the reader, his opponents had said he had an unclean spirit. Given the connections between madness (3:21) and unclean spirits

(3:30) in that symbolic world, and given the pattern of rejection found in both frame and middle—that those who reject Jesus are themselves rejected—the composite appears a powerful indictment. But of whom, exactly? The reader is left to wonder.

Mark also leaves the reader to puzzle out the connection between the healing of a twelve-year-old girl (5:22–24, 35–43) and the healing of a woman twelve years ill, which Mark inserts into that episode (5:25–34). Similarly, the prophetic shadow of John's beheading in 6:14–29 separates the sending of the Twelve on mission in 6:7–12 and their return in 6:30. The transfiguration of Jesus (9:2–8) reveals Jesus in splendor with Moses and Elijah—between a saying about the kingdom's coming in power (9:1) and a question about the prior coming of Elijah (9:9–13) which that statement would logically have prompted. In a somewhat more alternating pattern, the fall of the temple is entwined in the fate of a fig tree: Mark has Jesus enter the temple (11:11); when departing, he seeks fruit from the tree, finds none, and curses it (11:12–14); he returns to cleanse the temple, which had failed its proper role (11:15–18); he departs the temple and finds the fig tree withered (11:20–25). Mark makes no comment on any of this. He leaves the juxtapositions for the reader to figure out.

Mark's framing technique can be observed as well on a bigger scale. He places larger portions of the narrative between compositional signals. In Mark's Gospel, for example, Jesus heals two and only two blind men. The first is healed only gradually, since Jesus' first touch brings only hazy sight. This healing occurs immediately before the question is put to the disciples concerning Jesus' identity (8:22–26). The second man's healing is immediate, and leads to Bartimaeus's following Jesus "on the way" (10:46–52). Between these healings, which symbolize the turn from blindness to sight and from sight to commitment, Mark has placed Jesus' most explicit instructions to his followers on his identity and their call.

Even the overall narrative of Mark can be seen to have a triadic structure. It has often been observed that a critical turning point in Mark's story occurs when Peter declares Jesus to be Messiah (8:27–30). Before that point, the question, Who is Jesus? dominates. After Peter's confession, the journey to Jerusalem becomes the Messiah's self-revelation to his disciples as the suffering Son of man. The transfiguration account is an essential part of this turning in the story. When Jesus is shown to his closest followers as glorified, the voice from heaven identifies him, "This is my beloved son; listen to him" (9:7). The command "Listen" sets up the instructions on discipleship that follow (chaps. 9—10).

This announcement of Jesus as Son of God, however, is the middle one of three such declarations—abstracting from the cries of demons. The first occurs at Jesus' baptism, when the voice from heaven tells Jesus alone, "You are my beloved son, in whom I am well pleased" (1:11). The last occurs at Jesus' death, when one of his executioners says, "Truly this was God's son" (15:39). This triad of declarations at critical points in the narrative establishes a frame for the reader's perception of Jesus as Son of God. The three aspects are held in a tension that is left unresolved: Jesus, the chosen servant of the Father; Jesus, the glorified Lord and revealer; Jesus, the executed criminal. It is within this tension that the reader understands Jesus' prayer to the Father, Abba, in the garden (14:36), and his response to the high priest's question "Are you the Christ, the Son of the Blessed?"—a simple "I am" (14:62).

Later in this chapter, I will return to still another structural triptych, in the peculiar designation of Jesus as the stronger one (1:7). First in the Beelzebul controversy (3:23–27), last in the empty-tomb account (16:1–8), and in the middle, in the exorcism of the Gerasene demoniac (5:1–20).

The Open Ending

Typical of the difficulties Mark presents the reader is the understanding both of the end and of the beginning of his Gospel. A consideration of each in turn can lead us further into Mark's dense narrative and his particular shaping of the "good news."

The canonical text of Mark offers three different endings. The oldest and best manuscripts end at 16:8: the women who had come to the tomb to anoint Jesus fled, "and they said nothing to anyone, for they were afraid." Other manuscripts contain a series of appearance accounts (16:9–20). Still others insert a coda after 16:8, either as conclusion or as a bridge to the longer ending of 16:9–20. Which is the original Markan conclusion?

Some argue for the longer ending. They note that the Greek text of 16:8 ends in a conjunction, "for," *gar*, which appears to demand another clause. They think it odd to end a sentence, much less a whole book, so indeterminately. They add that 16:7, "There you will see him," calls out for the fulfillment the longer ending supplies.

The arguments for the shorter ending are stronger. The basic rules of textual criticism say that the best-attested, shorter, and harder readings are generally to be preferred to readings that are longer, smoother, and less well attested in manuscripts. Now, the ending in 16:8 certainly qualifies as the most difficult. While it is true that sentences and even whole books have been known to end with conjunctions, Mark's ending is not for all that any less truncated. Next, the shorter ending is far and away the best attested in the oldest and most reliable Greek manuscripts. Finally, it is much easier to explain the origin of the longer ending than it is to explain its loss: Mark 16:7, as we observed, does open a way for scribes to supply what they saw as the natural fulfillment of the prophecy, especially if these scribes knew the endings of Matthew and Luke. That this happened seems more likely since the longer ending weaves together traditions found in the other canonical Gospels (16:9 = John 20:11–18; 16:12 = Luke 24:13–35; 16:15 = Matt. 28:16–20; 16:19–20 = Acts 1:9–11). Finally, it seems likely that Matthew and Luke read Mark in this shorter version, since they both have an empty tomb account close to his but after that diverge dramatically in their appearance narratives.

The longer ending of Mark remains part of the canonical text, is read in the assembly as such, and contains a venerable tradition about the resurrection that should not be entirely reduced to its sources. But the distinctive Markan witness to Jesus is seen more clearly when we work with the shorter ending.

A puzzling finale it is. The women approach with amazement (16:5) and leave in fear (16:8). They do not pass on the message of a future appearance. The identity of the young man who delivers the message to them is left unspoken (16:5). What are we to make of this? Mark obviously believes Jesus was raised from the dead; such is the presupposition of the book and of its readers. Indeed, such also is the burden of the young man's message: Jesus is not among the dead, but "goes before them." He will appear, but at his own choosing. But if Mark and his readers knew traditions of Jesus' having appeared—traditions, we have seen already, that are very old (see 1 Cor. 15:3–8)—then why didn't he narrate them?

We can only guess. Perhaps the stories of Jesus' appearance in the past to witnesses enabled early Christians to regard his lordship as a reassuring fact rather than as a demanding call to "follow after." Perhaps Mark wanted his readers to examine again the grounds of their experience of Jesus: was it in past visions or in present power and conviction? Because Mark declares Jesus to be alive and ready to appear but does not attach his appearing to any specific times and places in the past, he leaves open for his readers the imaginative possibility of new encounters with the risen one. He thereby reminds them that the one who rose did not simply take up again his former life but lives now as powerful Lord who continues to place their life in question.

In a way completely consonant with the rest of his narrative, Mark insists that as risen Lord, Jesus remains the Holy One of God (1:24), the alien strong man (3:27), the mystery of the Kingdom (4:11), who cannot be understood or controlled but only followed in fear and trembling (4:41; 5:15, 33; 9:32; 10:32). Mark's ending is really an opening. The "good news" about Jesus' resurrection does not reduce the mystery but heightens it. Readers are invited once more to wonder, Who is this man?

The Sudden Beginning

The beginning of Mark's narrative also suggests the special character of this Gospel. Another textual difficulty requires a decision. The canonical version reads, "Beginning of the good news [*euaggelion*] of Jesus Christ,

Son of God" (1:1). Some manuscripts lack the phrase "Son of God." The best ones contain it. Which should we read? Here is a case where the shorter ending is not the best. Not only does the manuscript evidence heavily support the inclusion of "Son of God" but this title plays a significant thematic role in the narrative as a whole. I have already indicated its presence at the baptism, transfiguration, and crucifixion, as well as the repeated identification of Jesus as God's Son by demons (3:11; 5:7). The climax of Jesus' trial before the Sanhedrin is reached when he responds, " I am," to the high priest's question "Are you the Messiah, the Son of the Blessed One?" (14:62), a question, we notice, that combines the two titles found in 1:1. The reading "Son of God" is surely correct.

What, then, does Mark mean by "beginning of the good news"? The question is made more difficult by the lack of clear syntactical connection to the verses that immediately follow and by the generally very compressed character of Mark's first fifteen verses (1:1–15). Perhaps by "beginning," Mark means the chronological start with the ministry of John (see Acts 1:21–22; 10:37) or the theological rooting of John's ministry in prophecy (see the mixed citation from Exod. 23:20, Mal. 3:1, and Isa. 40:3 in Mark 1:2–3). Despite Mark's overall reticence regarding Torah, he begins his story with a literary cross-reference, alerting his readers to the fact that Jesus' story should be heard as the continuation of a longer one.

The "beginning of the good news" may also refer simply to the chronological start of what Jesus said and did, so that this verse forms a bracket with verse 15. In a still deeper but not impossible reading, the beginning (*archē*), with its almost unavoidable suggestion of the *archē* in Gen.1:1 (LXX), may have a specifically religious reference to the whole story of Jesus that Mark is about to relate: what happened in the words, deeds, death, and resurrection of Jesus is the absolute *archē*—both the beginning and continuing origin—of belief and discipleship. If the text can be read this closely, then 1:1 stands as a title for the Gospel as a whole. It marks off the narrative's major sections, the first ending with Peter's declaration of Jesus as Christ (8:29), the second with the declaration by the gentile centurion that Jesus was God's Son (15:39).

With whatever nuances, it is clear that the readers of this Gospel know from the beginning that Jesus is both Messiah and Son of God. Mark's *narrative* mystery—Jesus' being known at first only to demons, then vaguely to the disciples, then paradoxically to the soldier—is known already by the readers in 1:1. In the strictest sense, therefore, the Gospel as a whole is intensely ironic. The readers always know more than the characters in the story. This observation, however, needs further development.

Apocalyptic and Irony

The symbolism of Mark's Gospel is fundamentally that of apocalyptic. The greatest concentration of it is found in Jesus' secret discourse to his closest followers (chap. 13) which is often called the little apocalypse. In this chapter, we find private revelation (13:3) of things that are to happen (13:4), portrayed in terms of cosmic upheaval and conflict (13:7–8, 24–25), including persecution of the elect of God (13:9–13), which will cause apostasy from the true way (13:21–23). Those who persevere to the end will be saved (13:13). The end will be signaled by the coming of the Son of man, "with great power and glory" (13:26). These features are classically apocalyptic, with symbols that can be traced back to the Book of Daniel (see chap. 2, above, pp. 48–51).

If the discourse were straightforwardly apocalyptic, however, its function would be simply to comfort the hearers: they know the course of history, whereas the outsiders, the evil ones, do not. Indeed, the very reception of this sort of revelation would mark its hearers as insiders and the elect.

But Mark puts a twist on this apocalyptic theme. The insiders (Peter, James, John, and Andrew) are informed that they really do not know when all this is to happen but that they are to "take heed and watch" (13:32–33). More than that, Mark explicitly opens this "secret" discourse to all the readers. They are invited to overhear what Jesus says to the disciples and understand it more clearly than they do: "Let the reader understand"(13:14). Then, the readers of the Gospel are also warned: "And what I say to you I say to all: Watch!" (13:37). Apocalyptic is here worked into a literary irony. Apocalyptic aims at insiders and is understood by them. But Mark is warning his readers, If you think you understand, if you think of yourself as an insider, beware, you may not be. If those insiders, the disciples, could find themselves on the outside, so could the readers.

Apocalyptic symbolism is scarcely confined to chapter 13. Mark's entire Gospel can be considered an apocalypse in narrative form, but one with a distinctive ironic element. The symbolism of apocalyptic enables us to understand how Jesus' ministry is one of conflict with cosmic forces. He is the stronger one who enters the house ruled by Satan, binds him, and releases his captives (3:27). Within this symbolic structure, we recognize how this conflict expresses the essential proclamation of Jesus, "The kingdom of God is at hand" (1:15), because Jesus himself is the content of that proclamation.

Mark's presentation of Jesus is not itself without ambiguity. From one point of view, Jesus is clearly a thaumaturge, filled with the Spirit (1:10), whose works of healing and exorcism enable demons to recognize him as a "Holy One of God" (1:24), radiating an urgent power (5:30; 6:2). Yet, he cannot always use it (6:5). From another point of view, Jesus is a teacher. Mark has given Jesus this designation more often, proportionately, than has any other Gospel. He is called *didaskalos* or *rabbi* by both friend and foe. But what a strange sort of teacher he is! He calls people to follow him with no preamble, and with little apparent reason they do so (1:17, 20). He demands of them complete renunciation (10:17–31) and promises in return only that they will face suffering (10:39). When he is questioned, he does not seek to persuade but issues abrupt pronouncements (2:1—3:6; 7:1–23). When he speaks in parables, he does not invite understanding but deflects it. Indeed, his parables might be called instruments of attack (see 3:23). He tells the disciples that the parables are "so that they may indeed see but not perceive" (4:12). Jesus' words in this Gospel are few and hard. So is his fate. He is obviously the one meant by the "Son of man" who will come in glory (8:38; 13:26; 14:62) and who now speaks with authority (2:10), yet this Son of man is above all one who must suffer and die (14:21, 41) and, before he does so, must experience the extremes of human anguish (14:33–34). It is not much easier for the present-day reader than for Jesus' first disciples to completely understand this paradoxical Messiah.

Mysterious Revelation

Why is Mark's narrative so difficult and his presentation of Jesus so deflecting? The clue to this may be found in the explanation Jesus gives for speaking in parables (4:11). When the disciples ask him why he speaks in parables, he says that the parables are for those "outside." As for the disciples, they "have been given the mystery [*mystērion*] of the kingdom of God."

This statement is as important for what it does not say as for what it says. At first, it would appear that insiders and outsiders are distinguished on the basis of understanding or the lack of it. So we would expect the insiders, the disciples, to understand. But Jesus immediately asserts that they do not understand either: "Do you not understand this parable? How then will you understand all the parables?" (4:13). Knowledge or the lack of it does not distinguish insiders and outsiders. But how can the insiders both be given the mystery and fail to understand?

Here is a case where a comparison with Matthew's parallel passage helps us see what Mark means. In Matthew, Jesus tells the disciples, "To you has been given to know the mysteries of the kingdom of heaven" (Matt. 13:11). We notice two important differences: the disciples "know," and they are given "mysteries" to know, in the plural. The word can justifiably be translated "secrets" (RSV). As we shall see later, it is important in Matthew's Gospel that the disciples understand and communicate the revelations of Jesus to others (see Matt. 28:20).

But Mark's point is different. The disciples are not given the gift to know, and what they have been given is in the singular, *mystērion*, not a secret but a mystery. This may well be the key word in Mark's narrative. One can scarcely miss the associations it suggests with the *mysterium tremendum ac fascinosum.* Jesus himself is the singular "mystery of the kingdom," and he is so as the Holy One. He is recognized fully only by God and other spiritual forces. He radiates an intense and fearful power. It is a power, furthermore, that at once attracts and repels, so that some are drawn to him and some reject him. Most of all, the *mystērion* resists understanding. It cannot be deciphered, controlled, or reduced to formula. The mystery of the holy, *even when revealed*, remains ungraspable.

This presentation of Jesus as the Holy One helps us appreciate Mark's two-edged portrayal of the disciples. One side of the portrayal is positive: they are specially called by Jesus to be with him and share his work (3:14); they are given the mystery that is himself (4:11); to them is revealed his identity as suffering Son of man (8:31) and glorious Son of God (9:2–8); they hear his secret discourse on the tribulation and triumph to follow (13:5–37). The other side of the portrayal is almost unrelievedly negative. They do not in fact understand (4:13, 41; 6:52; 7:17; 8:21). They reject a suffering messiah (8:32), seeking instead a place of honor in a glorious kingdom (9:34; 10:37). One betrays Jesus for money (14:10–11), Peter denies even knowing him (14:66–72), and none of them stays with him to the end: "They all fled" (14:50).

These literary observations suggest something of Mark's religious purpose in shaping the story of Jesus and the disciples in this fashion. Mark's readers would naturally, as we still do, identify themselves with the disciples. Mark therefore uses that relationship to teach his readers. The message is mainly one of warning against smugness and self-assurance. He seems to be saying "If you think you are an insider, you may not be; if you think you understand the mystery of the kingdom and even control it, watch out; it remains alive and fearful beyond your comprehension. If you think discipleship consists in power because of the presence of God, beware; you are called to follow the one who suffered and died. Your discipleship is defined by his messiahship, in terms of obedience and service."

We do not need to postulate a distinct group of heretics or leaders in the Markan community at whom this message was aimed. Mark's sharp delineation of a paradoxical Jesus and an inadequate community of followers needed only readers who were human and, therefore, also with "spirit willing but flesh weak" (14:38).

These notes on Mark's method and message can prepare us for the reading of his text, preferably aloud and in the sequence of its verses, as Mark's first "readers" heard it. I turn, then, to a schematic reading of the Gospel, seeing in Mark an apocalyptic narrative in which the anticipated categories of insider and outsider are redefined in terms of response to the mystery of the kingdom who is Jesus.

FOLLOWING JESUS THROUGH THE STORY OF MARK

The Prologue: 1:1–15

We see at once that this is no biography or history. No account is given of John's origins or Jesus' childhood. The narrative is dense and deeply allusive. John's baptism fulfills Torah's promise of a forerunner (1:2–3), but his message is reduced to a single announcement, "After me comes one stronger than I" (1:7). As we read, the full implications of this designation for Jesus will become clearer. But now we see that the one who is to baptize with the spirit (1:8) is himself baptized and declared God's beloved Son (1:11). The one who is to drive out demons is himself driven out (the term *ekballō* is the one used in exorcisms) into the desert to grapple directly with Satan (1:12–13).

When Jesus returns from that testing, therefore, he comes as one who has already bound the strong one in single combat (see 3:27). There now remains for him only the loosing of his captives. Now, in Jesus' battle with cosmic forces, the outcome is not in doubt. Because the Stronger One has entered human history, the reign of evil is at an end. Jesus announces the effective rule of God, which the rest of Mark's narrative will spell out in such paradoxical fashion: "The kingdom of God is at hand; repent and believe in the good news" (1:15).

In these opening verses, Mark's readers encounter not the story of Everyman but that of God's unique Son, who spins history on its axis and calls for conversion, a change of heart and mind. In the story of this man the mystery of God is at work.

Conflict and Selection: 1:16—3:34

Between Jesus' proclamation of the kingdom in 1:15 and his declaration in 3:35 that "whoever does the will of God is my brother, and sister, and mother," three patterns structure Mark's narrative. The first is the demonstration of Jesus' authority and power in healings and exorcisms (1:21–28, 29–34, 40–45; 2:1–12), which is summarized in 3:7–12. The second is a positive response to Jesus by those whom he calls (1:16–20; 2:13–14), which is brought to a head by the choosing of the Twelve in 3:13–19. The third is the rejection of Jesus by his opponents (2:1–12, 15–28), which reaches a climax in the Sabbath conflict that issues in the resolve of the Pharisees and Herodians to seek Jesus' death (3:1–6).

Mark weaves these patterns together artfully. At the level of human history, we see the Messiah beginning his career of open preaching and healing. His powerful message and presence cause some to follow him, and from among their growing number he chooses an inner group to be "with him" in a special fashion. But his assumption of authority also causes religious leaders to reject him and seek his death. While this is taking place at the historical level, Mark also shows his readers that at the level of cosmic conflict, the Holy One of God is a mystery that at once attracts and repels.

Two paradigmatic stories illustrate the two levels of conflict. First, the cosmic conflict is illustrated by the exorcism in 1:21–28. Here is Jesus' first revelation of power. Mark characteristically fits the exorcism itself (vv. 23–26) into an account of Jesus' teaching in the synagogue (vv. 21–22, 27–28) by his intercalation technique. Jesus rebukes and expels the spirit who recognizes him as the Holy One, showing that in fact he is the Stronger One promised by John, through whom God's Spirit is at work to bind Satan. The reaction of the crowd combines astonishment at both wonderworking and teaching: "What is this? A new teaching! With authority he commands even the unclean spirits and they obey him" (1:27). We see that for Mark, the essential teaching of Jesus is going to be connected to his personal presence. The second paradigmatic story is the synagogue controversy caused by Jesus' healing on the Sabbath (3:1–6). His opponents seek to accuse him of breaking Torah, just as they have challenged his practices in the previous stories. Although Jesus now once more silences them—just as he can silence demons—they leave with the intent to kill him. Thus early on, Mark shows his readers the eventual outcome of this conflict of the power "to do good or harm, to give life or to kill" (3:4).

The two levels of conflict are joined in the complex intercalation of 3:20–35 (see above, pp. 151–52). Jesus has already chosen those who will be with him (3:13–19); from now on, they will be his family (3:35). His natural family shows itself to be against him by seeking his arrest and finds itself on the outside quite literally (3:21, 31–35). The scribes from Jerusalem, who accuse him of casting out demons by demonic collusion, show themselves as sinners against the Holy Spirit (3:22, 28–30). At the heart of this complex passage, Jesus' parable—the first he tells—interprets the cosmic implications of this human conflict: he is the Stronger One who has entered the house of the strong one and overcome him.

This opening plot sequence has established that Jesus' open preaching has already created a division between insiders and outsiders. Jesus prepares for a new mode of teaching by choosing a select audience to be with him. Those who have rejected his open speech and healing powers have already put themselves on the outside, and Jesus has already begun to speak to them in parables!

Teaching in Parables: 4:1–41

Mark's peculiar use of parables becomes more intelligible in light of this plot sequence. In the Jewish wisdom tradition a parable (*mashal*) could be a dark and ambiguous saying like a riddle, but the dominant use of parables among contemporary Jewish teachers was as a means of clarifying scriptural difficulties. As an analogy in narrative form, it could lead someone from an understanding of the familiar to an understanding of the strange. This is also the dominant function of parables in both Matthew and Luke. In Mark, the case is different. Although the character of the parables themselves is no more difficult in this Gospel than in others, Mark exhibits a different use of them. Mark suggests that Jesus used parables to confound rather than to instruct.

If we have followed Mark's story, however, we see that it was because Jesus' open preaching caused a violent opposition and threat of death that he began to speak in a veiled way. Doing so, of course, accentuated further the distinction between insider and outsider. Now, to those outside, everything is in parables, simply because they do not have the single necessary hermeneutical key: the acceptance of Jesus. So we find the parables of chapter 4 hedged about with apocalyptic warning signs: "Listen!" (4:3); "He who has ears to hear let him hear!" (4:9); "Whoever has ears to hear, let him hear" (4:23). There is, as well, talk about things now told in secret being made manifest (4:21–25). To the outsiders the parables make obvious their previous failure to accept Jesus as the personification of the kingdom; the parable serves to repel those who had already decided not to be attracted. These "may indeed hear but not understand, lest they should turn again and be forgiven" (4:12). If this stood as a comprehensive statement of Jesus' mission, it would show an extraordinarily harsh discrimination against the outsider. But it must be understood explicitly in light of the story Mark has already told; only in the face of massive rejection does Jesus turn to his inner group with language clear to them but repelling to outsiders. The parables here function like the coded insider language of apocalyptic.

In the light of Mark's plot development, the parable of the sower (4:3–8) is also easy to understand. For those, like the readers of the passage, who have just heard of Jesus' open preaching and its acceptance and rejection, the parable is a transparent commentary on that story. Like the parable of the vineyard at the end of Mark's Gospel, this parable calls out for an allegorical interpretation. The code is supplied by the previous narrative itself. As the seed sown meets various fates, so does the word preached by Jesus.

But now, Mark's irony begins to work. Those on the inside were supposed to understand the parables. The disciples were supposed to be insiders. But they do not understand; they seek an *interpretation* of the parable (4:10). When Jesus gives his interpretation, the commentary character becomes even more obvious, for the sower now sows "the Word" (see Mark 2:2; 4:16–17, 33; 8:32). But the disciples should not have needed this interpretation. They were given the hermeneutical key, the *mystērion* of the kingdom, who is Jesus himself.

As readers, we begin to suspect that those who were intended to be on the inside possibly were not. We recognize that when Mark says that "he did not speak to them without a parable, but privately to his own disciples he explained everything" (4:34), we are to understand by this not an absolute distinction but, rather, various degrees of being outside. The disciples, we shall shortly see, grasp little more than others about Jesus. But are they, on account of that, culpable? Isn't it precisely the nature of a *mystērion* to resist understanding?

Mark now shows his readers what kind of understanding he wanted from his followers. It was the sort that came from the commitment of the heart, from being with Jesus, in loyalty and fidelity. He shows us this with a parabolic story that concludes this chapter on parables (4:35–41). Jesus demonstrates his power privately before his disciples and in their behalf. He speaks to the raging winds as he did to the demons (4:39; compare 1:25). And like the demons, the winds are "bound" (4:39). Then, in the question Jesus puts to the fearful disciples, we discover what it is that Mark regards as the key to understanding the mystery of Jesus: the commitment of *faith*. The disciples' manifest lack of this loyalty is shown by their fear and by their question, which is programmatic for the next section of the narrative: "Who is this, then, that even the wind and sea obey him?" (4:41). The readers already know, and by now the disciples should know. By hearing those on the inside ask the same question asked earlier by those on the outside (see 1:27), the readers are instructed and warned.

To Caesarea Phillipi: 5:1—8:26

This part of Mark's narrative is given structure by its series of doublets (see above, p. 151). The story line, however, is carried by the various responses to Jesus' wonderworking. As intimated in the stilling of the storm, the positive response is that of faith, the negative, that of disbelief.

Mark had early established a connection between healing, the forgiveness of sins, and faith: "When Jesus saw their faith, he said to the paralytic, 'My son, your sins are forgiven' " (2:5). Now, the connection is made even more explicitly (5:21–43). Mark inserts the story of the healed woman into that of the raising of the young girl, so that the readers understand that the same power (5:30) and response were at work in both: "Daughter, your faith has made you well; go in peace and be healed of your disease" (5:34); and "Do not fear, only believe" (5:36). Likewise when Jesus is rejected in Nazareth by his townsfolk (6:1–6), "he could do no mighty work [*dynamis* = power, as in 5:30] there, except that he laid his hands on a few sick people and healed them; and he marveled because of their faithlessness" (6:5–6).

Jesus heals a wild demoniac, who then goes into gentile territory (Decapolis; 5:20) to preach the word (5:1–20). We will return to him later. Jesus also heals the daughter of a Greek woman from Syro-Phoenicia, because of her bold faith (7:24–30). In the Decapolis region, a deaf mute is healed (7:31–37). In short, ordinary needy people even from among the Gentiles recognize the power at work in Jesus and seek him out in faith (6:30–31; 7:35–36). In contrast, he is rejected by his townsfolk (6:1–6) and opposed by Pharisees and scribes (7:1–23). Only the reprobate Herod gives ironic testimony to the power the reader—seeing the story from the perspective of Jesus' resurrection—could see at work in Jesus: "John the baptizer has been raised from the dead; that is why these powers are at work in him" (6:14).

All this time, however, the disciples remain dull and imperceptive. The ailing woman reaches out in faith to touch Jesus' garment, but the disciples around him say, "You see the crowd pressing about you and yet you ask, 'Who touched me?' " (5:31). After Jesus speaks with utter clarity on obedience to God rather than to human custom, the disciples ask for an explanation of "the parable" (7:17). Even plain speech is dark to them! Jesus responds, "Are you then also without understanding?" (7:18). After Jesus walks on the water (6:45–51), "they were utterly astounded, for they did not understand about the loaves, but their hearts were hardened" (6:52). The passage of Isa. 6:9–10, which in 4:12 had been applied to outsiders, is here applied to the disciples. The application is made again, without equivocation, in the dialogue between Jesus and the disciples after the second feeding, this one on gentile territory (8:1–10). Jesus asks them, "Do you not yet perceive or understand? Are your hearts hardened? Having eyes do you not see, and having ears do you not hear, and do you not remember? Do you not yet understand?" (8:17–21).

This harsh question is followed immediately by the healing of the blind man in two stages (8:22–26). This is one of the few Markan stories not taken over by Matthew and Luke, and it clearly serves a special symbolic role in Mark's narrative. It anticipates the progression of the disciples from a state of complete blindness to a state of feeble sight—to be shown in the succeeding narrative.

To Jerusalem: 8:27—10:52

Peter learned something from Jesus' multiplication of the loaves. He was able to extract from the sight of one who like a shepherd fed the sheep (6:34), the recognition of a messianic figure (see 2 Sam. 5:2; Ps. 23:1; Isa. 40:11; Ezek. 34:12; Zech. 10:2): "You are the Christ" (8:29). But like the vision of the man who saw humans walking about as trees (8:24), Peter's vision is still blurred. A messiah could mean many things in that world (see chap. 2, p. 46), and the working definition of the disciples, we quickly learn, has to do with power and prestige. Their sight needed correction, and Mark devotes the next section of his narrative to that task.

As Jesus moves inexorably toward Jerusalem and his own death, he reveals himself as the Son of man who is to be rejected, will suffer and die (8:31; 9:31; 10:33–34). After each of these announcements, his disciples betray a fundamental misunderstanding of his messiahship and therefore also of their discipleship (8:32; 9:33–34, 38; 10:35–37). In response to each misunderstanding, Jesus clarifies the nature of discipleship, making clear that it demands following after him in service even to death (8:34–38; 9:35–37, 39–41; 10:38–45).

The first instance is paradigmatic. Peter objects to Jesus' talk of suffering, by "rebuking" him. The word used here is the same used when Jesus "rebukes" the demons; Peter seeks to "bind" Jesus as Jesus "bound" Satan. But Jesus now in turn rebukes Peter and identifies him as representing precisely the cosmic forces that resist God's rule; he calls Peter, simply, Satan. Peter wants the mystery to match his own perceptions, but Jesus tells him, "You are not on the side of God but of men" (8:33), and reminds him of the proper place for a disciple, following after: "Get behind me."

Throughout the journey the disciples are not only fearful (9:6, 32; 10:32) and confused (9:28, 34, 38; 10:26, 37), they consistently try to tailor the mystery to their own measure. They do not want a suffering messiah (8:32). They use human standards of greatness (9:34). They divide the world easily into us and them (9:38); they want power over others in the kingdom (10:37). They do not perceive that the mystery of the kingdom *is* Jesus and that resisting his path toward death means resisting the kingdom of God.

Mark makes this teaching explicit. To be a disciple of Jesus, one must "take up the cross and follow" (8:34), be willing to lose one's life (8:35), be "last of all and servant of all" (9:35), allow others to perform wonders with no personal gain for oneself (9:39), be initiated into the death of Jesus, and be spent as slaves of all (10:39–44). In short, to learn from this teacher, that is, to be a disciple, one must walk in the way that Jesus is taking, following after him.

The transfiguration (9:2–8) alerts the readers to the proper understanding of this whole narrative sequence. The closest companions of Jesus see him proleptically in glory and they seek to preserve that condition. Peter says, "Lord, it is good for us to be here. Let us make three booths, one for you, one for Moses, one for Elijah" (9:5). Mark immediately lets the readers know that Peter's response is wrongheaded: "He did not know what to say, for they were exceedingly afraid." Peter's error was twofold. First, he wanted to control and domesticate the mystery by reducing it to ritual expression (the tents). Second, he saw Jesus as just another "man of God" on an equal level with Moses and Elijah. The voice from the cloud pronounces correction to these errors, not only for the three disciples, but above all for Mark's readers. First, Jesus is not like other prophets and thaumaturges: "This is my beloved [or, unique] Son." Second, he will not be pinned down or controlled but himself leads the way: "Listen to *him*." If we are to learn *how* Jesus is Christ and Son (1:1), Mark tells us, and if we are to learn what it means to be "with him" as a disciple, then we cannot listen to Peter and these others, who think just as we do, but we must listen to, look to Jesus only (9:8).

Jesus in Jerusalem: 11:1—13:37

While Mark has kept our attention focused on Jesus and the disciples, he has not let us forget entirely the opposition to Jesus from those who are truly outsiders, the Jewish leaders. Their opposition reaches a climax in the Jerusalem narrative, providing a dramatic prelude to the description of Jesus' death. Mark has another purpose in showing Jesus rebutting a whole series of Jewish opponents: through the teaching of Jesus, he situates his Christian readers with respect to Judaism and Torah.

We have seen how the active conflict between Jesus and Jewish leaders began in the series of controversies of 2:1—3:6, resulting in the resolve to kill Jesus. We have seen how scribes from Jerusalem accused Jesus of demonic possession (3:22–27) and how scribes and Pharisees challenged him on purity regulations (7:1–13), while the Pharisees alone questioned him on divorce (10:2–9). In these last two cases, Jesus turns from a rebuttal of the opposition to a private instruction of his followers (7:17–19; 10:10–12). For his followers also he corrects the scribal view of Elijah's return (9:11–13). Similarly, when the Pharisees ask for a sign from heaven after the multiplication of the loaves, he rebukes them (8:12), then warns his disciples, "Beware the leaven of the Pharisees and the leaven of Herod" (8:15).

When Jesus enters Jerusalem publicly proclaimed as Messiah, the readers therefore know that he is entering the home of his enemies. The people who recognized the signs of a Davidic messiah in his feedings (6:34) and heard him called Son of David by blind Bartimaeus, who upon being restored to sight, "followed him on the way" (10:52), now cheer him as he enters the city as well as "the kingdom of our father David that is coming" (11:9–10). The leaders, however, do not cheer. They gear themselves for the final and open battle.

We have already seen how Mark weaves together the fate of the fig tree and the temple (see above, p. 152). Neither the tree nor the temple yielded what God willed. Both will be destroyed. So also, we are clearly to understand, will those who reject God's kingdom in Jesus, themselves be rejected. Indeed, the parable of the vineyard, placed in the middle of the Jerusalem sequence, plainly offers the reader this interpretation of events (12:1–11). The temple from this point forward plays an important thematic role. Although Jesus predicts the temple's end only in private discourse (13:2), it is the only charge made explicitly against him in the Sanhedrin trial (14:58). And when Jesus dies on the cross, "the curtain of the temple was torn in two, from top to bottom" (15:38). Mark thereby signals that the old separation between insider and outsider, between sacred and profane, is gone. Jesus is the place of the mystery and where the holy is revealed. Mark anticipates the replacement of the temple by Jesus as cult center for Christians, by having Jesus prophetically cleanse it (11:15–17)—thus also sealing his own fate (11:18)—and then taking it over as the place for his confrontation with his enemies (see 11:27).

Representative Jewish leaders approach Jesus as he teaches in the temple. Each asks a question appropriate to the group's concerns; each is bested by Jesus. Sanhedrin members question his authority (11:28–33); Pharisees and Herodians try to trip him on taxes to Caesar (12:13–17); Sadducees challenge him on the resurrection life (12:18–27). The scribes have been Jesus' chief tormentors throughout the narrative and the temple scene closes with Jesus' interaction with them. A scribe who identifies love of God and neighbor as the first commandments of Torah is said by Jesus to be "not far from the kingdom of God" (12:28–34). But the scribes who think the Messiah is nothing more than David's son and not also Lord are said to be wrong (12:35–37). Jesus' last words in the temple form an attack on the rapacity of scribes who steal from widows (12:38–40) and who provide a sharp contrast to the widow who puts "all her living" into the poor fund of the temple (12:41–44).

Since the conflict with Jewish leaders took place in the temple precincts, the transition to Jesus' apocalyptic discourse is all the more striking. Here the contrast between insider and outsider is again expressed in spatial terms. Jesus withdraws from the temple, sits with his close companions on the mount facing the temple, and predicts the temple's fall (13:1–4). The insiders with Jesus are themselves in danger of becoming outsiders. The motif of taking heed and watching, which runs through this discourse, takes on a special poignancy at this place in the narrative, for we shall shortly see that those told to watch will prove incapable of doing so. Mark wants them to be a warning to his readers, for he closes the discourse with this opening to the readers, "What I say to you I say to all, watch!" (13:37).

The Passion: 14:1—15:47

Mark's whole narrative has moved steadily toward Jesus' death. In the Passion narrative, the dialectic between the inner and outer becomes intensified, as Mark shifts the readers back and forth from the outer plot to its inner meaning.

The outer plot shows Jesus caught up in the machinery of official rejection, condemnation, and death. The chief priests and scribes seek his death (14:1–2), arrest him in the garden (14:43), try him (14:53–65), and as Jesus had predicted, hand him over to Gentiles (15:1–15). And those who should have been with Jesus become part of the machinery of betrayal. Judas was chosen to be with Jesus, though even then Mark warned the reader to expect betrayal by him (3:19). Now he conspires with Jesus' enemies (14:10–11) and leads them to him (14:44). The enormity of his betrayal is emphasized by the repetition of "one of the Twelve" in 14:10 and 14:43. Peter had always resisted Jesus' suffering. Now, despite his foolish boasting (14:29), he denies Jesus three times (14:66–72). When Jesus is arrested, "all forsook him and fled" (14:50). At this point Mark adds a provocative statement, to which we will return: "And a young man followed him [this is a suggestive phrase] with nothing but a linen cloth about his body. And they seized him; but he left the linen cloth and ran away naked" (14:51–52). Here is the real failure of the disciples: not lack of knowledge but lack of loyalty. They were chosen simply to "be with him," to "follow," and in this they all failed.

While the outer plot unravels, Mark draws his readers into three scenes that reveal its inner meaning: the anointing, the supper, and the garden. In the anointing (14:3–9), an anonymous woman's action symbolizes Jesus' messiahship as one inextricably bound up with his death (14:8) and memorializes herself "wherever the good news is preached" (14:9). Typical of the women in this Gospel (cf. 5:25; 7:25), she shows more insight into Jesus' identity than those with him. Only women stay anywhere near the scene of Jesus' death, from among those who "followed him and ministered to him" (15:41). They did what disciples were supposed to do, follow, and they did for the Messiah what he did for others, minister. Women also witness the burial (15:47) and are the first entrusted with the message of the resurrection by the young man (16:1–8). And although the shorter ending has them flee in fear, telling no one, Mark's longer ending has Mary Magdalene report to the disciples, who refuse to believe her (16:11), for which they are severely rebuked by Jesus (16:14).

At the supper (14:12–25), the mystery of the kingdom is revealed in ritual. The broken bread recalls the loaves shared on the mountains, and the body to be shattered on the hill; Jesus is the body language of servanthood. The cup recalls the suffering promised the disciples (10:39), which Jesus himself must now face (cf. 14:36). The Passover meal is transformed by his impending death "for many" (see 10:45). But even here, the presence of his betrayer and of his denier renders the symbolism of the bread ambiguous (14:17–21). Nevertheless, the supper points to a future beyond his betrayal and death: "I will drink it new in the kingdom of God"

(14:25). And at the moment of entering the garden to face his agony, Jesus tells them, "You will all fall away, for it is written, 'I will strike the shepherd and the sheep will be scattered.' But after I am raised up, I will go before you to Galilee" (14:27–28).

In the garden, the mystery is not mediated by ritual but is exposed in the naked encounter of the Holy One alone and in fear. He asks that the cup be taken away, but the final words of his prayer reveal him to be truly the obedient son and the pattern for discipleship, "Abba, . . . not my will but yours be done" (14:36). Even as Jesus thus prays, his closest companions whom he had asked to "watch with him" (14:34, 37; cf. 13:37) fall asleep three times, emphatically failing him, remaining outsiders to that lonely place where Jesus accepts the Father's will.

Having revealed by these three scenes the inner meaning beneath what appears to be a meaningless execution, Mark sweeps his readers back to the turmoil of the outer plot, moving them quickly through the arrest, hearing, trial, and at last, the crucifixion. How that climactic scene is made meaningful through scriptural midrash I have tried to demonstrate earlier (see chap. 6, pp. 135–39). But Mark does not thereby relieve the desolation of Jesus' death. Jesus is surrounded at the end by triumphant and mocking enemies. He is abandoned by his followers. Only the women from Galilee watch from afar, bearing witness (15:40–41). Jesus, the *mystērion* of the kingdom is at last alone before the still more awesome mystery of God. Only the Markan readers can recognize in the apparent cry of desolation "My God, my God, why have you forsaken me?" the faint anticipation of hope offered by Ps. 22:1. With consummate irony Mark chooses this moment to have the ultimate outsider, Jesus' executioner, become the only human character in the narrative to identify Jesus properly: "Truly this was God's son" (15:39). This is hidden revelation, indeed.

The Empty Tomb: 16:1–8

We return again to the ending, and this time, having followed Jesus all through Mark's narrative, find it surprisingly full of hope. The disciples who had abandoned Jesus will see him again "in Galilee" (see 14:28). Jesus is alive and goes before them; they are called once more to "follow after" him.

Now, we look more closely at the young man who delivers the message. He is dressed in a white robe. He sits at the right hand of the tomb. The white robe tells us that he has been transformed. But from what? Where have we seen this young man before? We remember him as the naked young man in the garden, who fled (14:51–52). And remembering this, we understand that those who fail can also be restored and that this very "good news" traces its origin to such a source.

Hearing the young man's message, we are also moved to ponder again the meaning of this Galilee where they are to see Jesus. Where is it? For those who read now—and possibly for Mark's first readers—there remains only the Galilee of the text. The reader is therefore invited by the young man to follow Jesus there, to "see him there." The invitation is to read the story again, this time slowly.

When we read the text slowly, seeking the resurrected one in the story, we encounter another one who was "in the tombs" (5:2–5), the naked demoniac. He was so strong because of his demonic possession that no one could bind him. But he recognized the "Son of the most high God," and when he was freed from his self-alienation, he was found clothed, and seated next to Jesus, and in his right mind (*sōphronounta;* 5:15). That man wanted to "be with" Jesus as his disciple (5:18), but Jesus did not allow him. Rather he was told to "go and tell all" that the Lord had done for him (5:19), just as these women at the tomb are told to "go and tell" by a young man, newly clothed, sitting at the side of the tomb. The healed demoniac did not keep silence, but "he went away and began to proclaim [*kerys-sein* = preaching] in the Decapolis [= gentile territory] how much Jesus had done for him" (5:20).

Because Mark forces us to reconsider all his story by the openness of his ending, we discover that not fear and silence but proclamation of Jesus continued the Gospel story, a proclamation announced by those who, however inadequate or even faithless, had come to be "in their right minds" by knowing that the Stronger One lives.

BIBLIOGRAPHICAL NOTE

The Synoptic Gospels

The classic argument for the two-source solution to the Synoptic problem is that of B. H. Streeter, *The Four Gospels: A Study of Origins* (London: Macmillan & Co., 1924); a more compressed treatment can be found in W. G. Kümmel, *Introduction to the New Testament*, trans. H. C. Kee (Nashville: Abingdon Press, 1975), 38–80. Matthew's priority is argued by B. C. Butler, *The Originality of St. Matthew* (Cambridge: At the Univ. Press, 1951), and W. R. Farmer, *The Synoptic Problem* (New York: Macmillan Co. 1964). A more accessible introduction to the Synoptics as a whole is K. H. Nickle, *The Synoptic Gospels: An Introduction* (Atlanta: John Knox Press, 1980).

On the genre of the Gospels, see W. Schneemelcher, "Gospel," in E. Hennecke, *New Testament Apocrypha*, ed. W. Schneemelcher, trans. R. McL. Wilson (Philadelphia: Westminster Press, 1963), 1:71–48; C. W. Votaw, *The Gospels and Contemporary Biographies* (Philadelphia: Fortress Press, 1970 [1915]); C. H. Talbert, *What is a Gospel? The Genre of the Canonical Gospels* (Philadelphia: Fortress Press, 1977); J. Z. Smith, "Good News Is No News: Aretalogy and Gospels," in *Christianity, Judaism, and Other Greco-Roman Cults: I. New Testament*, ed. J. Neusner, Studies in Judaism in Late Antiquity 12 (Leiden: E. J. Brill, 1975), 21–38.

A balanced treatment of the evangelists' purposes in writing is that of C. F. D. Moule, "The Intention of the Evangelists," in *New Testament Studies: Studies in Memory of T. W. Manson*, ed. A. J. B. Higgins (Manchester: Univ. of Manchester Press, 1959), 165–79. On the notion of "realistic narrative," see E. Auerbach, *Mimesis*, trans. W. Trask (Princeton: Princeton Univ. Press, 1953), and A. Wilder, *Early Christian Rhetoric* (Cambridge: Harvard Univ. Press, 1971), 18–70.

The Gospel of Mark

Mark's peculiar use of secrecy was first explored by W. Wrede, *The Messianic Secret*, trans. J. C. Grieg (Cambridge: James Clark, 1971 [1901]). For the hypothesis that Mark was the earliest source for the life of Jesus, see A. Schweitzer, *The Quest of the Historical Jesus*, trans. W. Montgomery (New York: Macmillan Co. 1964 [1906]), 121–36. Representative of early form critics' appreciation of Mark as an editor is R. Bultmann, *The History of the Synoptic Tradition*, rev. ed., trans. J. Marsh (New York: Harper & Row, 1963 [1921, 1931]), *337–51. Even less complimentary is J. Meagher, *Clumsy Construction in Mark's Gospel: A Critique of Form and Redaktionsgeschichte* (TorSTh 3; New York: Edwin Mellen Press, 1979). For the possible relation of Mark to the primitive kerygma, see C. H. Dodd, "The Framework of the Gospel Narrative," *ExpTim* 43 (1932): 396–400.

Mark's theological purposes were taken seriously in the pioneering studies by R. H. Lightfoot, *History and Interpretation in the Gospels* (New York: Harper & Brothers, 1934), and idem, *Locality and Doctrine in the Gospels* (New York: Harper & Brothers, 1937). Of far greater influence was the study in redaction criticism by W. Marxsen, *Mark the Evangelist* (Nashville: Abingdon Press, 1969).

The community-crisis approach to Mark's Gospel is exemplified by W. Kelber, *The Kingdom in Mark: A New Place and a New Time* (Philadephia: Fortress Press, 1974); E. Trocmé, *The Formation of the Gospel According to Mark*, trans. P. Gaughan (Philadelphia: Westminster Press, 1975); and T. Weeden, *Mark: Traditions in Conflict* (Philadelphia: Fortress Press, 1971). A fuller attempt to sketch the Markan community on the basis of the text is found in H. C. Kee, *Community of the New Age: Studies in Mark's Gospel* (Philadelphia: Westminster Press, 1977). A recent argument for taking the historical traditions of Mark seriously was made by M. Hengel, *Studies in the Gospel of Mark*, trans. J. Bowden (Philadelphia: Fortress Press, 1985).

A thoroughly literary approach to Mark was pioneered by A. Farrer, *A Study in St. Mark* (Westminster: Dacre Press, 1951), and has become very influential in recent scholarship, as represented in such studies as R. M. Fowler, *Loaves and Fishes: The Function of the Feeding Stories in the Gospel of Mark*, SBLDS 54 (Chico, Calif.: Scholars Press, 1981); T. E. Boomershine and G. L. Bartholomew, "The Narrative Technique of Mark 16:8," *JBL* 100 (1981): 213–23; N. Petersen, *Literary Criticism for New Testament Critics*, GBS (Philadelphia: Fortress Press, 1978), esp. 44–80; D. Rhoades and D. Michie, *Mark as Story: An Introduction to the Narrative of a Gospel* (Philadelphia: Fortress Press, 1982); R. C. Tannehill, "The Disciples in Mark: The Function of a Narrative Role," *JR* 57 (1977): 386–405; and E. S. Malbon, "Fallible Followers: Women and Men in the Gospel of Mark," *Semeia* 28 (1983): 29–48. A comparative literary analysis is carried out by V. Robbins, *Jesus the Teacher* (Philadelphia: Fortress Press, 1984).

Markan scholarship is proliferating rapidly. Three helpful collections of essays are these: J. L. Mays, ed. *Interpreting the Gospels* (Philadelphia: Fortress Press, 1981), on all four Gospels; C. Tuckett, ed. *The Messianic Secret*, IRT 1 (Philadelphia: Fortress Press, 1983); and W. Telford, ed. *The Interpretation of Mark*, IRT 7 (Philadelphia: Fortress Press, 1985).

Among the studies that are congenial to the reading found in this chap. are R. Meye, *Jesus and the Twelve* (Grand Rapids: Wm. B. Eerdmans, 1968); J. R. Donahue, *The Theology and Setting of Discipleship in the Gospel of Mark* (Milwaukee: Marquette Univ. Press, 1983); T. A. Burkill, *Mysterious Revelation* (Ithaca, N.Y.: Cornell Univ. Press, 1962); N. A. Dahl, "The Purpose of Mark's Gospel," in his *Jesus in the Memory of the Early Church* (Minneapolis: Augsburg Pub. House, 1976), 52–65; F. Kermode, *The Genesis of Secrecy: On the Interpretation of Narrative* (Cambridge: Harvard Univ. Press, 1979); J. M. Robinson, *The Problem of History in Mark and Other Marcan Studies* (Philadelphia: Fortress Press, 1982 [1957]); N. Perrin, *What Is Redaction Criticism?* (Philadelphia: Fortress Press, 1969), 40–57; idem, "The Interpretation of the Gospel of Mark," *Int* 30 (1976): 115–24; L. E. Keck, "The Introduction to Mark's Gospel," *NTS* 12 (1965–66): 352–70; H. C. Kee, "The Terminology of Mark's Exorcism Stories," *NTS* 14 (1967–68): 232–46; J. D. Crossan, "Mark and the Relatives of Jesus," *NovT* 15 (1973): 81–113; G. H. Boobyer, "The Secrecy Motif in Mark's Gospel," *NTS* 6 (1959–60): 225–35. The notion of Mark as apocalyptic drama can be found in N. Perrin, *The New Testament: An Introduction* (New York: Harcourt Brace Jovanovich, 1974), 143–67.

To date we have no really first-rate critical commentaries on Mark. On specific linguistic points, V. Taylor, *The Gospel According to St. Mark*, 2d ed. (London: Macmillan & Co., 1966) may be consulted; otherwise, there are available the straightforward guides of E. Schweizer, *The Good News According to Mark* (Richmond: John Knox Press, 1970), and C. E. B. Cranfield, *The Gospel According to St. Mark*, 2d ed. (Cambridge: At the Univ. Press, 1963).

8

The Gospel of Matthew

MATTHEW IS THE GOSPEL OF THE CHURCH. NOT ONLY IS IT THE ONLY Gospel to use the term "church," *ekklēsia* (16:18; 18:17) but both its contents and structure indicate an interest in providing clear and coherent guidance to a community of believers. In contrast to the Gospel of Mark's rather marginal early existence, Matthew has been from the beginning the Gospel most used by the church in its worship, and in consequence, it has provided the text for the most preaching and commentary. Already quoted directly by Ignatius of Antioch (ca. 115), it was given a full-scale commentary by Origen (ca. 185–254). So far as ecclesial use is concerned, Matthew is the most successful edition of Mark's Gospel.

The patristic writers did not see it that way. They all regarded Matthew as the first of the Gospels to be written. Along with the Gospel's inherent excellence and usefulness, this putative priority gave Matthew a favored place. If Matthew was written first, and if its author was the apostle Matthew, then the earliest Gospel could claim apostolic and even eyewitness authority, a claim Mark obviously could not make. Papias is again our earliest source for this traditional attribution. He says, "Matthew organized 'the sayings' *[ta logia]* in the Hebrew dialect, but everyone has translated them as best he could" (Eusebius *Ecclesiastical History* III.39, 16). It is not at all clear what "the sayings" really were, or what the "Hebrew dialect" was. It is not clear that Papias had any decent historical information at all. But Irenaeus (*Against Heresies* III.1.1–2) and Origen (*Eccl. Hist.* VI.25.3–6) understood that Matthew, one of Jesus' apostles, first wrote a Gospel in Hebrew that was later translated into Greek. Such also was the opinion of Jerome (*Commentary on Matthew*, pref. 5–7) and of Augustine (*On the Harmony of the Evangelists* II.4, III.6) who reduced Mark to the status of "a lackey and abbreviator" of Matthew (*Harmony* I.2).

Some internal evidence supports the tradition. The manuscripts of the Gospel uniformly bear the heading "According to Matthew" and twice in the text itself this name is supplied. The tax collector whom Mark calls

Levi of Alphaeus, and Luke simply Levi, is named Matthew by this Gospel (9:9). More significant, in the list of the Twelve (10:3), he reappears as "Matthew the tax collector" (contrast Mark 3:18 and Luke 6:15). The conviction of Matthew's priority may also have influenced its consistent placement as first in the canonical collection.

Those who support Matthean priority today claim tradition as their ally and insist as well that their version of the Griesbach hypothesis (1787)— which updates Augustine by having Mark at once conflate and reduce *both* Matthew *and* Luke—simplifies the issue by eliminating needless constructs like Q. But even if part of the prehistory of this Gospel goes back to an apostle, which is certainly possible, the present Greek text of Matthew does not suggest a direct translation from Hebrew or Aramaic. When compared with Mark, for example, it shows a consistently clearer, more concise and correct, use of Greek. Matthew incorporates most of Mark and follows Mark's order for the most part, and when he does not, Luke does. When passage after passage is carefully compared, it remains far easier to explain the differences as Matthew's commentary on and correction of Mark than as Mark's clumsy omission of fifty percent of Matthew. Finally, the Jewish quality of Matthew's language is due not to Matthew's early date or original language but to the social context and symbolic world of the community within which it was composed.

STYLE AND STRUCTURE

Matthew is much longer than Mark, and its length is especially impressive because of the considerable compression it has forced on the ninety percent of Mark it uses. Matthew shortens all of Mark's narratives, generally needing a third fewer words to tell a parallel story (cf., e.g., the story of the Gerasene demoniac, Mark 5:1–20 and Matt. 8:28–34). Additional length comes from the extension of the story line. Matthew includes a genealogy and birth narrative (chaps. 1—2) and resurrection appearance accounts (28:9–10, 16–20). Most of the additional bulk, however, comes from the rich collection of discourse material that Matthew includes.

The story line of Mark therefore gives Matthew its basic structure (see chap. 7), and Matthew does not fundamentally disagree with Mark's understanding of Jesus. The Passion narrative still holds the same prominent and climactic place. Matthew follows Mark particularly closely in the Passion account, making only minor changes. He does, however, provide additional structural elements in the rest of the narrative.

Four of these elements deserve mention. First, he uses stereotyped *summary transitions* between discourse material and narrative: "When Jesus had finished these words . . ." (7:28–29; 11:1; 13:53; 19:1; 26:1). These transitions accentuate the alternation between kinds of material. The effect is similar to saying "Now, to pick up the story again . . ." Second, Matthew uses two *temporal transitions*, which mark stages in Jesus' ministry: in 4:17, "From that time, Jesus began to preach . . . ," and in 16:21, "From that time, Jesus began to show his disciples . . ." Third, he introduces many of his direct quotations from Scripture with the stereotyped formula "This was to fulfill what was spoken. . ." (1:22; 2:6, 15, 17, 23; 4:15–16; 8:17; 12:17–21; 13:14, 35; 21:4; 27:9–10). These are conventionally called *formula citations*, and they offer an authorial commentary on the narrative. Fourth, Matthew also puts materials within literary brackets, using the technique called *inclusio*. The effect is less dramatic than in Mark, but provides the reader important clues in reading the Gospel. The entire narrative, for example, is framed between the angelic announcement in 1:23, ". . . his name shall be called Immanuel, which means 'God with us,' " and the messianic announcement in 28:20, ". . . lo, I am with you always, to the close of the age."

Matthew's Gospel lacks Mark's dramatic force because of the way the evangelist has arranged the sayings of Jesus he found in Q and M. Although called Teacher proportionately less often in this Gospel than in Mark—we will see the reason for that—Jesus here does much more teaching. Matthew collects the sayings of Jesus into the form of sermons or discourses and inserts them block fashion into Mark's narrative structure. The result is a much slower, and sometimes even a distracted, dramatic development.

The sayings collections are by no means random. First, they tend to be grouped topically. Thus, we find separately treated the law (5:17–48), piety (6:1–18), demands of discipleship (10:1–42), parables of the kingdom (13:1–52), relations in the church (18:1–35), polemic against opponents (23:1–39), and eschatology (24:4—25:46). Second, Matthew uses similar formal elements within each discourse: parables in chapter 13, beatitudes and antitheses in chapter 5, woes in chapter 23. Third, Matthew uses numerical groupings. He is even fonder of threefold structures than Mark. The genealogy has three sets of fourteen generations, thereby including the number 7 in the calculation as well (1:1–17). There are three angelic messages for Joseph (1:20; 2:13, 19), three temptations of Jesus (4:1–11), three modes of piety (6:1–18), and more. He uses other numerical groupings as well, such as six (the antitheses, 5:21–48), seven (parables and woes, chaps. 13 and 23), and ten (miracles, chaps. 8–9).

The discourse material in Matthew is, in sum, characterized by fullness, order, and symmetry. Matthew is a systematizer. In the abstract, it is possible that Jesus spoke all his blessings in one sermon or all his woes in another. It is also possible that, as in the rabbinic tradition, sayings could be organized mnemonically during oral transmission. But when we observe the tendency to systematize not only in the sayings material but also in the narrative, it becomes more likely that it is owed to Matthew's literary technique.

Two major and meritorious proposals have been advanced for the overall structure of Matthew's Gospel. The first pays closest attention to the summary transitions between discourse and narrative, which establish a definite alternating pattern throughout the Gospel. A narrative of beginnings (chaps. 1—4) leads to the discourse called the Sermon on the Mount (chaps. 5—7). The narrative of messianic words and wonders (chaps. 8—9) precedes a discourse on mission and discipleship (chap. 10). The narrative telling of growing opposition to Jesus (chaps. 11—12) is followed by parabolic discourse (chap. 13). A narrative of miracles and predictions (chaps. 14—17) leads to the discourse on life in the community (chap. 18). The narrative of the Judean ministry (chaps. 19—23) is followed by a discourse on the coming kingdom (chaps. 24—25). The Gospel concludes with the narrative of the Passion, death, and resurrection (chap. 26—28).

On this reading, there are five discourses set off by the transition formulas. This reminds some scholars of the second-century fragment that reads, "Matthew curbs the audacity of the Jews, curbing them in five books, as it were with bridles," and suggests that Matthew has deliberately structured his Gospel in five books corresponding to the five books of the Pentateuch, the heart of Torah. He seeks thereby to provide his community with the messianic equivalent of Torah. This has been an enormously popular hypothesis, and it has considerable strength. Matthew does give Jesus a Mosaic shading, and his Gospel definitely reflects dialogue with a developing Pharisaic Judaism for which Torah was the central symbol (see above, chap. 2, pp. 41–43, 51–57). Taken alone, however, the analysis also has weaknesses. It effectively reduces the beginning and end of the narrative to prologue and epilogue; indeed, it neglects the narrative generally. More tellingly, the discourse of chapter 23 does not fit the pattern and can be saved for the hypothesis only if it is regarded less as instruction to the disciples, in the manner of the other discourses, than as polemic against opponents.

A second structural analysis places greater emphasis on the narrative, particularly on the temporal transitions of 4:17 and 16:21. These establish within the narrative, it is suggested, a three-stage presentation of Jesus as Messiah: the person of Jesus Messiah (1:1—4:16); the proclamation of God's kingdom by Jesus Messiah (4:17—16:20); and the revelation of Jesus Messiah to his disciples through his suffering, death, and resurrection (16:21—28:20). Such an analysis has the virtue of recognizing that 1:1—4:16 is an integral literary unit with a specific thematic development, and it respects the shifts in emphasis on Jesus' ministry that the transitions indicate. It is an analysis complementing that which isolates the five books.

Both summary transitions and temporal transitions provide the reader clues to Matthew's purposes.

SETTING

The massive amount of teaching material in this Gospel and the systematic way in which it is presented have suggested two ecclesial contexts for its composition. The first is broadly catechetical. Matthew provides instructions for missionaries, discipline in the community, and forms of piety in a way that anticipates later church writings called church orders, the earliest of which is the *Didache* (usually dated ca. 90). An even more specific setting has been suggested: such teaching was developed in something like a Christian "scribal school" where reflection on the words and deeds of Jesus included demonstrations of how they fulfilled Torah. A second plausible church setting for the development of at least some of Matthew's materials is liturgical. It has long been noted how much more liturgical some of Matthew's renditions are when compared to Luke's (cf., e.g., the Lord's Prayer in Matt. 6:9–13 with that in Luke 11:2–4). This quality could owe something to liturgical use. Some have suggested that the Matthean tradition developed as a form of homiletic expansion of Mark; others, that a specific kind of midrashic activity accounted for the shape of Matthew. Both the catechetical and liturgical settings could have helped influence the shape of this Gospel; certainly the plausibility of those suggestions reminds the reader again of the community orientation of this Gospel. In the end, however, we must recognize that we have to do not only with the product of a school but with the artistry and religious perceptions of an evangelist.

Is there anything we can learn from Matthew about the larger social context within which it was composed? As always in the case of ancient writings whose precise provenience is unknown and that bear signs of conscious literary fashioning, we need to be cautious. The very shape of this Gospel and its obvious attention to community concerns, however, as well as the character of its symbolization, make such speculation more plausible than in the case of Mark. These factors suggest a community that was in contact with, and sought to define itself in response to, a developing Pharisaic tradition within Judaism. We will see shortly many individual details in the text that support this suggestion. Matthew may not have been providing his church with a new Moses or a new Torah, but his Gospel does define Jesus and the church by using the symbols specifically associated with what in its later developed form is called rabbinic Judaism.

An imaginative extrapolation may help us see the situation the Gospel's form seems to presuppose. In the Mesopotamian border city of Dura-Europas (destroyed in 250 C.E.), archaeologists discovered along the same street three houses dedicated to worship. One was a Mithraeum, another a Christian house church, the third a synagogue. Devotees attending each were close enough for mutual comparison and contrast. Matthew's Gospel seems to demand something like that sort of situation: the Christian sect not only was aware of the older and better-established Jewish tradition but also found itself required to explain and understand—first of all for itself—why it came to worship here and not in the synagogue down the street. Matthew's Gospel makes a great deal of sense if this pluralistic context is assumed, one in which rival and persuasive claims demand interpretation of one's own. In order to distinguish the story of Jesus and that of the church from that of Pharisaic Judaism, Matthew must appropriate the very symbols of that tradition. The movements of both separation and appropriation are evident in the text of the Gospel.

If Mark can fairly be read as an apocalyptic narrative, Matthew's shaping of the story of Jesus owes most to the symbols of the rabbinic tradition. And if this suggested setting makes sense, the time and place of Matthew's final composition are easier to locate. Both the scribal quality of the Gospel and its knowledge of Pharisaic traditions suggest an urban setting, and nothing in the text disputes this. We cannot be sure which city, of course, though Antioch is the traditional favorite guess and remains so today. As for dating, we remember that the Pharisaic movement really emerged as dominant—becoming eventually normative—after the fall of the temple. Hostility between messianist and nonmessianist Jews grew more fierce after that point and reached a crystallization in the *Birkat-ha-minim,* which brought curses on heretics and made it impossible for Christians to pray in synagogues any further. That benediction is usually, though not definitively, dated ca. 85 C.E. Further precision is not possible, and the date could be even earlier.

I am not suggesting that the Matthean church was necessarily Jewish-Christian demographically. It knows of the gentile mission and may itself be one of its fruits. But it is a church that must define itself in terms of a more dominant Jewish movement. This accounts both for the thoroughly Jewish (i.e., rabbinic) tone of the Gospel and for its intense hostility toward those who "sit on the seat of Moses" (23:2).

The interpretive remarks on Matthew that follow must be—because of the limits of space—only suggestive. The frame of the Markan narrative is presupposed, and I will not repeat here the parts of Matthew that are taken over from Mark without substantial alteration. Matthew's distinctive appropriation of Mark is often to be detected only in the cumulative effect of many minute additions and alterations. The careful reader is advised here above all to make use of a synopsis, so that the textual basis for my assertions can be checked. Because Matthew is so large and the space available here so small, some observations will be supported only by strings of references. The reader can pursue them.

WHO IS JESUS? SON OF DAVID, SON OF GOD (1:1—4:16)

The opening of the Gospel shows how the Markan understanding of Jesus as Son of David and Son of God is in Matthew distinctively influenced by the reading of Torah and interaction with Pharisaic Judaism. For the sake of convenience I am here treating chapters 1—2 separately as an "infancy account." In fact, chapters 1—4 form a coherent literary unit. Matthew lacks the solemn transition to the ministry of John provided by Luke 3:1, and it is really only the fact that Mark begins with the Baptist that leads us to think of Matthew's first chapters as prologue.

The Infancy: Jesus as Son of David (chaps. 1—2)

The infancy narratives of Matthew and Luke have little in common beyond the characters of Jesus, Mary, and Joseph; and in Matthew, Joseph is more dominant than Mary. The two Gospels interpret Torah midrashically but in very different ways. They use distinct literary devices and divergent geographical emphases. Each, in short, is fitted to the distinctive witness of the Gospel it begins.

Matthew's version is distinguished by its genealogy (1:1–17) and dense clustering of formula citations (1:23; 2:6, 15, 23). They help define the place of Jesus within traditional Jewish messianic expectation. For Christians in conversation with an aggressive Pharisaic movement (see 23:15), proclaiming Jesus as resurrected Messiah was insufficient; the credentials of a Davidic king required demonstration. For this, Jesus' dubious parentage and lowly place of origin were problematic (see John 1:46; 7:27). The formula citations prove that Jesus meets prophetic expectations; the genealogy connects him to the royal line. Together, they answer, at least to this community's satisfaction, who Jesus is and whence he comes.

The genealogy (1:1–17) fits Jesus into the literary forms and family lineage of Torah. By its arrangement into generations, furthermore, it shows his birth to be the "fulfillment of the times." He is immediately identified as "Messiah, son of David, son of Abraham" (1:1). As son of Abraham, he is connected to the people as a whole. This is an important link for other NT authors, but Matthew does not exploit it (see only 3:9; 8:11; 22:32). The Davidic connection is stated first, and it is the more significant for Matthew. It establishes Jesus' messianic credentials "according to the flesh" (see Rom. 1:3) within Judaism. The stress in the genealogy falls on David the king in 1:6; Joseph is called son of David in 1:20;

and the child's kingly status is made clear by 2:2, "Where is the king?" and 2:6, "For from you shall come a ruler" (Mic. 5:2).

Matthew's emphasis on this identification is found in many references to David not found in the text of Mark (see 9:27; 12:3, 23; 15:22; 20:30–31). It is made most explicit at Jesus' entry into Jerusalem. Matthew, which has a formula citation from Zech. 9:9 that identifies Jesus as your king, has Jesus awkwardly fulfill the letter of that citation by using both colt and ass in procession (21:2, 7). The populace twice cries out: "Hosanna to the son of David" (21:9, 15). Precisely this stress makes more climactic the controversy—in Matthew, it is with the Pharisees—over whether the Messiah is David's son or Lord (22:41–45). As we shall see shortly, Jesus is definitely Lord for Matthew, but he is also assuredly a Davidic messiah.

The genealogy also helps Matthew deal with Jesus' suspect parentage. Included among Jesus' ancestors are four women: Tamar (1:3), Rahab (1:5), Ruth (1:5), and Bathsheba ("wife of Uriah"; 1:6). All were outsiders to Israel; all were sexually suspect; through all of them God had worked surprisingly for the salvation of the people. They prepare for the surprising birth of a messiah by the virgin Mary.

Baptism and Testing: Jesus as Faithful Son of God (chaps. 3—4)

The formula citations of chapter 2 show that Jesus' hometown, as everyone knew, was Nazareth (2:23) but that his birthplace was the Davidic city of Bethlehem (2:5–6). Matthew draws his readers, however, into a deeper understanding of Jesus' origins and, therefore, his identity. Jesus is more than David's son, he is also Son of God. The strength of Matthew's use of the term is indicated by the citation of Isa. 7:14. Jesus is able to "save all the people" because he is Immanuel: he makes God truly present among them (1:23). Since 1:23 stands with 28:20 as an *inclusio* for the whole Gospel, a glance at that passage is appropriate here.

In this distinctive Matthean appearance account (28:16–20), Jesus shows himself to the disciples on a mount in Galilee, and they worship him (28:17). He claims "all authority" (28:18) and commissions them, "Go, make disciples of all nations, baptizing them . . . teaching them to observe all that I have commanded you; and, Lo! I am with you always, to the close of the age" (28:19–20). Jesus continues to be present through his resurrection. More striking, though, is the suggestion that his presence will be mediated by the commandments he had taught. Because we know that Jesus makes God present (1:23) as his Son, the commandments of Jesus mediate God's presence as the Word of God. This perception of Jesus and his words has important implications for other Matthean motifs.

What Matthew means by "Son of God" in his Gospel, however, owes less to ontology than to Torah. His understanding of the title is shown already in the formula citation of 2:15, "Out of Egypt I called my son" (cf. Exod. 4:22; Hos. 11:1). The prophet, of course, had referred to the people Israel in the exodus. By using this citation, Matthew not only interprets Jesus' journey, he identifies him as the faithful child whom God had desired in Israel. Matthew's image of Jesus as God's Son is therefore primarily relational. Jesus is the human being who is fully faithful and obedient to the will of God.

Several aspects of the infancy account, in fact, echo the exodus story in Torah and help create the image of Jesus as a Mosaic figure or one who represents the people Israel. Jesus is miraculously born to "save his people" (cf. Exod. 3:10), he is saved from a wicked king (2:13–14; cf. Exod. 1:22—2:10), and he is "called out of Egypt" (2:15). Now, if we read straight on to Jesus' baptism (3:13–17), we cannot help noticing that it corresponds to the crossing of the people through the sea (see Exod. 14:21–25; cf. 1 Cor. 10:1–5). Here the heavens open and the voice proclaims, "This is my beloved Son, in whom I am well pleased" (3:17).

The allusion is by no means far-fetched. It is in fact confirmed by Matthew's version of Jesus' testing (4:1–11). Both he and Luke use Q material to expand Mark's terse account, thereby making the demonic temptations and Jesus' responses explicit. Matthew has Jesus led up to be tested just as Israel was in the desert. Israel's hardships, however, led to its "testing of the Lord" by rebellion and faithlessness (see Num. 11:1; 14:1; Deut. 1:26; Exod. 16:2; Pss. 95:8–11; 106:13–25). Jesus' testing will also determine his fidelity. The devil makes the issue explicit, saying twice, "If you are God's Son . . . " (4:3, 6). He holds out to Jesus the possibilities of pleasure, power, and divine protection. Jesus, however, answers with the very words of Torah: "It is written, 'Man shall not live by bread alone, but by every word that proceeds from the mouth of God' " (4:4; cf. Deut. 8:3; cf. also the citations for Deut. 6:13 and 6:16 in Matt. 4:7 and 4:10). Jesus is the faithful, obedient son of God. He represents the child God always wanted in Israel, and he perfectly fulfills the righteousness demanded by Torah (see 3:13–15).

Now his mission to Israel can begin. Those who hear his proclamation of the kingdom (4:17) and hear him teach from the mountain like Moses (5:1–2)—those at least who hear him in this narrative—recognize one who, like Israel, was called, passed through the water, and was tested in the wilderness.

A haunting echo of the temptation account occurs in Matthew's crucifixion scene. Matthew makes few alterations to Mark's Passion narrative. One of them places blame for Jesus' death on the populace as a whole (27:25). Another has the passers-by at the cross cry out to him derisively, "If you are the Son of God, come down from the cross" (27:40; cf. 27:43). We hear in their taunt an eerie reprise of Satan's "If you are Son of God, throw yourself down" (4:6). A Son of God, surely, was one who exercised power. But Jesus accepts his father's will (26:39) and is obedient to the end. When the centurion confirms, "Truly this was God's Son" (27:54), Matthew's readers understand that this is because of Jesus' fidelity and obedience.

JESUS AS TEACHER AND LORD

Jesus' most prominent activity in Matthew's Gospel is teaching. As God's Son, he uniquely knows the Father's will, and can reveal it to others (11:25–30). For the Matthean church, moreover, Jesus is now risen Lord, whose teachings mediate God's presence. By the resurrection, he has "all authority." It is given by God, not grasped (see 4:9). The readers of the Gospel hear the words of Jesus not as those of just another sage from the past but as the living words of the commanding Lord. For Matthew, Jesus is teacher precisely as Lord of the church.

Evidence for this observation (as well as an indication of how carefully Matthew adapts Mark) is given by Matthew's precise use of the terms "teacher," whether in the form of *rabbi* or *didaskalos*, and "Lord," *kyrios*. We have seen (chap. 7, p. 156) that in Mark's Gospel everybody calls Jesus Teacher, whether opponents (Mark 12:14, 19, 32), those who encounter Jesus but fail to follow (10:17–31), those who encounter him and believe (9:17), or the disciples (4:38; 9:38; 10:35; 13:1). On the other hand, Mark never has disciples or opponents call Jesus Lord; only the afflicted give him that title. Matthew's discrimination is finer. Who calls Jesus Teacher? Always outsiders, whether opponents such as the scribes (8:19; 12:38), Pharisees (12:38; 22:16, 36), Jewish tax collectors (17:24), Herodians (22:16), Sadducees (22:24), or those who encounter Jesus but do not follow, like the rich young man (19:16). Jesus is never called Teacher by the disciples, the afflicted, or those coming to faith in him. The disciples (8:25; 17:4; 14:28; 16:22; 18:21) and those coming to faith in Jesus (8:2, 6, 8; 9:27–31; 15:22, 25, 27; 17:15; 20:30) call him Lord.

If Matthew's community is in truth one defining and defending itself against a Jewish scribal tradition, this distinction is dramatically effective. Those outside—as in the synagogue down the street—see Jesus as just another rabbi, whose opinions have only human authority. But those inside hear his words as those of the Lord, "God with us," filled with "all authority." The only apparent exception to this rule confirms it. The term "Lord" is never found on the lips of the betrayer, Judas. When Jesus predicts his betrayal at the last supper, the other disciples ask, "Is it I, Lord?" (26:22). Judas asks, "Is it I, Rabbi?" (26:25). And when he greets Jesus in the garden to arrest him, it is with these words, "Hail, Rabbi" (26:49). Matthew subtly but effectively shows Judas as outside.

The Parables of Jesus in Matthew

Matthew's distinctive understanding of Jesus as teacher affects his presentation of Jesus as parable speaker. As in Mark, Jesus begins telling parables because his open preaching meets hostility and rejection. In chapters 8—9, Jesus works ten miracles, interpreted by a "servant" citation from Isa. 53:4: "He took our infirmities and bore our diseases" (8:17). In chapters 11—12, Jesus is rejected repeatedly by family and opponents, driving him to a more veiled mode of teaching. This is interpreted by a second servant citation from Isa. 42:2: "He will not wrangle or cry aloud, nor will anyone hear his voice in the streets" (12:19). When Jesus begins speaking in parables, this too is in fulfillment of the prophecy "I will open my mouth in parables" (Ps. 78:2, in 13:35).

In contrast to Mark, however, Matthew's parables are truly intelligible to the insiders. The disciples have been given "to know the mysteries of the kingdom of heaven" (13:11). Outsiders do not perceive; the prophecy of Isa. 6:9–10 about blindness and deafness applies to them. The disciples do "see and hear" (13:16–17). The division between insiders and outsiders is here lacking irony. The role of knowledge, furthermore, is central for Matthew in a way it is not for Mark. This is indicated by the interpretation of the parable of the sower (13:18–23). In the parable itself, Matthew already made the seeds plural rather than singular, and the growth of the seed distributive, "some a hundredfold, some sixty, some thirty." These changes invite a more individualizing interpretation, which Matthew provides. Now, it is "anyone who hears" the word of the kingdom, and the point of differentiation is "understanding." The one who hears but "does not understand" has the word taken away (13:19). The one who "hears and understands" will yield fruit (13:23).

What is this proper understanding? It is the recognition that Jesus is not just another scribe but the Lord of the church. For Matthew as for Mark, understanding is fundamentally that commitment called faith. Such faith enables the disciples to grasp the significance of Jesus' teachings. Since Jesus' presence in the church is mediated by his words, it is also essential that those who hear them in faith understand, so that they can pass them on to others. At the end of this first series of parables, therefore, Jesus asks his disciples, "Have you understood all this?" They said to him, "Yes." Then Jesus tells them, "Therefore every scribe who has been trained for the kingdom of heaven is like a householder who brings out of his treasure what is new and what is old" (13:51–52). It is the disciples, we see, who are defined in terms of the rabbinic category of the scribe. They are to perform the scribal function for the messianic community, teaching the church what Jesus first taught them. They need, therefore, to understand.

As a consequence, the parables of Jesus in Matthew are more than defense weapons in his fight against opponents, and even more than the author's interpretation of the narrative; they are genuine instruments for teaching the church. Matthew includes some seventeen parables, many more than Mark. Three of them come from Mark, four from Q, the source shared with Luke, and ten from M, his own source. They fall into three clusters within the narrative. The first is the secret teaching of the disciples in chapter 13. The second occurs in the context of controversy in 18:23— 22:14. The third is in the eschatological discourse to the disciples in 24:45—25:46.

The parables of Matthew 13 reveal "the mysteries of the kingdom" in threefold fashion. They show that the kingdom is one that emerges suddenly and inexplicably in the world by God's will; this is expressed by the parables of growth—the mustard seed and the leaven (13:31–33). The kingdom demands a decision for or against it; this is expressed by the parables of decision—the pearl and the treasure (13:44–46). The kingdom involves judgment. Depending on one's choice, there is reward or punishment; this is expressed by the parables of judgment—the weeds, and the net and the fishes (13:24–30 and 13:47–50). The parable of the sower is programmatic, for it combines all three elements of growth, decision, and judgment (13:3–9).

The parables of chapters 18—22 are dominated by the theme of acceptance and rejection, pointing to the destiny of Jesus and Israel. The parables of the two sons (21:28–30), the vineyard (21:33–43), and the wedding feast (22:1–14) all rather transparently indicate the rejection of those who reject Jesus and the transfer of the kingdom to others. But there is judgment for those within the church, as well, as is shown by the denouement of the wedding feast (22:11–14) and the parable of the wicked servant (18:23–35): "So also will my heavenly father do to each one of you, if you do not forgive your brother from the heart."

The parables in Jesus' eschatological discourse all center on the theme of judgment in some fashion: the wicked householder (24:45–51), the ten virgins (25:1–13), the talents (25:14–30), the sheep and the goats (25:31– 46). Although the parables are intended for insiders and are understood by them, they by no means only comfort and confirm. They warn those already in the church that their decision for the kingdom requires constant renewal.

JESUS AND TORAH

The central religious symbol of the Pharisaic tradition was Torah (see chap. 2, pp. 51-57). It was the source of wisdom and the measure of righteousness, the reflection of the mind of God, the blueprint for creation, the ideal frame for humanity. Though revealed through Moses on

Sinai, Torah was eternal; though dwelling among humans, it would live forever. Taking upon oneself the observance of Torah was to "take on the yoke of the kingdom of heaven."

Since the Matthean community interpreted its life in reference to this tradition, it was required both to separate itself from the actual synagogue with its teachers and to reinterpret the symbols it shared with that tradition. Both movements find their focus in Jesus. Because messianists confessed him as Christ and Lord, they were regarded as heretics (minim) by the synagogue. The figure of Jesus therefore also organizes the Christians' appropriation of the rabbinic symbolic structure. We can approach this dialectic in four stages: (1) Jesus as polemist against scribes and Pharisees; (2) Jesus as the authentic interpreter of Torah; (3) Jesus as the fulfillment of Torah; (4) Jesus as the personification of Torah.

Polemic Against Scribes and Pharisees

The developing rabbinic tradition joined the religious ideals of the Pharisees to the legal expertise of the scribes. The groups here attacked by Jesus are the exact historical representatives of the Judaism Matthew's church confronted in its life. The polemic is not, consequently, an attack by Jesus on the Jewish people generally, much less an expression of anti-Semitism. The polemic establishes distance and distinction between rival claimants to be the authentic realization of Judaism, God's people. Some of the polemic, furthermore, such as the charge of saying but not doing (23:3, 13), is standard for disputes between ancient philosophical schools.

The attack is strategically placed within Matthew's narrative. It follows the series of Jerusalem controversy stories in 22:15–46 and precedes the eschatological instruction of the disciples in private (24:1—25:46). The placement dramatically expresses separation and distance. The discourse is given structure by its seven woes (23:13, 15, 16, 23, 25, 27, 29), which form a counterpart to the blessings spoken to the disciples in 5:3–12. The actual polemic is prefaced by an instruction to Jesus' disciples ("you") in 23:1–12: they are told what attitude to have toward the opponents and what view they should have toward their own leadership.

Valuable historical information on the Matthean setting can be gleaned from the polemic. We first notice the activities and preoccupations of the Pharisaic tradition: the title Rabbi for teachers (23:7), the aggressive missionary travels (23:15), the careful discrimination among commandments by means of midrash (23:16–22), the concern for tithing (23:23–24) and ritual purity (23:25–26). Apart from the honorific Rabbi, these match what we know of the early Pharisaic period from Paul and Mishnah Demai 2. The time period may be indicated by "your house left desolate" (23:38), though the reference to the temple is not certain. As for the Christians, they are being excluded from and persecuted in the synagogues (23:34). This is precisely the sort of setting that makes the symbolic texture of Matthew intelligible.

The passage gathers together elements of polemic against scribes and Pharisees found in other places within the narrative, such as the polemics against swearing (23:16–22; cf. 5:33–37), neglect of mercy (23:23; cf. 9:13; 12:7), purity regulations (23:25–26; cf. 15:1–9), and hypocrisy (23:5–7, 28; 6:1–16).

The polemic against teachers is not an attack on Torah itself. The scribes and Pharisees, in fact, are condemned for preaching but not practicing (23:3), or practicing for people's approval (23:5–7) without a corresponding inner disposition (23:26, 27). Their casuistry distorts Torah by preferring lighter matters to the weightier ones of justice, mercy and faith (23:23). Their midrash does not liberate but lays heavy burdens that keep people from the kingdom (23:4, 13). The allusion to "the yoke of the kingdom" cannot be missed here. Their real religious attitude is shown by their treatment of those who do follow God's word. They killed the prophets in the past (23:29–31); they persecute Christians today (23:34–37).

Christians, in turn, are to keep Torah ("Do as they say") but are not to imitate their behavior (23:3). Within the messianic community, therefore, no one is to bear the title of Rabbi, or Father. They have one father, God, and one teacher, the Messiah (23:10). The emphasis on God as father we will meet again shortly. As for the title Teacher given to the Messiah, it does not contradict Matthew's usage, for here only, he uses the term "master," *kathēgētēs*. Authority within the messianic community is not expressed by honor and titles but by service (23:8–12). The Messiah is their teacher.

Jesus as Teacher of Torah

One form of messianic expectation within Judaism looked for the Messiah to interpret Torah definitively: "They shall not depart from any commandment of the law . . . until there should come a prophet and the Messiahs of Aaron and Israel" (CD 9.9–11). Such an interpretation of Torah is one of the essential messianic functions given to Jesus in Matthew's Gospel. It is expressed programmatically in the Sermon on the Mount (chaps. 5—7). Matthew has prepared the reader to see in the one who speaks from the mountain a faithful representative of Israel, even a Mosaic figure. But Jesus is no new Moses and delivers no new law. He is God's Son who through Torah shows the real intent of God's word. He is messianic interpreter.

The term "sermon" is a misnomer, for these chapters contain a collection of sayings material brought together by the evangelist. Some of it is paralleled in Luke's Sermon on the Plain (Luke 6:17–49; cf. Matt. 5:3–12, 38–48; 7:1–5, 15–20, 24–27). Other sayings are found within different contexts in Mark or Luke (see Matt. 5:13–16, 22–26, 31–32; 6:9–13, 19–23, 25–34; 7:7–11, 13–14). The rest is distinctively Matthean (5:17–20, 27–30, 33–37; 6:1-8, 16–18; 7:6). The sermonic turn Matthew gives these traditions is seen by comparing two of the shorter sayings to their parallels in Mark and Luke. The parallels have, "Salt is good" (Mark 9:50; Luke 11:34), but Jesus says in Matthew, "*You* are the salt of the earth" (5:13). Mark 4:21 has, "Is a lamp brought in to be put under a bushel?" (cf. Luke 11:33–36). But in Matt. 5:14, Jesus says, "*You* are the light of the world." We find here direct teaching to the disciples. Messiah Jesus teaches the church, which hears his words as those of the powerful resurrected one.

The Beatitudes that open the sermon (5:3–12) establish the conditions of entry into the kingdom proclaimed by Jesus (4:17) and remind us again of the giving of the Torah by Moses: it too was accompanied by blessings and curses (Deut. 27–28). In contrast to Luke's version (Luke 6:20–26), Matthew individualizes and interiorizes the Beatitudes. The kingdom is made up of those who are poor in spirit, lowly, sorrowing, meek, pure in heart, and persecuted. The Matthean community could certainly see itself at least in the last of these categories; its members were part of God's kingdom. Their inclusion, however, is less for their sake than for the world's. They are to be in the world like seasoning or like light, to the glory of their "father in heaven" (5:16). With this last phrase, we strike the essential note of the sermon. The kingdom is not Jesus' own or that brought about by human effort or demonic pretense (see 4:1–11). It is God's kingdom.

The phrase "father in heaven" runs throughout the sermon as the constant point of reference (5:16, 45, 48; 6:1, 4, 6, 14–15, 18, 26, 32; 7:11, 21). And if it is God's effective rule that Jesus announces, then God is the only adequate measure of it: "Be perfect as your father in heaven is perfect" (5:48). The words of Jesus, therefore, do not present a program capable of human fulfillment, but a measure for all Christian existence. A measure less ultimate than God would mean a kingdom less ultimate than God's. This is the essential framework for understanding the messianic interpretation of Torah by Jesus.

Jesus' statement in 5:17–20 is programmatic for all his words and deeds throughout Matthew's Gospel:

Think not that I have come to abolish the law and the prophets; I have come not to abolish them but to fulfill them. For truly I say to you, till heaven and earth pass away, not an iota, not a dot, will pass away from the law until all is accomplished. Whoever then relaxes one of the least of these commandments and teaches men so, shall be called least in the kingdom of heaven; but he who does them and teaches them shall be called great in the kingdom of heaven. For I tell you, unless your righteousness exceeds that of the scribes and Pharisees, you will never enter the kingdom of heaven.

How has Jesus come to fulfill and accomplish Torah? Matthew has already shown us how Torah as witness is being brought to completion by the deeds and words of Jesus. But the term "fulfill" in this place also bears the sense of "reveal." By his teaching, Jesus will show the true and "full" meaning of God's Torah. The proper understanding of "these commandments" here is critical. The keeping of them will make people lesser or greater in the kingdom. We know that the kingdom in question is precisely that announced by Jesus. The phrase, "these commandments," then, does not refer to the Torah taken alone or to the Torah as interpreted by the Pharisaic tradition but *to the Torah as it is interpreted by Jesus Messiah.* Remember Jesus' final commission, "teaching them all that I have commanded you" (28:20).

These messianic teachings describe a "righteousness" that exceeds that of Pharisees and scribes (see 5:20). This is in direct contradiction to the Pharisaic claim to define "righteousness" (see chap. 2 above, pp. 54–57). But how do Jesus' teachings exceed those of the Pharisees? Certainly not in the multiplication of commands, for we are here presented with only a suggestive sample. The exceeding is to be found in the radical nature of Jesus' interpretation; radical in the sense of getting to the root. Jesus' interpretations assert God himself as the only adequate and ultimate norm for the kingdom (5:48). For the Matthean community, then, Torah meant the words of Scripture as interpreted by Jesus Messiah.

The six antithetical statements in 5:21–47 exemplify the messianic interpretation of Torah. Even in form, they show familiarity with the tradition they oppose. Jesus begins each with "You have heard it said," followed by a text of Torah. Then he responds, "But I say to you," and gives his interpretation. This pattern is formally similar to that relation of Mishnah to Gemara in the compilation of the halachic tradition, the Babylonian Talmud. In its finished state, the Talmud is centuries later than Matthew, but it only makes more formal a relation between text and interpretation that was much older. Matthew's use of this form is distinctive for two reasons. First, he has Jesus quote Torah directly, rather than traditional oral teaching, though Matt. 5:43 expands Lev. 19:18. Second, Jesus does not cite other authorities to support his own interpretation as the essential protocol in talmudic circles would dictate. He assumes a direct and unique authority to interpret: "Amen, I say to you." He claims direct knowledge of the original intent of Torah and, therefore, of God's mind.

How does the Messiah interpret Torah? He radicalizes it in three different ways. In the case of murder and adultery (5:21–30), he demands an *interior disposition* corresponding to outer action. For the prohibitions of swearing and divorce (5:31–37), he demands an *absolute adherence* rather than a mitigating casuistry (though cf. 19:9). In matters of human relationships (5:38–47), he demands a *response that goes beyond* the letter of the commandment. These antitheses serve to assert Jesus' authority to interpret for the kingdom. They also provide directions for the understanding of Torah within God's kingdom. They do not provide a complete code of ethics and certainly not a full interpretation of Torah. The Sermon on the Mount remains a sketch, not a system.

Throughout the rest of his narrative, Matthew presents Jesus as the authoritative interpreter of Torah. In the controversy stories Matthew characteristically refers to the proper understanding of Torah (see 8:4; 12:12; 15:1–9; Markan pars.). With some regularity, Jesus challenges his opponents' understanding of Torah, asking them rhetorically, "Have you not *read* in the Law (or Scripture) . . . " and following with a direct citation of Torah (see 12:5; 19:4; 21:16, 42; 22:31). The scribes and Pharisees, we are to infer, do not understand the very Torah to which they cling, for they do not recognize its full expression in the words and deeds of Jesus. They are told by him, "Go and learn what this means, 'I desire mercy and not sacrifice,' for I came not to call the righteous but sinners" (9:13; cf. 12:7 and Hos. 6:6).

Jesus the Fulfillment of Torah

Matthew makes the pattern of scriptural fulfillment far more explicit and prominent than Mark does. He cites Scripture directly some fifty-seven times, compared with Mark's thirty. His citations are also fuller and more deliberately set off. This is found above all in his formula citations. By means of them, Matthew brings specific texts of Torah and specific moments in the Messiah's life together, so that they are mutually interpretive. From seeing Jesus, we understand the real meaning of Torah; by reading Torah, we discover the full meaning of Jesus' ministry. From these citations alone, we learn a great deal about Matthew's understanding of Jesus and how he "fulfills" Torah.

From these citations, we learn that Jesus is Immanuel, God with us (1:23; cf. Isa. 7:14) and that he is God's Son (2:15; cf. Hos. 11:1). We learn that he is a Nazarene (2:23; cf. Judg. 13:5; Isa. 11:1?) but was born in Bethlehem as a ruler of the people (2:6; cf. Mic. 5:2). His kingship was made manifest at his entry into Jerusalem (21:5; cf. Zech. 9:9). But he is also God's chosen servant who bears the ills of others (8:17; cf. Isa. 53:4), a hidden servant (12:18–21; cf. Isa. 42:1–4) who speaks in parables (13:35; cf. Ps. 78:2). He is one betrayed by a companion, for money (27:9–10; cf. Jer. 18:1–3). His significance is not confined to Israel. He will proclaim justice to the Gentiles and in his name the Gentiles will hope (12:18, 21; cf.

Isa. 42:1–4). For Galilee of the Gentiles, as for all nations (28:19), he is the great light that has dawned, to shine on those who dwelt in darkness (4:15–16; cf. Isa. 9:1–2). The formula citations represent the explicit reflection of the "scribes of the kingdom" within Matthew's community on the messianic implications of Torah.

Jesus the Personification of Torah

We have seen Jesus as the focus both for the separation from the synagogue and for the appropriation of its symbolic system. Matthew shows Jesus to be interpreter and fulfiller of Torah. But does he go further in his shaping of the image of Jesus, to suggest that Jesus virtually personifies Torah—is, in effect, God's Word? It is more than a little likely, because of the way certain functions and attributes of Torah current in the Pharisaic tradition are suggested by Matthew's presentation of Jesus.

We find the personification of wisdom already in the Book of Proverbs, where Wisdom "calls out" in her own voice (8:4–20), claiming to be at once the first of God's creations present with him in the beginning (8:22–30) and the companion of humankind, "delighting in the sons of men" (8:31). In its praise of Sophia (Wisdom), the Wisdom of Solomon calls her the reflection and image of God. She passes from generation to generation into the souls of "holy people and prophets" (Wis. 7:25–27). The Book of Sirach explicitly connects this personified Wisdom to Torah: "All this is the book of the covenant of the Most High God, the law which Moses commanded us" (Sir. 24:23).

In the Pharisaic tradition, the identification of Wisdom with the study of Torah was well established. Those who studied Torah were wise men (*hakamim*), as those who did not were sinners. Haggadic speculation on Torah and its attributes led to the conclusion that Torah, too, was from the beginning and had no end; that those who took its yoke upon them took on the yoke of the kingdom, which meant freedom and a share in God's rest; that the study of Torah itself mediated God's presence by means of the *Shekinah* (see chap. 2 above, p. 56). These images provide a backdrop against which some of the statements that Matthew places in the mouth of Jesus become highly intriguing.

We have already seen the astounding authority claimed by Jesus when he says, "You have heard it said, but I say to you. . . ." Such language asserts a virtual equality with Torah. In the midst of controversy with opponents, moreover, Jesus claims in turn to be greater than the temple (12:6), greater than Jonah (12:41), and greater than Solomon (12:42). Are these assertions of superiority chosen at random? Do the three things with which Jesus compares himself stand only for themselves? Or do they stand for the three parts of Torah: Law, Prophets, and Writings?

That such a suggestion cannot be entirely dismissed is shown by Jesus' statement "I came not to call the righteous but sinners" (9:13). As Wisdom called to life, so does he. And as Wisdom "delighted in the sons of men," so do we find Jesus defending himself when attacked for consorting with undesirables: "Wisdom is justified by her deeds" (11:19). And in his own voice, Jesus says, "I will send out prophets and wise men and scribes" (23:34). We know from 5:48 that the Father is the measure of what is perfect; but Jesus tells the rich man who wanted eternal life (19:16) first to "keep the commandments" (19:17). But when the man said this had been done, Jesus tells him, "If you want to be perfect, sell all you possess . . . and come, follow me" (19:21). In 5:18, Jesus says of Torah, "Until heaven and earth pass away, not an iota, not a dot, will pass from the law until all is accomplished"; but in 24:35, he says of his own words, "Heaven and earth will pass away, but my words will not pass away"; and he commissions his disciples to teach all nations "all that I have commanded you. Lo, I am with you till the close of the age" (28:20).

The foregoing examples are suggestive and only that; it would be impossible to make a case from them alone. In the following passages, however, there is no mistaking the equation of Jesus and Torah. Jesus had attacked the scribes and Pharisees for placing heavy burdens on people (23:4). In 11:28–30, after declaring his unique capacity to reveal the Father, Jesus says:

> Come to me all who labor and are heavily burdened and I will give you rest. Take my yoke upon you, and learn from me, for I am gentle and lowly in heart, and you will find rest for your souls; for my yoke is easy and my burden light.

Several points require comment in this extraordinarily rich passage. First, because he is gentle and lowly, Jesus personifies membership in God's kingdom (cf. 5:3–5). Second, as Torah revealed God's will, so Jesus reveals the Father to whom he wishes (11:27). Third, in contrast to scribes and Pharisees—the "wise" from whom the revelation is hidden, 11:25—Jesus gives a light burden. Fourth, his "yoke" corresponds exactly to the symbol of Torah as "yoke of the kingdom of God." Fifth, as the Pharisees looked to Torah to learn God's ways, so those whom Jesus calls are to "learn from me." Sixth, the commandment that, above all, defined Jews in society was the Sabbath observance, which was regarded as participation in God's own Sabbath rest; here, learning from Jesus brings rest for the soul.

Finally, the *Shekinah* was said to dwell among even two or three who studied Torah together. We hear Jesus tell his community in 18:20: "Where two or three are gathered in my name, there I am in the midst of them." In Matthew's Gospel, Jesus is teacher of Torah, fulfillment of Torah, and the very personification of Torah.

THE CHURCH OF THE MESSIAH

I have mentioned that Matthew is the only Gospel to use the term "church" (*ekklēsia;* 16:18; 18:17) and that this Gospel shows a constant concern for the identity and integrity of the messianic community. This focus makes more intelligible the Gospel's hostility toward Jewish leaders. Jesus' polemic gives voice to a community's struggle to define itself against an older, more powerful, and antagonistic tradition.

Jew and Gentile

The struggle for self-definition was all the harder for the Matthean community, since it was caught in a tension between particularity and universality. In what way were they part of Judaism and in what way were they from among the Gentiles? Part of the community's traditions made it clear that the mission of Jesus and his first disciples had been meant only for Israel (2:6; 9:36; 10:23; 19:28). Twice, however, a strange phrase is used to express this. Jesus tells the Syro-Phoenician woman that "I was sent only to the *lost sheep* of the house of Israel" (15:24), and he tells the Twelve whom he sends out, "Go nowhere among the Gentiles . . . but go rather to the *lost sheep* of the house of Israel" (10:5–6).

The sayings material in this Gospel also reveals a pronounced animus toward Gentiles. They are like dogs (6:32) and even swine (7:6). Their manner of pleasure (6:32), power (20:25), prayer (6:7), and hospitality (5:47) are all criticized. As Jesus was handed over to the Gentiles (20:19), furthermore, so would the disciples give testimony before all nations (10:18), even though they be hated by them (24:9). Perhaps the most revealing instance of how this community appropriated to itself the symbolic structure of Judaism is this remark concerning a community troublemaker: "If he refuses to listen to the *church,* let him be to you as a Gentile and tax collector" (18:17).

At the same time, the community knew that its Messiah had been rejected by the Jewish leadership and the populace of Jerusalem (27:25), and that he continued to be rejected by those who worshiped in the synagogue down the street. The community remembered the moral of the parable of the two sons, that tax collectors and sinners entered the kingdom first (21:28–32), as well as the words of Jesus, "Many will come from the east and west and sit at the table . . . while the sons of the kingdom will be thrown into outer darkness" (8:11–12). It recalled how the parable of the vineyard made this point: "The Kingdom of God will be taken away from you and given to a nation producing the fruits of it" (21:43). And it recalled how in the parable of the wedding feast, "the king was angry and he sent his troops and destroyed those murderers and burned their city"

(22:7), and that Jesus had told the scribes and Pharisees, "Behold your house is forsaken and desolate" (23:38).

The community scribes had also pondered the texts of Torah that spoke of the Messiah as a servant who would be a hope and a light to Gentiles (4:15–16; 12:18–21). They saw hints of the Messiah's universal significance already in his birth (2:2). And the community knew stories of Gentiles who had shown faith in the Messiah when Jews had not. "I have not seen such faith in Israel," said Jesus of the centurion (8:10), and he told the Syro-Phoenician woman, "O Woman, great is your faith" (15:28). The community knew above all that Jesus' promise of the gospel's being preached to all nations (24:14) so that all nations might come before him in judgment (25:32) had been given as an express command in the words of the risen Lord to the Eleven, "Go, make disciples of all nations" (28:19). That commission had begun to be fulfilled, and this church included Gentiles in its membership, with virtual certainty. But it was also a community that was forced to work out its particular identity—perhaps as the lost sheep of the house of Israel—in confrontation with a developing Pharisaic Judaism and that so thoroughly appropriated the symbols of Judaism to itself that it called those outside the messianic community, simply, Gentiles (18:17).

The Disciples in Matthew

Matthew treats the disciples—he is fond of the term "the twelve disciples" (10:1; 11:1; 20:17; 26:20)—far more favorably than Mark does. We have already seen the reason. The disciples must pass on the words of the Lord to others; they cannot be totally faithless and unintelligent. We know that they understand and both "see and hear" (13:51–52; 13:10–17). Matthew by no means hides the hard facts about Jesus' first followers: they all still abandon him (26:56), and even at his resurrection appearance "some doubted" (28:17; cf. 14:31). But Matthew consistently softens Mark's harsher portrait in scenes such as the stilling of the storm (8:23–27), the hemorrhaging woman (9:18–26), the transfiguration (17:1–8), and the second Passion prediction, where the disciples are not "afraid," as in Mark, but only "greatly distressed" (17:23). Matthew defines their problem as one of having little faith (17:20), and the phrase "men of little faith" is effectively his epithet for the disciples (6:30; 8:26; 14:31; 16:8).

Matthew's treatment of the disciples is most noteworthy for the prominent role played by Peter. Much more than in Mark, Peter here emerges as the representative of the other disciples. In the story of the walking on the water, a whole section is devoted to his individual response (14:28–31). Jesus' prediction of twelve thrones for the twelve disciples within Israel is given in response to a question from Peter (19:27–30). In the garden of

Gethsemane, it is twice emphasized that Peter (not "Simon," as in Mark) was sleeping (26:37, 40).

The positive and negative sides of Peter's prominence are exemplified by his confession of Jesus and his denial of him. Peter's recognition of Jesus at Caesarea Philippi is fuller than in Mark: "You are the Christ, the Son of the living God" (16:16). Jesus responds in kind with a blessing specifically directed to Peter. He is the rock of the church, and in a community of scribes, he has the power to "bind and loose," that is, he has decision-making authority. The scribes and Pharisees "shut up" the kingdom, but Peter is given "the keys to the kingdom" (16:19). Since the whole community is also said to "bind and loose" in 18:18, Peter's authority is not isolated from that of the community but articulates it. He is once more a representative figure. And Matthew shows immediately that the greatness of his confession is matched by the depth of his resistance to God's will. When he hears of Jesus' suffering, he says, "God forbid, Lord!" (16:22), and Jesus calls him, "a stumbling block to me" (16:23).

With a small but telling detail, Matthew also heightens the enormity of Peter's denial of Jesus (26:69–75). Peter denies him three times, as in Mark, but in two of his denials, he takes a curse upon himself and swears (26:72, 74). By this, Matthew shows that Peter denied not only Jesus but also his teachings (see 5:34). Peter represents the disciples at their best and worst.

Instructions to the Church

In one sense, all of Jesus' words in this Gospel teach the church. In chapters 10 and 18, however, there is a more obvious focus on the life and activity of the community. Jesus sends out the Twelve on mission in 10:1–42. Matthew, like Mark, allows the shadow of rejection and persecution to fall over this enterprise, by placing the discourse in a part of the narrative where Jesus is being rejected (see chaps. 8—9, 11—12). So are they to expect rejection, persecution (10:14–25), and division within their households because of him (10:34–36). They are not, in these circumstances, to fear (10:26–33). Not only do they bear the authority to carry out the tasks of the Messiah (10:1, 7–8), as his representatives they make him present. They can therefore expect the same reception and rejection that were his (10:40–42). In Matthew's scribal context, this saying would be heard distinctly: "A disciple is not above his teacher, nor a servant his master; it is enough for the disciple to be like his teacher, and the servant his master" (10:24–25).

Chapter 18 addresses the inner life of the church. There is a remarkable concentration on humility and service. Rebuke, correction, and even excommunication may be necessary for the messianic community, as they are for other communities. But this is not a community that defines itself first of all in terms of power. Greatness is measured by smallness, and the model for receiving the kingdom is a child (18:1–4). In similar fashion, the community as a whole is to show an active concern for "the little ones." They are to be received (18:5) and not scandalized (18:6–9) or despised (18:10). They are to be searched out and saved: "It is not the will of my father that one of these little ones should perish" (18:12–13). As so often in Matthew, the note of forgiveness becomes the characteristic attitude of those in the church (18:21–35; cf. 6:12–15; 9:2–6). And if discipline and forgiveness are necessary, this means Matthew does not regard the church as an assembly of the perfect. The parable of the weeds, with its interpretation (13:24–30, 37–43), the parable of the net and fishes (13:47–50), and the parable of the wedding feast (22:11–14) have already made it clear that continual reform and response are required even for those in the church. No parable makes plainer how the community stands under judgment than that of the sheep and goats (25:31–46). It states unmistakably that the criterion for reward or punishment will be what one has done "for one of these least of my brethren" (25:40, 45). The Torah of Jesus demands "mercy, not sacrifice" (12:7).

BIBLIOGRAPHICAL NOTE

References to the discussion of Matthean priority can be found in the bibliographical note to chap. 7. The five-book hypothesis for Matthew was developed most fully by B. W. Bacon, *Studies in Matthew* (New York: Henry Holt, 1930). An analysis based on the temporal transitions is J. D. Kingsbury, *Matthew: Structure, Christology, Kingdom* (Philadelphia: Fortress Press, 1975). Aspects of Matthew's literary technique can be found in J. C. Fenton, "Inclusio and Chiasm in Matthew," *SE* 1 (TU 73, 1959): 174–79, and C. H. Lohr, "Oral Techniques in the Gospel of Matthew," *CBQ* 23 (1961): 403–35.

Matthew's systematic use of Scripture is examined by R. H. Grundy, *The Use of the Old Testament in St. Matthew's Gospel* (Leiden: E. J. Brill, 1967), and by K. Stendahl, *The School of St. Matthew and Its Use of the Old Testament* (Philadelphia: Fortress Press, 1968). Stendahl suggests a school context for this exegetical enterprise. The way Matthew's use of Torah can shape his narration is shown by J. H. Neyrey, "The Thematic Use of Isaiah 42:1–4 in Matthew 12," *Bib* 63 (1982): 457–73. The liturgical context of Matthew is stressed by G. D. Kilpatrick, *The Origins of the Gospel According to St. Matthew* (Oxford: At the Clarendon Press, 1946), and M. D. Goulder, *Midrash and Lection in Matthew* (London: SPCK, 1974).

On Matthew's first chaps., see K. Stendahl, " 'Quis et Unde?' An Analysis of Mt 1–2," in *The Interpretation of Matthew*, ed. G. Stanton, IRT 3 (Philadelphia: Fortress Press; London: SPCK, 1983 [1961]), 56–66; and R. E. Brown, *The Birth of the Messiah* (Garden City, N.Y.: Doubleday & Co., 1979). For the Passion, see

N. A. Dahl, "The Passion Narrative in Matthew," in *The Interpretation of Matthew*, ed. Stanton, 42–55. Matthew's very special use of the titles of Jesus is studied by J. D. Kingsbury, "The Title 'Son of David' in Matthew's Gospel," *JBL* 95 (1976): 591–602; idem, "The Title 'Kyrios' in Matthew's Gospel," *JBL* 94 (1975): 246–55.

For the parables generally, see J. Jeremias, *The Parables of Jesus*, rev. ed., trans. S. Hooke (New York: Charles Scribner's Sons, 1963); J. D. Crossan, *In Parables: The Challenge of the Historical Jesus* (New York: Harper & Row, 1973); and esp. M. Boucher, *The Mysterious Parable: A Literary Study*, CBQMS 6 (Washington, D.C.: Catholic Biblical Assn. of America, 1977). For the Matthean use of parables, see J. D. Kingsbury, *The Parables of Jesus in Matthew 13* (Richmond: John Knox Press, 1969).

For attempts at deciphering the Matthean context from the polemic in chap. 23., see D. R. A. Hare, *The Theme of Jewish Persecution of Christians in the Gospel According to Matthew* (Cambridge: At the Univ. Press, 1967); S. Van Tilburg, *The Jewish Leaders in Matthew* (Leiden: E. J. Brill, 1972); O. L. Cope, *A Scribe Trained for the Kingdom of Heaven* CBQMS 5 (Washington, D. C.: Catholic Biblical Assn. of America, 1976); D. E. Garland, *The Intention of Matthew 23*, NovTSup 52 (Leiden: E. J. Brill, 1979). The polemical intention of chap. 7 is examined by D. Hill, "False Prophets and Charismatics: Structure and Interpretation in Matthew 7:15–23," *Bib* 57 (1976): 327–48.

No section of Matthew has received more attention than chap. 5. For various aspects, see J. Jeremias, *The Sermon on the Mount*, trans. N. Perrin (Philadelphia: Fortress Press, 1963); W. D. Davies, *The Setting of the Sermon on the Mount* (Cambridge: At the Univ. Press, 1963); J. Meier, *Law and History in Matthew's Gospel: A Redactional Study of 5:17–48* (Rome: Biblical Inst. Press, 1976); B. Przybylski, *Righteousness in Matthew and His World of Thought*, SNTSMS 41 (New York and Cambridge: Cambridge Univ. Press, 1980); H. D. Betz, *Essays on the Sermon on the Mount*, trans. L. L. Welborn (Philadelphia: Fortress Press, 1985).

The literary relationship between Torah and Jesus in Matthew is explored by J. M. Gibbs, "The Son of God as Torah Incarnate in Matthew," *SE* 4 (TU 102, 1968): 38–46; M. J. Suggs, *Wisdom, Christology, and Law in Matthew's Gospel* (Cambridge: Harvard Univ. Press, 1970); F. Burnett, *The Testament of Jesus-Sophia* (Washington, D.C.: Univ. Press of America, 1981). The special role played by Peter among the disciples is examined in R. Brown, K. P. Donfried, J. Reumann, eds., *Peter in the New Testament* (Minneapolis: Augsburg Pub. House, 1973).

Collections of essays touching on a number of Matthean themes are G. Bornkamm, *Tradition and Interpretation in Matthew* (Philadelphia: Westminster Press, 1963); J. L. Mays, ed., *Interpreting the Gospels* (Philadelphia: Fortress Press, 1981); and G. Stanton, ed., *The Interpretation of Matthew* IRT 3 (Philadelphia: Fortress Press; London: SPCK, 1983). An attempt to read Matthew from the standpoint of reader-response methodology is R. A. Edwards, *Matthew's Story of Jesus* (Philadelphia: Fortress Press, 1985).

As with Mark, there are no excellent critical commentaries in English. Some benefit may be derived from those of D. Hill, *The Gospel of Matthew*, NCB (Grand Rapids: Wm. B. Eerdmans; London: Oliphants, 1972); J. C. Fenton, *The Gospel of*

St. Matthew (Baltimore: Penguin Books, 1963); E. Schweizer, *The Good News According to Matthew* (Atlanta: John Knox Press, 1975). More technical is R. H. Gundry, *Matthew: A Commentary on His Literary and Theological Art* (Grand Rapids: Wm. B. Eerdmans, 1982).

9

Luke-Acts

LUKE-ACTS IS A CONVENTIONAL ABBREVIATION FOR THE GOSPEL OF LUKE and the Acts of the Apostles. The hyphenated title calls attention to the conviction that the two documents separated in the canon by the Fourth Gospel are two volumes of a single literary composition.

The separation must have taken place early. We have no manuscripts in which they appear joined, and the patristic writers, who know of their common authorship, treated them separately. Reasons for their separation may have been straightforward. The first volume fits well among the other Gospels, but Acts looks unlike any of the other NT writings. On the other hand, Acts provides a fine introduction to the letters of Paul. We notice that Acts ends with Paul in Rome, and the Pauline collection ordinarily began with his Letter to the Romans. Acts also presents a portrait of Paul that emphasizes his place within the larger mission of the church. This may have helped make that more dangerous writer acceptable within the canon.

CHARACTER OF THE WRITING

The literary unity of the work is indicated by the prologue to each volume. The Gospel prologue (Luke 1:1–4) is longer and offers valuable clues to the author's intentions:

> Inasmuch as many have undertaken to compile a narrative [*diēgēsis*] of the things that have been accomplished [or, fulfilled: *plērophoreō*] among us, just as they were delivered to us by those who from the beginning were eyewitnesses and ministers of the word [*logos*], it seemed good to me also, having followed all things closely for some time past, to write an orderly account [*kathexēs*] for you, Most Excellent Theophilus, that you may know the truth [or, that you may know security: *asphaleia*] concerning the things of which you have been informed [or, instructed: *katēcheō*].

The prologue to Acts (1:1–2) follows convention by providing only a rapid résumé of the first volume:

In the first book [*logos*], O Theophilus, I have dealt with all the things that Jesus began to do and teach, until the day when he was taken up, after he had given commandment by the Holy Spirit to the apostles whom he had chosen.

In addition to the clear evidence of the prologues, a variety of structural, stylistic, and thematic elements conspire to convince nearly all contemporary scholars that Luke-Acts is a single witness within the NT canon. The implications of that recognition for interpreting Luke-Acts, however, are seldom fully developed.

A composition dedicated to an individual would ordinarily bear his or her name. Luke-Acts, then, would be called *Ad Theophilum*, "To Theophilus." A formal prologue also often indicated formal publication, with the addressee being the sponsor. The identity of this "God lover" (the etymology of Theophilus) is unknown to us; we are not even sure whether he was an individual or the symbol for Luke's readers. The implication of "the things of which you have been informed" (Luke 1:4) is that the reader knows of the Christian movement. If translated more stringently as "the things in which you have been instructed," the phrase suggests that the reader is a member of the Christian movement, one prominent enough, perhaps, to merit the honorific Excellent and one wealthy enough to sponsor publication.

According to the superscription of the Gospel and the consensus of tradition, the author is someone called Luke. Ancient authorities identified him with the physician Luke who was Paul's co-worker (see Phlm. 24; Col. 4:14; 2 Tim. 4:11). The Pauline connection seems strengthened by the fact that substantial portions of Acts dealing with Paul are written in the first-person plural, thus suggesting the presence of an eyewitness (see Acts 16:10–18; 20:5—21:18; 27:1—28:16). The traditional attribution is often challenged because of a perception of Luke-Acts as a second-generation writing (see esp. Luke 1:2; Acts 20:17–35). A designation such as second-generation, however, does not lead to precise dating, nor does it automatically preclude authorship by a Pauline companion. The traditional attribution may be correct. It is not significantly supported, however, by supposed textual evidence of a physician's insight or vocabulary. The data adduced for such claims show only that Luke shared an educated vocabulary in no way unusual for his time, not that he used the technical language of a physicians' guild. The question of authorship does not in any case greatly help us in interpreting the work.

We have then a two-volume work by an otherwise unknown Christian to an otherwise unknown patron sometime in the latter part of the first century. It is later than Mark, for it uses him as a source. How much later is impossible to determine. The readers were in all likelihood Christian. They could read a rather higher level of Greek than that found in most other early Christian writings. We assume that they appreciated Luke's often somewhat subtle stylistic touches and literary allusions. Beyond these general conclusions, we have only the text itself to guide our investigation into its destination and intentions. Luke-Acts has been categorized and catalogued many ways. Mention of some major diagnoses can accompany our preliminary probe of the text's anatomy.

We notice first its length. By classical standards not a writing of great proportions, it is by far the longest in the NT collection, with its fifty-two chapters occupying a full quarter of the canon. The length is not due to verbosity. Luke's Greek style is spare and effective. He has aroused deserved admiration as a teller of short stories who in a few words can evoke a whole world. Luke-Acts is studded with vivid vignettes. They range in Acts from the hearty humor of Rhoda dithering at the door (12:12–17), through the irony of the secret and scared Sanhedrin session (5:33–39) and the polish of Paul's preaching to philosophers (17:16–34), to the simple humanity of the story of Eutyches's fall from a window (20:7–12). In the Gospel are the parables of compassion and mercy, the prodigal son (15:11–24), and the good Samaritan (10:30–35). The sense of satisfying fullness given by these stories is due not to length but to artistry.

The length of Luke-Acts is due to the scope of Luke's vision. He writes "an orderly account" of "the things that have been fulfilled," and his narrative reaches back to the very beginning of humanity. Matthew's genealogy begins with Abraham; Luke's with Adam (3:23–38)! Luke tells us more than Matthew about Jesus' birth and childhood (see esp. 2:39–51) and much more about his resurrection appearances (24:1–53). The "things fulfilled" do not even stop there. They reach up to Luke's own day, "among us."

Here is Luke's decisive contribution to the development of early Christian literature. He tells as the one story of God's fulfilling his promises to Israel *both* the life, death, and resurrection of Jesus *and* the birth and spread of the church. Herein also is the real significance of hearing Luke-Acts as a single witness. Luke grasps the meaning of Jesus and the church for the world in a single vision, and he tells that story so that what happens with Jesus foreshadows the church's experience and what happens in the church finds meaning as the continuation of Jesus' story.

It witnesses to Luke's literary skill that for two millennia people thought he told the story just the way it happened, indeed, had to have happened. The story of the church's beginnings need not, however, have been told at all. It might also have been told very differently. That we read it as a continuation of Jesus' story is the accomplishment of Luke.

Over the two volumes, his narrative covers some sixty years. The text gives an initial impression of completeness and consecutiveness. The impression owes more to literary skill than to an abundance of materials.

In the first seven chapters of Acts, for example, Luke has only a handful of specific stories with which to work: the election of Matthias, Pentecost, the healing of a lame man, the death of Ananias and Sapphira, the gift of Barnabas, a dispute, the stoning of Stephen. Likewise, in the ministry of Paul recounted in chapters 15—18 of Acts, Luke has available only a few anecdotes beyond a bare-bones itinerary. When we read these sections, however, we gain a sense of detailed amplitude. How does he do it? He fills out his few specific stories by means of summaries that amplify and generalize the details of the accounts. And he extends dramatic moments with speeches that comment upon and interpret the events recounted in the narrative.

GENRE AND PURPOSES

If Luke is a storyteller, is he then simply and straightforwardly a maker of fiction? Or is he in some sense what he was so long considered, a historian? This question leads to a consideration of his composition's genre and purposes.

Traditionally, the question was answered, Yes, Luke is a historian and intends to be one; and the discussion could then move to the issue of whether he was a good or bad historian. There are reasons for taking this answer seriously: (1) His prologue tells us that he is writing an "orderly account." Historians of his age used such language to describe their work. He refers as well to oral and written sources; he knew others had written narratives before him. He had sources; therefore, he regarded them as such, and he used them critically. (2) He tries to relate his story to the broader historical context. He does this first by providing chronological references for pivotal events (see Luke 1:5; 2:1–2; 3:1–2; Acts 18:12). In addition, he identifies power blocs and governing agents, not only in Palestine (Acts 12:20–22) but in Asia Minor (Acts 19:31) and Europe (Acts 18:12–17). (3) Above all, Luke has the historian's instinct for chronology and causality; he makes connections between events, so that a thread of purpose runs through his narrative.

If Luke is a historian, what kind is he? And how good? These questions impinge on each other. To a considerable extent, a historian is dependent on his or her sources. Luke tells us he had some reports from eyewitnesses (Luke 1:2). Perhaps his unusually good information on Herod's household came from such a source (8:3). The "we" source in Acts could also have been based on an eyewitness, whether the author or another. Since the first-person plural was sometimes used conventionally in travel narratives, however, we cannot be certain. Luke also had written sources (Luke 1:1). In the Gospel, he used Mark, materials from Q, and other distinctive materials designated L. We can check his use of a source only in the case of

Mark (Q is harder because its original form must be abstracted from the Lukan *and* Matthean variations).

Luke uses Mark differently from the way Matthew does. When he follows Mark's order, he does so more closely, although he tends to eliminate blatant doublets, such as the feeding stories, whereas Matthew multiplies them. Instead of inserting blocks of discourse material into the narrative framework, he alternates narrative and sayings more subtly. Jesus' sayings in Luke have an air of biographical plausibility (see, e.g., chaps. 9—19). So far as we can tell, then, he is faithful to his Gospel source. But that is the real problem: telling where there *is* a source. If Matthew and Mark were not both extant and available for comparison, I doubt we could be really sure, even in the Gospel, just where Luke was using a source. Like many ancient historians, he rewrote as he borrowed from his sources. He even adjusted the Greek of Mark, bringing it closer to his own.

The real problem in discovering Luke's sources is his capacity of writing convincingly in a variety of styles. Take the Greek of the Gospel prologue and contrast it against that of the infancy account; add Peter's Pentecost sermon and Paul's defense speeches from Acts. Place them side by side. One could easily be convinced that they come from different books and different writers. Luke follows the ancient rhetorical ideal of "writing in character," *prosōpopoeia*, which fits style to character and occasion. In the infancy account of the Gospel, for example, his Greek has a Semitic coloration. Some have concluded he was using Hebrew or Aramaic sources. Was he? When we observe other places where he shows a flair and fascination for a biblical or, more accurately, septuagintal style, the determination becomes difficult in the extreme.

In Acts, the search for Luke's sources is even more frustrating, since we have no way to check his usage. It appears that he had fewer written sources and more literary control in Acts than in the Gospel. Apart from the "we" sections—which are otherwise stylistically consistent with the material around them—we cannot identify any certain sources. Attempts to identify a Jerusalem source or an Antiochean source for the first fifteen chapters of Acts have proved in the main to be more complex than useful.

How reliable is Luke as a historian? Taking into account his fidelity to the one source we can check, his general accuracy in matters we know about from archaeological or documentary sources, and the overall agreement between his description of Paul's movements and the descriptions in the Pauline letters, we conclude that Luke is accurate in what he tells us. The phrase "what he tells us" is critical. Luke writes selectively. The Gospel, for example, contains none of Matthew's infancy material, no Sermon on the Mount, no promise of keys to Peter, no parables of virgins or of sheep and goats, no Galilean appearances of the risen Lord. In Acts,

Luke either does not know some things or chooses to ignore or minimize them. He describes no Galilean mission of the church (notice the conspicuous absence in Acts 1:8 and 15:3) nor any rural evangelization; the cities are his focus. Of the first missionaries, he concentrates on Peter and Paul to the virtual neglect of all others. Although Paul's arrival in Rome is the climax of Acts, he never, for example, bothers to inform us when the Christian movement itself reached there (see Acts 28:14–16).

Luke so concentrates on Jesus and on a few of his followers that some consider him less a historian than a biographer. It has been shown that the biographies of some Hellenistic philosophers, such as those found in Diogenes Laertius, fall into a twofold form similar to that of Luke-Acts. First, the life of the founder is considered, together with an account of his deeds and teachings; then a succession narrative tells of the deeds and teachings of his students. This attractive hypothesis accounts for some features of Luke's work. Unfortunately, it omits consideration of one of the most important "characters" in Luke's work: the people Israel. Because Luke shows a constant concern through both volumes for the fate of this historic people, his writing is properly if roughly categorized as a form of history.

This pushes us closer to a consideration of what kind of historian he might be. He was obviously not a disinterested observer, nor was he attempting to set down a comprehensive record of the Christian past. He was neither Bishop Eusebius nor Leopold von Ranke. The possibility of open publication suggested by the prologue, however, may indicate some interest in influencing the outside, non-Christian world. Perhaps Luke-Acts is the first example of Christian *apologetic* literature?

Noting Luke's positive view of Gentiles generally—he entirely lacks Matthew's xenophobia—and of Roman officials in particular, some have concluded that Luke was writing an apology for the Christian movement. Why? He sought to demonstrate the political harmlessness of the movement so that magistrates might give Christians the same freedom enjoyed by "other Jews." In this light, Luke's description of Christianity as rooted in Judaism makes an important political point. The proconsul Gallio's decision in Acts 18:14–15 is therefore exemplary: in matters of dispute among Jews, magistrates need not meddle.

Others have noted the abrupt ending of Acts with Paul under house arrest (Acts 28:30–31) and have considered Luke-Acts to be an apology for Paul, perhaps even a defense brief for use in his trial. Certainly, Luke's concentration on Paul and his defense requires explanation. But the rest of his long narrative would ill fit such a narrow role. Luke-Acts has been considered to be an apology for Paul in yet another direction. To appease a significant and theologically vocal minority of Jewish believers within the Christian community, it is suggested, Luke presents Paul not as one opposed to Torah but as a true teacher of Israel. Once again, however, that undoubted emphasis does not help us grasp the purposes of Luke-Acts as a whole. The problem of these suggestions concerning Luke-Acts' apologetic character is that they understand apologetic literature itself too narrowly.

We remember that Jewish apologetic literature had a double function (see chap. 3 above). Outwardly, it defended Jews against attack and misunderstanding. But it also had a function for the community of Jews. It reinterpreted the tradition within a pluralistic context. Luke-Acts has a similar double-edged function. It presents the Christian movement to a hypothetical outside reader as enlightened, harmless, and beneficent. Its more immediate and important function, however, points inward, to the reinterpretation of the gospel within the context of a pluralistic environment composed of both Jews and Gentiles. To see this, another and closer look at the prologue of the Gospel is required.

The Gospel prologue (Luke 1:1–4) shows that although it may have been published and therefore available to outside readers, Luke-Acts is addressed first of all to the Christian community. Theophilus has already been "instructed" in the Christian story. Why, then, does Luke write still another version for him? Luke writes to give him "security" in his knowledge of the "things brought to fulfillment among us." Not only the distant past, therefore, but also present circumstances require interpretation: the "among us" reaches to Luke's own day. The expression "fulfilled" is in the passive voice. In the biblical idiom, this equals "realities that *God* brought to fulfillment." The narrative, we begin to see, is about the fulfillment of God's promises, right up to the present. But why is security (*asphaleia*) required? And how will a narrative written "in sequence" provide it?

The text of Luke-Acts overwhelmingly suggests that Luke's audience was almost entirely gentile. There may still have been Jewish members of his churches. But the Jewish mission, which Acts shows us so repeatedly failing, appears to be less than vigorous. In contrast, the closing statement regarding the Gentiles is "They will listen" (Acts 28:28). And for Luke's readers, that statement has come true. But precisely these two facts of gentile acceptance and Jewish rejection of the Gospel message create a severe "uncertainty" for thoughtful gentile Christians.

God's promises, after all, had been made to the people Israel, through Abraham (Gen. 12:1–3). If that historical people was not *now* in possession of the promised blessings, and someone else was, what did that signify for God's reliability? Did God keep his word, or did he utterly betray Israel? And what were the implications for *gentile* believers in this God? Could they rely on "the things fulfilled among them" any more than the Jews could? If God's word failed Israel, could it not fail the Gentiles as well?

The problem addressed by Luke's narrative is precisely and properly one of *theodicy*, that is, of defending God's work in history. By telling how each thing happened "in order," he wants to show that God in fact did *first* fulfill his promises to Israel and *then* extended the blessings to the gentile world. Therefore, the word that had reached the Gentiles was trustworthy. Here we see the importance of the "in order," or consecutiveness, of Luke's narrative. The saving of Israel was required precisely for the security of gentile faith.

Luke is therefore a historian, but of a special kind. He is required to write the continuation of the biblical narrative. By showing the story of Jesus to be rooted in that of Israel and by demonstrating how God's promises were realized in a restored Israel, Luke could assure gentile Christians that they could trust the "good news" that had reached them. Luke's purposes are not determined by a momentary crisis or a fleeting misunderstanding. They are generated by the fundamental mystery posed by a messianic sect's existing among gentile people. So successful was Luke that his narrative has become the etiological or foundational myth of gentile Christianity.

Many of the distinctive literary features of Luke's work, furthermore, can be best appreciated when seen as serving his overall purpose: his emphasis on the fulfillment of prophecy and the spirit of prophecy in the church, his development of a prophetic Christology and model of authority, his use of the story of Moses for the structuring of the two volumes. It is to these literary dimensions of Luke-Acts we must now turn.

LITERARY STRUCTURE AND INTERPRETATION

Luke-Acts so clearly bears the marks of literary skill and intentionality that attempts to isolate its dominant literary patterns have not been lacking. Among them are studies that emphasize the cyclical structure of the work. Events in Acts clearly do parallel those of the Gospel. Mary, for example, appears at the beginning of each volume; the apostles work wonders remarkably similar to those of Jesus; Paul's final journey to suffering resembles Jesus' journey toward suffering. Intricate analyses of these correspondences, however, lack plausibility when raised to the level of a central organizing principle. The cyclical patterns in Luke-Acts are placed within a story that is essentially and intentionally linear. Things really change in Luke-Acts: the story begins in the OT priesthood and ends in a Roman apartment. Luke tells us that he is writing a narrative "in order." For the understanding of Luke-Acts, *where* something occurs in the narrative is almost as important as *what* occurs.

Geographical Structure

Luke uses geography as a literary and theological instrument. The center of his story is the city of Jerusalem. The whole movement of the

Gospel is *toward* Jerusalem. Thus, the infancy account leads to the presentation of Jesus in the temple (Luke 2:22) and to his discovery there after being lost (2:41–51). The Lukan temptation account reverses Matthew's order for the last two temptations, so the climax is reached in Jerusalem (4:9). The transfiguration at the end of the Galilean ministry explicitly prepares for the journey to Jerusalem and Jesus' death (9:31). The journey itself begins with a solemn announcement (9:51), followed by multiple references, during the journey, to Jesus' destination (13:22, 33–34; 17:11; 18:31; 19:11, 28). After Jesus' resurrection, all his appearances take place in the environs of Jerusalem, the last of them ending with his instruction "Stay in the city" (24:1–49).

The movement of Acts is *away from* Jerusalem. Jesus' instruction in Acts 1:8, "You shall be my witnesses in Jerusalem and in all Judea and Samaria and to the end of the earth," is fulfilled by the narrative: the ministry centered in Jerusalem (chaps. 1—7) is followed by the evangelization of Judea and Samaria (chaps. 8—12), then Asia Minor and Europe (chaps. 13—28). Each outward movement circles back to Jerusalem, before reaching out still further (see Acts 12:25; 15:2; 18:22; 19:21; 20:16; 21:13; 25:1).

Jerusalem is therefore the *center* of the narrative. The middle twelve chapters of Luke-Acts narrate events in and around the city. Why is Jerusalem so central? The city and its temple were obviously of historical importance for Judaism, and the city was also historically important for the Christian movement. Jesus was killed and the church born there, after all. The importance of Jerusalem for the Church is abundantly noted by Paul (1 Thess. 2:14–15; Gal. 1:17—2:1; Rom. 15:19, 26–28). More than historical recollection is at work for Luke. The city and the temple, for him virtually identical, symbolize the people Israel. The death of Jesus and the birth of the church in that place are the paradigmatic expression of the Jewish people's acceptance or rejection of God's prophet. Jerusalem is the place of pivot in the story of the prophet and the people. This brings us to the second major literary pattern.

Prophecy as Literary Device

We have seen that proof from prophecy was a standard element in early Christian apologetic. Matthew used a highly developed form of it in his formula citations. Luke expands and refines the notion of prophetic fulfillment. Not only the events of Jesus' ministry, death, and resurrection fulfill the Scripture but also stages of the church's life and mission: they are among the things "fulfilled among us" (Acts 3:24; 13:40; 15:15; 28:25–27). Unlike Matthew, Luke does not mechanically align texts and events. His references are more general and inclusive. He often uses the phrase "it must," *dei*, of various situations, indicating how outcomes were determined by prophecies: the suffering and glorification of the Messiah (Luke

9:22; 17:25; 24:7; Acts 3:21; 17:3), the apostasy of Judas and the election of Matthias (Acts 1:16–22), the sufferings of Paul (Acts 9:16) and those of all Christians (Acts 14:22).

Specifically Lukan is the use of literary prophecy. Things predicted by characters within the story are later shown to be fulfilled explicitly in the narrative. Only Luke combines with Jesus' three Passion predictions (Luke 9:22, 44; 18:32) the clear announcement in the resurrection accounts that they had been fulfilled (24:6–8, 44). Jesus' prediction of the tribulations of his witnesses (Luke 21:12–15) is literally fulfilled in the narrative of Acts (4:3–5, 14; 5:17–42). His instruction about proper responses to unbelieving cities (Luke 9:5; 10:11) is carried out by the missionaries in Acts (13:51). Jesus says the Twelve are to be judges over Israel (Luke 22:30), and we find them exercising judgment among the people in Acts (5:1–11). The prophet Agabus predicts sufferings for Paul (Acts 21:10–14), which speedily come true (21:30–35).

Of particular importance for interpreting Luke's narrative are his programmatic prophecies. These are spoken by characters at critical junctures within the narrative and provide an interpretation of the narrative that follows. The reader understands that the plot development fulfills the prophecy. We have seen already how Jesus' commission in Acts 1:8 functions as a guide to the whole book of Acts. I have also suggested that the final announcement of Acts 28:28, "This salvation of God has been sent to the Gentiles; they will listen," is understood as having been fulfilled among Luke's readers. The prophecies at the end and beginning of the Gospel are equally important. Jesus' promise of a "power from on high" (Luke 24:49) enables the reader to perceive the "ascension" (Luke 24:50–53; Acts 1:9–11) not as an absolute departure but as a transformation of presence, and to understand the outpouring of the Holy Spirit in Acts 2:1–4 as the fulfillment of Jesus' saying, "I will send the promise of my father upon you." Likewise, the prophecy of Simeon at the start of the Gospel, "This child is set for the fall and rising of many in Israel and for a sign that is spoken against" (Luke 2:34), prepares the reader to understand the subsequent Gospel narrative as the story of a prophet whose ministry creates a division among the people.

A similar fulfillment pattern is found within smaller units. Luke arranges speech and narrative so that a narrative immediately following a saying fulfills the saying, often ironically. Here are some examples: Jesus declares that a prophet is not acceptable in his own country, and his own townspeople reject him who is a prophet (Luke 4:16–30). After declaring that sinners accepted God but that the Pharisees rejected God's plan, and after quoting the charge that he was a friend of tax collectors and sinners, Jesus is accepted by a woman who is a sinner and rejected by a Pharisee (Luke 7:36–50). Stephen, who we know is a prophet filled with the Holy

Spirit, accuses the Jewish leadership of rejecting prophets and the Holy Spirit; they reject him (Acts 7:51–60). Paul warns the Jews of Antioch in Pisidia not to reject the gospel lest they be rejected and it be given to others; they do reject it and it goes to Gentiles (13:40–48). Speech and narrative are often mutually interpretive in Luke-Acts. That Luke uses speeches in Acts as means of interpreting the narrative (Acts 2:14–36; 3:11–26; 17:22–31) has long been recognized. But Luke uses this technique of the Hellenistic historian in his Gospel narrative as well.

Interpreting the Gospel Through Acts

The prophetic structuring of Luke's work is seen in the relationship between his two volumes. The observation requires considerable development, but the essential points can be made at once. First, the Book of Acts both continues the story of the Gospel and fulfills or confirms it. What is found only by way of implication in the story of Jesus is made explicit in the story of the apostles. The pertinence of this for the reader? In Acts, Luke gives us the first and authoritative *interpretation* of his Gospel. The perspective given by Acts is even more important than that given by Synoptic comparison, for understanding the specific shape of Luke's Gospel. Second, the two volumes are parts of a two-stage prophetic model. Here I will argue these points in order, moving from a consideration of the prophetic image of the main characters in Acts to the implications of the theme of a "prophet like Moses."

Acts has appropriately been called the Book of the Holy Spirit. The Holy Spirit is an active power intervening in the progress of the mission, both impelling and guiding it (8:29, 39; 10:19; 11:15; 13:2; 15:28; 16:6; 20:22). There are five separate accounts of an "outpouring" of this power on believers (2:1–4; 4:28–31; 8:15–17; 10:44; 19:6). Although for Luke all Christians definitely "have" the Holy Spirit, he describes his important characters as "men of the Spirit" in a special way. Although he never calls them by the title, he describes them as *prophets*.

Scholars have noticed the similarity between Peter and Paul in Acts. They preach the same sort of message (chaps. 2 and 13). They perform similar miracles (3:1–7; 14:8–11). It has less often been remarked that *all* the characters in Acts who advance the plot in significant ways are described in stereotypical terms. Whether Peter and John, or Philip and Stephen, or Barnabas and Paul, they share all, or nearly all, these characteristics: They are "filled with the Holy Spirit" (4:8; 5:32; 6:3; 7:55; 11:24; 13:9). They are bold (*parrēsia*) in their proclamation (4:13; 13:46; 28:31). What they proclaim is "good news" (5:42; 8:4, 12, 25, 40; 11:20; 13:32; 14:7; 15:35) or the Word of God (4:29; 8:14; 13:5). They are, furthermore, witnesses (2:32; 10:41; 13:31; 22:20). They work signs and wonders (*sēmeia kai terata;* 4:30; 6:8; 8:6; 14:3; 15:12). They preach and

perform these wonders among the people *(laos)*, that is, the Jewish populace considered as God's people (3:12; 4:1; 6:8; 13:15). Because of their
activity, they create a division among the people; some accept their message, others do not (4:1–4; 6:1–11; 8:6, 19; 13:40–50). Taken together,
these characteristics suggest a specific image within the biblical tradition,
that of the prophet. The witnesses to Jesus' resurrection in Acts are
portrayed as prophets among the people Israel.

In Peter's speech at Pentecost, in which he interprets the first outpouring of the Spirit for his listeners—and Luke's readers—he cites the
prophecy of Joel 2:18–32 about the Spirit's being poured out on all flesh
(Acts 2:17–21). Luke makes three significant alterations in this citation.
By changing Joel's "after these things" to "in the last days," he indicates
that this outpouring of the Spirit is an eschatological event. By adding the
words "and they shall prophesy" to verse 17, he accentuates the prophetic
character of this Spirit already suggested by the citation. By adding the
phrase "and signs on the earth below" in verse 19, he forms the combination "signs and wonders." He has, therefore, brought together three
elements—an eschatological prophetic spirit manifested by signs and wonders—that suggest a very specific image in the biblical tradition, that of
Moses, the first and greatest of prophets (see, e.g., Ps. 78:11–12, 32, 43).
Messianic expectation for a "prophet like Moses" was not unknown in first
century Judaism (cf. 4Q *Testimonia*, 1–5) and was based on texts such as
the following (Deut. 34:10–12):

> There has not *arisen a prophet* since in Israel like Moses, whom the Lord knew
> face to face, none like him for all the *signs and wonders* which the Lord sent
> him to do in the land of Egypt . . . and for all the mighty power and all the
> great and terrible deeds which Moses wrought in the sight of *all Israel.*

We notice at once the potential of a phrase such as "a prophet arisen" for
the interpretation of a resurrected Messiah. And immediately after the Joel
citation, Peter describes Jesus in this way (Acts 2:22–24):

> Jesus of Nazareth, a man attested to you by God with *mighty works and
> wonders and signs* which God did *through him* in *your midst* . . . this Jesus you
> crucified . . . but God *raised him up.*

Jesus is described in terms that explicitly recall the prophet Moses.

As we read further, we find it repeated that the Spirit active in the
prophetic witnesses is the Spirit of Jesus (Acts 2:33; 3:13; 4:10; 30; 33).
The rejection of these witnesses by the people? That too is anticipated by
Jesus, as is shown by the kerygmatic passages that recall his rejection by
humans and his vindication by God in the resurrection (2:23, 36; 10:39).
The longest of these kerygmatic statements (3:13–15a) says that the people
were not entirely to blame, because they were ignorant. They were not
fully aware of what they were doing when they killed Jesus (3:17). In the

offer of repentance extended to them, Peter draws an explicit connection between Moses and Jesus (Acts 3:22–23; cf. Deut. 18:18–19):

Moses said, "The Lord God will *raise up a prophet* among your brethren as he raised me up. You shall listen to him in whatever he tells you. And it shall be that every soul that *does not listen* to that prophet *shall be destroyed from the people.*

Both Jesus and the apostles are described in terms reminiscent of Moses. The connection, moreover, is made even firmer in the description of Moses found in Stephen's speech (Acts 7:17–44). His discourse at first sight appears to be a straightforward retelling of the biblical version. Closer examination shows that Luke has selected and structured the Moses story so that it matches exactly the story of Jesus and his witnesses.

Moses' story falls into three stages. At the time when the promises to Abraham were about to be fulfilled (Acts 7:17), Moses is sent by God to "visit" the people, to "save" them. They are "ignorant" of his identity and role, so they reject him a first time. He must flee into exile (7:23–29). While in exile, Moses is empowered by God and sent back to the people a second time. He leads them out of Egypt and through the desert with "signs and wonders." But they reject him and his words a second time, preferring an idol made with their own hands. As a result, those who reject him this time are themselves to be rejected (7:39–43).

Here we have two sendings by God, the first with Moses in weakness, the second with him in power. Here are two offers of salvation made to the people. The first is rejected out of ignorance, and so leads to a second chance; when this is refused in full knowledge of the signs and wonders, God rejects the people. This is striking enough, but the connection between Jesus and Moses is made absolutely clear. At the heart of the Moses story we find the same sort of kerygmatic statement made elsewhere of Jesus (Acts 7:35–37):

This Moses, whom they refused, saying, "Who made you ruler and judge?" God sent as both ruler and deliverer by the hand of the angel that appeared to him in the bush. He led them out, having performed wonders and signs in Egypt and at the Red Sea and in the wilderness for forty years. This is the Moses who said to the Israelites, "God will raise up for you a prophet from your brethren as he raised me up."

Some implications of these observations can now be spelled out. We cannot be sure whether Luke's perception of Jesus' death and resurrection affected his portrayal of Moses or whether the influence moved in the opposite direction. It is clear, however, that the story of Moses as Luke understood it shows how he saw the "necessity" of a prophet's suffering before glory (see Luke 13:33–34; 24:25–26, 44–46). The Moses connection also reveals the typology and succession of spiritual authority important for Luke. Moses provides the type of prophetic authority. Jesus is the prophet like Moses. But Jesus has not only been "raised up" in the sense of "elected." He is "raised up" by the resurrection as Lord (Ps. 110:1; Acts 2:34–36). As Moses "received the living words and gave them" to the people in the desert (7:38), so did Jesus receive from God the Holy Spirit and poured it out on his witnesses (2:33). In their testimony, the message of Jesus is filled with power. The offer of salvation now bears with it an equally great threat: those who do not listen to the voice of "this prophet" will be "cut off from the people" (3:23).

The pattern of the Moses story provides the fundamental structure for Luke's two-volume work. In the Gospel, we read the story of God's first sending of the prophet Jesus to "visit" his people for their "salvation" (Luke 1:68; 7:16; 19:44); of their initial rejection of the salvation, out of ignorance; and of Jesus' being "raised up" from death. In Acts, we find his establishment in power signified by the outpouring of the Holy Spirit, the sending of his witnesses filled with that Spirit, and the second offer to Israel of salvation "in his name" (Acts 4:12; 5:31). This time, the cost of a refusal is separation from the people. The pattern also shows us the precise reason the Jerusalem narrative is so dominant and critical. It is in Jerusalem that the first rejection, the empowerment, the second offer, and either acceptance or rejection by the people all occur.

Luke clearly had more freedom to craft this image in Acts. But if Acts gives us Luke's interpretation of his Gospel narrative, then we can expect to find there, within stricter constraints, the same understanding of Jesus as a prophet like Moses. Only a full reading could make this plausible, but three small details can be anticipated here. When Jesus raises a widow's son from the dead (Luke 7:11–15), the story concludes (7:16):

Fear seized them all, and they glorified God, saying, "A great *prophet has arisen among us!*" And, "God has *visited* his people!"

The alert reader hears definite echoes of that identification, when reading Acts 3 and 7. At the conclusion of the transfiguration story, the voice from heaven identifies Jesus as Son, and says, "Listen to him" (Luke 9:35). Commentators on Matthew and Mark see there a possible allusion to Deut. 18:19 and the prophet like Moses. In the light of Acts 3:22, the allusion is clearly certain and deliberate in Luke. Finally, Gospel readers hear the disciples on the road to Emmaus (Luke 24:19) describe "Jesus of Nazareth, who was a *prophet mighty in deed and word* before God and *all the people.*" When they hear in Acts of the "prophet whom God has raised up," they will realize how that description was accurate. The shape of Luke's story in Acts enables us to detect subtle shadings in his Gospel narrative. To a fuller consideration of his first volume we can now turn, presupposing once more the basic Markan story line and paying closest attention to the Lukan redaction.

THE GOSPEL NARRATIVE

The Infancy Stories

Luke's infancy account (chaps. 1—2) is a form of haggadic midrash. His language evokes both specific texts from Torah and a general atmosphere of the biblical world. After the elegant Greek period of the prologue (1:1–4), the reader is plunged suddenly by the septuagintal style of 1:5 into the world of the Judges and Ruth. The speech of both angels and humans resonates passages of Scripture. Gabriel's annunciation to Mary (1:28–33) recalls at once the annunciation in Judges 13:2–5, the oracles of Zeph. 3:14 and Zech. 2:10, and the prophecy of 2 Sam. 7:12–16. Mary's Canticle (Luke 1:46–55) adapts and alters the Song of Hannah from 1 Sam. 2:1–10. The very description of characters suggests the piety associated with the "poor of Yahweh" in Zeph. 3:11–16 and Psalms 34 and 40 (cf. 1:6; 2:25, 36–37). The infancy account, in short, roots the story of Jesus in the longer story of Israel. At the same time it points forward to the ministry of Jesus and beyond, by establishing motifs that are later developed and by means of programmatic prophecies.

The infancy account has a complex internal structure. It contains two sets of contrasting diptychs. The annunciation to Zechariah (Luke 1:8–23) is contrasted to the one made to Mary (1:26–38). The birth of John (1:57–67) is placed against that of Jesus (2:1–21). The first diptych is followed by the visitation of Mary to Elizabeth (1:39–45) and the Canticle of Mary, the Magnificat (1:47–55). The second diptych is flanked on one side by the Canticle of Zechariah, the Benedictus (1:67–79), and on the other side by the purification, the Canticle, and the prophecy of Simeon (2:22–35) and by the praise of the prophetess Anna (2:36–38). The narrative reaches a climax with the discovery of Jesus in the temple (2:41–51). Short panels describing the growth of John (1:80) and Jesus (2:52) point the reader to their future roles. As always in Luke, the geographical movement centers on Jerusalem, both beginning (1:8) and ending (2:42) there.

From the prophetic announcements and canticles we learn of the significance of John and Jesus. They are both prophetic figures. John will "go before him in the spirit and power of Elijah . . . to prepare a people for the Lord" (1:16–17). Luke does not later need to make an explicit connection between John and Elijah after the transfiguration (cf. Luke 9:36 with Matt. 17:11–13), because he has already made it here. In his canticle, Zechariah says of John, "You, child, will be called prophet of the most high, for you will go before the Lord to prepare his ways, to give knowledge of salvation to his people in the forgiveness of their sins" (1:76–77). John, we see, will be "great before the Lord" (1:15). But Jesus "will be great and will be called Son of the Most High" (1:32). John and Jesus both stand in the line of prophets, but Jesus is Messiah and Son and Lord. John remains precursor (see also 7:24–35).

Luke makes clear that Jesus is also a Davidic messiah. The oracle of 2 Sam. 7:12–16 is applied directly to him by Gabriel. Jesus will be given "the throne of his father David" (Luke 1:32–33). The Davidic link is forged securely by 2:4 ("city of David . . . lineage of David") and 2:11 ("born this day in the city of David"). In Luke's genealogy, too, Jesus is son of David (3:31), and Luke incorporates the other son-of-David passages from Mark (Luke 6:3; 18:38–39), in addition to exploiting this lineage in Acts 2:25; 13:22-23; 15:16. Like Matthew, however, Luke also stresses that Jesus is more than David's son; he is also Lord (Luke 20:41– 44; cf. 7:13; 10:1; 17:6; 18:6; 19:8; but this is found much more frequently in Acts, after the resurrection). And because Mary is overshadowed by the Holy Spirit, Jesus is also Son of God (Luke 1:35; 3:22; cf. 4:3; 8:28; 10:22; 22:70; but in Acts, only 9:20; 13:33).

Luke's characteristic preoccupation is with the meaning of John and Jesus *for Israel*. John, we have seen, will "prepare a people for the Lord." In the Benedictus, Zechariah praises God for the "visitation" of his people for their redemption in fulfillment of the promises to Abraham (1:68–69; cf. Acts 7:17). The story of Jesus now brings to completion the ancient and fundamental promises of God that gave birth to a people. The figure of Abraham and the fulfillment of the promises to him play a more central role in Luke-Acts than in the other Gospels (see, e.g., Luke 16:22–31; 19:9; Acts 3:25; 7:2-8; 13:26), precisely because Luke is concerned to connect the church's story to Israel. The language of "God's visitation" here is echoed later (Luke 7:16; 19:44; Acts 7:23; 15:14); it is God's intervention to save his people. In Mary's canticle, this action of God reverses the fortunes of rich and poor, powerful and weak; the birth of the Messiah transforms the measure of the world even as it brings the promises to Abraham to their completion (1:55).

The significance of Jesus for the people, and for *all* people, goes far beyond that of John. In Jesus is the dawn of *salvation*. Zechariah praises God for "raising up a horn of salvation for us in the house of his servant David" (1:68–69), and at Jesus' birth the angels announce "a savior who is Christ the Lord" (2:11). The understanding of Jesus as one who brings salvation is a specifically Lukan emphasis. By it he makes explicit a conviction found already in Mark, which is shared also by Matthew. Luke uses the vocabulary of "saving" with great frequency. In the Gospel, he increases Mark and Matthew's thirteen uses of the verb "to save" to seventeen, adding thirteen more in Acts. He is also fond of substantives for "salvation," using *sōtēria* in Luke 1:69, 71, 77; 19:9; and Acts 4:12; 7:25; 13:26, 47; 16:17; 27:34; and reserving *sōtērion* for the critical passages of Luke 2:30; 3:6; and Acts 28:28. The last is the prophecy with which Acts ends: the Gentiles will listen to "this salvation from God." Luke also gives the title Savior (*sōtēr*) to Jesus in Luke 2:11 and Acts 5:31; 13:23. As Moses went to "visit" his people (Acts 7:23) to bring them "salvation" (Acts 7:25), so does God visit the people Israel in the offer of salvation made through Jesus. In contrast, however, to the salvation and redemption of old, which was a freeing from slavery and an inheritance of a land, this salvation is a redemption from sins, leading to the capacity of worshiping God "without fear," because of the inheritance of the Holy Spirit (Luke 1:73–77; Acts 2:38–39).

Jesus' ambiguous relationship to his people is suggested by his presentation in the temple. The "righteous and devout" Simeon had been awaiting the "consolation of Israel." When he takes the child Jesus in his arms, he praises God for allowing his eyes "to have seen thy salvation." This salvation will be "a light of revelation unto the Gentiles and for glory to thy people Israel" (2:29–32). The reader is here prepared for the spread of the word to the gentile world (Acts 13:47), but Luke's primary interest is the fate of Israel. The salvation brought by Jesus is to be its "glory." But there is more. In the prophecy made to the child's parents, Simeon predicts a division within the people, caused by Jesus (2:34). This programmatic prophecy interprets the subsequent narrative. The pattern of the prophet like Moses would lead us to expect a complete rejection of the prophet sent by God, and there are elements of that in Luke. But his most consistent presentation is of a division within the people of God. Some accept the prophet, and some do not.

Luke's infancy account is also noteworthy for the important role played by Mary. Luke is generally observant and appreciative of the life and activity of women. Most of his male characters have a female counterpart (see e.g., Luke 1:6–7; 2:36–38; 4:25, 38; 7:11–15, 36–50; 8:1–3, 19–21, 43–56; 10:38–42; 11:27; 13:10–17; 15:8–10; 17:29–32; 18:1–8; 23:28–31, 49, 55–56; 24:1–11, 22–24; Acts 1:14; 2:17–18; 5:1–11, 14; 6:1–2; 8:12; 9:36–43; 12:12–17; 13:50; 16:1, 11–18, 40; 17:12, 34; 18:1–4, 18, 26; 21:5, 8–9; 22:4; 23:16; 24:24–25; 25:13; 26:30). Mary is far more than a representative woman, however; she represents the faithful people of Israel. The reversal of her condition symbolizes the great reversal that God's visitation will bring upon the whole people. As a woman she was lowly and an outcast, a member of the poor in a patriarchal society (see 6:20; 7:22). And as a virgin, she was powerless even to produce valued offspring. But God "raised her up" by choosing her to be the one filled with grace, just as he lifted up the poor; and by overshadowing her with the Holy Spirit, God showed that out of apparent powerlessness comes strength, for "nothing is impossible with God" (1:37; cf. 18:27). Mary also represents Israel in her anguish. Jesus will be a sign of contradiction, causing a division within the people; so will Mary have a sword piercing her soul (2:35). Finally, Mary represents the restored Israel, for she is present at the definitive outpouring of the Holy Spirit at Pentecost (see Acts 1:14). With other women, she is among the daughters and women servants who prophesy (Acts 2:17–18).

Mary is also an individual person of faith. She identifies herself as a "servant of the Lord" (Luke 1:38). By saying, "Let it be done to me according to your word," she shows a response to God structurally identical to that of Jesus (see Luke 22:42). She is a model of the faithful acceptance of God's will. Elizabeth cries out to her, "Blessed is she who believed there would be a fulfillment of what was spoken to her by the Lord" (1:45). Jesus later identifies as "blessed" and as his "mother and brothers" those "who hear the word of God and keep it" (8:19–21; 11:27–28). Last but surely not least, Luke shows Mary to be one who reflected on the Word of God, turning it over in her heart (1:29; 2:19, 51), and one who was able to interpret the new experience of God through the symbols of God's word in Torah (1:47–55).

The Prophetic Messiah

The relationship between John and Jesus continues into the ministry narrative. John's prophetic role is immediately made clear: "The word of the Lord came to John" (3:2). From this point forward, "the word of God" is thematic in Luke-Acts. It contains an explicit theological valuation given to the speech of John, of Jesus, and of Jesus' followers, linking them together in a succession of prophetic authority. In Luke's parable of the seed, "the seed is the word of God" (8:11; cf. 5:1; 8:21; 11:28). In Acts, "the word of God" is virtually a synonym for the Christian mission: "So the word of God grew and prevailed mightily" (Acts 19:20; cf. 4:31; 6:2; 6:7).

Jesus' baptism by John also suggests a prophetic anointing. Luke gently removes John from the actual scene, to show that it is God who bestows the Spirit on Jesus (Luke 3:21–22). The reality of the bestowal is signified by the bodily descent of the dove. The Spirit descends, furthermore, while Jesus is praying (3:21), just as the disciples pray when the Spirit is bestowed at Pentecost (Acts 1:14). Indeed, Jesus prays in this Gospel at every critical turn in his ministry (see Luke 6:12; 9:18, 28–29; 10:21; 11:1; 22:32, 41–46; 23:46). We understand by this that Jesus' sonship to God is not a matter of physical descent from Adam (see 3:23–38) but above all a matter of faithful obedience. In Acts, Jesus' followers also pray for guidance and for power (Acts 1:14, 24; 2:42; 3:1; 4:24; 6:6; 8:15; 10:9; 12:12; 13:3; 14:23; 16:25; 20:36; 28:8).

That Jesus is a prophetic messiah is shown clearly in the story of his rejection in Nazareth (Luke 4:16–30). Luke moved this story from the later position it holds in Matthew and Mark to the very beginning of the ministry. He has also expanded it into a programmatic statement on the nature of Jesus' mission. The reader has learned already that Jesus received the Spirit bodily (3:22) and that "full of the Holy Spirit . . . he was led away by the Holy Spirit forty days in the wilderness" (4:1). After his testing, Jesus began preaching "in the power of the Spirit" (4:14). Now he reads from Isaiah, "The Spirit of the Lord is upon me because he has anointed me to preach good news to the poor. . . . " (Luke 4:18; cf. Isa. 61:1–2; 58:6). He then announces, "Today this Scripture has been fulfilled in your hearing" (4:21). Luke understands the title Messiah (anointed) literally. Jesus is Christ, "the anointed," because he has been anointed *(chriō) by the Holy Spirit* (see also Acts 4:27; 10:38). The nature of his messiahship is to proclaim deliverance to the outcast and afflicted, bringing to completion (or, fulfillment) the prophetic ministry of the Isaianic herald. Jesus is a prophetic messiah.

The story points as well to the second aspect of this prophetic ministry. His townspeople at first hear him gladly, but they turn against him when he compares himself to Elijah and Elisha (Luke 4:25–27). Why? They were prophets through whom God worked salvation for those *outside* the historical people Israel. The townspeople represent those Jews who do not accept the prophet who offers God's "visitation" to any but themselves. They seek to kill him. This prophet's preaching creates a division within the people, and "the designs of many hearts will be revealed" (2:35).

The next section of the Gospel showing intensive Lukan redaction continues the prophetic motif. In Luke's Sermon on the Plain (6:17–49), Jesus proclaims both blessings and woes (6:20–26). The programmatic prophecy of 4:18 is here fulfilled as the Messiah brings "good news" to "you poor, you who are hungry, you that weep, you that are persecuted." In contrast, he speaks woes over those who are rich, well fed, joyful, and approved by others. These "have their consolation now" (6:24) and do not need the "consolation of Israel" brought by Jesus (Luke 2:25). Mary's canticle established a pattern of divine reversal. The rich are sent away empty and the powerful brought low, while the poor are lifted up. Luke's blessing of the poor fits within this pattern of messianic reversal. He does not prescribe a "spiritual attitude" for his followers but announces that God is upsetting the measure of the world: those outcast and excluded from the "consolation" of full membership in God's people are accepted by God. The "good news" to them is that the standards of humans are not those of God: "Yours is the kingdom of God."

Luke similarly has Jesus signal this nature of his messiahship in 7:21–22, when he sends word to John of his messianic deeds, the list of which culminates in Jesus' mention that "the poor have the good news preached to them." In the parable of the great banquet, likewise, Jesus suggests that those preoccupied with possessions could not respond to the kingdom invitation and therefore were rejected, so that the call went out to "the poor, and maimed, and blind, and lame" (14:21; cf. 14:13). The Lukan parable of the rich man and Lazarus, finally, brings the theme to completion. In language that deliberately echoes that of the Beatitudes, this parable reverses fortunes: he who was rich is lost; he who was poor is received "in the bosom of Abraham" (16:25). Although Luke is concerned throughout his work with the role of material possessions in symbolizing one's response to the call of God (see, e.g., Luke 12:13–40; 14:26–33; 16:1–13; 17:22–35; 18:18–30; Acts 2:41–47; 4:32–37; 20:17–35), the language of the "rich and poor" does not serve primarily such a teaching function. It functions first of all to demonstrate that Jesus is a prophetic messiah who proclaims "good news" to the outcast among the people and that he is a prophet rejected by the well-established and powerful. In his narrative, the role of the poor is played by sinners and tax collectors, and the role of the rich by the Pharisees and lawyers. Because in his ministry the visitation of God to his people is effective, those who reject him are rejected from the people; those who accept him are accepted by God.

Jesus had compared himself to Elijah and Elisha in Luke 4:25–27. In 7:1–16, he imitates them. Elisha had healed the Syrian general Naaman (2 Kings 5:1–14) through the intercession of a young Jewish girl. In Luke 7:1–10, Jesus heals the slave of a gentile centurion through the intercession of Jewish elders. The prophet Elijah had raised to life the son of the widow of Sarephath (1 Kings 17:17–24). In Luke 7:11–15, Jesus raises from the dead the son of the widow of Naim. Luke makes the connection clear by using the same phrase in 7:15 that appears in 1 Kings 17:23 (LXX): ". . . and he gave him to his mother." The people recognize the identification, for they proclaim Jesus as a great prophet and praise God for visiting his people (Luke 7:16). It is at this point that John sends from prison seeking confirmation of Jesus as the awaited one and Jesus responds with the message, "The poor have good news proclaimed to them" (7:22).

The discourse and narrative that follow this scene sharpen our understanding of the division within the people created by the prophet. Jesus praises John as a prophet and as more than a prophet (7:26). But John had been accepted as such only by "the people and the tax collectors." In contrast, the Pharisees and lawyers ("lawyers" is Luke's term for scribes) had "rejected the purpose of God for themselves, not having been baptized by him" (7:29–30). They rejected John as a prophet on the charge that he had a demon. Now quite a different sort of prophet appears in Jesus. He is no ascetic. But he too is rejected because "he is a friend of tax collectors and sinners" (7:34). Immediately after this, Jesus is accepted by a woman who is a sinner, and she is forgiven her sins; and he is rejected by a Pharisee who cannot recognize in him a prophet sent by God (7:36–50).

The division in Israel is between, on the one hand, the ordinary people of the land—in particular those made marginal or outcast by ritual law—who accept this prophet and are thereby accepted into the people God is forming, those who are poor, lame, blind, maimed, women (and in Acts, eunuchs, Samaritans, Gentiles) and, on the other hand, the leaders of the people who already had their consolation in their power and prestige and did not accept either John or Jesus and would not later accept Jesus' emissaries, that is, those who were rich, powerful, and arrogant, and who "sought to justify themselves" (see Luke 16:15; 18:9).

The Formation of the People

Already in the Gospel's first eight chapters, we catch glimpses of the people of God forming around Jesus. He calls disciples who are sinners (5:1–11) and tax collectors (5:27), who leave all to follow him (18:28–30). From among them, he chooses twelve, who are explicitly called apostles (6:13; the term is very frequent throughout Luke-Acts: see, e.g., 9:10; 11:49; 17:5; 22:14; 24:10; Acts 1:2; 1:26). After the story of the sinful woman, we begin to see the nucleus of the people gathering: Jesus and the Twelve are preaching in Galilee. With them is a group of women, who support them (8:1–3). Here is the core of the restored Israel, merely a small band of followers from Galilee.

Beginning in Luke 9:1, Jesus prepares a ministry of authority within the people to replace the erstwhile leaders who refused the prophet. He sends out the Twelve with "power and authority" to preach the kingdom and to heal (9:2)—to engage, that is, in precisely the activities of Jesus himself (see, e.g., 9:11). When they return, Jesus has them distribute the food when the five thousand are fed (9:10–17). Luke thereby establishes a connection, which he consistently makes, between authority among the people and service at table fellowship. That these Twelve will take over the leadership of Israel is suggested in the Lukan parable of the pounds (19:11–27) and parable of the vineyard (20:9–18). Jesus explicitly bestows authority (*basileia*) on the Twelve to judge the twelve tribes of Israel, at the last supper (22:30), which is fulfilled in their exercise of leadership in the Jerusalem community in Acts (2:41–47; 4:32—5:11).

In the meantime, we are shown the people itself in process of formation, particularly in that distinctive section of Luke's Gospel (9:51—19:44) called the journey narrative. The movement towards Jerusalem dominates the section. At the transfiguration, Jesus converses with Elijah and Moses about the exodus he was going to accomplish in Jerusalem (9:31). His turn toward the city is solemnly announced in 9:51: "When the days drew near for him to be received up, he set his face to go to Jerusalem." Some seventeen times in the succeeding chapters we are told that Jesus is "on his way." This travel motif gives the entire section a dynamic quality and renders more dramatic the calls to discipleship (see 9:57–62).

More than a journey, than even a journey toward suffering and death (Luke 9:22; 18:31), is taking place here. Luke places within the journey's framework the largest portion of his sayings material. Jesus is always speaking. As he travels, furthermore, he is surrounded by three groups. There are the amorphous crowds (ochloi), his opponents (above all the Pharisees in this section), and his disciples (mathētēs occurs twenty-two times in chaps. 9—19, compared with sixteen in the rest of the Gospel). Luke takes considerable pains to note, moreover, exactly what Jesus says to whom in these sayings.

As for the substance of the sayings, the words addressed to each group have a distinctive character. Jesus attacks his opponents and tells them parables that warn of their rejection. To the crowd, he gives warnings of judgment and he calls them to discipleship. To the disciples, in contrast, he gives specific instructions on prayer, hospitality, suffering, and possessions. Luke arranges these sayings in an alternating pattern: Jesus turns from one group to another as he journeys. A short review of one section will indicate the pattern.

He speaks parables to the crowd on the growth of the kingdom and the reality of selection and judgment in the kingdom (13:18–30). Then, he turns to the Pharisees with a lament over Jerusalem and its rejection of prophets (13:31–35) and, while at dinner with them, rebukes their seeking of higher places (14:1–14) and tells the parable of the great banquet (14:15–24), which suggests their rejection of God's invitation and the call of the outcast. Jesus then turns again immediately to the crowd and, in terms that pick up the parable, calls them to discipleship and spells out its demands (14:25–35). Next, he tells to the Pharisees the three parables of the lost (sheep, coin, son) because they had objected to his attracting sinners and tax collectors around him (15:1–32). Then, turning to the disciples, he gives instructions on the use of possessions in almsgiving, by telling the story of the unjust steward, with its appended morals (16:1–13). This teaching of the disciples is rejected by the Pharisees, who are called lovers of money and ones who justify themselves (16:14), and Jesus tells them the parable of the rich man and Lazarus (16:19–31), with its clear threat of rejection for those who heed neither the demands of the Torah on almsgiving nor the voice of the prophet: "They will not be convinced if someone should rise from the dead" (16:31). Finally, Jesus turns again to the disciples with teaching on scandal and faith (17:1–10).

A subtle but effective point is made by this alternating pattern of sayings. On the way to Jerusalem to face his rejection and death at the hands of the leaders, the prophet Jesus is forming the true people of God around himself. The crowds are being called to repentance, and those who respond are being instructed in the nature of discipleship. But those who reject the prophet are being warned of their own rejection by God. When the Pharisees ask him when the kingdom of God will come, Jesus answers, "The kingdom of God is in the midst of you" (Luke 17:21). In this context, his answer can be taken literally: the people obedient to the prophet's call are being formed all around the Pharisees; they alone cannot see the signs of what is happening.

The journey reaches an end with Jesus' triumphant entry into Jerusalem. The small band of followers we spotted in Luke 8:1–3 has now swelled, so that "the whole multitude of disciples" (19:37) greets Jesus as king. The Pharisees? They tell Jesus, "Rebuke your disciples" (19:39). Jesus then voices a solemn lament over the city of Jerusalem. It will face destruction because it did not recognize the "time of its visitation" (19:44). The Lukan parable of the pounds (19:12–27), which is told just before the entry into the city, interprets the larger narrative. The one who is king will reward his faithful followers with authority in the kingdom. But those who resisted his kingship will be utterly cut off.

The Passion Narrative

Matthew follows Mark's Passion narrative closely, but Luke significantly deletes from and adds to his Markan source. He deletes the anointing at Bethany (7:36–50 is another story altogether), the shepherd citation from Zechariah, and the mocking of Jesus by the soldiers. He shifts two elements of the Passion to Acts: the death of Judas (see Acts 1:16–20) and the false witnesses who accuse Jesus of speech against the temple (see Stephen in Acts 6:11–14). Luke also adds significant materials. He attributes Judas's betrayal to Satan's entering his heart (22:3). He expands the last-supper sayings to include a discourse on leadership as service within the community (22:24–38). He includes a separate hearing before Herod (23:6–12). The entire crucifixion scene is richer, with Jesus addressing both the crowds about him as he carries his cross (23:28–31) and the two criminals crucified with him (23:39–43). The cry of abandonment from the cross found in both Mark and Matthew becomes in Luke a prayer of acceptance (23:46), and it is preceded by words of forgiveness (23:34) and promise (23:43).

These alterations make Luke's Passion narrative the closest of the Synoptics to John's Passion account. Two emphases emerge, however, that are distinctively Lukan: the image of Jesus as *sophos*, and the role of the populace in his death.

Luke does not deny the scandal of the cross, but he shades the image of

Jesus to more closely resemble the *sophos* of Hellenistic moral ideals, whose self control, freedom from fear, and courage are a model to his followers. At the last supper, Jesus disposes of his heritage. As he had received authority *(basileia)* from God, so he bequeaths it to the Twelve (22:29–30). Jesus also provides them with a model for this authority: "I am among you as one who serves" (22:27). He instructs his disciples and prepares them for the future (22:35–38). In the Garden of Gethsemane, he tells them to pray lest they fall into temptation (22:40; cf. 8:13). When he withdraws from them to pray, he is not overcome with sorrow *(lupē)*, but they are—a sign of their weakness and lack of courage (22:45). Jesus is comforted by an angel in his bloody sweat (22:43), which reworks a theme from the temptation account (4:9–13; cf. Mark 1:13). When Peter strikes the high priest's servant, Jesus heals the man's ear (22:51). At the end he is not powerless but goes willingly to do his father's will (22:42). His self-control is further shown by his words of comfort and warning to the women of Jerusalem (23:28–31) and his offer of a place in paradise to the thief (23:39–43).

The *sophos* is also one who is just *(dikaios)*. That Jesus is innocent of any crime deserving death is emphasized by Pilate's threefold declaration of his innocence (23:4, 14, 22), a verdict confirmed by Herod as well (23:15). Jesus' "righteousness" is demonstrated by the forgiveness he extends to his executioners (23:34) and the entrusting of his life to God: "Father, into your hands I commit my spirit" (23:46). The image of Jesus as the Just One is confirmed by the statement of the centurion at the cross. Rather than identify Jesus as God's Son (as in Matthew and Mark), he declares, "Truly, this man was righteous" (23:47). The term "righteous," *dikaios*, is often translated "innocent" in this place. Although that agrees with one of Luke's emphases, it is too weak to capture the full significance of Jesus as the Righteous One. Throughout his Gospel, Luke shows that righteousness is found in the total devotion to God here demonstrated by Jesus (see Luke 1:6, 17; 2:25; 16:15; 18:9, 14; 20:21; 23:50), and Jesus is three times given the title the Just One in Acts (3:14; 7:52; 22:14).

Luke's sharpest contrast with Matthew's Passion narrative concerns the role of the populace in the death of Jesus. Matthew explicitly involves all the people of Jerusalem: "His blood be upon us and upon our children" (Matt. 27:25). Luke also knows traditions that implicate "all the people" (Acts 3:14), but in the narrative itself he does all he can to minimize the participation of the people as such in the rejection and death of Jesus. In the Passion narrative, the split between the ordinary people and the leaders, now represented by the Sanhedrin, Sadducees, and priestly classes, is sharply delineated.

The postresurrection declaration of the men on the road to Emmaus accurately summarizes Luke's view of this division (Luke 24:20–21):

. . . how our *chief priests and rulers* delivered him up to be condemned to death, and crucified him. But *we* had hoped that he was the one to redeem Israel.

One place only in the narrative finds all together "the chief priests, and the rulers, and the people" (23:13). So anomalous is the appearance of the people here that some scholars seek the desperate remedy of an emendation to "rulers *of* the people." The solution is wrong, but the fact that it was felt to be needed points to the way Luke otherwise removes the people from the proceedings. To accomplish that removal, he makes many small alterations in Mark's text.

After Jesus cleanses the temple (19:45–46), the "priests and scribes and leaders of the people" try to destroy him, but the common people hang onto his words (Luke 19:47–48). Jesus is in the temple teaching "the people" when the leaders begin their attack (20:1–2). In 21:38, again, "the people" come early in the morning to the temple to hear him teach. The leaders, by contrast, must be circumspect in their plot against Jesus, "for they feared the people" (22:2). Judas must carry out his betrayal "in the absence of the multitude" (22:6). The crowd that comes to arrest Jesus is made up not of the general population but entirely of chief priests and captains and elders (22:47, 52). It is they who take Jesus to trial (23:1) and accuse him before Pilate (23:2). On the way to the crucifixion, women lament him and a great crowd follows him (23:27). At the cross, Mark (15:29) and Matthew (27:39) have *all* the passers-by mock Jesus. Luke has only the *rulers* mock him (23:35). At the point of Jesus' death, Luke pays particular attention to the common people. They had come as though witnesses to a spectacle, but now, they turn away, "beating their breasts" (23:48). With this sign of distress and remorse, Luke suggests a preparation for the repentance of the people in Acts. They will become part of the restored people of God.

The Resurrection and Ascension

Moses was vindicated by God after his first rejection and sent back with new power (Acts 7:34–38). So is Jesus vindicated by his resurrection, becoming the "prophet whom God raised up" in power (Acts 2:24; 3:13–15). Luke-Acts has a rich and complex presentation of Jesus' resurrection. By no means is it confined to the empty-tomb and appearance accounts of the first volume.

Unique to Luke is the ascension motif (Luke 24:50–51; Acts 1:9–11; cf. Luke 9:31, 51). According to Acts 1:3, the ascension occurred after forty days of appearances to Jesus' witnesses. According to Peter's speech in Acts 10:40–41, "God raised him up on the third day and made him manifest; not to all the people, but to us who were chosen by God as

witnesses, who ate and drank with him after he rose from the dead." At
first the ascension appears to be a temporary withdrawal (Acts 1:11):

> This Jesus, who was taken up from you into heaven, will come in the same
> way as you saw him go into heaven.

But it does not in the least make him absent in the narrative of Acts. He is
seen by Stephen "standing at the right hand of God" (7:55–56) and by
Paul in a blinding light (9:1–9). These are appearances of the resurrected
one to his chosen witnesses. Ananias told Paul, "The God of our fathers
has appointed you to know his will, to see the Just One, and to hear a voice
from his mouth" (Acts 22:14). More significant, Jesus' presence continues
palpably through the words and deeds of his witnesses. The power of the
Holy Spirit operative in them comes from him, so that they preach and
heal "in the name of Jesus" (Acts 2:33; 3:6, 16; 4:10, 29–31; 5:32; 10:43;
16:18; 19:13). Indeed, Jesus is even more powerfully present through the
signs and wonders worked by them "among all the people."

The ascension, therefore, does not signal a removal of Jesus from the
story, but symbolizes his presence in a new mode. The ascension accounts
provide a bridge between the appearances to witnesses and Jesus' presence
to the community through the Holy Spirit. The reader can hardly miss the
prophetic typology at work in this spiritual empowerment. Elijah, too, was
carried up into heaven by a whirlwind (2 Kings 2:1–12). Before he left, his
disciple Elisha asked to inherit a double share of his prophetic spirit (2:9).
Because he was able to see Elijah depart in the chariot of fire, it was
granted to him (2:11–12). He then performed a miracle fully as impressive
as Elijah's, or Moses': he too parted the waters (2:13–14). The response of
those who witnessed his power? "The spirit of Elijah rests on Elisha"
(2:15).

As for Luke's appearance accounts, they have several distinct characteristics. I have already mentioned their geographical concentration on
Jerusalem. The women at the tomb are not told, "Go to Galilee," but
"Remember how he told you in Galilee" (Luke 24:6). The disciples are
told to "remain in the city" for the bestowal of power (24:47–49). Luke
also makes the fulfillment-of-prophecy motif more explicit. Jesus' Passion
predictions are fulfilled (24:6), as are "all the Scriptures" (24:25–26, 44).
The content of these Scriptures was that "the Christ must suffer first
before entering his glory" (Luke 24:26, 46; cf. Acts 3:18; 17:3). Luke's
appearance accounts combine matter-of-factness with mystery. On one
side, the reality of Jesus' bodily resurrection is stressed, above all in 24:39.
This is one of the functions of his eating and drinking with the disciples
(24:30, 41–43; Acts 1:4; 10:41); another is to suggest the way in which
Jesus continues to be present for the Christian assembly "in the breaking
of the bread" (24:35). On the other side, although the one who appears to

the disciples is the same Jesus—"It is I myself"—he is difficult to recognize. He is mistaken for a stranger on the road (24:13–35); reports of his appearance are met with incredulity (24:11, 24). Even his palpable appearance causes them to "disbelieve for joy" (24:41).

Finally, the appearances point forward to the story's continuation in Acts. In Jesus' last Gospel appearance (24:47–49), the basic plot of Acts is sketched:

> Repentance and forgiveness of sins should be preached in his name to all nations, beginning from Jerusalem. You are witnesses of these things.

The period of the church is a period not of Jesus' absence but of his presence in a new and more powerful way. Through his apostles, the offer of salvation will be made once more to Israel (Luke 24:49):

> Behold, I send the promise of my father upon you. But stay in the city until you are clothed with power from on high.

THE ACTS NARRATIVE

The Restored Israel in Jerusalem

Luke's Gospel shows the reader a prophet like Moses who is rejected despite his offer of salvation. His preaching creates division within the people. At the end of this first volume, the common people are ready for repentance, and the leadership Jesus has prepared await in the city the power that will make them ministers of the word and leaders over Israel.

The next part of the story is most critical. In the Jerusalem narrative of Acts (chaps. 1—8), Luke must answer the fundamental question of God's fidelity to his promises, so that his readers will know security (*asphaleia*). He must show that God kept his promise to Israel and can be trusted to keep his word to the Gentiles who now believe in him. To do this, Luke must show that there was a restored Israel, which received the blessings God had promised to Abraham, blessings that reached the gentile world as well. His story must make clear the identity of the authentic people, the nature of the leadership over it, and how the Gospel was transferred with essential continuity from Jew to gentile believer.

Luke's concern for the church as the restored Israel is made clear at once by the account of Matthias's election (Acts 1:15–26). Luke has steadily built up an expectation for the outpouring of the Spirit: "I send the promise of my Father upon you" (Luke 24:49); "Wait for the promise of the father" (Acts 1:4); and "You will receive power when the Holy Spirit comes upon you" (Acts 1:8). Luke's natural tendency is to have fulfillment follow prophecy as rapidly as possible. The delay of this particular fulfillment is significant. It tells us that Judas's betrayal of Jesus was not simply a personal failure; it was a defection from the ranks of the apostolic office. It is necessary to replace Judas before the gift of the Spirit is given. Why? Because the Twelve, as we have already learned in Luke 22:30, are to rule over Israel, and themselves symbolize the Twelve Tribes of the restored Israel. They are the nucleus of the people that is to be empowered by the Holy Spirit. When the circle is filled, the leadership of the people is in place. Then all those who had come up from Galilee and devoted themselves to prayer (Acts 1:13–14) could welcome the long-awaited promise of the Spirit.

The People Restored

The Pentecost story describes by means of external symbolization the witnesses' internal transformation (Acts 2:1–4). The mighty wind and tongues of fire signal the presence of God (see, e.g., Exod. 19:18; 24:17; 1 Kings 18:38; 19:11–13). The essential work of this Spirit is transforming eyewitnesses into "ministers of the word" (Luke 1:2): "They began to speak in other tongues as the Spirit gave them utterance" (Acts 2:4). Already in fact they are "witnesses to the end of the earth" (1:8), since Jews from all over the Diaspora had gathered in the city for the feast and hear them proclaim "the mighty acts of God."

The many tongues at Babel had shown how arrogance had dispersed people into nations and confusion (Gen. 11:1–9). Because of that scattering, God had selected one man with whom he could make a people for himself, Abraham (Gen. 12:1–3). Now, in this gift of the Holy Spirit, the promise to Abraham was finally fulfilled, and those who heard in their own tongues of the praise of God, were drawn together (Acts 2:11). Even in this highly charged symbolic moment, however, Luke does not fail to note the mixed reception: some of those who heard marveled, but others simply mocked (2:12–13). Without interpretation, experience is ambiguous and witness obscure.

Peter's speech (Acts 2:14–36) interprets the event and makes the witness explicit. The Joel citation shows that the outpouring of the Spirit is one of eschatological prophecy exercised by all the faithful. The "prophet whom God raised up" is now more powerfully present than before. The conclusion of Peter's speech is particularly important. It shows us Luke's understanding of the first messianic community. After demonstrating that the messianic texts of Pss. 16:8–11, 110:1, and 132:11 applied not to David but to Jesus, Peter declares (Acts 2:36):

> Let all the *house of Israel* therefore know assuredly that God has made him both Christ and Lord, this Jesus whom you crucified.

The focus is on Israel. They had rejected the prophet, and now they are called to repentance. This is their second offer of salvation, "Save yourselves from this crooked generation" (2:40), now issued by the prophetic word of the Messiah's witness. And as the people had responded to the prophet John by asking, "What shall we do?" (Luke 3:10), so also do they respond to Peter's prophetic proclamation with "What shall we do?" (Acts 2:37).

Peter's response makes Luke's perception of the first community clear. If the people repent and are baptized, they also will receive the Holy Spirit (Acts 2:38). And what is this Spirit? It is "the promise" (2:39). Here the visitation of God according to the promises made to Abraham is brought to fulfillment. For whom is this promise? "To you and to your children." First of all, then, for the Jewish population of Jerusalem and, as with Abraham, "their descendants." But for them only? No: "And to all that are far off, every one whom the Lord God calls to him (2:39; cf. 2:21). Those who respond make up the restored people of God.

In his idyllic picture of the first community (Acts 2:41–47), Luke stresses its Jewish character. The believers attend the temple together and they enjoy favor with all the people. Their beginning number of three thousand steadily increases. In principle, therefore, the people of God within the historical Israel has been restored. Indeed, it already has a universal character, since it includes Jews from all over the Diaspora. For some of his purposes, Luke could have stopped his story at this point, for part of the theodical problem had been solved. God in fact did keep his promise to Abraham, and the Jewish people enjoyed the blessings of the Spirit. But still another issue must be resolved: Who are the real leaders over this people? The infant community is devoted to the apostles' teaching (2:42). Will the Jewish leadership that opposed Jesus and had him put to death allow his prophetic successors to succeed where he did not? The story takes up that point next.

Leadership Over the People

Peter's speech after his healing of a lame man (Acts 3:11–26) interprets the next part of the narrative. The healing, Peter tells us, was done "in the name of Jesus" (3:6, 16). We see that the signs and wonders worked by the witnesses are evidence that the prophet's power is active among the people (see 2:43). Peter's speech ends with a promise and a warning. These provide the reader with a programmatic prophecy for understanding the succeeding narrative. The promise? Those who join the messianic movement will participate in the "times of refreshment" (3:19) within the restored people of God (Acts 3:25–26):

> You are the sons of the prophets, sons of the covenant which God gave to our fathers, saying to Abraham, "And in your posterity shall all the families of the earth be blessed." God, having raised up his servant, sent him to you first.

The warning? Those who reject this final proclamation will definitively be separated from God's people (3:22–23):

Moses said, "The Lord God will raise up a prophet from among your brethren as he raised me up. You shall listen to him in whatever he tells you. And it shall be that every soul that does not listen to that prophet shall be destroyed from the people."

The narrative following this programmatic prophecy focuses squarely on the apostolic witnesses. From the outside, their authority over the restored people is threatened by opposition from the Sanhedrin. Twice they are brought to trial (4:1–22; 5:17–42). Within the community, however, they are established in power and rule over Israel (4:23—5:16). The progression deserves closer examination.

The people who heard Peter's speech are divided between leaders and populace. Many who heard are converted (Acts 4:4), but the leaders arrest the apostles and put them in prison (4:1–3). At this first hearing, the apostles directly accuse the leaders of responsibility for Jesus' death: "This is the stone which *you* the builders rejected" (4:11; cf. Luke 20:17). The Sanhedrin is still very much in charge. They find no way to contradict the healing (Acts 4:14), but they can threaten the apostles (4:21). They unwittingly testify, however, to the slipperiness of their hold over the people, in the phrase "in order that it may spread no further among the people" (4:17). Will the official warning stop Jesus' witnesses or lessen their authority over the people?

The answer is given in Acts 4:23—5:12. The apostles pray for power, and another gift of the Spirit is given (4:23–31). Then, they stand as authorities within the community of goods. All who sell their possessions "lay them at the feet of the apostles" (4:35, 37; 5:2). And the apostles make distribution according to their perception of need (4:35). Their prophetic spirit and authority is forcibly brought home for the whole church (Luke's first use of the term "church" occurs in 5:11) when Ananias and Sapphira counterfeit the sharing of Spirit symbolized by the sharing of possessions, are prophetically tested by Peter, and fall dead "at his feet" (5:1–11). They have not obeyed the prophet's voice and have been literally cut off from the people (see 3:22–23). Now, the power of the apostles is greatly extended (5:12–16). The healing deeds performed by Jesus are performed by his witnesses (5:16), just as their boldness in speech had made their association with him evident (4:13).

When the Sanhedrin tries to stop the apostles a second time, a great reversal has taken place. They are now "jealous" of the apostles' success among the people (Acts 5:17). They cannot hold them in prison, for an angel frees them (5:19). They fear using coercion to bring them to trial, "for they were afraid of being stoned by the people," and they are reduced to inviting them to a hearing (5:26). With delicate irony, Luke has a Pharisee, one of those who had opposed every deed of Jesus, interpret the narrative. He gives a fine theological explication: if the movement is from God, nothing can stop it; if merely human, it will collapse. What is ironic about this interpretation is that the reader already knows the movement is from God, and knows as well that Peter's challenge at the hearing—heard by Gamaliel—was not for theology but for conversion. Gamaliel proves he does not have "the Holy Spirit whom God gives to those who obey him" (5:32).

Despite receiving a beating, therefore, the apostles continue to preach Jesus as the Messiah (Acts 5:42). Luke has made his essential point clear. Whatever political manipulations might still be available to the Sanhedrin, effective religious authority over Israel, considered as God's people, has passed to the apostles. They rule over the Twelve Tribes of the restored Israel in Jerusalem.

Luke could once again have stopped there. But another question still required an answer. Granted that God had remembered Israel and had made the Twelve to be leaders over the people, how did that blessing reach the gentile world? Was the community represented by Theophilus *in continuity with* Israel or was it a new thing altogether, and therefore only artificially connected to the story of Abraham? As he has done twice before, Luke first prepares a leadership for the transfer of the Gospel to the Gentiles, to show that there was continuity between the Twelve and those who preached to pagans. He uses a fragmentary tradition about a dispute in the Jerusalem community over the feeding of widows to make this point. The seven chosen by the community and ratified by the apostles to serve over the distribution of goods (6:1–6) were in reality those who, themselves filled with the prophetic spirit, preach the word to Hellenists in Jerusalem and to the pagan world. As the apostles had their spiritual authority symbolized by their function of feeding the people (see Luke 9:10–17; 12:42–48; 22:25–30; Acts 4:32–37), so the seven have their spiritual authority for the Hellenistic mission signified by their charge to feed the Hellenistic widows.

The arrest, trial, and murder of Stephen, which combine elements of a mob action with a judicial proceeding, close the Jerusalem narrative. With his death, the missionaries, except for the Twelve, are scattered, to begin spreading the word beyond the city. As we have seen repeatedly, Stephen's speech offers an interpretation of Luke's entire narrative structure. But its conclusion also contains a startling and effective element of irony. Here is Stephen, who we know is one filled with the Spirit and who works signs and wonders among the people. He preaches about Moses who worked signs and wonders and was twice rejected. In closing, he attacks the leaders—he is before them—for always rejecting prophets and opposing

the Holy Spirit and for killing Jesus, the Just One. At that moment, he is
filled with the Holy Spirit and sees Jesus at the right hand of God. And at
that moment, he is killed.

The Gentile Mission

God had always willed in principle that Israel's blessing should be
extended to the Gentiles as well. Such is the clear implication of the
allusion to Isa. 42:6 in Simeon's canticle, when he calls the salvation
brought by Jesus a light for revelation to the Gentiles (Luke 2:32). So also
is the import of the full citation from Isa. 40:5 (only in Luke) that
introduces John's ministry: "All flesh shall see the salvation of God" (Luke
3:6). John himself warned his hearers that God could raise children to
Abraham out of stones (Luke 3:8). Jesus had compared himself to prophets whose work had reached outside Israel (4:25–27). In his journey to
Jerusalem, Luke alone has Jesus send out a second group of seventy (-two)
before him; given Luke's avoidance of doublets, the extra mission suggests
an anticipation of the later sending out "two by two" of missionaries to the
Gentiles (Luke 10:1–12; cf. Acts 13:1–3). The resurrected Jesus told his
disciples that repentance would be preached in his name "to all nations"
(Luke 24:47) and that they would be his witnesses "to the end of the
earth" (Acts 1:8).

In the narrative of Acts, however, the gentile mission proceeds in a more
haphazard and human fashion than these intimations might suggest. Gentiles are preached to in the first place because of Jewish rejection of the
gospel. That rejection is never total; some Jews, even in the Diaspora,
convert to the messianic sect. What is most striking about Luke's perception is that believing Jews and Gentiles together make up the authentic
Israel, the people of God.

Stephen had already debated Hellenistic Jews in Jerusalem (Acts 6:9).
After his execution, a persecution drove all but the Twelve from the city
(8:1). Philip carried the gospel to Samaria, working signs and wonders
there (8:13) as well as in Gaza (8:26–40). His mission is confirmed by
representatives from Jerusalem (8:14–24). Luke thereby shows that the
mission maintained continuity with Jerusalem. Why? Because for him, the
primitive Jerusalem church is the restored people of Israel. Continuity
with it is critical if the gentile church is to be rooted in the Israel of the
promise.

The gospel is carried to Antioch on the Orontes and preached to Greeks
by others scattered in the Stephen persecution (11:19–26). Barnabas, who
had shown himself doubly submissive to the authority of the Twelve (he
had placed his possessions at their feet and had received a new name from
them, 4:37), was sent to confirm the Antiochean mission (11:22), a certification all the more important because Paul will come from that church.

In the meantime, Peter works wonders in the coast towns of Lydda and Joppa (9:32–43) and ends up in Caesarea. In his conversion of the centurion Cornelius (chap. 10), we have the first *narrative* description of gentile conversion and its consequences.

It is from within this context that Luke's hero Paul emerges. Glimpsed first as a collaborator at the death of Stephen (Acts 8:1) and as a rabid persecutor of the church, he encounters the risen Lord on the road to Damascus (9:1–9). After being baptized and instructed by Ananias, he preaches Jesus in Damascus, is persecuted there, is given access to the Jerusalem community through the offices of Barnabas (9:27), debates and is persecuted there, and is sent off to Tarsus (9:30). From there, Barnabas recruits him to work with the church in Antioch (11:25). They carry a collection to the Jerusalem church (11:30). After they complete that task (12:25), they are sent by the Antiochean church on mission (13:1–3). This summary, it should be noticed, is culled from a considerably more complex narrative, in which the emergence of Paul is intermixed with the mission of Philip, Peter, and John in Samaria and Judea, the conversion of Cornelius, with the trouble it causes, and the imprisonment of Peter.

Both literary art and theological purpose are here interwoven. Peter, Barnabas, and Paul appear and reappear as central figures. The complexity of their movements not only reinforces the impression of fullness in Luke's narrative but also places Paul squarely within the overall missionary effort of the church. So carefully has Luke crafted this account that it undoubtedly serves to make two apologetic points concerning Paul. The first is that his mission to the Gentiles is not idiosyncratic but part of the Spirit's guidance of the entire church. The second is that his mission is intimately connected—the role of Barnabas is crucial here—to the believing community in Jerusalem, and therefore to the restored Israel.

Luke's continuing concern for Israel is demonstrated further by the first missionary tour of Barnabas and Paul. They do not intend to convert Gentiles. Only when their message is rejected in Antioch of Pisidia do they turn away from the Jews of that place. Paul's sermon there is remarkably like Peter's at Pentecost, with its emphasis on the promise to the Jewish people carried by Jesus (Acts 13:32):

> We bring you the good news that what God promised to the fathers, this he has fulfilled to us their children by raising Jesus.

When the offer is rejected, Barnabas and Paul turn to the Gentiles. At this point, Luke explicitly applies to Paul the phrase from Isa. 49:6, "light of the Gentiles" (Acts 13:44–48; cf. 26:17; Luke 2:32). In Iconium and Lystra, the pattern is repeated (Acts 14:1–21): the Jews' failure to accept the gospel drives the missionaries to the more receptive Gentiles. Paul and

Barnabas therefore return to Antioch with the report of how God "had opened a door of faith to the Gentiles" (14:27).

Before describing Paul's distinctive and far-ranging mission to the Gentiles, however, Luke first must address the issue of the legitimacy of gentile inclusion within the messianic community. God had willed their salvation, and the Spirit had guided the proclamation of the gospel to them, but what were the implications for the church's identity as the people of God? The Council of Jerusalem (15:1–35) takes up that issue. It also forms a watershed in the Acts narrative. Before it, all the apostles were at least ostensibly in view. After it, Paul's work totally dominates. The council brings Peter back into the narrative for the last time. James is the chief spokesperson for the Jerusalem church during the council, and he only reappears once more, to confirm its decision and confront Paul (21:18). The narrative of the council itself forms the climax of a complicated plot development that has quietly been providing the background for Paul's emergence. Acts 15 is unintelligible unless read continuously from the conversion of Cornelius. In this narrative, Luke shows how the decision to recognize the full status of Gentiles within the messianic community resulted from a complex interaction of divine intervention and human obedience.

Peter had preached to Cornelius's household in the first place only because his own deeply ambiguous personal vision received clarification from the experience of the gentile Cornelius as it was reported to him (Acts 10:1–28). When he preached about Jesus, the Holy Spirit fell on the whole household (10:34–44). The witnesses of the event, who included Jewish believers, recognized that the same gift given to them in the beginning was now shared by these Gentiles. Because God had acted, so could the church. The Gentiles were baptized (10:44–48). The decision is immediately challenged by the Jerusalem leadership. Peter's defense of his action consists simply in the narrative "in order" (*kathexēs;* as in Luke 1:1–4) of his experience and that of Cornelius, showing how these experiences had led him into a deeper understanding of his own vision and indeed of the very words of Jesus (Luke 11:15; cf. Acts 1:5).

The Jerusalem leadership ratified the decision (Acts 11:18). But the issue was not fully settled. Even if Gentiles were accepted into this church, the question of fellowship was not thereby decided. This was critical above all for Jewish believers. They already belonged to God's special people, and symbolized that by circumcision and the observance of laws of ritual purity and diet. Are Gentiles also fully equal members of this people of God? The members of the Pharisaic party of believers from Jerusalem attack the very foundations of the gentile membership in the church, claiming that one cannot be saved except by observance of Torah (15:1–2). This attack coincides with Barnabas and Paul's return to Antioch with the news of how God had done great deeds through them among the Gentiles

(14:27–28). Luke effectively draws his main characters from their diverse missions, to this one critical decision. The reader already knows God's will in the matter; will the church ratify God's action by its decision?

In the end, yes. No further burden is placed on gentile believers beyond the norms known to them already through the diffusion of Mosaic values in the Diaspora (Acts 15:19–21). More significant, these regulations were not conditions of membership in the people but were intended to enable table fellowship with Jewish believers. The decision was made by the assembly as a whole and was communicated to the church in Antioch. It was a decision of fundamental importance. It opened the way for a free gentile mission. In the narrative of Acts, it opened the way for a full concentration on the missionary work of Paul.

We note in passing the consistent viewpoint Luke brings to his description of this great decision. The narrative of the experience of God within the assembly enables the community to discern the working of the Spirit. The experience also gives the community's members deeper insight into the meaning of Scripture. The text of the prophet Amos is said to agree with the experience of God among them, not the experience to conform to a previous understanding of the prophet (15:15–18). And the gentile mission itself is understood as a restoration of Israel. James's words resonate many individual notes within Luke's story (15:14–18; cf. Amos 9:11–12):

> Simeon has related how God first visited the Gentiles, to take out of them a people for his name. And with this the words of the prophets agree, as it is written, "After this I will return, and I will rebuild the dwelling of David which has fallen; I will rebuild its ruins, and I will set it up, that the rest of men may seek the Lord, and all the Gentiles who are called by my name, says the Lord, who has made these things known from of old."

Finally, Luke suggests that the experience of God's free gift of the Spirit among the Gentiles led even these Jewish witnesses to a new understanding of their own salvation (Acts 15:11):

> We believe that we shall be saved through the grace of the Lord Jesus, just as they will.

THE PICTURE OF PAUL IN ACTS

The last thirteen chapters (16—28) of Acts are devoted to Paul. Since Acts gives us the only sustained narrative account of Paul's ministry, critical questions inevitably arise concerning its reliability. I made the point earlier that when we can check him against his sources, Luke is generally reliable, as in the movements of Paul checked against his letters. More must be said on this subject, in order to sharpen our perception of

Luke's presentation of Paul. The version of Paul found in Paul's own letters will be treated in its turn.

Considered as historical evidence, Acts is a secondhand primary source for the life and thought of Paul. It is also a later source. Even if it relies at least in part on eyewitnesses, it looks back on Paul's career as past (see esp. 20:17–35). How much distance is involved is impossible to determine. Acts is also a source that, apart from some speeches that reflect distinctively Lukan concerns, focuses entirely on Paul's actions.

In contrast, the letters of Paul, leaving aside for the moment the issue of which are authentic, are firsthand primary sources. They are also obviously contemporary to the events they describe. Paul speaks at greater or lesser length on his past and present activities in 1 Thessalonians, 1 and 2 Corinthians, Galatians, Romans, Philippians, and 2 Timothy. These letters would ordinarily have much greater value as historical sources. Two considerations, however, must temper enthusiasm about their objectivity. First, Paul was less obsessive about biographical accuracy—with a possible exception in Galatians, where he takes an oath on some points—than he was about the development of his argument and the instruction of his community. Second, Paul has biases. He was often under attack, and many of his autobiographical remarks—as in Galatians—have an apologetic if not polemical edge to them. Nevertheless, his letters must be given great weight, particularly in disputed cases.

If the sources agreed completely about what Paul did and said and thought, there would, of course, be no problem. In fact, however, there are three major types of divergence between the sources that force the reader to make choices, some not at all easy.

Chronology

Only because of a fortuitous correlation between Acts 18:12, telling us that Gallio was proconsul of Achaia when Paul encountered him in Corinth, and an inscription found at Delphi, telling us that Gallio was proconsul of Achaia in 50–51 C.E., can we work toward an absolute and not only a relative chronology for the Pauline mission. In at least that sense, Acts is the indispensable starting point for a Pauline chronology, despite some scholars' protestations that they use only the letters. The attempt to erect even a relative chronology on the letters alone is futile, for their internal evidence is insufficient to support supposed lines of development. However little acknowledged, it is only the narrative of Acts 16—19 that enables us to date with reasonable accuracy 1 Thessalonians, 1 and 2 Corinthians, and Romans.

How wide is the disparity between Acts and the letters concerning what happened when and in what sequence? We have already seen part of Acts' version. Paul's conversion (Acts 9:1–9) is followed by his preaching in

Damascus (9:10–25), a first visit to Jerusalem with Barnabas (9:26–27), and work in Jerusalem, Cilicia, and Antioch (9:28–30; 11:25–26). After being recruited by Barnabas, Paul carried a collection to Jerusalem with him from the Antioch church (11:29–30; 12:25). Then Barnabas and he were commissioned by the Antioch community for a first "missionary journey" (chaps. 13—14). A third visit to Jerusalem was for the Jerusalem Council (15:1–29), which was followed by a second "missionary journey" with Silas (15:36—18:21) overland through Asia Minor into Europe. He made a fourth trip to Jerusalem to "greet the church," in 18:22. He then went on a third "missionary journey" from Antioch, once more through Asia Minor to Europe (18:23—21:14). His fifth visit to Jerusalem led to his arrest, a transfer to Caesarea for a two-year imprisonment, a long sea voyage to Rome, and a final two-year house arrest there (21:15—28:31). From this account, we have the picture of an apostle who goes on well-structured missionary journeys. At the end of each, he touches base with the Jerusalem church, making five visits there in all. Jerusalem is the center of his missionary work as it was for all the apostles.

The information in the letters is much skimpier. Paul's call as an apostle (Gal. 1:15–16) is not followed by a journey to Jerusalem, but by a three-year period of ministry in Syria and Arabia (Gal. 1:17), which is then followed by a short trip to Jerusalem (Gal. 1:18–20). Next Paul spent some eleven years in missionary activity "in the regions of Syria and Cilicia" (Gal. 1:21). Then came a second journey to Jerusalem—the "after fourteen years" of Gal. 2:1 is variously computed—for a conference with the "pillars" of that community (Gal. 2:1–10). This was followed by activity in Galatia, Asia Minor, Macedonia, and Achaia, and possibly in Dalmatia, as indicated by his cryptic references to his movements in Galatians, 1 and 2 Corinthians, and Romans. He planned to visit Jerusalem a final time to bring it a collection he had taken up from his churches (Rom. 15:25–32); then he wanted to visit Rome and use it as the base for a ministry to the West.

Paul stresses his independence from Jerusalem with regard to his status as an apostle of God (Gal. 1:11–12; 2:5–11), although his visits there also pay testimony to the importance he accorded that community. He mentions three such visits. From his letters, it is difficult to detect journeys of the sort suggested by Acts. Paul rather seemed to use various urban centers for greater or lesser periods as the base of his missionary operations; Acts 18:11 and 19:10 give some support to this impression. By the measure of ancient historical writings, the disparity between the sources is not remarkable and confirms more than it calls into doubt. But two critical cases point us to some deeper difficulties.

Was there an apostolic council? If so, who took part? When was it? Paul (Gal. 2) says a conference took place after fourteen years of missionary work; Acts, at least on the face of it, would suggest a much shorter period before the conference. In Acts, Barnabas and Paul are sent to Jerusalem as part of a community delegation; in Galatians, Paul's companion is Titus, and he goes up in response to a revelation (Gal. 2:1–2). Was there a full gathering of the church (Acts) or was it a private meeting between peers? More critically, did it come before the encounter between Peter and Paul in Antioch (recounted in Galatians 2:11–14) or after? Galatians could be construed either way. If it came after, then Paul and Acts might agree that the meeting in Jerusalem resolved differences caused by an Antiochean dispute. But if before, then the meeting settled nothing about fellowship that did not remain troublesome. Did the meeting issue a decree concerning dietary regulations (Acts), or only an agreement about areas of missionary work (Galatians)? If there was a decree, why didn't Paul refer to it when discussing idol meat in 1 Cor. 8—10? These historical questions have proved incapable of sure resolution.

A second difficulty concerns the collection of money for the Jerusalem church taken up by Paul. According to his letters, the collection was a major task of the latter part of his ministry (Gal. 2:10; 1 Cor. 16:1–4; 2 Cor. 8—9; Rom. 15). But the Acts account of Paul's fateful last journey to Jerusalem mentions nothing of such a collection. Acts does say that Paul was accompanied by delegates from the very places where the collection was taken up (Acts 20:4–5) and that Paul was taking with him a large amount of money (24:17, 26). But although Paul saw the collection as an act of reconciliation and fellowship between gentile and Jewish churches, Acts has James suggest to Paul on his arrival in the city quite another gesture of reconciliation (21:23–25). On the other hand, Luke has both Paul and Barnabas take part in a collection for the Jerusalem church, sponsored by the Antiochean community, at the very beginning of Paul's career (11:29–30). Again, it is extremely difficult to put these versions together.

Ultimately, both Acts and the letters are of limited value when it comes to establishing a sequence of Paul's letters. Letters such as 1 and 2 Thessalonians, 1 and 2 Corinthians, and Romans fit well within the Acts narrative. Those written from captivity, however—Colossians, Philemon, Philippians, Ephesians, 2 Timothy—could come from Paul's imprisonment in Caesarea (Acts 24:27) or in Rome (Acts 28:30), or even from some detention Acts does not mention (see 2 Cor. 11:23–27). Still other letters are virtually impossible to place with any confidence within the Acts framework (Galatians, 1 Timothy, Titus). All this means is that both the letters and Acts are about another business than biography. A more telling point is that in all the Acts narrative, Paul is never said to write a single letter. Paul the preacher and founder of churches is the subject of Acts. And this brings us to the next point of difference.

The Apostolic Style

Differences between Acts and the letters in the presentation of Paul's apostolic style have often been noticed. In his letters, Paul confesses to little eloquence (2 Cor. 11:6), but in Acts, he is a masterly talker in every situation, whether speaking before Jews in the synagogue (13:16–40), to sophisticated philosophers in Athens (17:22–31), or before rulers in self-defense (24:10–21). Although Paul in his letters acknowledges the ability to work signs and wonders as certifications of his power (2 Cor. 12:12; Rom. 15:19), he downplays such displays in favor of a preaching of the cross (1 Cor. 2:1–5). In Acts, however, Paul works signs and wonders, performing both healings and exorcisms (Acts 19:11–20; 20:7–12; 28:1–10) and showing himself clever and resourceful in crisis (16:25–30; 27:21–25). Acts stresses Paul's relationship to, and even his dependence on, Jerusalem; Paul in the letters minimizes both. In Acts, Paul is portrayed as an observant Jew, taking a vow (18:18), purifying himself in the temple (21:24–27), and even having his close follower Timothy circumcised (16:3). In his letters, Paul says he is a "Jew to the Jews" (1 Cor. 9:20–23), but he also refuses to circumcise Titus when that act might be construed as a submission to the demands of Torah (Gal. 2:3). These are significant differences. They should be placed, however, within the intentions and literary conventions of the respective sources. Luke-Acts sees Paul as part of the prophetic tradition that emphasizes the work of God by signs and wonders and the speaking of God's word with boldness. It therefore stresses Paul's rhetoric and wonders. Paul in his letters contrasts his suffering ministry to the arrogance of the "superapostles" who oppose him. He is therefore concerned to minimize rhetoric and miracles in favor of a paradoxical weakness.

Theology

Luke-Acts contains little of what is distinctively Pauline theology. It is easy, in fact, to contrast individual points within Acts and the letters, such as the treatment of natural law in Acts 17:27 and in Rom. 1:18–32, or the powerful presentation of righteousness by faith in Galatians and the mild echo of that argument in Acts 13:39: "By him everyone that believes is freed from everything from which you could not be freed by the law of Moses." Such point-by-point comparisons are almost meaningless. The Paul of Acts, like the Peter and Stephen of Acts, does not speak in his own voice. He gives expression in his speeches to the religious perceptions— the theology—of Luke. Through the speeches of his characters, Luke interprets the story for his readers. There are some differences between them, for Luke uses prosopopoeia: his characters are given speeches appropriate to their circumstances. Paul before the philosophers sounds more like Dio Chrysostom, whereas Paul in the synagogue sounds more like Peter. Given the prophetic typology with which Luke works, which demands the minimizing of individual characteristics in favor of a common literary presentation, the small element of the distinctively Pauline that does emerge within Acts is all the more remarkable.

The Lukan Presentation of Paul

We have been trying to sharpen our perception of Luke's understanding of Paul. At each point of comparison, we find that divergence results from specifically Lukan literary and religious concerns that affect Luke's treatment not only of Paul but of all his major characters: the connection to Jerusalem and to Judaism; the powerful works and rhetoric; the stereotypical teaching.

What, then, is Luke's positive appreciation of Paul? He calls him an apostle together with Barnabas (14:4) and—more tellingly for him—a witness (22:15; 26:16). Like the other major figures of the church's mission, Paul is described in specifically prophetic terms (14:3). The prophetic imagery is made sharper when Paul is called a chosen instrument, in 9:15 (cf. Jer. 1:5 and Gal. 1:15), and light to the Gentiles, in 13:47 (cf. Isa. 49:6; Luke 2:32).

Paul was not alone in bringing the "good news" to the Gentiles, nor even the first. For Luke, however, he was preeminent in that mission. It was a ministry, furthermore, carried out in obedience to Jesus' command, which is emphasized in Luke's three versions of Paul's apostolic call. The first is found in direct narrative (Acts 9:1–9), the others in Paul's speeches of defense (22:6–21; 26:12–23). All three versions tell the same story, with some variations: his companions, for example, hear the voice but see nothing in 9:7, but in 22:9 they see the light and are deaf to the voice. The element of shining light is constant in all three accounts and is connected to his commission to be light to the Gentiles. The climax of each version is reached with the command to go to the Gentiles (9:15; 22:21; 26:23). In the defense speeches, this creates a negative response (22:22; 26:24). As with the rejection of Jesus in Nazareth, the Jewish refusal of the prophet's message has something to do with its universal scope.

Yet, Paul's preaching in Acts is by no means exclusively to Gentiles. He turns to them only upon repeated rejection in the synagogue. The first time it happens, Paul solemnly announces a redirection of his efforts to Gentiles (Acts 13:46), but we still see him preaching to Jews and converting some, even though twice more he declares a turn to the Gentiles (18:6; 28:23–29). Even the last and most somber of these pronouncements, which is made to the Jewish leaders of Rome with whom Paul debates and which uses the blindness passage from Isa. 6:9–10, is made in the face of less than total rejection. Even there, some Jews believe (Acts 28:24–25). Indeed, throughout Paul's ministry in the Diaspora, Luke shows us a division within the people; some accept the gospel, others do not (see 17:11; 18:4; 19:9–10). The emphasis in Paul's ministry is definitely on those who do not. This circumstance is indicated linguistically by the overwhelming dominance of the distancing characterization "the Jews" in the narrative devoted to Paul. It is used, except in titles, only once in the Gospel (Luke 7:3) and nine times in Acts apart from Paul. But in reference to those who oppose Paul, the term "Jew," *Ioudaios*, occurs some seventy times.

The Paul of Acts never sees his mission as separated from God's concern for Israel. In the defense speeches above all, Paul defines himself in terms of Jewish messianic expectation, specifically the Pharisaic hope in the resurrection, which he insists has come to fulfillment in the resurrection of Jesus (see 22:3–4; 23:6; 24:14–21; 26:4–11). To the Jewish leaders in Rome, this apostle of the Gentiles declares (Acts 28:20):

> For this reason, therefore, I have asked to see you and speak to you, since it is because of the hope of Israel that I am bound with this chain.

However much Paul carried the gospel to the "end of the earth" he remained for Luke the teacher of Israel.

That the gospel reached the gentile world through the ministry of Paul is made plain by Luke's literary mastery. Just as surely as he took his readers back into the world of ancient Israel by the style of his infancy account, so does he lead them, bit by bit, into the world of Greek religious and philosophical perceptions. This is not a matter of sources but of prosopopoeia; Luke writes appropriately to the circumstances of his characters. Down to the minutiae of style, his Greek becomes less biblical and more secular in the vignettes that show us the gospel's impact on pagans, scenes among the most lively in all his engrossing story.

When Paul heals a cripple in Lystra (Acts 14:8–18), the pagan population thinks "the gods have come down to us in the likeness of men." They call Barnabas Zeus, since he is the leader and possibly more prepossessing in appearance, and Paul, Hermes, since he is the speaker. They try to offer them sacrifice and can only barely be restrained. Paul tells them that the message he and Barnabas bring is precisely that pagans should turn "from these vain things to a living God" (see also 1 Thess. 1:9). The scene would fit comfortably within Apuleius's *Golden Ass;* the wandering sages have such impressive thaumaturgy that they are regarded as immortals and need to teach their would-be worshipers the true nature of piety and the divine.

The turbulence at Ephesus caused by the success of Paul's mission there (Acts 19:11–40) could have sprung from the pages of Philostratus's *Life of Apollonius of Tyana*. Paul's thaumaturgic powers are extraordinarily active. Demons come to prefer being exorcised by him to being exorcised by rival Jewish exorcists (19:11–15). The defeated magicians burn their books, acknowledging the superiority of this new power abroad: "So the Word of God grew and prevailed mightily" (19:20).

The carefully crafted scene of Paul preaching at the Areopagus in Athens (Acts 17:16–34) shows the gospel fully clothed for the gentile world. Luke accurately evokes the world of the wandering philosopher or sophist like Dio Chrysostom, who builds on the native piety of his listeners a higher understanding of the one divine power (see Dio *Oration* 12). Here are the Epicureans and Stoics with their characteristic Greek interest in barbaric deities and novelty and debate, just as we find them in the pages of Lucian (see *The Eunuch* 1–13). In Paul's preaching we hear not only a rhetorically effective use of pagan images for the divine (17:26–29) but quite possibly an authentic echo of the sort of gentile preaching carried out by Paul and his companions (17:30–31; cf. 1 Thess. 1:9–10; Heb. 6:1–2):

> The time of ignorance God overlooked but now he commands all men everywhere to repent because he has fixed a day on which he will judge the world in righteousness by a man whom he has appointed, and of this he has given assurance by raising him from the dead.

Luke also indicates in this scene that Gentiles as well as Jews could refuse God's invitation and turn away in mockery (17:32). But some do believe, and from among them, as from among believing Jews, God fashioned "a people for his name" (15:14).

BIBLIOGRAPHICAL NOTE

Still a classic introduction to Luke-Acts as a literary unity, and unsurpassed for grace and comprehension is H. J. Cadbury, *The Making of Luke-Acts* (New York: Macmillan Co., 1927). For a whole battery of critical issues, see F. J. Foakes-Jackson and K. Lake, eds., *The Beginnings of Christianity, Part I: The Acts of the Apostles*, 5 vols. (London: Macmillan & Co., 1920–27). The pioneering redactional study of Luke that initiated serious attention to its theology was H. Conzelmann, *The Theology of St. Luke*, trans. G. Buswell (Philadelphia: Fortress Press, 1982 [German, 1957; ET, 1961]). The best collection of essays devoted to the two volumes remains L. Keck and J. L. Martyn, eds., *Studies in Luke-Acts* (Philadelphia: Fortress Press, 1980 [1966]), although there are also some useful pieces in C. H. Talbert, ed., *Perspectives on Luke-Acts* (Danville, Va.: Assn. of Baptist Professors of Religion, 1978). A brief survey of recent scholarship is available in E. Richard, "Luke—Writer, Theologian, Historian: Research and Orientation of the 70's," *Biblical Theology Bulletin* 13 (1983): 3–15.

For stylistic aspects of the writing, see H. J. Cadbury, *The Style and Literary Methods of Luke*, HTS 6 (Cambridge: Harvard Univ. Press, 1920); J. Dupont, *The Sources of the Acts*, trans. K. Pond (New York: Herder & Herder, 1964); M. Dibelius, *Studies in the Acts of the Apostles*, trans. H. Greeven (New York: Charles

Scribner's Sons; London: SCM Press, 1956); W. C. Van Unnik, "The 'Book of Acts' Confirmation of the Gospel," *NovT* 4 (1960): 26–59. Much of the literary analysis of this chapter is based on L. T. Johnson, *The Literary Function of Possessions in Luke-Acts*, SBLDS 39 (Missoula, Mont.: Scholars Press, 1977), and idem, "The Lukan Kingship Parable (Lk 19:11–27)," *NovT* 24 (1982): 139–59. For the importance of the Gospel prologue for understanding Luke-Acts as a whole, see R. J. Dillon, "Previewing Luke's Project from His Prologue," *CBQ* 43 (1981): 205–27. On the Stephen speech in Acts, see esp. E. Richard, *Acts 6:1—8:4: The Author's Method of Composition*, SBLDS 41 (Missoula, Mont.: Scholars Press, 1978). For the Moses typology, see H. Teeple, *The Mosaic Eschatological Prophet*, SBLMS 10 (Philadelphia: Soc. of Biblical Literature, 1957), and P. S. Minear, *To Heal and to Reveal: The Prophetic Vocation According to Luke* (New York: Seabury Press, 1976).

Luke-Acts as a historical writing is discussed by C. K. Barrett, *Luke the Historian in Recent Study* (Philadelphia: Fortress Press, 1970 [1961]); I. H. Marshall, *Luke: Historian and Theologian* (Grand Rapids: Zondervan Pub. House, 1970); and M. Hengel, *Acts and the History of Earliest Christianity* (Philadelphia: Fortress Press, 1979). As a form of biography Luke-Acts is discussed by C. H. Talbert, *Literary Patterns, Theological Themes, and the Genre of Luke-Acts*, SBLMS 20 (Missoula, Mont.: Scholars Press, 1974). Aspects of apologetic in Luke-Acts were found by B. S. Easton, *The Purpose of Acts* (London: SPCK, 1936), and D. L. Tiede, *Prophecy and History in Luke-Acts* (Philadelphia: Fortress Press, 1980). The apology for Paul within Judaism is advanced by a work important for its consistent appreciation of Luke-Acts within an intra-Jewish dialogue, J. Jervell, *Luke and the People of God* (Minneapolis: Augsburg Pub. House, 1972). A similar emphasis is found in the essays by N. A. Dahl, "A 'People for His Name' (Acts 15:14)," *NTS* 4 (1957–58): 319–27, and idem, "The Story of Abraham in Luke-Acts," in *Studies in Luke-Acts*, ed. Keck and Martyn, 139–58. For the use of Scripture, see B. Lindars, *New Testament Apologetic: The Doctrinal Significance of Old Testament Quotations* (Philadelphia: Westminster Press, 1961). On some Lukan theological emphases, see R. F. O'Toole, *The Unity of Luke's Theology*, Good News Studies 9 (Wilmington, Del.: Michael Glazier, 1984). Valuable for its treatment of both Luke's use of Scripture and his rhetorical technique is W. S. Kurz, "Hellenistic Rhetoric in the Christological Proof of Luke-Acts," *CBQ* 42 (1980): 171–95.

On Luke's infancy account, see P. S. Minear, "Luke's Use of the Birth Stories," in *Studies in Luke-Acts*, ed. Keck and Martyn, 111–30, and R. E. Brown, *The Birth of the Messiah* (Garden City, N.Y.: Doubleday & Co., 1979), 235–495. For aspects of the ministry narrative, see G. W. H. Lampe, "The Lukan Portrait of Christ," *NTS* 2 (1955–56): 160–75; S. Brown, *Apostasy and Perseverance in the Theology of Luke*, AB 36 (Rome: Biblical Inst. Press, 1969); B. Reicke, "Instruction and Discussion in the Travel Narrative," *SE* 1 (TU 73, 1959): 206–16; D. P. Moessner, "Luke 9:1–50: Luke's Preview of the Journey of the Prophet like Moses of Deuteronomy," *JBL* 102 (1983): 575–605. On the Passion, see J. H. Neyrey, "The Absence of Jesus' Emotions: The Lukan Redaction of Luke 22:39–46," *Bib* 61 (1980): 153–71; J. Kodell, "Luke's Use of *laos* 'People' Especially in the Jerusalem Narrative," *CBQ* 31 (1969): 327–43; R. J. Karris, *Luke—Artist and Theologian:*

Luke's Passion Narrative as Literature, Theological Inquiries (New York: Paulist Press, 1985). For the resurrection accounts as they relate to the whole narrative, see P. Schubert, "The Structure and Significance of Luke 24," *Neutestamentliche Studien für R. Bultmann,* BZNW 21 (Berlin: Töpelmann, 1954), 165–86, and R. J. Dillon, *From Eyewitnesses to Ministers of the Word,* AB 82 (Rome: Biblical Inst. Press, 1978).

The gentile mission in Luke-Acts is considered by J. Dupont, *The Salvation of the Gentiles,* trans. J. Keating (New York: Paulist Press, 1979), and S. G. Wilson, *The Gentiles and the Gentile Mission in Luke-Acts,* SNTSMS 23 (Cambridge: At the Univ. Press, 1973). The apostolic council is read for its historical perspective by S. G. Wilson, *Luke and the Law,* SNTSMS 50 (Cambridge: At the Univ. Press, 1983), and for its narrative structure by L. T. Johnson, *Decision Making in the Church: A Biblical Model* (Philadelphia: Fortress Press, 1983), 46–87.

For the problems of Pauline chronology, see R. Jewett, *A Chronology of Paul's Life* (Philadelphia: Fortress Press, 1979), and G. Luedemann, *Paul, Apostle to the Gentiles: Studies in Chronology,* trans. F. S. Jones (Philadelphia: Fortress Press, 1984). The contrasting images of Paul in the two sources are considered by P. Vielhauer, "On the Paulinism of Acts," in *Studies in Luke-Acts,* ed. Keck and Martyn, 33–50; and G. Bornkamm, "The Missionary Stance of Paul in I Cor 9 and in Acts," in *Studies in Luke-Acts,* 194–207.

The need for a critical commentary and rich bibliography for the Gospel of Luke has now been met by J. A. Fitzmyer, *The Gospel According to Luke I-IX,* Anchor Bible (Garden City, N.Y.: Doubleday & Co., 1981), and idem, *The Gospel According to Luke X—XXIV* (1985). A generally solid treatment of the Greek text of the Gospel is found in I. H. Marshall, *The Gospel of Luke,* NICNT (Grand Rapids: Wm. B. Eerdmans, 1978); for a more popular reading, see E. E. Ellis, *The Gospel of Luke,* 2d ed. NCB (Grand Rapids: Wm. B. Eerdmans; London: Oliphants, 1974). The standard commentary on Acts remains that of E. Haenchen, *The Acts of the Apostles: A Commentary,* trans. B. Noble et al. (Philadelphia: Westminster Press, 1971).

PART FOUR

PAULINE TRADITIONS

THE CHRISTIAN MOVEMENT FOUND ITS FIRST AND MOST VIVID VOICE IN THE letters of the apostle Paul. The evangelists remained anonymous behind their shaping of Jesus' story, letting it speak for them. Paul's letters reveal a human personality so forcibly yet complexly that, for some, coming to grips with Christianity means first of all coming to grips with Paul.

Paul's personality appears at first to be full of contradictory elements. He can be gentle (2 Cor. 10:1) and also harsh (1 Cor. 4:21). He is full of restless energy (2 Cor. 2:12–13) yet also of firm resolution (2 Cor. 1:17). He claims to be weak rather than strong (2 Cor. 12:5) even as he boasts of power (2 Cor. 12:11). He is sublime in the expression of ideals (Rom. 12:14) but very human in his lack of them (Gal. 5:12). So various and even violent do the shifts of his moods sometimes appear that some have thought him mentally unbalanced. The first impression of a volatile and perhaps unhinged ego, however, requires qualification by some other observations.

Paul had remarkable organizing ability. His missionary work did not result from impulsive gestures but from sustained and coordinated expeditions. He worked side by side with other missionaries, male and female, during the rapid spread of the Christian movement, during its first thirty years, to the gates of Rome. His letters do show something of Paul's heart and mind. But close examination also shows that the letters are scarcely the result of raw, unprocessed emotion. To the contrary, they are composed with considerable art, often in cooperation with fellow workers. There is certainly as much rhetoric as ego to be found in them. The Hellenistic world did not exalt self-expression as an ideal of style but rather valued the capacity to write appropriately to circumstances in a variety of "selves."

An equal caution must be applied to characterizations of Paul's thought. It is sometimes called radical. There is no doubt he is fond of the either/or, and he develops antitheses such as death/life, sin/righteousness, flesh/spirit, law/grace, works/faith, wisdom/folly, power/weakness. At the same time, however, more than any other NT writer, Paul seeks to make opposites meet: in his letters we find the reconciliation of God/world, Jew/Greek, female/male, slave/free, rich/poor.

Much of the history of the interpretation of Paul has consisted in construing one part of his multifaceted literary presentation as the whole. More often than not, this results from treating him as a thinker or theologian, a writer who had a center to his system. But Paul was first of all a founder and pastor of churches. His thought was forged on anvils of various controversies and needs, some personal, some communal; and his thought was given expression through a complex process of composition.

Every construal of Paul requires decisions on certain basic questions. The first is, Where is the real Paul? Some decision must be made from the beginning concerning the weight to be accorded the treatment of Paul in Acts and in the letters. And once that is done, a harder issue still remains: Which of the letters traditionally attributed to Paul are written by him and which by his followers? Deciding between authentic and inauthentic letters is not possible, however, on purely objective grounds; it requires some prior sense of what the "real" Paul is. Even those letters acknowledged as authentic, furthermore, look quite different if they are read in continuity with the presentation of Acts and the Pastorals, from how they look if they are read in isolation from the developments of the Pauline tradition, often regarded largely as a betrayal of Paul himself.

A second major issue concerns Paul's historical importance for earliest Christianity. Does the dominance given him in the NT canon reflect historical reality or a theological decision? Was Paul the most important of the missionaries to the Gentiles or only the one whose writings happened to be preserved? Did his influence die out quickly, or was it still active in radical and conservative forms throughout the second century? Decisions concerning the authentic and inauthentic letters, and the way to understand a Pauline "school" obviously are important for that discussion.

A third issue concerns Paul's religious significance. What is the relation between Jesus and Paul? Is Paul a solitary religious genius, the second founder of Christianity, or is he a man of tradition, the heir to and hander-on of communal understanding? Does Paul fundamentally pervert the message of Jesus, or does he faithfully interpret it for changed circumstances? Is Paul the heart of the NT canon? If so, why? And if so, *which* Paul?

All such questions are about Paul's place in history. They are sufficiently compelling to draw attention away from the individual literary documents that alone can provide answers. In this book, however, it is Paul's *letters,* as witnesses to and interpretations of the experience of the crucified and raised Messiah Jesus in the continuing life of the church, that will be our concern. No attempt is made here to decide on the shape of a Pauline theology or to reconstruct Paul's place in earliest Christianity. These issues are discussed only as they are necessary for an intelligent reading of the letters themselves.

Preliminary to that reading, some general remarks should be made on the overall pattern of Paul's ministry and the ways he communicated with his churches.

10
Paul's Ministry and Letters

O F PAUL'S EARLY LIFE WE KNOW ONLY LITTLE. HE IS CALLED A YOUNG MAN (*neanios*) at the death of Stephen (Acts 7:58) and refers to himself as an old man (*presbytēs*) in one of his letters (Phlm. 9). According to consistent tradition, he was martyred under Nero (54–68 C.E). Correlating these points of reference with his encounter with Gallio (ca. 50–52) in Corinth, we can place his date of birth about 5–15 C.E. He was born in Tarsus of Cilicia (Acts 22:3), which truly was "no mean city" (Acts 21:39). It was a center for Hellenistic culture. Popular philosophers and rhetoricians preached in its streets (Dio *Oration* 33.3–4), and important Stoic teachers such as Athenadoras, the tutor of Caesar Augustus, lived and taught there (see Lucian *Octogenarians*; Plutarch *On Stoic Contradictions* 1033D). Mystery cults were also known to have flourished there. In Tarsus, Paul the Jew could breathe the same Hellenistic air as could his older contemporary Philo Judaeus in Alexandria.

Paul had a particularly impressive Jewish heritage, in which he showed considerable pride: "I was circumcised on the eighth day, of the people of Israel and the tribe of Benjamin, a Hebrew of Hebrew origins" (Phil. 3:5; cf. Rom. 11:1). He grew defensive if his pedigree was challenged: "Are they Hebrews? So am I! Are they Israelites? So am I! Are they descendants of Abraham? So am I!" (2 Cor. 11:22).

According to Acts 22:28, Paul was born with Roman citizenship, a fact that enabled him to appeal to Caesar (25:11–12) and that astonished his jailer, who had purchased his own citizenship (22:28). Citizenship in the city was considerably extended in the first century, but for provincial Jews to have this privilege for at least two generations suggests that Paul's family was socially prominent. His original social status may give some edge to his awareness of all he gave up for the Messiah (Phil. 3:8) and to his complaints about his manual labor (1 Cor. 4:12; 1 Thess. 4:11; 2 Thess. 3:7–9). During his ministry, he probably worked as a tentmaker (Acts 18:3). Such manual labor was practiced by Pharisees as well as by Cynic philosophers who did not want to take payment for preaching. It enabled Paul to be self-sufficient (Phil. 4:11) and to share with others (Acts 20:34–35).

Paul's specific religious commitment was to Pharisaism—"as to the law a Pharisee, . . . as to righteousness under the law, blameless" (Phil. 3:5–6). His dedication to that strict brotherhood was intense, even fanatical: "I advanced in Judaism beyond many of my own age among my people, so extremely zealous was I for the traditions of my fathers" (Gal. 1:14). The importance of Paul's Pharisaism cannot be overestimated. Involved was an understanding not only that observance of Torah was the absolute measure of righteousness before God but also that the study of Torah was the way to wisdom. Paul was a scholar in the symbolic world of Torah. Of all first-generation Christians, he was the most aware of the issues posed for the Jewish symbolic world by a crucified Messiah.

It was possible to be a Pharisee in the Diaspora, but the movement was centered in Judea. This raises the question of the place where Paul was reared and educated. Did he come to Jerusalem as a young man and receive technical scribal training? He clearly says so in Acts 22:3:

> I am a Jew, born in Tarsus of Cilicia, but I was brought up in this city [Jerusalem]. Here I sat at the feet of Gamaliel and was educated strictly in the laws of our fathers.

Some scholars think that Gal. 1:22–23 argues decisively against this:

> I was still not known by sight to the churches of Christ in Judea; they only heard it said, "He who once persecuted us is now preaching the faith he once tried to destroy."

But even Judea is large and populous enough for a former Pharisaic student and persecutor, however notorious, to be unknown by sight to small messianic communities. If we take seriously all the evidence—Acts' general agreement with the letters on Paul's background; the use of technical biographical vocabulary by Luke in Acts 22:3; the indications of Paul's having some relatives in the city (Acts 23:16); the greater probability of scribal training's being available in Jerusalem than in the Diaspora, and the plain fact that Paul *knew* and *used* such scribal techniques in his letters—it suggests that Paul went to Jerusalem as a young man, was educated in the study of Torah, and there first encountered and persecuted the deviant messianic sect.

Paul's place of upbringing and education has usually been considered important because it would seem to determine the relative strength of cultural influences on his thought. Those who understand Paul in terms of apocalyptic or rabbinic categories would like to place his roots in Palestine. Those who see Paul as a Hellenist of the Hellenists, interpreting him from the standpoint of Hellenistic philosophy (Stoicism, Cynicism, Epicureanism) or religion (the mystery religions) exploit the Tarsus connection. We have already seen, however, that geographical and symbolic worlds do not neatly coincide in the first-century Hellenistic world (see pp. 22, 67 above). In Paul as in Philo we find creative reshaping of a complex symbolic world by a single thinker responding to the multiform needs of a Diaspora community. No one aspect of that symbolic world will completely explain Paul, for his creativity consists precisely in his realignment of that world's elements. Far more important in the process is the personal religious experience that distinguishes Paul among all the first witnesses: he was a persecutor of the church and was then called by the risen Lord to be an apostle. Paul is paradigmatic for the way a religious experience can re-create a symbolic world.

Paul's persecution of the church is emphasized both in his letters and in Acts: "You know how I persecuted the church of God violently and tried to destroy it" (Gal. 1:13; cf. Phil. 3:6). Even after twenty years his call still seemed remarkable to him: "I am the least of the apostles; unfit to be called an apostle because I persecuted the church of God" (1 Cor. 15:8). Paul contrasts the mercy shown him in his call of Jesus' service, with his former behavior as the first of sinners: "I formerly blasphemed and persecuted and insulted him, but I received mercy because I acted ignorantly in unbelief" (1 Tim. 1:12–13). According to Acts, Paul colluded in the stoning of Stephen (7:58), persecuted the Christians in Jerusalem (8:3), and was traveling to Damascus to continue his persecution of "the way" (9:1) when he met Jesus.

Why did Paul seek to extirpate the messianic sect? Our best clues are his self-designation as one zealous for the law, together with his subsequent polemic against the ultimacy of Torah (see esp. Gal. 3:10—4:10, 5:1–4). By the norms of Torah, Jesus could not be righteous, much less Messiah, since he was a sinner and cursed by God (see Deut. 21:23). If God was truly at work through Jesus, the whole symbolic framework of Pharisaism was threatened; Torah could not be the ultimate norm of righteousness. In Paul's messianic theology, the same either/or is carried through consistently, only in reverse. If Jesus is Messiah and Son of God, then Torah cannot be regarded as the ultimate norm of God's activity for righteousness, for Jesus does not fit. Before Paul's call and after, the categories remain the same, they are simply transvalued. No wonder his theology is markedly dialectical, and that his habitual contrast is between the then and the now; for such was his own life.

The experience that turned him from persecutor to apostle was both a prophetic call and a direct encounter with Jesus. According to Gal. 1:15,

when he who had set me apart before I was born and had called me through his grace, was pleased to reveal his son to me [or, in me] in order that I might preach him among the Gentiles.

Paul stresses that his call did not come from human beings, but directly from Jesus, "by revelation from [or, of] Jesus Christ" (Gal. 1:12). Formally, the experience was a resurrection appearance: "Last of all, as to one untimely born, he appeared also to me" (1 Cor. 15:8). "Am I not free? Am I not an apostle? *Have I not seen* Jesus our Lord?" (1 Cor. 9:1; cf. 2 Cor. 12:1–3). The experience almost certainly provides the context for the remarkable statement in 2 Cor. 4:6:

> It is the God who said, "Let light shine out of darkness," who has shone in our hearts to give the light of the knowledge of the glory of God in the face of Christ.

The Acts narratives of Paul's call also emphasize the personal encounter with Jesus. They indicate that the call was not a result of logical deduction but of an unexpected and shattering collision. It reversed Paul literally in midstride. The identification of the risen Jesus with the community persecuted by Paul is made clear. Both Acts and the letters see the experience less as a conversion, although as a radical turning it is properly so designated, than as a resurrection experience issuing in a command to be apostle to the Gentiles (Acts 9:15; 22:21; 26:23; Gal. 1:15). For the Pharisee Paul, to be assigned this specific task was not the smallest of paradoxes in his life, but it was a task he gladly acknowledges and spends his life in carrying out (see Rom. 1:5; 11:13; 15:16; Eph. 3:1; 1 Tim. 2:7; 2 Tim. 4:17).

The direct impact of Paul's experience is obvious: it impelled him on the mission of proclaiming Jesus as Messiah. But the experience also indirectly affected his interpretation of that proclamation. Paul's starting point is never the memory of Jesus' deeds or words but the transforming experience of the risen Lord: "Even if we once knew Christ according to the flesh, we no longer so know him" (2 Cor. 5:16). For Paul, Jesus is not so much the past founder of a messianic community as the present source of its life and power (2 Cor. 3:17–18):

> Now the Lord is the Spirit, and where the Spirit of the Lord is, there is freedom. And we all, with unveiled face, beholding the glory of the Lord, are being changed into his likeness from one degree of glory to another; for this comes from the Lord who is the Spirit.

Because the Lord is its life force, the community is the Messiah's "body" (1 Cor. 12:12–27; Eph. 4:12–16), "the fullness of him who fills all in all" (Eph. 1:23). It is also the "temple of the Lord," sanctified by the presence of his Holy Spirit (1 Cor. 3:16; 2 Cor. 6:16; Eph. 2:21).

Because Paul was plunged, in a moment, from hostility toward a false messiah to belief in a risen Lord, his thought is dominated by the turning of the ages. What he and his fellow Jews had expected was now accomplished in the resurrected Jesus. But the fulfillment was far more profound and paradoxical than could have been expected. Jesus *did not* inaugurate an age of righteousness and messianic rule within Israel alone. Through his resurrection, God inaugurated a renewal of humanity and of the world itself, with Jesus as the firstborn from the dead and the new Adam: "If any one is in Christ, there is a new creation; the old has passed away, behold, the new has come" (2 Cor. 5:17; cf. 1 Cor. 15:42–50; Rom. 5:12–21; Eph. 1:9–10; Col. 3:10–11). And since Paul was a Pharisee zealous for Torah, he above all had to resolve the cognitive dissonance between belief in a crucified, cursed Messiah as Lord and the words of Torah, which were "holy, just, and good" (Rom. 7:12).

PAUL'S MINISTRY

The difficulties presented by the sources for reconstructing Paul's ministry have already been recounted (see chap. 9). Even when the biases of the sources have been taken into account, much of what we would like to know they simply cannot tell us. Neither Acts nor the letters say much about the important years before Paul began his collaboration with Barnabas. Neither source is helpful on his method of actually founding communities. Acts is preoccupied with patterns of preaching and with the turning from Jew to Gentile; the letters are written to communities already established. We do not learn what first steps Paul took to establish the movement in a new place. Did he, as Acts suggests, always begin in the synagogue, or is that just a reflection of Acts' apologetic interest? Paul does retain some of the "Jew first, then Gentile" perspective on the mission (see Rom. 1:16; 11:11–12), but we cannot know whether this stemmed from or affected his practice.

The sources do, however, agree on some important patterns in his ministry. Paul's mission was almost entirely an urban one. He tended to use the most important city of a territory as his base of operations, accepting also from churches of that city financial support for the work of evangelization. That Antioch on the Orontes was the sponsor of his first venture to the West is stated by Acts (13:1–3). From the letters, we know that Philippi, his first European community, was active in his support (Phil. 4:15–16; 2 Cor. 11:8–9) and that Paul hoped to find the Roman church an equally committed sponsor of his mission to Spain (Rom. 1:13; 15:28—16:2). Paul worked with his hands to support himself, but his mission required considerable support. Travel and lodging, particularly for an entourage, were expensive.

The sources show clearly that Paul worked not alone but as the head of a team. Acts lists these significant associates in the mission of Paul: Barnabas (13:2), John-Mark (13:5; 15:37), Silas (15:40), Timothy (16:3), Priscilla and Aquila (18:2–4), Apollos (18:24–28), Erastus (19:22), Sopater, Aristarchus, Secundus, Gaius, Tychichus, and Trophimus (20:4)—fourteen people. In his letters, Paul also makes frequent mention of associates and co-workers. In the Roman church, which he had never seen, he could greet twenty-six people by name—ten of them explicitly designated as workers for the gospel—and pass on greetings from nine others with him (Rom. 16:1–23). The Corinthian congregations could recognize references to these workers for the mission: Cephas (1 Cor. 1:12; 9:5), Apollos (1 Cor. 3:6; 16:12), Barnabas (1 Cor. 9:6), Sosthenes (1 Cor. 1:1), Timothy (1 Cor. 16:10), Aquila and Priscilla (1 Cor. 16:19), Titus (2 Cor. 8:16) as well as other local workers (1 Cor. 16:15–17; 2 Cor. 8:23). The Philippians knew the fellow workers Euodia, Syntyche, Clement, and Epaphroditus (Phil. 4:2–3, 18). At Colossae, we find Epaphras (Col. 1:7), Luke and Demas (Col. 4:14), Tychichus and Onesimus (Col. 4:7–9), Aristarchus (Col. 4:10), Nympha (Col. 4:15), and Archippus (Col. 4:17). Second Timothy adds Onesiphorus (1:16) and Crescens (4:10), while Titus contributes Artemas and Zenas (Titus 3:12–13). This list contains only field agents, not local leaders, though at this distance it is obviously impossible to distinguish between them accurately. The list is therefore a rough one but must also, given the random nature of this evidence, be considered conservative. We can estimate that the Pauline mission involved at least forty persons, female and male.

The effort and organization required to mobilize and coordinate these co-workers must have been considerable. Paul's daily care for the churches was not an insignificant entry in his catalogue of sufferings (2 Cor. 11:28). A corollary of this complex network is that Paul could not do everything himself. Some tasks needed to be delegated. His letters show how Paul frequently used delegates to handle important and delicate missions when he himself could not make a visit (1 Thess. 3:2; 1 Cor. 4:17; 2 Cor. 8:23; Eph. 6:21; Phil. 2:19, 25; Col. 4:7–8; 1 Tim. 1:3; Titus 1:5). His letters were another way of maintaining contact in place of a personal visit.

A precise chronology of Paul's ministry is impossible to determine. Acts and the letters sufficiently overlap to allow us a plausible insertion of some letters into the Acts narrative. Because of the coincidence of Paul's stay at Corinth from the winter of 50 to spring of 52 and of Acts' close attention to his movements before and after, these letters can be dated between 50 and 58, and in a reasonable sequence: 1 and 2 Thessalonians, 1 and 2 Corinthians, and Romans. These are, however, only five letters out of thirteen. The letters written from captivity could come from a Caesarean (Acts 24:27) or Roman (Acts 28:30) imprisonment or from some earlier detention about which Acts is silent. It is therefore impossible to give a definite date and sequence to Philemon, Colossians, Ephesians, Philippians, and 2 Timothy. Three remaining letters presuppose Paul's active ministry but contain too little circumstantial information to place them in the Acts' framework: 1 Timothy, Titus, Galatians. Informed guesses are possible, but they remain guesses. The largest portion of Paul's correspondence, in sum, cannot be placed with certainty during what we know of his career!

There is not sufficient evidence, therefore, to trace accurately the development of Paul's thought within the corpus of his extant letters. There are two reasons for this. The first is that our first letter from Paul was written some dozen years after he began his missionary work; in all likelihood, his basic ideas were already well established. The second is that, apart from the letters that fall within an eight-year range, we cannot fix the date of the remaining letters. There may have been some development or change in thought or in attitude. Old age and imprisonment and discouragement have left their mark on the writings of others. But our evidence is not such as would allow us to make such determinations with confidence. Other factors, as we shall see, were as important in the process of composition as Paul's personal development.

Since Paul worked for many years before writing the first of the letters still in our possession, he had available to him the community traditions of his own and other churches—both Palestinian and Diaspora. As a leader in an extensive and complex missionary endeavor, Paul could not be, and does not show himself to be, purely charismatic and idiosyncratic. The customs and traditions of the churches were important to him, since lack of order and peace were dangerous. In choices between spontaneity and structure, Paul chose structure with perhaps surprising frequency (see, e.g., 1 Cor. 5:1–5; 7:17; 11:16; 14:33–36; 2 Cor. 6:14—7:1; Gal. 6:7–10; Titus 1:3).

THE PAULINE CORRESPONDENCE

In the NT canon, Paul's letters are arranged in order of length, from Romans to Philemon. Several conventional categories are used to group letters. Travel Letters are those written during Paul's active ministry. They include 1 and 2 Thessalonians, 1 and 2 Corinthians, Galatians, and Romans; 1 Timothy and Titus also fit this category. Captivity Letters are those written from prison: Philippians, Philemon, Colossians, Ephesians, 2 Timothy. First and Second Timothy and Titus are usually called Pastoral Letters; a better designation would be Letters to Delegates. The term Great Letters is sometimes used for Romans, 1 and 2 Corinthians, and Galatians, especially by scholars who regard Paul's teaching on freedom and justification by faith as the heart of his theology; it is obviously a value-laden designation.

Paul's correspondence was carried out in a cultural setting that both valued and had highly developed the art of writing letters (*epistulae*). Philosophers and statesmen and poets alike used the epistle as a literary vehicle for moral and aesthetic exposition (cf. Horace, Seneca, Cicero). Such epistles were often self-consciously literary and aimed at a readership beyond the addressee; posterity was as much in mind as the correspondent. Not only the learned used letters. Archaeologists have uncovered thousands of letters, scrawled on papyri or even shards of clay, from the Hellenistic period—genuine correspondence dealing with business and personal affairs. Employing a rather rigid distinction between literary epistles and nonliterary letters, as well as on the presumed sociological distance between the writers of each, many have considered Paul's correspondence a collection of letters. As a result, the literary features of his correspondence were for a long time neglected. The classification of Paul's correspondence as letters has also supported the picture of the low social standing of the first Christians.

The distinction between epistle and letter is helpful but overly sharp. Even popular letters followed the norms appropriate to letter types, which were later described in considerable detail in rhetorical handbooks. Such handbooks give examples of how certain epistolary types should be written: the friendly letter, the parenetic letter, the protreptic letter: each had its appropriate conventions and stylized expressions. Such letter forms provide valuable literary guidance to the reader of Paul's letters.

The choice of function for the Hellenistic correspondent was not so restricted as that between literature and life, either. Letters were composed for a variety of purposes. Perhaps the only universal function was that of making one who was absent, present: in a real sense, the letter was viewed as bearing the presence of the sender. Epicurean and Jewish communities used letters both to instruct and to propagandize. Christians inherited from Diaspora Jews the custom of writing letters of commendation between communities (see 2 Cor. 3:1), examples of which survive in the NT (see Romans 16; Philemon, 3 John).

The Pauline correspondence is marked by great variety. Philemon is essentially a personal note, and 1 and 2 Timothy and Titus are personal letters to delegates in the field. In contrast, Ephesians is the most public sort of letter, an encyclical. Colossians and Romans are written to churches founded by others that Paul does not know firsthand. In contrast, Philippians is a letter of friendship to Paul's dearest and closest community. Galatians is a letter of rebuke and argument. The Thessalonian and Corinthian letters probably come closest to being genuinely pastoral letters, whose contents and shape are determined above all by the current needs of the addressees.

Despite their variety, the Pauline letters have some shared characteristics. All have a certain degree of occasionality. They are written not for publication or posterity but for the contemporary addressees. In this sense, they are genuine letters. For all that, however, even the shortest of them does not lack literary artistry. All of them show care in their composition. Paul's letters also have an official character. He never writes simply as a friend or colleague but always as Paul the apostle. With the probable exception of Philemon and the Pastorals, furthermore, all his letters were intended to be read aloud to the community (see 1 Thess. 5:27; 2 Thess. 2:2, 15) and even to be exchanged between communities (see Col. 4:16). Finally, it is clear that Paul wrote letters not as a hobby or pleasant diversion but out of a sense of need and because he could not attend to a problem in person. The more we can recover the occasion for a letter, therefore, the more we are aided in understanding Paul's purpose in writing. This is not to say that the meaning of a letter will always be reducible to such purposes.

Epistolary Structure

The Hellenistic letter had a simple structure. The addressee's name was usually written on the outside of the papyrus roll. A greeting opened the letter. Its normal form was "From A to B, greetings [*chairein*]" (see 1 Macc. 10:25; 11:30; 12:6; Acts 15:23; 23:26). The body of the letter followed, and a short farewell normally consisted of a wish for health or good fortune. Paul's letters follow this basic structure, with each of the elements characteristically expanded.

1. In the *greeting*, for example, Paul changes the secular *chairein* to *charis*, "grace," and he adds the normal Jewish greeting *eirēnē*, "peace." In effect, the letter begins with a prayer as well as a greeting. Paul also sometimes expands any one of the three basic elements of the greeting, giving further information about the senders (Rom. 1:1–6; Gal. 1:1–2; 1 Tim. 1:1; 2 Tim. 1:1; Titus 1:1–3) or the recipients (1 Cor. 1:2; 2 Cor. 1:1; Phlm. 2) or the wish he has for the recipients (Gal. 1:3–5). Such expansions can provide clues to later developments in the letter.

2. Paul follows the greeting with a *prayer*. He ordinarily uses a thanksgiving formula ("I give thanks," *eucharistō*), as in Rom. 1:8; 1 Cor. 1:4; Phil. 1:3; Col. 1:3; 1 Thess. 1:2; 2 Thess. 1:3; 1 Tim. 1:12; 2 Tim. 1:3; Phlm. 4. Twice he uses the familiar Jewish blessing formula ("Blessed be God," *eulogētos ho theos;* 2 Cor. 1:3 and Eph. 1:3). In only two letters (Gal. 1:6; Titus 1:5) does Paul omit the prayer, and the alteration is striking. The prayer often anticipates themes developed later in the body of the letter and therefore functions as instruction and persuasion as well as prayer. There is considerable variation in the length of the prayer and some in its placement. Thus, the prayer in 1 Thessalonians takes up much of the first three chapters; in 2 Thessalonians, there are two formal thanksgivings

(1:3–4; 2:13–17), and in 1 Timothy, the prayer follows a preliminary exhortation.

3. In the *body* of the letter, Paul addresses the specific difficulties of the community or begins to develop his argument. The body is introduced with one of a variety of transitional formulas, including "I exhort you" (1 Cor. 1:10; 1 Thess. 4:1; 1 Tim. 1:3; 2:1; Phlm. 9), "We ask you" (2 Thess. 2:1), "I do not want you ignorant" (2 Cor. 1:8), "I want you to know" (Phil. 1:12), and "On this account . . ." (Eph. 1:15; Col. 1:9; 2 Tim. 1:6; Titus 1:5). Similar formulas often introduce new topics within the body of the letter or mark transitions (see, e.g., 1 Cor. 7:1; 8:1; 10:1; 12:1; 15:1; 16:1).

4. The body of the Pauline letter eases imperceptibly into the *final greetings* and *farewell*. The greetings are often fairly extensive, showing us the complex and communal nature of the mission. The letters characteristically close with a prayer formula, wishing, with considerable variations, grace from God on the readers (see Rom. 15:33; 16:25–27; 1 Cor. 16:23–24; 2 Cor. 13:14; Gal. 6:18; Eph. 6:23–24; Phil. 4:23; Col. 4:18; 1 Thess. 5:28; 2 Thess. 3:18; 1 Tim. 6:21; 2 Tim. 4:22; Titus 3:15; Phlm. 25). Within this basic structure, the Pauline letter contains many variations of form that are important for interpretation.

Elements of Composition

Paul's letters could not be simply a direct expression of emotion because of the complexity of their composition. Paul "authors" all his letters, in the broad sense that they were composed under his authority and direction. But it is sometimes difficult to determine how direct a role he played in the writing. There are several considerations.

Since writing on parchment or papyrus was awkward and physically tedious, particularly in the case of letters as long as Paul's, the job of writing was often given to a trained secretary (*amanuensis*). Cicero, for example, often dictated his letters to Atticus (see, e.g., VII.13a; VIII.13; X.3a; XI.24; XIII.25). We know that Paul also used a secretary for at least some of his letters. The scribe appears explicitly in Romans, "I Tertius, the writer of this letter, greet you in the Lord" (Rom. 16:22). At other times, Paul indicates that he is penning the greeting in his own hand, which indicates that he had dictated the rest (see 1 Cor. 16:21; Col. 4:18; 2 Thess. 3:17; and possibly Gal. 6:11). Why is this important? Because skilled and trusted secretaries were sometimes given considerable latitude in the actual composition of letters. Given the main point to be made, they could work up an appropriate treatment consonant with the author's thought and often his style as well. We have no direct evidence for this happening in Paul's correspondence, but the wide variety of styles within the Pauline corpus forces us at least to take the possibility seriously.

Many of Paul's letters were also cosponsored. He did not write in his name alone, but also in the name of Timothy (2 Cor. 1:1; Phil. 1:1; Col. 1:1; Phlm. 1), of Silas and Timothy (1 Thess. 1:1; 2 Thess. 1:1), of Sosthenes (1 Cor. 1:1), and of the brethren with him (Gal. 1:2). Only Romans, Ephesians, and the three letters to his delegates Timothy and Titus are sent out in Paul's name alone. How seriously should this be taken? Was cosponsorship merely a formal matter, or did the cosponsor contribute to the thought or style of the letter?

The question becomes sharper when we consider the social setting presupposed by some passages in Paul's letters. Scholars have long recognized elements of an oral-diatribal style in parts of Paul's letters, notably in the Roman and Corinthian correspondence. This style is highly dialogical, with the readers being addressed directly, and with frequent use of apostrophe and rhetorical questions, employment of stock examples for illustration, citation of written authorities, and use of stereotypical moral commonplaces, such as virtue and vice lists, tables of household responsibilities, and polemics against opponents. Until recently, this style was associated with public preaching. More recent study has shown its primary social setting to be the classroom; diatribe is above all a style of teaching. Elements of diatribe in Paul's letters therefore represent a literary transposition of the vivid dialogical exchanges between teacher and student. The diatribe comes from a communal activity of study. Such teaching could have been engaged in by Paul with Timothy and Titus and Sosthenes and Silas even at the workbench—other philosophers had taught from there.

Other portions of his letters contain elaborate midrashim (see esp. Galatians 3—4; Romans 9—11; Ephesians 2) in which scriptural texts are carefully expounded within a sometimes highly technical argument. Once again, for the Pharisaic tradition in which Paul was schooled, midrash was never a private but always a communal activity. It was what teacher and students did together over the text of Torah. There is the strong probability, therefore, that in these parts of the letters, we find set pieces worked out by Paul and his co-workers in their midrashic study together. The literary forms and the accustomed social contexts together suggest this. The corollary? Paul's "school" was operative in the production of his letters even during his lifetime. Although Paul authorized each of the letters that bore his name, it is highly probable, therefore, that many hands and minds contributed to their final composition. The social setting for the Pauline correspondence is as complex as for his ministry.

The composition of his letters, furthermore, involved the use of many traditional materials. By a kind of literary inertia, these materials affect the style and vocabulary of the contexts within which they are found. In some of his letters, (e.g., Romans, 1 and 2 Corinthians, Galatians), Paul makes extensive use of explicit citations from Torah. In other letters (Ephesians, Colossians, 1 and 2 Thessalonians, 1 and 2 Timothy, Titus, Philemon), he uses Torah scarcely at all. Paul also uses confessional formulas (Rom. 10:9; 1 Cor. 12:3), kerygmatic statements (1 Cor. 15:3–8; Rom. 4:24–25; 1 Thess. 1:9–10; Titus 3:4–7), hymns (Phil. 2:6–11; Col. 1:15–20; 1 Tim. 3:16; 2 Tim. 2:11–13), liturgical formulas (Eph. 5:14; 1 Cor. 6:11; Gal. 3:28; 4:6) and even—occasionally—the words of Jesus (1 Cor. 7:10; 9:14; 11:24–25; 1 Thess. 4:15; 1 Tim. 5:18). These elements affect the setting in which they are found because Paul comments or elaborates upon them. They also indicate his profound involvement in the wider Christian movement into which he himself had been baptized and instructed, since he adopts and reinforces shared symbols.

Authentic and Inauthentic Letters

Since the eighteenth century, the authenticity of some Pauline letters has been debated. At one time or another, virtually all thirteen letters have had to prove their authenticity to critics. As a result of these debates, a broad consensus has developed. Nearly all critical scholars accept seven letters—Romans, 1 Thessalonians, 1 and 2 Corinthians, Philemon, Galatians, and Philippians as written directly by Paul. There is almost equal unanimity in rejecting 1 and 2 Timonthy and Titus. Serious debate can occasionally be found concerning 2 Thessalonians, Colossians, and Ephesians, but the clear and growing scholarly consensus does not accept them as Pauline.

If some of the letters are not from Paul, then who wrote them? The consensus view of the Pauline corpus sees a radical and embattled Paul writing the seven undisputed letters. After his death, his followers, sometimes called the Pauline school, continue to write in his name. Soon after his death, Colossians is written, pushing Paul's thought in a cosmic, even mystical, direction; Ephesians is written later, perhaps on the basis of Colossians. At a considerably later time, perhaps in the second century, more conservative admirers of Paul perpetuate his tradition in 2 Thessalonians and the Pastorals, combatting Gnosticism and misunderstandings of Paul himself. Almost half the Pauline corpus is therefore to be regarded as pseudonymous literature. It may have been written in the spirit of Paul, but it cannot be taken into account when assessing his ministry or his thought. It is of value primarily for showing the permutations of the Pauline tradition through succeeding generations.

What are the criteria used for deciding on authenticity or inauthenticity? The first criterion is style. This includes not only vocabulary but also sentence length and structure. It can be extended to include variations in epistolary form, modes of argumentation, and density of scriptural use. The second criterion is broadly theological. It concerns consistency in content. This is usually measured by certain standard categories, including view of the law, eschatology, and Christology. Other content considerations are the view of the church: What is the role of structure and authority? What is the relation of the church to Christ, and to the world? Another subcategory is ethics: Is it defined by radical freedom tempered by service, or by the fulfilling of household responsibilities? The third major criterion is fit within Paul's ministry: Is there a place for the composition of this letter within the narrative of Acts or Paul's other letters?

A full discussion of the issue of authenticity is too complex to serve our present needs. Some methodological remarks, however, are in order. They are especially appropriate since I do not agree with the consensus opinion in this matter, and the reader deserves to know why.

Of the criteria, only the last is really "hard." If we really had a full biography of Paul and there were simply no place for the writing of a particular letter, then the criterion would be decisive. In fact, however, a full biography is exactly what we lack! We cannot pin down with precision most of Paul's letters. The sources leave us as ignorant of the circumstances surrounding Galatians as they do in the case of Titus. Yet if Paul wrote Galatians to north Galatia rather than to the churches Acts says he founded in south Galatia (cf. Acts 14:1–21; 16:1–6; 18:23), it is never, on that account, considered inauthentic. And properly so, for our sources do not tell us all about Paul's activities, only a little bit. The other criteria are therefore more determinative.

They are also much softer. Both the style and content criteria presuppose a fixed center of consistency as a norm for measuring deviance. But precisely such a center does not exist! Even in the seven unquestioned letters there is great variety in both style and content. If 1 Thessalonians were held to the same standards as the Pastorals, it would be judged equally inauthentic: it is not diatribal, it lacks Scripture citations, it has no significant teaching on sin or grace or faith or righteousness or Torah, it has a suspiciously un-Pauline anthropology. In its case, of course, a place within Paul's career is magnificently confirmed by Acts, so the criteria of style and content are waived.

If there is a significant range of style and content even within the undoubted letters, how do the criteria work? Largely subjectively: appeal is made to the reader's sense of what constitutes acceptable deviance from a presumed norm. Statistical analyses, sometimes invoked as support for this appeal, are not at all reliable, since the sample is too small and cannot take into account the most critical factors determining style in ancient writing: genre, topic, audience, and occasion.

The discussion of authenticity has been distorted by doubtful premises. It has yet to deal satisfactorily with the complexity of the composition process within the *undoubted* letters, a complexity that suggests already in the lifetime of Paul, the activity of a "school." It has also failed to reckon with the great variety of style and theme within the genuine letters. It is seldom noted that the very act of separating three similar documents, for example, the Pastorals, from a collection and comparing them together against the corpus as a whole already predetermines the result. They are different. The result is even clearer when they are compared not with all the letters but with an already reduced authentic core. One rarely finds 2 Timothy compared stylistically with the whole of the corpus; rather, the three Pastorals together are compared not against ten but against seven letters already determined to be authentic. Ephesians, likewise, is rarely compared with all the remaining twelve letters to test its style, but to the seven already determined to be authentic. If one isolated 1 and 2 Thessalonians and compared them as a set with all the rest of the corpus, they would also be found inauthentic on stylistic and content grounds.

In the present treatment of Paul's letters, issues pertaining to the genuineness (the authenticity) of each letter will be treated only briefly, since our purpose is the understanding of the writings in their literary integrity, not the reconstruction of Paul's career or theology. The issue of authenticity will always remain secondary. The reader may be surprised at my positive bias for the authenticity of all the letters. It is based on the persuasiveness of their literary self-presentation, the ability to find plausible places for them in Paul's career, and a conviction that the whole Pauline corpus is one that Paul "authored" but did not necessarily write.

BIBLIOGRAPHICAL NOTE

For a convenient treatment of Paul, combining primary texts with critical notes and essays, see W. A. Meeks, ed., *The Writings of St. Paul* (New York: W. W. Norton & Co., 1973). For the history of Pauline interpretation, see A. Schweitzer, *Paul and His Interpreters*, trans. W. Montgomery (New York: Macmillan Co., 1912), and E. E. Ellis, *Paul and His Recent Interpreters* (Grand Rapids: Wm. B. Eerdmans, 1961). On Pauline chronology, see chap. 9 above and J. Knox, *Chapters in a Life of Paul* (Nashville: Abingdon Press, 1950); R. Jewett, *A Chronology of Paul's Life* (Philadelphia: Fortress Press, 1979); and G. Luedemann, *Paul, Apostle to the Gentiles: Studies in Chronology*, trans. F. S. Jones (Philadelphia: Fortress Press, 1984). A conservative treatment of Paul within the framework of Acts is found in W. Ramsey, *St. Paul the Traveller and the Roman Citizen* (London: Hodder & Stoughton, 1925), and in J. A. T. Robinson, *Redating the New Testament* (Philadelphia: Westminster Press, 1978).

Among the classic appreciations of Paul's life and work, see A. Fridrichsen, *The Apostle and His Message* (Uppsala: Almqvist and Wicksell, 1947); A. D. Nock, *St. Paul* (New York: Harper & Row, 1938); A. Deissman, *Paul: A Study in Social and Religious History*, 2d ed. (New York: Harper & Row, 1927); M. Dibelius and W. G. Kummel, *Paul*, trans. F. Clarke (Philadelphia: Westminster Press, 1953); G.

Bornkamm, *Paul*, trans. D. M. G. Stalke (New York: Harper & Row, 1971); J. Munck, *Paul and the Salvation of Mankind*, trans. F. Clarke (Richmond: John Knox Press, 1959); K. Stendahl, *Paul Among Jews and Gentiles* (Philadelphia: Fortress Press, 1976); N. A. Dahl, *Studies in Paul* (Minneapolis: Augsburg Pub. House, 1977); and E. Käsemann, *Perspectives on Paul*, trans. M. Kohl (Philadelphia: Fortress Press, 1971).

On the issue of Paul's place of upbringing, see W. C. Van Unnick, *Tarsus or Jerusalem: The City of Paul's Youth*, trans. G. Ogg (London: Epworth Press, 1962). Paul's Hellenistic background is emphasized by Deissmann, *Paul*; A. J. Malherbe, "Hellenistic Moralists and the New Testament," in *ANRW*, forthcoming; W. Heitmueller, "Hellenistic Christianity Before Paul," in *The Writings of St. Paul*, ed. Meeks, 308–19; N. W. DeWitte, *St. Paul and Epicurus* (Minneapolis: Univ. of Minn. Press, 1954). The influence of Hellenistic Judaism is stressed by H.-J. Schoeps, *Paul: The Theology of the Apostle in the Light of Jewish Religious History*, trans. H. Knight (Philadelphia: Westminster Press, 1961), and S. Sandmel, *The Genius of Paul: A Study in History* (Philadelphia: Fortress Press, 1979 [1958]). The importance of apocalyptic categories is exploited by A. Schweitzer, *The Mysticism of Paul the Apostle* (New York: Seabury Press, 1931), and J. C. Beker, *Paul the Apostle: The Triumph of God in Life and Thought* (Philadelphia: Fortress Press, 1980). Paul's Pharisaic background is highlighted by W. D. Davies, *Paul and Rabbinic Judaism: Some Rabbinic Elements in Pauline Theology*, 4th ed. (Philadelphia: Fortress Press, 1980 [1948]), and E. P. Sanders, *Paul and Palestinian Judaism: A Comparison of Patterns of Religion* (Philadelphia: Fortress Press, 1977).

Helpful sketches of Paul's theological perspectives are found in H. N. Ridderbos, *Paul: An Outline of His Theology*, trans. S. R. Derrett (Grand Rapids: Wm. B. Eerdmans, 1975), and J. Fitzmyer, *Pauline Theology: A Brief Sketch* (Englewood Cliffs, N.J.: Prentice-Hall, 1967). For a full exposition of Pauline theology, the work of R. Bultmann, esp. *Theology of the New Testament*, vol. 1, trans. K. Grobel (New York: Charles Scribner's Sons, 1951), remains fundamental.

For the social dynamics of Paul's ministry, see E. A. Judge, "The Early Christians as a Scholastic Community," *Journal of Religious History* 1 (Sydney, 1960–61): 4–15, 125–37; A. J. Malherbe, *Social Aspects of Early Christianity*, 2d enl. ed. (Philadelphia: Fortress Press, 1983); W. A. Meeks, *The First Urban Christians: The Social World of the Apostle Paul* (New Haven: Yale Univ. Press, 1983); R. Hock, *The Social Context of Paul's Ministry: Tentmaking and Apostleship* (Philadelphia: Fortress Press, 1980); E. E. Ellis, "Paul and His Co-Workers," *NTS* 17 (1970–71): 437–52.

Discussion of the authenticity of specific Pauline letters will be found in the appropriate chapters. Here, one can simply note the quite different perspectives on the issue of style found in A. Q. Morton, "Statistical Analysis and New Testament Problems," in his *The Authorship and Integrity of the New Testament*, Theological Collections 4 (London: SPCK 1965), 40–60; and R. Longenecker, "Ancient Amanuenses and the Pauline Epistles," in *New Dimensions in New Testament Study*, ed. R. Longenecker and M. Tenney (Grand Rapids: Zondervan Pub. House, 1974), 281–97.

On the literary features of the Pauline letter, see W. G. Doty, "The Classification of Epistolary Literature," *CBQ* 31 (1969): 183–99; idem, *Letters in Primitive*

Christianity (Philadelphia: Fortress Press, 1973); N. A. Dahl, s.v. "Letter," IDBSup, 538–41; A. J. Malherbe, "Ancient Epistolary Theory," *Ohio Journal of Religious Studies* 5 (1977): 3–77; J. L. White, *The Body of the Greek Letter,* SBLDS 2 (Missoula, Mont: Scholars Press, 1972); P. Schubert, *The Form and Function of the Pauline Thanksgiving* (Berlin: Töpelmann, 1939); and P. T. O'Brien, *Introductory Thanksgivings in the Letters of Paul* (Leiden: E. J. Brill, 1977). A useful tool for the study of the formal aspects of Paul's letters is F. Francis and J. P. Sampley, eds., *Pauline Parallels,* 2d ed. (Philadelphia: Fortress Presss, 1984 [1975]).

11

1 and 2 Thessalonians

THE THESSALONIAN CORRESPONDENCE MARKS THE PROBABLE BEGINNING
of Christian literature. In these two short letters, we already find characteristic features of the Pauline mission and correspondence. Paul's overrid-
ing concern is the identity and integrity of the community. He writes
because he is not able personally to visit the church or because his
delegate's work needs further support. He needs to clarify misunderstanding or confront disaffection. We also find in this young community what
we discover elsewhere in churches founded by Paul: that an enthusiastic
reception of his message did not necessarily mean a thorough grasp of it.

Our sources give a fairly full picture of the events preceding the letters.
Paul was imprisoned in Philippi at the start of his first European campaign
(Acts 16:19–24; 1 Thess. 2:1–2). He then went to the capital city of
Macedonia, and proclaimed Jesus as Messiah in the Thessalonian synagogue (Acts 17:1–3). Some Jews were converted, but even more God-
fearing *(sebomenoi)* Greeks, together with "not a few" of the city's prominent women (Acts 17:4). This success stirred other Jews of the city to a
jealous rage; seeking Paul, they hauled the convert Jason and some others
to the city magistrates, charging Paul with treason in absentia because he
said, "Jesus is a king" (17:7). Paul was then sent by the community to
Beroea (17:10). There, he enjoyed further success until the enraged Jews
from Thessalonica came and again interfered (17:13). Paul left Timothy
and Silas there and went on to Athens (17:14–15). After a mixed reception
in that city, he went to Corinth, which became his new center of operations
(18:1–4; see esp. 18:11).

During his stay there, Silas and Timothy join him from Macedonia
(Acts 18:5). According to 1 Thess. 3:2–6, Paul had sent them to the
Thessalonians because of his anxiety for that community, and they had just
returned to him. The sending of delegates in this situation shows us the
function of Paul's emissaries. Timothy was sent "to establish you in your
faith and to exhort you" (3:2). These are exactly the goals Paul also hopes
to accomplish by his letter (see 3:13; 4:1). Because of the persecution

being experienced by this young church, Paul had feared that the tempter would seize the opportunity to sway them (3:5). Timothy's report gave Paul some reassurance, and he thanks God, "for we now live, if you stand fast in the Lord" (3:8). The real issue, we see, is stability in the face of oppression. Paul does not write his first Thessalonian letter in response to an acute crisis but he wants to give support to the work already done by Timothy, exhorting the Thessalonians "to live and please God just as you are doing" (4:1). Such support is all the more necessary since a harsh persecution can shake the convictions of a young and immature community.

The major point of confusion in the sources concerns the makeup of the church at Thessalonica. Acts tells us there were Greek converts but says the church contained Jews as well. Paul's conversion language in 1 Thess. 1:9–10, however, suggests a pagan, not Jewish, background: " . . . turning from idols to the living and true God." The Jews in 2:14 are spoken of in a manner suggesting that they are completely outsiders. The precise identity of the persecutors is also obscure. Acts makes it clear they are Jews. But 1 Thess. 2:14 says that the Thessalonians are suffering at the hands of their own countrymen *(tōn idiōn symphuletōn)*. This could mean Jews, if there were Jewish members of the community. But it could also mean Greeks, or simply fellow Macedonians. A decision would rest on whether or not one wanted to see the parallelism in 1 Thess. 2:14 between "your own countrymen" and "the Jews" (in Judea) as a contrast. The internal evidence strongly suggests a gentile majority in the community, with at best a Jewish minority. The issue is clouded by Acts' consistent concern for some success among the Jews in the Diaspora mission (see chap. 9, above).

FIRST THESSALONIANS

The agreement between the sources is far greater than the disagreement, and the neat fit keeps the authenticity of 1 Thessalonians free from serious challenge. The letter's structure is simple. A short, classic greeting (1:1) is followed by an extended thanksgiving (1:2—3:13). The thanksgiving passage is actually transformed into a long recollection of Paul's first preaching to this community and its response (1:6), returning to explicit prayer again only in 3:11–13. A series of moral exhortations (4:1—5:22) concludes with a prayer (5:23–24). The final greetings are general (5:25–27), and the farewell is short (5:28).

First Thessalonians has features resembling the Hellenistic epistolary form called the parenetic letter, though less impressively than 2 Timothy. The term "parenesis" means traditional "moral exhortation." It is sometimes used broadly of loosely arranged moral maxims. In a narrower sense, parenesis involves the interplay of three elements, which can be variously combined: memory, model, and maxims. Moral instruction was thought to be best accomplished by imitation of an example. The model was brought to life by memory, but since it was only an outline, it required filling out by means of maxims. These are often arranged antithetically, as in 1 Thess. 5:21–22: "Hold fast to what is good, abstain from every form of evil." The specific moral instructions begin in 4:1, but the elements of memory and model appear in the first three chapters.

The Self-Presentation of Paul

First Thessalonians is remarkable for its reminiscence of Paul's first preaching to the community. He reminds the Thessalonians of their beginnings, in order to strengthen their sense of identity. He recalls not only his manner of preaching but also their mode of response. In both, the distinctive Christian reshaping of symbols can be found.

Paul recalls his sojourn among the Thessalonians in terms similar to the self-characterization of wandering Hellenistic philosophers (e.g., Dio *Orations* 32.8–11, 35.8). He first contrasts himself to charlatans. Unlike them, he did not teach error, nor did he speak out of motives of uncleanness or guile (2:3). He was not out to flatter people or to get their money or to win their praise (2:5). He thus claims freedom from the three classic vices of charlatans: love of pleasure, love of possessions, and love of glory. Paul belonged to the tradition of philosophers who preached because of a divine call (see Dio *Orations* 13.9–10, 32.12), "not to please men but to please God who tests the hearts" (2:4). Paul also characterizes himself positively. He was "gentle as a nurse" among them (2:7). This phrase has two important aspects. The image of nurse coincides with the frequent understanding of philosophy as a spiritual medicine: healthy teaching cures the illness of the soul, which is vice (see chap. 1, above). Second, Paul's gentleness places him in a tradition unlike that of the harsh "surgical" methods of the Cynics, who called people to reform by reviling and vituperation. He was one who taught by positive example and instruction (see Dio *Oration* 77-78.38–45; Lucian *Demonax*).

Paul also calls himself a father to this church (2:11). He thereby establishes the accustomed social relationship for parenesis: the moral teacher stands in the place of a father with his children. Paul asserts this claim to a special authority with other churches as well (e.g., 1 Cor. 4:15). Finally, he presents himself as a model to the community: they are to imitate him (1:6). This has nothing to do with arrogance; such imitation is the normal mode of moral education in Paul's world. The Thessalonians also imitate the churches in Judea, insofar as they suffer like them (2:14). And they have become, in turn, examples to all the communities in Macedonia and Achaia, because of the way they accepted the gospel (1:7).

The message of Paul, Silas, and Timothy was not, however, simply another form of moral instruction; it was the word of God in power. They brought a message from God and about God (see the use of the phrase "gospel of God" in 2:2; 2:8; 2:9). Their proclamation did not simply express an abstract ideal; it was powerful and it could transform its hearers. It came to them "not only in word but also in power and in the Holy Spirit and with full conviction" (1:5). Paul rejoices that the Thessalonians recognized and accepted the gospel "not as the word of men, but as it really is, the word of God which is at work in you believers" (2:13). Paul and his fellow workers are therefore more than sophists and philosophers; they are "apostles of Christ" (2:6).

The Call of the Church

The "good news" from God is first of all that he has "called" these people "into his kingdom and glory" (2:12; cf. 4:7; 5:24). By his call, this segment of the world has become part of God's people: "He has chosen you" (1:4). The call of God demands a "turning" from their former way of life (4:7) to one appropriate to a world ruled by God. Before, they had been "those who do not know God" (4:5), those "without hope" (4:13), "sons of darkness who sleep in the day and are drunk at night" (5:7). Now, as the assembly of God (*ekklēsia tou theou;* 1:1; 2:14), they must "lead a life worthy of God" (2:12). Futhermore, since God is holy, they too are to be "established in holiness before God" (3:13), for "this is the will of God, your sanctification" (4:3). To be holy is to be different. God's holiness is marked by his complete difference from the world; what can be thought is not God. The task of the Thessalonians is to express their "differentness" behaviorally while remaining very much part of the world.

The norm is set by their first conversion, which established them as a community (1:9–10):

> You turned to God from idols, to serve a living and true God, and to wait for his Son from heaven, whom he raised from the dead, Jesus who delivers us from the wrath to come.

The kerygmatic statement establishes the framework for all of Paul's parenesis in this letter. The Thessalonians had turned their lives toward a "true" and "living" God. Their behavior, therefore, must be measured by God's own life. A share in this had in fact been given them by the power of the Holy Spirit. The gospel had been proclaimed in the power of this Holy Spirit (1:5) and had been received in the joy of the Holy Spirit (1:6). Whoever in the community, therefore, chooses not to live by this norm of holiness "disregards not man but God, who gives his Holy Spirit to you" (4:8). Their lives are to manifest this life and power and not stifle the work of the Spirit (5:19).

Living by such a measure inevitably involves affliction (*thlipsis*). Obedience to God is difficult, the turn from death to life painful. But more than that, in a world of falsehood and death, allegiance to a transcendent truth and life is threatening, leading almost inevitably to rejection and persecution: "You received the word in much affliction" (1:6). The Thessalonians suffered at the hands of their neighbors as the Judean churches were persecuted by "the Jews" (2:14). One should note that Paul uses the distancing term "Jews" in just this context, although he ordinarily avoids such usage (but cf. 1 Cor. 1:22–23; 2 Cor. 11:24; Gal. 2:13). Paul warned them from the beginning that this would happen: "We told you beforehand that we were to suffer affliction, just as it has come to pass, and as you know" (3:4). In this, too, they have an example in Paul (2:15–16) and above all "in the Lord Jesus and the prophets," who were killed for speaking God's word (2:15).

Life Between Times

The Thessalonians' suffering stemmed in part from the tension created by the distance between their convictions and their circumstances. They knew that they were beloved by God and chosen by him (1:4). They knew that Jesus was raised from the dead and would deliver them from the wrath to come (1:10). But the deliverance had not visibly occurred, and the wrath seemed to be very much on them (2:16). They seemed to be more under the promise than within the fulfillment (5:9–10):

> God has not destined us for wrath but to obtain salvation through our Lord Jesus Christ, so that whether we wake or sleep we live with him.

The last part of this conviction—that awake or asleep they lived with Christ—was exactly what those in the Thessalonian church did not grasp. Paul must therefore pay particular attention to their shaken confidence in the triumph of God, caused by the death of some community members.

Paul's initial preaching may, as in other cases, have helped create the problem. On the evidence, this was a young community, only recently turned from paganism. When Paul promised that they would wait "for his son from heaven" (1:10), they apparently understood this climactic triumph to happen *very soon*, surely in their lifetime. But now, some in the community have died. They may even have been killed in the persecution. Have they missed out on the full realization of the kingdom? It would seem so, if the revelation of God's power was future only, and not already present. Because those who died apparently missed out on the "not yet," the members of the community mourned, forgetting their more significant participation in the "already" of God.

Paul responds to the problem at three levels. First, he sketches a picture of the end time (4:16–18) that makes clear that those already dead will not in any way be disadvantaged at the coming of the Lord. Second, he warns that the time of this coming is not a matter of timetables or calculation but is in God's hands (5:1–3). But Paul's third point is the most important for him. The crisis in the community arose only because its members had forgotten a fundamental part of their identity. The essential victory over death and evil had *already* been won in the resurrection of Jesus. In it, God already showed himself triumphant. The God who raised Jesus to life is not a powerless projection of human desires, like idols, but a "living and true God" (1:9–10). The God preached by Paul lives. The members mourning for the dead is therefore both a loss of hope and a fall from faith.

The Christian identity of the members of the Thessalonian assembly was shaken, since they were responding like those outside the distinctive understanding of God gained by the resurrection of Jesus. Those who "did not know God" in this way lived in the world "with no hope," for their gods were dead. But those who had come to know the God who raised Jesus from the dead had hope rooted in reality. They knew that just as he had raised Jesus, so could he also raise them to life: "God will bring with him those who have fallen asleep" (4:14). The timing may be uncertain, but the outcome is sure: "We shall always be with the Lord" (4:17).

Paul does not use eschatological language for its own sake but to serve as a support to exhortation. Paul wants the Thessalonians to live appropriately within this in-between time. Their lives should be filled with alertness and watchfulness (5:5–10). They are not to be on the lookout for an external event—like trying to spy a thief creeping up in the night (5:2)—but are to be attentive to the transcendental measure of their existence as people called by God. In a series of contrasts stereotypical both for moral and eschatological discourse in his world, Paul opposes the life symbolized by darkness, night, sleep, and drunkenness—a life of oblivion and forgetfulness—to the life symbolized by the light, day, wakefulness, and sobriety, that is, a life lived on eschatological edge (5:4–9). This contrast, in turn, points to the exchange worked by God in the death and resurrection of Jesus, "who died for us, so that whether we wake or sleep, we might live with him" (5:10). This reversal was possible, finally, only because the power with which Christians have to do is that not of human projection but of the living God (1:9–10).

But what does Christian existence look like during this in-between time? How is watchfulness behaviorally expressed? Perhaps surprisingly, Paul's moral exhortations are not in the least innovative. He explicitly calls them traditions in which the Thessalonians have already been instructed (4:1–2; 11). We may have here, indeed, elements of an early Christian catechism. Certainly, the exhortations that spell out implications of holiness resemble the moral standards of Hellenistic Judaism. This is hardly surprising, since the primitive Christian communities existed in exactly the same

Diaspora context. They too had to work out the meaning of being God's chosen people in a pluralistic setting and to decide how to live within worldly structures without being utterly defined by them.

Paul exhorts the Thessalonian assembly to abstain from sexual immorality. As they had turned from idols to the living God, so must their behavior also turn from the "passion of lust like heathen who do not know God" (4:5). The proper context for sexual activity is a chaste marriage; adultery wrongs a brother and breaks covenant (4:6). This sexual ethic is not extraordinary. What is striking is the way Paul invokes the divine retribution: the community lives under the judgment of God (4:6–8).

Since they have turned from the ethos of the outside world, they require strong positive attitudes toward other members of the church. Paul praises them for their brotherly love (*philadelphia*). They have been taught it by God (4:9–10). Do we have here (as in 4:15) a memory of the teaching of Jesus? Paul also gives advice that was advanced by other philosophers of his age, notably the Epicureans, when he tells the Thessalonians to "live quietly, mind your own affairs, and work with your hands" (4:11). Avoidance of political activity in part strengthens the cohesion of the community and in part assures outsiders that they have nothing to fear from the church (4:12). Paul emphasizes the need for mutual edification: "Comfort one another with these words" (4:18), and "Encourage one another, and build one another up, just as you are doing" (5:11; cf. 5:14). As an intentional community, the church lives by mutual confirmation of its shared knowledge and convictions. Leaders are to be esteemed (5:12), and the community is to live at peace (5:13).

The same tone of sober reasonableness governs Paul's remarks on the working of the Spirit in prayer and prophecy. The Spirit is not to be quenched and prophecy is not to be despised, but everything is to be tested (5:21). The pertinence of this will be apparent when we turn to 2 Thessalonians. The community is responsible to God for its life during the in-between time. Its eschatological tension should lead not to an obsessive reading of signs but to a calm community life. Within the period between Jesus' resurrection and the final triumph of God, this people still needs to "hold fast to what is good and abstain from every form of evil" (5:21–22).

SECOND THESSALONIANS

Second Thessalonians is sometimes considered inauthentic, although it is difficult to make that case convincing. There is no problem placing the letter in Paul's career; the internal evidence presupposes a situation naturally following upon that of the first letter. The style is so close to that of 1 Thessalonians that the argument against authenticity must claim a direct and deliberate imitation of that letter. Second Thessalonians explicitly bears the personal signature of Paul as a mark of authenticity (3:17), an emphasis understandable in context (see 2:2). Those otherwise convinced of the letter's pseudonymous character, of course, see this validation as a sign of forgery. Paul is less gentle toward opponents than one might like (2 Thess. 1:6–9; 2:10–12) but not less gentle than in some other letters (cf. 1 Thess. 2:15–16). The only real difficulty concerns consistency in content. The description of the end time in 2 Thessalonians is thought by some to contradict that in 1 Thess. 4:13—5:3, especially since it seems to imply a schedule of events whereas 1 Thessalonians explicitly eschews any set sequence. There is unquestionably some difference between the two eschatological accounts. They are best understood, however, as successive responses by a pastor to stages in a community's panic rather than the subtle calibrations of a systematic theologian. The suggested reasons for a pseudepigrapher's imitating the first letter so closely and yet altering it so subtly, some generations later, are quite unconvincing.

The structure of 2 Thessalonians is not unusual. The short, unadorned greeting (1:1–2) is followed by an equally short thanksgiving (1:3–4), which, as in 1 Thessalonians, shifts imperceptibly into the body of the letter (1:5—2:12). A second thanksgiving passage (2:13–17) becomes a request for mutual prayer and support (3:1–5). A series of rather sharp exhortations (3:6–15) concludes with a prayer (3:16), the signature (3:17), and farewell (3:18).

The Crisis

The tone of 2 Thessalonians is definitely sharper than that of the first letter. The persecution is spoken of in more explicit terms (1:3–5). The judgment awaiting the persecutors is more dramatic (1:6–9). People in the community who have left their normal occupations are severely rebuked: "If anyone will not work, let him not eat" (3:10). Disobedience to the letter's instructions make one liable to shunning by other community members, so that the deviant might be made to conform (3:14–15). The letter indeed appears to be responding to a crisis.

The nature of the crisis is suggested by 2 Thess. 2:1–2:

> Now concerning the coming of our Lord Jesus Christ and our assembling to meet him, we beg you, brethren, not to be quickly shaken in mind or excited, either by spirit or word, or by letter purporting to be from us, to the effect that the day of the Lord has come.

The church is in a state of panic, thinking that the end time is upon them. Some have dropped their work altogether, devoting themselves to waiting for Jesus to come, in an event they apparently expect very soon. But why should they have thought the end so imminent? Three things have contributed to shaping the crisis: the immaturity of the community, Paul's instructions in 1 Thessalonians, and the classic apocalyptic scenario of the end time. To this already volatile mixture was added an intensification of the church's suffering through persecution: the crisis is catalyzed.

Paul, we remember, had used the term "affliction," *thlipsis*, in reference to the persecution the Thessalonians were enduring (1 Thess. 1:6; 3:3–4, 7). He also associates with their suffering the term "wrath," *orgē* (1 Thess. 1:10; 2:16; 5:9). Both terms were part of the apocalyptic end-time scenario. The Day of Affliction was sometimes thought to be the cataclysmic suffering by the saints that would usher in the definitive intervention of God (see, e.g., Dan. 12:1; *1 Enoch* 45.2; 48.8; 50.2; Matt. 24:21, 29; Mark 13:19, 24). The suffering is combined with persecution *(diōgmos)* in Matt. 13:21 and Mark 4:17 (see also Rom. 2:9, 8:35; Rev. 1:9; 2:9–10; 7:14). The term "wrath" could likewise point to the coming of God for judgment, as Paul elsewhere employs it (see Rom. 2:5; 5:9; Rev. 6:17; 14:10). For those already confused concerning when "the Son from heaven" would come to relieve them from their suffering and bring them salvation (1 Thess. 1:10), the temptation would be great to see in every increment of persecution the final progress of affliction toward that climactic moment.

The advice Paul gave in 1 Thessalonians would not have turned them definitively from that temptation. In his brief sketch of the Lord's coming (4:13—5:3), he assured them that all would be saved, and thus relieved them of their concern for their dead. But when he refused to give a timetable for the end and only called for alertness and watchfulness, he fed a preoccupation that apparently was already well established. What Paul meant by watchfulness, as we have seen, was a steady attentiveness to life in the community according to the measure of God's holiness. But the members of the community could easily have heard it as an encouragement for an increased obsession with the time of the thief's coming. No sleep or rest for them, no ordinary toil of life to distract them. They would give up all their activity and devote themselves to just this one thing.

If we imagine a group seized with such a conviction, gathered in assembly where there is prophetic utterance, it is easy to see how a "word of the Lord" or even a "spirit letter" from Paul (see Rev. 2:1—3:22) could precipitate a panic with the pronouncement "The end is upon us; the affliction has reached its outermost extreme; the Son of man is coming on the clouds." Such a catalyst seems presupposed by Paul's reference to their being shaken "by spirit or word or by letter purporting to be from us" (2:2). The effect of the pronouncement was to throw this fragile church into a deeper crisis than that posed by the death of its members; now its very life had ground to a halt.

The Time Before the End

Once more, Paul responds to the crisis in three steps. First, he reaffirms a basic understanding that he shares with the community's members: this intense affliction will lead to their salvation and to the punishment of their oppressors (1:6–10). But Paul subtly alters their perception of this reality. He shows them that the affliction is not simply an external fact to be endured but is a positive factor in the strengthening of their identity. It enables them to grow in faith and love (1:3), in steadfastness and endurance (1:4; cf. Rom. 5:1–5). They suffer for the kingdom of God (1:5), and the affliction makes them worthy of that kingdom (1:5, 11). Their experience leads to the goal that "the name of Jesus Christ might be glorified in you, *and you in him*" (1:12). As in his first letter, Paul calls them back to a sense of their identity. He insists that the in-between time is not empty but is a period during which the work of God and their lives are inextricably connected. What they experience is already a glorification of God and a preparation for his rule.

Second, Paul corrects the narrowness of the Thessalonians' vision. Their local affliction is not necessarily the climax to world history. More is at stake in God's work than their experience. Paul reminds them that he had already touched on this when he was with them (2:5). They are freed from preoccupation about the coming of the end, for its advent will be unmistakable. Paul does not really give here a schedule for the end. Rather, he suggests factors that traditional apocalyptic expectation say must be in place before the grand reversal can occur: the reign of lawlessness will be personified in a "son of perdition" who as a minion of Satan (2:9) will claim divine status and seek a place in the temple (2:4) and by working signs and wonders (2:9) will lead all the wicked astray (2:10–12). He will be destroyed by the coming of the Lord (2:8). The effect of this panoply is a simple point: the end will be more cosmic than the persecution of a single Thessalonian church.

Paul says that the general period of the lawless one's dominance has begun (2:7), so they are in time of the end but they are not at the climax. Indeed, Paul refers in 2:7 to a person or thing that is keeping the whole process in check: the restrainer *(ho katechōn)*. Nothing is murkier than apocalyptic, and this passage is no exception. We no longer know what some of Paul's terms meant or to what events or persons he alluded. Some have suggested that the restrainer was the Roman Empire; others that it was God; others, that Paul's own ministry was conceived by him as holding back the final retribution. Without further information, we will not know. The pastoral intent of the passage, on the other hand, seems clear: Paul wants to move the Thessalonians away from self-preoccupation and obsession about the end. Far from giving them further signs to discern, he deflects them from that enterprise by suggesting an indefinite period that must be endured. The work of the restrainer could last any length of time. Their vocation is not to drop everything and wait at the windows for the possible coming of a thief.

Third, Paul tries to direct their attention away from apocalyptic scenarios to their own lives. He suggests their proper focus in two prayers. In the first, he asks ". . . that God may fulfill every good resolve and work of faith by his power" (1:11), and in the second, he prays, "May our Lord . . . comfort your hearts and establish them in every good work and word" (2:17). Paul also expresses hopeful "confidence in the Lord about you, that you are doing, and will do, the things which we command" (3:4). The first thing required is that the members of the assembly attend to their own identity: "May the Lord direct your hearts to the love of God and the steadfastness of Christ" (3:5). To this end, Paul sharply rebukes those who have given up their worldly occupations, telling them to get back to work (3:6–12). And he warns others to avoid people who have stopped their normal lives. Why? Because for those already shaky in their grasp of Christian identity, such influence will be harmful. In his exhortation to work, Paul presents himself as a model of one working with his hands. He strikes a note (3:9) we will see again in the Corinthian correspondence:

It was not because we did not have that right [to support] but to give you in your conduct an example to imitate.

As in his first letter, Paul sees the time between the resurrection and the second coming not as one of meaningless waiting but as a time enriched by the presence of the Lord through the Holy Spirit, shaped by his call to holiness (2:13). His harsh demands for obedience and community pressure on deviance (2:3; 3:6; 3:14–15) stem from a fear that the very identity of this immature community is threatened by external oppression and internal misunderstanding. Paul reminds them as he had done before that even when part of the great eschatological drama, the call of God is simple: "Brethren, do not weary in well-doing" (3:13).

BIBLIOGRAPHICAL NOTE

The most useful studies of 1 Thessalonians as a parenetic letter are A. J. Malherbe, "Gentle as a Nurse," *NovT* 12 (1970): 203–17; and idem, "Exhortation in First Thessalonians," *NovT* 25 (1983): 238–55. See also idem, "Ancient Epistolary Theorists," *Ohio Journal of Religious Studies* 5 (1977): 3–77. Formal elements of the letter are discussed in H. Koester, "I Thessalonians—Experiment in Christian Writing," in *Continuity and Discontinuity in Church History* (Leiden: E. J. Brill, 1979), 33–44; and H. Boers, "The Form-Critical Study of Paul's Letters: I Thessalonians as a Test Case," *NTS* 22 (1975): 140–58.

Interpolation of the anti-Jewish sentiment in 2:13–16 is argued by B. A. Pearson, "I Thess 2:13–16: A Deutero-Pauline Interpolation," *HTR* 64 (1971): 79–94; and D. Schmidt, "I Thess 2:13–16: Linguistic Evidence for an Interpolation," *JBL* 102 (1983): 269–79. Further fragmentation is accomplished by

W. Schmithals, *Paul and the Gnostics*, trans. J. Steely (Nashville: Abingdon Press, 1972), 123–218.

Not surprisingly, the eschatology of 1 Thessalonians receives a disproportionate amount of attention. Useful discussions are found in C. L. Mearns, "Early Eschatological Development in Paul: The Evidence of First and Second Thessalonians," *NTS* 27 (1980): 137–57; R. N. Longenecker, "The Nature of Paul's Early Eschatology," *NTS* 31 (1985): 85–95; B. N. Kaye, "Eschatology and Ethics in First and Second Thessalonians," *NovT* 17 (1975): 47–57; J. H. Neyrey, "Eschatology in I Thess: The Theological Factor in 1:9–10; 2:4–5; 3:11–13; 4:6; and 4:13–18," in *SBL Seminar Papers 1980*, ed. P. J. Achtemeier (Chico, Calif.: Scholars Press, 1980), 219–31; C. F. D. Moule, "The Influence of Circumstances on Paul's Eschatology," *JTS* n.s. 15 (1964): 1–15; J. Plevnik, "The Taking Up of the Faithful and the Resurrection of the Dead in I Thessalonians 4:13–18," *CBQ* 46 (1984): 274–83; J. Gillman, "Signals of Transformation in I Thessalonians 4:13–18," *CBQ* 47 (1985): 263–81; and W. A. Meeks, "Social Functions of Apocalyptic Language in Pauline Christianity," in *Apocalypticism in the Mediterranean World and the Near East*, ed. D. Hellholm (Tübingen: J. C. B. Mohr [Paul Siebeck], 1983), 687–705.

Other features of 1 Thessalonians are touched on by I. H. Marshall, "Pauline Theology in the Thessalonian Correspondence," in *Paul and Paulinism*, ed. M. D. Hooker and S. G. Wilson (London: SPCK, 1982), 173–83; J. Munck, "I Thess 1:9–10 and the Missionary Preaching of Paul," *NTS* 9 (1962–63): 95–110; D. M. Stanley, "'Become Imitators of Me': The Pauline Conception of Apostolic Tradition," *Bib* 40 (1959): 859–77.

A representative discussion of the inauthenticity of 2 Thessalonians is by J. A. Bailey, "Who Wrote II Thessalonians?" *NTS* 25 (1978–79): 131–45. The peculiar problems presented by its eschatology are treated by J. Townsend, "II Thessalonians 2:3–12," in *SBL Seminar Papers 1980*, ed. Achtemeier, 233–46; C. H. Giblin, *The Threat to Faith: An Exegetical and Theological Re-Examination of II Thess. 2*, AB 31 (Rome: Biblical Inst. Press, 1967); and J. M. Bassler, "The Enigmatic Sign: 2 Thessalonians 1:5," *CBQ* 46 (1984): 496–510. For some of the background to Paul's statements on manual labor, see R. F. Hock, "The Workshop as a Social Setting for Paul's Missionary Preaching," *CBQ* 41 (1979): 438–50. Surely the most positive use made of 2 Thessalonians for the construal of Paul's theology and his understanding of his mission is that found in J. Munck, *Paul and the Salvation of Mankind*, trans. F. Clarke (Richmond: John Knox Press, 1959), 36–68.

There remains a need for a contemporary critical commentary on the Thessalonian letters in English. In the meantime, the two most serviceable are those of E. Best, *The First and Second Epistles to the Thessalonians*, HNTC (New York: Harper & Row, 1972), and F. F. Bruce, *1 & 2 Thessalonians*, Word Biblical Commentary (Waco, Tex.: Word Books, 1982).

12

The Corinthian Correspondence

OUR KNOWLEDGE OF EARLIEST CHRISTIANITY WOULD BE CONSIDERABLY diminished without Paul's two Letters to the Corinthians. We find in them a portrait of a community whose life together was a mixture of confusion, pettiness, and ambition, as well as enthusiasm and fervor. The community struggled to define its identity as the church of God in a complex and sophisticated urban setting. The letters also show us Paul's relationship with a beloved but refractory community founded by him, which forced him to expose both himself and his self-understanding as an apostle. We are thus enabled to meet here Paul the pastor, the father of a community.

The Corinthians first faced the problems that have proved to be perennial for all Christian communities: how to live in holiness and freedom within the very real structures of a given social world. They met these issues in culturally conditioned cases: Could they eat meat offered to idols? Could their women wear veils while prophesying? Those ancient cultural dilemmas, however, provide structural analogies to situations faced by churches in every generation. In this correspondence, we discover the difficulty of defining an identity within a pluralistic context. Rather than the specific conclusions offered by Paul, it is his way of thinking about these issues and the principles he invokes that remain of contemporary interest.

THE CHURCH AND THE CORRESPONDENCE

The restored city of Corinth was the capital of Achaia, a port city with harbors to the east, at Cenchrae, and to the north. It hosted a large transient population, which typically brought its cults as well as its trades to the city. Archaeology confirms the presence of both synagogue and Isis shrine. Like most ports ancient and modern, Corinth enjoyed a reputation for sexual immorality. It was, in short, the New Orleans of ancient Achaia.

Paul founded Christianity there (1 Cor. 4:15). The evidence of Acts is generally confirmed by that in the letters. Paul came to Corinth from

Athens and met Aquila and Priscilla (see 1 Cor. 16:19), who had recently been expelled from Rome with other Jews by Claudius (Acts 18:2). Paul joined them in tentmaking and preached in the synagogue. Rejected there (18:6) and rejoined by his Macedonian delegates (1 Thess. 3:6), Paul moved next door to the house of Titus Justus. He converted the ruler of the synagogue, Crispus (18:8; cf. 1 Cor. 1:14) and stayed in Corinth some eighteen months (18:11). During that period, he was brought before Gallio (18:12). When the proconsul dismissed the case, the Jews beat Sosthenes. Acts calls Sosthenes a "ruler of the synagogue" (18:17). He appears as their "brother" and Paul's co-writer in 1 Cor. 1:1.

When Paul left Corinth to return to Antioch, he stopped at Cenchrae to shave his head, and he took Aquila and Priscilla with him as far as Ephesus (18:18–21). In his absence, they encounter the charismatic Apollos in Ephesus (18:24–28), convert and instruct him and send him to Achaia (19:1). Apollos worked in Corinth, therefore, after Paul. Acts gives special attention to his eloquence (18:24), and Apollos plays a significant role in the life of the Corinthian church (1 Cor. 1:12; 3:4–7, 21–23; 4:6; 16:12).

In Acts 19:21–22, we find Paul planning to return to Macedonia and Achaia before going to Jerusalem and then Rome (1 Cor. 16:5; 2 Cor. 1:15). One of his delegates at that point is Erastus, identified in Rom. 16:23 as treasurer of the city (cf. 2 Tim. 4:20). Paul then spends three months in Achaia before departing for Macedonia (Acts 20:3). The letters basically agree with this sketch, but fill it out considerably with frequent visits by Paul and his delegates Timothy and Titus (1 Cor. 2:1; 4:19; 16:3–10; 2 Cor. 1:15; 8:6; 9:3; 12:14). Paul also wrote the letters to the Thessalonians and Romans from this city.

The church had members from both Jewish and gentile backgrounds. The issues treated in the first letter highlight the difficulties of former pagans, but the overarching symbolism by which the whole community understood itself came from Torah (see esp. 1 Cor. 10:1–13). The community also had a mixed social background. Paul says, "Not many of you were of noble birth" (1 Cor. 1:26), but some enjoyed a more prominent status than others—for example, Erastus (Rom. 16:23) and the heads of households where the community assembled (1 Cor. 1:11, 16; 16:15–17). One cause of strife in the young church came from the diverse social origins, expectations, and perspectives that were carried over from the world into the assembly of God.

The Corinthians' faults came from over-enthusiasm, not tepidity. Impressed by the powers given them by the Spirit (1:5–7), they were less concerned with understanding them (2:12) than with using them. They were fascinated by the specious and spectacular. Although restive under Paul's guidance, they were very much a Pauline church in that they reduced to slogans and catchwords (see 6:12–13; 7:1; 8:1; 14:22) some distinctive elements of his gospel. Paul had the uncomfortable task of reaffirming his premises while trying to lead them to better conclusions.

A form of spiritual elitism infected the community. Some were so awed by their new knowledge and freedom and capacities for ecstatic speech that they considered themselves fully mature, perfect (2:6—3:4). They tended to judge each other and even their mentors (4:1–5); at the same time, they neglected the moral demands of their calling (5:1—6:20). These tendencies seem to have been rooted in an understanding of the resurrection that stressed its present power within them but denied its completion in a future life; they had no need of transformation, for they enjoyed the life of glory now. They collapse the delicate tension between the "already" and the "not yet," by regarding themselves as already rich and ruling in God's kingdom (4:8). Such attitudes are also found in varieties of Gnosticism, which became a recognizable Christian variant in the second century C.E. Ideas like those of the Corinthians were developed in later gnostic texts. Congregations like this one, indeed, may have provided the connection between a diffused dualistic malaise and later Gnosticism. We find here, however, only the possible first seeds of that astonishing many-branched growth.

Spiritual elitism led to factionalism. The Corinthians tended to define themselves by their differences rather than by their common life. From the beginning of 1 Corinthians, we find groups identifying themselves by their allegiance to a particular apostle—"I belong to Paul," "I belong to Apollos," "I belong to Cephas"—or claiming the need of no teacher at all: "I belong to Christ" (1:12). Much scholarship has been devoted to these groups as representatives of competing factions within earliest Christianity—Jewish-Christian against gentile Christian, for example. Little in the letters supports such hypotheses. Not even in 2 Corinthians, where disputes between teachers become explicit, does any teaching show a clear delineation of disparate factions. Paul certainly does not align himself with a Pauline group but rejects such groups entirely, asserting his role as teacher of the whole community (4:14–21). The factions, in fact, may have been spontaneous creations of the circumstances leading to the first letter.

The canonical collection contains two Letters to the Corinthians. Paul's correspondence with this church, however, was considerably more extensive. It involved five and possibly more letters: (1) Paul alludes in 1 Cor. 5:9 to an earlier letter, now either lost or, as some think, found in 2 Cor. 6:14—7:1. (2) In 1 Cor. 7:1, Paul refers to a letter full of questions written to him by the Corinthians. (3) He writes 1 Corinthians—the unity of this letter is sometimes questioned but without cause—in response to their questions and other problems in the church. (4) Paul mentions in 2 Cor. 2:4 a "letter in tears," now lost, or found in 2 Corinthians 10—13, or simply identical with 1 Corinthians. (5) Paul wrote 2 Corinthians, which may be not a literary unity but an edited composite of several notes. The most significant aspect of this sequence is the testimony it offers, confirmed by the frequent personal visits of Paul and his delegates, to his close and careful concern for his communities. It is no accident that the Corinthian correspondence is extraordinarily lively, for the relationship that generated it was genuinely alive.

THE FIRST LETTER TO THE CORINTHIANS

After Paul left Corinth, problems developed concerning the maintenance of community boundaries: some in the church thought they could continue their former associations and practices. Even after Paul wrote a first note warning them not to associate with immoral people (1 Cor. 5:9), the situation was not resolved. Relations within the community were strained because of the diverse approaches to moral behavior. At this point, some wanted to ask Paul's advice (see 7:1). This suggestion, however, did not meet unanimous approval. Why should they turn to Paul? What authority did he possess? Was he an original apostle like Cephas (1:12; 9:5), or a great preacher like Apollos (1:12; 2:1)? Why not turn to them for guidance? The need for definitive advice brought already latent allegiances and disaffections into the open.

At least some in the community decided to send Paul a letter asking advice on the disputed issues. It may have been delivered by Stephanus, Fortunatus, and Achaichus (16:17), or by the domestic servants of Chloe (1:11). "Chloe's people" in any case brought Paul news of further developments: how some were flagrantly sinning, some were initiating lawsuits against others in the community, and some questioned Paul's authority to teach them. If Paul hoped to instruct them, therefore, and correct their distorted perceptions, he first had to reestablish his credibility as father of this community.

The outline of the letter corresponds to this sequence of events. After the greeting (1:1–3) and thanksgiving (1:4–9), Paul immediately turns to the divisions within the community, and reminds its members forcefully of his own authority to teach (chaps. 1—4). Next, he deals with the problems reported to him orally: sexual immorality and litigation in pagan courts (chaps. 5—6). Paul then treats the questions posed by their letter, dealing in turn with virginity and marriage (chap. 7), food offered to idols (chaps. 8—10), and problems in worship (chaps. 11—14). In chap. 15, he provides the theological teaching on the resurrection, which undergirds his treatment of specific issues. Finally, Paul raises his personal project, the collection of money for the saints in Jerusalem (16:1–4).

The Church of God (1 Corinthians 1—4)

Paul anticipates his basic message to the Corinthians already in the greeting. They are "sanctified in Christ Jesus [*hēgiasmenoi*]," but they are also "called to be saints [*klētoi hagioi*]" (1:2). Throughout the letter, Paul affirms their gifts but insists that they contain a mandate: the Holy Spirit, which enlivens them, must also lead to their behavioral transformation. Likewise in the thanksgiving, Paul acknowledges that they have been "enriched" with every spiritual mode of speech and knowledge. He then prays that the gift that has been made "secure" among them might remain secure but also "blameless" until the end (or, until they become perfect) "in the day of our Lord Jesus Christ" (1:4–8). The eschatological reference is deliberate: God's kingdom has not yet been fully accomplished; neither, therefore, can they yet be perfect. When Paul tells them in 4:8, "Already you have been filled, already you are rich, already apart from us you have come into your kingdom," he is sarcastic: their "rule" is illusory. The last verse of the thanksgiving sets the proper perspective: they have been called into a fellowship with Jesus. Neither the call nor the growth is their own doing, but both are the work of God, who is faithful (1:9). Fellowship with Jesus means conformity to his measure; the place where this happens is the church of God.

Although they were called into a fellowship (*koinōnia*) with Jesus, they are in fact destroying that unity by their factiousness. Paul exhorts them therefore to have the same mind (*nous*) and judgment (*gnōmē*) among themselves (1:10). Paul means something more here than mere unanimity. The same mind they should have is that formed by the one with whom they have been joined; they should have the "mind of Christ" (2:16). Their party spirit has "divided Christ" (1:13). Factions and rivalries are characteristic of human gatherings in which people define themselves by their knowledge, power, or prestige. In God's church, such measurings do not apply.

Their calling is not an invitation to a club or a cultic association, which would demand of them allegiance to their patron or mystagogue (see 1:13–14). Those are the perceptions of the world and not of the gospel. The Corinthians have been called into God's convocation (*ekklēsia*), in an invitation and command apart from natural abilities or predilections. God's call transcends human status (1:26), exceeds human strength (1:25), and confounds human wisdom (1:18). It is a call that reverses all human norms, for it is based not on the persuasiveness of human rhetoric but on the preaching of the cross (1:17). The identity of the church is indelibly marked by the one who remains scandal to the Jews and fool to Gentiles (1:18–23). Even to accept this invitation means to regard the measure of the world as inadequate for one who is "the power of God, the wisdom of God" (1:24).

Life in the church therefore demands measuring all of reality in a new way: not by the "wisdom of this age" (2:6) but by the "secret and hidden wisdom of God" (2:7). This wisdom is not the revelation of esoteric cosmic realities but a profound, even connatural, learning of the ways of the Spirit's working among the people (2:12). Those who use spiritual realities as a means of self-aggrandizement are not really spiritual people but immature (3:1). Those who truly have "the mind of Christ" (2:16) and know even the depths of God (2:10) have learned to use these gifts appropriately for the building up of God's community in the world.

So far from being rivals, Paul and Apollos together provide an example of the attitudes the Corinthians should have toward the community (4:6). They have each been given a separate function by the Lord, but both regard themselves as servants (3:5) and fellow workers (3:9) who cooperate in their efforts, knowing that "God gives the growth" (3:6). So also the Corinthians should not "be puffed up in favor of one against another" (4:6), lest they forget that everything they have comes as gift (4:7). If they treat the church as though it were simply a human institution, they profane and destroy the temple of God, because this community lives not by contract but by the life breath of the Holy Spirit (3:16–17). Paul therefore concludes (3:21–23):

> Let no one boast of men. For all things are yours, whether Paul or Apollos or Cephas or the world, or life or death or the present or the future, all are yours; and you are Christ's; and Christ is God's.

Although Paul is only a servant and workman, he has been given a special role in the Corinthian community; it was his task to "plant" (3:6) and to "lay the foundation" (3:10). He is more than a pedagogue; since he gave this community its birth through the preaching of the Gospel, he deserves to be regarded as its father (4:15). And as a father, it is his responsibility to instruct the community in morals. He will therefore, despite the Corinthians' reluctance, teach them both by his words and by his example: "I urge you then, be imitators of me" (4:16).

The Church in the World
(1 Corinthians 5—10)

The "mind of Christ" must be applied to the very real problems of life in a pluralistic society. Like Jews of the Diaspora, the Corinthians are pulled between the movements of separation and assimilation. Paul insists on the need for separation from the world's values; there must be real boundaries between the inside and the outside. But he denies the need to withdraw from society into alternative structures. The church is to be holy or it is not God's people but is only another part of the world. The church's holiness, however, is found not in flight from, but rather in a quality of life within, the structures of the world. Paul leaves much ambiguous at the level of directive, for he wants the Corinthians to learn to think; they must "understand their gifts" (2:12) within the context of society and the community.

Paul's advice must move in a delicate space between two extreme tendencies in the congregation. Both wanted to avoid ambiguity and thought, by reducing norms to slogans. Some pushed Paul's gospel of freedom to a virtual antinomianism: "All things are lawful for me" (6:12). For them, spiritual identity is secure and unassailable; material and social realities are strictly irrelevant: "Food for the stomach, the stomach for food" (6:13). They put great store in their knowledge—"All of us possess knowledge" (8:1)—and considered their spiritual state to be sufficiently secure to enable them to engage the world indiscriminately. Paul calls them the strong (4:10; 10:22); they tended to be arrogant and contemptuous of those who worried about behavioral norms to safeguard identity, the weak (8:7–10). The weak were convinced that Christian identity was fragile and required definite social practices different from those of society. Sexual activity should be distinctive and radical: "It is good not to touch a woman" (7:1). Food and drink could contaminate; better to maintain a diet that did not involve contact with pagan practices (10:28).

Paul agrees intellectually with the position of the strong. His bias is always for freedom. But his understanding of this freedom or power (*exousia*) is different. If one's identity is secure, it is because it is based in God (1:6), not in one's own accomplishments. It is not that the Christians have come to know God but that God has known them, which has given them freedom (8:1–3; 13:12). In this sense, "food will not commend us to God" (8:8). But the strong are naive about the social dimensions of human existence; spiritual life does involve physical entanglements. In fact, their vaunted freedom and knowledge have led to a neglect of others. They have become spiritual solipsists and have forgotten they are part of a community. Rather than boast of their superiority, they should build up the weak. Paul's focus is always the community. The primary gift of the Spirit is love (13:1–13); its main manifestation is the building up (*oikodomē*) of others in faith and understanding (8:1, 10; 10:23; 14:3, 12).

The Holiness of the Church (5:1—6:20)

When Paul turns to the problems reported by Chloe's people, his basic principles are clear. The church must maintain its integrity. Since the people have been "washed . . . sanctified . . . justified in the name of the Lord Jesus Christ and in the Spirit of our God" (6:11b), they can no longer live by their former standards (6:9–11a). But unless they are to go out of the world altogether—an option Paul does not recommend—they must continue to associate with those who do not share their perceptions

(5:9–10). The community must therefore exercise discernment in its internal life. Its task is not judging apostles (4:3–5) or outsiders; that sort of judgment is God's work (5:13). They must judge themselves and the quality of their life together (5:12). While they had been evaluating everyone else, they had let their own critical awareness of themselves as a community become slack (6:2–5).

How was the community failing? Boundaries between the world and the church were collapsing. Members sued each other in pagan courts (6:1–5). Such litigiousness was not only contrary to community spirit—better to suffer fraud than to defraud others (6:1–7)—it also indicated an abdication of responsibility for judging within the community. Such matters should be settled within (6:2). Boundaries had been virtually destroyed by the community's willingness to allow a man committing incest to remain in communion (5:1–2). This holy church allowed behavior even pagans detested (5:1). Since the community failed to exercise even a rudimentary self-discipline, Paul orders it to excommunicate the wrongdoer (5:2), both for his own sake (5:5) and for the sake of the community's integrity: "Cleanse out the old leaven" (5:7). A church that so ill maintained its separation from the world's standards, Paul says, is indeed presumptuous and arrogant when it judges apostles (5:2).

Freedom within the Christian church is therefore limited in several ways. The first limit is established by the appropriateness of its exercise. A freedom that leads to the slavery of vice is not from the Lord (6:12). Another limit is due to our bodily existence. The disposition of the body creates new spiritual combinations that must be taken seriously. Sex is not like food, for it demands a deeper level of human intentionality; sexual intercourse with a prostitute, therefore, is wrong not because it is physically contaminating but because it counterfeits the physical and spiritual exchange that is at the heart of the sexual—because in it one becomes "one flesh" without the commitment of the "spirit."

For Paul, Christian freedom is determined most of all by relationship to the Lord. Christians are already united to the Lord through the Spirit (6:17). Therefore they must dispose their bodies in a manner fitting to that relationship. They are not "their own" but live by the gift of another (6:20). When Paul tells them that their bodies are "the temple of the Holy Spirit," he establishes the two fundamental coordinates for Christian behavior: the primary relationship with the Lord, by whom the Christian lives by the gift of the Spirit, and the network of relationships that constitutes the community (6:19). Far from regarding physical existence as irrelevant for the spiritual life, Paul gives it a positive function: "Glorify God in your body" (6:20). This can be understood in two ways, which are mutually reinforcing: "Glorify God in your individual bodily lives," and "Glorify God within this body that is your community."

Marriage and Celibacy as God's Gifts (7:1–40)

In Paul's treatment of the community's questions, he must do what the sloganeers least want: he must make distinctions. He starts with their slogan "It is good not to touch a woman" (7:1). He agrees with it at one level, but for reasons other than those of Corinthians' wanting to express separation by a celibate lifestyle. Paul's partial agreement derives from the eschatological perspective he gives to the entire discussion. When he says that "the frame of this world is passing away" (7:31), he makes not only a temporal statement, "The end is coming soon" (7:29), but also an axiological one, "All created things are contingent and therefore transitory." Christians must live as people both engaged with and detached from worldly structures. They cannot flee them, but neither can they treat them as though they were permanent or ultimate. They are to live within them "as though not" (7:29–31), a difficult feat for anyone, and particularly for people attracted to simple solutions. But Paul refuses simple answers. He forces his readers to move through a serious reflection on the meaning of sexual existence in the kingdom of God.

His first and most important step is distinguishing between the call of God and different states of life (7:17–24). Since all human beings are called by God, no station in life can either impede or abet one's response. Male and female, Jew and Greek, slave and free are all called to a life of righteousness. Therefore, neither sexual nor social nor ethnic divisions can matter before God. In the church, therefore, stations in life are properly *adiaphora*; that is, they are not essential and can be understood as matters of free choice. Paul thinks of them as gifts consonant with each one's dispositions and capacities. Like all gifts, they are intended not for self-gratification but for the good of the entire community. Marriage and celibacy are both such gifts from God, ordered to the common welfare: "Each one has his special gift from the Lord, one of one kind, and one of another" (7:7).

Paul's personal preference for celibacy does not reflect a dualistic distaste for the physical or procreation. Celibacy is not advanced as an intrinsically superior mode of life. It is appropriate because of the situation of the church in the world. In a period of tribulation, Paul considers married people to be torn with anxiety between their legitimate care for spouses and children, and the service of the Lord in the mission. In such a setting, celibacy has a functional superiority: it frees a person for the service of the whole community.

Not everyone has the gift of celibacy, and marriage is equally to be valued. Paul enumerates two negative reasons to marry. Celibate people who fall into sexual immorality (7:2) or who are so preoccupied with passion that they too are "anxious" may as well be married (7:9). For them, celibacy has lost its purpose. Paul also sees the marriage relationship as having positive community functions. Marriage is more than a contract; it is a fully sexual engagement. Husbands' and wives' bodies belong to each other (see 6:19), and abstinence should be only temporary for attention to prayer (7:2–4). Just as sexual relations with a prostitute had negative spiritual implications (6:16), the sexual bonding of husband and wife has positive spiritual implications: they can sanctify each other and their children (7:14). Marriage is as serious as covenant; there is no divorce (7:10). The only exception is the separation—with freedom—that results from a fundamental spiritual estrangement that makes it impossible for a man and woman to live in peace (7:15).

Paul carefully notes the authority he invokes for each stage of his discussion. The prohibition against divorce in 7:10, for example, is backed by a command of the Lord (Mark 10:11; Matt. 5:32; 19:9; Luke 16:18), whereas the questions pertaining to mixed marriages are answered with Paul's own counsel (7:12). Paul has no command for the unmarried, only counsel (7:25). And for widows no command, only the advice of one who also has "the Spirit of God" (7:39–40).

Conscience and Freedom: The Issue
of Idol Food (8:1—11:1)

Meat was not a staple in the diet of ordinary first-century people. For those who could afford it, the most accessible source was the meat market connected to pagan temples. In idol shrines, one could also enjoy a festive meal involving meat dishes. But the Christian conversion was from "idols to the living and true God" (see 1 Thess. 1:9). How could the Corinthians have any further contact with idolatry? On the other hand, how could they avoid it? For the wealthier and socially more active members of the congregation, there could be serious disadvantages if they avoided shrine meals, since these often had more serious civic connotations than sacred. Here we meet again the problem of separation and assimilation. Must Christians abstain from meat altogether as they abstain from immorality? Or must they operate their own meat markets to ensure purity from idolatrous contaminations?

Some of the "strong" Corinthians claimed that since idols were not real, no harm was done by participation in these purely social contacts. But the "weak" are not convinced that the contacts are innocuous. They see them as collusion in idolatry. Beneath their conflict lies the issue of legitimate plurality of practice in the Christian community and the relative importance of right knowledge and love. There are four major stages to Paul's argument.

Stage One: Initial Distinctions (8:1–13). Paul distinguishes immediately between a knowledge that "puffs up" (synonymous with "boasts"; see 4:6, 18, 19; 5:2; 13:4) and a love that "builds up" (8:1). The distinction controls his whole argument. For Paul, theoretical correctness without community sensitivity is useless. Conceptually, he agrees with the strong: there is no ultimate power in the world but the one God (8:4–6); idols are nothing but human projections. This knowledge, however, is of no value to the one who cannot be convinced of it. Paul insists on the primacy of the individual conscience in moral choice. If some in the church think idols are real and eating idol meat acknowledges that reality, then for them, such eating is wrong. Their conscience is defiled if they act on what they truly consider wrong.

What obligation does this place on the strong? Paul again agrees with their basic understanding: eating and drinking are not by themselves determinative of our relation with God (8:8)—even though this position was distorted by some (see 6:13)—but the liberty (or, power: *exousia*) this knowledge grants must not be used in a way that is a "stumbling block" (1:23) to the weak (8:9). Christ identified himself with strong and weak alike (8:11–12); the strong, therefore, must limit their freedom for the sake of others. Willingly giving up a position of strength for one of weakness is the pattern of exchange that becomes shorthand for the gospel of the crucified Messiah (see 1:17–25), a pattern Paul himself exemplifies (8:13).

Stage Two: The Apostolic Example (9:1–27). Paul shows how the pattern is operative in his apostolic style. He, too, has *exousia:* he has seen Jesus, he is an apostle (9:1–2). He has a "right" to be supplied food and drink, a wife as a companion, and support for his ministry (9:3–7). Such rights are specified by Torah (9:8–11), the custom of Israel (9:13), and are ratified by Jesus himself: "Those who proclaim the gospel should get their living by the gospel" (9:14; cf. Luke 10:7; 1 Tim. 5:18). But Paul does not use this *exousia*, lest he place an obstacle to the proclamation of the "good news" (9:12–18). His freedom will not become a stumbling block *(scandalon)* to others. He is an example of power emptied out in service to others. He extends this to being available to all people, "that I might by all means save some" (9:22). He sees his ministry as a "life for others." So should their life together be one of mutual service and not one of competitive claiming of rights. Paul teaches them by example (see 4:16).

Stage Three: The Warning of Torah (10:1–13). The Corinthians should consider another example, one pertinent to more than this single issue. In a midrash of the exodus and wilderness narratives from Torah (see Exodus 14—34; Numbers 11—20). Paul compares the Christians in Corinth to Israel in the desert. He wants them to consider the earlier story as part of their own. That earlier generation had also been greatly gifted by God (10:1–5) just like the Corinthians (cf. 1:5–7). In spite of its great gifts, however, the desert generation was overthrown (10:5). Paul says they are a warning: what happened to them were *types* (10:6) of the dangers facing this present generation. The stories were written, indeed, to provide such examples (10:11). Why did Israel fall from God's favor despite its gifts? Because it was not faithful to its call. It did not live appropriately to its identity. Those people were idolators (Exod. 32:6) and were sexually immoral (Num. 25:1–3). They tested the Lord (Num. 21:5) and grumbled (Num. 14:2). There is a lesson here for both strong and weak. To the strong, a warning: "Let anyone who thinks he stands take warning, lest he fall" (10:12). To the weak, a consolation: "With the temptation [God] will also provide the way of escape" (10:13).

Stage Four: Freedom Is for Edification (10:14—11:1). Paul now turns to the subject of fellowship meals at idol shrines. Those having knowledge are warned to "shun the worship of idols" (10:14). They may be involving themselves in ways they cannot anticipate or control. Paul insists that even only bodily participation leads to spiritual entanglement. His argument? Think of the Christian sharing in the Eucharist, which leads to a participation in the body and blood of Jesus (10:16–17). Food eaten at the table of idols can therefore also involve participation in spiritual forces that operate for evil within that context. Idols may not be real, but the spiritual atmosphere of distortion characteristic of idolatry (cf. Rom. 1:18–32) is real and dangerous. Participants in fellowship meals at idol shrines may find themselves unwittingly the partner of demons (10:20–21).

Paul again asserts the essential freedom of the strong conscience. No one should be governed utterly by another's perceptions, but one should be governed by one's own informed judgment (10:25–27, 29–30). And if circumstances allow, one must act on that judgment. But if the good of a neighbor is involved, one's freedom is conditioned: "Let no one seek his own good, but the good of his neighbor" (10:24). Such service is not a denial of one's rights, but a self-emptying for the sake of a weak brother or sister (10:28–29) in order to "build them up" (10:23). Paul closes his argument with the simple exhortation to do all for the glory of God (10:31; cf. 6:20), which is shown most clearly by seeking the advantage of others rather than oneself. In Paul, the Corinthians can find both an example of this and a pointer toward a still more fundamental model: "Be imitators of me, as I am of Christ" (11:1).

The World in the Church
(1 Corinthians 11—14)

The attitudes that divide the Corinthians in their dealings with the world also affect their common worship and draw into sharp focus when the members "come together as church" (11:18). A community's identity is expressed by its communal activities. In the worship of the spiritual (*pneumatikoi*), their fleshly (*sarkikoi*) attitudes are revealed (see 3:1–3).

The structure and circumstances of the Corinthian assemblies are difficult to reconstruct. We know that the Corinthian Christians came together at least on the first day of the week (16:2), probably in a large room of a household (see 11:22, 34). They celebrated a ritual meal called the Lord's Supper (*kyriakon deipnon;* 11:20). Its cup of blessing and bread of breaking were regarded as a participation (*koinōnia*) in the body and blood of the Messiah (10:16). The meal contained a recital of Jesus' words at the last supper (11:23–25). We don't know how this cultic action was connected to the meals that provided the occasion for abuse (11:21, 33–34). Still less are we able to determine the circumstances of other liturgical activities involving various forms of speech: teaching (14:26), prophesying (14:1), speaking in tongues (14:2), interpretation of tongues (14:13), hymns, revelations, and prayers (14:14, 26).

It is obvious that the congregation was extraordinarily active and perhaps even spectacularly successful in its cultivation of spiritual utterances. Paul admits that it lacks no gift of knowledge or speech (1:5–7). The Corinthians' use of the gifts, however, is as a means of self-aggrandizement rather than as a means of building up (*oikodomē*) community identity. The attitudes of the world have infected the assembly of God. Its members have "gifts of the spirit" but they do not show the deeper wisdom of the "mind of Christ" (2:12–16), which teaches that gifts are for sharing.

They act as though blind to the implications of their liturgical behavior for others in the community, for outsiders, and for the identity of the church as a whole. We find in these discussions a tension between individualism and community consciousness, and between enthusiasm and tradition. Paul invokes the tradition of the churches four times in order to correct the Corinthians (11:16, 23; 14:33–36; 15:1–3). His appeal to tradition is especially striking because some of the Corinthians' perceptions undoubtedly came from him. Once again, he must assert the intrinsic value of an activity (e.g., the speaking in tongues, 14:18) while shifting the perception of it from an individual to a communal level. Not the prestige of this person or that but the health of the whole body is Paul's preoccupation. The integrity of the church as church is his concern. This also accounts for his attention to the impression outsiders have of the community (14:20–25; cf. 1 Thess. 4:12). Good order in the assembly is important not only because the continued stability of the community depends on it and because untrammeled spontaneity can lead to the subtle enslavement of spiritual manipulation but most of all because the source of all the spiritual gifts is "not a God of confusion, but of peace" (14:33).

The Prayer and Prophecy of Women (11:2–16)

The extraordinary complexity and confusion of this passage is itself the most important clue to its interpretation. Paul begins to commend the Corinthians for holding to traditions (11:2) but then launches into ways they do not, beginning with one that apparently bothered him emotionally. He questioned the way in which women were prophesying and praying in the assembly. This is obviously something that is happening, for no one would struggle as grimly as Paul does here against a mere hypothesis. Nor is there any doubt that ecstatic utterance is at issue. In 14:34–36, Paul says women are to be silent in the assembly. But that passage suggests a context of teaching, an activity culturally associated with males, particularly in Judaism. Here, it is not teaching but the charismatic gifts and prayer and prophecy. Paul has no problem with women's doing these things; the gifts, after all, come from the Spirit. But the manner of their performance upsets him. Unfortunately, like so much in this passage, the precise nature of their offense is not clear. Did they pray or prophesy without veils over their heads? Or did they, like mantic prophetesses, unbraid their hair and let it fly freely while they spoke? We cannot tell. In Paul's eyes, however, a fundamental sense of social decency has been offended. His position, however, was difficult. He was convinced, as they were, that in Christ, there is neither female nor male (Gal. 3:28), and he was not eager to set external constraints on prophets (14:32). But whether the lack of a veil suggested insubordination or the unbraiding suggested pagan prophecy, Paul is disturbed.

Paul wants to establish order and decency in the liturgical assembly. Like everybody in his age, he understood social order as intimately connected to cosmic order. As a male in a hierarchically structured society, therefore, he could invoke a series of arguments: the cosmic hierarchy of female, male, Christ (11:3); the order of creation, with male first and female second (11:7–8); an obscure reference to the angelic role in worship (11:10); and Hellenistic social sensitivities (11:5, 14–15).

The intrinsic weakness of Paul's position is indicated by the number of arguments he must invoke and his constant need to qualify them. He does not really believe, for example, that in Christ women are fundamentally subordinate to men (cf. 11:11). He is for once unable to argue from first principles to social behavior, for the very good reason in this case that the social norm has nothing to do with Christian first principles. It is just a matter of custom and customary perceptions. Paul at last recognizes that this is the only argument left to him: "If anyone is disposed to be contentious, we recognize no other practice, nor do the churches of God" (11:16).

Abuses at the Lord's Supper (11:17–34)

Once more, the exact nature of the problem is not completely clear. Because "each one goes ahead with his own meal," Paul says that some are filled while others go hungry (11:21). Are people bringing their own food and proceeding without waiting for the ritual actions that join them together? Are their uneven resources being selfishly and privately consumed, so that not everyone has enough? Or are those providing the meal taking larger portions for themselves and their clients, like patrons of clubs and cults? We cannot be sure. What is clear is that Paul perceives a sacred meal infiltrated by the attitudes of the world (11:20). Divisions between people on the basis of wealth or position threaten the common identity of the church. Paul berates those responsible for "humiliating those who have nothing," and by so doing, "despising the church of God" (11:22). Their party spirit is contrary to the very notion of church.

Paul responds with his most extensive and explicit citation of Jesus' words, introduced by the technical language of scribal tradition: "I received . . . what I also delivered to you" (11:23). The words are close to the Synoptic version of the last supper, providing an important clue to the development of the gospel traditions. Paul agrees with Luke 22:19 by including the command "Do this in memory of me," but he attaches it to both loaf and cup (11:24–25). He also makes explicit the connection of this broken bread to the crucifixion: "You proclaim the Lord's death until he comes" (11:26). By the words "until he comes," he reminds them that the ritual life of the church is framed by the "already" of the death and resurrection and the "not yet" of the Parousia. In such a context, the liturgical cry with which he ends the letter would have been most natural: "Lord, come [*maranatha*]" (16:22).

Paul draws a direct theological and behavioral inference from the tradition (11:27). By sharing loaf and cup Christians participate in the body and blood of the Lord—this is axiomatic (see 10:16). And if that sharing establishes them as "the body of the Lord" (10:17), those who are contemptuous of other members of the assembly also profane "the body and blood of the Lord" (11:27). Everyone, therefore, should "discern the body," lest eating and drinking lead to judgment (11:28–29). The consequences Paul draws for failure to do this (e.g., the death of people in the community or being disciplined by the Lord) are obscure (11:30–32), but his main point is clear. When the Corinthians "come together as church" they do not eat a worldly meal; that they can eat at home (11:22, 34). They enter into a ritual fellowship meal that establishes the community as "the body of the Lord." The worldly attitudes of self-aggrandizement and rivalry are not only inappropriate, they destroy the church and call down God's judgment (11:34).

The Spiritual Gifts (12:1—14:40)

In the Corinthians' use of their gifts of speech, the attitudes of elitism, rivalry, and individualism are painfully present. To grasp Paul's concern and argument, it is necessary to appreciate how active the pneumatic phenomena were in the congregation, as well as how highly esteemed the forms of ecstasy were in the Hellenistic world. That form of prophecy called mantic was particularly favored. It was thought to result from a direct inspiration, a virtual possession of the psyche by the divine Spirit, leading to *enthusiasmos*. Rapt in ecstasy, the prophetess or prophet cried out in unintelligible speech, which required translating and interpretation (see above, chap. 1). Just this form of spiritual utterance seems to be what the Corinthians called tongues. And consonant with the views of their world, they considered such ecstatic babbling to be the highest manifestation of the Spirit. Teaching and the rational discourse Paul calls prophecy seem to have been lightly regarded by them. With their characteristic capacity for making gifts from another into badges of their own worth, the Corinthians ranked the gifts, declaring that the sign of a spiritual person (*pneumatikos*) was tongues (see 14:22). Paul does not challenge the divine origin of this gift and claims to possess it himself (14:18). But he wants the Corinthians to begin to "understand the gifts given them by God" (2:12) within the context of their community function.

He warns them first that not all "spiritual powers" are necessarily good. When they had been pagans, they had been caught up in rapture, (*agomai*), but this had only resulted in their alienation (*apagomai;* 12:2). He wants them to understand, therefore, that he is not talking about spiritual realities (*ta pneumatika;* 12:1), but gifts from God (*ta charismata;* 12:4). The first work of God's Holy Spirit is to bring a human being into relationship with the Lord, enabling him or her to say, "Jesus is Lord"; likewise, any impulse that denies that relationship cannot be from God (12:3).

Since the Spirit they have received comes from the God who called them into a community, the diverse manifestations of this Spirit serve functions within the community. Paul insists on two reciprocal aspects of this community context: first, since all the gifts come from the same God, there is a fundamental unity and equality between them (12:4–11). All the gifts have been given for the common good (12:7; cf. 6:12), not by the random selection of a dumb force but by the direction of a personal spirit, the activity of the living God (12:11). Second, within this unity, there is a proper diversity of function within the church, which Paul here explicitly identifies as the "body of Christ." As eating the same loaf and drinking the same cup made them "one body" (10:16–17), so here the drinking of one spirit in baptism makes them one body (12:13). The parts of a human body exist in mutual interdependence (12:14–26). So should the members of the church: "You are the body of Christ and individually members of it" (12:27). All the functions are required for the body to be complete; there is no place for comparison or conflict between them.

Chapter 13 is not a digression but serves the parenetic function of presenting Paul as a model of "seeking the higher gifts" (12:31; cf. 9:1–27). The highest expression of the Spirit is self-donating love *(agapē)*. In contrast to passionate love *(erōs)*, a drive that seeks the other in order to fulfill the self, this *agapē* means having the disposition toward others that God had first toward them. It transcends all differentiating gifts; they represent the partial whereas it is the perfection (13:10). This is because *agapē* is the essential articulation of the life of the Spirit, which is to say, the life of God. The gifts of speech are transitory; only *agapē* will be the bond between God and humans in the life to come, when "we shall know even as we have been known" (13:12). Without *agapē*, the other gifts are meaningless (13:1–3). With it, the other gifts are ordered toward mutual edification, and life together can become "life for the other" (13:4–7). This is the "more excellent way" that Paul demonstrates in his apostolic ministry (13:1).

In Paul's discussion of the separate gifts, he concentrates only on tongues and prophecy. His preference for prophecy is plain. An utterance in tongues is ecstatic and unintelligible and requires interpretation. As a mode of prayer, it can glorify God and "build up" the one who prays (14:4), but it can become solipsistic: the church is not built up by it. Prophecy, in contrast, is a rational mode of speech that, even when a revelation, is intelligible to all by the way it addresses the community with the demands of the gospel and convicts it. Paul prefers prophecy because it engages the mind (14:14) and edifies the community (14:4). In fact, he reverses the slogan of the elitists who had claimed tongues as a sign of believers. With a midrash on Isa. 28:11–12 ("By mean of foreign tongues and by the lips of foreigners will I speak to this people and even then they will not listen to me") Paul shows that tongues can actually be a sign of disbelief. The implication that such was the case with the Corinthian elitists is palpable.

Prophecy, however, is a sign that calls people to belief, and builds on the foundation of Christ first laid by the apostolic preaching (see 3:10–15; 12:28). If outsiders came to the assembly and heard only tongues they would naturally identify the church as one more form of Hellenistic cult involving mantic prophecy; they would say, "You are raving *[mainesthe]*." But if they heard prophecy, they would be moved to say, "God is among you" (14:25). Paul therefore demands of the Corinthians responsibility, maturity, and thought (14:20). Even in the context of spiritual worship, the whole community must exercise judgment: "Let all discern" (14:29). The prophets should control their utterances (14:32), speech should be orderly and in turn (14:26–31), women should not teach publicly (14:34–36). Everything should be done with an eye to edification (14:26) but also "decently and in order" (14:40).

The Church and the Kingdom
(1 Corinthians 15)

Paul's long and carefully constructed treatment of the resurrection is neither an afterthought nor unconnected to the Corinthian problems. In it, he provides the theological underpinning for his practical directions. The Corinthians' attitudes of arrogance and self-aggrandizement are based on the conviction that they are already in full possession of God's life. They know God (8:2; 13:12), they have all spiritual gifts (1:5–7), they are "spiritual people" (3:1) and mature (2:6; 14:20), they are strong (10:12), they are already filled, rich, and reigning in the kingdom (4:8). From that perception comes their contempt for others who appear to be less well endowed and their neglect of their own entanglements. Because they are already perfect, there is no need for discernment in their behavior.

When Paul reminds them of the "fundamental" (15:3) message of the resurrection, he does more than recall historical facts. He reminds them of the structure of their existence "by which you are *being saved* if you hold it fast" (15:2), making that salvation both progressive and conditional. He needs to remind them of the pattern of the Spirit's work, which they see in Jesus. Jesus first died, then rose to a new life (15:3–5) and became in fact "life-giving Spirit" (15:45). With Jesus, there was first the sowing of the mortal body, *then* the spiritual (*to pneumatikon;* 15:44). So with them, the full reality of the spiritual life is not now but only with their resurrection.

More significant still, Jesus' resurrection and the outpouring of his spirit are not yet the fulfillment of God's work. They are still in the in-between time. Jesus is only the first fruits (15:20); death must still be overcome for all others as well (15:21). Not yet has everything been brought into subjection to the Lord (15:28), and therefore not yet can the kingdom be handed over by Jesus to the Father. And only then "comes the end" (15:24). The point of this is clear: the Corinthians cannot be now "ruling" (4:8), for there is as yet no kingdom of God. They are like fools sitting on fantasy thrones.

Paul points them inexorably toward the future. If the present were already the fulfillment, then they would be the most miserable of creatures. Their grandeur is self-deception made possible only by ignoring the fact of death. In fact, people in the community continue to die (11:30). If there is no future resurrection, if the present were all there was, then they would be fools to suffer for their faith (15:29–32). Paul now reverses the argument. If Jesus is the pattern of their life before God (2:16; 11:1) and

if there is no resurrection, then neither did Jesus rise from the dead
(15:13–16). But if he did not rise, then he could not be the life-giving
spirit—all their gifts would be absent and their faith a delusion (15:14).
And if that were so, then they would be still in their sins (15:17) and those
who have already died would be utterly lost (15:18). There is a sharp point
being made here. Paul suggests that precisely their neglect of the future
and their selfish grasping of their present gifts leaves them open to sin:
"Come to your right mind, and sin no more. For some have no knowledge
of God. I say this to your shame" (15:34).

When Paul speaks of the future life, he must shift to metaphor (15:35–
49), since neither does he "know" in these matters (cf. 13:12). His message
is nevertheless clear: "Flesh and blood cannot inherit the kingdom of
God" (15:50). We are reminded of the other "kingdom" formulation: "The
unrighteous will not inherit the kingdom of God" (6:9). There is an
infinite qualitative difference between the existence of all created beings,
however sanctified, and the Holy God. Although the Corinthians share in
the Spirit, they are still merely human. The kingdom, however, means a
share in God's glory (15:42–43, 49). For this they must be radically
changed: "We shall not all sleep, but we shall all be changed" (15:51). The
change required, furthermore, is not only metaphysical but moral (15:34,
58). The future kingdom will be glorious (15:51–58), but the Corinthians
are not yet there. The Spirit's work among them is not for their self-glory
but to change them in preparation for God's glory.

THE SECOND LETTER TO THE CORINTHIANS

Second Corinthians has many major historical and literary problems,
making the reconstruction of the situation faced by Paul more hazardous
than in the case of 1 Corinthians.

It is difficult, first of all, to piece together what happened between the
two letters. Although Paul's relations with the community were strained,
he had planned to visit it after passing through Macedonia (1 Cor. 16:5), to
pick up the collection on the way to Jerusalem (1 Cor. 16:3). In the
meantime, he had anticipated sending Timothy and expected an early
return of that delegate (1 Cor. 16:10–11; cf. 4:17).

There is no lack of biographical data in 2 Corinthians, but the sequence
of events remains elusive. In 1:8, Paul refers to an "affliction" he had
experienced in Asia, which threatened his life (1:9). Was this in any way
connected to his "fighting the beasts in Ephesus" (1 Cor. 15:32)? In 1:15,
he speaks of a visit that he had planned to make to the Corinthians in
connection with travel to Macedonia (the same itinerary as in 1 Cor.
16:3–5) but that he had called off since he did not wish another "painful
visit" (2:1). But what visit is this? He then speaks of a "letter written out of

much affliction and anguish of heart and with many tears" (2:4). Is this 1 Corinthians or another letter? It certainly caused considerable distress (2 Cor. 2:5–11; 7:8–13).

In 2 Cor. 2:12, Paul begins to speak of his actual movements rather than of his plans. He had gone to Macedonia not through Corinth but by way of Troas. Not finding his delegate Titus in Troas, he did not linger but went straight on to Macedonia. Here, the travelogue stops momentarily. It is resumed in 7:5, where we find Paul recounting the comfort he had received in Macedonia by the arrival there of Titus, who bore Paul news of the Corinthians' zeal for him (7:7). At this point, therefore, he appears reconciled with them (7:6–16).

Now, for more plans: In 8:6, Paul says that Titus had already begun work for the collection among them, and in 8:16–18, he is about to send Titus and "another brother" to complete that work. There is, however, a slight but troubling shift in 9:3–5, where Paul indicates that he is sending "brethren" for the collection. Is he simply collapsing together Titus and the "brethren" (cf. 8:23)? Things get even murkier when we find in 12:18 that Paul had already sent Titus and "the brother" to Corinth to work for the collection. Is this a reference to the earlier (8:6) or the later (8:16–18) visit of the delegate? Finally, Paul says in 12:14, "Here for a third time I am ready to come to you," whereas we would have expected this to be only a second visit.

It is not impossible to establish a sequence, although some filling in of spaces is required. Specifically, we must postulate a second "painful" visit to the community (2:1), and correlate it with at least three other factors: the excommunication of an erring member of the community, Paul's collection plans, and the popularity of other teachers. We remember that Paul threatened to come "with a rod" already in 1 Corinthians, if the community did not heed him (1 Cor. 4:21). That threat immediately preceded his command to excommunicate the brother living in incest (1 Cor. 5:1–5). It is plausible to suppose that Paul did come to the community, did demand obedience in this matter, and was rebuffed. This would obviously be a "painful visit." He could then have returned to Ephesus and penned the "letter in tears," which once more demanded obedience. The letter, probably delivered by Titus who went to Corinth on business for the collection, worked. It caused resentment, however, precisely because Paul had been forced to exert his authority so baldly. The growing estrangement between Paul and the community cannot have been decreased by the demand for money made by Titus. And Paul's authority over this church was still more tenuous because the Corinthians were increasingly fascinated with other apostles, whether those they had known earlier (see 1 Cor. 1:12) or newer visitors, who were more impressive than Paul and were straightforward in their demands for support, not devious like him. Paul therefore writes this letter at a point when he wants the Corinthians to cooperate in his great effort of reconciliation, while he himself is not sure of his reconciliation with them!

This historical reconstruction must remain tentative because of the serious reservations that are held by many scholars concerning the literary integrity of 2 Corinthians. They surmise that our canonical document is not a single composition but an edited composite of several notes by Paul written at various times. No manuscript evidence supports the hypothesis, but a number of seams in the letter appear to some readers incompatible with its being a unitary composition. These scholars detect a striking difference in tone, for example, between chapters 1—9, which are irenic and conciliatory, and chapters 10—13, which are polemical and defensive. Chapters 10—13, in fact, are sometimes thought to be the "letter written in tears" sent to the Corinthians *before* chapters 1—9. But since that letter dealt with an act of discipline, whereas 2 Corinthians 10—13 makes no mention of any disciplinary action, the suggestion is not convincing.

Even within the first nine chapters, moreover, there seem to be gaps. The detailed itinerary of 1:15—2:13, for example, breaks off without warning, only to be picked up as though nothing had intervened, in 7:5. The small segment 6:14—7:1, furthermore, appears to contain non-Pauline vocabulary and thought patterns, as well as to break the coherent and natural sequence of 6:13—7:2. Is this a pre-Pauline or even anti-Pauline fragment interpolated by a later editor? Finally, both chapters 8 and 9 deal with the collection. But chapter 9 begins with such an independent tack—"Now it is superfluous for me to write to you about the offering for the saints" (9:1)—that some see in the two chapters separate notes on the collection.

Second Corinthians is therefore commonly regarded as an edited collection of Pauline letter fragments. The case is not, however, absolutely conclusive. The shift in tone between chapters 9 and 10 can be accounted for on rhetorical rather than editing grounds. The disparity between chapters 8 and 9 is not so great as it at first appears. The broken itinerary is difficult but not impossible. Even in what appears to be a clear instance of interpolation (6:14—7:1), the insertion may have been done by Paul himself. If, in fact, he wrote something like this in his first letter to the Corinthians warning them to avoid the immoral (see 1 Cor. 5:9), it is not impossible that he used it again here to make a definite point: if the Corinthians reject him in favor of other teachers, it is tantamount to "yoking themselves with Belial."

Still, in view of the literary complexity of the writing, it is prudent not to insist on a sequential development of argument. Nor is such a linear reading required to make good sense of the writing. Whatever the precise historical situation, Paul's relationship with the Corinthians is shaky. They are more attracted to other teachers than to him. The apostolic work of the collection has only exacerbated the tension, making the Corinthians think Paul is defrauding them. Whether Paul wrote one or a series of letters, he is clearly a man trying to build a bridge across a rapidly widening gulf. His task is therefore one of reconciliation. Even as he seeks to advance his own great project of reconciliation with the Jerusalem church (in the collection), he must try to reestablish peace with his own community.

For Paul, to think about reconciliation means thinking about the nature and style of his apostleship. It is possible, then, to see the three major sections of this letter as addressing that issue from slightly different angles: apostleship negatively defined, in his self-defense (10—13); apostleship positively defined, in the ministry of the new covenant (2:14—7:4); apostleship symbolized in the collection (8—9).

Apostleship Negatively Defined:
Paul and the Superapostles
(2 Corinthians 10—13)

It may finally be impossible to determine the historical identity of Paul's rivals in Corinth. Were they representatives from Jerusalem claiming superior apostolic credentials and fidelity to the commands of Jesus? Was their teaching significantly different from his? Our knowledge comes only from Paul's self-defense, which is impassioned and polemical. Where Paul claims a plus we may be tempted to attribute a minus in the rivals and thus construct a portrait. In the end, however, it will be a portrait only of Paul's perceptions, which were not necessarily fair or accurate. There is no reason to regard his rivals as representing a part of an organized Jewish-Christian resistance to Paul's ministry, for the issue of observance of Torah never enters the discussion. Nor is it certain that they had a distinct Christology along the lines of a Divine Man, although Paul says, in 11:4,

> If someone comes and preaches another Jesus than the one we preached, or if you receive a different spirit from the one you received, or if you accept a different gospel from the one you accepted, you submit readily enough.

It is not at all clear what this owes to rhetoric and what to reality.

The major issue in the debate is apostolic style and rival claims to authority over the Corinthians. Paul insists on a direct connection between style of ministry and the kerygma. We cannot assume that the rivals make the same connection. Indeed, it is somewhat misleading to think of them as opponents, since Paul does not directly attack them, except in the slander of 11:13–15. His anger and frustration are directed more at the Corinthian congregation, which is so easily led from sobriety and stability by the spectacular. Paul's perception of his rivals is important mostly for leading us to his perception of his own ministry as an apostle.

Paul says his rivals claim to be apostles of Christ, as he is, rather than apostles of churches. He dismisses this claim with direct slander: they are in reality "false apostles, deceitful workmen, disguising themselves as apostles of Christ" (11:13). But he grudgingly admits their surface plausibility, for he calls them superapostles (*hyperapostoloi*; 11:5, 12:11). They claim a Jewish pedigree sufficiently impressive to arouse Paul's defenses (11:22). They engage in self-commendation and measure themselves over against others (10:12). They also travel with letters of recommendation from churches to validate their authority (3:1). They claim to work on the same basis Paul does, preaching the gospel for free (11:12), but they accept money for their preaching (11:7–10). They are peddlers of God's word (2:17), and they tamper with it (4:2).

Some other characteristics of his rivals may be guessed from the emphases of Paul's self-presentation—the things he feels the need to stress in his comparison with them. They seem to have been rhetorically gifted, placing great stock in their knowledge and speech (10:10; 11:6). They are able to work miracles to back up their claims (12:12). They have mystical experiences (12:1–5). They are spiritual athletes who have endured great hardships as "servants of Christ" (11:23–27). In all these things, they "boast" (11:21).

In response, Paul first matches them boast for boast. Everything they claim, he is and has. He does not need letters from churches, for the Corinthians are a letter "written by the spirit in the heart" (3:2–3). Or at least they should be. In fact, Paul knows they are turning away from him, and he rebukes them for forcing him to sing his own praises: "I ought to have been commended by you" (12:11). Ultimately, however, Paul and his co-workers do not need certification from any human source. Their competence comes from God (3:5). Paul's authority comes not from humans but from God (10:8, 18); he "belongs to Christ" (10:7). He is weak in speech but not deficient in knowledge (11:6). As they can testify, he has worked among them the signs of an apostle: wonders and mighty works (12:12). His Jewish background is better than any his rivals can claim (11:22). His visions are more impressive, for he has "heard things that cannot be told, which man may not utter" (12:1–5). And if they boast of hardships endured for God, he has an unparalleled catalogue of sufferings. He is truly a "servant of Christ" (11:23–27).

Paul is well aware of the delicate position in which this boasting puts him. In his theological lexicon, boasting is a mode of self-assertion he everywhere condemns as the epitome of "fleshly" behavior (see 1 Cor. 1:29; 3:21; 4:7; 5:6; 13:3). By so exposing his "divine jealousy" for the Corinthians to see, Paul appears "foolish" (11:1, 16–18). But he does not stop boasting. Why? Because he is really boasting of the work of God in him, rather than of his human capacities. He repeats here his principle from 1 Cor. 1:31: "Let him who boasts boast in the Lord, for it is not the man who commends himself who is accepted, but the man whom the Lord commends" (10:17–18; cf. Jer. 9:24). And God has commended Paul, so that his boasting is in effect a praise of God. To deny his qualifications would be to deny God's work. This, indeed, is what so upsets Paul about the Corinthians' fascination with other teachers. If they dismiss Paul, they also dismiss the adequacy of their experience of God, which Paul mediated to them. They reject their own past by choosing a Christianity of show rather than of service. And because his gospel is one of service, Paul's greatest boast is in his weakness: "If I must boast, I will boast in the things that show my weakness" (11:30; 12:5, 9–10). Paul stresses his weakness to show that it is really God's power at work, not human prowess. Paul attaches this perception directly to Christology, in 13:3–4:

> Since you desire proof that Christ is speaking in me, he is not weak in dealing with you, but is powerful in you. For he was crucified in weakness but lives by the power of God. For we are weak in him, but in dealing with you we shall live with him by the power of God.

In 1 Corinthians, Paul taught that the pattern of exchange between wisdom and foolishness, strength and weakness, was the way of living together according to the "mind of Christ." Now, he demonstrates that pattern in his apostolic style: "We are glad when we are weak and you are strong" (13:9).

Apostleship Positively Defined: Treasure in Earthen Vessels (2 Corinthians 2:14—7:4)

This long section of the letter, which bears some marks of having been worked out separately either as a distinct letter or as a midrashic argument, describes the apostolic ministry of Paul and his co-workers. It is dominated by the contrast between the glory of the message and the inadequacy of the messengers.

The ministry itself comes directly from God, according to 1:21–22:

> It is God who establishes us with you in Christ, and has commissioned us; he has put his seal upon us and given us his Spirit in our hearts as a guarantee.

The mission can therefore be described in terms of glory and power. It is like a triumphant march of conquerers (see also 1 Cor. 4:9). The apostles, however, do not lead the procession. It is God in Christ "leading us in triumph" (2:14). The images here are difficult to sort out, but the essential point is that the gospel is a message that calls for a decision with life-and-death consequences (2:15–16).

In Paul's insistence on the apostles' having been commissioned by God rather than by human assemblies with their "letters of recommendation" (3:1), his language moves toward his major metaphor of the ministry. They don't have letters "written on tablets of stone" but have letters written "with the spirit of the living God . . . on tablets of human hearts" (3:3). The opposition in 3:6 between spirit and writing, and in 3:3 between stone and heart, becomes a contrast between covenants, perhaps suggested by the same sort of contrast in Jer. 31:31–34. According to 3:6,

> [God] has made us competent to be ministers of a new covenant, not in a *written code*, but in the *spirit;* for the written code *kills,* but the spirit *gives life.*

For Paul, as we shall see again in Galatians, the code kills because by it Jesus is condemned, and the Spirit gives life because by it Jesus was raised. In a complex midrash of Exod. 34:29–35, Paul now opposes the glory of this new covenant to the old. "Glory" in this passage obviously bears the connotation of "radiance," as well as that of "presence" (3:7–11). The revelation of God in Christ is so much more powerful than in Torah, that only in its light can Torah itself be understood (3:12–16). Only by "turning to the Lord," that is, to Jesus, can the veil of blindness be removed, and the "dispensation of condemnation" become a figure for the "dispensation of righteousness" (3:9). Paul does not speak idly when he calls his midrash of Exodus bold (3:12), for it makes him the superior of Moses. Moses had to veil his face to hide from the Israelites the fading glory (3:13; but cf. Exod. 34:35). Such is not the case for Paul and his co-workers, who (3:18)

> with unveiled face, beholding the glory of the Lord, are being changed into his likeness from one degree of glory to another. For this comes from the Lord, who is Spirit.

The glory of Paul's gospel, therefore, comes not from rhetoric or worldly wisdom but from the presence of God's power working through it. The Spirit of the Lord is working to reveal "the glory of Christ, who is the likeness of God" (4:4). The same God who called light out of darkness (Gen. 1:3) "has shone in our hearts to give the light of the glory of God in the face of Christ" (4:6).

Paul does not deduce from the glory of the message that the messenger also should be powerful. Indeed, he draws an absolute distinction between the power of the gospel and the dignity of the minister (4:5):

> What we preach is not ourselves, but Jesus Christ as Lord, with ourselves as your servants for Jesus' sake.

The message is powerful, the messengers are not: "Who is sufficient for these things?" (2:16). The messengers' weakness serves to show that it is God at work and not simply human skill. The apostles are like clay pots, through whose cracks the divine light shines to enlighten others (4:7). And like such disposable pots, they are rejected and afflicted (4:8–9). In them is the paradox of Jesus' death and resurrection found in a new bodily expression (4:10–11): "Death is at work in us, but life in you" (4:12).

The apostles hope for a future glory; they do not enjoy it now. They know that "he who raised the Lord Jesus will raise us also with Jesus and bring us with you into his presence" (4:14). And they are convinced that the present suffering is meaningful for that future (4:17). But in the meantime, they feel the anguish of being pulled between the desire for God and the need to serve others (5:1–10). The apostles find their lives defined by two relationships. Because of the gift of love given them by God in Christ, they pour themselves out for their brethren: "It is all for your sake" (4:15). They replicate the pattern of Jesus' life and death for others (5:14–15):

> For the love of Christ controls us, because we are convinced that one has died for all; therefore all have died. And he died for all, that those who live might live no longer for themselves but for him who for their sake died and was raised.

So revolutionary is this new life given by the Spirit that it amounts to more than a new covenant; it is a "new creation" (5:17), which demands viewing human life in an altogether different way. The Spirit shapes them into the likeness of Jesus (3:18) who himself reveals the image of God (4:4). No longer is life to be defined by individual happiness and fulfillment, but by service; no longer by individual rights, leading to alienation, but by self-emptying, leading to reconciliation. The model? "In Christ, God was reconciling the world to himself" (5:19). How? "For our sake he made him to be sin who knew no sin, so that by him we might become the righteousness of God" (5:21).

Paul's style of ministry is therefore based on the pattern of God's reconciling work. The crucified and raised Messiah is the paradigm for ministry, which bodies forth in the world its paradoxical revelation of God's power. When Paul characterizes that style (6:1–10), he falls naturally into the same pattern of exchange. According to 6:9–10, the apostles are

> dying, and behold we live; as punished and yet not killed; as sorrowful, yet always rejoicing; as poor, yet making many rich; as having nothing, and yet possessing everything.

The Apostolic Fellowship: The Collection (2 Corinthians 8—9)

Paul's fund-raising project for the Jerusalem church was a major preoccupation of his ministry (see Gal. 2:10; 1 Cor. 16:1–4; Rom. 15:25–29).

Despite the fact that his asking the Corinthians for money exacerbated the alienation between them, he continued to seek their cooperation. The Corinthians saw his collection as a surreptitious way of exploiting them for personal gain. Despite his care to avoid misunderstanding (8:20–24), by sending delegates for money he was misconstrued (12:16–18). His rivals may well have seized on Paul's "inconsistent" monetary policy as a sign of his lacking proper apostolic credentials. Even Paul's boast of preaching to them freely (1 Cor. 9:15–18) is now twisted to appear as a lack of love for this church (2 Cor. 11:7–11). It is more than a little ironic that as Paul tried to establish a worldwide reconciliation, he was stymied by a local alienation. The importance of the project is indicated by his persistence in it even in the face of opposition and rejection.

Why was the collection so important? In part, it was simply a response to need (Gal. 2:10). For the first Christians, as for other Jews, the mandate of sharing possessions with the needy was binding on all (9:12). But Paul also wanted the collection to serve a symbolic function: to establish a reconciliation between his gentile communities and the Jerusalem church. This reconciliation was now the more needed, since Paul's ministry had stirred considerable hostility. Paul does not stand on his "rights" as an apostle to the Gentiles, but "empties himself out" in this complicated, arduous, and thankless enterprise. He asks his gentile communities to do the same.

If they join in the collection, they will give thanks to God for all that they have been given (9:12; cf. 4:15). They will also fulfill the Hellenistic ideals of friendship by establishing a fellowship *(koinōnia)* with the Jerusalem church (8:4; 9:13) and an equality *(isotēs)* that is reciprocal in nature (8:14). The reciprocity is expressed more fully in Romans: the Gentiles had received spiritual things *(ta pneumatika)* from the Jewish Christians; now they owed them material things *(ta sarkika)* in return (Rom. 15:27). The same principle is found in 1 Cor. 9:11: "If we have sown spiritual things [*ta pneumatika*] among you, is it too much to reap your material things [*ta sarkika*]?" Here, the material generosity of the Corinthians is answered by the Jewish Christians' prayer for them (9:14).

Paul does not call for a community of possessions in any structural sense. He does not demand a contribution as an obligation or "temple tax" (8:12; 9:5). He has, however, engaged in some competitive rhetoric that now threatens to embarrass him. He has told the Macedonians that the Corinthians were extremely generous in their pledges (9:2), just as he now boasts of the Macedonians' generosity in order to stimulate the Corinthians (8:2–5). The Macedonians have fulfilled their pledges, but the Corinthians have not, and Paul might appear a liar (9:3–4). More than his personal embarrassment is at stake. Paul sees giving as a demand of the Christian life. Sharing is an act of obedience to the gospel (9:13). How can this be?

Because when Christians "give out of poverty" (8:2), they express with the body language of material possessions the pattern of "life for others" that Paul has been trying to engender among them. They have the opportunity to show toward other communities the attitudes he has been urging them to have toward each other: gifts are not for clinging and boasting but for sharing freely to build up others. The pattern for this is again found ultimately in the "mind of Christ" (2 Cor. 8:9):

> For you know the grace (or, gift: *charis*) of our Lord Jesus Christ, that though he was rich, yet for your sake he became poor, so that by his poverty you might become rich.

Did the Corinthians reconcile with Paul and respond? We have two signs that they did. When writing to the Romans, Paul later reports: "For Macedonia *and Achaia* have been pleased to make some contribution for the poor among the saints in Jerusalem" (Rom. 15:26). And they saved his letters.

BIBLIOGRAPHICAL NOTE

Literature on the Corinthian correspondence is immense and always growing; the works mentioned here are but a sample.

Helpful for the historical and social setting are G. Theissen, *The Social Setting of Pauline Christianity: Essays on Corinth*, ed. and trans. J. H. Schütz (Philadelphia: Fortress Press, 1981); W. A. Meeks, *The First Urban Christians: The Social World of the Apostle Paul* (New Haven: Yale Univ. Press, 1983); A. J. Malherbe, *Social Aspects of Early Christianity*, 2d enl. ed. (Philadelphia: Fortress Press, 1983), 71–91; R. Banks, *Paul's Idea of Community: The Early Christian House Churches in Their Historical Setting* (Grand Rapids: Wm. B. Eerdmans, 1980); A. Ehrhardt, "Social Problems of the Early Church," in his *The Framework of the New Testament Stories* (Cambridge: Harvard Univ. Press, 1964), 275–312.

Of the multiple profiles of the community and its outlook, see W. Schmithals, *Gnosticism in Corinth*, trans. J. Steely (Nashville: Abingdon Press, 1971); B. A. Pearson, *The Pneumatikos-Psychikos Terminology in I Corinthians*, SBLDS 12 (Missoula, Mont.: Scholars Press, 1973); A. C. Thiselton, "Realized Eschatology in Corinth," *NTS* 24 (1977–78): 520–26; D. J. Doughty, "The Presence and Future of Salvation in Corinth," *ZNW* 66 (1975): 61–90; R. A. Horsley, " 'How Can Some of You Say There Is No Resurrection of the Dead?' Spiritual Elitism in Corinth," *NovT* 20 (1978): 203–40.

For the immediate occasion of 1 Corinthians, see J. Munck, "The Church Without Factions," in his *Paul and the Salvation of Mankind*, trans. F. Clarke (Richmond: John Knox Press, 1959), 135–67; J. C. Hurd, Jr., *The Origin of I Corinthians* (London: SPCK, 1965); N. A. Dahl, "Paul and the Church at Corinth According to I Corinthians 1:10—4:21," in his *Studies in Paul* (Minneapolis: Augsburg Pub. House, 1977), 40–61.

Consideration of special issues in the first letter can be found in B. Fiore, " 'Covert Allusion' in I Corinthians 1—4," *CBQ* 47 (1985): 85–102; A. Collins, "The Function of 'Excommunication' in Paul," *HTR* 73 (1980): 251–63; S. K. Stowers, "A 'Debate' over Freedom: I Corinthians 6:12–20," in *Christian Teaching: Studies in Honor of L. G. Lewis,* ed. E. Ferguson (Abilene, Tex.: Abilene Christian Univ. Bookstore, 1981), 59–71; R. Scroggs, "Paul and the Eschatological Woman," *JAAR* 40 (1972): 283–303; R. A. Horsley, "Gnosis in Corinth: I Cor 8:1–6," *NTS* 27 (1980): 32–51; J. Murphy-O'Connor, "The Non-Pauline Character of I Cor 11:2–16?" *JBL* 95 (1976): 615–21; E. Schweizer, "The Service of Worship: An Exposition of I Cor 14," *Int* 13 (1959): 400–408; J. Sweet, "A Sign for Unbelievers: Paul's Attitude to Glossolalia," *NTS* 13 (1966–67): 20–28; and J. Lambrecht, "Paul's Christological Use of Scripture in I Cor 15:20–28," *NTS* 28 (1982): 502–27.

The issue of the integrity of 2 Corinthians always means a discussion of interpolations. For two views, cf. H. D. Betz, "2 Cor 6:14—7:1: An Anti-Pauline Fragment," *JBL* 92 (1973): 88–108; and N. A. Dahl, "A Fragment and Its Context: II Cor 6:14—7:1," in *Studies in Paul,* 62–69. On the wider questions of literary unity, see R. Batey, "Paul's Interactions with the Corinthians," *JBL* 84 (1965): 139–46; and W. H. Bates, "The Integrity of II Corinthians," *NTS* 12 (1965–66): 56–69.

For a series of penetrating essays on both epistles, but particularly on Paul's rivals, see C. K. Barrett, *Essays on Paul* (Philadelphia: Westminster Press, 1982). Very influential has been the study of D. Georgi, *The Opponents of Paul in 2 Corinthians: A Study of Religious Propaganda in Late Antiquity,* 1st Eng. ed., enl. (Philadelphia: Fortress Press, 1985); see also C. J. A. Hickling, "Is the Second Epistle to the Corinthians a Source for Early Christian History?" *ZNW* 66 (1975): 284–87; R. E. Hock, *The Social Context of Paul's Ministry: Tentmaking and Apostleship* (Philadelphia: Fortress Press, 1980).

For Paul's defense of his apostleship, see J. H. Schütz, *Paul and the Anatomy of Apostolic Authority* (Cambridge: At the Univ. Press, 1975); G. G. O'Collins, "Power Made Perfect in Weakness: II Cor 12:9–10," *CBQ* 33 (1971): 528–37; and now, J. T. Fitzgerald, *Cracks in an Earthen Vessel: An Examination of the Catalogues of Hardship in the Corinthian Correspondence* (Ph.D. diss., Yale Univ., 1984). Paul's midrash on a ministry superior to Moses' is analyzed by T. E. Provence, "Who Is Sufficient for These Things," *NovT* 24 (1982): 54–81; and W. C. Van Unnik, "With Unveiled Faces: An Exegesis of II Cor 3:12–18," *NovT* 6 (1963): 153–69. See also J. D. G. Dunn, "2 Corinthians III.17—'The Lord Is the Spirit,' " *JTS* 21 (1970): 309–20. For the collection, see A. J. Malherbe, "The Corinthian Collection," *Restoration Quarterly* 3 (1959): 221–33; and K. F. Nickle, *The Collection: A Study in Paul's Strategy* (London: SCM Press, 1966).

A critical commentary on 1 Corinthians with full bibliography is H. Conzelmann, *1 Corinthians,* trans. J. W. Leitch, Hermeneia (Philadelphia: Fortress Press, 1975). More accessible yet careful guides through the text are C. K. Barrett, *A Commentary on the First Epistle to the Corinthians,* HNTC (New York: Harper & Row, 1968), and C. R. Holladay, *The First Letter of Paul to the Corinthians,* The Living Word Commentary (Austin, Tex: Sweet Co., 1979).

For 2 Corinthians a critical commentary with full and recent bibliography is V. P. Furnish, *II Corinthians*, Anchor Bible (Garden City, N.Y.: Doubleday & Co., 1984). Helpful again is the readable commentary by C. K. Barrett, *A Commentary on the Second Epistle to the Corinthians*, HNTC (New York: Harper and Row, 1973).

13

The Letter to the Galatians

IN PAUL'S LETTER TO THE GALATIANS, WE FIND THE APOSTLE AT HIS MOST difficult and exhilarating. In the face of opposition and rejection, he pushes the scandalous implications of the gospel to their limits, leaving Christianity its "charter of freedom." Here is a brave intelligence that moves beyond an apparently narrow parochial problem to the deepest questions concerning life before God. In the process, he allows his own and the community's personal religious experience to reshape their shared symbolic world in a radical way.

The interpretation of the letter is difficult not only because of the density of Paul's arguments but also because the circumstances to which he was responding are not entirely clear. We have only the information of the letter itself, and are reminded again just how helpful Acts is in other cases. Paul is writing to a group of churches (Gal. 1:2) whose members he can call Galatians (3:1). They could be descendants of Celtic tribes who inhabited the territory whose major city was Ancyra or people who lived in the southern part of the same land mass, which bore the name of the Roman province Galatia. The cities of Iconium, Lystra, and Derbe, evangelized by Paul and Barnabas (Acts 14:1–21), were in that province, though Luke does not identify it by its name. When he does speak of Galatia, he joins it with Phrygia. He has Paul make a short trip through this territory, without mentioning the foundation of churches (Acts 16:6). Later, Paul swings through both territories again to visit churches there (Acts 18:23; cf. 20:4).

It is doubtful we would be much helped even if we could decide where the addressees of Paul's letter lived. The dating of the letter is equally uncertain. Paul says the troubles there began "so quickly" (Gal. 1:6) and he recalls his first visit to them (4:13–14; cf. 1 Thess. 2:1–16); these might be indications of an early date. Some place Galatians later because of its thematic resemblance to Romans. It could be any time during Paul's active career. We also know nothing about the provenience: Ephesus is a convenient candidate because it is close enough to both regions and a known Pauline residence.

The tone of the letter is distinctive. Its rhetoric is emotional and polemical from its beginning, "Paul an apostle not from men but from God" (1:1), to its end, "Henceforth let no man bother me, for I bear on my body the marks of Christ" (6:17). Paul drops his characteristic thanksgiving period, and replaces it with "I am astonished! [*thaumazō*]" (1:6). Against those who are causing trouble he twice levels a curse (*anathema*; 1:8, 9). He accuses the congregation of stupidity (3:1) and is anguished by its fickleness: "I am afraid I have labored over you in vain" (4:11); "You were running so well, who has hindered you from obeying the truth?" (5:7). He is openly hostile toward the troublemakers: "I wish those who upset you would mutilate themselves" (5:12). Equally sharp is the opposition Paul establishes in this letter between slavery and freedom, between spirit and flesh, between law and faith, and between death and life. The theological vocabulary that in Romans is placed within the frame of a magisterial statement is here forged in combat and is all the sharper because of it. Yet this letter is by no means simply an outpouring of raw emotion. Its polemic is not random but carefully aimed, and the largest part of Galatians is a carefully constructed argument. Both the polemic and the thought of Galatians can best be appreciated when we try to reconstruct the situation they addressed, within the limits of the text itself.

THE OCCASION AND THE ISSUES

In spite of a physical weakness, Paul had founded these churches: "You know that it was because of a bodily ailment that I preached the gospel to you at first; and though my condition was a trial to you, you did not scorn or despise me, but received me as an angel of God, as Christ Jesus" (4:13–14). The term "angel of God" may also be rendered "messenger from God" and shows us again how Paul appropriated the sort of self-designation Hellenistic philosophers also used (see Epictetus *Diss.* III.22.49, 63,72). There may also be implied in the term a contrast to other messengers (see 1:8; 3:19). When the Galatians received him "as Christ Jesus," they recognized an intimate, even mystical, identity between the Messiah and his emissary. Paul's mystical bonding with Jesus is distinctive in this letter (see 1:16; 2:20; 6:14, 17), though not unique to it (cf. 2 Cor. 5:16–21).

In order to grasp the problem and Paul's response, it is crucial to understand that the Galatians were converted directly from paganism (2:8, 14; 3:8, 14; 4:8–9; 6:13). Paul's preaching was probably the first they had ever heard of Torah; certainly they had not lived by it (3:2; 4:21; 5:4). Second, when Paul preached a crucified Messiah to them (3:1) and they accepted this message as "good news" in faith, they received a palpable outpouring of the Holy Spirit, manifest in wondrous deeds (3:2–5). They had thereby come "to know God, or rather to be known by God" (4:9). Their "life in the Spirit" (5:25) had come about precisely through the preaching of the cross (3:1). The community, however, did not have a mature grasp of this identity "in Christ." Events in the churches since their conversion and his departure have made Paul anxious: "My little children, with whom I am again in travail, until Christ be formed in you! I wish I could be present with you now and change my tone, for I am perplexed about you" (4:19–20). What has happened to make these churches, which formerly would "pluck out their eyes" for Paul (4:15), now doubt both him and his message?

Paul is not at all certain who is responsible for their "turning to another gospel" (1:6). He asks them, "Who has bewitched you?" (3:1), and "Who hindered you from obeying the truth?" (5:7). He is certain that at stake is the "truth of the gospel" (2:5, 14; 4:16; 5:7). Since Paul is vague, and perhaps even ignorant, concerning the troublemakers' identity, we have no definite knowledge of them, either. The methodological problems of identifying the rivals in Corinth face us here as well. There are real people whom Paul opposes, but we know not *their* understanding but only Paul's perception of it. Many suggestions about the opponents in Galatia have been made. Were they representatives of the "James party" from Jerusalem (2:12) or "Gnostics" (4:9)? The problem is made more complex because the real difficulty seems to lie within the community. A stimulus may be coming from the outside ("They make much of you," 4:17), but individuals within the church are agitating for a different version of the gospel ("those *being* circumcised," 5:3). Although Paul is against those who "compel you to be circumcised" (6:12–13), he may himself not know whether they are insiders or outsiders. His energy is consequently directed at those likely to be seduced, the "foolish Galatians" themselves. From ancient times, the deviance Paul struggles to correct has been called judaizing (from "to live like a Jew," 2:14), a term appropriate not for Jews but for Gentiles who wish to imitate them. It indicates in broad terms the question agitating the young gentile communities: Did they need Torah as well as Christ?

The agitators have two interrelated complaints. First, like the rivals in Corinth, they question Paul's apostolic credentials. Paul is not one of the original apostles but is dependent on Jerusalem (and therefore should obey Jerusalem!). He is inconsistent in his teaching and practice, trying to please people rather than God; indeed, he has even circumcised one of his closest delegates, Titus (2:3). But second, just as Paul's apostolic credentials are deficient, so is his "good news." He has preached only of God's work in the crucified Messiah. He therefore delivers to the Galatians an incomplete, inadequate form of Christianity. In order to be truly right-eous—to be in a proper covenantal relationship with God—it is necessary as well to observe the commandments of Torah.

The Messiah is, after all (we can hear them say), a Jewish savior. Being "in the Messiah" therefore demands as well becoming part of the historic people, the "Israel of God" (6:16). Circumcision is the ritual symbol for "taking on the yoke of Torah" (see 5:1), which initiates one into this people. Paul deceived the Galatians by foisting on them merely the ritual washing of baptism. Like commitment to Christ, it is a beginning, but more is required for full maturity. Obedience to the gospel without obe-dience to Torah's commandments is, according to Paul's opponents, a superficial and distorted version of Judaism. The ultimate norm for God's righteousness, and therefore for human righteousness, is now as always Torah. If they are circumcised, the Galatians signal their willingness to advance to this more mature station within the people of God (5:2).

So much of their argument seems clear. Some details are hard to pin down, because we do not know whether they or Paul injected them into the debate. Did they, for example, make a point of the angels' role in the giving of Torah, or did Paul (3:19)? Did they advocate obeisance to angelic forces, the "elements of the universe," or did Paul draw that polemical equation (4:3, 9)? Did they or he make the connection between the observance of "days and months and seasons and years" and the obser-vance of Torah (4:10)?

In any case, the religious issues raised by this dispute over circumcision go far beyond proper ritual procedure. They touch on the adequacy of the experience of God in Jesus, and on whether Torah or "the law of Christ" is the ultimate norm for Christian existence. These questions lead in turn to the relationship between God and humans: Is it established by human effort or always by God's gift? Is God constrained by human ways of measuring his consistency, or must humans measure themselves by the ways God shows himself to be consistent? This in turn leads to the question of God's nature: Is God ultimately a passive bookkeeper who, after shaping the world, lets it alone, concerned only to tally the relative merits of his creatures? Or is God one who is at every moment creating anew, redeeming, sanctifying, the source of all that is, and the goal toward which all things tend? Does God act in strange and unexpected ways, or is God locked into his own past?

Paul perceives such questions as implicit within the seemingly in-nocuous gentile desire for "something more" than Christ. By their desire for more, the Gentiles will lose what they already have (5:2–4). Paul's defense of his apostolic office is intimately connected to his defense of the adequacy of his gospel, for on both does the "truth" of the Galatians' experience of God rest.

Much in Paul's response is difficult to understand, not only because we hear only one side of the conversation but also because the symbols presupposed by both parties, and their modes of argumentation, are sometimes obscure. But Paul's basic theological method is clear. He begins with his personal experience (1:1, 4, 11–12, 15; 2:11–20; 4:12; 6:14, 17) and the personal experience of his community (1:4; 3:1–5; 4:13–15; 5:24–25). And in the light of these mutually confirming experiences, he reinterprets the very Torah that is the point of disputation (3:6—4:31). In his manner of presentation, therefore, Paul already answers the basic question: the experience of God in Jesus Messiah is the ultimate norm for life before God. Even Torah itself must henceforth be understood in the light of this new experience of God.

APOSTOLIC APOLOGIA

Against insinuations that his apostleship is derived and dependent, Paul insists that it came by a direct call (1:1) and election (1:15) from God, who in a revelation of Jesus Messiah (1:12) turned Paul's life around. He has not been dependent on the Jerusalem community. He did not confer with its leadership after his call (1:16). His only meeting was private and a full three years after the start of his ministry (1:18–20). When he had a full meeting with the "pillars" of that church fourteen years later, he was recognized by them as their full equal. They agreed to divide the mission between him and Peter (2:9); Titus was not required to be circumcised (2:2–3) and their only request concerned a matter he had already begun: the care for the poor (2:10). All this, despite the "false brethren" who had tried to "spy out our freedom" (2:4). Paul wants the Galatians to grasp this analogy to their present situation. Paul had not then submitted to the false brethren, "so that the truth of the gospel might be preserved for you" (2:5). So now, he wants them to resist any threat to their freedom. The final evidence for Paul's independence as an apostle, as well as his consistency, is his confrontation with Cephas. When even Paul's partner Barnabas (see 2:1) had capitulated to the pressure exerted by "certain men from James" (2:12) and stopped eating with Gentiles in Antioch, Paul opposed Cephas to his face (2:11), because he and Barnabas and all the Jews had not been "straightforward about the truth of the gospel" (2:14). Paul's consistency is also shown by the opposition he had to face in the past and continues to face: "If I were still pleasing men, I would not be a slave of Christ" (1:10). The sign of the servant is suffering and rejection: "But if I, brethren, still preach circumcision, why am I still persecuted?" (5:11); "I bear on my body the marks of Jesus" (6:17).

Paul turns the charge of insincerity back on his opponents (2:13). Those upsetting the Galatians are like the "false brethren" who had bothered him both in Jerusalem and Antioch (2:4, 12). They are deceivers: "They make much of you, but for no good purpose; they want to shut you out, so that you may make much of them" (4:17). Paul suggests in 6:12–13 that their real motivation is not only to gain prestige but to avoid persecution from the Jews:

> It is those who want to make a good showing in the flesh that would compel you to be circumcised, and only in order that they may not be persecuted for the cross of Christ. For even those who receive circumcision do not themselves keep the law, but they desire to have you circumcised that they may glory in your flesh.

What stake did community members have in circumcision? It made them appear to be normal members of Israel rather than candidates for persecution and martyrdom. Why was there such persecution? Because the crucified Messiah was a stumbling block to those who saw Torah as the ultimate norm of righteousness (3:13)—as Paul's own past experience showed (1:13–14). The choice of circumcision was, in Paul's eyes, both cowardly and a rejection of the experience of God through the preaching of the crucified Messiah (3:1). Paul himself utterly rejects (6:14) that choice:

> But far be it from me to glory except in the cross of our Lord, Jesus Christ, by which the world has been crucified to me, and I to the world.

The Galatians outrage and puzzle (4:15) Paul all the more because of their willingness to deny their own experience, something he refuses to do. In their hearing of the gospel, they had already powerfully experienced the Holy Spirit (3:2–5). In their baptism, they had already been joined to the Messiah as children of God and heirs of the kingdom (3:26–27) and could call God, Father (4:6–7). To seek now another form of initiation is to denigrate the first. To seek righteousness by the norm of Torah means denying the righteousness they received from the faith of the Messiah. The Galatians resemble healthily breathing people who are told the *only* way to breathe is by means of an artificial respirator. No one can deny the efficiency of a respirator for those who cannot breathe for themselves. But if the Galatians are now breathing by the life of the Spirit, to choose a respirator is to choose slavery.

THE GOSPEL IN OUTLINE

Paul's defense of the gospel is so dense and elliptical that it is helpful to review some of his presuppositions, such as we are able to pick out from his argument here as well as from the fuller exposition of Romans.

A person is established in a right relationship with God not by external observance of commandments but by a fundamental response called faith

(2:16; 3:11). Such faith is a yes to the transcendent Holy One. It means a turning away from the no that is idolatry—the refusal of God's claim on human existence in favor of lesser and more easily managed powers (4:8–9). God calls all human beings to this form of righteousness. In whatever circumstances God becomes manifest, the human being must respond. In Torah, Paul finds the primordial pattern of this dialogue in God's promise (3:22). God promised a blessing to Abraham and his descendants, which elicited faith (3:8, 16–18), and that promise has come to fulfillment in Jesus (3:16b, 22, 26, 29).

But whose faith is now at work? There is great dispute over this stage of Paul's perception because of the ambiguity of his language, particularly in the elliptical expression *pistis christou*. The expression can be translated either "faith *in* Christ" or "faith *of* Christ." What makes the case difficult is that Paul seems to mean both, at different times. He can speak clearly about the Christians' "faith in Christ" (Phil. 3:9; Col. 1:4). This kind of faith is confessional: those who have faith in Christ acknowledge that God has manifested himself in the Christ and commit themselves to that revelation. But Paul also uses faith language with God as the object, as in "Abraham believed God" (3:6). The difficult question is whether he speaks of Jesus' responding in this way to God—whether he speaks of the "faith *of* Christ"—and if so, what the significance of that response is. In almost all contemporary translations and commentaries, there is a clear bias toward only one understanding, that of "faith *in* Christ." If this is correct, then Paul opposes two principles of salvation: that which seeks to win God's favor by observance of Torah and that which responds to God by "faith in Christ."

I am convinced that the minority opinion is in this case correct, and that Paul sometimes uses the expression *pistis Christou* to speak of the human response of the man Jesus to God: the "faith of the Messiah." This response of Jesus, furthermore, is part of the salvific act. What Paul means by it is the faithful *obedience* that Jesus showed to the Father in his life and death (see Phil. 2:6–11; Rom. 5:18–19). The "faith of Jesus" is Jesus' human response to God, which enables others to "have faith" and to "be made righteous by faith." The fundamental gift of righteousness, in other words, is established by God in the cross through Jesus' obedience, and is then appropriated by humans as they trust and obey this manifestation of God, answering as did Jesus, Yes.

It is in this sense that Paul speaks of faith, in 2:20 (against the RSV): "I live by the faith of the Son of God who loved me and gave himself for me." Throughout this letter, Paul emphasizes that in accordance with the will of God (1:4) Jesus was active in the bestowal of the gift to humans. He gave himself and delivered humans from the present age (1:4; 4:5). If this faith of Jesus establishes righteousness, those who accept the gospel accept such righteousness in obedience and trust, receiving as a result the Holy Spirit (3:2, 5; 4:6, 29; 5:5). In this, the promise to Abraham is fulfilled for both Jews and Gentiles (3:8, 28).

Since this Spirit is the very life and power of God, it brings freedom from death, slavery, flesh, and the law (4:1–7, 31; 5:1, 13). The source of life determines the shape of life. If persons live by the Spirit of God, then their existence is given its norm by the same Spirit. Both power and norm, the Spirit relativizes the ultimacy of Torah as the measure of life before God (5:16–18, 25; 6:8). Nor is the work of the Spirit random. It replicates in individual human lives the pattern of life for others that is found in Jesus. This pattern is "the law of the Messiah" (6:2; cf. 2:20; 4:6–7, 19; 5:24; 6:14). God's life has come to the Galatians entirely unmediated by Torah.

What, then, is the status of Torah? It is both annulled and fulfilled by the Messiah. It is annulled as an absolute norm for God's activity and human righteousness. If the only measure of righteousness is Torah, then Jesus cannot be the source of God's life? Why? Because Jesus is not righteous by that norm. He is a "sinner," one "cursed by God" because he "hangs on a tree" (Deut. 21:23). The cross is therefore pivotal, for Torah will not allow a crucified messiah. But if the Galatians have come to know, or to be known by, God through Jesus, something has to give: Torah can no longer be ultimate.

The necessary choice between Jesus and Torah as *ultimate* norm for life shows why Paul calls the desire for circumcision apostasy from Christ (5:4) and an attempt to avoid persecution for the cross (6:12). When Paul declares that "Christ redeemed us from the curse of the law, having become a curse for us" (3:13), the corollary is that Torah's power is annulled. Jesus cannot at once be their righteousness and cursed by God. But Paul goes further: those baptized into the Messiah have also "died to the law" (2:19) since their life comes from the spirit of the resurrected Jesus. Paul therefore can conclude: "I do not nullify the grace of God, for if righteousness were through the law, then Christ died to no purpose" (2:21).

Torah is also fulfilled in the Messiah. It was always more than law, being also God's revelation and wisdom. Paul cannot even speak of righteousness without using Torah's narratives and prophecies. Only in Romans does he more fully state Torah's function as witness to the Messiah (see Rom. 3:21), but even here, we see that the problem is less with Torah than with the claims that it is a source of life (3:12). Torah as the definitive norm of God's work is superseded. God did something new in Jesus' death; he revealed righteousness outside the norm of Torah. This calls for a new response of faith, which shows that Torah as the bearer of promise is also fulfilled. Before Jesus, one could think of Torah as ultimate, as Paul himself had when he persecuted the church of God (1:13). But it never gave life (3:21). Paul could not understand Jesus without the symbol of Torah; but neither could he rightly understand the symbols of Torah without Jesus.

Before the Messiah, the Torah had two functions. It helped reveal the slavery to sin under which all humans labored before the heir came (3:19). It also functioned as a pedagogue, holding humans under the restraint of minimal moral observance until faith was revealed (3:23). But in the light of God's revelation in the cross and resurrection of Jesus, "circumcision means nothing, uncircumcision means nothing, but [there is] a new creation" (6:15).

THE ARGUMENT OF GAL. 2:15—4:31

Some observations on the stages of Paul's argument can now be made. Paul's use of midrash in the heart of this letter is technical and complex. His Pharisaic teachers would applaud his methods, although they would be appalled by his conclusions. His argument is not convincing, unless one agrees with his starting point, the experience of God's life through Jesus.

The argument begins directly from his apologetic narration without transition. He begins with a series of dialectical assertions much like those of 5:2–6, which recapitulate the argument. Paul insists on the opposition between the faith that comes through the Messiah and observance of the law, as principles of righteousness (2:15–16). This does not mean, however, that the one who chooses faith is a sinner (2:17–18). Why? Because Paul and other Christians are mystically united to the Messiah and live through him (2:19–21). This is not yet explained, though we later learn that baptism is an initiation into the Messiah's life (3:27). At this stage, Paul stresses the connection between (a) the present life of Christians, (b) its origin in God, and (c) its mediation through the cross of Jesus.

The appeal to experience (3:1–5) is critical to his argument. If the Galatians agree, then his argument is cogent. But if they disagree, then they deny their own experience. They have been given life through the Holy Spirit. It was mediated through the preaching of the cross and it was a preaching received in faith, not by observance of law. If they were already breathing, then why should they need a respirator?

If their shared experience is granted, then Paul can begin to reinterpret Torah in the light of it. His first appeal to Scripture takes the form of a balanced series of propositions. He uses two statements about Abraham in Genesis: that all nations would be blessed in him (Gen. 12:3), and that his righteousness came by faith (Gen. 15:6). On this basis, Paul can conclude that all nations (that is, Gentiles) who had faith were also children of Abraham and shared his blessing (3:6–9). The value of Torah as a witness is implicitly asserted here, but its meaning is only unlocked by the present experience of God; in the narrative of the promise the Galatians find the beginning of their own story.

Paul's second appeal to Scripture (3:10–14) forms a tight midrash on Torah. Paul uses the midrashic rule that when two texts of Scripture contradict each other, a third text can resolve them. Here, we see that the prophet Habakkuk says that life comes from the righteousness of faith (Hab. 2:4). But Lev. 18:5 claims that life comes by observing the commands of law. Paul sharpens the contradiction by citing in favor of Leviticus the text of Deut. 27:26, which levies a curse (the opposite of life) on those who do not keep the commandments. But then he says that this curse was redeemed by Jesus. How? First, in that his death was one cursed—according to Deut. 21:23—since he was hanged on a tree. Second, however, in that Jesus' crucifixion did not lead to a curse but led to a blessing, did not end in death but led to life: Jesus above all *lives*! It follows, therefore, that in this conflict between texts, the one stands that says, "The righteous one will live by his faith" (Hab. 2:4), and it is fulfilled first in the faithful death and resurrection of Jesus Messiah.

Paul's third appeal to Scripture (3:16–18) is a midrash on the promise to Abraham in Gen. 12:3–7. It is complicated and depends on the technique of reading a collective noun (*sperma*, "seed" or "offspring") as a singular and referring it not to all of Abraham's descendants but to a single individual—the Messiah (see also 2 Sam. 7:14)—and then to those who belong to him. Paul has thereby shown that the Messiah is the ratification of the essential covenant (*diathēkē*, also "will") between God and humans, thus leaping over the Mosaic covenant as though it were only a digression.

But was the Mosaic covenant simply a mistake? Only in its claims, not in its purposes. Torah was not eternal but only a temporary agreement; it was not given directly by God but only through the mediation of Moses, and angels; it did not, above all, lead to life (3:21). It could reveal transgression and teach morality, but it could not empower or transform. The law did not contradict but neither did it fulfill the promise (3:21–22). Only in the Messiah's faith is the promise fulfilled (3:22). And Christians are joined to the Messiah by the response of faith and by the ritual of baptism; they become thereby "one in Christ Jesus . . . heirs according to the promise" (3:29).

Paul now moves to the contrast between slavery and freedom. Both Jews and Gentiles were like slaves before the coming of the Messiah. As children under the guardianship of the law, the Jews were no better off than the pagans who were subject to cosmic forces (4:1–4, 8–9). Only the Son can give them both a "share in the inheritance" that is his by nature and that will enable them to enjoy the freedom of the children of God (4:6–7):

And because you are sons, God has sent the Spirit of his son into our hearts crying, Abba, Father! So through God you are no longer a slave but a son, and if a son, then an heir.

The same contrast between slavery and freedom provides the perspective for Paul's fourth appeal to Scripture, addressed by way of rebuke to those who "wish to be under the law" (4:21–31). In an allegorical interpretation worthy of his contemporary Philo Judaeus, Paul works with Genesis 16 and 21 together with Isaiah 54 from the vantage point of the conviction that Christians as the "children of Abraham" enjoyed the freedom of sons, whereas the Jews were still enslaved. As Isaac was formerly persecuted by Ishmael, so are the present children of the free woman being persecuted by the Jews (4:29). In a very bold move, Paul says (4:30; cf. Gen. 21:10):

But what does the Scripture say? "Cast out the slave and her son; for the son of a slave shall not inherit with the son of the free woman."

Jews persecuted Christians because of the cross. But the cross brought the Christians life and freedom, made them children of the promise. They can therefore "cast out" those in their midst who advocated a flight from the cross to circumcision.

In Gal. 5:2–6, Paul presents a summation of the argument. Those who seek circumcision deny their experience of God and turn away from Christ. Within the community of the Messiah, distinctions between Jew and Gentile are meaningless, "for in Christ Jesus, neither circumcision nor uncircumcision is of any avail, but faith working through love" (5:6).

LIFE ACCORDING TO THE SPIRIT

The Spirit is both the power and the norm for life before God (5:25). Rejection of Torah as an ultimate norm for righteousness does not mean its rejection as a moral guide, much less an opening to antinomianism. Self-aggrandizement, living according to the flesh, is always part of the human predicament before God's rule is finally established (5:21). Those given the Spirit, however, are called to conform their behavior to *its* impulses rather than to those that arise from self-seeking. The impulse of the flesh based on rivalry and competition leads to boasting in one's own accomplishments and contempt of others; such an attitude is not foreign to those wishing to impose Torah observance and circumcision as a measurement of righteousness: "If you bite and devour one another, take heed that you are not consumed by each other" (5:15).

Like the Corinthian elitists, the Judaizers must be reminded of the community context of their lives. The gift of God's Spirit enables them to live by the "law of the Messiah," which requires a life lived for others rather than oneself: "Bear one another's burdens and so fulfill the law of Christ" (6:2). Although each person must answer to God individually (6:4–5), care and compassion are demanded for others (6:1). Christians are to "do good to all men, especially to those who are of the household of the faith" (6:10).

The flesh leads to rivalry, dissension, and party spirit; it wages war against the Spirit (5:19–21). The Spirit's work, in contrast, is manifested in attitudes of community upbuilding, beginning with love (agapē): "Against these, there is no law" (5:23). The Galatians by God's gift have been freed from the power of the flesh even though they must continue to resist it (5:13). And they are enabled by the Spirit to have the disposition to resist it: "Those who belong to Christ Jesus have crucified the flesh with its passions and desires" (5:24).

The full meaning of Torah is found only in Jesus. Torah never ceases to provide a norm for Christian existence. But it does so only as understood through the pattern of Jesus' life for others: "Through love be servants of one another. For the whole law is fulfilled in one word: 'You shall love your neighbor as yourself' " (5:13–14; cf. Lev. 19:18). Those who "walk by this norm" are the true "Israel of God," and upon them by the gift of the Spirit comes peace (6:16).

BIBLIOGRAPHICAL NOTE

Despite our lack of real information about the Galatian churches, there have been many attempts to reconstruct the situation faced by Paul. A sampling: W. Schmithals, *Paul and the Gnostics*, trans. J. Steely (Nashville: Abingdon Press, 1972), 13–64; J. Tyson, "Paul's Opponents in Galatia," *NovT* 10 (1968): 241–54; R. Jewett, "The Agitators and the Galatian Community," *NTS* 17 (1970): 198–212; A. E. Harvey, "The Opposition of Paul," *SE* 4 (1968): 319–32; R. McL. Wilson, "Gnostics—in Galatia?" *SE* 4 (1968): 358–67. The most convincing rendering is that by J. Munck, "The Judaizing Gentile Christians," in his *Paul and the Salvation of Mankind*, trans. F. Clarke (Richmond: John Knox Press, 1959), 87–134.

The most thorough attempt to deal with Galatians within the canons of ancient epistolary rhetoric has been made by H. D. Betz, "The Literary Composition and Function of Paul's Letter to the Galatians," *NTS* 21 (1974–5): 353–373; see also J. D. Hester, "The Rhetorical Structure of Galatians 1:11—2:14," *JBL* 103 (1984): 223–33. For the Jerusalem visit and meeting with Cephas set against the background of legal norms, see J. P. Sampley, "Societas Christi: Roman Law and Paul's Conception of the Christian Community," in *God's Christ and His People*, ed. J. J. Jervell and W. A. Meeks (Oslo: Universitetsforlaget, 1977), 158–74.

The basic lines of Paul's position are well sketched by M. Barth, "The Kerygma of Galatians," *Int* 21 (1967): 131–46; and L. Cerfaux, "Christ Our Justice," in his *Christ in the Theology of St. Paul* (New York: Herder & Herder, 1959), 205–29.

For the issues concerning Torah, see J. Tyson, "'Works of Law' in Galatians," *JBL* 92 (1973): 423–31; J. A. Sanders, "Torah and Paul," in *God's Christ and His People*, ed. Jervell and Meeks, 132–40; W. D. Davies, *Paul and Rabbinic Judaism: Some Rabbinic Elements in Pauline Theology*, 4th ed. (Philadelphia: Fortress Press, 1980 [1948]), 17–57; H.-J. Schoeps, "Paul's Misunderstanding of the Law," in *The Writings of St. Paul*, ed. W. A. Meeks (New York: W. W. Norton & Co., 1972), 349–60; E. P. Sanders, "On the Question of Fulfilling the Law in Paul and Rabbinic Judaism," in *Donum Gentilicum*, ed. E. Bammel, C. K. Barrett, and W. D. Davies (Oxford: At the Clarendon Press, 1978), 103–26.

The complexities of Paul's scriptural argument are touched on in N. A. Dahl, "Contradictions in Scripture," in his *Studies in Paul* (Minneapolis: Augsburg Pub. House, 1977), 159–77; idem, "The Atonement—Adequate Reward for the Akedah?" in his *The Crucified Messiah* (Minneapolis: Augsburg Pub. House, 1974), 146–60; B. Lindars, *New Testament Apologetic: The Doctrinal Significance of the Old Testament Quotations* (Philadelphia: Westminster Press, 1961), 232–37; M. Wilcox, "'Upon the Tree'—Deut 21:22–23 in the New Testament," *JBL* 96 (1977): 85–99; T. Callan, "Pauline Midrash: The Exegetical Background of Gal. 3:19b," *JBL* 99 (1980): 549–67. For the significance of the Galatian experience for Paul's argument, see D. J. Lull, *The Spirit in Galatia*, SBLDS 49 (Chico, Calif.: Scholars Press, 1980).

The "faith in/of Christ" issue is discussed from the traditional standpoint by A. Hultgren, "The *Pistis Christou* Formulations in Paul," *NovT* 22 (1980): 248–63. My treatment in chap. 13 of this book agrees more with the position of M. Barth, "The Faith of the Messiah," *Heythrop Journal* 10 (1969): 363–70; G. Howard, *Paul: Crisis in Galatia*, SNTSMS 35 (Cambridge: At the Univ. Press, 1979); and esp. R. B. Hays, *The Faith of Jesus*, SBLDS 56 (Chico, Calif.: Scholars Press, 1983).

Questions of Pauline anthropology are almost inevitably raised by Galatians. For the argument that it was conditioned by the polemical context, see R. Jewett, *Paul's Anthropological Terms: A Study of Their Use in Conflict Settings*, AGJU 10 (Leiden: E. J. Brill, 1971). For more systematic presentations, see R. Bultmann, *Theology of the New Testament* (New York: Charles Scribner's Sons, 1953), 1:259–88; J. A. Fitzmyer, *Pauline Theology: A Brief Sketch* (Englewood Cliffs, N.J.: Prentice-Hall, 1967), 53–74.

Galatians has not lacked commentaries, particularly of a theological character. For a recent critical commentary with full bibliography and careful attention to literary form, see H. D. Betz, *Galatians: A Commentary on Paul's Letter to the Churches in Galatia*, Hermeneia (Philadelphia: Fortress Press, 1979). A thoroughly theological treatment is found in G. Ebeling, *The Truth of the Gospel: An Exposition on Galatians*, trans. D. Green (Philadelphia: Fortress Press, 1985). An accessible commentary is that of C. B. Cousar, *Galatians*, Interpretation (Atlanta: John Knox Press, 1982).

14

The Letter to the Romans

Romans is generally considered the central writing in the Pauline corpus for its subject matter as well as the length, power, and clarity of its argument. Unlike those letters whose responses to specific problems are virtually sketched in shorthand, Romans is an epistle both ample and magisterial. It is unmistakably scholastic, with an air of detachment that puts severely to the test easy equations between purpose and meaning. Paul's reasons for writing Romans are not obscure, but there is a great gap between his prosaic purpose and the beauty of the instrument he crafted to meet it.

He had neither established (see Acts 28:15) nor ever met the Roman churches (Rom. 1:10–13). He does not write in response to a crisis within the community. His treatment of differences between the "strong" and the "weak" is general (14:1—15:6). There may have been differences in practice within—or between—the Roman assemblies, but Paul's knowledge of them does not appear either detailed or intimate; there is no urgency to his discussion. He is careful throughout the letter not to assert the same role he thought he could assume with the Corinthians (1 Cor. 4:15), since he was neither a founder nor father. He qualifies his desire to "impart some spiritual gift to them," for example, by adding quickly, "that is, that we may be mutually encouraged by each other's faith, yours and mine" (1:12). Although he wrote "on some points very boldly by way of reminder" (15:15), he does not suggest that the Romans deserve rebuke for any deficiency: "I myself am satisfied about you, my brethren, that you yourselves are full of goodness, filled with all knowledge, and are able to instruct one another" (15:14; cf. 16:17–20).

Paul's purpose in writing is practical and has to do with the future of his mission. In the thanksgiving, he says he had wanted to visit the Romans for a long time but had been delayed (1:10–11, 13). He explains at the end of the letter why he had not come earlier (15:22): he had been preaching throughout the East, "from Jerusalem to Illyricum" (15:19), always in places no one else had gone (15:20). Now he has completed that circuit and hopes to begin a mission to the West, toward Spain (15:24), using Rome as his point of departure (15:24). Before he can do that, he plans to complete delivery of his collection from the gentile churches to Jerusalem (15:25–29). He is not sure of success and asks for prayers that his gift be accepted (15:30–31).

Paul is at a juncture in his ministry, marked by the completion of his reconciling work between Jew and Gentile. With the symbolism of that enterprise in his mind, he writes to the Romans, preparing the way for them to become his new base of operations in the West, as Philippi had been for his Macedonian and Achaian mission (Phil. 4:15; 2 Cor. 11:9). He hints at his financial expectations in the thanksgiving; he had wanted to visit earlier "to reap some harvest among you as well as the rest of the Gentiles" (1:13). He had wanted, in other words, to include the Romans in the collection effort. Now he offers them another chance to provide support. The end of the letter makes his desire plain. He hopes "to be sped on my journey there [to Spain] once I have enjoyed your company for a little" (15:24). The term "be sped on my journey," *propempo*, is used technically for outfitting expeditions (cf. 3 John 6). His expectation to be refreshed *(synanapauomai)* among them also suggests monetary support (15:32; cf. the use of "refreshed," *anapauō*, in Phlm. 7).

This expectation enables us to make good sense of Romans 16, which at first sight seems a strange appendix; indeed, some scholars have questioned whether it originally belonged to Romans. But the chapter admirably serves Paul's purpose. The greetings demonstrate Paul's extensive contacts within the community and thus serve to recommend him. More pertinently, Paul recommends to the Romans the deacon of the church at Cenchrae, Phoebe (16:1–3). Paul says that "she has been a helper of many and of myself as well." The term "helper," *prostatis*, is often used of financial patrons. Paul now expects the Romans in turn "to help her in whatever she may require from you." His language unmistakably refers to financial matters. Phoebe has helped support Paul's mission in the East, and he now sends her to Rome, to organize and prepare for his expedition to the West. The end of Romans is a letter of recommendation for Phoebe to the Roman church.

But if Paul's purpose is so practical, why did he write so long and elaborate a letter? Because he was known to this church only by name, his understanding of the gospel and of his mission was not known. Before he could ask a new community to support his mission financially, he had to let it know what it would be backing. Romans is therefore Paul's letter of recommendation *for Paul*. It is true he had rejected such letters from local churches (2 Cor. 3:2), but that was when he had founded such communities. On the other hand, who could recommend a "servant of Jesus Christ," one "called to be an apostle, set apart for the gospel of God" (1:1), except the apostle himself, through his teaching? For Paul to recommend his ministry is to recommend the gospel in which he "boasts" (1:16).

Romans is by no means a systematic summary of Paul's theology. Many of his distinctive ideas about Jesus, the end time, wisdom, and reconciliation are at best only touched on. Instead, the letter brings to mature expression Paul's religious interpretation of his work of evangelization and reconciliation among the churches of the East. The teaching on justification by faith shaped by the polemic of Galatians is here placed on a more explicit anthropological basis and made the principle for interpreting the relations between Jew and Gentile in history. The pastoral response to community conflicts in Corinth is here placed within the same overarching framework.

The epistolary structure of Romans is unexceptional. In terms of content, however, the letter at first appears to be divided between a theological argument devoted to justification by faith (chaps. 1—8) and an appendix devoted to scriptural midrash (chaps. 9—11), with general ethical teaching added on (chaps. 12—15). In fact, however, chapters 9—11 are not an appendix but the climax to the opening argument, and chapters 12—15 are not as separate from the thesis of the letter as at first appears. Notice how 15:1-3 makes a transition from parenesis back to history. There is, furthermore, thematic unity in the three discernible sections of the letter. Paul first demonstrates God's way of making humans righteous; the premise underlying his argument is the lack of partiality in God (chaps. 1—8). He then shows God's righteousness being worked out in the history of Jews and Gentiles. The principle here is the same: there is no partiality in God (chaps. 9—11). He then applies that same principle as a paradigm for life together in any Christian community (chaps. 12—15). The argument of Romans is therefore theological in the proper sense. It describes and praises the work of the one from whom, and through whom, and to whom are all things (11:36).

ROMANS AS SCHOLASTIC DIATRIBE

The affinity between Romans and the Hellenistic rhetorical style known as the diatribe has long been observed. A vivid, dialogical form of discourse, the diatribe uses many separate stylistic devices that are detectable in Romans: apostrophe (2:1, 3, 17); rhetorical questions (2:3-4, 21-23; 7:1; 8:31-35; 9:19-21, 30; 10:14-15; 11:34-35); questions answered by abrupt answers like "By no means" (3:2-9; 6:1-2, 15; 7:7, 13; 11:1, 11); hyperbole (8:37-39; 9:3); vice lists (1:29-31); exemplars from the past (4:1-25); citation of written texts as authorities (9:1—11:36). All these devices help place the reader within a literary dialogue between a speaker and an imagined audience. The concentration of these elements outside

Romans is strongest in the *Discourses* of Epictetus, but the elements are found in other philosophers and rhetoricians as well.

Because of the oral character of the diatribe, it was long thought to be a style of public preaching such as that carried out by Cynic philosophers on street corners. By analogy, Romans would be a sample of Paul's preaching sent to the Romans in epistolary form. Recent investigation has shown that the life setting for the diatribe was not public preaching but the classroom. Epictetus, for example, ran a school for would-be philosophers. By analogy, then, Romans is a sample of Paul's teaching within his school of delegates and fellow workers. The diatribe is not a formless rant but a structured form of argument with the following features: *(a)* a statement of thesis (e.g., "Every good person is free"); *(b)* a demonstration by means of antithesis (e.g., of how vice leads to slavery); *(c)* a restatement of the thesis; *(d)* a demonstration of the thesis by example (e.g., that Heracles was free because of his virtue even though he was a slave); *(e)* an exposition of the thesis; *(f)* an answering of objections to the thesis (e.g., to the objection "Aren't there virtuous people who are prisoners?"). These components are not always found together, but they are often enough to support the suggestion that Romans is such a scholastic argument worked out by the Pauline school and sent to the Roman church as a commendation of Paul's gospel.

The pattern of argumentation also provides the key to reading Romans. Paul states his thesis in 1:16–17 and follows immediately with its antithesis in 1:18—3:20. He then restates the thesis in 3:21–31 and demonstrates it by example in 4:1–25, before completing his exposition in 5:1–21. Objections to the thesis are raised as early as 3:1–8 but are not picked up and answered systematically until 6:1—11:3.

THE "GOOD NEWS" OF GOD'S RIGHTEOUSNESS

The letter's greeting already commends Paul and anticipates important elements of his teaching: *(a)* he is an apostle of God (1:1); *(b)* the Gospel was promised already in the prophetic writings (1:2; cf. 10:14–21); *(c)* what he preaches fundamentally agrees with the traditions of the churches, as the traditional kerygmatic formula of Jesus as the Davidic messiah raised as Son of God by the Spirit of holiness shows (1:3–4); *(d)* Paul's distinctive missionary call is to work among Gentiles, among whom he includes the Romans (1:5–6); *(e)* the gospel demands a response Paul calls obedience of faith (1:5). This last phrase is both difficult and critical to Paul's thought (see 5:12–21; 16:26). It makes "faith" and "obedience" mutually defining terms: "the obedience which is faith," and "the faith which is obedience."

Announcement of Thesis (1:16–17)

For I am not ashamed of the gospel: it is the power for salvation to every one
who has faith, to the Jew first, and also to the Greek. For in it, the righteousness of God is revealed through faith for faith [ek pisteōs eis pistin]; as it is
written, "He who through faith is righteous shall live."

The thesis is properly dense. Paul uses litotes, understatement for
effect, when he says that he is "not ashamed," for the "good news" is
actually his basis for *boasting*, in contrast to any basis in human accomplishment (3:27; 5:2–3; cf. 1 Cor. 1:31; 2 Cor. 10:17; Gal. 6:13–14). The
"good news" is not merely verbal. It is a power *(dynamis)* for salvation (see
1 Cor. 1:18–21; 2 Cor. 2:15) at work universally, if dialectically, among
both Jew and Greek (see chaps. 9—11). In this "good news," God's
righteousness (or, "justice": *dikaiosynē*) is revealed. The phrase is poly-
valent. It refers both to a quality of God (he is just) and to God's activity
(he establishes humans in right relationship with him; see esp. 3:26). That
God is righteous was inarguable in Judaism; that humans could be righteous before him was equally unexceptionable. The edge of Paul's thesis
comes in the assertion that these propositions are "revealed in the good
news," that is, by free gift (3:24; 5:15), and appropriated by the response
of faith.

The revelation of righteousness itself is qualified by the elliptical phrase
ek pisteōs eis pistin, literally, "out of faith to faith." The phrase might
simply be adverbial: "thoroughly faithwise," or "beginning and ending in
faith." It might also specify the dynamic of gift and response: the revelation of righteousness begins in God's faithfulness to humans and is answered by their obedient acceptance. A third possibility is even more
specific and quite likely correct: God's righteousness is revealed *out of the
faith of Jesus* and *leads to the faith of Christians*. If the "faith of the
Messiah" is thus an essential part of the free gift from God, and Paul
explicitly says it is (3:25–26; 5:12–21), then the text of Hab. 2:4 refers first
of all to Jesus. He is the one who through faithful obedience is righteous
and lives (see above, 1:4). Such is the compressed statement Paul argues
through this letter.

The Antithesis: Faithless Humanity
and the Power of Sin (1:18—3:20)

By means of the antithesis, Paul seeks to show the logical need for his
thesis. The thesis argues that God's righteousness comes by gift; he
therefore wants to show that every form of human grasping misses the
mark.

He begins with an attack on idolatry borrowed from Hellenistic Judaism (see Wisdom of Solomon 13—19), giving it (in 2:17–24) a distinctive twist. Paul is also much harsher than the Wisdom of Solomon, which made allowance for the seductive beauty of created things. For Paul, "there is no excuse" (1:20; 2:1); idolatry is rebellion.

If the gospel "reveals" righteousness, the "revelation of God's wrath" comes through sin (1:18). God's wrath (*orgē tou theou*) is not a psychological category but a symbol for the retribution that comes to humans because of their willful turning away from God (2:5; 3:5; 4:15; 5:9; 12:19; 1 Thess. 1:10; 2:16; 5:9; and also Isa. 51:17; Jer. 6:11; 25:15; Hos. 13:11; Zeph. 1:15); for those alienated from God, even the face of mercy is hateful. The retribution here results from the very distortion of their existence that they chose.

That God can be known from the very shape of creation is axiomatic (1:19; Wis. 13:1). But humans can refuse to acknowledge that reality, that is, refuse to allow it to make a claim on their lives. Idolatry begins in the refusal to "glorify God as God" (1:21, 28). But to reject contingency and dependence on God is to lie about human existence and the very structure of reality. It is as though someone should die in the middle of a crowded room, but because recognition of that obvious fact would demand some response from the bystanders, they choose to ignore the undeniable fact that there is a dead body in the room with them. And if they stay in that room, their lives together become increasingly and compulsively falsified by their first great lie; they collude in ignoring the palpable fact of a dead body in the room.

So does idolatry tend toward the systematic distortion and corruption of social life. The great lie is itself a "suppression of the truth" (1:18) and leads to progressive deterioration even of the capacity to know truth (1:25). Sight itself becomes crooked ("Their senseless minds became darkened," 1:21); they begin to see the world awry according to the way they have constructed it (1:21–22). Each stage of degradation is marked by the phrase "God handed them over" (1:24, 26, 28), but it is clear that the process results from the misuse of human freedom: "They receive in their own person the due penalty for their error" (1:27). The polemic ends with the vice list in 1:29–31, which is remarkable most of all for its number of antisocial, hostile vices. Paul essentially asserts again the lesson of the Fall: rupture of the relationship with God through rebellion leads to the rupture of relations between humans, and the reign of envy and murder. Now, Jewish listeners would ordinarily be cheered by such a stock attack on pagan vice, thinking that as worshipers of the true God, they were exempt from its sting. Paul will shortly challenge that assumption.

Before turning to his self-confident Jewish hearer (real or imagined), Paul argues in 2:1–16 that God is utterly fair in his judgment. We meet here the first enunciation of the principle that "there is no partiality in

God" (2:11). The axiom is rooted in Israel's ancient legal procedures: those who sat at the gate as judges between rival claims were not to be "respecters of persons," that is, they were not to take "appearances" into account but were to consider only the merits of the case. They were not, in short, to take bribes of any kind, as Lev. 19:15 makes clear:

> You shall do no injustice in judgment; you shall not be partial to the poor or defer to the great; but in righteousness shall you judge your neighbor.

If God is such a fair judge, which is certainly also axiomatic (2:5), he must hold all people to the same standard. What is this standard? The response of the human heart to God. Using common pious vocabulary rather than the language of disputation, Paul speaks here of "works" (2:6), meaning that humans are judged by God not on the basis of their origin or ritual allegiances, but on the basis of what they in fact do, the way they live (2:9–11):

> There will be tribulation and distress for every human being who does evil; Jew first and also the Greek. But glory and honor and peace *for everyone* who does good, the Jew first and also the Greek. God shows no partiality.

And if this is so, it means that a positive response to God is also available to pagans and that God accepts such a response. This is just what Paul argues: not membership in a nation or ritual observance but the response of the heart in obedience establishes humans before God, whether they have Torah or not; the same response is required of all (2:12–16).

Paul now turns this leveling principle on any who might be smug because they possessed Torah. The Jews enjoyed tremendous privileges because of Torah (2:17–20), but if these became simply a means of measuring themselves over against others, of self-assertion (or boasting, 2:23), while they themselves did not observe the law's commandments, the privileges did not matter at all (2:25–28). According to 2:29, the Jew is one

> who is one inwardly, and real circumcision is a matter of the heart, spiritual and not literal. His praise is not from men but from God.

Paul does not deny the advantages given the Jews by Torah (3:1; cf. 9:4–5). His point is that these do not fundamentally give them an advantage with regard to their relationship with God—i.e., righteousness. Even though they have Torah, they are as much under the power of sin as pagans (3:9)—an assertion supported midrashically by a chain of verses from Torah (3:10–18; cf. Pss. 14:1–2; 53:1–2; 5:9; 140:3; 10:7; Isa. 59:7–8; Ps. 36:1), which show that "none is righteous, no not one; no one understands, no one seeks for God" (3:10; Ps. 14:1–2). The texts of Torah are addressed to those who have the "advantage" of Torah, so "that every mouth may be stopped" (3:19). The antithesis concludes in 3:20 with a paradox for Jewish understanding that will only be resolved in 7:7–12:

For no human being will be justified in his sight by works of the law, since through the law comes knowledge of sin.

The argument of the antithesis has been so compressed that some interpretive remarks might enable the reader to follow the next steps of Paul's argument more securely. Sin, as Paul speaks of it, is not first of all a moral category but a religious one. He does not suggest that every pagan and Jew is locked in vice. He would grant—if pushed to it—that both Jews and Greeks could be virtuous. Immorality is a sign and consequence of sin, but it is not itself sin. The opposite of sin is not virtue but faith. Sin and faith denominate the two fundamental responses of a human being to God: "Whatever does not proceed from faith is sin" (14:23). In such contrasts, Paul speaks of sin in the singular, because it is a rebellion found not in multiple acts of moral failure, but in a basic disposition, or orientation, of human freedom. It is a turning away from God.

At root, sin is the disposition that strives to establish one's own existence and value apart from the claims of God. It is a refusal to acknowledge contingency and dependency on an absolute other; it is idolatry. This disposition is what Paul terms "life according to the flesh," for it measures reality apart from the transcendence of spirit. He calls it boasting, for it involves a self-aggrandizement that asserts the value of the self at the expense of others. But such self-assertion arises from a deep well of fear, a primitive and pervasive terror at nonbeing and worthlessness. Refusing that side of contingency which is the gift of being from another, the idolater seeks to eliminate fear by constructing life and worth out of his or her own effort. This requires such ceaseless toil and vigilance that it becomes slavery. Compulsion is the child of fear. It is the direct corollary of idolatry.

If the human person is locked into this orientation, morality itself, virtue itself, even the observance of Torah's commandments, can be an expression of sin. They all can articulate the human attempt to establish life and worth on one's own terms. Virtue can therefore be a source of boasting over another person who is immoral. But such judgment is itself a hostile expression of the flesh, and an expression of sin (2:1–3). Observance of God's commandments can become a form of boasting (2:23), even of bribing God for a reward. Paul virtually makes of *sin* a personified entity, giving it at times an almost mythical coloration (see 5:12–14). This is because he sees human freedom as inevitably in allegiance (service, obedience) to some greater spiritual force, whether the spiritual systems of idolatry or of the one true God (6:15–23). But the capacity for choice remains as a potential, even when the human being is "enslaved" by the "power of sin." If liberated by the gift of knowledge and love from the

Other who was once refused, the human being can be made truly free in faith.

The Thesis Restated (3:21–31)

The human efforts at self-assertion that "fall short of the glory of God" (3:23) are now reversed by "God's way of making humans righteous" (3:21), which is, in short, through gift (3:24). The gift is through Jesus. Paul's language here is again extraordinarily dense, and I should stress that my reading of the Greek differs considerably from that of the RSV. God put forward Jesus as a sacrifice to establish unity between himself and humans (cf. Lev. 16:12–16)—thus, "by his blood" (3:25). The death of Jesus, however, was not a mechanical offering but the faithful death of a living human being: it was an act of obedience to God. Thus it was an act "through faith" (3:25). Since Jesus is God's son, in him the gift was at once given from God and received by humans. In the body language and freedom of a single human being, God has acted in behalf of all (3:22). God thus showed both his nature (he is righteous) and his activity for humans (he makes others righteous, 3:26).

God makes human beings righteous on the same basis. The gift is for all who will have it, both Jews and Greeks; there is no distinction between them (3:22). There is one basis for judgment (2:11); there is one gift; and there is one mode of acceptance, "by faith." On the cross, Jesus relinquished any claim to life or worth apart from God's gift. Thus, he is the "righteous one by faith," and thus "he lives" by virtue of resurrection (see Hab. 2:4; Rom. 1:17). Those who have been empowered by the Spirit that comes from him to have "the faith of Jesus" (the RSV rendering in 3:26 of "the one who has faith in Jesus" should instead be read as "the one who has faith like Jesus") are established in right relationship with God. They do not seek to assert their own life and worth but accept in obedience the "free gift" of God in Jesus.

God's revelation of his righteousness in the body and freedom of a crucified Messiah has taken place apart from, even against, the norm of Torah. But this does not make Torah totally irrelevant. It is a witness to God's way of making humans righteous (3:21). Paul will next show how. But first, he makes three rapid assertions. First, that all human boasting is now excluded; one can glory (or, boast) only in the gift of God. No human achievement, even the observance of commandments, can place a claim against God (3:27–28). Second, that Jews do not have privileged access to God's gifts or to righteousness (3:29–30). Such partiality would contradict God's very being, and would reduce the one God of heaven and earth to the level of a tribal deity. If God is Lord of all creation and if God is fair, then there must be one principle by which all humans can be righteous before him. It is in fact the principle of faithful obedience. Known already in

Torah, it was crippled by the power of sin. But now, it has been made powerfully available through the faithful death and life-giving resurrection of Jesus. Third, that Torah itself is therefore properly established in its true status as a witness to God's righteousness when it is read as showing its basis in faithful obedience (3:31). To that demonstration, Paul now turns.

The Example of Abraham (4:1–25)

Paul uses Abraham as his example in the diatribal argument and as proof that Torah is "established" on the principle of faith. He does this through a midrash on Gen. 15:6, "Abraham believed God and it was reckoned to him as righteousness." In contrast to what he did in Gal. 3:6–18, he here concentrates on Abraham himself and the structure of his faith. His presentation relies on two midrashic premises: (1) The textual sequence of events is significant; thus, Abraham was called righteous in Gen. 15:6 *before* he was circumcised in Gen. 17:11. (2) The meaning of a term in Torah can be clarified by use of the same term elsewhere in Scripture (here, the term "reckon" used in both Gen. 15:6 and Ps. 32:1 shows that God is not a passive "keeper of the book" but one who "makes righteous" even the ungodly). Paul's presentation of Abraham as the father of all who believe (4:11) is the more striking because of the praise of Abraham within contemporary Judaism as one whose righteousness was proved by his "works" (see, e.g., *Aboth de Rabbi Nathan* 7, 33; Jas. 2:18–26).

First, Paul argues that Abraham was called righteous not because of his accomplishments but because of his faith (4:1–12). He did nothing that could give him reason to boast (4:2) or that earned him wages (4:4–5). His righteousness was a gift of God received by faith; God makes humans righteous (4:5, 6–8). That he was declared righteous before his circumcision shows that his righteousness derived from his obedient yes to the promise. He thus manifested the principle of faith for all and became the "father" both of Gentiles ("who believe without being circumcised and who thus have righteousness attributed to them") as well as of Jews ("the circumcised who are not merely circumcised but also follow the example of the faith of Abraham"; 4:11–12).

Second, Paul asserts that the law played no role in making humans righteous (4:13–15). He deliberately twists the implication of 3:31 that the principle of faith would destroy (*katargeō*) Torah. Here, Paul asserts that if law were the principle of righteousness, *faith* would be empty (*kenos*) and destroyed (*katargeō;* 4:14).

Third, Paul declares that the structure of Abraham's faith is the same as the Christians', involving trust, hope, and obedience. Despite all the appearances of death (his age, her "dead" womb—*nekrōsis*, 4:19) Abraham had faith in the God "who gives life to the dead and calls into existence things that do not exist" (4:17; cf. 1 Cor. 1:28). Abraham was not an idolater who refused to glorify God (1:21); as he waxed strong in faith, he "gave glory to God" (4:20). So is the structure of Christian faith specified, not by the birth of Isaac from the dead womb of Sarah but by the resurrection of Jesus from the dead. They also hope in the same God "who raised from the dead Jesus our Lord; who was put to death for our transgressions and was raised for our righteousness" (4:25).

The Consequence of the Gift: Peace and Reconciliation (5:1–21)

Paul's presentation has its hinge in 5:1–21, where he concludes the exposition of the thesis that began in 3:21 and sets up the objections that will begin in 6:1. The chapter in turn is itself hinged. The consequences of righteousness are stated in 5:1–11: peace and reconciliation with God. In 5:12–21, the thesis of 3:21–31 (that humans are made righteous through the faithful death of Jesus) is reargued, now explicitly in terms of *obedience*. Paul uses the argument *qal we chomer* (light and heavy) borrowed by the scribes from Hellenistic philosophy ("from the lesser to the greater"). Thus, in 5:9, 15 and 17, the expression "how much more" contrasts a previous state with the present one. For the argument to work, one must grant more than a purely symbolic function to representative figures in history. For Paul, they are persons whose actions determine, or at least fundamentally condition, the existence of others. The contrast in this case is absolute, between the first human being, Adam, and Jesus, the firstborn of a new creation (cf. 1 Cor. 15:20–22). Their respective responses to God provide a range of possibility for those who follow them.

In Rom. 5:1–11, the objective nature of the gift is stated: once made "righteous," humans are "reconciled with God" (5:10–11; cf. 2 Cor. 5:16–21). God's gift is real. Justification is not simply a decree, but a transforming action: "God's love poured into our hearts through the Holy Spirit which has been given to us" (5:5). The gift is all the more astonishing because given to those alienated from (5:8) and hostile toward (5:10) God. Because God has in Jesus reached across that space of alienation, he has brought about a state of covenantal "peace" (5:1) in which humans have free access to the gift (5:2). Now they can indeed "boast," not on the grounds of their accomplishment, but on the basis of God's love; boasting itself becomes praise of God (5:2, 11)!

Paul now describes the way the gift has come to humans through the faith of Jesus. Because of Adam's transgression, people lived under the power of sin and experienced death as alienation from God (5:12–14). But the free gift has destroyed the reign of sin and death, being infinitely more powerful in its effects (5:15–21), as Paul demonstrates in a series of five antithetical contrasts: (1) Although many died because of Adam, even more the free gift "of the one man Jesus Christ" has abounded for many (5:15). (2) The judgment of God after the trespass led to condemnation, but the free gift brings a decree of righteousness (5:16). (3) One man's trespass made death rule, but now those made righteous "through the one man Jesus Christ" reign in life (5:17). (4) One man's trespass led to condemnation for all, but one man's "act of righteousness" led to acquittal and life for all (or, to the acquittal that is life: *dikaiōma zoēs;* 5:18). (5) One man's disobedience "established" all humans as sinners, Jesus' obedience leads to the possibility and reality ("they will be established") of being righteous people (5:19).

The formal parallelism between 5:12–21 and 3:21–26 makes clear that the gift of righteousness is brought about by the "faith of Jesus" considered as obedience to God. The "righteous one who by his faith will live" is first of all Jesus. His faith established the possibility for others to be righteous through faith, since his life has been given to them by the Spirit (5:5). A new power rules in the world, "so that as sin reigned through death, grace also might reign through righteousness to eternal life through Jesus Christ our Lord" (5:21).

Implications of the Gift (6:1–23)

Paul must now answer objections to his thesis. He begins with the question raised first in 3:8, "Are we to continue in sin, that grace may abound?" (6:1) and shifts slightly in 6:15 to "Are we to sin since we are not under the law but grace?" His emphasis on the free gift that has "exceeded" human sin has obviously left him open to antinomian inferences. Paul regards them, however, as essentially trivial, because they misunderstand completely the point he has been making: the gift is real and effective; it changes things. Grace is not an external judgment about humans but a gift of knowledge and love from God that transforms them. To suggest that sin is compatible with this new life and empowerment is to miss the point entirely.

Paul reminds his readers of the implications of their baptism (6:2–14). In it, they were identified with Christ's death, so that they might "rise" to a new form of life (6:3–4). Since they now live by the spirit of the resurrected Jesus, they must, in their behavior, "die" to sin (6:6–7). Like Jesus, they are to be "alive to God" (6:11). To return to a pattern of idolatry would mean again "refusing to acknowledge" what God has done for them, and would treat grace as an external status rather than internal change.

The mention of law in 6:14 shifts Paul's language from the contrast between death and life to that between slavery and freedom. To continue in sin is to forget that it is slavery. When Paul's readers considered themselves "free" from God's claim, they were self-deluded: their own compulsions imprisoned them (6:20–21). Now that through faith they are "obedient from the heart" to God (6:17; cf. 2:15, 29), they are "slaves of righteousness, having been set free from sin" (6:18). But obedience to the Lord of all, the source of all, is actually true freedom, for in it the creature is established in "right relationship." Each form of obedience brings a reward. Slavery to sin wins *wages* which are death (cf. 4:4); but obedience to God (faith) enabled by "the free gift in Christ Jesus our Lord" receives eternal life (6:22–23). Something has happened to them; it has reversed their lives; to turn back to any other power, or to measure their lives by any other norm but that of the gift, is to lose it.

The Problem of the Law (7:1–25)

Paul has spoken of this change in terms of death and life in 6:1–14 and in terms of slavery and freedom in 6:15–23. He now shifts explicitly if awkwardly to the contrast between law and freedom, by means of a tangled analogy: as a marriage contract is broken by the death of a partner, so has "a death" broken their obligation to any contract with the law (7:1–3). However tortuous, the example is intended to remind them that their identification in baptism with the death of Christ has made them (with him) "dead" to the claims—and curse—of Torah (6:6; cf. Gal. 2:19; 3:13). Christians live by his new resurrection life and are quit of the law's claims (7:4). They are no longer under an "old written code" but serve God in the "new life of the Spirit" (7:6; cf. esp. 2 Cor. 3:7–18). Paul frames the problem of the Torah, therefore, in terms of a contrast between written prescription and power for life.

Throughout the letter, Paul has hinted at a collusion between sin and law: "Through the law comes knowledge of sin" (3:20); and "For the law brings wrath, but where there is no law, there is no transgression" (4:15); and "Sin is not counted where there is no law" (5:13); and "Law came in to increase trespass" (5:20); and "Sin will have no dominion over you, since you are not under the law but under grace" (6:14). These statements, in turn, remind us of some others, above all "Why the law? It was added because of transgressions" (Gal. 3:19) and "The sting of death is sin and the power of sin is the law" (1 Cor. 15:56). The climactic assertion of 7:5, "While we were living in the flesh, our sinful passions, aroused by the law, were at work in our members to bear fruit for death," demands of Paul a more comprehensive explanation.

It is necessary to stress, if we are to understand this discussion of Torah, that Paul is not describing the situation of those who have the "new life of the Spirit" (7:6). His whole point, after all, is that grace has changed things. He speaks here, rather, of the perplexity faced by those "living in the flesh" (7:5). At the same time, there is no reason to detect in these remarks an autobiographical account of Paul's preconversion struggles. Paul never suggests that he had trouble keeping the commandments, and insists that he is, by the measure of Torah, righteous (see Phil. 3:6). He addresses here the state of humanity enslaved by the power of sin, and above all the inability of Torah to change that state by itself. He argues for the distinction between prescription and power.

Paul insists that Torah is good (7:13) and reveals God's will for humans (7:7). And as God's word it is by definition spiritual (7:14), "so the law is holy and the commandment is holy and just and good" (7:12). Indeed, the commandments reveal wrongdoing precisely as sin. They show that wickedness is not just "immorality" but a rupture of the religious relationship with God—transgression (7:7, 9, 13). An analogy may help. A child may feel an irresistible urge to tease the cat. Only when her mother says, "Don't tease the cat," however, does the child know the deed as transgression of a commandment. Now, teasing the cat is not only wrong but disobedience.

The commandment paradoxically potentiates the sin by consciousness. Another analogy: Suppose I have a mild tickling between my shoulder blades. I am told: "Don't scratch." The commandment not only does not take away the itch, it makes it worse, by isolating and magnifying what had been only a latent symptom. So Paul sees the commands of Torah. They are only verbal. They cannot empower new behavior in a person and heal the impulse toward the old: "I am in the flesh, sold under sin" (7:14). The power of sin (7:8, 9, 11) continues to drive one's actions. The commandment, therefore, is powerless really to change a person and in fact exacerbates the situation. Torah as revelation is good, but if it pretends to give life, it is deceitful (7:10; cf. Lev. 18:5). If these claims are believed, the prescription can in fact kill (7:11). So in the case of one critically ill, having a doctor's diagnosis, or even a script for medicine, does not help; what is wanted is medicine.

The conflict of 7:15–25 is one between the perception of the good made available through Torah and the lack of power to do it, because of the self-aggrandizing power of sin. The tension is there, we should note, *even when the commandments are observed.* This point is essential to Paul's argument, though it becomes evident only in 9:32—10:4: the Jews could reject obedience to God precisely because they regarded Torah as the only norm for God's action as well as their own. The conflict is stated succinctly: "I serve the law of God with my mind, but with my flesh I serve the law of sin" (7:25; cf. 8:7). What is needed is a power from the outside, a gift that can create the capacity for freedom from fear and compulsion (7:24). Because that gift has been given, Paul gives thanks in return (7:25).

The Fruit of Righteousness: Life
in the Spirit (8:1–39)

Paul now picks up the programmatic statement of 7:6, "We serve in the new life of the Spirit," to develop more fully the meaning of the righteous life. What humans could not accomplish, God has accomplished (8:3). Because of the gift of life by the Spirit, human behavior can now correspond to the empowerment, "in order that the just requirement of the law might be fulfilled in us who walk not according to the flesh but according to the Spirit" (8:4; cf. Gal. 5:25). In his description of this new direction of life, Paul more fully expounds the two options available to freedom (8:5–10) and makes clear that because of the reality of the new power that has come to persons from the resurrected one (8:11), they must in their behavior also "put to death the deeds of the body" (8:13). And this is truly possible, because they have been freed from the power of sin. God's Spirit is not one of "slavery leading back to fear" but one of Sonship, enabling them to greet God as Jesus did with the filial cry "Abba, Father!" (8:15).

Paul reminds his readers as well, however, that just as the gift is real, for "the love of God *has* been poured into their hearts" (5:5), so also its full realization is not yet manifest. They still live in the in-between time. The Spirit, then, is a "pledge" of their future redemption (8:23). Their human suffering is not eliminated by the resurrection life, but it is transformed, since they are sustained in it by the Spirit (8:17–21). And since the Spirit is at work in the world to bring about a radical renewal of all creation, there is genuine hope for the future (8:22–25). So do Christians live, like Abraham, who despite the signs of death, hoped in the one who calls into being the things that are not; although the evidence looks like death, the Christians see the suffering of the world as birth pangs of a new world (8:21). And this is possible because even now, the Spirit is at work transforming their lives (8:12–14) into "the image of his son that he might be the firstborn of many brothers" (8:29) and even in their suffering prays for them "according to the will of God" (8:12–14). It is not blind optimism but the paradox of hope in suffering that enables Paul to declare that there is meaning even in the reverses of history, even in blindnesses and hurt. Only on the basis of their own deeply ambiguous experience can they assert: "We know that in everything, God works for good with those who love him" (8:28).

Abraham had shown faithful obedience to God by being willing to offer his only son Isaac in sacrifice (Gen. 22:12–13). So has God shown himself faithful in return, to Abraham, to his own Word, to his own history. Measure for measure, he too, "did not spare his own Son but gave him up for us all" (8:32). In praise of this gift, Paul's argument reaches its first conclusion by climbing to poetry: "If God is for us, who is against us?" (8:31). Since it is God who has acted for us, the gift is final and absolute; nothing can threaten it, nothing can "separate us from the love of God in Christ Jesus our Lord" (8:39).

God's Plan for the Salvation of
Jew and Greek (9:1—11:33)

Paul has asserted that God works for the good of those who love him (8:28) and also that his call to humans has been effective: "Those whom he called he justified, and those he justified he also glorified" (8:30). But when those assertions are taken together with the principle that God has made no distinction between Jew and Gentile (2:9; 3:22, 29), Paul is forced to defend the working out of God's will in history. Paul therefore provides the messianic community its first "history of salvation" in a sustained midrash on some thirty texts from Torah. Paul reinterprets Torah from the perspective of messianic belief: Jesus is Messiah. The questions first raised earlier are now treated in turn (9:4 = 3:1–4; 9:6 = 3:3; 9:14 = 3:5; 10:12 = 3:22; 11:26 = 3:29; 11:32 = 3:19–26).

Despite the invitation these chapters appear to issue for discussions concerning free will and predestination, Paul's concern is not with the ultimate fate of any individual before God, still less philosophical issues of fate versus freedom. Pharaoh's soul is not the issue! Paul rather praises God's work in the history of peoples, as he can discern its traces in the stories of his own tradition. His discernment is governed by *(a)* the contemporary Jewish rejection of the "good news" about Jesus as Messiah and Lord, and *(b)* the acceptance of that same proclamation by contemporary Gentiles. These contemporary events, in which Paul's mission itself plays the most pivotal role, raise hard questions. What is the meaning of "God's people"? Has God been faithful to his word? Is Israel as a people rejected, and if so, can God be trusted? These are far from abstract considerations for Paul. He is filled with anguish for his kinsmen (9:2). In a striking contrast to "Nothing can cut us off from the love of God" (8:39), Paul declares that he would wish to "be accursed and cut off from Christ" for their sake, taking on the role of Moses for the people, "if thou wilt forgive their sin—and if not, blot me out of the book thou hast written" (Exod. 32:32).

Paul asserts from the start the blessings of the Jews, which include the Messiah (9:4–5). But these great blessings of God only make the present situation of the Jews more critical and puzzling. The question must be raised whether God's word has failed (3:3; 9:6). Paul's reinterpretation of Torah is therefore a defense of God's word and work in history, and is therefore ultimately praise of his glory.

He first distinguishes between the "people of God" and historical Judaism (9:6–13). Israel as a people was never simply conterminous with the Jews as an ethnic or national group. In the stories of the patriarchs, it is God's election that establishes the line through which the promises are fulfilled (9:6–9). Election has everything to do with God's gift and nothing to do with human accomplishment (9:11). Paul has little patience for the objection that such choices are arbitrary and make God an unjust despot (9:14–23). To think of God's justice in terms of human concepts of fairness shows but little grasp of the infinite distance between creator and creature, a distance measurable only in terms of the creator's mercy, not the creature's justice. Everything comes from God. From what independent standpoint does the critic question God (9:19–21)? Paul also insists, in turn, that however ambiguous particular cases appear, the face God shows toward the world is always one of mercy rather than wrath. But it *is* all God's doing. For the second time he asserts, "It depends not on man's will or exertion but upon God's mercy" (9:16; cf. 9:11). The prophets show God's mercy reaching out to people who were not part of the historical nation; already in Torah, God calls into being a people from among the nations (9:24). The prophets also show that many of the Jews were obdurate and heedless of God's call to repentance. Israel as a religious reality was both larger and smaller than the nation. It was a remnant defined by faith (9:25–29).

The critical part of Paul's argument is its middle (9:30—10:21), in which he must account for the contemporary rejection of the Jews and the call of the Gentiles. Now the argument of chapters 1 through 8 appears pertinent. The Gentiles have become part of the righteous people on the basis of faith (9:30). That is easy enough (see 3:30; 4:11). But why have so many Jews fallen away? Because they treated righteousness as a matter of accomplishment, not of gift. By so doing, they missed "fulfilling Torah" (9:32). How can Paul say this? Only on the basis of the rejection of Jesus by some Jews. Here is the case above all where God's call has come outside (and even against) the norms of Torah, in a crucified Messiah. For some Jews, the cross remains only a stumbling block, not the cornerstone of belief (9:32). In the present choice between God's unexpected call through Jesus and the precedents of Torah, they choose Torah. It is a safe and sure norm for righteousness. Their zeal for God has not slackened, but it is blind (10:2). They have tragically made their understanding of God's consistency the measure of their own consistency. By so doing, they have refused God the freedom to speak in new ways (10:3–4):

> Being ignorant of the righteousness that comes from God, and seeking to establish their own, they did not submit to God's righteousness. For Christ is the end of the law, that everyone who has faith may be justified.

In a stunning midrashic move, Paul now collapses the historical distance between the time of Torah and the present completely. He reads Torah totally as a messianic text. First, the claim of Moses that righteousness by law will give life (10:5; Lev. 18:5) is opposed by reading Deut. 30:12–13 as messianic: the word that God placed close to the people was the word of faith concerning the Christ; what Torah intended from the beginning was the Messiah (10:6–9). He is the Lord (cf. 2 Cor. 3:17–18) who, when called upon, saves (10:13). All humans can therefore have equal access to God (10:12):

> For there is no distinction between Jew and Greek; the same Lord is the Lord of all and bestows his riches upon all who call upon him.

Second, Paul says that the rejection of the Messiah is found already in the prophet Isaiah. When he says, "They have not all obeyed the good news," he does not mean only the Jews of his own generation (10:16), for the "good news" was also proclaimed by the prophets: "How beautiful are the feet of those who preach good news" (Isa. 52:7). Paul has insisted from the beginning of this letter that the "good news" was "announced ahead of time (*proepangellomai*) by the prophets in the holy writings" (1:2). He also asserted that it was "witnessed to by the law and the prophets" (3:21). The prophet that Paul particularly had in mind is Isaiah. Throughout this letter, full citations or allusions to the latter part of that prophet play an important thematic role. It is clear that Paul has pondered his ministry in the light of a careful reading of Isaiah 49—60 (Isa. 49:18–Rom. 14:11; Isa. 50:8–Rom. 8:33; Isa. 51:1–Rom. 9:31; Isa. 51:5–Rom. 1:17 and 3:21; Isa. 51:7–Rom. 2:15; Isa. 51:8–Rom. 1:17; Isa. 52:5–Rom. 2:24; Isa. 52:7–Rom. 10:15; Isa. 52:15–Rom. 15:21; Isa. 53:1–Rom. 10:16; Isa. 53:5–Rom. 4:25; Isa. 53:11–Rom. 5:19; Isa. 53:12–Rom. 4:24; Isa. 54:16–Rom. 9:22; Isa. 59:7–Rom. 3:15–17; Isa. 59:20–Rom. 11:26).

Now when he quotes Isa. 53:1, "Lord who has believed what he has heard from us? (10:16), we know that Paul has in mind precisely the proclamation of Christ in Isa. 52:13—53:12, the Song of the Suffering Servant. It is an allusion too obvious for his readers to miss. There in the text of Isaiah is proclaimed one who died for others and was the source of their righteousness (Isa. 53:11):

> By his knowledge shall the righteous one my servant make many to be accounted righteous; and he shall bear their iniquities.

Even before Jesus, therefore, the Jews had heard the "good news." They should have recognized from their reading of Torah that one who was "numbered with transgressors" (Isa. 53:12) could be God's righteous servant. They could have recognized in Jesus, even on the basis of Torah, not one cursed by God but one who made others righteous through his faithful obedience. In this sense Isaiah fairly says, "All day long I have held out my hands to a disobedient and contrary people" (10:21; Isa. 65:2).

The third part of Paul's argument shows that, despite some Jews' rejection of the gospel, God has not rejected his people. Indeed, Paul and his fellow Jewish messianists are proof that there is, even now, a believing remnant within Judaism (11:5–6):

> So too at the present time there is a remnant chosen by grace; but if it is by grace, it is no longer on the basis of works; otherwise grace would no longer be grace.

As for the Jews of the present who reject Jesus, their blindness is only temporary and serves God's larger purpose in history (11:7–10). God wants all Israel to be saved (11:26). God will bring this about dialectically. The "good news" was preached to the Gentiles at all only because of Jewish rejection (11:11–12). In like manner, the conversion of the Gentiles—and Paul's own ministry!—has as its main purpose the stimulation of the Jews to envy, so that they too will "turn to the Lord" (11:13–14). Gentiles therefore should not boast. Their inclusion had nothing to do with their merits. They can more easily be cut off and the Jews restored, for the Jews were there from the beginning (11:17–24). Paul makes the Jews' priority plain (11:28–29):

> As regards the gospel they are enemies of God for your sake; but as regards election, they are beloved for the sake of their forefathers. For the gifts and the call of God are irrevocable.

God's word has not failed, but neither has it finished. The Gentiles are called to recognize, as the contemporary Jews had failed to, that God's working is mysterious and never ending. They must remain open to new and surprising manifestations of his will in the world. All that is sure is the fidelity and mercy of God, which have been shown in all his works, even those that appear most harsh: "For God has consigned all people to disobedience that he might have mercy on all" (11:30–32).

In his prayer of praise, Paul again asserts the infinite distance between human knowledge and God's action. Humans do not counsel God; they can only struggle to follow after the traces of his thoughts (11:33–34). So great a distance also obtains between human effort and divine gift. At the end Paul alludes to Job 41:11: "Who has ever given a gift to him that he might be repaid?" (11:35). God is not a human judge who can be bribed. God is always and everywhere the source of all being and beauty, "for from him, and through him, and to him are all things." So the argument concludes with the obedience of faith, not idolatry (cf. 1:21): "To him be glory forever. Amen" (11:36).

LIFE IN THE CHRISTIAN COMMUNITY

Paul's practical directives in Romans 12—13 appear at first to have no connection to the magnificent theological argument that preceded them, for they are thoroughly commonplace and traditional in their treatment of gifts in the community (12:3–8), attitudes of reciprocity (12:9–21), attitudes toward ruling authorities (13:1–7), the law of love (13:8–10), and the eschatological dimension of Christian existence (13:11–14). This collection of parenetic materials shows the Roman church that if it supports Paul's mission, it will not be sponsoring a renegade or idiosyncratic version of the Christian life. Although there is much in this parenesis that could be found in both pagan and Jewish moralists, there are some distinctive emphases. The injunction to be "lowly" (12:16), for example, could only be considered a virtue in light of a Messiah who was "lowly" and a slave; for pagan moralists, the attitude was a vice, not a virtue. Likewise, the Romans are told to have brotherly love *(philadelphia)* rather than love for humanity *(philanthrōpia)*, in 12:10 (cf. 1 Thess. 4:9). We notice as well the emphasis on hospitality and contributing to the needs of the saints (12:13). All in all, however, the classic parenetic summary works here as well: "Avoid evil, cling to what is good" (12:9).

Paul does not, however, leave the parenesis entirely without his distinctive touch. He begins (12:1–2) with a call for a transformation of mind that will enable one to test what is good (see also 1 Cor. 2:12–16). The gift of the Spirit empowers the capacity to measure reality differently than by the measure of the world, and to discern in concrete circumstances the appropriate response by which God will be praised (12:1). At the end of this section, Paul also tells his readers to "put on the Lord Jesus Christ, and make no provision for the flesh" (13:14; cf. Gal. 5:13). They are to "put on" their identity symbolized by the new clothing of their initiation in such manner that their behavior follows from it naturally. They are to live by the pattern of the Messiah's "life for others" rather than by the pattern of the flesh's self-seeking. And the pattern of the Messiah is found already in Torah (13:8–10):

> He who loves his neighbor has fulfilled the law. The commandments, "You shall not commit adultery, you shall not kill, you shall not steal, you shall not covet," and any other commandment are summed up in this sentence, "You shall love your neighbor as yourself." Love does no wrong to a neighbor; therefore love is the fulfilling of the law.

Here is a deliberate echo of 10:4: "Christ is the end of the law, that everyone who has faith may be justified."

In Rom. 14:1—15:13, Paul calls for this measure of discernment and love in the tensions caused within a community with a pluralism of practices. The situation resembles that of 1 Corinthians 8—10, but with much less detail. The "weak in faith" (14:1) find it necessary to have stricter observance in matters of diet (14:20) as well as calendar (14:5). They "judge" those who are less observant. Those who are "strong," on the other hand, "despise" the weak (14:3).

Paul agrees with the strong that the kingdom of God is not a matter of observance (14:17; cf. 1 Cor. 8:8), but he also allows for diversity of practice within the same community. The important thing is that God be given praise (14:6). God alone is master and Lord; all humans must answer to God alone (14:4, 10–12). There is, therefore, no place among them either for condemnation or contempt (14:3–4, 10, 13). Freedom of conscience stands as the norm for individual decisions (14:14, 20), but service to one another is a superior norm. When the norms conflict, life for the other should prevail (14:15, 20).

Paul provides specific theological backing for these guidelines and by so doing establishes a connection to the earlier argument. Christians should accept one another in their diversity, because God has accepted all of them, Jew and Greek alike: all humans have been accepted in Christ (14:3). How were they accepted through Christ? The Messiah died and lived again, so that he might be Lord of all, and so that whether they lived or died, they would belong to him (14:7–8). Christ died for all, and this must be the pattern of their life together: "Do not let what you eat cause the ruin of one for whom Christ died" (14:15). Christ is therefore the effective cause of their being accepted by God (15:8–9) and the model (15:2–6) of how they are to accept one another in mutual service: "Welcome one another, then, as Christ has welcomed you, for the glory of God" (15:7).

Now, Paul returns to the argument of chapters 9—11. God's work in history should guide Christians' actions toward one another. Messiah became a servant to the circumcised, to show God's truth (alētheia), so that the promises to the patriarchs might be secured (15:8). And the mission to the Gentiles in Christ's name (15:9–13)? That is so Gentiles might glorify God for his mercy (eleos; 15:9). Paul has here brought together the very attributes of God: "truth and mercy" translates the Hebrew emeth we chesed, the attributes of the Lord revealed to Moses (Exod. 34:6):

> The Lord, the Lord, a God merciful and gracious, slow to anger, and abounding in steadfast love and faithfulness.

"Truth and mercy" can also be translated as "faith," pistis, and "love," agapē. Paul suggests three closely connected truths in this allusion. First, in the dispensation of history, humans come to know God as he really is, a God of fidelity and loving kindness. Second, the perfect expression of the nature of God is found in Messiah Jesus, whose faithful obedience to God was expressed in his loving service to humans. Third, such is the pattern of life for all who belong to the Messiah. Their faith in God is also expressed in their mutual love and acceptance of one another, "that together you may give glory [cf. 1:21] to the God and Father of our Lord, Jesus Christ" (15:6).

BIBLIOGRAPHICAL NOTE

For the history of the interpretation of Romans, see J. D. Godsey, "The Interpretation of Romans in the History of the Christian Faith," *Int* 34 (1980): 3–16; and R. Jewett, "Major Impacts in the Theological Interpretation of Romans Since Barth," *Int* 34 (1980): 17–31.

Whether the letter was sent only to Rome or was a circular letter, whether Romans 16 belongs with this letter or not, whether the letter's substance is determined more by the Roman situation or by Paul's plans—these are matters of endless discussion. For a taste of the debates, see P. Minear, *Obedience of Faith* (London: SCM Press, 1971), and the essays in K. P. Donfried, ed., *The Romans Debate* (Minneapolis: Augsburg Pub. House, 1977). On Romans 16, see H. A. Gamble, Jr., *The Textual History of the Letter to the Romans: A Study in Textual and Literary Criticism* (Grand Rapids: Wm. B. Eerdmans, 1977); E. J. Goodspeed, "Phoebe's Letter of Introduction," *HTR* 44 (1951): 55–57; and C. H. Kim, *Form and Function of the Familiar Greek Letter of Recommendation* (Missoula, Mont.: Scholars Press, 1972), 132–42.

On Romans as a scholastic diatribe, the indispensable reference is S. K. Stowers, *The Diatribe and Paul's Letter to the Romans*, SBLDS 57 (Chico, Calif.: Scholars Press, 1981). Also useful for critical stages in Paul's argument are these studies: K. Grayston, "'Not Ashamed of the Gospel,' Rom. 1:16a and the Structure of the Epistle," *SE* 2 (1964): 569–73; N. A. Dahl, "Romans 3:9: Text and Meaning," in *Paul and Paulinism*, ed. M. D. Hooker and S. G. Wilson (London: SPCK, 1982), 184–204; L. E. Keck, "The Function of Rom. 3:10–18: Observations and Suggestions," in *God's Christ and His People*, ed. J. J. Jervell and W. A. Meeks (Oslo, Universitetsforlaget, 1977), 141–57; S. K. Stowers, "Paul's Dialogue with a Fellow Jew in Romans 3:1–9," *CBQ* 46 (1984): 707–22; R. B. Hays, "Psalm 143 and the Logic of Romans 3," *JBL* 99 (1980): 107–15; L. T. Johnson, "Romans 3:21–26 and the Faith of Jesus," *CBQ* 44 (1982): 77–90; C. T. Rhyne, *Faith Establishes the Law*, SBLDS 55 (Chico, Calif.: Scholars Press, 1981); R. B. Hays, "'Have We Found Abraham to Be Our Forefather According to the Flesh?' A Reconsideration of Rom. 4:1," *NovT* 27 (1985): 76–97; R. Schnackenburg, *Baptism in the Theology of St. Paul* (New York: Herder & Herder, 1964), 105–70; K. Stendahl, "The Apostle Paul and the Introspective Conscience of the West," in *Paul Among Jews and Gentiles* (Philadelphia: Fortress Press, 1976 [1963]), 78–96; J. Munck, *Christ and Israel: An Interpretation of Romans 9—11* (Philadelphia: Fortress Press, 1967); G. E. Howard, "Christ the End of the Law: The Meaning of Romans 10:4ff," *JBL* 88 (1969) 331–37; N. A. Dahl, "The Atonement: Adequate Reward for the Akedah?" in *The Crucified Messiah* (Minneapolis: Augsburg Pub. House, 1974), 146–60; idem, "The Future of Israel," in his *Studies in Paul* (Minneapolis: Augsburg Pub. House, 1977), 137–58; C. K. Barrett, "Romans 9:30—10:21: Call and Responsibility of Israel," in his *Essays on Paul* (Philadelphia: Westminster

Press, 1982), 132–53; H. E. Stoessel, "Notes on Romans 12:1–12: The Renewal of the Mind and the Internalizing of Truth," *Int* 17 (1963): 161–75; E. Käsemann, "Principles of Interpretation of Romans 13," in his *New Testament Questions of Today* (Philadelphia: Fortress Press, 1969), 196–216; J. Knox, "Rom. 15:14–33 and Paul's Conception of his Apostolic Mission," *JBL* 83 (1964): 1–11.

Interpreting Romans inevitably involves theology, often enough controversial theology. For an opening statement, see R. P. Martin, "The Kerygma of Romans," *Int* 25 (1971): 303–28. For a range of issues, see the following sample: E. Käsemann, "The Righteousness of God in Paul," in his *New Testament Questions of Today*, 168–82; K. Barth, *Christ and Adam* (New York: Collier Books, 1962); N. A. Dahl, "The Missionary Theology in the Epistle to the Romans," in his *Studies in Paul*, 70–94; J. Bassler, *Divine Impartiality: Paul and a Theological Axiom* SBLDS 59 (Chico, Calif.: Scholars Press, 1981); S. K. Williams, "The Righteousness of God in Romans," *JBL* 99 (1980): 241–90; idem, *Jesus' Death as Saving Event: The Background and Origin of a Concept*, HDR 2 (Missoula, Mont.: Scholars Press, 1975); W. D. Davies, "Paul and the Law: Pitfalls in Interpretation," in his *Jewish and Pauline Studies* (Philadelphia: Fortress Press, 1984), 91–122; R. Bultmann, "Romans 7 and the Anthropology of Paul," in his *Existence and Faith*, ed. and trans. S. M. Ogden (New York: Meridian Books, 1960), 147–57; idem, *Theology of the New Testament* (New York: Charles Scribner's Sons, 1953), 1:288–306; H. Moxnes, *Theology in Conflict: Studies of Paul's Understanding of God in Romans*, NovTSup 53 (Leiden: E. J. Brill, 1980).

Because of their peculiar importance in the history of theology as well as of exegesis, two older theological commentaries on Romans should be noted: M. Luther, *Lectures on Romans*, trans. W. Pauck (Philadelphia: Westminster Press, 1961), and K. Barth, *The Epistle to the Romans*, 6th ed., trans. E. Hoskyns (London: Oxford Univ. Press, 1933). This line of interpretation is continued vigorously by E. Käseman, *Commentary on Romans* (Grand Rapids: Wm. B. Eerdmans, 1980). The older critical commentary of W. Sanday and A. Headlam, *The Epistle to the Romans*, 5th ed., ICC (Edinburgh: T. & T. Clark, 1902), still has valuable observations. For accessible and careful guides through the text, there are C. H. Dodd, *The Epistle of Paul to the Romans* (London: Hodder & Stoughton, 1932), and C. K. Barrett, *A Commentary on the Epistle to the Romans*, HNTC (New York: Harper & Row, 1957).

15

The Letter to the Philippians

THE CHURCH PAUL FOUNDED AT THE ROMAN COLONY OF PHILIPPI WAS HIS first in Europe (Acts 16:12–40; Phil. 4:15) and financially supported his mission (4:15–16; cf. 2 Cor. 11:7). The gentle tone of the letter conveys the special relationship between Paul and the community. When Paul wrote (with Timothy, 1:1), he was in prison (1:12–14). The work of the ministry, however, continued, if not entirely to his satisfaction (1:15–17; 4:2–3), and Paul fully expected to be released (1:19; 2:24). So much is clear. There is less unanimity among scholars concerning Paul's locations, the situation he addressed, or even the literary integrity of this letter.

It is impossible to decide from which of Paul's several imprisonments he wrote the letter. Mention of the whole praetorium (1:13) and those of Caesar's household (4:22) would naturally if not necessarily suggest captivity in Rome or Caesarea (Acts 24:26–27; 28:30). Those who question the letter's unity and see in it an edited version of several letter fragments, add the observation that there is movement between Paul and his readers by means of delegates (2:19–30; 4:18). They conclude that Ephesus would be an appropriate provenience simply on the basis of geographical convenience. If the literary unity is not in doubt, no hypothetical imprisonment is required.

The authenticity of Philippians is not seriously questioned, but changes of tone within the letter, the presence of apparent editorial seams, and conflicting information lead some to doubt its literary integrity. Here is the basis for that conclusion: The letter seems to have several endings, since Paul uses the phrase "finally," *to loipon*, which usually signals a conclusion, twice without stopping, but in moving to another discussion (3:1; 4:8). Such are the seams. The shift in mood is found only in one place, when Paul moves from an encouragement to rejoice in the Lord (3:1) to a warning against "the dogs" (3:2). As for biographical details, in 2:25–28 Paul plans to send Epaphroditus back to the Philippians after their emissary had been sick nearly to death; but when he mentions Epaphroditus' delivery of their monetary gift in 4:18, no mention is made of a lengthy stay. Some also consider Paul's delay in thanking them for their gift unconscionable if he first mentions it in 4:10–20, whereas if this were a separate letter, Paul's thanks would be direct and his mention of Epaphroditus intelligible.

Such literary observations are joined to a reconstruction of the Philippian situation that emphasizes the role of the "opponents" (1:28). Paul says that some preach the gospel out of envy and rivalry (1:15–17), that there is murmuring and grumbling in the community (2:14), and that some of the mission workers are not getting along (4:2–3). He also mentions some who are "enemies of the cross" (3:18) and refers to some "dogs" and "evil workmen" who put their pride in circumcision (3:2–4). The conclusion is reached that the fragments of Philippians reveal stages of a conflict developing in the community, generated by Pauline opponents and answered by Paul in a series of notes.

On this reading, three separate letter fragments are later sewn together, which accounts for the unevenness in the final version. The first is 4:10–20, a note thanking the Philippians for their gift of money. The second warns against divisions in the church (1:1—3:1; 4:4–7, 21–23). The third sharply attacks the false teachers who have fomented dissension (3:2—4:3; 4:8–9). The history of the community troubles follows the same progression. There is no hint of trouble in the first letter. In the second, there is rivalry and grumbling, which Paul thinks he can contain by exhortation. The third letter shows the situation more dangerous than he had supposed, requiring a direct rebuttal of the opponents.

The hypothesis is needlessly complex and not required by the evidence of the text itself. The literary breaks in the letter are not so severe as those in 2 Corinthians. Paul's thanks for the money in 4:10–20, for example, is clearly anticipated by the language of the epistolary thanksgiving (1:3–11). The "outbreak" of 3:2—4:3 has been well prepared by 1:15–17, 28; and 2:21–22. This supposed polemic furthermore is bracketed on both sides by exhortations to "rejoice" (3:1; 4:4), which suggests literary framing rather than clumsy editing. The discrepancy regarding Epaphroditus is only apparent. There is no reason, therefore, to treat Philippians as a composite of three letters.

The attempt to reconstruct a historical sequence is even more hazardous. Even if there were a series of letters, the progression could have gone in the opposite direction, from severe trouble to moderate grumbling to fellowship and the sharing of money. Without controls, why not? Finally, atomizing the letter distracts the reader from discovering the way the writing works as a text. Is the section 3:2—4:3 really a polemic, or does it have another literary function? Is there a coherent thematic and structural pattern being followed through chapters 2 and 3? Unless the text is read in its integrity as a single composition written with some degree of literary consciousness, such questions cannot be answered, or even asked.

THE CHARACTER OF PHILIPPIANS

Philippians challenges any monochromatic portrait of the Pauline corpus. It contains side by side and sometimes intertwined, elements that are often considered logically opposite. Its authenticity is not seriously questioned. Yet it has a surprising number of features ordinarily associated only with inauthentic letters. With Philemon, Philippians is the only unquestioned letter written from captivity, yet it has certain small touches found most frequently in other "inauthentic" captivity letters. Stylistically, for example, it is "flatter," without the dialogical vigor of the diatribe; it lacks any scriptural citations; and it has some expressions found elsewhere only in other captivity letters (see, e.g., "the praise of glory," Phil. 1:11 and Eph. 1:6, 12, 14). Substantively, Paul here calls Jesus, Savior (3:20), a title otherwise found in the so-called nongenuine letters (Eph. 5:23; 2 Tim. 1:10; Titus 2:13; 3:6). The perception of his sufferings in Phil. 1:16–18 finds its clearest echo in 2 Tim. 1:8–12; 2:9. The emphasis on the cosmic implications of Christ's resurrection (Phil. 2:6–11; 3:21) is matched most neatly by Col. 1:15–20 and Eph. 1:19–23.

Alone of the unquestioned letters, Philippians mentions in its greeting, bishops and deacons (1:1). The term "overseer," *episkopos*, is elsewhere found in Paul only in the singular, in 1 Tim. 3:2 and Titus 1:7. The term "deacon" or "servant," *diakonos*, on the other hand, is used often with reference to his own (1 Cor. 3:5; 2 Cor. 3:6; Eph. 3:7) and others' ministry: the ministry of Phoebe (Rom. 16:1), Apollos (1 Cor. 3:5), Tychichus (Eph. 6:21), Epaphras (Col. 1:7), and possibly Timothy (cf. the variant readings in 1 Thess. 3:2 and 1 Tim. 4:6). Of members of a local community the term is used only here and in 1 Tim. 3:8, 12; 4:6. Without using either term, Paul often refers to the local leaders of churches (see 1 Thess. 5:12; Gal. 6:6; 1 Cor. 6:5–6; 12:28; 16:15–17; Rom. 12:8; Phlm. 1–2).

The eschatology of Philippians is complex. Paul expresses a definite future expectation like that of 1 Thess. 4:13—5:3 in Phil. 1:10; 2:16; 3:11, 20–21, and he even gives that expectation a note of urgency: "The Lord is at hand" (4:5). On the other hand, he expects to experience a union with Jesus before "the day of the Lord" (1:6) if he should die. He will then "be with" Christ, (1:21–23), a hope that more closely resembles that expressed in 2 Cor. 5:1–5. Paul also sees the Christians' "homeland" in spatial rather than temporal terms: it is "in heaven" (3:20; as also in 2 Cor. 5:1–2; Eph. 6:9; Col. 1:5; 4:1). The Christology of this letter places equal stress on the "cosmic Christ" (2:5–11; 3:21; cf. above), on "Christ the righteousness from God that depends on faith" (3:9; cf. Rom. 3:22; 1 Cor. 1:30; 2 Cor.

5:21), and on Christ the exemplar of faith (2:5; cf. 1 Cor. 11:1; 2 Tim. 2:8–13).

Philippians also contains diverse aspects of Paul's self-understanding as an apostle. Suffering is a sign of genuine ministry (1:15–25; 2:17; 3:8–10), as it is of all Christian existence (1:29–30). Paul presents himself as a model *(typos)* for the community to imitate (3:17; cf. 1 Cor. 4:16; 11:1; 1 Thess. 1:6; 2 Thess. 3:9; 1 Tim. 1:16; 2 Tim. 1:13). His delegate Timothy is "like a son" and "genuinely concerned" for the members of the community as he labors with Paul for the gospel (2:19–24; cf. 1 Cor. 4:17; 1 Tim. 1:2; 2 Tim. 3:10). In contrast to his usual claim of independence from community financial support (2 Thess. 3:6–9; 1 Cor. 9:15–18; 2 Cor. 11:7–12), Paul here gladly admits that from "the beginning of the gospel" he has been in a relationship of "giving and receiving" with his church (4:14–15). At the same time, he emphasizes his personal contentment or self-sufficiency *(autarkeia)* with respect to possessions (4:11–13). That he accepts financial support from this community is a symbol of the fellowship he enjoys with them.

Philippian's emotional warmth is often and justly remarked. Not here the warmth of outrage and anger as in Galatians; rather we find the warmth of affection and tenderness, even of sweetness. Positive expressions of feeling abound: "I hold you in my heart" (1:7); "I yearn for you with all the affection of Christ Jesus" (1:8); "I am glad and rejoice with you all; likewise you should be glad and rejoice with me" (2:18); "My brethren whom I love and long for, my joy and my crown" (4:1); "It was kind of you to share my trouble" (4:14). Above all, a quality of quiet joy pervades the letter (1:4, 19; 2:2, 17–18, 19, 28, 29; 3:1; 4:1, 4, 10), a joy deriving from their special fellowship (1:5; 2:1; 3:10; 4:15). This leads us to the most distinctive thematic element in Philippians, as well as the letter's organizing principle: it is a letter of friendship.

In calling Philippians a letter of friendship, I do not suggest that it precisely follows a letter form for the friendly letter *(epistolē philikē)* in a rhetorical handbook like that of Pseudo-Demetrius. I mean, rather, that Paul uses the rhetoric of friendship to evoke appropriate responses in his readers. To appreciate the force of his language, it is necessary to remember how the topic of friendship fascinated Greek moralists, finding distillation in a series of proverbs universally used and endlessly expounded. Friendship could be defined simply as fellowship *(koinōnia)*. Everyone agreed that "friends hold all things in common [*tois philois panta koina*]." Such sharing included both material and spiritual goods. Friendship was a form of equality *(isotēs)*. So close was the spiritual unity between friends that a friend was "another self." Friends were one soul *(mia psychē)* and thought the same *(to auto phronein)*. Friendship language employed many compound words using the prefix "with," *syn-*, since fellowship always involved some sort of "life together." The proverbs are so well known that they are reversible. To speak of being one soul or holding all in common automatically implied as well equality, friendship, and fellowship (for a condensed treatment, see Aristotle *Nicomachean Ethics* 8–9).

The friendship language of Philippians is easily observed in the Greek, though it is less obvious in English translation. Paul uses forms of the term "fellowship," *koinōnia*, in 1:5; 2:1; 3:10; and 4:15. These occur, it will be noted, in all four "fragments" of the letter. The same distribution obtains for Paul's heavy use of the *syn-* prefix. He attaches the prefix to verbs like "struggle" (1:27; 4:3); "rejoice" (2:17, 18); "be formed" (3:10); "receive" (4:3); and "share," *synkoinōneō* (4:14); and to nouns like "sharer," *koinōnos* (1:5); "soul" (2:2); "worker" (2:25; 4:3); "soldier" (2:25); "imitator" (3:17); "form" (3:21); and "yoke" (4:3). If one consistently translated each instance with "fellow," the repetitive force of the Greek would be evident. Paul also works variations on the motif of unity, speaking of one soul (*mia psychē;* 1:27), one spirit (1:27), and thinking the same thing (2:2). So also he rings changes on expressions for "the same thing," *to auto,* in 1:6, 30; 2:2, 18; and 4:3. Finally, he mentions equality (*isos*) once of Jesus (2:6) and once of Timothy (2:20).

The power of this friendship language for a community that was from the beginning of Paul's ministry a "fellow sharer" with him in the work of the gospel is obvious. It evokes the positive connotations of the relationship between the community and him. More significant, it serves a real parenetic function for a community experiencing dissension because of envy and rivalry (1:15). Quite apart from the possible influence of outside agitators, whose presence is not certain, the Philippians have among them some who are grumbling and bickering (2:14; 4:2–3). With its emphasis on equality and unity, friendship language counters the impulses of self-assertion. Paul's rhetoric is even more powerful, however, because he has made fellowship the organizing principle of the letter.

FELLOWSHIP IN THE GOSPEL

The fellowship binding the Christian community is not, as for a Hellenistic club or benevolent association, based on like interests or mutual material benefits. It is not, as in some Hellenistic philosophical schools, based on convictions concerning the metaphysical unity of all beings. Like such schools, the Christians are of "one mind" (1:27) and "share their possessions" (4:15), but the "spirit" joining them together is the Holy Spirit of God. Theirs is a "fellowship of the Spirit" (2:1). They "stand in the one Spirit" (1:27) and they worship God "in spirit" (3:3). This spirit is not theirs by nature but by gift (4:23). It is "the Spirit of Jesus Christ," who is at work both in Paul and in them (1:19).

Since the Spirit came to them through the hearing of the "good news," theirs is also a "fellowship in the gospel" (1:5). The "good news" has bound them together from the beginning (4:15). They have supported it financially (4:10–20) and have labored together in its proclamation (2:22; 4:3). They have suffered together in its defense (1:7, 12, 16, 29–30; 3:10). If they are "one soul" it is because they "struggle together in faith for the gospel" (1:27). That "good news," furthermore, demands from them a response consonant with the gift: "Let your life be worthy of the gospel of Christ" (1:27).

The vice of envy *(phthonos)* is a vice in which one seeks one's own good at the expense of others. For Paul, it is unthinkable that rivalry and envy and competition should arise over the preaching of the gospel (1:15), when that is precisely the focus of Christian unity. The language of fellowship therefore rebukes those members of the community who forget the common good because they seek their own interests. If they are grumbling and complaining against each other (2:14), they will no longer "shine like lights in the world" (2:14), for they will be just like the world, seeking unity on the illusory basis of utopian dreams rather than on the face of God's activity: "God is at work in you, both to will and to work for his good pleasure" (2:13).

THE FORM OF FELLOWSHIP IS SERVICE

Philippians 2:1—4:3 is an extended demonstration of how Christian fellowship should shape the community's identity. A statement of principle (2:1–4) is followed by a series of examples that illustrate it: Jesus (2:6–11), Paul (2:17), Timothy (2:19–24), Epaphroditus (2:25–30), and Paul in contrast to self-seekers (3:2–16). A call to the imitation of these examples (3:17–21) is followed by the specific application to individual disputants (4:2–3).

Paul begins with a rich compilation of terms evoking friendship (2:1–2): the members of the community are to be "like-souled," to "think the same thing," and "have the same love." But their fellowship is based on their being "of the spirit," and "in Christ." The form of their fellowship is therefore given by the way the Spirit works in the Messiah. Paul contrasts this form with its opposite, then explicates the proper attitude. Their fellowship cannot be based on party spirit *(eritheia)* or conceit *(kenodoxia)*. These are forms of self-seeking. They are, rather, to have an attitude of lowly-mindedness *(tapeinophrosynē)* toward each other. They count or reckon *(hēgeomai)* others over themselves. This is a delicate statement easily corrupted. What does Paul mean? He does not call for a denial of self or personal projects. He calls for a functional "reckoning" that relativizes individual interests for the sake of others—the same communal consciousness, in short, that he advocated for the Corinthians. Paul spells it out when he says, "Let each one of you look not only to his own interests but also [or, more: *mallon*] to the interests of others" (2:4).

Three examples illustrate the proper attitude in action. The first and most important is that of Jesus. Paul's language in 2:6–11 is dense and rhythmic, possibly indicating reliance on a traditional hymn about Jesus. The correspondence in structure and language to the rest of this section is so close that it is also possible that Paul himself wrote the hymn or conformed the rest of his language to match it. Certainly of greater significance is the content of the hymn, and how Paul uses it. Before looking at it more closely, a final reminder is in order about the flexibility of friendship proverbs. If friends are equal and hold all things in common, their sharing of possessions also points to equality. Possession language can be used to symbolize spiritual relations. Throughout the hymn and the following section, in fact, it is crucial that this function of possession language be recognized. Paul writes of Jesus (2:6–11),

> who, though he was in the form of God did not count equality with God a thing to be grasped, but emptied himself, taking the form of a slave, being born in the likeness of men. And being found in human form he humbled himself and became obedient unto death, even death on a cross. Therefore God has highly exalted him and bestowed on him the name which is above every name, that at the name of Jesus every knee should bow, in heaven and on earth and under the earth, and every tongue confess that Jesus Christ is Lord to the glory of God the Father.

Here is one who was in the form of God (*morphē tou theou*) but did not reckon (*hēgeomai*) equality with God (*isos*) something to be seized (*hapargmon;* the word suggests "booty"). Rather, he "emptied himself" and took on another form (*morphē*), that of a slave (*doulos*). This is the essential exchange.

Then, being found (*heuretheis*) in this form of a human being, he still humbled himself (*etapeinōsen*) by his obedience, all the way to death, death on the cross (2:8). The cross is the ultimate symbol of self-emptying and of the obedience that is faith. The hymn has moved downward, in "dispossession." It also clearly corresponds to the command to "reckon" and "be humble," in 2:3.

Now, the movement is reversed. The one who did not "grasp at" equality with God has been gifted (*charizomai*) by God (2:9) and exalted as Lord. He is greeted and worshiped as Lord by all creation (2:10–11). The pattern is therefore clear. For the very reason (*dio,* "therefore," in 2:9, is emphatic) that Jesus gave up his "legitimate interest" of equality with God, he was gifted with exaltation.

Scholars debate whether the pattern describes the mythological descent and ascent of the incarnation; the preexistent Christ "emptied himself out" of his divine status by becoming human only to receive it back in resurrection. This would not be foreign to Paul, who is fond of cosmic exchanges (cf. 2 Cor. 5:21; 8:9; Gal. 4:4–7). Others argue that the focus is less on the incarnation than on the manner of Jesus' messianic activity. Paul here interprets the story of Jesus through a midrash on Isaiah 52—53, the Song of the Suffering Servant, showing how in his lifetime Jesus refused any status claiming equality with God and consistently "emptied himself out" in service. This reading too is intelligible and corresponds to Paul's sensitivity to the faith of Jesus as the cause and shaper of Christian identity. There is, however, no need to choose between the options. For Paul, both the gift of God that was the coming of the Messiah and the "Messiah's faith" that was spelled out in obedience take the form of "self-emptying for others."

Jesus is a model to the Philippians of how they should not "grasp after equality" by seeking their own interests, but "empty themselves" in service to one another, with the expectation that, like Jesus, they will be gifted by God. The work of the spirit in them replicates the pattern of its work in Jesus. So Paul introduces the hymn: "Have this mind in you which is yours in Christ Jesus" (2:5). The RSV translation nicely catches the ambiguity of the Greek, which can be read both indicatively and imperatively. They have this mind already because of the Spirit (cf. 1 Cor. 2:16); but they must live it out in imitation of Jesus. The hymn is concluded, "Therefore my beloved, as you have always obeyed, so now" (2:12). Otherwise, Paul's work among them is in vain (2:16). God's work among them (2:13) leads not to divisiveness (2:14) but to mutual service.

In 2:17, Paul anticipates his self-presentation as a model by referring to his own work for the Philippians: "Even if I am to be poured out as a libation upon the sacrificial offering of your faith, I am glad and rejoice with you all." He rejoices *with* them because he spends his life *for* them; the similarity of "poured out" to "emptied out" is striking. They should respond in kind: "You also rejoice the same [*to auto*], and rejoice with me [*synchairein*]" (2:18).

Timothy also is an example of the proper "mind of Christ." He is "equal minded" with Paul (2:20). Why? Because he is "genuinely anxious" for the welfare of the Philippians. His service is defined by their needs, not his desires (2:21–22):

> They all look after their own interests, not those of Christ Jesus [cf. 2:4!]. But Timothy's worth you know, how he served with me [*edouleusen*] in the gospel.

As Jesus was a slave (2:7), so Paul and Timothy have slaved not for their own glory, but for the good of the Philippians in the gospel. Thus they imitate the slave Jesus and can themselves therefore bear the title of slave (cf. 1:1).

Epaphroditus, too, is an example of life for others (2:25–30). He is Paul's fellow worker, fellow soldier (2:25). He was sent by the Philippians as a supplier (*leitourgos;* cf. 2:17) of his needs. Because his illness was so serious, he was almost literally "obedient unto death," since he "risked his life to complete your service to me" (2:30).

Paul finally presents himself as an example of the same attitude. Such repetition of the same point is for their benefit (3:1). The literary function of 3:2–16, which is so often considered a polemic against false teachers is that of a counterexample, used to highlight the positive model. One reason the historical delineation of Paul's opponents in Philippians is so difficult is that they may not be *his* opponents at all. The only explicit mention of opponents refers to those standing against the Philippians themselves (1:28). Paul's descriptions lack much specificity. He speaks of "dogs" and "evil workmen" (3:2; cf. 2 Cor. 11:13) who "mutilate the flesh" (*katatomē* being a pun on *peritomē*, "circumcision"). Using stereotypical slander, he says, "their end is destruction, their god is their belly, their glory is their shame" (3:19; cf. Rom. 16:18). Otherwise, they are simply "enemies of the cross" (3:18). In Gal. 6:12, this expression referred to those who made the choice of circumcision to avoid persecution as a Christian. That is also possible here. But in the light of 2:6–11, the cross also stands as a symbol of self-emptying obedience and service, in contrast to those who glory in their own accomplishments and status.

Paul does not directly attack these opponents or argue against them. He simply tells the Philippians to look at *(blepete)* them. The term *blepete* can be used as "beware," but it can also mean "observe" (cf. 1 Cor. 1:26; 3:10; 10:18). They are to "consider" those who glory in the flesh as the contrasting image of Paul's positive example. When 3:2–16 is read according to the pattern of the Christ hymn of 2:6–11, the parallelism is patent, and Paul's parenetic use of the counterexample becomes clear.

The hymn contrasted a status once held "by right" with a new status as a slave, brought about by obedience. So also does Paul contrast his former and his present status. In every respect, he had reason for "confidence" in his Jewish background. He was, indeed, "as to righteousness under the law, blameless" (3:6). In his portrayal of the reversal, he uses possessions language like that in 2:6. In 3:7–8, he says.

> Whatever gain I had, I counted [*hēgeomai*] as loss, for the sake of Christ. Indeed, I count [*hēgeomai*] everything as loss because of the surpassing worth of knowing Christ Jesus my Lord.

His conversion to the Messiah involved the same sort of loss of status and paradoxical gain as in the case of Jesus (3:8):

I have suffered the loss of all things for his sake, and count [*hēgeomai*] them as refuse in order that I might gain Christ.

Paul wants to be found [*heurethō*] in him, just as Jesus was found [*heuretheis*] in the form of a human being (3:9; cf. 2:8). Because he is so found in Jesus, he also is gifted by God (3:9),

not having a righteousness of my own based on law, but that which is through the faith of Christ, the righteousness from God which depends on faith.

Now, Paul shows how the pattern is empowered and manifested (3:10). Because he "knows the power of the resurrection," he experiences the Spirit that comes from the risen Lord. That Spirit works in him, however, so that he "might share in his sufferings, becoming like him in his death, that if possible I might attain the resurrection from the dead." The term "being like him" is stronger in the Greek. Literally, it is "formed together into his death." It explicitly picks up the language of form [*morphē*] from 2:6–8.

Paul has therefore allowed the form of Christ's self-emptying to be the form of his own existence. Unlike those who preach circumcision, he does not cling to a status of which he can boast but receives the gift of righteousness that comes by faith. So also should the Philippians regard themselves (3:15–16). The process has not yet been completed in Paul; he still must struggle as an athlete (3:12–14); he has not reached the resurrection glory. He is still being conformed to the suffering of Christ. This is their call as well, since "Christ Jesus has made [them] his own" (3:12–14).

Paul calls them to imitation in 3:17–21. They can look to Jesus, Paul, Timothy, and Epaphroditus as examples of "the mind of Christ": "Brethren join in imitating me, and mark those who so live as you have an example in us." As often in parenesis, Paul provides another contrast to this positive command (3:18–19) before picking up the language of the hymn once more and drawing his readers with him into the Spirit's work of transformation (3:20–21):

Our commonwealth is in heaven, and from it we await a savior, the Lord Jesus Christ, who will change [*metaskēmatizō*] our lowly body [*sōma tapeinōseōs*] to be like [or, formed with: *symmorphē*] the body of his glory, by the power which enables him to subject all things to himself.

Paul at last turns this demonstration to its practical end. He exhorts— notice how the double *parakalō* brackets the *paraklēsis* of 2:1—his "fellow laborers" Euodia and Syntyche and the "genuine yokefellow" to "think the same thing in the Lord" (4:2). There can now be no doubt what this "one thing" can be. The fellowship of the Christian community rests not in the assertion of rights but in the relativization of them for the sake of others (3:15–16):

Let those of us who are mature be thus minded; and if in anything you are other minded, God will also reveal this to you. Only let us hold true to what we have attained.

In fact, Paul finds in the relationship between the Philippian community and himself just such a living fellowship. We see, as further evidence for the literary unity of this letter, that the central argument of chapters 2:1— 4:3 is framed by precisely the same pattern of "life for others." In the beginning of the letter (1:21–26), Paul shows how he gave up the gain (*kerdos*) that would be his by dying to go "be with Christ," for the sake of the Philippians' "progress and joy in the faith." Likewise at the end of the letter, the Philippians themselves have "thought in behalf of Paul" (4:10, with the Greek rendered literally) and have "shared his affliction" (4:14). Paul wants them to be toward each other the way he is toward them and the way they show themselves toward him.

BIBLIOGRAPHICAL NOTE

As so often in the Pauline correspondence, scholarship has focused almost exclusively on the critical issues of integrity and the opponents. For the place of Philippians in Paul's career, as well as the issue of literary integrity, see, among many, G. S. Dungan, "Paul's Ministry in Asia—The Last Phase," *NTS* 3 (1956– 57): 210–18; W. Schmithals, *Paul and the Gnostics*, trans. J. Steely (Nashville: Abingdon Press, 1972), 65–122; B. D. Rahtjan, "The Three Letters of Paul to the Philippians," *NTS* 6 (1959–60): 167–73; V. P. Furnish, "The Place and Purpose of Phil III," *NTS* 10 (1963–64): 80–88; R. Jewett, "The Epistolary Thanksgiving and the Integrity of Philippians," *NovT* 12 (1970): 40–53; and T. E. Pollard, "The Integrity of Philippians," *NTS* 13 (1966–67): 57–66. Pollard demonstrates some significant thematic connections. In particular, see W. J. Dalton, "The Integrity of Phil," *Bib* 60 (1979): 97–102; Dalton convincingly establishes the literary unity of chaps. 2 and 3. In contrast, see the continuation of the fragment motif in J. Reumann, "Philippians 3:20–21—A Hymnic Fragment?" *NTS* 30 (1984): 593– 609.

On the opponents, besides Schmithals (above), there is A. F. J. Klijn, "Paul's Opponents in Phil 3," *NovT* 7 (1964–65): 278–84; H. Koester, "The Purpose of the Polemic of a Pauline Fragment," *NTS* 8 (1961): 317–32; R. Jewett, "Conflicting Movements in the Early Church As Reflected in Philippians," *NovT* 12 (1970): 361–90.

Among very many studies of the Christ hymn in 2:6–11, the following are representative: R. P. Martin, *Carmen Christi: Philippians ii 5–11 in Recent Interpretation and in the Setting of Early Christian Worship* (Cambridge: At the Univ. Press, 1967); G. Bornkamm, "On Understanding the Christ-Hymn, Phil 2:6–11," in his *Early Christian Experience* (New York: Harper & Row, 1969), 112–22; L. Cerfaux, "The Christological Hymns," in his *Christ in the Theology of St. Paul* (New York: Herder & Herder, 1959), 369–401; C. F. D. Moule, "Further Reflexions on Phil 2:5–11," in *Apostolic History and the Gospel*, ed. W. Gasque and R. P. Martin (Grand Rapids: Wm. B. Eerdmans, 1970), 264–76; C. H. Talbert, "The Problem of Pre-Existence in Phil 2:6–11," *JBL* 86 (1967): 141–53; J. Murphy-O'Connor, "Christological Anthropology in Phil II, 6–11," *Revue Biblique* 83 (1976): 25–50; G. Howard, "Phil 2:6–11 and the Human Christ," *CBQ* 40 (1978): 368–87. Most of these studies isolate the hymn from its literary context; an exception is that by M. D. Hooker, "Philippians 2:6–11," in *Jesus und Paulus*, ed. E. E. Ellis and E. Grässer (Göttingen: Vandenhoeck & Ruprecht, 1975), 151–64.

For some discussion of Philippians 1, see D. W. Palmer, "To Die Is Gain (Phil 1:21)," *NovT* 17 (1975): 203–18; and V. J. De Vogel, "Reflexions on Philipp 1:23–24," *NovT* 19 (1977): 262–74.

The reading of the central section of Philippians in this chapter owes much to W. Kurz, "Kenotic Imitation of Paul and Christ in Phil 2 and 3," in *Discipleship in the New Testament*, ed. F. Segovia (Philadelphia: Fortress Press, 1985), 103–26. For a lead to the use of possession language in connection with friendship, see F. Hauck, s.v. "koinos," *TDNT* 3:789–810; and L. T. Johnson, *Sharing Possessions: Mandate and Symbol of Faith* (Philadelphia: Fortress Press, 1981). It will be noticed that I take a different approach to this language from that of J. P. Sampley, who derives it from the Roman legal uses of *societas*; see "Societas Christi: Roman Law and Paul's Conception of the Christian Community," in *God's Christ and His People*, ed. J. Jervell and W. A. Meeks (Oslo: Universitetsforlaget, 1977) 158–74; and idem, *Pauline Partnership in Christ: Christian Community and Commitment in Light of Roman Law* (Philadelphia: Fortress Press, 1980).

16

The Letter to Philemon

THE SHORTEST OF PAUL'S LETTERS POSSESSES AN IMPORTANCE BEYOND
itself as a key to deciphering a larger part of the Pauline collection. Itself of
unquestioned authenticity, Philemon has literary links to Colossians and
Ephesians, whose authenticity is always discussed and frequently rejected.
A consideration of each of these three writings will be helped by a
preliminary display of the connections between them and a discussion of
the ways in which scholars have construed them. Such historical detection
does not bear on the literary worth or religious message of the writings.
But the issues raised help sharpen the literary character and religious
dimensions of these Pauline traditions.

CONNECTIONS AND CONSTRUALS

Connections

The three letters share several features. Each claims to be written by
Paul from captivity (Phlm. 1; Col. 4:10, 18; Eph. 3:1; 4:1; 6:20). Phi-
lemon is cosponsored by Timothy (v. 1), and Paul writes at least part of the
letter in his own hand (v. 19). Colossians also claims to come from Paul and
Timothy (1:1), with Paul adding at least the final greeting himself (4:18).
Ephesians makes no mention of an amanuensis or cosponsorship (1:1).

There is a considerable overlap in the names mentioned in each letter.
With Paul in prison, according to Philemon, is Epaphras, his "fellow
prisoner," and Mark, Aristarchus, Demas, and Luke (vv. 23–24). Paul is
sending the slave Onesimus back to his owner, Philemon (v. 10). In the
assembly that meets in Philemon's household, Paul greets his "sister
Apphia" and Archippus, his "fellow soldier" (v. 2). We meet the same cast
in Colossians. Paul mentions Onesimus as "the faithful and beloved
brother who is one of yourselves" (Col. 4:9). He is being accompanied by
Tychichus, who will report to the community about Paul (4:7). Paul's
fellow prisoners are Aristarchus, Mark, Jesus Justus (4:10–11), Luke and

Demas (4:14), and Epaphras, "one of yourselves" (4:12). With the exception of Tychichus and Jesus Justus, the names match exactly. Among those in the church at Colossae, Paul has a message only for Archippus: "See that you fulfill the ministry which you have received in the Lord" (4:17). He greets the brethren at Laodicea, and "Nympha and the church at her house" (4:15). He expects the Colossians and Laodiceans to exchange letters (4:16). He regards the communities of Hierapolis, Colossae, and Laodicea as part of a circuit of churches bound by communication (4:13). The coincidence of names suggests that these letters were written at the same time from the same place by the same person. Ephesians lacks any personal references, except in 6:21–22:

> Now, that you may also know how I am and what I am doing, Tychichus, the beloved brother and faithful minister in the Lord will tell you everything. I have sent him to you for this very purpose, that you may know how we are, and that he may encourage your hearts.

Tychichus links Colossians and Ephesians. In each, he is the deliverer of personal information about Paul. This chain of names corresponds furthermore to the little we know from other NT writings. Mark the cousin of Barnabas was a companion of Paul for a time (Acts 15:37–39) as were Tychichus (Acts 20:4; 2 Tim. 4:12; Titus 3:12), Aristarchus (Acts 19:29; 27:2), Demas (2 Tim. 4:10), and Luke (2 Tim. 4:11). The local personalities Epaphras, Philemon, and Onesimus, in contrast, are attested only in the two letters. Paul's companion Jesus Justus is found only in Colossians.

Philemon is so short that not a great deal can be said about its style. Colossians and Ephesians, however, share much common vocabulary and have similar sentence structures and thematic emphases. Their similarities can be overdrawn, for their shared terms often occur in different contexts and with distinct nuances. But when the documents are viewed side by side, one would easily conclude that some literary relationship, though not necessarily one of dependence, connected the two letters.

The three letters differ most in their intended audiences and function. Philemon is basically a personal note. It greets others in the church but is written throughout in the second-person singular. The letter also has a very personal purpose. Paul wants Philemon to receive back his runaway slave Onesimus. The injunction "Receive him as you would me" (Phlm. 17) makes the note, in effect, a letter of recommendation. Onesimus is no longer simply property. He is a brother in the faith and should be received as such.

Colossians is written not to an individual but to a community. Paul writes to a church founded by his fellow prisoner Epaphras (Col. 1:7). He responds to a crisis of confidence in that young community resembling the one in Galatia, except that fewer details are known or revealed in this case and that Paul must instruct a church he does not know personally and that has never met him (Col. 2:1).

In Ephesians, a community of indeterminate character is addressed. The themes and images of Colossians are placed within the framework of a theological exposition concerning God's reconciling work in the world. The relation of Ephesians to Colossians is almost precisely that of Romans to Galatians; the issues forged in controversy are elevated to the level of a magisterial statement. Ephesians, however, lacks almost all personal references and is even more general in its teaching than Romans.

Each letter raises its distinct problem, whether taken individually or together with the others. The authenticity of Philemon is not seriously questioned. But why would such a personal note, and one with so little apparent general appeal, be preserved and made part of a collection? Was it therefore sent by itself, or as part of a larger packet? Colossians is obviously related to Philemon. But because its authenticity is often challenged on other grounds, the network of names becomes a possible indication of pseudepigraphy, which in this case comes close to forgery. A later author may have used the names found in Philemon to give the impression that Colossians was written by Paul. But this suggestion is also less than satisfactory. Why should imitation of random biographical details from an obscure private note, which was not likely to have had wide circulation, have been expected to mark the letter as Pauline?

The authenticity of Ephesians is most often challenged on grounds of style and theology. Some think it represents a Pauline understanding as filtered through a mystical, possibly even gnostic, sensibility. Also a later one: in Paul's time, one could not speak thus, it is suggested, of the reconciliation between Jew and Greek as an accomplished reality in the church. Paul's ethics could never have been so domesticated as these lists of household duties. Nor could Paul ever have written to a church so well known to him in such an impersonal and distant fashion.

On this last point, however, a further complication simplifies things. The incompatibility of Paul's manner with the general teaching of Ephesians was long ago noted. The second-century Paulinist Marcion thought this letter was the one "to the Laodiceans" (Col. 4:16) of which otherwise we have not a trace. Marcion's solution is not likely, but manuscript evidence suggests he was not altogether wrong. Some good and early manuscripts lack the name Ephesians in the title, having only "to the saints" (1:1). The omission is all the stranger, since the form of the Greek sentence calls out for a place name: "to the saints at ___." When these observations are taken together, it is not surprising that many scholars consider Ephesians not a letter written to a specific community but a *circular letter* to be delivered to several communities.

Construals

The pieces could be put together in several different ways. First, one could regard all three letters as an elaborate literary hoax, much as some regard the Pastorals. But there is no reason at all to doubt the genuineness of Philemon. Second, either Colossians or Ephesians could be regarded as inauthentic, and the literary relations among the letters explained on the basis of copying and imitation. Finally, all three could be seen as genuine, and their differences explained on the basis of their audience, form, and function. Since the present discussion serves simply to place Philemon within each scheme, I leave aside further consideration of authenticity until I treat Colossians and Ephesians in turn.

If, as a respectable number of scholars still think, Colossians is authentic, the situation is considerably clarified. If Colossians and Philemon were sent together by Paul to Colossae, the preservation of Philemon is explained, and only the production of Ephesians remains needing explanation. One suggestion is that Onesimus, stirred by the reading of Colossians, undertook, after Paul's death, the collection of all his letters. Having read those he collected, he borrowed liberally from their substance if not their style and, in an act of filial loyalty to Paul, undertook the composition of Ephesians. He intended it to be a compendium of Paul's theology and a frontispiece to the Pauline collection. This is an ingenious theory. It takes care of pseudonymity and the literary relation to Colossians: Onesimus simply lifted portions of Colossians when writing Ephesians. The hypothesis lacks any manuscript evidence for thinking that Ephesians headed up the collection, and it greatly oversimplifies the stylistic similarities between Colossians and Ephesians. But it does cover the data.

But if Colossians is also considered inauthentic, a more complex accounting is required. Does Onesimus write Colossians as well, lifting from the authentic letters, themes—and from the note written about him by Paul, names—to cover his literary tracks? Does someone else besides Onesimus write Colossians after Paul's death, while also writing Ephesians but omitting in the second case the clever network of names that certified the first?

It is also possible to regard all three letters as authentically Pauline in the sense used in this book. They are all written in Paul's lifetime under his authorization. The major difficulty to this hypothesis is not stylistic but thematic, and the cases of Colossians and Ephesians will each require discussion. But if a Pauline sponsorship in the broad sense can be granted, then the literary relationship of the three letters is clear and the figure that emerges as a key to the correspondence is not Philemon or even Onesimus but Tychichus.

Here is a possible reconstruction. Paul is in prison with the founder of the Colossian community, Epaphras. He is joined by the runaway slave Onesimus. The slave or someone else brings news to Paul and Epaphras of a crisis of confidence in the Colossian church. Epaphras asks Paul to support his ministry and work there by writing a letter to his troubled community, and Paul obliges him. He takes advantage of the occasion of sending Onesimus back to his master to have the Colossian letter delivered. He also has composed a circular letter employing many of the themes of Colossians but cast in a distinctive and general exposition about God's work in the church. He wants this letter to be delivered to the circle of gentile churches associated with his mission though not necessarily founded by him personally. Tychichus is both the companion of Onesimus and the mailman. He carries three or four letters in his packet. The first is a letter of recommendation for Onesimus. The second is the letter to the Colossian church which he expects to be read aloud at the assembly. Another possible letter is that to the local assembly at Laodicea. Finally, he carries the circular letter, which he will deliver to Hierapolis, Ephesus, and other cities in Asia Minor, at the same time carrying to them personal information concerning Paul's condition while in prison. This is the simplest of the hypotheses, and it covers the data. It is the imaginative picture I carry with me when I read these three letters.

THE LETTER

In spite of its brevity, Philemon is a carefully crafted witness to an emerging Christian ethos, showing at once its power to transform symbols and attitudes, as well as its struggle to transcend social forms. It also reveals a Paul who is unexpectedly diplomatic, urbane, and even witty. Within its classic epistolographic form—greeting (vv. 1–3), thanksgiving (vv. 4–7), body (vv. 8–20), greetings (vv. 21–24), and farewell (v. 25)—the letter is a masterpiece of suggestion.

Paul needs considerable diplomatic skill (whether he calls himself an old man, in v. 9, or ambassador), for his situation is awkward. Toward Philemon, the slave owner, he owes the legal rights of the society, and since Paul is the cause of Onesimus's defection, he is to blame. But he is also convinced that Onesimus—now that he is a Christian—cannot be considered simply property. He is an equal before the Lord and a "brother." By accepting Onesimus among his companions, Paul has brought some financial harm to Philemon, which he promises to repay (v. 18). At the same time, he is Philemon's benefactor. Through the Pauline mission, Philemon has been given life, so that Paul can say to him, "You owe me even yourself" (v. 19).

The situation is even more complex, since Paul does not really want to lose the assistance of Onesimus. He would like Philemon to send him back. But is he in a position to command this? Why yes, "in Christ" (v. 8), but the delicacy of his position demands that he "appeal" rather than "command" (v. 9). He wants Philemon to read between the lines and follow his wishes, without having to risk his fragile authority by making them explicit.

The letter contains a number of elegant puns. The name Onesimus means "useful" in Greek. Paul tells Philemon that Onesimus had formerly been "useless," *achrestos*, to him but now had become "useful," *euchrestos*; (v. 11), since he had been "begotten" by Paul as a son in the faith (v. 10). The pun is actually double, since the Greek *chrēstos* suggests *Christos*, "Christ." So, before his conversion, Onesimus was useless because he was *a-Chrestos*, "without Christ," but now he was useful because he was *eu-Chrestos*, a "good Christian"! Onesimus, in other words, found his true identity in the gospel, as did Philemon himself (v. 19)!

A second pun is suggested in the thanksgiving. Paul remembers Philemon had "refreshed the hearts [*ta splanchna*] of the saints" (v. 7). The expression undoubtedly refers to the hospitality and financial support Philemon had made available to the messianic movement from the resources of his household (see, e.g., v. 22). But when Paul speaks of returning Onesimus to him, he virtually sighs, "I am sending my very heart" (the same term in Greek; v. 12). The two levels of pun are intertwined in v. 20. Paul tells Philemon, "Yes brother, I want some benefit [a play on Onesimus's name again] from you in the Lord; refresh my heart in Christ." No wonder Paul can then add, "Confident of your obedience, I write to you, knowing that you will do even more than I say" (v. 21)!

Philemon opens a small but light-filled window on the Pauline mission. It shows us the close network of fellow workers (vv. 2, 23–24) and of hospitality (v. 22), the leadership role of women (v. 2), the understanding of the community as "the holy ones" (vv. 4, 7), the church meeting in households (v. 2). We find the fellowship (*koinōnia*) of the Christian community to be one of faith active in sharing (v. 6), in service (v. 13), and in reciprocity (v. 17). The fellowship "in Christ" (vv. 8, 20) and "in the Lord" (v. 16) transcends natural kinship relationships and social stratification. Paul is a "father" to Onesimus because he converted him to the "good news" (v. 10), and that new status makes him also now a "beloved brother" to his master Philemon (v. 16). We begin to see how this new sort of fellowship will strain ever more urgently against the framework of ancient social structures, so that not even tact and diplomacy will resolve the tension between "There is neither slave nor free," and "Slaves be submissive." And at last we see again the paradox of Paul who is in chains (vv. 1, 10) giving freedom to both slaves and masters by the "good news."

BIBLIOGRAPHICAL NOTE

Understandably, Philemon by itself has not enjoyed a great deal of scholarly attention. Concerning its role in the Pauline corpus, see P. N. Harrison,

"Onesimus and Philemon," *ATR* 32 (1950): 268ff. Above all, see J. Knox, "Philemon and the Authenticity of Colossians," *JR* 18 (1938): 144–60; and idem, *Philemon Among the Letters of Paul*, rev. ed. (Nashville: Abingdon Press, 1959). The role of Onesimus in the composition of Ephesians is also proposed by E. J. Goodspeed, *The Meaning of Ephesians* (Chicago: Univ. of Chicago Press, 1933), and is taken up by C. L. Mitton, *The Formation of the Pauline Corpus of Letters* (London: Epworth Press, 1955). See also C. P. Anderson, "Who Wrote the Letter from Laodicea?" *JBL* 85 (1966): 436–40. His answer is Epaphras. F. C. Baur showed his usual consistency by stating that the authenticity of all three rose or fell together and then rejecting all of them as inauthentic. Philemon he called "a Christian romance serving to convey a genuine Christian idea," in his *Paul the Apostle*, trans. R. A. Menzies (London: Williams & Norgate, 1875), 2:1–44, 80–84.

In contrast, Philemon is used as a key to Paul's world in N. R. Petersen, *Rediscovering Paul: Philemon and the Sociology of Paul's Narrative World* (Philadelphia: Fortress Press, 1985). See also J. H. Elliott, "Philemon and House Churches," *The Bible Today* 22/23 (1984): 145–50. For a rhetorical analysis, see F. F. Church, "Rhetorical Structure and Design in Paul's Letter to Philemon," *HTR* 71 (1978): 17–33. A recent exegetical study is by H. Riesenfeld, "Faith and Love Promoting Hope: An Interpretation of Philemon v. 6," in *Paul and Paulinism*, ed. M. D. Hooker and S. G. Wilson (London: SPCK, 1982), 251–57.

For Philemon as a letter of recommendation, see C. H. Kim, *Form and Structure of the Familiar Greek Letter of Recommendation* (Missoula, Mont.: Soc. of Biblical Literature, 1972), esp. p. 123; and A. J. Malherbe, "Ancient Epistolary Theory," *Ohio Journal of Religious Studies* 5 (1977): 63–71.

In commentaries, Philemon is most often teamed with Colossians, as in E. Lohse, *Colossians and Philemon*, Hermeneia (Philadelphia: Fortress Press, 1971 [1968]), and C. F. D. Moule, *The Epistles of Paul the Apostle to the Colossians and to Philemon*, CGTC (Cambridge: At the Univ. Press, 1962).

17
The Letter to the Colossians

THE SITUATION PRESUPPOSED BY COLOSSIANS IS UNCOMPLICATED. PAUL IS A prisoner (1:24; 4:3, 18) with Epaphras (4:12), the founder of the Colossian community (1:7) as part of Paul's mission among the Gentiles (1:23–24). Paul does not know the community personally (2:1). He and Epaphras hear of problems caused in the young church by troublemakers. Paul takes the occasion of the return of Onesimus to his owner Philemon (4:7–9) to have Tychichus report to the Colossians and Laodiceans on his condition (2:1; 4:13) and to deliver this letter to be read aloud (4:16) to the troubled church in Colossae.

THE ISSUE OF AUTHENTICITY

Although a significant number of scholars think Colossians is authentic, a growing majority consider it inauthentic. As a result, it has fallen out of serious discussions of Paul's mission and thought, being treated instead as a witness to traditions developing after the apostle's death. Sometimes appeal is made to the widespread practice of pseudonymity in the Hellenistic world or to the first Christians' lack of interest in distinguishing between the sources of spiritual teaching. These observations are without either general or specific pertinence. Pseudonymity was practiced, but most often as a transparent fiction employing the name of a person long dead and known to be so (Enoch, for example in Apocalypses, or Socrates in the Cynic letters). Here, in contrast, we have a school producing a letter shortly after Paul's death, deliberately using signals—his autograph, the network of names—that make the enterprise much more like a deliberate forgery. The first generations of Christians, furthermore, were very much concerned with the sources of spiritual teaching and with distinguishing between true and false teachers; they did not live in a charismatic fog (see only 1 Cor. 7:10–12; 14:29; 2 Cor. 11:13–15; 2 Thess. 2:2).

Is there textual evidence for the charge of inauthenticity? Stylistic criteria are not determinative here. The Greek is well within the range Paul displays elsewhere, especially if the sample of comparison includes the Captivity Letters. As in Philippians and Philemon, he does not cite Torah. As in Philippians and 2 Timothy, he uses hymnic material (see 1:15–20). Much of his vocabulary is affected by the use of liturgical traditions, above all those associated with Baptism (see 2:20; 3:1–5, 9–12).

Colossians presupposes no elaborate or hierarchical church order. The governing image for the church is that of the body of Christ (1:18, 22, 24; 2:17, 19; 3:15). The similarity to 1 Cor. 12:12–27 is strong, although in Colossians, as in Eph. 4:4–16, Christ is imaged as the head of the body. Colossians makes no reference to authority, apart from calling Epaphras a slave (4:12) and commanding Archippus to fulfill his ministry (*diakonia;* 4:17) and greeting Nympha, the head of a household where the assembly met (4:15).

Does the ethics of Colossians lack the distinctive Pauline eschatological edge? The table of household ethics in 3:18—4:6 is offered in evidence. The use of this stereotypical teaching, however, has less to do with the passage of time and the "routinization of charism" than it does with Paul's audience. He is writing to a community not known to him personally. As in Rom. 12:1—13:7, therefore, and Eph. 5:21—6:9, his moral exhortations fall into the general frame of household ethics, the variations on which we will later note. His other ethical admonitions depend in large part on the baptismal traditions shared by gentile churches (3:1–17; cf. Rom. 6:1–14; 1 Cor. 6:9–11).

Does the theology of Colossians deviate dramatically from the recognizably Pauline? Not with respect to Paul's view of his own ministry. He calls himself an apostle (1:1) and a servant (1:25). His suffering is in behalf of the church (1:24). His preaching is based on the revelation of a "mystery" hidden in the past but now made known (1:26; 4:3; cf. Rom. 11:25; 16:25–26). His work is above all among the Gentiles (1:27). His goal is to present people as mature in Christ (*teleios;* 1:28; cf. 1 Cor. 2:6; 14:20; Phil. 3:15). Paul understands Jesus as the source of wisdom and understanding (2:3; cf. 2 Cor. 6:16). Because of his resurrection, Christ rules over angelic forces (2:10, 15; cf. Phil. 2:10–11). He also played a role in creation (1:15–16; cf. 1 Cor. 8:6). The instrument of salvation is the cross and Jesus' redemptive blood (1:14, 20, 22; 2:14). The Pauline character of this emphasis requires no documentation.

The most serious charge of inconsistency is leveled at the eschatology of Colossians. On the basis of 2:12, "you were buried with him in baptism, in which you were also raised with him through faith in the working of God"; 2:13, "You were made alive in him"; and 3:1, "If then you have been raised with Christ," it has been suggested that Colossians has a "realized eschatology" that destroys the delicate tension between the "already" and the "not yet" typical of Paul. Apart from the issue of how much latitude an author has before he reaches self-inconsistency and the rather obvious shifts in eschatological emphasis in the undisputed letters, this charge simply misreads the text of Colossians. It is clear from 2:20 and 3:1–4 that the "death" to sin in baptism leads to a "resurrection life" not of glory but of faith, which requires of the Colossians a conversion of their behavior. Their "life" indeed is "hid with God in Christ." Only at the end, "when Christ our life appears" will they themselves be in a state of "glory" (3:4). The language is slightly different, but the thought is virtually identical to that in Rom. 6:1–14.

Neither the stylistic nor the substantive reasons for doubting the authenticity of Colossians are convincing. And if one credits the letter to an associate of Paul during his lifetime, then one has agreed that it is authentic in the sense of the present book.

THE CRISIS IN COLOSSAE

Colossae was in Phrygia, a region renowned in the ancient world for its fascination with all things magical and mysterious. From Phrygia came the cult of the mother goddess Cybele, as well as the later enthusiastic version of Christianity known as Montanism. We can understand how a recently founded intentional community, the cult of the Christ, which had lost its founding figure to imprisonment, was placed in the difficult and vulnerable position of making comparisons with other cults, and other claims to ultimate worth. Fascinated by the charms of those who could offer them more, these half-formed Christians were easy prey to instability. Their all too palpable immaturity made them vulnerable to the offer of a greater perfection (or, maturity: *teleios*) than that available in their cult.

Hints of Paul's concern are subtly suggested even in his praise of the Colossians. Using the metaphor of plant maturity, Paul acknowledges that the "good news" is "bearing fruit and growing" among them (1:6), but he prays immediately after, that they "might bear fruit in every good work and increase in the *knowledge* [*epignōsis*] of God" (1:10; cf. 2:2). The significance of "knowledge" we will see shortly. At the very end of the letter, Epaphras also prays that "they stand mature [*teleios*] and fully assured in all the will of God" (4:12). Furthermore, Paul wants them to be "stable in the good news" (1:23) and to be "mature [*teleios*] in Christ" (1:28). He rejoices because of their good order and the "firmness of the faith in Christ" (2:5). The issue that begins to emerge from these hints concerns the nature of perfection (maturity) before God. In what does it consist? On what is it based?

Paul's fundamental position is clear even from these first hints. He wants the Colossians to be mature "in Christ" (1:28). Their further growth and perfection will come through an ever-deepening recognition of what they already have been given and who they already are. Thus Paul prays that they have "recognition of the gift [grace] of God in truth" (1:6) and follows this immediately with, "just as [*kathōs*] you learned it from Epaphras" (1:7). Paul wants them to have recognition (*epignōsis*) of "Christ the mystery of God" (2:2), as a protection against the wiles of false teaching (2:4). The crisis in Colossae was one of confidence (or, assurance; 4:12). Is what they have been given in Christ enough for perfection, or do they require more for maturity? The crisis is exacerbated by the efforts of troublemakers.

Once more we meet the problem of identifying the "opponents" and their influence in Paul's mission. Are they visitors from the outside? Are they local representatives of rival cults? Or are members of the church itself—as perhaps the reprimanded Archippus—agitating for alliances propagated since the forced departure of Epaphras? We cannot know for certain, since we are totally dependent on Paul's secondhand information. His characterizations tend to be general. He calls their teaching a "philosophy" based on human traditions according to "the elemental spirits of the universe" and not Christ (2:8), which tells us at once too little and too much. This "philosophy" generates a desire to observe festivals and a special diet (2:16). It involves an admiration for physical asceticism (2:20–22). This philosophy in fact would appear to be some variety of Judaism, since the role of Torah (2:14) and of circumcision (2:11) figure in Paul's response. The most problematic piece of the puzzle is provided by the troublesome text in 2:18:

> Let no one disqualify you, insisting on self-abasement [or, humility: *tapeinōphrosynē*] and worship of [or, with] angels, taking his stand [*embateuōn*] on visions, puffed up without reason by his sensuous mind.

The pieces have been put together in many ways. Some scholars have detected advocates of pagan mysteries, others an esoteric and rigorous form of Judaism, such as Essenism. Still others have found Judaizing Gentiles, as in Galatia (see Gal. 3:19; 4:3, 9). The mention of visions, however, suggests Jewish mystics of the Merkabah variety. These were fond of esoteric traditions and demanded strict observance of Torah and sexual asceticism as prerequisites for their flights of prayer to the heavenly throne chariot (*merkabah*) where they "worshiped with angels" (see also 2 Cor. 12:1–5).

More important than their specific identity, however, is the way the agitators understood perfection or maturity before God, and the attitude they adopted toward others in the Colossian community. They saw perfection as the achievement of new levels of spiritual status, marked by observance of law and sexual asceticism, and above all by initiation into the higher mysteries of visionary experiences. By such marks, they could identify who was "fleshly" and who was "spiritual." Christ was for them only a beginning; to be fully mature before God meant taking on more elaborate and visible forms of religious observance, and the experience of higher planes of ecstasy. On the basis of their greater spiritual maturity, furthermore, they could "judge" others (2:16) and even seek to "disqualify" them (2:18, the word suggesting disqualification from a race).

Such attitudes outrage Paul. All their spiritual athleticism and theosophy only show them to be "puffed up (cf. 1 Cor. 8:1) without reason in their sensuous mind" (2:18). Their "love of wisdom" is nothing of the sort but only a cover for fleshly behavior (2:23), for as we learned in 1 Cor. 3:1–3, the "flesh" above all means the hostile judgment of others. This self-regard and contempt of others is the exact opposite of genuine spiritual maturity, which has to do not with the cultivation of the human psyche, but with obedience to God's Spirit, and which expresses itself in love and mutual support. Paul will not debate these spiritual dilettantes, for his concern is for the confidence of those whom they are corrupting. He wants to remind them that what they have already been given: the "gift of God" gives them the only real basis for maturity.

The troublemakers Paul treats with contempt, as self-deluded charlatans. In Christ, the Colossians already have "all the treasures of wisdom and knowledge" (2:3), even though they are riches that are not obvious but hidden. The seducers in contrast dangle before their eyes shiny coins, seeking to "defraud" them (*paralogizetai;* 2:4), and if they succeed, they will make the Colossians their booty (*sulagōgōn;* 2:8). The monetary metaphor running through this section is unmistakable in the Greek. Paul's point is that the Colossians have the true wealth that comes from God; they should not be taken in by counterfeit coinage. To show how the attempt to achieve spiritual maturity on the basis of human accomplishment is illusory, Paul uses another metaphor: it is like reaching after a shadow (*skia*), when the body (*sōma*) that casts the shadow is at hand (2:17). The shadow, of course, is their quest; the body (or, reality) is Christ. Their growth, therefore, must be illusory. In 2:19, Paul indicates that this is

> because they do not hold fast to the head, from whom the whole body is nourished and knit together through its joints and ligaments, and grows with a growth that is from God.

That the "growth comes from God" is critical and reminds us of Phil. 1:6: "I am confident that he who began a good work in you will bring it to completion at the day of Jesus Christ" (cf. Gal. 3:1–5).

Paul uses yet another mixed metaphor of growth (2:6–7):

> As therefore you received Christ Jesus the Lord, so live in him, rooted and built up in him and established in faith, just as you were taught, abounding in thanksgiving.

The sentence is carefully constructed. As (that is, in the manner) they received Christ, so (again, in that manner) are they to grow. The phrase "just as you were taught" echoes 1:7, "... just as you learned from Epaphras." Paul reminds them that maturity will come not by taking on esoteric lore and rituals but by increasing in awareness *(epignōsis)* of the gift already given by God in Christ (cf. 1 Cor. 1:12), "to recognize the grace of God in truth" (1:6; cf. 1:9, 10; 2:2; 3:10).

THE GIFT OF GOD IN TRUTH

The Colossian congregation is to learn that because they are "in Christ" they are also "in God." When they meet Jesus, they encounter the ultimate power in the universe. There is no more to be had, for the "fullness" is in him. To show this, Paul cites the christological hymn of 1:15–20. Possibly liturgical in origin, it reworks the traditions associated with the preexistent wisdom of God (Prov. 8:22–31; Wis. 7:22—8:1) and with Adam as the "image and likeness of God" (Gen. 1:26–27; 2 Cor. 4:4), in light of the conviction that in the "beloved son" Jesus, ultimate reality was touched. So he is the "image of the unseen God" (1:15), and all things came to be through his agency (1:16)—even those angelic powers with whom they would like to worship!—all things are sustained by his power (1:17). Indeed, in him "all the fullness of God was pleased to dwell" (1:19). This means, of course, that when he acts, God is at work. Through him, therefore, God reconciled the world to himself (cf. 2 Cor. 5:16–21) "making peace by the blood of his cross" (1:20; cf. Rom. 5:1). This ultimate power has not, moreover, gone away. It is still active in the world, for "he is the head of the body, the church" (1:18). Those who are incorporated into the church, then, are in touch with the power of God. The pretensions of these spiritual adepts are hollow, for "they do not cling to the head from whom the whole body ... grows with a growth that is from God." They only chase after shadows (2:17).

Paul is talking not about abstract convictions but about present experience. By initiation into the church in baptism, Christians have in fact passed over into God's kingdom. Paul frames the hymn by these two statements:

> He has delivered us from the realm of darkness into the kingdom of his beloved Son, in whom we have redemption and forgiveness of sins, (1:13)

and

> You who were once estranged and hostile in mind ... he has now reconciled in his body of flesh by his death. (1:21)

The passing over and reconciliation are real, because they were worked by

God. Now Paul's readers know why they should not allow anyone to "judge" them (2:16) or "disqualify" them (2:18) on the basis of human achievements, for God has already "qualified" them to "share in the inheritance of the saints in light" (1:12).

Why should they need another ritual of initiation such as circumcision? In their baptism, they have been initiated into the ultimate "mystery," into the very "working of God" (2:12). The triumph of Jesus' death and resurrection together with his annulment of the power of law exercised by the inimical spiritual powers (2:14–15) have been made powerfully available to them (2:12):

> You were buried with him in baptism, in which you were also raised with him through faith in the working of God who raised him from the dead.

Such is the basis of their confidence that enables them to "grow and bear fruit," to "continue in the faith, stable and steadfast, not shifting from the hope of the gospel which you heard" (1:23): it is their insight into the "knowledge of God's mystery in Christ" (2:2). For in Christ, Paul says (2:9–10),

> the whole fullness of deity dwells bodily, and you have come to fullness of life in him, who is the head of every rule and authority.

They need only to realize their new identity and translate it into appropriate behavior within the community.

A NEW FORM OF HUMANITY

Maturity is not yet in the Colossians' possession. They have "died to the elemental powers of the universe" (2:20) and live by the power of a new life (2:13), and are therefore called to shape their behavior in accordance with that identity. This does not mean new rules for asceticism or flights of mystic ecstasy. In contrast to the spiritual solipsism that seeks the self in a lonely leap to the divine, their growth in God is one that comes through their way of living together in community.

The images Paul uses to remind them of their identity come from the ritual of Baptism, which was their initiation into a "messianic body." It is within that body that their growth will come. As baptism was a "dying and rising" with Christ, so are they to "put to death" their former practices (3:5) and "seek the things that are above where Christ is" (3:1). At baptism they signified a change of identity with a change of clothes. Paul reminds them therefore (3:10) to "put off" their old self with its attitudes, so that they can "put on the new nature which is being renewed in knowledge [*epignōsis*] after the image of its creator" (3:10). Their call, therefore, is to abandon the actions and attitudes "in which they once lived" (3:7) and to adopt new attitudes and behavior.

Since they have come to know "the gift of God in truth" (1:6), which came to them through "the word of truth, the gospel" (1:5), they are able in the community to speak truth to each other; they need no longer lie (3:9). Neither do they need to discriminate on the basis of origin or status (3:11):

> Here there cannot be Greek and Jew, circumcised and uncircumcised, barbarian, Scythian, slave, free man, but Christ is all, and in all.

Since they have been brought into contact with the ultimate power of the world, they need no longer be governed by the forces of idolatry that bring upon them God's wrath (3:5–6). Rather, they can be compassionate toward others and forgiving (3:12–13). The "new humanity" is one that is being shaped in the community itself. Here, then, is the goal of Christian maturity: not the self-assertion and pride of the ascetic or mystic, which leads to the judgment of others, but the patient service of love in the community (3:14–15). It is not spectacular. Indeed, their life is "hidden in Christ" (3:3), just as all the treasures of God are "hidden" in him (2:3). But just as "the fullness of God dwelt in Christ bodily" (2:9), so will this manner of life "in the body" allow the "word of Christ to dwell in them richly" (3:16) and make of all their lives a praise of God (3:17).

The Colossians do not live "above, where Christ is" (3:1) but only anticipate the "hope laid up for them in heaven" (1:5). They must live in the very real social structures of the world, which never correspond precisely to the shape of God's kingdom. When Paul, then, turns to the mutual duties owed by members of a household (3:18—4:6), he by no means proposes a revealed Christian social order. Rather, he reminds the Colossians that "maturity in Christ" does not mean fleeing the world in visions or in alternative social structures of a purely "religious" character, but in coming to grips with the real and resistant structures of the world. He takes for granted the societal framework of the Hellenistic world, which had as its basic unit the extended patriarchal household, with lines of authority running downward from paterfamilias on top, to slaves and clients at the bottom, and with its glue being the submission shown at each level to the level above. Paul could no more have envisaged another kinship system than he could have proposed a Jeffersonian democracy in place of the Roman Empire. Social worlds, after all, exist at all only because for the most part humans treat them as natural (see Introduction, pp. 12–15 above).

To this structure of the household, Paul applies the best available philosophical teaching specifying the duties (*ta kathēkonta*) owed by each tier in the hierarchical power structure. The Pauline version is noteworthy, however, for its emphasis on reciprocity between the members. Wives are to be submissive to their husbands (not to all males), but husbands are to "love" their wives. The term means not simply erotic affection but *agapē*, the self-emptying affirmation of the other as other (3:18–19). Children are to obey both parents, but fathers—who are responsible for discipline—are to show them understanding in return (3:20–21). Paul gives most attention to the relations between slaves and masters, undoubtedly because of the circumstances in which the letter was written: singleness of heart is expected of the slave, but masters are to show justice and also equality (*isotēs*) toward slaves. This means more than the RSV's "justly and fairly." It is a recognition that subtly subverts the social stratification itself (3:22—4:1).

Indeed, Paul relativizes the entire social system by placing it within the critical framework of the "good news" from God. It is not simply that any stratification will be in tension with the community ideal of "neither slave nor free, neither Jew nor Greek" (3:11) and "neither male nor female" (Gal. 3:28). Paul also brings the measure of transcendence to bear on the social arrangements and attitudes themselves. Submission is conditioned by whether it is "fitting in the Lord" (3:18). Obedience to parents is to "please the Lord" (3:20). Slaves are to serve as "fearing the Lord" (3:22) and as "serving the Lord not men" (3:23), for they are in fact "serving the Lord Christ" (3:24). They can know that every wrongdoer, including a master, will be repaid, "for there is no partiality" with God (3:25). Masters, too, have a "master in heaven" to whom they must answer (4:1).

Each of these expressions can be—and have been—taken as legitimations for the social structure itself, and as strengthening the response of submission. But this interpretation subverts Paul's clear intention. By placing all these relations "in the Lord," he demands of all an allegiance and obedience first and always to God. No social structure and no authority can claim an idolatrous, absolute allegiance from anyone, whether wife or child or slave. And any submission that would oppose the more fundamental obedience owed to God must be resisted. The phrase "in the Lord," therefore, places this social structure itself, as well as all social structures, under the critical distance of the gospel.

A tension, of course, remains and will always remain, for the gospel is incapable of being translated into any specific social arrangement. At the same time, some sort of social structure will always prove necessary, for Christians must go on living in the world no less than, but not like, other people. So Paul wants them to live both in the assembly of faith and in their households "wisely toward outsiders," knowing that as they share in the riches of Christ, they can in fact "purchase the time" (4:5).

BIBLIOGRAPHICAL NOTE

A general statement on the issues relevant to pseudonymity is found in K. Aland, "The Problem of Anonymity and Pseudonymity in Christian Literature of the First Two Centuries," *JTS* n.s. 12 (1961): 39–49; and B. M. Metzger, "Literary Forgeries and Canonical Pseudepigrapha," *JBL* 91 (1972): 3–24.

Arguments against the authenticity of Colossians are marshaled from the side of literary connections by E. P. Sanders, "Literary Dependence in Colossians," *JBL* 85 (1966): 28–45; and from the standpoint of theological consistency by E. Lohse, "Pauline Theology in the Letter to the Colossians," *NTS* 15 (1969): 211–20. An extensive and positive position on authenticity is argued by G. E. Cannon, *The Use of Traditional Materials in Colossians* (Macon, Ga.: Mercer Univ. Press, 1983).

The crisis in Colossae has been variously interpreted. For a fine collection of essays representing various hypotheses, see W. A. Meeks and F. O. Francis, ed., *Conflict at Colossae*, rev. ed., SBS 4 (Missoula, Mont.: Scholars Press, 1975). The essay by F. O. Francis, "Humility and Angelic Worship in Col 2:18," *Studia Theologica* 16 (1963): 109–34, best covers the data, and is finding increasing acceptance. See, e.g., A. J. Bandstra, "Did the Colossian Errorists Need a Mediator?" in *New Directions in New Testament Study*, ed. R. Longenecker and M. C. Tenney (Grand Rapids: Zondervan Pub. House, 1974), 329–43; C. A. Evans, "The Colossian Mystics," *Bib* 63 (1982): 188–205; and W. Carr, "Two Notes on Colossians," *JTS* 24 (1973): 492–500.

On the overall symbolism of Colossians, see E. W. Sanders, "The Colossian Heresy and Qumran Theology," in *Studies in the History and Text of the New Testament*, ed. B. L. Daniels and M. J. Sugg (Salt Lake City: Univ. of Utah Press, 1967), 133–45; J. C. O'Neill, "The Source of the Christology in Colossians," *NTS* 26 (1979–80): 87–100; and N. A. Dahl, "Christ, Creation, and the Church," in *Jesus in the Memory of the Early Church* (Minneapolis: Augsburg Pub. House, 1976), 120–40.

Various aspects of the letter are covered by F. O. Francis, "The Christological Argument of Colossians," in *God's Christ and His People*, ed. W. A. Meeks and J. Jervell (Oslo: Universitetsforlaget, 1977), 192–208; H. Weiss, "The Law in the Epistle to the Colossians," *CBQ* 34 (1972): 294–314; E. Käsemann, "A Primitive Christian Baptismal Liturgy," in his *Essays on New Testament Themes* (Philadelphia: Fortress Press; London: SCM Press, 1964), 149–68; B. Vawter, "The Colossian Hymn and the Principle of Redaction," *CBQ* 33 (1971): 62–81; T. E. Pollard, "Col 1:12–20: A Reconsideration," *NTS* 27 (1980–81): 272–75; B. Hollenbach, "Col 2:23: 'Which Things Lead to the Fulfillment of the Flesh,'" *NTS* 25 (1978–79): 254–61; A. T. Hanson, "The Conquest of the Powers," in his *Studies in Paul's Technique and Theology* (Grand Rapids: Wm. B. Eerdmans; London: SPCK, 1974), 1–12.

For the household ethics, see J. E. Crouch, *The Origin and Intention of the Colossian Haustafel* (Göttingen: Vandenhoeck & Ruprecht, 1972). For a more extensive treatment of the Hellenistic background, see D. Balch, *Let Wives Be Submissive: The Domestic Code in I Peter*, SBLMS 26 (Chico, Calif.: Scholars Press, 1981).

In addition to the commentaries listed in chap. 16 (on Philemon), see also these reliable guides to the letter: P. T. O'Brien, *Colossians, Philemon*, Word Biblical Commentary (Waco, Tex.: Word Books, 1982), and R. P. Martin, *Colossians: The Church's Lord and the Christian's Liberty* (Grand Rapids: Zondervan Pub. House, 1973; Exeter: Paternoster Press, 1972).

18

The Letter to the Ephesians

EPHESIANS IS THE LEAST PERSONAL OF PAUL'S LETTERS. THE STANDARD epistolary elements of greeting (1:1–2), blessing (1:3–14), thanksgiving (1:15–23), body (2:1—6:20), and final greeting (6:23–24) are all formal. The letter is almost devoid of references to the circumstances either of the writer or the readers. About Paul, we learn only that he is a prisoner (3:1–13; 4:1; 6:19–20). He does not know the community firsthand but has only heard of its "faith in the Lord Jesus and love toward all the saints" (1:15). No community crisis motivated the letter; its two brief references to false teaching (4:14; 5:6) serve as warnings against any possible deviance. The only person mentioned by name is Tychichus who appears, as in Colossians, as one delivering personal news from Paul (6:21–22).

This would indeed be a strange document if written by Paul to a church with which he had spent over two years (Acts 19:10) and whose elders he could tell, when leaving them, "You yourselves know how I lived among you all the time from the first day I set foot in Asia . . ." (Acts 20:18). If written pseudonymously, the author in this case failed to create a plausible impression of intimacy between Paul and a church he knew so well. As noted earlier, however, important early manuscripts lack the name Ephesians in the greeting (1:1). Ephesians is a letter only in the broadest sense, being generated not by the immediate circumstances of Paul or a specific community but by the desire to communicate to a wider circle of gentile churches his insight into the implications of his mission for their self-understanding, and being sent out as a circular letter. But since the authenticity of Ephesians is so widely rejected, we must ask whether the evidence of the text itself forces us to see in it not the work of Paul but that of a devoted follower after his death.

THE ISSUE OF AUTHENTICITY

If the authorship of Paul's letters is understood in the way it is in this book—if it means the production by Paul *and his fellow workers*—then the criterion of style is by itself less pertinent than if we were comparing a sample of writings produced totally by a single hand. Still, a short discussion of stylistic factors helps define the character of this writing.

Ephesians is stylistically closest to Colossians, except that it is even more expansive and hyperbolic, with a tendency to heap substantives for effect (see, e.g., 1:19; 3:7). Some phrases are almost identical in the two writings (Eph. 1:4 = Col. 1:22; Eph. 1:15 = Col. 1:4; Eph. 2:13 = Col. 1:20; Eph. 4:2–3 = Col. 3:12–13; Eph. 6:21–22 = Col. 4:7–8). More often, similar terms are used in slightly different ways or in slightly different combinations (cf. Eph. 1:18 to Col. 1:9; Eph. 2:15 to Col. 2:14; Eph. 3:2 to Col. 1:25; Eph. 3:16 to Col. 1:11). A good example is Eph. 5:19, which has the same words in the same order as Col. 3:16, yet with quite a different effect, since the framing before and after the series is in each case distinctive.

Some expressions characteristic of Ephesians are found both in Colossians and other Pauline writings, if not in the same concentration. "Powers and principalities," *archai kai exousiai*, is used as a term for cosmic forces in Eph. 1:21; 3:10; and 6:12, as well as in Col. 1:16 and 2:10, 15. The combination is also found, however, in Rom. 8:38 and, possibly, 1 Cor. 15:24. A similarly obscure designation, however, "the elemental powers of the universe," *stoicheia tou kosmou*, is found in Col. 2:8, 20, as well as in Gal. 4:3, 9, but not in Ephesians at all. The patterns are not always what we would expect. The term "surpass," *hyperballō*, might seem almost a summation of the style of Ephesians (1:19; 2:7; 3:19), but it does not occur in Colossians. On the other hand, it is found elsewhere in an even more concentrated fashion in 2 Cor. 1:8; 3:10; 4:7, 17; 9:14; 11:23; and 12:7. Likewise the combination "praise of glory" (Eph. 1:6, 12, 14) does not occur in Colossians but occurs, in a variant form, in Phil. 1:11.

Ephesians at first glance seems to be particularly rich in language about knowledge and enlightenment, but a closer look reveals that the concentration is not remarkable for a Pauline letter. "Knowledge," *gnōsis*, is used once (3:19; cf. Col. 2:3; Rom. 15:14; Phil. 3:8; 1 Cor. 1:5; 2 Cor. 4:6). "Recognition," *epignōsis*, (Eph. 1:17; 4:13) is a favorite expression in Colossians (1:9, 10; 2:2; 3:10) but is used in a similar way in Rom. 10:2; Phil. 1:9; 1 Tim. 2:4; 2 Tim. 2:25 and Phlm. 6. The expression "to be enlightened," *phōtizō*, occurs twice (Eph. 1:18; 3:9) and also in 1 Cor. 4:5 and 2 Tim. 1:10. "Light," *phōs*, as a metaphor for revelation (5:8–9, 13), is found also in Col. 1:12; 1 Thess. 5:5; 1 Tim. 6:16; Rom. 13:12; 2 Cor. 4:6; 6:14. In summary it can be said that the vocabulary and syntax of Ephesians is not anachronistic, and its stylistic idiosyncrasies decrease when the letter is compared to all the captivity letters (Philemon, Philippians, Colossians, and 2 Timothy) or to those parts of the travel letters that are specifically devoted to prayer (e.g., Rom. 16:25–27; 2 Cor. 1:3–7).

Trying to decide authorship on the basis of style is always hazardous, as the endless disputes concerning the real Shakespeare attest. Subjective judgments are always involved: how much range is an author to be allowed? What circumstantial factors are to be considered? Is the *Laws* of Plato to be considered as authentic as *The Republic*, even though the dialogical form is almost nonexistent and the style flat? And if these differences can be attributed to factors like age and disappointment in a life relatively free from stress, can we allow similar factors, such as imprisonment and abandonment, to affect a Paul? We are fortunate that we are not called on to decide the genuineness of Lucian's *On the Writing of History*, having as a standard of comparison only his more scurrilous dialogues and tales.

If the style of Ephesians is regarded as too far from Paul's own to allow for authenticity, what account can be given of its production? If Colossians is thought to be authentic, then a forger (pseudepigrapher) lifted parts of that letter in order to convince his readers that it was Paul writing, while at the same time enriching the vocabulary by extensive excavation of other genuine letters. The relation between Ephesians and Colossians would then be much like the relation between 1 and 2 Thessalonians. The very similarity of style between two letters argues against the authenticity of the one already suspect on other grounds. This account, however, has two major weaknesses. If Colossians was followed so assiduously, why does the usage even of the shared vocabulary differ in such interesting ways? And if the forger had available to him other genuine letters, why weren't they used in a more effective and convincing way?

A second option for those who reject the authenticity of Ephesians is to regard Colossians as also nongenuine. This, of course, calls for a rather complicated effort. First, Colossians must be viewed as a deliberate forgery, using the information derivable only from Philemon to certify its authenticity, even though Philemon is only a private note. Then, Ephesians must be thought written in a style very similar, but not identical, to that of Colossians, by the same pseudepigrapher. Only this time the impulse to certify authenticity by the use of personal references will have been mysteriously neglected. And, if the letter was entitled "To the Ephesians," the author will not have known enough about the Pauline mission to be aware that the Ephesians were well known to Paul. Altogether a clumsy job.

If the style of Ephesians is not so diverse as to demand authorship by another writer than those available in the Pauline circle during Paul's life, (that is by the "school" of Paul active in his ministry), then the relation to Colossians obviously strengthens rather than weakens the case for authenticity. The similarities between the writings are to be accounted for by the circumstances that obtained in the production of Colossians, Philemon, Philippians, and 2 Timothy. The differences between the writings are accounted for by their diverse audiences and functions, their shared relationship to the rest of the Pauline corpus by their shared authorship: the same mind and heart authorized and directed their production.

What was said about Colossians with regard to church structure and ethics applies as well to Ephesians. There is no attention to church order apart from the list of apostles, prophets, evangelists, pastors, and teachers (4:11). The gifts of the spirit articulate the community life (4:11–12). Behavior derives from the transforming power of the Holy Spirit (4:15–16, 23–24). Ephesians has a distinctive twist to the Pauline imitation motif (4:20–21; 5:1–2) and devotes much of its treatment of household responsibilities (5:21—6:9) to the marriage relationship.

The real challenge to Ephesian authenticity comes—or ought to come—from its distinctive theological perspective. It is just sufficiently different on a number of points to raise questions as to whose mind is at work. Here are a few examples. Paul does not often talk about the kingdom of God, but when he does, it is always, "God's kingdom" (Rom. 14:17; 1 Cor. 4:20; 6:9; 15:50; 2 Thess. 1:5; Col. 4:11). Yet in Col. 1:13, he speaks of "the kingdom of his beloved Son," and in Eph. 5:5, it is "the kingdom of Christ and God." It is true that 1 Cor. 15:24 states that Christ will rule until he hands over the kingdom to his father, and there is the intriguing fact that Ps. 8:6, "He has put all things under his feet," is used in a remarkably similar way in 1 Cor. 15:27 and Eph. 1:22, but there is that slight difference to be taken into account. Likewise, it is certainly Pauline to call the church the body of Christ. In Col. 1:18 and Eph. 1:23 and 4:16, however, Christ is said to be the head of this body from which it derives growth, an anatomical complication not specified by 1 Cor. 12:27. In Eph. 5:23, furthermore, Christ is called the Savior of the body, using a title found only in Phil. 3:20 (of the undisputed letters).

When the author of this letter speaks of "mystery" (3:3–4; 6:19), he refers first of all to the relationship between Jews and Gentiles in God's plan, which is certainly a Pauline reference (Col. 1:27; Rom. 11:25; 16:25), but he can also apply the word "mystery" to marriage (5:32), giving that relationship a positive connotation only implicit in 1 Cor. 7. The author of Ephesians also refers to the dispensation (*oikonomia*) of God's will (1:10; 3:2, 9). The term "dispensation" is found otherwise only in Col. 1:25 and 1 Cor. 9:17, even though Paul can elsewhere refer to himself as a dispenser (*oikonomos*) of the mysteries of God (1 Cor. 4:1–2). Where does what is different turn into what is strange?

More troublesome are differences in perspective that would at first appear to derive from a lapse in time between the career of Paul and the writing of this letter. Paul, for example, ordinarily uses the term "church," *ekklēsia*—often in the plural—to refer to local communities (Rom. 16:4, 16; 1 Thess. 2:14; 1 Cor. 1:2; 4:17; 2 Cor. 8:1; Gal. 1:2; Phil. 4:15). In the singular, he uses it of the assembly as such (1 Cor. 11:18; 12:28) or when he speaks of his persecution of the "church" before his call to be an apostle (Phil. 3:6; 1 Cor. 15:9). In Ephesians, only the singular usage is found, with reference not to the local assembly but to the whole association of Christians, as in "Christ is the head of the church" (5:23; cf. 1:22; 2:10; 21; 5:23–32). Only Col. 1:18 and 1:24 are close to this. Does the difference reveal the perspective of a Pauline successor who looked back to the joining of many local assemblies into a self-consciously worldwide movement? Or was the perspective available as well to the Paul who engaged in a collection precisely to engender such a sense of church as something more than a local aggregation?

A similar question is raised by the treatment of Jews and Gentiles (2:11–22). As we shall see, the exposition is in some respects remarkably close to Romans 9—11. In Romans, however, the reconciliation of Jew and Greek is dialectical and spoken of as a future hope. Ephesians appears to see it as a present reality. Does the shift result from a different *temporal* perspective? We could say so only if there were more evidence for a growing state of harmony between Jews and Gentiles after Paul's death than is available to us. Or is the difference due to a shift in *focus*, with Romans addressing the grand view of history, and Ephesians the realization of it within the actual community? Or, does the difference derive from a new *function*, allowing Ephesians to speak in the indicative to say something in the imperative? The number of possibilities makes a decision difficult.

Finally, Ephesians speaks of the church as a temple (*naos;* 2:19–22), which is certainly a Pauline designation (cf. 1 Cor. 3:16; 2 Cor. 6:16), as is terming the members of the community, members of a household (*oikeioi;* 2:19; cf. Gal. 6:10). But when it says that this temple is "built up on the foundation of the apostles and prophets, with the cornerstone being Christ Jesus," does this represent an unacceptable metaphoric shift from 1 Cor. 3:11, which says that "no other foundation can be laid except that which has been laid, Jesus Christ"? And does the reference to apostles and prophets represent a backward look to an "apostolic age" by one who was not a member of it? Or is the language addressed not to Paul's own apostolic role but to the whole missionary enterprise of the church, so that here (as in 1 Cor. 12:28—and Eph. 4:11!) the author can say unselfconsciously that "God has placed in the church first apostles, second prophets, third teachers"?

The decision concerning the authenticity of Ephesians is much more difficult than that concerning the authenticity of Colossians. But there is nothing in it that cannot be accounted for by the special circumstances and purpose of the letter. If, in fact, Ephesians is a circular letter written to Gentile communities under the authorization of the captive Paul, then the lack of personal references, the distinctive stylistic traits, the use of tradition, and the perspective on the church are not only all intelligible but virtually necessary.

THE CHARACTER OF EPHESIANS

If not written by Paul or under his direct supervision, Ephesians is the work of Paul's best disciple, one whose religious perceptions and theological vision are not inferior to Paul's own. In Ephesians we find a masterly statement on the work of God in the world and church, expressed not by the passion of polemic or the logic of argumentation but by prayerful meditation. Ephesians has variously been described as homiletic or a wisdom discourse. But it is the pervasive atmosphere of prayer that is its most distinctive feature. The peculiar effusiveness of its Greek derives not from a mindless enthusiasm but from the traditional rhythms of liturgical prayer. The best analogies to its enthusiastic style are found in the grand *berakoth* and *tefilloth* of synagogal worship (see chap. 2, pp. 57–59) and of the Christian eucharistic prayers *(anaphora)* which were its successors. Here we find the interpretation of faith itself leaping to worship. In Ephesians, theology informs the prayer, and the prayer itself is the vehicle for theology.

In this letter are found distinctive elements of the Pauline gospel placed within a symbolic framework only suggested in other Pauline writings but here explicitly formulated. Here we have the Pauline emphasis on justification by God's free gift (grace) accepted by humans with faith (1:13; 2:5, 8–9), and the conviction that the gift came above all through the cross of Jesus (2:15–16), whose sacrificial death brought redemption (1:7). Here is the perception of the Holy Spirit as a transforming (1:13–14; 4:17—5:2) and reconciling (2:17–18) power, which manifests itself in the community by diverse gifts (4:1–13). Here we find as well the Pauline emphasis on the relation between Jew and Gentile in God's plan (1:12–13; 2:11–12; 3:6) expressed as always from the point of view of one who is himself a Jew (1:12; 2:11–14; 3:1)—the conviction that Paul's ministry came about by revelation from God (3:3–5) to preach the "good news" to Gentiles (3:7–8).

The "good news" is placed, however, within the framework of cosmic battle, in which the conflict between truth and falsehood, good and evil, light and darkness, is represented by spiritual powers active in the world (see above all 6:10–18). These "powers and principalities" appear as superior to humans, yet related to the dispositions of human freedom (see 1:21; 2:2; 3:10). Such a symbolization of religious reality was not infrequent in the Hellenistic world. It is impossible, therefore, to determine whether the author tapped specific sources that fed groups like the sectarians at Qumran or other proto-gnostic movements, or simply gives a sharper definition to elements drawn from the broadly apocalyptic symbolic framework universally available to the earliest Christian movement (cf., e.g., 1 Thess. 5:6–11; 2 Cor. 6:14—7:1). More important than the origin of the symbols is the use to which they are put in this writing. They place human freedom within the context of a struggle for the cosmos. Human alienation from God is expressed by an enslavement to forces fighting God. Alienation from God is also manifested in hostility and alienation between human beings. The prime example of this hostility is the division of humanity into "two races," the historical competition between Jew and Gentile.

The "good news" in Ephesians announces God's work to reverse this state of cosmic-historical hostility. God has revealed his mysterious plan to reconcile all reality to himself, to establish unity between himself and humans, and therefore he has revealed the possibility of unity between humans themselves. The agent of reconciliation is the Messiah, whose paradoxical death heals the rupture between God and humanity, reduces the cosmic forces that have enslaved humans to captivity, and reveals the possibility of a new way of being human, not divided by hostility but united in peace.

The sign of this reconciliation is the unity of Jew and Greek in the church. In the messianic community, the one Spirit gives all humans equal access to God and draws them into a humanity based on the Messiah himself. Such is the gift that creates the church. Such also, however, is its mandate. If the church is to be the sign of God's reconciling power at work in the world, then it must actually manifest that unity in its life. The church is "the fullness of him who fills all things" (1:23). The church is therefore the central focus of this writing (see 1:22; 2:21; 3:5–6), precisely because it is, as a living community, the revelation to the world and to the cosmic powers of God's work and of the world's possibility (3:10),

> that through the church the manifold wisdom of God might now be made known to the principalities and powers in the heavenly places.

It is also in the church that God's work is recognized and acknowledged (3:21):

> To Him be glory in the Church and in Christ Jesus to all generations, for ever and ever. Amen.

THE GIFT: THE CHURCH AS THE
PLACE OF RECONCILIATION
(EPHESIANS 1—3)

The special tone of Ephesians is struck at once. Unlike other Pauline letters, except 2 Cor. 1:3–7, it opens not with the thanksgiving but with a prayer of blessing (1:3–14), which resembles the Jewish *berakah* formula and shares its threefold structure: *(a)* God is blessed (1:3); *(b)* the reasons for this blessing are recounted; and *(c)* there is a periodic response of praise (1:6, 12, 14). In this prayer Paul announces the major themes of the letter: the "mystery" (1:9) that God is working out in history according to his purpose and will (1:5, 9, 11) through the redemptive death of his son Jesus (1:7) and that he made available to humans by free gift (1:6): his plan is to unite all reality with himself (1:10). The first sign (seal) of its realization among them is the Holy Spirit (1:13), whose present activity among them guarantees their future inheritance (1:14). The gift, furthermore, has been made available not only to those Jews who had awaited a messiah but to the Gentiles who had never heard of him (1:12–13). The prayer is, in effect, an expansion of the condensed praise of God's purpose in Rom. 8:28–30.

Paul uses the thanksgiving passage (1:15–23) to remind his readers of the reality of this gift, so that they might come to a deeper understanding of what was being accomplished among them (1:17–18). They should become aware not only of what lies before them, the "hope to which they have been called" and their eventual "inheritance among the saints" (1:18), but above all, of the present reality: "the immeasurable greatness of his power in us who believe." It is the actuality of God's power among them, "the working of his great might" (1:19), and the ultimacy of that power, that Paul wants them to appreciate. It is the same power by which God raised Jesus from the dead and established him over all spiritual beings (1:20–21). Precisely this power is at work in their experience within the community (1:22–23):

> He has put all things under his feet and has made him head over all things for the church, which is his body, the fullness of him who fills all in all.

The thanksgiving passage moves imperceptibly into the theological exposition (2:1–22) that forms the heart of this letter. In it Paul continues to describe the effect of the gift for humans, first in their relationship with God (2:1–10), and then in their relations with one another (2:11–22). The argument worked out by diatribe in Romans is here laid out in a highly condensed fashion. In 2:1–2, Paul sketches briefly the state of humanity as subject to the power of evil (cf. Rom. 1:18—3:20). Here, the spiritual alienation is expressed in terms of subjection to spiritual forces, "the prince of the power of the air, the spirit that is now at work among the sons of disobedience" (2:2). But Paul does not exclude those who had Torah from the power of sin (cf. Rom. 2:17—3:20), for "we," the Jews, were in the same state of alienation (2:3): "We were by nature children of wrath [cf. Rom. 1:18] like the rest of mankind." As Rom. 3:21—5:21 argued that God had reversed a state of alienation by bringing about reconciliation and peace through the faithful death of Jesus, so does Eph. 2:4–10 state that God brought those who were "dead" in sin (2:1, 5) to life through the resurrection of Jesus (2:5). Again, there is an emphasis on the cosmic implications of the reconciliation (2:6–7), but the human response is unmistakably Pauline (2:8–9):

> For by grace you have been saved by faith, and this is not your own doing, it is the gift of God—not because of works, lest any man should boast.

The cosmic alienation of human beings from God was expressed through "trespasses and sins" (2:1). The alienation between humans is expressed by the perversion of religious symbols, in the division between Jew and Greek. We come now to the densest and most difficult part of the letter. In a daring haggadic midrash, Paul reworks the argument of Romans 9—11 in a new way by combining the images of Torah and temple. He suggests that although these gifts from God were the basis of Jewish claims to a distinctive access to God (cf. Rom. 9:4–5), they were thereby a sign of the power of sin, for they separated rather than united human beings. The imagery here is very complex. It depends on the physical arrangement of the Jerusalem temple, which had a wall dividing the court of the Gentiles from the Holy Place, and on that wall a sign threatening death to any Gentile who transgressed. Since the Holy Place promised "access" to God, moreover, this physical arrangement symbolized at once the wall between humans and the cosmic wall between God and humanity. Those who were circumcised and who observed Torah supposed that they had special access to God, because they could enter into the Holy Place, whereas those who did not have these symbols were excluded from such access, under literal pain of death. The problem lay not with Torah or temple as such but with the human hostility that perverted even the gracious gifts of God into signs of self-aggrandizement and rivalry and boasting—all the signs, in short, of hostility (2:14).

Paul drastically restructures these symbols by the figure of the crucified Messiah. Through his death on the cross, he "brought the hostility to an end." First of all, the enmity between God and humans, then, the hostility between Jew and Greek. The blood of the rejected one was the new bond of unity for all (2:13, 15–16), reshaping in the process the entire Jewish symbolic structure (2:14–15):

> He is our peace who has made us both one, and has broken down the dividing wall of hostility, by abolishing in his flesh the law of commandments and ordinances.

Paul asserts that in Jesus there is not only the revelation of God's gift but the model for a new humanity. Jew and Greek both find in him the new way of access to God (2:15–16), that he might create in himself one new man in place of the two, so making peace, and might reconcile us both to God in one body through the cross.

What Torah and temple offered to Jews, Jesus gives not only to one part of humanity but to all humans, on the basis of God's free gift (2:17–18):

And he came and preached peace to you who were far off and to those who were near; for through him, we both have access in one spirit to the father.

Paul now reappropriates the symbolism of the temple for the messianic community. The church is founded on the "cornerstone" of Jesus. But since he is living Lord and "head of the church," it is a living entity, "joined together and growing into a holy temple of the Lord." The church is the place of reconciliation in the world. Those who were once "without God and hope in the world" (2:12) are no longer "sojourners and strangers" but "fellow citizens with the saints and members of the household of God" (2:19). Jews and Greeks together form this living place of united worship, "for a dwelling place of God in the Spirit" (2:22).

Paul interprets his own call and ministry (3:1–3, 7–8) along the lines of this same symbolization: the church is the place where God's reconciling will for the world is made manifest. Such is his special insight (3:4) into the "mystery of the Messiah." Gentiles (3:6) were

fellow heirs, members of the same body, and partakers of the promise in Christ Jesus through the gospel.

The church, therefore, has both a salvific and a revelatory function in and for the world. It is to be the place where the world can see reconciliation as a reality (3:10),

that through the church, the manifold wisdom of God might now be made known to the principalities and powers in the heavenly places.

When people in the world see what the possibility is for a humanity based not in rivalry and boasting (enmity) but in the gift of God (reconciliation), they will themselves be drawn into the community of peace. The church does not, in Ephesians, exist for itself, but as a sacrament of the world: it offers both a sign and a realization to the world of its own future possibility, so that in the church, God might be "glorified," that is, his presence might truly be acknowledged in the world (3:20–21).

THE MANDATE: LIVING A RECONCILED LIFE

The moral exhortation of Ephesians is closely tied to its theological exposition and makes clear that the letter's emphasis on the "realized" victory of Jesus over the cosmic forces (2:5–8) does not imply that members of the messianic community have no further struggle. In Christ, there has been given the possibility of a new form for humanity (2:15). And the same Spirit that works to give humans access to God in him (2:18) is active in transforming their perceptions, so that their behavior will be consistent with this new identity: "Be renewed in the spirit of your minds, and put on the new nature, created after the likeness of God in true righteousness and holiness" (4:23–24). This call goes out not only to individuals but to the church as such. The community as a whole is to "grow up in every way into him who is the head, into Christ," by love (4:15–16). Since the gift given by the Spirit is one of peace and unity, we are not surprised to find the mandate to be the living out of those gifts. Paul's listing of the Spirit's gifts in 4:1–13 emphasizes the unity that underlay their diversity, and this unity is based ultimately in the oneness of him who gives the gifts, the "one God and Father of all, who is above all and through all and in all" (4:6).

If the church is to manifest God's work in the world and reveal his mystery to the principalities and powers (3:10), it must also do battle against those forces in the world that continue to resist truth and light. Its members require all the "armor" of God if they are to stand "against the devil" in this cosmic battle (6:10–18). Above all, they require the power of the Spirit (6:17–18) to enable them to "live in a way worthy" of their call (4:1).

The power at work in them is the Spirit, but the measure of their transformation is Jesus himself. They are to "attain to mature manhood, to the measure of the stature of the fullness of Christ" (4:13). Using baptismal imagery, Paul tells them to "take off" all their hostile attitudes and actions that formerly characterized them when "they were darkened in their understanding, alienated from the life of God, because of their ignorance" (4:18), and to live by this new measure. If they no longer live in the darkness but in the light, they should act accordingly (5:6–14):

> Look carefully then how you walk, not as unwise men but as wise, making the most of the time, because the days are evil (5:15).

When they reject their former pattern of life, they are to adopt the pattern they see in Jesus. When Paul speaks of their former ways, he explains (4:20–21):

> You did not so learn Christ—assuming that you have heard about him and were taught in him, as the truth is in Jesus.

He follows this programmatic statement with a series of contrasting commandments. They are to give up falsehood (4:25), hostility (4:26), stealing (4:28), evil talk (4:29), bitterness, wrath, anger, and malice (4:31). We notice how fundamentally antisocial all these are. In exchange, they are to speak the truth, for they are members of each other (4:25); they are to do honest work so that they can share their possessions with each other (4:28); they are to speak so as to build one another up in their identity (4:29); they are to be kind to each other (4:32—5:2),

> forgiving one another, as God in Christ has forgiven you. Therefore be imitators of God as beloved children, and walk in love, as Christ loved us and gave himself up for us, a fragrant offering and sacrifice to God.

The whole life of the community, therefore, is to be based on those attitudes of "lowliness, meekness, patience" (4:2) that they learned from the Messiah Jesus. With these attitudes, they will approach that "mature humanity" (4:13) which is created after the likeness of God himself (4:24). They will be able to "forbear one another in love, eager to maintain the unity of the Spirit in the bond of peace" (4:3).

Households, too, should demonstrate the same sort of attitudes in their members. In the Ephesian table of household duties (5:21—6:9), we find the same notes of reciprocity and relativization as in Col. 3:18—4:6, but the attitudes of submissiveness are here broadly generalized. These are the very attitudes by which the assembly itself is to live; by carrying them into the forms of social life, they begin to "reveal" the mystery of God in the world. When Paul begins, therefore, "Be subject to one another out of reverence for Christ" (5:21), he deliberately echoes his earlier statement "Walk in love as Christ loved us and gave himself for us" (5:2).

The most remarkable feature of this household ethic, however, is the lengthy and positive attention given to marriage. Although the wife is plainly told to be submissive to her husband, the strongest admonitions are made to the "higher" member of the relationship, the husband. He is called to leave all other ties (5:31) in order to "love his wife as Christ loved the church and gave himself up for her" (5:25). Paul says in effect that the pattern of strength becoming weak, and love being manifest in submission to the needs of others, that we find revealed in Jesus, is above all incumbent on the "higher" members on the social scale. Paul's language must be taken seriously here; he does not say the husband is to "love" his wife only in the sense of having erotic or affectionate feelings for her; he is to "love" her with *agapē*, the self-emptying disposition that God himself revealed in Jesus.

It is this connection that enables Paul to conclude the treatment of marriage with this remarkable statement (5:32):

> This mystery is a profound one, and I am saying that it refers to Christ and the church.

We remember that Paul's "mystery" is that Jews and Greeks are reconciled and made one in the church. The relationship between husband and wife, therefore, symbolizes the mystery of unity in plurality and makes it present within the community. This completes the Pauline perception of "neither Jew nor Greek, neither male nor female." It also suggests that, as the church is the sacrament (i.e., the effective sign) of the world's possibility as a place of peace and reconciliation, so is marriage a sacrament to the church of what it should progressively become. Man and woman submit to each other in respect and love and service, finding unity and peace not in a false identification but in a pluralistic unity. So should Jew and Greek celebrate their unity in service to each other, so that God's purpose might be fulfilled, "to unite all things in him, things in heaven and things on earth" (1:10).

BIBLIOGRAPHICAL NOTE

A classic expression of the difficulties posed by Ephesians is H. J. Cadbury's "The Dilemma of Ephesians," *NTS* 5 (1958): 91–102.

The case against authenticity is argued in various ways by E. J. Goodspeed, *The Meaning of Ephesians* (Chicago: Univ. of Chicago Press, 1933); J. Coutts, "The Relationship of Ephesians and Colossians," *NTS* 4 (1957–58): 201–7; idem, "Ephesians 1:3–14 and I Peter 1:3–12," *NTS* 3 (1956–57): 115–27; J. A. Allen, "The 'In Christ' Formulations in Ephesians," *NTS* 5 (1958–59): 54–62; E. Käsemann, "Ephesians and Acts," in *Studies in Luke-Acts*, ed. L. Keck and J. Martyn (Philadelphia: Fortress Press, 1980 [1966]), 288–97; A. E. Barnett, *Paul Becomes a Literary Influence* (Chicago: Univ. of Chicago Press, 1941). The most elaborate treatment of the issue came to a decision in favor of authenticity: A. Van Roon, *The Authenticity of Ephesians*, NovTSup 39 (Leiden: E. J. Brill, 1974).

For the textual problem in 1:1, see M. Santer, "The Text of Ephesians 1:1," *NTS* 15 (1968–69): 247–48; R. Batey, "The Destination of Ephesians," *JBL* 82 (1963): 101; E. Best, "Ephesians 1:1 Again," in *Paul and Paulinism*, ed. M. D. Hooker and S. G. Wilson (London: SPCK, 1982), 273–79.

Aspects of Ephesian's liturgical tone are touched on in P. T. O'Brien, "Ephesians 1: An Unusual Introduction to a New Testament Letter," *NTS* 25 (1978–79): 504–16; and J. C. Kirby, *Ephesians, Baptism, and Pentecost: An Inquiry Into the Structure and Purpose of the Epistle to the Ephesians* (Montreal: McGill Univ. Press, 1968).

The specific symbolic structure of Ephesians is discussed in F. Mussner, "Contributions Made by Qumran to the Understanding of the Epistle to the Ephesians," in *Paul and Qumran*, ed. J. Murphy-O'Connor (Chicago: Priory Press, 1968), 159–78; and N. A. Dahl, "Cosmic Dimensions and Religious Knowledge," in *Jesus und Paulus*, ed. E. E. Ellis and E. Grässer (Göttingen: Vandenhoeck & Ruprecht, 1975), 57–75. The background and identity of the cosmic forces so important for both Colossians and Ephesians are discussed by G. B. Caird, *Principalities and Powers: A Study in Pauline Theology* (Oxford: At the Clarendon Press, 1956); H. Schlier, *Principalities and Powers in the New Testament* (New York: Herder & Herder, 1961); and W. Wink, *Naming the Powers: The Language of Power in the New Testament*, vol. 1: *The Powers* (Philadelphia: Fortress Press, 1984).

Other thematic elements in the letter are treated in R. Schnackenburg, *The Church in the New Testament* (New York: Herder & Herder, 1965), 77–85; L. Cerfaux, "The Revelation of the Mystery of Christ," in his *Christ in the Theology of St. Paul* (New York: Herder & Herder, 1959), 402–38; A. T. Lincoln, "The Use of the OT in Ephesians," *JSNT* 13–15 (1981–82): 16–56; idem, "Ephesians 2:8–10: A Summary of Paul's Gospel?" *CBQ* 45 (1983): 617–30; R. A. Wild, "The Warrior and the Prisoner: Some Reflections on Ephesians 6:10–20," *CBQ* 46 (1984): 284–98; idem, " 'Be Imitators of God': Discipleship in the Letter to the Ephesians," in *Discipleship in the New Testament*, ed. F. Segovia (Philadelphia: Fortress Press, 1985), 127–43; M. Barth, "Traditions in Ephesians," *NTS* 30 (1984): 3–25; J. P. Sampley, *"And the Two Shall Become One Flesh": A Study of Tradition in Eph. 5:21–23*, SNTSMS 16 (New York and Cambridge: Cambridge Univ. Press, 1971); and J. L. Houlden, "Christ and Church in Ephesians," *SE* 6 (1973): 267–73.

For a careful commentary from the standpoint of Pauline authenticity, see M. Barth, *Ephesians*, 2 vols., Anchor Bible (Garden City, N.Y.: Doubleday & Co., 1974); and from the standpoint of inauthenticity, see C. L. Mitton, *Ephesians*, New Century Bible (Grand Rapids: Wm. B. Eerdmans; London: Oliphants, 1976).

19

1 Timothy, 2 Timothy, Titus

PAUL'S LETTERS TO TIMOTHY AND TITUS HAVE BEEN CALLED THE PASTORAL Letters since the eighteenth century. They were accepted and cited as genuinely Pauline by early Christian writers. For two hundred years, however, scholars have debated their authenticity. The debate has slackened only because the great majority of scholars think the issue has been decided: all three are considered inauthentic, at best a later and derivative testimony to Pauline traditions. Some scholars persist in thinking that conclusion to be precipitous. Even those who like myself are not absolutely convinced that they come directly from Paul, think some of the reasons given for assigning their composition to a pseudepigrapher unconvincing.

Since these are letters and not narratives, a decision concerning their authenticity affects our picture of Paul's ministry, our understanding of the development of Paulinism, and most important, our reading of the letters themselves. Even though this debate already dominates the scholarship on these writings and threatens to obscure their distinctive and individual witness to early Christian experience and interpretation, a consideration of the issues can nevertheless lead to an appreciation of the special character of these canonical writings.

Strong tendencies among the disputants have a real impact on the debate. The first tendency derives from the primary and positive place most scholars accord Paul among NT writers. He is, after all, "the apostle." Scholars often want to find in him what confirms their perceptions of "genuine" Christianity, and consider inauthentic what contradicts these perceptions. Those who regard the heart of Paul, if not of the whole NT, to be the teaching of righteousness through faith tend to reject the Pastorals as moralizing. On the other hand, those committed to traditions within which doctrine and church structure and the inspiration of Scripture are important, tend to find these in the undisputed as well as the Pastoral Letters, which latter they therefore are inclined to regard as genuine. Scholarship is not utterly determined by bias, but neither is it entirely free of it. A second tendency also derives from Paul's place as the earliest and most exciting Christian writer. A judgment against authenticity of any letter means for some a judgment on its value as well. They implicitly measure the worth of a writing by its authorship, rather than by its content or its place within the community's canon. The tendency is found on both sides of the debate. Some fight the authenticity of the Pastorals, thinking such a recognition would inevitably mean as well an acceptance of their teaching. Others defend their authenticity for the same reason. These tendencies do not help the making of sober literary and historical judgments.

A third tendency in the debate does not come from bias but is an inevitable result of categorization. These three letters are invariably treated together as a group. Characterizations of "the Pastorals" are typically drawn from all three letters, although the contributions of the letters on separate points are very uneven. The Pastorals are often said, for example, to contain an elaborate church order. But 2 Timothy lacks any reference to order at all, and Titus contains only a bit more. Reference is also made to "the opponents in the Pastorals," even though they have a distinct profile in each of the letters. Such generalizing descriptions dull our perception of the individual letters, and this heightens our sense of their isolation from the rest of the Pauline corpus. A similar effect would result from treating the Thessalonians as a separate group without ever referring them to other Pauline writings. But if Titus is read with other travel letters, or 2 Timothy with other captivity letters, their strangeness is greatly diminished.

Even when such tendencies are taken into account, the Letters to Timothy and Titus present unique and difficult questions to every reader. No one denies that they represent a strain of Paulinism. They are written in his name, and seek to communicate teaching which is recognizably Pauline. But in each letter there is also just enough divergence from any reader's instinctive perception of what is Pauline that even those most sympathetic to their authenticity must wonder at this blend of the familiar and the strange so erratically distributed over three documents.

FACTORS TO BE CONSIDERED

Since the issues are so complex, a full discussion is impossible, but each criterion for determining genuineness is, in the case of these letters, called into play. Although the letters lack obvious anachronisms, they are thought by some not to fit into Paul's career as we know it from Acts and the other letters. First Timothy and Titus presuppose Paul's active ministry. In 1 Timothy, Paul has left his delegate in Ephesus for a time while he goes to Macedonia (1 Tim. 1:3); Timothy is to attend to affairs until Paul's return within a short period (3:14). In principle, such a letter could have been written any time during Paul's lengthy Aegean ministry. Titus is written to Paul's delegate in Crete (Titus 1:5). Paul's whereabouts are not revealed. He plans to winter in Nicopolis (3:12), which could be any of several cities of that name. That there should be a church in Crete is not surprising. The account in Acts, however, places Paul there only tangentially, and then as a prisoner (Acts 27:7–15). Could he have had the opportunity to found churches or to commission his delegate to found them? The phrase "I left you in Crete" is also ambiguous. Was Titus left there by Paul physically? Or was he left in his assignment?

Second Timothy is written from (probably the Roman) captivity (1:16–17). But does Paul's reference to a first defense (4:16) indicate that this is a second imprisonment, since he was released from the first (4:17)? In contrast to 1 Timothy and Titus, 2 Timothy contains information about fifteen of Paul's helpers (4:9–21). Nothing in their movements is in clear contradiction to what little we know of them elsewhere, although some scholars cavil over the apparent discrepancy between Acts 21:29 and 2 Tim. 4:20 in the matter of Trophimus. Other information is startlingly confirming, as the short remark "Erastus remained in Corinth" (4:20; cf. Rom. 16:23).

What can be done with this situation? It is obviously rendered more difficult by the attempt to place all the letters in the same time frame. The following options are possible. Some think the letters are pseudonymous and written at the same time after Paul's death. The biographical information in this case is only the internal decoration of pseudonymity and is irrelevant. A second option invokes the ancient tradition (cf. *1 Clem.* 5.7) that Paul was released from a first Roman imprisonment and preached in Spain before being made captive again and put to death. Supporters argue for a period of active work between the two imprisonments, such as is reflected in these letters. But the tradition spoke of work in the West, whereas the ministry here is in the East. A third option is to regard the letters as genuinely Pauline and to try to fit them into Paul's ministry as we know it from Acts and the other letters. This is not impossible, although it requires considerable ingenuity. A fourth option is the best, though rarely chosen. It admits that neither Acts nor the letters give us a full chronology of Paul, and that these letters do not by themselves account for their placement in his life. But it also suggests that they may give us important information those other sources do not about incidents in Paul's career and captivity. Just as 2 Corinthians tells us of imprisonments we would otherwise not suspect, so do these letters tell us of Pauline missionary endeavors—in Crete, Dalmatia—we would not otherwise know (but cf. Rom. 15:19).

The criterion of style is difficult to apply to the Pastorals. They obviously contain a large number of words not found in other Pauline letters and share other words not otherwise attested in the NT. But there are also real differences among the three letters. On the whole, 2 Timothy has a vocabulary remarkably close to that of other Pauline epistles, whereas the word usage in 1 Timothy and Titus varies more significantly. How much of this special vocabulary is due to the nature of the letters, the character of the addressees, and the subject matter is, however, difficult to determine. There is no indication that dictation was used for these letters, but an amanuensis cannot be altogether ruled out. Since a large amount of the vocabulary of 1 Timothy and Titus is found elsewhere in the NT only in Luke-Acts, Luke has been proposed as the amanuensis (2 Tim. 4:11) or even the author of the letters.

More than vocabulary is involved in stylistic analysis. The syntax of the Pastorals is generally flatter and smoother than in letters like Galatians and Romans. Sentences are longer and more regular; the use of particles is less varied and rich. Yet, one must ask how much the style of Romans and Galatians is itself affected by the adoption of the "diatribal" mode in those letters. If the Pastorals are compared to 1 Thessalonians or Philippians, in contrast, the differences are not so extreme. The issue of style is further complicated by the fact that the Pastorals do not reveal a different but consistent "hand," as do Colossians and Ephesians. Rather, the mixture of Pauline vocabulary and sentence structure with non-Pauline is complex and varied. Some indeed have suggested that the Pastorals may contain fragments of authentic Pauline notes, worked up later into new pseudonymous compositions. The close correlation of non-Pauline passages with the subject matters unique to the pastorals has largely gone unattended.

One of the early reasons for questioning the genuineness of the Pastorals was the nature of the opponents or "heresy" found in them. It was thought to be a form of "gnosis" (see 1 Tim. 6:20) such as was not known until the second century, which taught that the resurrection life was already accomplished (2 Tim. 2:17–18), scorned marriage, advocated physical asceticism (1 Tim. 4:3, 8), and emphasized a concern for law (1 Tim. 1:7; Titus 3:9). This picture is of course a composite. Even as such it does not preclude Pauline authorship, for there is nothing in this mix not already encountered in the undisputed letters (cf., e.g., 1 Cor. 8:1–3; 15:17–19; Gal. 4:8–10; 1 Cor 7:1, and above all, Col. 2:20–22). The composite sketch, however, ignores the very real differences between the letters themselves, each of which is internally consistent and need not be read with the others to be understood. But even if this be granted, some suggest that the manner of responding to the opponents is un-Pauline, since it relies on polemic rather than on refutation. This is slightly inaccurate, since 1 Timothy does clarify theological points several times (1:8; 4:3–5, 7–8; 6:5–10), and the genuine Paul is not immune from the use of slander against rival teachers (cf. 2 Cor. 11:13–15; Gal. 5:12; 6:13; Phil. 3:2). What is distinctive in the Pastorals is the amount of polemic, its largely stereotypical character, and the literary function it fills in 1 and 2 Timothy.

The authenticity of these letters has been challenged because of the church organization found in them. Here is not merely a shift in emphasis, such as making Christ the head of the body (as in Colossians) but an entirely different outlook. The organic sense of the church is lost, replaced by an organization, the "household of God," which has a hierarchical ministry of bishops, presbyters, and deacons, together with orders of deaconesses and widows. Such attention to structure, it is thought, results from the "routinization of charism" when eschatological expectations and initial enthusiasm diminish and the church grows used to being in the world and adapts to its ways. Others see in it a defensive reaction against a popular Paulinism that was more radically egalitarian. The Pastorals, on this reading, come from a time and situation like that found in the letters of Ignatius of Antioch (ca. 115) in which a monarchical episcopate and hierarchical order are essential to the well-being of the church (see Ign. *Eph.* 2.2; *Magn.* 3.1; *Trall.* 2.2; 3.1).

Such conclusions go considerably beyond the evidence of the letters themselves. First, it is inaccurate to speak of the church order of the Pastorals, since there is none in 2 Timothy, and the little found in Titus does not match precisely the fuller account in 1 Timothy. Second, what organization is spoken of is not elaborate. It corresponds rather well, in fact, to what we know of the synagogal structure of Diaspora Judaism in the first century. Third, the organizational structure is not legitimated in these letters; that is, it is neither theologically defended nor interpreted. There is nothing "sacral" about it. Fourth, the letters do not prescribe for order but presuppose it; they contain not job descriptions for new positions but moral and mental qualifications for those who are to fill established positions. Fifth, sociological studies of intentional communities in every era suggest that they do not survive for decades without strong structures for decision making and social control; a great time lapse between the birth of a community and the establishment of structure is counterintuitive; structure and charism, in fact, often coexist rather than follow each other. Sixth, the undisputed letters of Paul not only refer by title to office holders found here (bishops and deacons, Phil. 1:1; woman deacon, Rom. 16:1) but obviously recognize the role of authority figures in each community (cf. 1 Cor. 16:15–17; Gal. 6:6; Col. 4:17; 1 Thess. 5:12). Seventh, the structure found in the undisputed letters is much more closely related to that found in the Pastorals than either is to that found in the Qumran community, where an eschatological messianic, charismatic sect possessed not only a rigid hierarchical structure but one that was highly legitimated theologically. Eighth, the attention that is given to organizational matters in two of these letters owes a great deal to the nature of the writings and the identity of the addressees.

The most telling objection to the authenticity of the Pastorals is the criterion of theology and ethics. Even when full credit is given to Paul's great range, some elements in these letters appear to be marginal. Common Pauline terms such as "faith" and "law" and "righteousness" occur, but all with slightly different nuances. "Law" appears as something that can be used "lawfully" (1 Tim. 1:8), "faith" seems less an obediential response to God than the common body of conviction and commitment (Titus 1:1; 1 Tim. 5:8) or a virtue (2 Tim. 2:22). "Righteousness," *dikaiosynē*, does not signify a state of right relation with God but signifies a virtue in the Greek sense of "justice" (1 Tim. 6:11; 2 Tim. 2:22). Tradition is a deposit of truth that is to be protected (1 Tim. 6:20; 2 Tim. 1:12–14) rather than a process of transmission (1 Cor. 11:2, 23; 15:3). The Christology emphasizes the role of Jesus as Savior (2 Tim. 1:10; Titus 1:4; 3:6) and his "appearance" (1 Tim. 6:14; 2 Tim. 1:10). It must be said that each one of these elements can be found somewhere in the undisputed letters, but never in this concentrated combination; and therein lies the difference.

A similar point can be made about the ethical teaching of these letters. There is certainly nothing explicitly like Paul's command in 1 Corinthians 7 to live in the world "as though not." Here, the attitudes and aptitudes of household members are appropriate as well to the life of the community. The Pauline note of conscience (*syneidēsis*) appears, but now not in terms of weak and strong (cf. 1 Cor. 8:7–12) but in terms of "good" (1 Tim. 1:5, 19) and "pure" (1 Tim. 3:9; 2 Tim. 1:3) in contrast to "soiled" (Titus 1:15) and "cauterized" (1 Tim. 4:2). Here, too, is the contrast between "healthy teaching" (1 Tim 1:10; 6:3; 2 Tim. 1:13; 4:3; Titus 1:9; 2:1) and "sick" (2 Tim. 2:17; 1 Tim. 4:2), which expresses itself in a life of virtue (1 Tim. 1:10; 3:2–4, 11; 4:12; 2 Tim. 2:22, 24; 3:10; Titus 1:7–9; 2:7) and of vice (1 Tim. 1:8–10; 2 Tim. 3:2–5; Titus 3:3).

Listing these elements is easy; evaluating them is not. Neither appeal to the outlook of an aging apostle nor mention of a second generation seems adequately to account for them. It is clear, however, that there is a shift in these letters to a more Greek and less "biblical" mode of presentation. Before drawing conclusions from that, it is good to remember that the "biblical" style of Paul in Galatians and Romans is no more natural than his Greek style in 1 Thessalonians or Philippians. His style was very much affected by his subject matter, his audience, and the traditions he was using. Can the same factors help account for the moralizing tone of the Pastorals? Titus and Timothy, we recall, both have at least partially a Greek background. Both are portrayed in the role of teachers. Do these factors help us locate the kind of language used in letters to them? How did Paul speak and write when among his more educated Hellenistic associates?

ACCOUNTING FOR THE CORRESPONDENCE

Most scholars see the Pastorals as the production of a "Pauline school" at a period long after Paul's death, sometimes as late as the mid-second century. The personal aspects of the letters are thought to be entirely fictitious, imitations of genuine letters for the purpose of persuading readers of Pauline authorship. The three letters together make one point. They represent the beginning of church orders, a tradition of documents such as the *Didache*, the *Didascalia Apostolorum*, and the *Apostolic Constitutions*, which regulated church worship and ministry. Why were they written? As part of a conservative reaction within Paulinism, possibly to the use of Paul by heretics who radically extended Paul's ascetic tendencies. It has even been suggested that Polycarp of Smyrna wrote them as a weapon in his fight against Marcionism. Another stimulus that has been suggested is a growing egalitarianism, especially among women, which threatened the stability of communities.

The author of the Pastorals therefore sought to adapt the Pauline message for a new generation, emphasizing structure and order, while resisting ascetical and egalitarian excess. In the process, he revealed an acceptance of a diminished eschatological expectation, growth in church structure, and increased accommodation to the world, since the apostle's death. The Paulinism of the Pastorals is one refracted through the prism of second and third-generation concerns. Paul is a legendary hero, whose authentic genius is diminished, reduced to being part of the "deposit" of faith for future generations.

The obvious appeal of this reconstruction is testified to by its many adherents. It provides for development and conflict within Paulinism. It suggests that, with Acts and Ephesians, the Pastorals were part of the movement of "early Catholicism" that resisted Gnosticism and a normative asceticism, while domesticating the radical Paul, so that his letters might remain in the canon.

This reconstruction also has serious deficiencies. Even if the writing of epistolary pseudepigrapha soon after Paul's death be granted, the Pastorals were universally accepted as genuine by the ancient church, in contrast to other Pauline productions (*3 Corinthians, Letter to Laodiceans, Letters of Paul and Seneca, Acts of Paul and Thecla*) which were almost as universally rejected. A mid-second-century dating must dismiss the citation of 1 Tim. 6:7, 10 by Polycarp's *Letter to the Philippians* 4.1, and make it a touch of his own, which does not properly deal with its peculiar literary framing. The late dating must also reject the express statement of Tertullian

(*Against Marcion* V. 21) that Marcion rejected the Pastorals from his canon, apparently because he did not like their teaching.

The common reconstruction falters most by failing to provide a convincing life setting for the production of three such similar and yet quite different letters, and by paying too little attention to their self-presentation and literary form. It has been suggested, for example, that the letters were intended to rehabilitate a Paul fallen into disrepute because of his popularity among heretics. But Paul's authority is never at issue in the letters; it is always assumed. Nor is specific attention given to his "image." The suggestion also presupposes a consciousness of fine distinctions in doctrine such as may exist among scholars but not most others. For anyone seriously doubting or misplacing Paul's worth, furthermore, it is unlikely that the rather banal material in the Pastorals would prove an effective antidote. Were copies of Paul's entire correspondence available for comparison? The hypothesis moves inevitably from pseudonymity to forgery. An orthodox leader like Polycarp creates the letters, then hands them out as a Pauline discovery. Besides being inconsistent with Polycarp's character such as we know it, this hypothesis makes us wonder why more use was not made of this creation by Polycarp himself. Would such a ploy be successful at a time when Paul was apparently a figure of controversy and rival communities were compiling their lists of acceptable and nonacceptable writings, on the basis of apostolic origin?

Another suggestion places the letters' production within a school setting in which the imitation of literary models took place. This is a sensible solution, since it eliminates the unhappy options of a charismatic mist and deliberate forgery. It would be a stronger suggestion if we could be as confident about the existence of such a school after Paul's death as we are of its existence during his lifetime. However sensible, the suggestion is not altogether satisfying. If Pauline models were being imitated, why were not his letters to churches reproduced, rather than letters to individual delegates? Why was the style and form of the undisputed letters not followed more accurately? The fragment hypothesis (see p. 384) is of little help here. It is hard to see why tiny autobiographical notes would be preserved in the first place, and then lifted into new compositions so clumsily. And what is there about them that would convince a skeptic they are from Paul? If a pseudepigrapher had authentic fragments before his eyes, why could he not imitate their style on either side of the fragment?

An enduring difficulty for the conventional reconstruction is the variety in the Pastorals. Why would three such letters be produced, each of which was directed to a situation that was internally consistent yet very difficult to make consistent with the situations the other two were directed to? Here we would have a forger able subtly to create the verisimilitude of an established church (in Ephesus) and a new church (in Crete), together with the appropriate sort of directions to each, and yet not able to imitate more convincingly the Pauline samples available to him.

No real progress will be made in the understanding of the Pastorals until the attempt to treat them as parts of a whole is abandoned and they are restored to separate and equal status within the collection. It may well be, for example, that 2 Timothy can lay a far better claim to authenticity on every count than 1 Timothy. The first sustained questioning of their authenticity applied only to 1 Timothy and then only on one point. The declaration of inauthenticity for all three has been a more recent and unhealthy development. It is theoretically possible, for example, that 1 Timothy is pseudonymous, based on the authentic letter to 2 Timothy. Such possibilities must be entertained. More significant, however, renewed attention must be given to the literary self-presentation of each of the letters in turn and to their respective shapings of the Christian message within the Pauline tradition.

PAUL'S DELEGATES

The letters are written to Paul's most important delegates. We have repeatedly seen Timothy's prominence within the Pauline mission: co-sponsor of five letters (see 2 Cor. 1:1; Phil. 1:1; Col. 1:1; 1 Thess. 1:1; 2 Thess. 1:1), he was Paul's go-between with the Macedonian churches (see Acts 18:5; 19:22) of Thessalonica (1 Thess. 3:2) and Philippi (Phil. 2:19), as well as the Corinthians (Rom. 16:21). According to 1 Tim. 1:3, he played the same role for the Ephesian church. In Acts 16:1, he is said to have a Greek father, which would make it likely that he had some Greek education as well. From what Paul says of him in the undisputed letters, his special role and place in Paul's affections is obvious. When Paul (1 Cor. 4:16) wants the restive Corinthians to "imitate" him, he adds (4:17):

> Therefore, I sent to you Timothy, my beloved and faithful child in the Lord, to remind you of my ways in Christ, as I teach them everywhere in the church.

We notice the role of memory and imitation, and the portrayal of Paul as a teacher and Timothy as the "reminder" of Paul's teaching and example to a local community. Timothy may not have had an excess of personal presence and confidence, for Paul also tells the Corinthians (1 Cor. 16:10–11):

> When Timothy comes, see that you put him at ease among you, for he is doing the work of the Lord, as I am. Let no one despise him.

When writing to the Philippians (2:19–23) Paul says of him:

> I hope in the Lord Jesus to send Timothy to you soon, so that I may be

cheered by news of you. I have no one like him, who will be genuinely anxious for your welfare. They all look after their own interests, not those of Jesus Christ. But Timothy's worth you know, how as a son with a father, he has served with me in the Gospel. I hope therefore to send him just as soon as I see how it will go with me.

Finally, in 1 Thess. 3:2, Paul reports of Timothy:

And we have sent Timothy, our brother and God's servant in the gospel of Christ, to establish you in your faith and to exhort you, that no one be moved by these afflictions.

There is a remarkable agreement between these random characterizations and the portrayal of Timothy in the Pastorals. He is there young, and timid, and easily despised (1 Tim. 4:12; 2 Tim. 1:7). He is a "beloved" (2 Tim. 1:2) or "genuine" son (1 Tim. 1:2). He is a "servant of God" (*diakonos* in 1 Thess. 3:2; *doulos* in 2 Tim. 2:24 and Phil. 1:1). He is to "exhort" others (1 Tim. 6:2; 2 Tim. 4:2), and to "remind" churches of Paul's teaching (2 Tim. 2:14), and to provide to them an example of it (1 Tim. 4:12), just as he has an example to follow in Paul (2 Tim. 1:13). Two reasonable explanations can account for this close agreement. The first is that the letters accurately report Paul's habitual perceptions of his delegate. The second is that a pseudepigrapher had available to him the full range of such epithets when he drew up his imitation. The more important point is that 1 and 2 Timothy present Timothy in a role that corresponds exactly to that given him explicitly in the undisputed letters. He is Paul's troubleshooter.

The undisputed letters tell us much less about Titus. He was of Greek origin (Gal. 2:3), and Paul makes much of his not having to be circumcised when he accompanied Paul to Jerusalem (Gal. 2:1). Although it could never be proved, he may be the Titus (or Titius) Justus whom Acts 18:7 calls a God fearer and whose house Paul uses after leaving the synagogue. He is notably associated with Paul's Corinthian ministry (2 Cor. 2:13; 7:6, 13, 14), especially his collection efforts (2 Cor. 8:6, 16, 23; 12:18). He is not the representative of a local church but is Paul's associate (*koinōnos;* 2 Cor. 8:23). He is not pictured as being on intimate terms with Paul. The same sense is given by the Letter to Titus, in which he is called "genuine son" (Titus 1:4) but is not shown the sort of affection found in 1 and 2 Timothy. His duty in Crete may well also have included fund raising (see Titus 3:14). According to 2 Tim. 4:10, Titus also worked in Dalmatia, which would fit within the broad range of the Pauline mission (cf. Rom. 15:19).

What sort of letters would we expect Paul to write to delegates with such responsibilities? We would expect discussion of matters inappropriate for letters written for community consumption: personal encouragement for their hard task of dealing with lively Pauline communities; reminders of the ideal they should follow; hostile dismissals of rival teachers; ad hoc directions concerning local leadership positions and structural conflicts. We would expect not lengthy doctrinal treatises, but only formulaic allusions. For fellow workers of Greek education, we might expect a shaping of the gospel that emphasized its godliness (*eusebeia*) and a Christology in which the "appearance of a savior" figured dominantly, as well as ethical teaching that stressed virtue and the avoidance of vice. Such letters would likely combine attention to the delegates' personal dispositions, as well as to the attitudes appropriate to their office of teaching. As so often in the Hellenistic world, there were precedents for letters like these.

2 TIMOTHY: A PERSONAL PARENETIC LETTER

Paul writes to Timothy from prison (1:16; 2:9; 4:16). Although he still has workers around him, he is sensitive to the apostasy by others (1:15; 4:10, 16). He still struggles to proclaim the gospel (4:17) and to direct the mission through delegates (4:10–12) and correspondence (4:13). He still faces active opposition himself (4:14). Although he feels close to death (4:6–8), he writes to encourage and admonish his favorite delegate in *his* struggles. The letter is dominated by its unswerving attention to Timothy. Whatever is said about others is sooner or later turned back to him, "but you . . . " The most frequent verb form in the letter is the second-person singular imperative. Nothing new is being communicated to Timothy, only reminders of what he already knows, together with the exhortation to hold fast to it.

Because we find here an aging, even dying, religious figure who instructs his follower before his death on the struggles to come and the need for perseverance, many who regard these letters as pseudonymous find the most appropriate literary category for the understanding of 2 Timothy to be the farewell discourse, such as we find it in the *Testaments of the Twelve Patriarchs* or even Acts 20:17–35. But an even closer literary form, and one that does not demand pseudonymity, is the personal parenetic letter.

In the rhetorical handbooks, there is an *epistolē parainetikē*, which is written to "exhort someone advising him to pursue something and to abstain from something." The sample letter given by Pseudo-Libanius reads:

> Always be an emulator, dear friend, of virtuous men. For it is better to be well spoken of when imitating good men, than to be reproached by all for following evil men.

This short sample contains the elements of imitation, model, and the antithetic expression of options: do this, avoid that. In actual parenetic discourses such as the treatise *To Demonicus* of Pseudo-Isocrates, the form is followed exactly: the presentation of a model and appeal to memory (*Dem* 3–11) is followed by a series of moral maxims often expressed antithetically (12–49), and at the conclusion there is a representation of models for imitation (50–51). So also in 2 Timothy we find the elements of memory, model, and maxims.

A further element requires an accounting: the polemic against false teachers. We are given little specific information about them, despite the naming of Phygelus and Hermogenes (1:15), and Hymenaeus and Philetus (2:17). They claim that the resurrection is already past (2:18), but apart from that, they are characterized mainly by their methods, which involve harsh disputation (2:16, 23) and the intellectual seduction of uneducated women (3:6), as well as their morals, which are obviously poor. Much of this takes the form of stereotypical slander, like that used by Hellenistic philosophers when attacking each other. Yet Paul never attacks them directly. His concern is for his delegate. He alternates characterizations of them with direct commands to Timothy. In this parenesis, the false teachers thereby become the negative model Timothy is to avoid. The same use of polemic can be found in protreptic (i.e., exhortatory) discourses addressed to would-be philosophers. In them, too, the slander whose first life setting was open disputation is used as a counter type to the ideal teacher (cf. Dio *Oration* 77/78; Lucian *Demonax;* Epictetus *Discourses* III.22).

Second Timothy has the overall form of a personal parenetic letter. But since Timothy is being addressed in his role as a teacher, the elements of a protreptic discourse, and in particular the use of polemic as a foil to the ideal, are also found. The structure of 2 Timothy therefore is *(a)* the presentation of Paul as a model (1:3—2:13); *(b)* maxims for Timothy as a teacher, presented in contrast to the false teachers (2:14—4:5); *(c)* the re-presentation of Paul as a model (4:6–18).

Paul, the Model for Teaching and Suffering (2 Timothy 1:3—2:13)

The motifs of memory and model open the letter. In the face of the opposition and success of rival teachers, Timothy is discouraged and tempted to give up preaching, particularly since his "father" Paul has little hope for release from prison. The thanksgiving typically anticipates Paul's main point. He "remembers" Timothy (1:3) and "remembers" his tears (1:4) and "remembers" the sincere faith he had learned from his mother and grandmother (1:5). When Paul adds, " . . . and, I am sure, dwells in you" (1:5), however, he reveals his concern. He clearly needs to "remind" Timothy of the qualities and dispositions to which he was called. He was not given a spirit of timidity (or, cowardice: *deilia*) but was given one of "power and love and self-control." Paul wants to "stir up" in him this gift of power and confidence (1:6), so he will persevere in his ministry.

Paul presents himself as a model for Timothy, who can find in him the "pattern of healthy teaching" (1:13). Timothy can preserve it, since it has been entrusted to him by "the Holy Spirit dwelling in us" (1:14). Paul is more than a source of proper teaching. He is the example of how to suffer for the gospel in adversity. Timothy is told, "Don't be ashamed" of testifying to the Lord; he is to "take a share of suffering for the gospel" (1:8). Paul too had been appointed a "preacher and apostle and teacher" of this "good news" (1:11), and "therefore I suffer as I do, but I am not ashamed" (1:12). He suffers and is not ashamed. Timothy should not therefore draw back because of his suffering for the "good news." He is able to keep going because of God's power (1:8), the indwelling Spirit (1:14), and the certainty of God's promise (1:12).

The mention of Onesiphorus in 1:15–18 is not beside the point. Because he provided help ("often refreshed me") and did so despite Paul's captivity, he provides Timothy with another example: "He was not ashamed of my chains" (1:16). As Paul can look forward to a reward from God for his suffering (1:12), so he can pray, "May the Lord grant to him to find mercy from the Lord on that day" (1:18).

The second aspect of Timothy's role is suggested in 2:2. He is to entrust the "sound teaching" to others who in turn will be able to teach. Timothy is not only a Christian who lives the gospel and suffers for it. His suffering occurs precisely because he is a teacher of the "good news." The focus therefore turns to his ministry of teaching, the attitudes he himself should have and inculcate in others. Before turning to that role (2:14—4:5), however, Paul offers a series of models to which Timothy can look for encouragement. "Take your share of suffering as a good soldier of Jesus Christ" (2:3), suggests the first. The soldier, the athlete, and the farmer are all stock examples for moral exertion in Hellenistic moral teaching. Paul here emphasizes their attention to duty. The soldier does not get distracted by extraneous affairs; the athlete competes by the rules; the farmer works hard. Reward only follows upon this devotion: the soldier pleases his recruiter; the athlete receives the crown; the farmer enjoys the first fruits of the crop (2:3–6).

Paul saves his most important example till last: "Remember Jesus Christ, risen from the dead, descended from David, as preached in my gospel" (2:8). Once again, the note of memory; but what about Jesus should Timothy remember? The next line provides the clue: ". . . the gospel for which I am suffering" (2:9). Paul endures suffering so that others might attain salvation (2:10). The implication is that Jesus likewise suffered and died, "so that life and immortality might be brought to light through the gospel" (1:10). So Paul reminds Timothy of the "faithful word" (2:11-13):

> If we have died with him we shall also live with him. If we endure, we shall reign with him. If we deny him, he will also deny us. If we are faithless, he remains faithful, for he cannot deny himself.

The first three lines of this apparently traditional saying have perfect internal symmetry: as we are toward God, so will God be toward us. Suffering now with Jesus will bring glory later with Jesus; endurance will bring rule; denial, denial. But the final line is a surprise, and in it we find the typical Pauline emphasis: God is more faithful than human infidelity. God escapes perfect symmetry by his grace.

As Paul offered the Philippians a series of examples of "life for others" including Jesus and himself (Phil. 2:1—4:3), so here we find the same rhetorical technique. He provides Timothy with a series of concrete examples of suffering in the hope of reward: Onesiphorus, the soldier, athlete, and farmer; himself; and Jesus who rose from the dead.

The Ideal Teacher (2 Timothy 2:14—4:5)

Paul now fills out the model with maxims, set in a series of antitheses. The attitudes and actions of Timothy oppose those of the false teachers. They are given to disputatiousness (2:14) and godless chatter (2:16), which spreads like a gangrenous sickness (2:17). They have revolutionary impulses (2:22), engage in senseless and useless quarrels (2:23). They are filled with all manner of vice (3:2-5). Timothy and those he instructs (2:14) are to avoid such practices and people (2:14, 16, 22, 23; 3:5). The opponents are charlatans (3:13) who prey on the uneducated and curious (3:6-7). They are like the magicians of Pharaoh's court who opposed Moses, "men of corrupt mind and counterfeit faith" (3:8). Paul uses a spatial imagery throughout this section. The opponents are always on the move. They "go from house to house" (3:6); they fall away and turn away (2:18); they "stand against" (3:8); and they "advance" (2:16; 3:13). Against this advance, Timothy is to "remain" (3:14) and "stand fast" (3:14; 4:2). Although they "make progress," Paul assures Timothy, "they will not advance" (3:9). Such comfort is all the more welcome since the opponents are obviously enjoying considerable success. Paul characterizes these as the "last days," when stress will cause people to be "lovers of pleasure rather than lovers of God" (3:4). And it will only get worse. People will not even be willing to listen to sound teaching but will seek charlatans willing to shape their teaching to expectations (4:3).

Against the tide of indifference and apostasy, Paul can only tell Timothy to remain steady, to endure suffering, and to fulfill his ministry (4:5).

Timothy cannot cut truth to fit the season, but must remain constant (4:1–2):

> Preach the word; be urgent in season and out of season; convince, rebuke, exhort, be unfailing in patience and in teaching.

Timothy can once more look to Paul as a model of such endurance before adversity. Paul reminds Timothy (3:10–11):

> You have observed my teaching, my conduct, my aim in life, my patience, my love, my steadfastness, my persecutions, my sufferings, what befell me at Antioch, at Iconium, and at Lystra, what persecutions I endured; yet from them all the Lord rescued me.

Paul too faced resistance to the truth, and as Paul held on, so should Timothy. The gospel ministry bears with it the necessity of suffering. For a sick world, health is a threat: "All who would desire to lead a godly life in Christ will be persecuted" (3:12). But as Paul was delivered—"From them all the Lord rescued me" (3:11)—so will Timothy be delivered.

In light of the harshness and success of the opponents, the advice given Timothy by Paul is remarkable. The use of medical imagery was common in the contemporary moral literature, so it is not unusual for Paul to contrast "healthy" and "sick" teaching. Indeed, this is what gives the polemic against the moral behavior of the opponents its force, for the ancients had the correct perception that action does follow on perceptions, and bad ideas can lead to bad actions. Nor was Paul original in comparing the teacher to a physician (2:15). Philosophers who used such language disagreed, however, about the proper medical approach to "sick thought." Some, like the Cynics, advocated harshness and scorn. They operated like surgeons. Others considered gentleness and care to be more healing of moral illness. In 2 Timothy, that is the approach Paul advocates for Timothy. As Paul had characterized himself as being "as gentle as a nurse" (1 Thess. 2:7), so he wants Timothy to be gentle. Even when reproving, he is not to engage in harsh quarrels. Indeed, Paul sees such an attitude as holding open the possibility of the adversaries' conversion (2:24–26):

> The Lord's servant must not be quarrelsome but kindly to everyone, an apt teacher, forbearing, correcting his opponents with gentleness. God may perhaps grant that they will repent and come to know the truth, and may escape the snare of the devil.

What resources are available to the Christian teacher? Timothy can look to the education he has received in the faith from his maternal ancestors (1:5; 3:14). He has in Paul the source of sound teaching (1:13) and the example of steadfastness in the ministry (3:10) as well as of suffering for the "good news" (3:11; 4:6). And, like Paul, he has the guidance of the

Scriptures, which he has known from his youth. They instruct him "for salvation through faith in Jesus Christ" (3:15). And because they are inspired by God, they are (3:16–17)

> profitable for teaching, for reproof, for correction, and for training in righteousness, that the man of God may be complete, equipped for every good work.

Paul, Model of Suffering in Hope (2 Timothy 4:6–18)

Paul concludes by again presenting himself as a model for Timothy. Even in prison, Paul continues to be opposed (4:14). Despite that, he does not turn from his ministry (4:17):

> The Lord stood by me and strengthened me to proclaim the word fully that all the Gentiles might hear it. So I was rescued from the lion's mouth.

The point for Timothy is clear. He should not be cowardly but imitate the perseverance of Paul and take "his share of suffering for the gospel." He can count on the Lord's supporting him, as well, and must rely on that support, since Paul himself is about to die. He closes with his own hope, that "Henceforth there is laid up for me the crown of righteousness which the Lord, the just judge, will award to me on that day," and extends that hope to Timothy as well, "and not only to me, but also to all who have loved his appearing" (4:8).

If 2 Timothy is not authentic, it is written by someone whose knowledge of age and hardship and discouragement was such that he could write a letter of astonishing psychological verisimilitude. Beneath the poignancy, however, is the gospel. Here is truly the Paul who knew the one in whom he trusted (1:12) and was convinced in every circumstance that "the word of God is not fettered" (2:9).

1 TIMOTHY: LIFE IN GOD'S HOUSEHOLD

First Timothy comes closest to the stereotypical picture of the Pastorals. Elements of a personal parenetic letter are present in it: Paul is an example (now of God's mercy to sinners, 1:16), and Timothy is to be a model for the church (4:12). Timothy's attitudes are also contrasted antithetically to those of false teachers (1:3–20; 4:1–16; 6:2b–16, 20–21). The letter, however, has less overall literary coherence than 2 Timothy. It gives only the merest hint of personal circumstance: Paul left Timothy in Ephesus on his way to Macedonia (1:3). He hopes to return soon (3:14) but writes instructions to his delegate (3:15),

> so that you may know how one ought to behave in the household of God, which is the church of the living God, the pillar and bulwark of the truth.

These instructions give 1 Timothy its special character. They deal with prayer (2:2) and the role of women in the liturgical assembly (2:8–15); the qualifications for bishops (3:1–7), deacons (3:8–13), and women deacons (3:11); the care of widows (5:3–16); the payment of elders (5:17–19); the resolution of charges against elders (5:19–22); and the attitudes of slaves (6:1–2) and the rich (6:17–19). The most disconcerting feature of 1 Timothy is the way these elements are put together so haphazardly. If one isolated the passages concerned with Timothy and the opponents, a letter much like 2 Timothy would be the result. If one kept only the prescriptions, the writing would provide the nucleus of later "church orders," albeit with an air of the random and provisional about it.

The concern for community affairs is the most prominent feature of this letter, expressed not to a community as a whole or to a local leader but to a delegate who is expected to attend to the problematic aspects of a local church's life. What, then, was the situation in the Ephesian community? As always, a precise reconstruction is difficult. On the whole, the letter gives the impression of a relatively mature community, with its basic structures firmly in place. As so frequently, however, there is also the problem of deviance within the community. The names Hymenaeus and Alexander occur here again (1:20), now together (cf. 2 Tim. 2:17; 4:14). Of them, we are told little, except that "by rejecting conscience they have made shipwreck of their faith," so that Paul was forced to hand them over to Satan so that they might not blaspheme (1:19–20). They are, therefore, present or former members of the church. Otherwise, only "certain people," *tines*, are referred to (1:3, 6; 6:21). Timothy is to charge them not to teach other doctrines (*heterodidaskein;* 1:3). The reference to other doctrines is not clear. Some want to be considered "teachers of the law" (1:7) and are preoccupied with "myths and endless genealogies" (1:4). Some "liars whose consciences are seared" are against marriage for Christians and advocate dietary restrictions (4:2–3) and possibly other forms of asceticism (4:7–8). Some seek money for their teaching (6:5). Paul's final characterization is that they are involved with "godless chatter and contradictions of what is falsely called knowledge [*gnōsis*]" (6:20). The traits can be combined and aligned with those of opponents in other Pauline writings. When the elements of slander (e.g., the accusation of cupidity) are removed, however, they simply represent once more the sort of elitist esoteric groups we so often encounter in the religiosity of the Hellenistic world.

Several features distinguish 1 Timothy from 2 Timothy on the issue of the false teachers. (1) 1 Timothy makes no mention of their aggressive missionary tactics or what effect these might be having. (2) In 1 Timothy they do not appear as teachers from the outside, but rather as ambitious and elitist members of the community itself. (3) In contrast to 2 Timothy, this letter does not stress the rebuke or correction of them. They are simply to be commanded. There is neither the note of gentleness nor the hope for conversion. (4) On the other hand, more than polemic is used against them. Paul here clarifies the proper understanding of those things the opponents are distorting. In response to their wishing to be teachers of the law (1:7), he specifies the nature and function of the law (1:8–10). In response to the forbidding of marriage and food, he stresses the essential goodness of creation and its capacity to be sanctified by prayer (4:3–5). He counters the claims for physical asceticism with those of "training in godliness" (4:7–8). He clarifies exactly what sort of "gain" one can expect from godliness, in response to those who sought monetary rewards for their teaching (6:5–10). It is very difficult, however, to draw a direct or explicit connection between anything said of or in response to the troublemakers and the concrete directives concerning community life. Certainly, one can extrapolate from certain emphases to commotions caused by divergent teachings: from Paul's insistence that prayer should be free of disputation, from his refusal to give women a teaching role (2:8–15), and from his concern for widows' becoming gadabouts and gossips (5:13), his warning against the precipitate appointing of elders (5:22), and his injunctions to slaves to obey believing owners (6:2). But the explicit connections are more difficult to find.

First Timothy contains allusions to familiar Pauline teaching, particularly in its emphasis on God's salvific will for all humanity (see 1:15–16; 2:3–6; 4:9–10; 6:13–16). There is not only a fascinating version of Paul's conversion—seen as an example of God's mercy—(1:12–16) but there are also allusions to the trial and testimony of Jesus (2:6; 6:13). There is also this hymnic expression of the "mystery" in 3:16:

> He was manifested in the flesh, vindicated in the Spirit, seen by angels, preached among nations, believed on in the world, taken up in glory.

These elements are dominated, however, by the practical instructions, and the context of moral exhortation, with its "sound teaching" (1:10; 6:3) and "training in godliness" (1:4; 4:7); with its "good conscience" (1:5, 19; 3:9) contrasted to a "seared conscience" (1:4; 4:7).

The Household of God

It is not easy to derive from 1 Timothy a full and satisfying picture of the community structure of the church at Ephesus. The instructions deal with matters of immediate pertinence to the author and first reader, not to the historian's curiosity.

The author calls the church the household of God (*oikos tou theou;* 3:15). In other letters, Paul uses the expression "the church in the household of . . ." (cf. Rom. 16:5; 1 Cor. 16:19; Col. 4:15), although he can also speak metaphorically of community members as "household servants" (Rom. 14:4) or "members of a household" (Gal. 6:10; Eph. 2:19). It is important to note here that the church as intentional community is not completely assimilated to the household structure. A distinction is made several times between "one's own household" and the community (1 Tim. 3:4–5, 12; 5:4). The community does not appear to have, furthermore, the monarchical structure typically associated with the household. The most important function of the household in this letter, in fact, is to provide an analogy for leadership: administrative abilities and leadership skills demonstrated in one structure are applicable to another. However unclear to contemporary readers, there is also a distinction drawn between the life and responsibilities of individual households, and the life and responsibility of the church as such (see 5:4, 8, 16).

Paul's directions to Timothy apply to several different spheres of the community's life. Some are directed to the life of individual households and the community members living within them. Such are the remarks about slaves belonging to Christian masters (6:1–2) and those about rich members of the community who are not to rely on their wealth but use it for helping others (6:17–19). So likewise is the demand that individual children within households provide for widows (5:4, 8, 16) and the banal yet pertinent advice on the attitudes Timothy should display toward diverse age and gender groups (5:1–2). There is little dramatic in this advice and nothing implausible. The author wants order, propriety, and some graciousness in the domestic lives of believers.

There is not much attention to the liturgical life of the community, either, and what little there is has another focus than the instructions concerning the Lord's Supper and charismatic gifts in 1 Corinthians 11—14. Three very specific directives are given. First, prayers are to be said for all people, especially rulers (2:1–4). This is certainly unexceptionable, as is the second instruction, which is that the male members who pray with uplifted arms should not have anger or quarreling among them (2:8). The instructions about women, however, are somewhat more problematic. The contrast between luxurious external adornment and the life of internal virtue is a commonplace in Hellenistic and Diaspora Jewish moral teaching (2:9–10). The prohibition against women teaching in the assembly or having authority over men, on the other hand, sounds very much like the setting of Jewish synagogal worship, in which women had no function, although they had a role in the domestic liturgy (2:11–12). The command here lacks something of the tension found in 1 Cor. 11:2–16 and 14:34–36. There, the context was one of charismatic worship in which women were certainly prophesying and praying. Here, the instruction focuses narrowly on the cultural unacceptability of women teaching in public. They are to give instruction only in private for their children (2:15;

cf. 2 Tim. 1:5; Titus 2:3). The justification for the prohibition is harsh, and the account of the sin of Eve (2:13–14) is sharper than in Paul's other reference to this part of the Genesis story (2 Cor. 11:2–3). What we learn overall from these few remarks about worship is that it involves public prayer and teaching, and that both of these activities are male prerogatives. It sounds a great deal like the worship in Diaspora synagogues.

The most extended attention is given to the officers of the Ephesian church. The office of bishop (*episkopos;* 3:1–7) and deacon (*diakonos;* 3:8–10, 12–13) have been met, if briefly, before (Phil. 1:1), as have women deacons (3:11; cf. Rom. 16:1). The existence of women deacons indicates that although teaching was not allowed to women, some ministerial roles were given them in Ephesus. The office of elder (*presbyteros;* 5:17–22) is not found in other Pauline letters, although Acts associates elders with Pauline churches (14:23) and specifically with Ephesus in 20:17.

The instructions spell out not job descriptions but qualifications. The bishop (or overseer) is obviously an administrator above all, and his position demands appropriate capabilities, although the bishop is also expected to be an "apt teacher" (3:2). Sound moral qualities and leadership ability are most important (3:1–7). For those romantically inclined, the morality of marital fidelity and sobriety may appear dull; for those who live in the real world, their quiet heroism is recognized. The work of deacons is also such that administrative abilities (proved by the management of a household) are desirable (3:12). Because specific cases are raised, we learn a little more about elders. Those who "rule well" are to be paid double, "especially those who labor in the word and teaching" (5:17). This suggests a board of elders (*presbyterion,* 4:14) who perform administrative functions, among whose number some may also teach or preach. The other directives concerning elders are a reminder of human frailty in every position of authority. Charges can be brought against them and must be carefully considered (5:19). Timothy may be forced to rebuke an elder publicly—surely the role of a delegate, not of another in the same community (5:20). In the light of these possibilities, Paul gives the sound advice that appointment to such positions should not be made hastily (5:22). His concluding injunction is classically Pauline: "Keep these rules without favor; do nothing from partiality" (5:21).

The discussion of widows (5:3–16) is the most problematic for our understanding of the Ephesian community structure. The question clearly seems to be who should be supported by community funds, for a distinction is made on the basis of support available from private families (5:4, 8). The resources of the community as a whole are not unnecessarily to be burdened (5:16). The community's obligation is to help those who are "real widows" (5:16). But the discussion becomes more complicated on the point of who is a real widow. Paul distinguishes between those whose husbands have died and those who are truly "left alone and have hoped in God" (5:5). Some women whose husbands have died are self-indulgent (5:6)—which means they have resources—or are not wholeheartedly committed to the community's life. If they got the chance, they would like to remarry. Some of them are idlers on the community dole, using the community's resources without serving the community in return but being busybodies (5:13). Paul's solution would have widows of a marrying age remarry if possible. Only older widows, or those without other resources ("left alone") would be enrolled (5:9, 11). But does the term "enroll" indicate a special order of widows? Paul complicates the question by appearing to provide a list of qualifications as he does for other offices (5:9–10).

The simplest and best explanation is that the Ephesian church followed the model of Diaspora Judaism in providing assistance on a regular and organized basis for the needy of the community (cf. Acts 6:1–7). One of the most important tasks of every Jewish community was the carrying out of this obligation. It was never easy. The obvious categories of those who required aid were the strangers, orphans, and widows. Orphans and strangers were easy to identify and relatively easy to provide for. The case of widows was always far more ambiguous and difficult. Cheating and fraud were always possible. Paul wants Timothy in this case to be sure that only the truly needy be cared for by the community as a whole—and only those with no other resources available to them. They should be enrolled on a list that would certify their qualification for help. In return, they were to give themselves not to their own interests but to the service of the community as a whole. Women, however, who technically were widowed but who were primarily interested in their own pleasure or who had resources sufficient that they could be "busybodies and gossips" (5:13) should not be allowed to defraud the community of its funds.

The community structure at Ephesus according to 1 Timothy is not complicated. It resembles what little we know of the structure of Diaspora Jewish synagogues (see chap. 3, pp. 69–73 above). In them, a leader (archisynagogos) and a board of elders (gerousia) did administrative work and settled disputes. Their obligations included running the community charity efforts, both the raising of funds and their disbursement. They were helped in these functions by assistants (chazzan/diakonos) who performed more menial tasks in the liturgy and community charity functions. There is nothing in this that is not utterly compatible with Paul's lifetime. There is nothing in this letter that approaches a hierarchical, much less a monarchical, order. No office is theologized or otherwise legitimated. The community structure is task-oriented and practical. It breathes the air of plausibility.

Why, then, the attention given to these matters? The instructions themselves make it partially clear: there were problems with elders and with widows. But the need may also have come from the disruptions caused by those community members who "with ideas in their heads" unsettled others. Certainly, a concern for order, and also for the good reputation of the community with outsiders, runs through these instructions, a concern not alien to Paul elsewhere. The community's prayer for rulers is so that it may lead "a quiet life" (2:2). The bishop should not be a recent convert whose head will be turned, thus falling into Satan's trap and giving outsiders a negative view of the church (3:7). The bad behavior of would-be widows can make outsiders revile the community (5:14). Slaves who refuse to serve their Christian masters will cause the gospel to be defamed (6:1). Internal stability and external peace; here they are approached through the instructions given to a delegate. The motivation, however, is not much different from that expressed in the most charismatic of Paul's letters (1 Cor. 14:37–40):

> If anyone thinks that he is a prophet or spiritual, he should acknowledge that what I am writing to you is a command of the Lord. If anyone does not recognize this, he is not recognized. So, my brethren, earnestly desire to prophesy, and do not forbid speaking in tongues. But all things should be done decently and in order.

TITUS: AN INFANT CHURCH
IN THE OUTPOST

In Titus, the pieces that make up the Pastorals puzzle are fitted together in still another fashion. Unlike 1 Timothy, this letter gives a bit more autobiographical information. Paul is apparently in midcareer. We don't know his present whereabouts, but he expects to winter in Nicopolis (3:12) and expects Titus to return to him from his temporary duty in Crete when Paul sends Artemas and Tychichus to relieve him (3:12). Why has Paul "left" Titus on Crete? Two reasons are given: Titus is to amend what is defective, and he is to appoint elders in each city (1:5). Much of the letter is taken up with instructions on these matters.

There is nothing in this information that is itself implausible, except that we do not know of any Pauline mission in Crete, where Acts mentions Paul's being only as a shipboard prisoner (Acts 27:7–15). And if the Apollos of 3:13 is the same as the one in 1 Cor. 3:1–6, it is perhaps a little strange to see him as a helper of Titus (though cf. Acts 18:27; 1 Cor. 16:12). Tychichus, of course, we have met before (Acts 20:4; Col. 4:7; Eph. 6:21; 2 Tim. 4:12).

Stylistically, Titus is between 1 Timothy and 2 Timothy. It is not approximately Pauline throughout, as is 2 Timothy, nor only remotely Pauline throughout, as is 1 Timothy. Rather, it alternates short sections whose Pauline rhythms none would deny (see, e.g., 1:15; 2:11–14; 3:4–7) with longer stretches of quite a different style. In contrast to 2 Timothy, the parenetic elements are minimal. Titus is only told, in 2:7–8:

> Show yourself a model of good deeds and in your teaching show integrity, gravity, and sound speech that cannot be censured, so that an opponent may be put to shame, having nothing evil to say of us.

Much more than in 1 or 2 Timothy, there seems to be a direct relationship between the opponents and the instructions concerning "what is defective." In sum, Titus is best understood when considered by itself as a genuine piece of correspondence, addressing a specific and real situation.

The Situation of Titus

Everything in the letter supports the picture of a new, half-finished community suggested by 1:5. In 1 Timothy, the church at Ephesus already had bishops, elders, and deacons in place. Indeed, the provision could be made that the bishop not be a "recent convert" (1 Tim. 3:6). The community was therefore in existence for some years. In Titus, the elder or bishop (the transition in 1:5–7 is not altogether clear) should have children who are believers and should not be "open to the charge of being profligate or insubordinate" (1:6). The bishop in the community can therefore still have children who are unconverted. A further clue is offered in the list of this bishop's qualities. In addition to those mentioned in 1 Tim. 3:1–7, Titus adds some that are intriguing. The bishop is not to be "arrogant or quick tempered or violent" (1:7); in the Greek these terms are quite strong. We are led to wonder about the population among which Christianity is trying to strike roots. In the eyes of the author, the populace is not attractive: "Cretans are always liars, evil beasts, lazy gluttons" (1:12). In fact, such a view of the Cretan population seems to have enjoyed almost proverbial status in antiquity. Titus suggests that the gospel is trying to make a place for itself in an atmosphere of severe incivility.

The climate for evangelization is made stormier by opponents who are competing for the religious allegiance of the populace. In Titus, these opponents are outsiders and are clearly Jewish rivals. They are "from the circumcision" (1:10). They have "Jewish myths" (1:14). They are teaching Christians about the laws of purity (1:15). They claim to "know God" (1:16). They are concerned for the observance of the law (3:5; 3:9).

The opponents are quite successful, and the degree of their success provides an important insight into the emphasis of Titus: "They are upsetting whole households by teaching for base gain what they have no right to teach" (1:11). A fragile Christian community, therefore, is being threatened not only by the harsh and misanthropic character of its converts but also by the ability of rival Jewish missionaries to persuade the newly converted that they have a more attractive version of God's word. Here there is no possibility for dialogue. The survival of an infant church is at stake. Titus is therefore told by Paul, "They must be silenced" (1:11); and those being seduced by the Jewish myths are to be "rebuked sharply" so that "they may be sound in the faith" (1:13). Titus himself is to avoid "stupid controversies, genealogical discussions, and quarrels over the law" (3:9). If anyone in the community remains factious, that person is to be warned repeatedly, then cut off (3:10). These are rough remedies for a tough situation. The bishop, likewise, is not simply to be an apt teacher (*didaktikos*) as in 1 Tim. 3:2. He requires a more vigorous gift (1:9):

> He must hold firm to the sure word as taught, so that he might be able to give instruction in sound doctrine, and also to confute those who contradict it.

The Teaching of Titus

It is important to observe that the *only* specific element of "church order" in Titus are the remarks about the bishop. Otherwise, the focus of practical instructions is on the household and civic responsibilities of Christians. In 2:1–10, Paul gives a listing of attitudes that are appropriate, if somewhat bland, for older men (2:2) and women (2:3), younger women (2:4–5), and younger men (2:6) generally, and then an exhortation to slaves (2:9–10). In 3:1–2, general civic attitudes of submission to authority and good manners are recommended. All of these can be summed up as the doing of good deeds (*kala erga*; 2:14; 3:8, 14) that express their new identity, in contrast to the wicked deeds of the opponents (1:16).

A closer look at the specific instructions raises some interesting questions. Why should older women need to be told not to be winebibbers (2:3)? Do their daughters really require teaching to "love their husbands and children" (2:4)? Are Christian slaves in need of instruction not to pilfer their masters' goods and not be refractory (2:9–10)? Do Christians generally need to be told to seek "honest work" and that they should not be revolutionary (3:1–2)? The Greek in each of these cases indicates nuances that the English translations disguise. The problem is this: behavior this ordinary should fall in the category of "what goes without saying." But here we find basic instructions being given in civility, the rudiments of civilized behavior. If the bishop needs to be reminded not to be a violent man, and his children not to be revolutionaries, this is not an urbane setting. Still more is involved. We have seen that "households" are being overturned by the success of the Jewish missionaries. These instructions therefore, are intended to strengthen the basic familial unit of the household, so that the gospel teaching itself might be able to grow securely and to close off the opportunity for further damage being done by the opponents. In Titus, the gospel itself has a civilizing function: it teaches people how to be members of a society.

In this light, we can better understand the two remarkable kerygmatic statements in Titus in which the Pauline language is most pronounced. These statements, we should note, frame and interpret the concrete directives. In 3:3–7, the author quotes a "faithful saying" that takes the form of a before-and-after statement, with the point of pivot being people's baptism as a response to the "good news." Before, they had shared all the hostile attitudes of their neighbors, passing their days in malice and envy, "hated by men and hating one another" (3:3). But they had been given a new identity (3:4–7):

> But when the goodness and loving kindness of God our Savior appeared, he saved us, not because of deeds done by us in righteousness, but in virtue of his own mercy, by the washing of regeneration and renewal in the Holy Spirit, which he poured out upon us richly through Jesus Christ our Savior, so that we might be justified by his grace and become heirs in hope of eternal life.

Here we see that the qualities of God's gift—the goodness and kindness and mercy—should themselves shape Christians' identity, renewing it and regenerating it. This statement is followed by the final command, "Insist on these things, that those who have believed in God might apply themselves to good deeds" (3:8). In short, Christians' behavior should follow upon their new identity, which has been given by God.

The other statement (2:11–14) is found in the middle of the very elementary civic instructions we have already noted, and is even more illuminating:

> *For* the grace of God has appeared for the salvation of all men, training us to renounce irreligion and worldly passions, and to live sober, upright, and godly lives in this world, awaiting our blessed hope, the appearing of the glory of our great God and savior Jesus Christ, who gave himself for us to redeem us from all iniquity and to purify for himself a people of his own who are zealous for good deeds.

The most important word in this passage may well be the first, the "for" that connects it to the specific instructions. Paul here gives the basis for those instructions. It is the grace of God itself. But the next most important word is surely "training," *paideuousa*. The Greek sense of this participle should be given full strength. The grace of God itself has an educative function. It trains people in becoming human social creatures. This is really what Titus is about.

In a context where the populace both inside and outside the community is rough, and where civic order is in disarray, the gospel itself can provide a rooting in the world and the possibility of growth. The grace that comes to people in baptism can change their hearts from hostility to sweetness. And it can begin as well to shape their behavior in ways compatible with their new identity. Life together in the social structures of "this world" demands of Christians that they leave behind irreligion and worldly passions and hostility, and adopt sober, godly, and upright living. In some situations, what appears to be a domesticated virtue is actually an eschatological witness.

BIBLIOGRAPHICAL NOTE

A good summary of the issues pertaining to authenticity is found in W. G. Kümmel, *Introduction to the New Testament*, rev. ed., trans. H. C. Kee (Nashville: Abingdon Press, 1975), 366–87; and in E. E. Ellis, "The Authorship of the Pastorals: A Resume and Assessment of Recent Trends," in his *Paul and His Recent Interpreters* (Grand Rapids: Wm. B. Eerdmans, 1961), 49–57. For the discussion of specific points, see P. N. Harrison, *The Problem of the Pastoral Epistles* (London: Oxford Univ. Press, 1921), in which the fragment hypothesis was suggested; and idem, "The Authorship of the Pastoral Epistles," *Exp Tim* 67 (1955–56): 77–81. See also K. Graystone and G. Herdan, "The Authorship of the Pastorals in the Light of Statistical Linguistics," *NTS* 6 (1959–60): 1–15, where the principle, The style is the man, is twice misguidedly applied. See also the more recent vocabulary studies by D. Cook, "2 Timothy IV.6–8 and the Epistle to the Philippians," *JTS* 33 (1982): 168–71; and idem, "The Pastoral Fragments Reconsidered," *JTS* 35 (1984): 120–31. For well-balanced discussions, see C. F. D. Moule, "The Problem of the Pastoral Epistles: A Reappraisal," *BJRL* (1965): 430–52; and B. Metzger, "A Reconsideration of Certain Arguments Against the Pauline Authorship of the Pastoral Epistles," *Exp Tim* 70 (1958): 91ff. The most extensive recent attempt to place the Pastorals within the framework of Acts was by J. A. T. Robinson, *Redating the New Testament* (Philadelphia: Westminster Press, 1970), 67–85. The Lukan connection is pursued in different ways by S. G. Wilson, *Luke and the Pastoral Epistles* (London: SPCK, 1979), and J. Quinn, "The Last Volume of Luke: The Relation of Luke-Acts to the Pastoral Epistles," in *Perspectives on Luke-Acts*, ed. C. H. Talbert (Danville, Va.: Assn. of Baptist Professors of Religion, 1978), 62–75.

The standard view of the pastorals as pseudonymous and second- or third-generation productions is found (with variations) in R. Bultmann, *Theology of the New Testament* (New York: Charles Scribner's Sons, 1955), 2:95–118; J. M. Ford, "A Note on Protomontanism in the Pastoral Epistles," *NTS* 17 (1976): 338–46; H. von Campenhausen, *Ecclesiastical Authority and Spiritual Power in the Church of the First Three Centuries*, trans. J. Baker (Stanford, Calif.: Stanford Univ. Press, 1969); C. K. Barrett, "Pauline Controversies in the Post-Pauline Period," *NTS* 20 (1973–74): 229–45; E. Käsemann, "Paul and Early Catholicism," in *New Testament Questions of Today* (Philadelphia: Fortress Press, 1969), 236–51; W. Bauer, *Orthodoxy and Heresy in Earliest Christianity*, ed. and trans. R. Kraft and G. Krodel (Philadelphia: Fortress Press, 1971), 88–94, 222–228; M. C. de Boer, "Images of Paul in the Post-Apostolic Church," *CBQ* 42 (1980): 359–80.

For the argument that the Pastorals responded to the threat posed by the egalitarian demands of second-century women, see R. D. Macdonald, "Virgins, Widows, and Paul in Second-Century Asia Minor," in *1979 SBL Seminar Papers*, ed. P. Achtemeier (Missoula, Mont.: Scholars Press, 1979), 1:165–84; S. L. Davies, *The Revolt of the Widows: The Social World of the Apocryphal Acts* (Carbondale: Southern Ill. Univ. Press, 1980); J. Bassler, "The Widow's Tale: A Fresh Look at 1 Tim. 5:3–16," *JBL* 103 (1982): 23–41; R. D. Macdonald, *The Legend and the Apostle: The Battle for Paul in Story and Canon* (Philadelphia: Westminster Press, 1983). My reading of the evidence is obviously very different. For the structure of the synagogue, see above, chap. 3, incl. bibliography. For the effort of organized charity in Diaspora Judaism, see L. Frankel, "Charity and Charitable Institutions," *Jewish Encyclopedia* (1903), 3:667–70; and G. F. Moore, *Judaism in the First Three Centuries of the Christian Era* (New York: Schocken Books, 1971 [1927]), 2:162–79. A. E. Harvey, "Elders," *JTS* 25 (1974): 318–32, rightly points out the paucity of data for the title of elder associated with the Jewish synagogue. My argument depends less on the use of that title than on the overall sort of structure presupposed by the Pastorals, which matches best what little we do know about the workings of the synagogue.

The use of polemic in these letters is examined by R. J. Karris, "The Background and Significance of the Polemic of the Pastoral Epistles," *JBL* 92 (1973): 549–64; F. H. Colson, "Myths and Genealogies—A Note on the Polemic of the Pastoral Epistles," *JTS* 19 (1917–18): 265–71; and L. T. Johnson, "II Timothy and the Polemic Against False Teachers: A Re-examination," *JRS* 6/7 (1978–79): 1–26, which provides the basic framework for the analysis in this chapter. For the example of the parenetic letter, see A. J. Malherbe, "Ancient Epistolary Theorists," *Ohio Journal of Religious Studies* 5 (1977): 70–71.

On the community structure reflected in these letters, the following provide helpful guidance: R. Schnackenburg, *The Church in the New Testament* (New York: Herder & Herder, 1965), 94–102; B. Reicker, "The Constitution of the Early Church in the Light of Jewish Documents," in *The Scrolls and the New Testament*, ed. K. Stendhal (New York: Harper & Row, 1957), 143–56; J. P. Meier, "*Presbyteros* in the Pastoral Epistles," *CBQ* 35 (1973): 323–45.

For various thematic aspects of the three letters, see J. A. Allen, "The 'In Christ' Formula in the Pastoral Epistles," *NTS* 10 (1963): 115–21; N. J. McEleny, "The Vice-Lists of the Pastoral Epistles," *CBQ* 36 (1974): 203–19; J. G. Duncan, "Pistos ho Logos," *ExpTim* 35 (1923–24): 141; R. H. Gundry, "The Form, Meaning, and Background of the Hymn Quoted in I Tim 3:16," in *Apostolic History and the Gospel*, ed. W. Gasque and R. P. Martin (Exeter: Paternoster Press, 1970), 203–22; A. T. Hanson, *Studies in the Pastoral Epistles* (London: SPCK, 1968); M. J. Harris, "Titus 2:13 and the Deity of Christ," in *Pauline Studies*, ed. D. Hagner and M. Harris (Exeter: Paternoster Press, 1980), 262–77; A. J. Malherbe, "Medical Imagery in the Pastorals," in *Texts and Testaments*, ed. W. E. March (San Antonio: Trinity Univ. Press, 1980), 19–35; idem, " 'In Season and Out of Season': 2 Timothy 4:2," *JBL* 103 (1982): 23–41.

A critical commentary with full bibliography written from the point of view of pseudonymous authorship is M. Dibelius and H. Conzelmann, *The Pastoral Epistles*, ed. H. Koester, trans. P. Buttolph and A. Yarbro, Hermeneia (Philadelphia: Fortress Press, 1972). More positive toward authenticity with a clear reading of the text is J. N. D. Kelly, *A Commentary on the Pastoral Epistles*, HNTC (New York: Harper & Row, 1963).

PART FIVE

THE GENERAL EPISTLES

THE LIMITS OF THE HISTORICAL-CRITICAL MODEL ARE PERHAPS BEST ILLUS-
trated by its embarrassment at, and frequent neglect of, the writings we next
consider: Hebrews, 1 Peter, 2 Peter, Jude, and James. These writings are an
embarrassment because they are insufficiently connected to our single sure line of
chronology (the Pauline) to enable their placement within a developmental
scheme. But so strong is the developmental instinct (and so intrinsic to the model),
that these writings are almost always regarded as later, rather than simply as
different.

Their variety in style and substance also make difficult any attempt to fit them
into a developmental framework. The category usually applied to them is Early
Catholicism. This is an admirably flexible rubric, stretching to fit almost anything
that is thought to be non-Pauline: concern for church order and tradition, diminished eschatological expectation, and domesticated ethics. These writings provide
so little support for those characterizations, however, that the category's inadequacy is clear.

It must be confessed, however, that the same variety makes any sort of classification difficult. The substantive range is so wide that simple formal categories offer
the best possibility for grouping. These writings all present themselves, for example, as letters. This would be helpful were it not for the evidence that Hebrews and
James only approximately accommodate themselves to the epistolary form. Sometimes these writings (together with the three Johannine letters, which I consider
separately) are called general, or catholic, epistles. Certainly James and 1 Peter
address themselves to a readership wider than a single congregation. There is
nothing about Hebrews, Jude, and 2 Peter, however, that is incompatible with their
being writings aimed at specific individual churches. But since we do not know the
identity of the readers, we group these as general letters. They could also be called
letters to gentile churches, but while more or less plausible arguments can be made
that James and 1 Peter and Hebrews (and even 2 Peter and Jude) are written to
exclusively gentile churches rather than Jewish or mixed congregations, the assessment cannot be certain, and has as its main attraction its convenience.

The writings are also sometimes grouped together on the basis of their
pseudonymous character. But although few would challenge pseudonymity in the
case of 2 Peter, it is still possible to find supporters for the composition of 1 Peter
by the apostle himself. More important, very little is gained by saying that James
and Jude are pseudonymous. We know so little about their putative eponyms that
no light is shed on the meaning of the texts by the assertion. Hebrews, of course, is
pseudonymous only because of the tradition of Pauline attribution. The text does
not identify the author. It is, properly speaking, an anonymous composition.

The lesson may simply be that our compulsion to categorize does a fundamental
disservice to these writings. Their greatest contribution to our historical understanding of early Christianity may be the constant reminder that the movement was
never reducible to Paul and his opponents, and that these short messages from the
past represent many other voices whom the accidents of history have left silent.

The writings are of value, moreover, not simply for what they can tell us about
the past but also for each one's distinctive and irreducible witness to life before
God in the light of the experience of Jesus. In Hebrews we find one of the two or

three richest and most complex interpretations of the Christian experience in the canon; in 1 Peter, an exhortation of rare grace; in 2 Peter and Jude, the voice of outrage in the face of deviance and defiance, and a defense of community identity; in James, the unswerving and uncompromising translation of conviction into action. Each demands attention to its own voice. And together, their very capacity to slip the chains of easy categorization gives classifiers, too, some freedom.

20

The Letter to the Hebrews

LIKE ITS OWN DESCRIPTION OF MELCHIZEDEK (HEB. 7:3), HEBREWS APPEARS in the canon "without father or mother or genealogy," yet so impressively that its place seems due not to its author or circumstances but simply to its own extraordinary worth. Although the Western church was slower in allowing it a position in the canon, the East gave it immediate and lasting popularity, so that its imagery helped shape liturgical prayer and its substance provided disputants of the third and fourth century with a rich lode for christological mining.

Contemporary scholars find Hebrews fascinating for the subtle combinations it gives to diverse philosophical and religious symbols of the first century. For a writing of such beauty and power, however, Hebrews goes largely unread by ordinary Christians who are nourished by John and Paul. One reason might be that Hebrews is a sustained argument from beginning to end. Only a complete reading enables one to appreciate its full force. The few self-contained pericopes it can provide for liturgical lectionaries themselves lose a great deal by being excerpted. A second reason is that in Hebrews a truth that can remain implicit and unacknowledged in other NT writings cannot be ignored: the symbolism of the ancient world is alien to our own.

Despite its complex symbolization, Hebrews provides a witness to the Christian experience which is clear and compelling. No pretense of an adequate reading will be found in this treatment; I want only to provide sufficient clues so that the reader might distinguish what is merely unfamiliar from what is truly strange.

PRELIMINARY PROFILE

The author's apology for "writing briefly" (Heb. 13:22) is a literary convention (cf. 1 Pet. 5:12). Hebrews is shorter than only Romans and 1 Corinthians among NT epistles. But then Hebrews is not really a letter. Besides the lack of formal epistolary elements, the circumstances of the writer are only briefly mentioned, almost as an afterthought (Heb. 13:23–25). The author appears as a subject only in 13:18, with an assurance that he or she has a pure conscience and hopes for a rapid restoration to the readers. There is news that Timothy, called "our brother," has recently been released from prison (13:23), and the author sends greetings from "those who come from Italy" (13:24). These notes establish a rather obvious connection to the Pauline mission, but take us no farther.

If not a genuine letter, what kind of writing is this? As a theological treatise, it could comfortably stand next to Romans as a reflection on the mystery of God's work in Christ. But Hebrews also has an intense, immediate, and consistent pastoral orientation. *It most resembles a homily.* The author says he has written a word of exhortation (*logos tēs paraklēseōs;* 13:22). The style agrees with that description. Like any good preacher, the author uses throughout the first-person plural ("we"), only shifting to direct address for emphasis. References to speaking occur throughout: ". . . of which we are speaking" (2:5), " . . . about this we have much to say, which is hard to explain, since you have become dull of hearing" (5:11), " . . . though we speak thus" (6:9).

The rhetorical organization of the homily is masterly. Exposition and exhortation alternate throughout with greater or less rapidity. They build on each other inexorably, demanding of the reader at every point an assent of the mind and a commitment of the will, so that the cumulative impact is impressive. The exposition of 1:1–14, for example, leads directly to exhortation (2:1–4); the argument of 2:5–18 is turned directly to an application by 3:1; the discussion of 3:2–6 is driven home by the "therefore" of 3:7–13. Then, more rapidly, the exposition of 3:14–19 is applied in 4:1; that of 4:2–10 in the exhortation of 4:11–16; and so through the sermon. In the process, the writer early suggests themes that are only later developed, which also creates a wavelike, cumulative force. Thus, Jesus' fellowship with humans (2:14–18) is made thematic in 5:1–10; his faith (3:1–6) is made explicit in 12:1–3; his role as priest (4:14; 5:1–10) is developed by 7:1—9:28.

By designating Hebrews a homily I am not suggesting that it was necessarily delivered orally: I am suggesting only that it retains, as does Paul's "diatribe," the air of speech rather than writing. Homily or letter, it was intended to be read by someone. To whom was it addressed? The title "To Hebrews [*pros hebraious*]" was appended early but probably represents guesswork as much as the present remarks. It certainly does not mean (as was recently suggested) "against the Hebrews." Without any external controls, it is not surprising to find many candidates for the audience: the Colossians, the Corinthians, converted priests in Jerusalem (cf. Acts 6:7), converts from Qumran, converts from Alexandrian Judaism, Diaspora Jews in Jerusalem on pilgrimage. The suggestions all depend on the same internal evidence.

The audience certainly consisted of Christians (see 6:1–3) who knew the Scriptures rather well. One cannot always argue from a writer's use of texts to a reader's appreciation of them. In Hebrews, however, the argument relies so heavily on citations and the ability to recognize their import, that if the audience was deficient in this respect, the writer was a poor communicator. What else can we learn from thematic elements? The author puts the angels in their proper place (1:5–14; 2:2), much as Paul had to do in Galatia (Gal. 3:19; 4:9) and Colossae (Col. 1:16; 2:18). Hebrews also puts Moses in his place (3:2–6), as Paul did in Gal. 3:19 and 2 Cor. 3:7–18. Most of all, the Levitical (Aaronic) priesthood is put in its place (chaps. 5—10), reflecting a concern unparalleled in the NT, although rival claims to the priesthood are heard in contemporary Jewish writings. The author makes disparaging remarks about diverse teachings and about legislation dealing with food and drink (9:10; 13:9). These remind us of similar remarks in Col. 2:20–22, 1 Cor. 8:1–13, and Rom. 14:1–23. The comments here are made in passing, however, so that their significance is unclear. These thematic traces give us at once many possibilities and no certainties.

Of more importance for the overall presentation of the document are some clues concerning the social situation of the audience. The community has already experienced some suffering for their commitment to the Messiah (10:32–35; 12:3–13) and can look forward to more (13:13–14). What form did their suffering take? They had not yet suffered unto death (12:4), but they knew and had visited some who had been imprisoned (10:34). They had either themselves experienced or knew of those who had faced "public abuse and affliction" (10:33). Of most interest to us is the remark that the readers "joyfully accepted the plundering of [their] property, since [they] knew that [they themselves] had a better possession and an abiding one" (10:34). Like the sectarians at Qumran (see chap. 2, pp. 61–64), some of them had experienced despoliation of their property. This small clue is important. It enables us to appreciate some specific instructions to the hearers: they are to show hospitality (13:2), keep free from love of money and be content (13:5), and share what possessions they have (13:16). Even more, it helps us grasp much of the homily's imagery, which relies on many property metaphors. Already in 10:34, we notice the contrast between the property that was taken and their "better possession and more lasting." Throughout the writing, property language symbolizes relationships and realities (see, e.g., 2:14; 3:1; 6:13–18; 7:4–10; 9:16–22), most impressively and climactically in 11:1—12:17.

To the community's physical dispossession corresponded a spiritual condition of discouragement, even despair. The most obvious concern of the author is that the community's members are developing "drooping hands and weak knees" (12:12). Their discouragement puts them in temptation (2:18) of turning away from their commitment (12:16–17). The author fights the lassitude and inattention, the "dullness of hearing" (5:11) that leads to disobedience, the failure both of nerve and of faith (2:3; 3:12—4:1; 4:11, 14; 5:11–14; 6:4–8; 10:24–29).

The text gives us, therefore, a considerable amount of evidence about the readers. But we meet here again the methodological problem epistolary writing always involves. Can we pull these threads together into one hypothetical cloth? Do the thematic elements all point to one specific situation? Can we identify the hearers as, say, priestly converts from Qumran, whose loss of property and prestige as a result of their conversion shakes their confidence and tempts them to return to their former priestly order? The literary artistry of the writer gives us pause, for an accomplished rhetorician need not rely on the conditions of his hearers for the generation of themes. Some may derive simply from his imagination, others from the literary inertia created by his primary themes. We must in the end be content with the certain knowledge that his hearers were Christians who knew enough of the Scriptures to appreciate such a learned and literary tour de force and who were, in the estimation of the homilist, in need of such encouragement as might be given by this "word of exhortation" (13:22).

A search for the author of Hebrews is no less frustrating than the search for his audience. Attribution to Paul is reflected in canonical lists and manuscripts (such as P[46] where it appears after Romans) but was vigorously questioned by early writers like Tertullian, who thought the Timothy connection made Barnabas a likely candidate, and Origen, who suggested Luke might have translated Paul's thought, but then confessed that "only God knows" (Eusebius *Ecclesiastical History* III.38.2). Certainly Hebrews contains a number of touches that we would otherwise have considered Pauline, such as "access" to God given by Christ (4:16; 10:19–22; cf. Rom. 5:1; Eph. 2:18), God's promise to Abraham (6:13–18; cf. Gal. 3:16–18) and Abraham's response of faith (11:8–12; cf. Rom. 4:1–25), and the faith of Jesus understood as obedience (5:1–10; 12:1–3; cf. Rom. 5:12–21). In some other respects, Hebrews resembles the Gospel of John, as in its beginning with a preexistent word (1:2–5; cf. John 1:1–18) and its regarding flesh (2:14; 5:7; 10:20) not as an attitude hostile to God (as in Paul) but as a symbol of human mortality and frailty (see John 1:13–14; 3:6; 8:15). Hebrews puts all these elements together in an entirely distinctive fashion. The characterizations Pauline and Johannine are equally misleading.

If not Paul or John, then who? We need someone in the primitive church who was learned in the Scripture and knew technical modes of argumentation, those associated with both the rabbis and Philo, someone whose perceptions were influenced by the symbolic world of Alexandrian Judaism, who had argumentative clarity, rhetorical skill, fervor in exhortation, and moral severity. Martin Luther hit upon a rather obvious candidate: Apollos. We met him as an associate of Paul (Acts 19:1; 1 Cor. 1:12; 3:4–22; 4:6; 16:12; Titus 3:13). In Acts 18:24–28 there is a portrait of him that sounds like a job description for the writer of Hebrews:

> Now a Jew named Apollos, a native of Alexandria, came to Ephesus. He was an eloquent man, well versed in the Scriptures. He had been instructed in the way of the Lord; and being fervent in spirit, he spoke and taught accurately the things concerning Jesus, though he knew only the baptism of John. He began to speak boldly in the synagogue; but when Priscilla and Aquila heard him, they took him and expounded to him the way of God more accurately. . . . He powerfully confuted the Jews in public, showing by the Scriptures that the Christ was Jesus.

If Apollos was the author, several of the connections of Hebrews with 1 Corinthians would make more sense, for he was associated with Corinth: the question of foods (9:10; 13:9; cf. 1 Cor. 8:1–13); the comparison of the congregation to the people in the desert (3:7—4:13; cf. 1 Cor. 10:1–13); the contrast between infants' food and that of adults (5:11–14; cf. 1 Cor. 3:1–3). Paul's concern at once to associate Apollos with himself (1 Cor. 3:5–9; 4:6), yet to distance himself from a ministry based on rhetorical skill (1 Cor. 2:1–5), would also take on a sharper edge. The suggestion that Apollos might have written a letter like Hebrews to the Corinthian congregation before Paul wrote 1 Corinthians has just enough piquancy not to be dismissed entirely. It must remain, of course, purely conjectural. Indeed, the same evidence that supports the authorship by Apollos has been used to argue that Paul's staunch co-worker who had herself instructed Apollos was the author, the ubiquitous Priscilla. Whoever the author, the writing testifies to another fine intelligence in the Christian movement's first generation.

Hebrews was composed early enough to be quoted extensively by *1 Clement,* also written to the Corinthian church, around 95 C.E. The dating is sometimes thought to depend on the question of whether such temple imagery as used by Hebrews would be plausible before the destruction of the Jerusalem temple in 70. But this is a false issue on two counts. First, the appropriation of temple imagery by dissident groups was both possible and popular long before the temple's destruction, as both Qumran and Paul have shown us. Second, Hebrews does not focus on the physical temple in Jerusalem and the cult carried on there but focuses on the idealized rule for worship described in Torah (Exodus, Leviticus, Numbers, Deuteronomy) to be carried out in the "tent in the wilderness" (cf. Exod. 25:10–40). The argument is carried not by a comparison to a stone edifice but by a literary allusion. The sermon could therefore have been written any time between the death of Jesus and 95 C.E.

HEBREWS AS A CHRISTIAN WITNESS

Because the interpretation of Jesus' work that is offered by Hebrews is so distinctive, it may be helpful to begin with those aspects of the writing that connect it to the wider Christian movement. The author twice refers to matters he presupposes but will not treat. In Heb. 2:3–4 we find something like a kerygmatic statement, which sounds much like the story line of Luke-Acts: a great salvation first declared by the Lord and attested to by those who heard him (cf. Luke 1:2), attested to by signs and wonders and powerful deeds (cf. Acts 2:43; 5:12; 2 Cor. 12:12) as well as by gifts of the Spirit (Acts 2:1–4; 1 Cor. 12:11; Eph. 4:2–7). In 6:1, the author mentions the "elementary doctrine of Christ," which he presupposes as he moves on to more mature teaching. Here is an important clue to the nature of the writing. It is preceded by the same contrast between "milk for babes" and "solid food for the mature" (5:11–14) that Paul employs in 1 Cor. 3:1–3. But whereas Paul thought the Corinthians incapable of mature teaching since they were full of rivalry and strife (1 Cor. 3:3), this author chides his hearers for their "dullness" in order to push them toward a deeper understanding, one fit for "teachers" (5:12). Hebrews does not advance an interpretation that disputes shared traditions but advances one that builds on the traditions for those able to move to greater insight.

The author lists some elements of the common tradition: repentance from dead works and faith toward God (cf. 1 Thess. 1:9); instruction about "baptisms" (plural; or, ablutions; cf. 10:22); the laying on of hands; the resurrection of the dead; the eternal judgment. Surprising in this list of rudimentary messianic doctrine is the lack of Christology, but of course, that is the author's real theme. Another conviction shared with the rest of the Christian movement, but not requiring statement, is that the Scriptures are authoritative and inspired by the Holy Spirit: "The Holy Spirit says . . ." (3:7); and "The Holy Spirit also bears witness to us, saying . . ." (10:15). This is found most emphatically in the prologue: "In many and diverse ways, God spoke of old to our fathers by the prophets . . ." (1:1).

That statement of the prologue concludes with the real focus of Hebrews: "In these last days, God has spoken to us by a Son" (1:1). The Christology of Hebrews is extraordinarily full. It contains a clear statement of the Son's preexistence (1:2; 10:5), of his incarnation (2:14–18; 10:5–7), and of his sacrificial, atoning death (1:3; 2:9; 6:6; 7:27). The resurrection of Jesus is found explicitly in 1:3 but also provides the dominating presupposition of the sermon, so much at the heart of the exposition that it requires no direct statement. Hebrews is, indeed, largely a midrashic working out of the implications of Psalm 110, the classic resurrection psalm of the Christian movement. Finally, Hebrews has a definite statement that Christ will return again for judgment (9:28; 10:25). The range and grandeur of the Christology of Hebrews is suggested by its stark, yet strangely allusive, summary: "Jesus Christ is the same, yesterday, today, and forever" (13:8).

No less substantial is the teaching of Hebrews on Christian existence. In the first place comes faith, which finds in this sermon its fullest exposition next to that in Romans. As for Paul, faith is a kind of hearing that involves trust and obedience. But Hebrews puts emphasis above all on the "enduring" quality of faith, its "fidelity" (see, above all, chaps. 11—12). Fidelity is rooted in the reliability of God's promises, enabling Christians to have hope, all the more secure because it is "anchored" in the resurrection and exaltation of Jesus (see 6:18–20). Brotherly love is also touched on (13:1) and explicated in terms of hospitality (13:2), care for prisoners (13:3), respect for marriage fidelity (13:4), and the sharing of possessions (13:16). Little is said about the internal life of communities, apart from their holding regular assemblies (10:25) and saying prayers of praise as sacrificial offerings to God (13:15). The audience is exhorted to obey and submit to its leaders (13:17). They are also told (13:7):

> Remember your leaders, those who spoke to you the word of God; consider the outcome of their life, and imitate their faith.

The "imitation of faith," in Hebrews, inevitably involves suffering. This writing emphasizes the essential connection between the life of faith and the experience of suffering, and makes it thematic (see, e.g., 5:1–10; 12:3–13).

THE ARGUMENT OF HEBREWS

Hebrews contains the longest sustained argument in the NT. One form of midrashic logic structures the sermon as a whole, so that grasping it means grasping much of the writing's essential point. We met the basic argument before, most strikingly in Rom. 5:12–21. It was used widely in the Pharisaic tradition where it probably was borrowed from Greek rhetoric. It is the argument *a minore ad maius*, "from the lesser to the greater," or, in its Hebrew form, *qal we chomer*, "the light and the heavy." Reduced to its bare bones, the argument looks like this: If such and such is the case with x, which is a small matter, then it is even more the case with y, which is a greater matter.

The argument obviously relies on analogy. As in all analogy, two things are required: an element of similarity or continuity, and an element of dissimilarity or discontinuity. In the typical midrashic application of the argument, we find God's way with Israel compared to an earthly king's way with his people. The element of continuity is the relationship of rule and submission; that of discontinuity, the distance between God's rule over all creatures and a king's over a city. The logic then runs, If an earthly king acts such and so, how much more will the king of the universe?

The element of continuity in Hebrews is provided by the word of God spoken to his people. God spoke in the past and continues to speak in the present (1:1–2; 2:1–4; 3:5–7; 4:12–13; 7:28). The author speaks of the Christian confession as a word (6:1; 13:7), and his own discourse is such a word as well (4:13; 5:11; 13:22).

The element of discontinuity is the agent of speaking. The contrast is sharply drawn between the mediation of God's word by prophets, angels, Moses and Torah (with its cult) on the one hand, and Christ, on the other. The critical step in the argument is therefore to establish the "heavy" as opposed to the "light," the "greater" over against the "lesser." The linchpin of Hebrews is the supremacy of the word spoken through the Son of God. So, the author shows in sequence—from Torah itself—that although angels are God's ministering spirits, Jesus is God's Son (1:1–14); that although Moses was a servant within God's house (the people), Jesus is son and builder of the house (3:5–6); that the cultic acts of the Aaronic priests had to be repeated through time because of their inefficacy but that because by his resurrection he is eternal Son, the offering of Jesus endures forever (chaps. 5—10).

The Word spoken through the Son holds a greater promise and a more certain fulfillment than that spoken of old (12:22–24). The term *bebaios*, "fair, certain, reliable, sure," recurs frequently in characterizing this Word (2:2; 3:6; 6:19; 9:17; 13.9). Because the present Word is surer and more powerful, it demands a greater obedience than the word of old. Disobedience bears a greater punishment (see 2:2; 4:1–2; 6:6–8; 12:17). The logic of the argument moves toward that of exhortation. Now the contrast is between the *people in the desert* and the *people of God today.* The desert generation failed to hear and obey, so it did not enter the land of Canaan, which was the lesser "rest." The people of God today also have a "rest" promised it: the life of God into which the resurrected Jesus has entered once for all, which is the greater. This promise also demands a response of obedience, and failure will be more grievous than in the first case. Thus, the urgency of the exhortation in 4:11–13:

> Let us therefore strive to enter that rest, that no one fall by the same sort of disobedience. For the word of God is living and active, sharper than any two-edged sword, piercing to the division of soul and spirit, of joints and marrow, and discerning the thoughts and intentions of the heart. And before him no

creature is hidden, but all are open and laid bare to the eyes of him with whom we have to do.

THE SYMBOLISM OF HEBREWS

The symbolism of Hebrews is complex, deriving from a variety of traditions. The search for a perfect correspondence between one tradition and this writing is futile, for Hebrews reshapes the available symbols around the figure of a crucified and exalted Messiah. A discussion of the symbolic framework is valuable only insofar as it helps us understand that new shaping. It has recently been argued, for example, that Hebrews most resembles the thought world of the Qumran sectarians. Both there and here, we find a New Covenant community, separation from cult with appropriation of its symbols, the expectation of a priestly as well as kingly messiah, even an interest in the figure of Melchizedek. The elements of disagreement, however, are more impressive: Hebrews rejects the laws of purity and diet about which the sectarians were obsessive, has no mythic explanation for the world's division into good and evil, indeed lacks such dualism entirely. More important, the Qumran connection does not really help us grasp the author's basic conviction concerning what constitutes "the greater."

The long-standing opinion that Hebrews reflects a kind of Platonic world view is sufficiently accurate to include its author as first among the Christian Platonists of Alexandria. I use the term "world view," because by the first century, Plato's classic metaphysical theories, as expressed, for example, in the *Republic* 509D–521B, had filtered through many schools and permutations, becoming in the process as much a common consciousness as a theoretical doctrine.

In broad terms, this is a view of reality that draws a sharp distinction, indeed, a dividing line, between the *phenomenal* world, which is the realm of materiality, characterized by movement, change, and corruption—and, therefore, only partial knowledge—and the *noumenal* world, characterized by changelessness and incorruptibility because it is not material but spiritual. This is the world of pure "forms" or "ideas." The distinction is metaphysical: one realm of being is denser and more "real" than the other. It is epistemological: the world of change allows only approximate perceptions, therefore, "opinions"; but ideas can truly be "known." The distinction is also axiological: the noumenal world is "better" than the phenomenal.

That which we do not see, therefore, is more real and more worthwhile than that which can be seen. The perceived world, in fact, is only a "shadow" or "reflection" of the noumenal world. The idea of cat is finer and more real than any furry moving creature that catches mice. The two realms are related by a certain formal causality. Noumenal being is primordial; the phenomenal world is derivative. If the ideal world is the stamp, the phenomenal bears its seal. The spiritual realm is one of types; the material world has antitypes, which correspond only roughly to their ideal models.

The Platonism of Hebrews resembles that of Philo or the Book of Wisdom, a version well on its way to what is called middle Platonism, which forms a hybrid (found also in Hermetic literature) of Platonic metaphysics and Semitic cosmology as found in the Genesis creation accounts. There, the heavens *(ha shemaim)* is the realm where God dwells, and the earth *(ha aretz)* the place of human activity. A great distance lies between them: "As far as the heavens are above the earth, so great is his steadfast love for those who fear him" (Ps. 103:11); "God is in heaven, you are on earth; therefore let your words be few" (Qoh. 5:2); "Thus says the Lord, heaven is my throne and the earth is my footstool" (Isa. 66:1). In this understanding, the temple can be regarded as a place of access between the two realms: "The Lord is in his holy temple, the Lord's throne is in heaven" (Ps. 11:4).

Not a great step is required to identify the heavens with the world of forms, and the earth with the material world. Philo, for example, observes the double account of human creation in Gen. 1:26–27 and 2:7. He is innocent of source theories. He notices that the first account was "according to the divine image" and the second "from the dust of the earth." He not unnaturally sees the first creation as that of the ideal "form" of humanity and the second as its material realization. In Exod. 25:40, likewise, Philo read that Moses was told to construct a place of worship in the desert according to the pattern of what God showed him on the mountain. In Philo's Greek version (LXX), it said, ". . . according to the type [*typos*]" that Moses was shown. It followed that earthly worship was only an imperfect representation of that divine ideal or model (cf. Chap. 3, pp. 78–82).

The static, ahistorical character of Platonism has often been noted. In Philo's version, the "oracles of God" in Scripture are like the oracles at Delphi, timeless messages whose original context is not critical. God's word is spiritual and timeless but is clothed in human speech, which is temporal and changing. Human interpretation must take account, therefore, of diverse levels of meaning. The same words can at once bear a material (i.e., literal) meaning, a psychic (i.e., moral) sense, and a spiritual (i.e., allegorical) signficance. So Philo reads the exodus story at once as the literal freeing of Israel from Egypt, as a passage from vice to virtue, and as the ascent of the soul to spiritual freedom and ecstasy.

Hebrews shares not only the language of this outlook, but also some of its fundamental perceptions. The Son, for example, is said to "reflect the

glory of God and bear the very stamp of his nature" (1:3), which recalls
Wis. 7:26. The worship of priests in the tent is called a shadow and copy of
the real worship (8:5), and the authority given is the same LXX text from
Exod. 25:40 as used by Philo. The law is a shadow (*skia*) rather than the
real image (*autēn tēn eikona*) of "the good things to come" (10:1). Torah
provides "examples" that anticipate "the real" (4:11; 9:23). Jesus, for
example, enters the real tent (*skēnēs alēthinēs*) in his resurrection (8:2) and
is said to go into a sanctuary "not made by hand, a copy of the true one,
but into heaven itself" (9:24). In contrast to the repeated offerings of
earthly priests through time, his priestly act is one that is "once for all"
because it takes place in the realm of "true being," heaven.

Platonism is, however, entirely reworked by Hebrews. First, Hebrews
shows a very acute awareness of history: God spoke of old, and speaks
now, but differently. The past also serves as a type or example for the
present, which is "greater" and "more real" (see 4:11). Second, the
distinction between heaven and earth is not only cosmological, it is also
existential. "Heaven" describes God's existence and all that can participate
in it, whereas "earth" denotes merely human existence. Third, Hebrews
exalts rather than denigrates the physical. Only because Jesus was and had
a body could he be a priest. His body, furthermore, is not cast off at death
but exalted. Fourth, Hebrews emphasizes change: Christ came once and
will come again; he was, for a little while, lower than the angels but is now
exalted and enthroned. Platonism is here stretched and reshaped around
belief in a historical human savior whose death and resurrection made both
his body and time axiologically rich. Hebrews shows us what Philo might
have written had he become Christian and itself contributes to the transformation of Hellenism, which with the Christian Platonists Origen,
Clement, Athanasius, and Cyril fundamentally affected the development
of western philosophy.

THE USE OF SCRIPTURE IN HEBREWS

Hebrews quotes widely from Torah (mostly the LXX version), using the
Law, the Prophets, and the Writings. The author introduces the texts with
a variety of formulas (see, e.g., 2:5; 3:7; 4:4; 7:17). He particularly
exploits texts (e.g., Pss. 110:4 and 95:11) that have God swearing oaths,
for when God swears, a promise is doubly sure. Hebrews sometimes alters
a text to make a point. The LXX version of Ps. 40:6–8, "Sacrifices and
offerings thou hast not desired, but ears you have prepared for me,"
becomes ". . . a body you have prepared for me" (10:5), which nicely fits
the point in 10:10: "We have been sanctified through the body of Jesus
Christ once for all."

The longest citation is from Jer. 31:31–34 (in Heb. 8:8–12), which is used because it speaks of a new covenant unlike the one made in the wilderness. The author's comment: "In speaking of a new covenant, he treats the first as obsolete." Hebrews uses a variety of interpretive techniques. It follows the rule of aligning two texts in which the same word occurs so that they interpret each other (see, e.g., the use of Pss. 110:1 and 8:5–7 in Heb. 1:13 and 2:6). He sometimes makes elliptical citations, expecting his readers to catch their further implications (see, e.g., 2:12–13). Three examples illustrate the range of the author's technique and the way the scriptural interpretation carries his argument.

A Midrash on Ps. 95:7–11 (Heb. 3:7—4:13)

In this section, the author establishes his most dramatic image of existence before God, that of a pilgrimage. It stretches from the patriarchs to the present, and only in Jesus is the goal of that pilgrimage (access to God) finally accomplished. The key words from the psalm are "*today* if you hear my voice" and "as I *swore* in my wrath, they will never enter my *rest*." Here we have God speaking, and swearing, long after the event of the exodus, through David. The "today" of the psalm must, therefore, be an eternal call of God. Therefore, the word of Scripture addresses his present hearers directly. They are not to harden their hearts as the people did in the desert, for which reason God did not let them enter the "rest" of Canaan (3:19). But if God can still speak of a "today," his promise too must remain: "Therefore the promise of his rest remains" (4:1).

But what sort of "rest" could the Scripture mean? Here, the text of Gen. 2:2 provides the clue: ". . . and God rested on the seventh day from all his works." It is, then, the "Sabbath rest" of God himself (cf. Exod. 20:11) that the Scripture still extends, one the people of old did not achieve. They had entered the land, certainly, but they did not attain the rest that is God's life (4:8). The first "Jesus" (the Greek form of "Joshua") could not bring them so far; otherwise the "today if you hear his voice" would not still challenge them. Since the offer remains open, the promise must still be open as well: "So then, there remains a Sabbath rest for the people of God. For whoever enters God's rest also ceases from all his labors as God did from his" (4:9–10).

An Encomium on the Ancestors in the Faith (Heb. 11:1–40)

As in Romans 9—11, the history of the people is reread from the perspective of faith, now not the faith that justifies but the one that endures. As in the midrash of Rom. 4:1–25, Abraham appears here as the supreme example of faith among the patriarchs and matriarchs; the aspect of his faith that is stressed is its endurance even through testing. But also, Abraham exemplified the one who lived as though seeing things other men did not; he wandered homeless, yet was convinced that he was headed for a "city which has foundations, whose builder and maker is God" (11:10). In this, he showed by example how faith is "the assurance of things hoped for, the conviction of things not seen" (11:1). The term "conviction" is sometimes translated "substance" (from the Greek *hypostasis*), and it is a word with legal connotations: it is a down payment or a pledge of property. For those whose property had been plundered and who were told that they had a "better possession and an abiding one," the example of the ancestors was most pertinent. They all acted in view of what had not yet appeared (11:3, 7, 8, 13, 26–27). The repeated formula "by faith . . . by faith" has a powerful, almost hypnotic effect, culminating at last in the powerful exhortation of 12:1: "Therefore since we are surrounded by such a cloud of witnesses, let *us also* lay aside every weight and sin that clings so closely, and run with perseverance the race that is set before us." It is a stirring call to join in the pilgrimage to a heavenly homeland that was begun with Abel (11:4). The pilgrims are not to fall by the way (12:12–13).

An Allegory on Torah (Heb. 7:1–17)

Melchizedek appears only once in the narratives of Torah, when he meets Abraham after the slaughter of the kings (Gen. 14:18–22). He reappears in Ps. 110:4. The author of Hebrews is the only NT writer to read past the first verse of this resurrection psalm—"The Lord said to my Lord, sit at my right hand"—to find "The Lord has sworn and will not repent, you are a priest forever according to the order of Melchizedek" (Ps. 110:4). The author finds in this evidence that the resurrected Jesus is not only a kingly messiah—"the Lord sends forth from Zion your mighty scepter" (Ps. 110:2)—but a priestly one as well. In the light of this, he reads the story of Abraham and Melchizedek in Genesis.

Etymology is a favorite resource for allegorical interpretation. The name Melchizedek can be construed *melek-zedekah*, that is, "king of righteousness." And, since he is the king of Salem, he is also king of peace (*shalom*; Heb. 7:2). And this surely anticipates the messianic age, when "righteousness and peace shall kiss" (Ps. 85:10). Of all the important figures in Genesis, moreover, this king alone has no genealogy *(toledoth)*. But if something is not in Torah, neither is it in the world *(non in tora non in mundo)*. The author can legitimately conclude that Melchizedek had no ancestry (7:3, 6). And since Torah does not relate his death, neither did he die, "but resembling the Son of God, he continues as a priest forever" (7:3). Such an interpretation, of course, could come only from one who first knew of such a Son of God.

Abraham, moreover, gave *tithes* to Melchizedek, thereby recognizing him as "priest of God most High" (7:2, 4). But since Abraham bore the whole line of Levitical priests potentially in his loins, his gesture was, in effect, the recognition of Torah itself that the priesthood descended from Melchizedek was superior (7:6–10). A talmudic passage (Babylonian Talmud, *Nedarim* 32b) says God wanted to give the priesthood to Melchizedek, but because in his blessing he had named Abraham before God, the priesthood was taken from him and given to Abraham instead. In the citation of Ps. 110:4, the Hebrew that our letter understands as "according to the order of Melchizedek," the Talmud understood as "because of the words of Melchizedek." The psalm therefore declares that *he* is a priest, but not his descendants. Such a passage seems to respond to just the sort of use of Melchizedek that we find in Hebrews (cf. *Genesis Rabbah* 43.6–8).

THE CHRISTOLOGY OF HEBREWS

Hebrews is unusually full in its use of titles for Jesus. Many of them are traditional. The author has a predilection for the simple name Jesus, corresponding to his interest in the humanity of the Messiah (2:9; 3:1; 4:14; 6:20; 7:22; 10:19; 12:24; 13:12, 20), as well as for the simple title Christ, reflecting his interest in the messianic work (3:6, 14; 5:5; 6:1; 9:11, 14, 24, 28). He uses the combination Jesus Christ only three times, each solemn (10:10; 13:8, 21). He speaks often of the Son (1:2, 5, 8; 3:6; 5:5, 8; 7:28), as well as Son of God (4:14; 6:6; 7:3; 10:29) and Lord (1:10; 2:3; 7:14; 13:20). By implication, Hebrews also understands Jesus to be Son of man (2:6; cf. Ps. 8:4). We also find here one of the very few attributions of the title God (*theos*) to Jesus in the NT once by implication (3:4) and once by a citation (1:8, which cites Ps. 45:6–7).

Other titles in Hebrews are either unique or rare. Jesus is called an heir (1:2), the firstborn (1:6), the great shepherd of the sheep (13:20), the pioneer (2:10; 12:2), and the perfector (12:2). He is the sanctifier (2:11), the apostle (3:1), and the builder of the house (3:3). He is the cause of salvation (5:9), the forerunner (6:20), the guarantor (7:22), the minister (8:2), and the mediator (8:6; 9:15; 12:24). When viewed synoptically, these special titles illustrate two aspects of the Christology of Hebrews: Jesus is one who brings salvation from God to humanity (apostle, cause, sanctifier, shepherd, minister, builder, guarantor). He is also a human being who first reaches what all approach (heir, firstborn, pioneer, perfector, forerunner). As one who reaches from one end to the other, he is, preeminently, mediator.

Both aspects come together in the cluster of titles that are unique to this writing in the NT. Jesus is a priest (10:21), high priest (3:1; 4:14; 5:5, 10; 6:20; 7:26; 8:1; 9:11), and a merciful and faithful high priest (2:17). The priestly title, however, is everywhere associated with an imagery that is royal. The combination, of course, occurs in Ps. 110:1–4. Based on that psalm, the image of royal enthronement runs through the sermon (1:3, 8, 13; 2:5, 7, 9; 4:16; 7:1, 2; 8:1; 10:12; 12:2, 28). The Qumran sectarians and other apocalyptists expected a priestly as well as a royal messiah. For Hebrews, however, it is not descent from David that makes Jesus king, though he knows he comes from the tribe of Judah (7:14). His resurrection is the royal enthronement (1:13). This exaltation is also the completion of his priestly work that began with his death (9:11):

> But when Christ appeared as a high priest of the good things that have come, then through the greater and more perfect tent (not made with hands, that is, not of this creation), he entered once for all into the holy place, taking not the blood of goats and calves but his own blood, thus securing eternal redemption.

Priesthood and kingship are both culminated by resurrection (10:12):

> But when Christ had offered for all time a single sacrifice for sins, he sat down at the right hand of God, there to wait till his enemies be made a stool for his feet.

Death and resurrection together form the movement of Jesus to the Holy Place that is God's presence (9:23):

> Christ has entered, not into a sanctuary made with hands, a copy of the true one, but into heaven itself, now to appear before the presence of God in our behalf.

By his resurrection, Jesus enters into true being and real life. Because he continues to live as the resurrected one, his mediation of salvation is forever, once for all, the acceptable offering of humanity to God. Because this passage of a human being from death "through the veil of the flesh" into God's life is the organizing conviction of the author, the imagery of the tent and its furniture in Hebrews 8—9 becomes jumbled. It does not help to compare notes with the original in Torah, for the Christian confession stretches those symbols into almost unrecognizable forms. Precisely the confused state of the symbolism reminds us that the starting point of Hebrews, as for all the NT writings, is the paradoxical experience of a crucified and raised Messiah.

Because Jesus is priest, the Christology of Hebrews must be both "high" and "low." To offer a truly efficacious sacrifice, Jesus must be the eternal Word, the true Son of God, living "by the power of indestructible life" (7:16). But to be an effective mediator, he must be fully human as well. Thus we find the emphasis on the body of Jesus in 10:5–10, and this striking passage in 2:14–18:

> Therefore since the children share in flesh and blood, he himself partook of the same nature, that through death he might destroy him who has the power

of death, that is, the devil, and deliver all those who through fear of death were subject to life-long bondage. For surely it is not with angels that he is concerned but the children of Abraham. Therefore he had to be like his brothers in every respect that he might become a merciful and faithful high priest in the service of God, to make expiation for the people. For because he himself has suffered and been tempted, he is able to help those who are tempted.

From the side of God, he was a "merciful" priest; from the side of humans, he was "faithful."

The last line of the previous citation leads us to the most profound aspect of the Christology of Hebrews. The God-man Jesus was not a fleshly puppet worked by a divine *logos*. He was a full human being, who, because of his human response to God, was "made perfect" (5:7–10):

In the days of his flesh, Jesus offered up prayers and supplications, with loud cries and tears, to him who was able to save him from death, and was heard for his godly fear. Although he was a son, he learned obedience through what he suffered, and being made perfect, he became source of eternal salvation to all who obey him, being designated by God a high priest after the order of Melchizedek.

It is not certain that this passage shows awareness of the Synoptic Gospels' Passion accounts. It is clear that for Hebrews, Jesus' obedience is fully human and demands of him suffering. Indeed, the obedience itself is a form of suffering. From it Jesus learns ever more fully what it means to be a son. The author here plays on a commonplace of Hellenistic education: "Learning is suffering [*emathen, epathen*]."

As human, therefore, Jesus progressively became obedient son. He progressively moved by faith toward the God who called him. His perfection (maturity) as son was not a given, but was wrought in him by obedient faith. The humanity of Jesus was a continual opening to God. His death appeared to be a final closing of all possibility, but it was in reality (to the eyes of faith) the definitive opening of his whole being (body and spirit) to the presence of God. He stepped through the veil of the flesh into the Holy Place. The significance for those whose human lot Jesus shared totally, apart from sin, is that every human is thus capable of being perfected. The "capacity for God" which has been placed in humans by their creation according to God's image has been realized in a single and specific human being who has shown the way:

Consider Jesus, the apostle and high priest of our confession—he was faithful to him who appointed him. (3:1–2) . . . Being made perfect, he became source of eternal salvation. (5:9)

The Christology of Hebrews therefore also becomes the basis for its exhortation. At first, the insistence on God's discipline of those he loves in

12:5–11 appears jejune, or even a throwback to the moral insensitivity of Job's friends. Only when we remember one of the nuances of the word "discipline," *paideia*, in Greek, do we grasp the depth of the exhortation. The RSV translation says, "It is for discipline you have to endure." But what Hebrews means is, "Endure for the sake of an education [*eis paideian hypomenete*]" (12:7). Discipline is not punishment but an "education." The human experience of suffering shapes Christians in the pattern of him who "learned to be son" from what he suffered. It is the process of learning to become children of God, as Jesus was his Son. His is the way they are to go. He is the scout who plotted the path. He is also the "finisher" who gives them power to follow after. If they remain faithful as he did, then they will attain a full share in the inheritance he as heir (1:4) has obtained for them (Heb. 12:1–3):

> Therefore since we are surrounded by such a cloud of witnesses, let us also lay aside every weight and sin which clings so closely, and let us run with perseverance the race that is set before us, looking to Jesus, the pioneer and perfecter of our faith, who for the joy that was set before him, endured the cross, despising the shame, and is seated at the right hand of the throne of God.

BIBLIOGRAPHICAL NOTE

Hebrews has much good English-language scholarship devoted to it. The following studies represent a sample. For some discussion of authorship, destination, and the like, see T. W. Manson, *The Problem of the Epistle to the Hebrews* (Manchester: Manchester Univ. Press, 1949); F. F. Bruce, "'To the Hebrews,' or 'To the Essenes,'" *NTS* 9 (1962): 217–32; B. P. Hunt, "The Epistle to the Hebrews: An Anti-Judaic Treatise?" *SE* 2 (1964): 408–10; R. Hoppin, *Priscilla, Author of the Epistle to the Hebrews* (New York: Exposition Press, 1969); and C. P. Anderson, "The Epistle to the Hebrews and the Pauline Letter Collection," *HTR* 59 (1966): 429–38.

For genre and argument, see J. Swetnam, "On the Literary Genre of the 'Epistle' to the Hebrews," *NovT* 11 (1969): 261–69; idem, "Form and Content in Heb 1—6," *Bib* 53 (1972): 368–85; C. Mackay, "The Argument of Hebrews," *Church Quarterly Review* 168 (1967): 325–38.

On the general background are F. LoBue, "The Historical Background of the Epistle to the Hebrews," *JBL* 75 (1956): 52–57; C. J. A. Hickling, "John and Hebrews: the Background of Hebrews 2:10–18," *NTS* 29 (1983): 112–16. The Hellenistic aspects of Hebrews are emphasized by R. Williamson, "Platonism and Hebrews," *SJT* 16 (1963): 415–24; idem, *Philo and the Epistle to the Hebrews* (Leiden: E. J. Brill, 1970); J. W. Thompson, *The Beginnings of Christian Philosophy: The Epistle to the Hebrews*, CBQMS 13 (Washington, D.C.: Catholic Biblical Assn. of America, 1982). The symbolic world of Gnosticism and the anthropos myth are vigorously exploited by E. Käsemann, *The Wandering People of God: An*

Investigation of the Letter to the Hebrews, trans. R. A. Harrisville and I. L. Sandberg (Minneapolis: Augsburg Pub. House, 1984 [1957]). The connection to Qumran's symbols is pursued by F. C. Fensham, "Hebrews and Qumran," *Neotestamentica* 5 (1971): 9–21; and M. DeJonge and A. S. van der Woude, "11Q Mechizedek and the New Testament," *NTS* 12 (1965–66): 318–26.

The use of Scripture in Hebrews is analyzed by F. L. Horton, *The Melchizedek Tradition* (Cambridge: At the Univ. Press, 1976); A. T. Hanson, "Christ in the Old Testament According to Hebrews," *SE* 2 (1964): 393–407; F. Howard, "Hebrews and the Old Testament Quotations," *NovT* 10 (1968): 208–16; J. Fitzmyer, " 'Now This Melchizedek . . .' Heb 7:1," *CBQ* 25 (1963): 305–21; J. C. McCullough, "The Old Testament Quotations in Hebrews," *NTS* 26 (1980): 363–79; G. Hughes, *Hebrews and Hermeneutics*, SNTSMS 36 (Cambridge: At the Univ. Press, 1979).

For various thematic aspects to the letter and the treatment of specific passages, see F. F. Bruce, "The Kerygma of Hebrews," *Int* 23 (1969): 3–19; M. R. D'Angelo, *Moses in the Letter to the Hebrews*, SBLDS 42 (Chico, Calif.: Scholars Press, 1979); D. Worley, *God's Faithfulness to Promise: The Hortatory Use of Commissive Language in Hebrews* (Diss., Yale Univ., 1981). Worley's analysis of the possession language in Hebrews particularly influenced the reading in this chapter. See also C. K. Barrett, "The Eschatology of the Epistle to the Hebrews," in *The Background of the New Testament and Its Eschatology*, ed. D. Daube and W. D. Davies (Cambridge: At the Univ. Press, 1964), 363–93; J. Schaefer, "The Relationship between Priestly and Servant Messianism in the Epistle to the Hebrews," *CBQ* 30 (1968): 359–89; W. E. Brooks, "The Perpetuity of Christ's Sacrifice in the Epistle to the Hebrews," *JBL* 89 (1970): 205–14; A. J. B. Higgins, "The Priestly Messiah," *NTS* 13 (1966): 211–39; A. MacNeil, *The Christology of the Epistle to the Hebrews* (Chicago: Univ. of Chicago Press, 1914); D. Peterson, *Hebrews and Perfection*, SNTSMS 47 (Cambridge: At the Univ. Press, 1982); N. A. Dahl, " 'A New and More Perfect Way': The Approach to God According to Hebrews," *Int* 5 (1951): 401–12; H. Koester, " 'Outside the Camp,' Heb 13:9–14," *HTR* 55 (1962): 299–315; J. W. Thompson, " 'Outside the Camp': A Study of Hebrews 13:9–14," *CBQ* 40 (1978): 53–63; F. Filson, *"Yesterday": A Study of Hebrews in the Light of Ch. 13* (London: SCM Press, 1967); W. G. Johnson, "The Pilgrimage Motif in the Book of Hebrews," *JBL* 97 (1978): 239–51.

Lacking a first-rate critical commentary that incorporates all the research into the world of Hebrews done over the past decades, the older commentaries of B. F. Westcott, *The Epistle to the Hebrews* (London: Macmillan & Co., 1889), and J. Moffatt, *Epistle to the Hebrews*, ICC (Edinburgh: T. & T. Clark, 1924), still offer good insight into the language. G. W. Buchanan, *To the Hebrews*, Anchor Bible (Garden City, N.Y.: Doubleday & Co., 1972), has the merit of independence and close attention to the midrashic character of the letter, but it is far too one-sided in its reading. The commentaries of H. Montefiore, *A Commentary on the Epistle to the Hebrews*, HNTC (New York: Harper & Row, 1964), and F. F. Bruce, *The Epistle to the Hebrews*, NICNT (Grand Rapids: Wm. B. Eerdmans, 1964), are both reliable and readable.

21

1 Peter

First peter's place in the canon undoubtedly owes something to its attribution to the apostle who walked with Jesus and witnessed his resurrection. But since other writings bearing the same apostle's name did not enter the canon (*The Gospel of Peter, Apocalypse of Peter*), a greater reason is this letter's intrinsic quality. Martin Luther included it among the NT writings that "show thee Christ" (*German Bible*, 1522).

Our problem in understanding Hebrews was in coming to grips with the reshaping of a complex symbolic world so apparently different that its shared traditions were not immediately visible. First Peter presents the opposite problem. So much does it share common traditions that at first reading its distinctive voice can be missed. Here is a writing much like Paul's but equally like James's, yet claiming to come from Peter. The fact that another letter in the canon is also attributed to Peter (2 Peter) does not help, for its appearance is so drastically different as to raise more questions than it answers. The real character of 1 Peter yields only to repeated and careful reading, but in the space here available, certain critical questions can emerge from the description of the text itself.

LITERARY FORM AND RELATIONSHIPS

First Peter has the appearance of a real letter. Because of its heavy use of baptismal imagery, some have concluded that it originated in a paschal liturgy or even a baptismal ritual. It has also been considered a homily preached (on Psalm 34) at the occasion of baptism. Only the homily suggestion has real merit. Whatever its antecedents, 1 Peter bears the marks of a genuine piece of correspondence.

The greeting (1:1–2) is classic. The addressees are "exiles of the Dispersion [Diaspora]" and also the "elect." They live in the provinces of Pontus, Galatia, Cappadocia, Asia, and Bithynia. This is, then, a general letter. We do not expect to learn from it of local circumstances. The odd geographical sequence of provinces may indicate the route of delivery. The author identifies himself simply as Peter an apostle of Jesus Christ (1:1). He later calls himself a "fellow elder and witness of [or, to] the sufferings of Christ" (5:1).

A blessing formula, "Blessed be God" (1:3–9), follows the greeting (cf. 2 Cor. 1:3–7; Eph. 1:3–14). First Peter's style makes the exact determination of transitions difficult, but the blessing is followed by a statement (1:10–12), which leads to the body of the letter (1:13). The author's careful use of connectives throughout the letter makes it a fairly seamless fabric. The repetition of "I exhort"—the first time to all the readers (2:11), the second time to the leaders (5:1)—is probably of greater structural significance than the frequently observed transition in 4:11–12. The final remarks in 5:12–14 are brief but tell us something of the author's circumstances. He sends greetings from the "fellow-elect sister" in "Babylon," which probably means the church at Rome (cf. Rev. 17:1, 5). He has with him Mark, whom he calls "my son" (5:13), and he is writing "through Silvanus" (5:12). He characterizes his writing as one that "exhorts and bears witness that this is the true grace of God" (5:13).

However straightforwardly the letter presents itself, its origin and authorship are not entirely clear. An ancient tradition associates a Mark with Peter in Rome (see Eusebius *Ecclesiastical History* II.14–15). Mark is, of course, one of the most common names in the Roman Empire. Still, the only Mark we know in the NT is the cousin of Barnabas, an on again, off again companion of Paul (cf. Acts 15:37; Col. 4:10; Phlm. 24; 2 Tim. 4:11). How did he become a companion of Peter? We also know something of a Silvanus (or Silas). He began as a delegate of the Jerusalem church (Acts 15:22–24) and after Paul and Barnabas split (over Mark!), he became Paul's co-worker in the European ministry (Acts 15:40), part of the time with Timothy (Acts 17:14–15; 18:5). With them, he helped evangelize Corinth (2 Cor. 1:19). He co-sponsored the two Thessalonian letters (1 Thess. 1:1; 2 Thess. 1:1). Silvanus is part of the *Pauline* mission.

The connection to Pauline Christianity does not appear to be simply a matter of names. It has been said that if the letter did not claim to be from Peter, no one would doubt it came from Paul. What supports this (over-) assertion? The dense midrash of 1 Pet. 2:4–10 uses the same Scripture texts as Rom. 9:25–33. Language such as in the phrases "die to sin and live to righteousness" (2:24; cf. Rom. 6:2, 11) and "put to death in the flesh, but alive in the spirit" (3:18; cf. Rom. 6:10; Eph. 2:18) and "Jesus Christ, who has gone into heaven, and is at the right hand of God, with angels, authorities, and powers subject to him" (3:22; cf. Phil. 2:10–11; Col. 2:15; Eph. 1:20–21) certainly seems to echo Paul. So does the description of gifts in 4:10–11 (cf. Rom. 12:3–8). Despite these sometimes striking resemblances, however, Peter gives such language his own distinctive turn.

Besides, there are even more substantive contacts with the Letter of James. Among many small points, there is the remarkable parallelism in the discussion of "faith tested by trials" in 1 Pet. 1:6–8 and James 1:2–4 (though cf. Rom. 5:1–5). Even more impressive is 1 Pet. 5:5–9, in which there is a point-by-point correspondence to James 4:6–10, down to the identical citation from Prov. 3:34.

Do such literary similarities and parallels demand the hypothesis of literary dependency? Some scholars think so. They have either James or Peter dependent on Paul, then one dependent on the other. In such theories the concept of authorship tends to be very mechanical. First Peter is also thereby pushed well beyond the point of possible Petrine authorship, particularly if Ephesians is the Pauline letter thought to be copied and Ephesians is considered later than Paul. A more likely hypothesis, one increasingly adopted by scholars, is that Peter used liturgical, apologetic, and parenetic traditions in his composition, just as Paul and James used shared traditions when composing their letters. Thus, the concatenation of texts on the rejection of Israel (2:4–10) could be drawn by both Paul and Peter—and used somewhat differently by each—from an apologetic *testimonium*. So also with the use of liturgical and parenetic materials. First Peter need not be dependent on any Pauline writing. No conclusion can be reached on the composition's date on the basis of the traditions it uses.

The questions we have been considering obviously touch on the issue of the letter's authenticity. Could the Peter who was a follower of Jesus have written such a letter, or must we posit pseudonymity? The Greek style is sometimes thought to preclude Petrine authorship. It is spare but expressive, with a rich and sensitive use of participles, generally more subtle if less vivid than the Greek of the "typical" Pauline letter. Was such finesse within the range of the Peter we know in the Gospels? He appears there as something of a rustic, whose accent betrays his origins (Matt. 26:73). Luke goes out of his way to call him and John uneducated, common men (*agrammatoi kai idiōtai;* Acts 4:13). The issue of style is not decisive, however, for the following four reasons: (1) Acts makes a literary point by contrasting, in good Hellenistic style, the bold barbarians and the sophisticated authorities. The "Hebrew" learning of the "rulers, elders, and scribes" (Acts 4:5) is countered by the ignorant but possibly Greek-speaking Galileans. (2) As Galileans, John and Peter were, from every indication, successful small-time entrepreneurs, who would have had some command of at least marketplace Greek in order to do business. The regional accent detected in the courtyard would have had a Greek tonality if anything. (3) Peter could have improved his Greek during the years of his ministry. To deny him this capacity is cultural condescension. Two of the great English stylists of the twentieth century (Conrad and Nabokov) learned and mastered English only as adults. (4) The letter could have been dictated. The phrase "through Silvanus" (5:12) is ambiguous. It could mean simply that he was the postman. Or he could have been an amanuensis. And of Silvanus's accent we know nothing.

THE CONDITION OF THE READERS

The issues of authorship and dating hinge most of all on a decision concerning the situation to which 1 Peter was addressed. A proper assessment of that context is also necessary to appreciate the author's response. Peter speaks to his readers as if they came from a pagan background: "As obedient children, do not be conformed to the passions of your former ignorance" (1:14), and "You know that you were ransomed from the futile ways inherited from your fathers" (1:18). These remarks would ill befit those who had been observers of Torah! Peter also applies Hos. 2:10 to them: "Once you were no people, but now you are God's people" (2:10). Converts from Judaism, furthermore, would not need the reminder, "Let none of you suffer as a murderer, or a thief, or a wrongdoer, or a mischief-maker" (4:15). Alerting his readers to the change required of them, Peter says, "The time is past for doing what the Gentiles like to do. . . . They are surprised that you do not now join them in the same wild profligacy" (4:3; note the "no longer," *mēketi*, in 4:2). The statement has some ambiguity. Peter associates his readers with a pagan past of debauchery; on the other hand, "Gentiles" now offer a contrast to the Christians' own new identity. We will learn the reason for this soon.

If his readers are largely of gentile origin, however, we hit upon another problem for the attribution of Petrine authorship. In Paul's version of the Jerusalem Council, Paul was to preach to Gentiles, and *Peter to the circumcised* (Gal. 2:8). Why then would he be writing to gentile Christians? There are some indications that Peter's ministry was extensive (cf. Gal. 2:11–12; 1 Cor. 1:12; 9:4), and the tradition of his sojourn in Rome is solid. A circular letter to gentile churches from Peter in Rome may be surprising, but it is not impossible (cf. also Acts 10–15).

The believers to whom Peter writes are clearly undergoing some sort of suffering. "Various trials" are testing their faith (1:6). They are being "spoken against" as evildoers (2:12). They may "endure pain while suffering unjustly" (2:19); they may be abused and reviled and suffer (3:16). They are not to return "evil for evil or reviling for reviling, but on the contrary, bless . . ." (3:9; cf. Rom. 12:14). Even if they suffer for righteousness' sake, they will be blessed (3:14; cf. Matt. 5:10). They should not be surprised at the "fiery ordeal" they are experiencing (4:12). They "share Christ's sufferings" (4:13); they are "reproached for the name of Christ" (4:14); they may "suffer as a Christian" (4:16).

The fact of their suffering is clear, the nature of it is disputed. Some scholars take the expressions "for the name of Christ," *en onomati Christou* (4:14), and "as a Christian," *hōs Christianos* (4:16), as indicating an organized state persecution such as that carried out by Pliny the Younger in Bithynia (see 1:1) under Trajan (ca. 112). In fact, Pliny's letter to Trajan asks whether Christians should be punished for "the name itself" (*Letters* X.96) or only if they are guilty of other crimes as well. In such an imperial or otherwise state-sponsored persecution, Christians were forced to choose between Christ and death. Since the first such persecution was the local one in Rome under Nero, and we know of none in the East until Domitian (93–96), and since Peter was killed in Rome under Nero (64–68), the implications of this construal for both dating and authorship are obvious. The letter would date at the earliest from the end of the first century, and Peter the apostle could not have written it.

Taken as a whole, however, the letter does not support the hypothesis of a state persecution to the death. Apart from the "fiery ordeal," *pyrōsis*, in 4:12, which may well pick up the image of fire from 1:7 (*dia pyros*), the author's depiction of the believers' suffering points to a context of social ostracism. Except for the term "suffering," *paschō* (2:19–20; 3:14, 17; 4:15, 19; 5:10), the terms used suggest verbal rather than physical attacks: "speaking against" (or, "slandering," *katalaleō*, 11:24; 3:16), "insulting," *epēreazō* (3:16), "reproaching," *oneidizō* (4:14), and "reviling," *loidoreō* (2:23; 3:9). They are certainly experiencing hostility. The possibility of random local mob action cannot be excluded. But such was the lot of Jews everywhere in the Diaspora, and of Christians from the beginning (see Acts 18:12–17; 19:23–40; 1 Thess. 2:14; 2 Cor. 12:24). Those who insist on an identity that distinguishes them from others are liable at once to be admired and reviled, just as they themselves are both attracted to and repelled by the dominant social ethos. In 1 Peter, we find the internal stress experienced by intentional communities within a pluralistic context.

This perception is supported further by the nature of Peter's response. There is in this letter no trace of a martyr piety—a seeking of death in imitation of Jesus—or apocalypticism, both frequently stimulated by persecution. Christians are told, rather, to avoid conflict by their exemplary behavior (2:12). The presupposition is that such a tactic will be effective. Peter therefore assumes the reasonableness and essential good will of the outsiders. Members of the communities should be prepared to offer a reasoned account (*apologia*) of their convictions, with gentleness and reverence, "to anyone asking of you an account" (3:15). This does not suggest a formal hearing before a judge, but a response to the individuals who are reviling them. There is the hope that the Christians' good behavior "will put them to shame" (3:16).

Peter's attitude toward civil authority is utterly incompatible with a situation of state persecution. Civil government is, to say the least, viewed positively. We read in 2:13–14, 17:

> Be subject for the Lord's sake to every human institution, whether it be the emperor as supreme, or to governors as sent by him to punish those who do wrong and praise those who do right. . . . Honor the emperor.

This is not the description of the anti-Christ! While Christians were being killed simply for being Christians, one could not claim the government was "punishing those who do wrong and praising those who do right."

Suffering is no less real, however, for its not leading to death. Persecution and martyrdom, after all, have a certain clarity and comfort. Lines of allegiance are obvious. However painful the choice, it need be made only once. But scorn and contempt are slow-working acids that corrode individual and communal identity. Social alienation is not a trivial form of suffering. Persecution may bring death, but with meaning. Societal scorn can threaten meaning itself, which is a more subtle form of death. In the face of outside hostility or contempt, intentional communities can ordinarily preserve their distinctive identity only by portraying the outsiders as essentially and irredeemably evil. It is remarkable, therefore, that Peter advocates such an open attitude toward the larger society. Its reasonableness and openness to persuasion is assumed. It need only be shown that the Christian way is harmless. Peter's outlook may not be realistic, but it is refreshing.

THE FORM OF CHRISTIAN IDENTITY

Peter does not attack the outsiders. Instead, he calls his readers to a renewed sense of their own distinctive identity. I will touch on three aspects of his teaching: the basis of their hope in the power of God; the implications of their baptismal initiation; and the conformity of their identity to that of Jesus. Then we will look at the communal context for their new lives.

Faith and Hope in God

The opening prayer is a powerful reminder of their identity. The first period (1:3–5) is tightly structured. The complex implications of a single statement are elaborated. The statement? "God has given us a rebirth." This statement immediately implies that they live on a plane different both from their neighbors and from their own former selves. Peter goes on to state three specific implications. First, they have a "living hope." They do not share the futile fantasies of idol worshipers. Christian hope is secure because it is in a "living God," demonstrated "through the resurrection of Jesus Christ from the dead" (1:3). Second, they have by this birth come into an "inheritance." This is not the perilous gift of the land (cf. Deut. 4:38) but is "imperishable, undefiled, and unfading, kept in heaven for you" (1:4). They live in reference to a future that is already realized in the life and power of God. Third, their new life has a definite goal: the "salvation ready to be revealed in the last time" (1:5). Therefore, between their "already" (rebirth) and their "not yet" (salvation), they live in hope.

Peter immediately offers two further elements of encouragement. All of the prophecies of Scripture pointed to his readers' own time; Christians stand, therefore, within a history that continues and is legitimated by the sacred writings of Israel. Second, these writings certify that the Christians' "trials," (1:6) like those of the Messiah (1:11), will have the effect of leading—through the "refinement" of their faith—to the "salvation of their souls" (1:9). Just as Christ's sufferings led to "the subsequent glory" (1:11), so will his readers' lead to the salvation of their souls. Here is the characteristic outlook of 1 Peter: a serene confidence that what has been given is secure and what is hoped for is certain. Why? Because their entire existence is shaped by the overwhelming power of God revealed in the death and resurrection of Jesus: "Through him you have confidence in God, who raised him from the dead and gave him glory, so that your faith and hope are in God" (1:21–22).

Baptism

What happened in Jesus extends to all Christians: "He himself bore our sins in his body on the tree, that we might die to sin and live to righteousness. By his wounds you have been healed" (2:24). The power of Jesus' resurrection, in fact, has cosmic extension. Peter says, "This is why the gospel was preached even to the dead, that though judged in the flesh like men, they might live in the spirit like God" (4:6). But how could the gospel be preached to the dead? The statement is intelligible only by reference to 3:18–22: when Christ was made alive in the spirit, he went and preached to the "spirits" in prison—people who in the past had not obeyed God, all the way back to the days of Noah (3:20). The passage is notoriously obscure and appears to depend on the mythology elaborated in apocalyptic literature on the basis of Gen. 6:1–4 (cf., e.g., *1 Enoch* 10.5–15; 15.10–12; 18.15—19.1; 22.4). First Peter suggests a mass of unredeemed people who waited in captivity for God's definitive salvation. Because of their disobedience, they are farthest removed from God's presence. Yet, even they are touched by the power of resurrection life. Jesus' Spirit can reach across the deepest spiritual alienation, even into the prison of damnation, and save. From such a seed sprouts the apostolic conviction that "he descended into hell."

This mythic account, we notice, is fitted between two kerygmatic fragments. The *assertion* of universal salvation is framed by the *confession* of God's power manifest in Jesus' resurrection (3:18, 21–22):

> Christ died to sins once for all, the righteous for the unrighteous, that he might bring us to God, being put to death in the flesh but made alive in the spirit. . . .
>
> . . . through the resurrection of Jesus Christ who has gone into heaven, and is at the right hand of God, with angels, authorities, and powers, subject to him.

One more aspect of the passage calls for attention. Eight persons in Noah's time were "saved through water" (3:20). This seems somewhat odd, since in Genesis, the water destroyed, while it was the ark that saved (Gen. 7:17). The image, however, is governed by its immediate application, wherein water serves as an instrument: "Baptism, which corresponds to this, now saves you . . . through the resurrection of Jesus Christ" (3:21). The power of God released in the resurrection of Jesus and extending to all creation reaches also to these new believers through the ritual of Baptism.

Throughout 1 Peter we see an emphasis on the immediacy of the readers' experience of a transition from the past to the present (1:12), a stress on the now of their new identity (see 1:21; 2:10, 25; 3:21). Baptism is one moment in this transition from one state of identity to another, a transition that Peter calls rebirth (1:23). Its most extended treatment is in 1:22—2:3:

> Having purified your souls by your obedience to the truth for a sincere love of the brethren, love one another earnestly from the heart. You have been born anew, not of perishable seed but imperishable, through the living and abiding word of God. For all flesh is grass, and all its glory like the flower of the grass. The grass withers and the flower fades, but the word of the Lord abides forever. This is the good news which was preached to you. So put away all malice and guile and insincerity and envy and all slander. Like newborn babes, long for the pure spiritual milk, that by it you may grow up to salvation, for you have tasted the kindness of the Lord.

Here, obedience to the gospel proclamation and the ritual of Baptism are brought together as the pivotal experience of "rebirth" into a new identity. Peter's readers have been "purified" (1:22) and "reborn" (1:23). They have and should continue to "put off" their old qualities as one puts off clothing. Since they are only babes and have yet to grow into maturity, the pure spiritual milk (*logikon adolon gala*) is appropriate food (cf. 1 Cor. 3:1–3; Heb. 5:11–14). The allusion to Ps. 34:8 in 2:3 contains a deliberate pun. The Greek reads, "Taste and see that [or, because] the Lord is sweet [*chrēstos*]." The messianist sees here in Scripture the plain statement: "The Lord is *Christ*." The syntax of the verse is such that two construals are possible. Either the "guileless milk of the word" is to be the basis of their growth "in it," or Jesus himself is to be: they have tasted, now they can grow up "in him." In either case, the transformation before them is one that will shape them according to the pattern of Jesus as found already in the Scripture.

Imitation of the Suffering Jesus

The Christology of 1 Peter is in two ways closely tied to the experience of the believers. First is its affirmation of a personal love for Christ. Even love for God is rarely mentioned in the NT (cf. Matt. 22:37; Mark 12:30; Luke 10:27; Rom. 8:28; 1 Cor. 2:9; 8:3; 2 Tim. 4:8; Jas. 1:12; 2:5). Only in the Fourth Gospel (14:23–24; 21:15–16), however, do we find the equivalent personal response to the Messiah: "Without having seen him you love him; though you do not see him, you believe in him with unutterable and exalted joy" (1:8).

Second, Jesus is consistently portrayed as one who suffers (1:10, 19; 3:18; 4:1), just as they suffer. When Christians suffer, they share in his suffering (4:13). Jesus also left them an example (*hypogramma*) of his suffering, so that they might "follow in his footsteps" (2:21). Indeed, to this role they have been "called" (2:21). They are not called to replicate his death; there is no martyr piety in 1 Peter. Rather, they are to imitate the *manner of his endurance* before his death. They may have to suffer even though they have done nothing wrong (2:19). They can therefore look to Jesus, for when he suffered, he had "committed no sin; no guile was found on his lips" (2:22). And this was the manner of his suffering (2:23):

> When he was reviled, he did not revile in return; when he suffered, he did not threaten; but he trusted to him who judges justly.

Therefore, when *they* are reviled, they should not revile in return but bless (3:9) and place their trust in God (1:21). In this description of Jesus, we see once more the pervasive influence of the passage about the suffering servant, in Isa. 53:4–9, on the early Christian ethos. And although this passage is formally directed to those who are household servants (*oiketai*; 2:18), it is clear that the attitudes of patient endurance, submission, and fidelity contained in the image of the servant are intended to be ideals for the whole community.

THE CHURCH AS GOD'S HOUSE

First Peter has no elaborate church order. Ministries of speech and service are exercised according to the "gift of God" (4:9–11). Elders are instructed by their "fellow elder" (5:1), to "tend their flock" willingly. They are not to be domineering but to be "examples to the flock" (5:3). The flock image is extended by 5:4: "When the chief shepherd is manifested you will receive the unfading crown of glory" (cf. 2:25: "You were straying like sheep but have now returned to the shepherd and guardian [bishop] of your souls").

In the biblical tradition, the flock is an image for the people Israel (2 Sam. 5:2; Ezek. 34:12; Isa. 40:11; Jer. 31:10). One of the most distinctive aspects of this letter is its identification of *gentile* believers with Israel. The addressees are called "exiles of the Diaspora" and "elect" (1:1); they are to conduct their lives in fear "throughout the time of exile" (1:17); they are "aliens and exiles" (2:11). The scattered gentile Christians are the spiritual equivalent of the Jewish Diaspora. Diaspora was defined by contrast to the homeland, Palestine. From what are these gentile believers exiled? Their alien condition consists not in their geographical location or even, as recently suggested, in their social status, but in the stance they adopt toward the world. Wherever they live, they are not "at home," for they are fundamentally defined by their relationship to God. Their inheritance *(klēronomia)* is "kept in heaven for them" (1:4; cf. Heb. 13:14; Phil. 3:20). Christians live within the world but are not completely defined by it. They refuse to grow comfortable within its structures. They are called by one who transcends the world's measure. In this sense, the gentile Christians inherit the attributes of Diaspora Judaism.

First Peter sees no tension between believing and unbelieving Jews; the sort of historical tension that characterizes Romans 9—11 is not found in this letter. For the first time in the NT, we can speak accurately of the consciousness of a "new Israel." This is shown dramatically in 2:9–10, where Peter applies the most treasured epithets of Israel directly to gentile Christians. *They* are now the "chosen race" (cf. Isa. 43:20; Deut. 7:6; 10:15), the "royal priesthood" (cf. Exod. 19:6), "God's own people" (cf. Exod. 19:5; Isa. 43:21). The Gentiles have been called out of darkness (cf. Isa. 9:2), have now received mercy and become God's people (cf. Hos. 2:23).

The Christian community also appropriates to itself the image of the temple. It is a "house of the Spirit" where "spiritual offerings" are made to God (2:4–5). No less complexly than in Eph. 2:19–22, the church is here portrayed as a living place of worship built up on the "cornerstone" of Jesus. Rejected by men, he has been made a "living stone" by God (2:4, 7–8). Although with regard to the world these believers are aliens and exiles, they have a home in God's creation: they are the house built by the Spirit of the living Lord.

The image of a spiritual house wherein prayers are offered to God "through Jesus Christ" (2:5) corresponds to that of the household of God *(oikos tou thou)* that consists of those who believe the "gospel of God" (4:17). Peter provides a list of duties for this household (2:13—3:7). He begins with submission to the emperor, who was regarded as the paterfamilias or head of the extended household that was the empire (cf. Rom. 13:1), and to other civil authorities. We see at once the motivation that runs through these directives. Like the Jews of the Diaspora, Christians must show by their good behavior and domestic order that they are not dangerous—strange, perhaps, but not a threat to the social fabric.

Peter turns next to the attitudes of slaves (2:18–25), but he has no corresponding exhortation for masters. This could be an indication of the social status of many believers, but it could also be due to the author's desire that everyone in the community cultivate the attitudes of domestic servants (oiketai) within the "household of God," by following in the footsteps of Christ. Characteristically, women are to prefer internal to external adornment, and to obey their own husbands (not all men); their attention to male preachers should not be able to be seen as a threat to the family structure. Husbands, in turn, are to regard their wives as "fellow sharers in the gift of life" (3:5–7).

The household duties, though, are basically outward looking, a way for the Christian Diaspora to disarm its critics. The truer norm for its internal life is the concept of holiness, which also corresponds to the notion of a spiritual temple. Christians are measured not by the standards of others but by the one who called them and gave them their new identity: "As he who called you is holy, be holy yourselves in all your conduct, since it is written, 'You shall be holy, for I am holy' [Lev. 11:45]" (1 Pet. 1:15–16). That the church should be characterized by holiness was axiomatic in the Christian movement (cf. 1 Thess. 4:3; 1 Cor. 6:9–11; 2 Tim. 1:9). Christians could not adapt themselves completely to the world. Since they were always "called by God" and always "purified by the word of truth," they would always be different. Even in the "house of God," therefore, they were not totally at home, but remained "in exile," waiting for him who was to appear (1:7) and the salvation of their souls (1:9). They could maintain the tension in confidence and hope (1:21), knowing (1 Pet. 5:10) that

> after you have suffered a little while, the God of all grace, who has called you to his eternal glory in Christ, will himself restore, establish, and strengthen you. To him be the dominion forever. Amen.

BIBLIOGRAPHICAL NOTE

A survey of the NT data on Peter can be found in R. E. Brown, et al., *Peter in the New Testament: A Collaborative Assessment by Protestant and Roman Catholic Scholars* (Minneapolis: Augsburg Pub. House, 1973). Recent literature is summarized in J. H. Elliott, "The Rehabilitation of an Exegetical Stepchild: 1 Peter in Recent Research," *JBL* 95 (1976): 243–54. Idem, *A Home for the Homeless: A Sociological Exegesis of 1 Peter* (Philadelphia: Fortress Press, 1981), updates the literature further, and engages in a close examination of the social setting of 1 Peter in an analysis different from the one sketched in this chapter. Somewhat older general statements on 1 Peter that retain their value are those by C. F. D. Moule, "The Nature and Purpose of 1 Peter," *NTS* 3 (1956–57): 1–11; and W. C. Van Unnik, "Christianity According to 1 Peter," *ExpTim* 68 (1956–57): 79–83.

The possible liturgical background to the letter is explored by F. L. Cross, *1 Peter a Paschal Liturgy* (London: A. R. Mowbray & Co., 1971); A. R. C. Leaney, "1 Peter and the Passover: An Interpretation," *NTS* 10 (1963–64): 238–51; and T. C. G. Thornton, "1 Peter, A Paschal Liturgy?" *JTS* 12 (1961): 14–26.

On the possibility of Peter the apostle's knowing good enough Greek to write such a letter, see generally J. N. Sevenster, *Do You Know Greek?* NovTSup 19 (Leiden: E. J. Brill, 1968). The dependency approach to this letter's literary relations is suggested by C. L. Mitton, "The Relationship Between I Peter and Ephesians," *JTS* 1 (1950): 67–73; and J. Coutts, "Ephesians 1:3–14 and I Peter 1:3–12," *NTS* 3 (1956–57): 115–127. An approach closer to mine is found in P. Carrington, *The Primitive Christian Catechism* (Cambridge: At the Univ. Press, 1940); A. C. Sundberg, "On Testimonies," *NovT* 3 (1959): 268–81; and B. Lindars, "Books of Testimonies," *ExpTim* 75 (1963–64): 173–75. For the relation of 1 Peter to the gospel tradition, see R. H. Gundry, " 'Verba Christi' in I Peter: Their Implications Concerning the Authorship of I Peter and the Authenticity of the Gospel Tradition," *NTS* 13 (1966–67): 336–50; and E. Best, "I Peter and the Gospel Tradition," *NTS* 16 (1970): 95–113.

Some significant thematic aspects of the letter are treated in F. Filson, "Partakers with Christ: Suffering in I Peter," *Int* 9 (1955): 400–412; J. Knox, "Pliny and I Peter: A Note on I Pet 4:4–16 and 3:15," *JBL* 72 (1973): 187–89; E. G. Selwyn, "Eschatology in I Peter," in *The Background of the New Testament and Its Eschatology,* ed. D. Daube and W. D. Davies (Cambridge: At the Univ. Press, 1954), 394–401; J. H. Elliott, *The Elect and the Holy,* NovTSup 12 (Leiden: E. J. Brill, 1966); C. F. D. Moule, "Sanctuary and Sacrifice in the Church of the New Testament," *JTS* 1 (1950): 29–41; F. H. Agnew, "I Peter 1:2: An Alternative Translation," *CBQ* 45 (1983): 68–73; W. C. Van Unnik, "The Teaching of Good Works in I Peter," *NTS* 1 (1954): 92–110; W. J. Dalton, *Christ's Proclamation to the Spirits,* AB 23 (Rome: Biblical Inst. Press, 1965); B. Reicke, *The Disobedient Spirits and Christian Baptism* (Copenhagen: Munksgaard, 1946); H. Vorgrimler, "The Significance of Christ's Descent Into Hell," *Concilium* 11 (1965): 147–59; D. L. Balch, *Let Wives Be Submissive: The Domestic Code in I Peter,* SBLMS 26 (Chico, Calif: Scholars Press, 1981); and J. H. Elliott, "Backward and Forward in His Steps " in *Discipleship in the New Testament,* ed. F. Segovia (Philadelphia: Fortress Press, 1985), 184–209.

The commentary of F. W. Beare, *The First Epistle of Peter* (Oxford: Basil Blackwell, 1947) reads the letter as a late pseudonymous composition, but has some good notes on the text. Much more conservative is E. G. Selwyn, *The First Epistle of Saint Peter* (London: Macmillan & Co., 1958), most noteworthy for its fine appendixes. Readable and accessible are the newer commentaries by J. N. D. Kelly, *A Commentary on the Epistles of Peter and Jude,* HNTC (New York: Harper & Row, 1969), and E. Best, *I Peter,* NCB (Grand Rapids: Wm. B. Eerdmans; London: Oliphants, 1971).

22

2 Peter and Jude

THE SECOND LETTER OF PETER AND THE LETTER OF JUDE ARE STEP-
children in the NT canon, disliked when not disowned. Even those who
claim them do not rank them in a list of favorite NT writings. They are
seldom read and less often studied. Since there is almost surely a literary
connection between them, they are also invariably joined together, so that
even their distinctive ways of bearing a common witness are obscured.

They are most vigorously detested by those who see in them the
exemplification of "early Catholicism." They contain nothing about
church order, but most of the other themes that are typically associated
with a second-generation "decline" in Christianity are found in them: faith
not as existential response but as the shared belief of the community (2
Pet. 1:1, 5; Jude 3, 20); tradition as the transmission of a body of truth (2
Pet. 2:21; Jude 3); salvation as present possession more than future hope
(2 Pet. 3:15; Jude 3); God and Christ regarded almost exclusively as Savior
(2 Pet. 1:1, 11; 2:20; 3:2, 18; Jude 25); deviation from community norms
as a serious offense (2 Pet. 2:17–22; Jude 12–16); eschatology reduced to a
defense of the second coming (2 Pet. 3:4–13). This portrait is, of course, a
stereotype. Many of the same features are found in the earliest Christian
writings, and the qualities of Jude and 2 Peter are not so easily reduced to
formula. The list shows, however, that for these letters ignorance and
animus walk in step.

In truth, the letters are not easy to read. They are not, first of all,
pleasant reading, since they consist in large part of polemic and threat
against unsavory characters. Neither are they easy to understand. In broad
terms, they are simple enough: both defend the common heritage against
distortion and corruption. But they presuppose in their allusions traditions no longer fully available to us. Reading them requires a greater
cryptographic ability than is needed for other parts of the NT. Their
allusiveness is only exacerbated by their relative isolation within the NT
collection. They are clearly related to each other. Their connections to
other traditions are less easy to determine.

THE DOCUMENTS TOGETHER

The two letters are joined by the sharing of a substantial amount of material. Jude is much the shorter, consisting almost entirely in polemic. Much of Jude's material is also found in 2 Peter 2, altered and fitted within quite a different kind of letter. Was Jude written first and later incorporated into 2 Peter? Or was there dependence in the other direction, with Jude being an abbreviated version of 2 Peter 2? Despite the obvious points of contact between them, however, even the shared material is not used in an identical way, and there is the third possibility that they independently employed a common source. Most scholars think that there is a direct literary dependence, with the direction going from Jude to 2 Peter 2. Once that is said, little is learned therefrom about either writing. Each has its own voice, and Jude in particular is done a disservice by being reduced to the level of a source for 2 Peter.

Pseudonymity is generally asserted or assumed for both letters. The implications are clearly much weightier in the case of 2 Peter, since another letter attributed to Peter is also in the canon. A few scholars still support the attribution to "Simeon Peter, a servant and apostle of Jesus Christ" (2 Pet. 1:1) for both Petrine epistles. They point to 2 Pet. 3:1, which explicitly states that this is the second letter written "by way of reminder" to the readers. They observe that the autobiographical elements in 2 Peter (esp. in 1:1; 13–18) are so explicit that if it is not authentic the letter must be considered either a deliberate forgery or a transparent and presumably harmless fiction. They note the few thematic connections between the two letters, such as the role of prophecy in Scripture (2 Pet. 1:19–21; 1 Pet. 1:10–12) and the rescue of Noah from the flood (2 Pet. 2:5; 1 Pet. 3:20–21). Finally, they argue that the dissimilarity in the style of the letters could be due to the use of an amanuensis in 1 Peter (see 5:12).

The two Petrine letters have, however, so many and such great differences that a majority of scholars conclude that they come from different authors; and if not a necessary conclusion, this certainly seems plausible. Barring an amanuensis, the styles are significantly different. The Greek of 1 Peter is clear and direct; that of 2 Peter is convoluted and deliberately arcane in its vocabulary. More difficult are the several indications that 2 Peter is only fictionally written from within the first generation. The author speaks of "all the letters" of "our beloved brother Paul," and whereas the second phrase might be used by Peter, the first would be very unlikely, presuming as it does a Pauline collection of some sort. These letters, furthermore, are given the status of "the other Scriptures," and a history of interpretation and misinterpretation of them is presupposed. (3:15–16). The reference to the predictions made by Jesus and "your apostles" is also somewhat strange if this is itself written by an apostle

(3:2). Part of the problem addressed by this letter is caused by a lapse of time since those predictions sufficient to create doubts about their fulfillment. The phrase "since the fathers fell asleep" (3:4) need not refer to the first Christian generation, but it may; it certainly indicates the lapse of some time. The term "your apostles" in the mouth of Peter can be explained, but with some difficulty. Finally, the two letters have a different outlook. In the face of revilement from the outside, 1 Peter offered comfort but also the exhortation to be open to outsiders. Second Peter fights deviance within the community caused by teachers seeking their prey among "unsteady souls" (2:14). In response, 2 Peter is as bellicose as 1 Peter is irenic.

The letter closest in tone and outlook to 2 Peter is, of course, Jude. This has led to the hypothesis that the "first letter" referred to in 2 Peter 3:1 was really Jude. In fact, Jude 3 can be read as though a longer exhortation on "our common salvation" was interrupted by the pressing need to deal with troublemakers. In this theory, then, Jude was sent off as a stopgap response to a crisis, then had its material incorporated as chapter 2 of the longer treatment that had been planned from the start. The hypothesis is clever and complicated. It requires a confusion in attribution very early in the manuscript tradition. It also demands that 2 Peter and Jude both address fundamentally the same problem; and that may be to demand too much. The theory does remind us that we know so little about these writers and their relationships that we cannot be overly confident about who wrote them when.

The claim that Jude is pseudonymous is even less illuminating. The author is a "brother of James" and a "servant of Jesus Christ" (v. 1). His readers apparently knew which James this was, but we do not. Was it James "the brother of the Lord" (Gal. 1:19; 2:9) or James the son of Alpheus (Matt. 10:3; Mark 3:18) or James the Son of Zebedee (Matt. 4:21; Mark 1:19)? Was this Jude, then, himself the "brother of the Lord" (Matt. 13:55; Mark 6:3) or the apostle "Jude the son of James" (Luke 6:16; Acts 1:13; John 14:22)? There is, of course, no way of knowing. There is also no way to date the letter accurately. There is nothing about Jude that would prohibit its being a letter written by a follower of Jesus in Palestine during the first generation of the Christian movement. It was probably written before 2 Peter, whose date is equally uncertain. Certainly 2 Peter is one of the last of the NT writings to be composed, but it could well have been written before the end of the first century.

Both letters are usually included among the General Epistles, signifying that they were written for a broader readership than that of a specific community. The designation may not be accurate for either. Unlike James and 1 Peter, these letters simply do not identify their audience. But it is possible that each of them was written for a specific community.

JUDE

Despite the amount of space it devotes to polemic, Jude is not a direct attack on opponents. It is, rather, a letter of exhortation *(parakalōn)* to those who are "called" (v. 1) and "beloved" (vv. 1, 3, 17, 20), to struggle for *(epagōnizesthai)* the faith, "once for all delivered to the saints" (v. 3). Several components of a parenetic letter can be spotted. The author "reminds" his readers of what they already know (v. 5) but also calls them to "remember" (v. 17) both the apostolic words that predicted the troubles they now face and the examples *(deigma)* that Scripture provides of how wicked people are always punished by God (v. 7). These examples all point to the present situation (vv. 8, 10, 12, 16, 19). After characterizing the opponents, however, Jude twice turns to his readers, "but you, beloved" (vv. 17, 20), exhorting them to have attitudes opposite those of the opponents.

Jude does not lack literary grace. The repetition, " . . . these are the ones . . . [*houtoi eisin*]" (vv. 8, 10, 12, 16, 19), is rhetorically effective. A pleasing play on the concept of keeping (using both *tēreo* and *phylassō*) runs through the letter. The addressees are those God has "kept for Jesus Christ" (v. 1). The wicked angels did not "keep" their place and were punished by being "kept" in chains (v. 6). In similar fashion, the "nether gloom of darkness" is being "kept" for contemporary rebels (v. 13). The readers are to "keep" themselves in the love of God (v. 21). And God is the one who can "keep" them from falling (v. 24).

The identity of those disturbing the community is particularly hard to determine because of the stereotypical polemic. All opponents, we have by now learned, are pleasure seekers (vv. 7–8) and braggarts (v. 16), arrogant (v. 10), rapacious (vv. 11, 16), driven by desires (v. 16), and given to nastiness (v. 4). There is no indication in this letter of false teachers or of a specific doctrine supporting the immoral behavior. The closest thing to a doctrinal comment says that some ungodly people have sneaked in (cf. Gal. 2:4) and are "perverting grace into licentiousness" and "denying our only Master and Lord, Jesus Christ" (v. 4). The contemporary reader conditioned by Paul's letters may be tempted to understand perverting grace as involving a theological position, but it could also be simply a matter of behavior: the ungodly "twist the gift by licentiousness." The "denial" of the "Master and Lord" does not represent a christological position but, as in Titus 1:16, stands for a practical rejection. As ancient sinners did, so do these ungodly ones reject authority *(kyriotēta;* v. 8). They deny the implications of an allegiance to God and Christ by their faithlessness, arrogance, and rebellion.

The specific injury they do the church appears in their behavior at love feasts, in a way that is left unclear, except that they apparently have a very good time (v. 12). The phrase "looking after themselves" (v. 12) translates "shepherding themselves," which could mean either that they were themselves church leaders, or that they refused any guidance from authority. Otherwise, they are malcontent (v. 16) and, not surprisingly, divisive (v. 19). So inconsistent is their behavior with the life guided by the Spirit that Jude calls them "worldly people [*psychikoi*], not having the Spirit" (v. 19).

Jude's outrage is obvious. He wants to protect the church's "most holy faith" (v. 20). His readers can be comforted by the fact that the rebellious are already experiencing the consequences of their immoral behavior (v. 10) and they will surely also be punished like those God repaid in the past. Such were they who came out of Egypt but were destroyed for their faithlessness (v. 5; cf. 1 Cor. 10:1–13; Heb. 3:7—4:13). The angels (undoubtedly those of Gen. 6:1–4 and *1 Enoch*) were punished for not holding their proper place (v. 6). The cities of Sodom and Gomorrah combined lust with the breaking of natural boundaries (v. 7).

Jude's reference to the dispute between Michael and the devil over the body of Moses does not appear in Torah, but seems to come from an apocryphal work called the *Assumption of Moses*. The point of the reference is the "reviling speech" practiced by the opponents. Since they "walk in the way of Cain," we surmise that they are envious (cf. Gen. 4:5 LXX; 1 John 3:12). Because they are like Balaam in their desire for gain (Num. 22:7; 31:16), we know that they are avaricious. Since they also "perish in Korah's rebellion" (Num. 16:3–50), we know that they are arrogant and defiant of authority.

The symbols used by Jude derive from an apocalyptic context. In addition to the use of the *Assumption of Moses*, we find a direct citation from *1 Enoch* 1.9 (in vv. 14–15). The author obviously regarded him "who lived in the seventh generation after Adam" (cf. *1 Enoch* 60.8) as an inspired prophet (cf. Gen. 5:24; Heb. 11:5) and his writing as Scripture. He reminds his readers as well of Christian apocalyptic sayings, "the things said beforehand by the apostles of our Lord Jesus Christ": "In the last time there will be scoffers, following their own ungodly passions" (v. 17). The closest we come again to such a statement in the NT writings is in 2 Pet. 3:3 and 2 Tim. 3:2–5.

The troublemakers are rootless and spiritually wandering (vv. 12–13). In contrast, Jude wants his readers to root themselves in the "common salvation" (v. 3). They are to be "built up" in the most holy faith. They are, in contrast to those who have not the Spirit, to "pray in the Holy Spirit." They are to "keep" the love of God and wait for the mercy of the Lord Jesus (vv. 20–21). They are, in short, to stand fast, just as God will enable them to do (v. 24). While they maintain the integrity of their Christian identity, avoiding even the hint of corruption ("the garment spotted by the flesh"), they are also to reach out to those whom they might help (vv. 22–23):

> Convince some, who doubt; save some, by snatching them out of the fire; on some have mercy with fear.

If Jude is a limited witness, his witness is nevertheless honest and forceful, and perhaps a healthy reminder of the uses of outrage in the face of corruption.

2 PETER

The distinctive voice of 2 Peter can be detected immediately in the use he makes of the material he shares with Jude in chapter 2. In contrast to Jude, the moral condemnation here definitely serves as a polemic against false teachers, who propagate destructive doctrines (2:1). Peter also has a wordplay that shows his preoccupation throughout this section. His adversaries teach "destructive heresies," but they themselves are heading toward "destruction." Jude left the judgment of God largely implicit in his polemic, but it is this element that 2 Peter makes explicit and emphatic. His redaction is clear in 2:3: the opponents exploit others with false words, but the Scripture will show ("from of old") that their "destruction has not been asleep."

In the recitation of examples, we find that Peter stresses not the angels' rebellion but the fact that God did not spare them (2:4). A figure lacking in Jude is introduced in 2:5: Noah shows that God saves the righteous even while the ungodly are being destroyed. Lot shows the same thing. Jude saw only the evil cities. Peter shows us Lot "vexed in his righteous soul" and saved (2:7–8). Both figures appear as examples of eschatological judgment also in Luke 17:26–32. Peter wants to show that the divine judgment is both real and discriminate: the wicked are punished and the righteous saved (2:9).

After 2:10, much of the polemic matches Jude closely, but the distinctive Petrine touch is found in the donkey's voice (cf. Num. 22:21–35) by which Balaam was "rebuked for his own transgression" (2:16) and in the description of the opponents as teachers. They are trying to seduce the newly converted by promising them freedom (2:18). What sort of freedom? It appears that they offer a life free from the threat of God's presence and power. They deny the divine retribution. People can live as they please, for God is powerless to respond. Licentiousness now is joined to theory; practical atheism ("the fool says in his heart there is no God," Ps. 14:1) is linked to an intellectual posture claiming God's impotence to judge the world.

Peter closes in on the self-deception. This vaunted freedom is really a slavery to corruption (2:19). Christians who follow the false teachers end up worse off than when they were pagans (2:20). Before they converted, after all, they were ignorant. But once they have come to the knowledge of "our Lord and Savior," their apostasy is knowing and willful, and a denial of their own experience (2:21). Their supposed leap to freedom is in reality a habituated compulsion like that which drives dogs to eat their vomit (2:22).

Peter's use of this polemical material reveals both his situation and his method. A theoretical doctrine is now supporting the disruption of the newly converted. False teachers proselytize among the naive. Peter must not only slander them but he must also show their intellectual pretensions to be empty. He does this by showing from the scriptural examples how God's judgment was effective in the past, and that it was a judgment that responded to the actions of human beings: the good were rewarded and the evil punished. The clear implication is that he and his readers have to do with the living God, one for whom human actions are real and important. The point will be made even more explicit in the chapters that frame this middle section.

The Defense of God's Judgment
(2 Peter 3)

Peter now answers the intellectual challenge of the opponents. Not merely the delay of the Parousia (3:3–4) is at issue. The opponents question whether God judges at all. Both experience and reason, they claim, show that everything continues as it has from the beginning (3:4). Implied is a world outside the power of God. Peter says that they have forgotten already the point of his scriptural examples (3:5), which show God judging and punishing the wicked. Peter's argument in 3:5–7 depends on the validity of the scriptural witness as well, but with a deeper theological connection. First, the world we inhabit is not independent or accidental. It is created by God's word, that is by God's freedom and power (3:5). Second, the very stuff of its making (i.e., water) can be used by God for destruction, as the Genesis story of the flood shows (3:6). Third, the same word of God remains with power to judge those who scorn it. The judgment last time was by water; next time it will be by fire (3:7; cf. 3:10, 12). God's power to judge is defended on the basis of Scripture, experience, and reason. The rationalists are wrong; God is the source of all reality and continues to shape the world in accordance with his freedom. We are not on our own.

Peter turns next to the deficiency in the theological imagination of the opponents. They think of God and humans in univocal terms. God, however, cannot be "tardy," for temporal categories do not apply to divinity (3:8). If we as temporal creatures cannot avoid thinking in temporal terms, we must at least qualify our conclusions by a reminder of the qualitative distance between God and us. His measure is not ours (3:8). Even if the time seems long to us, the judgment is no less sure. Indeed, as the tradition knows, "the day of the Lord will come like a thief" (3:10; cf. Matt. 24:43; Luke 12:39; 1 Thess. 5:2; Rev. 3:3), and when it does, then there will certainly be judgment. Then, those whose only hope is in this world will find their hope dissolve with the world, in fire (3:10, 12).

Peter's argument makes sense not as a comfort to those dismayed at the delay of Jesus' second coming—there is no hint of that—but as a defense against rationalists who, for a life of "freedom," deny God's rule. Second Peter is fundamentally a Christian theodicy. On the basis of Scripture and logic, Peter shows that the "scorning of Lordship" (2:1) leads to a corrupt life that also calls down on itself the very judgment it denies.

The debate here resembles that in Hellenistic philosophy between upholders of divine providence (such as the Stoics) and its deniers (such as the Epicureans). Among Jewish sects, the Epicurean position was associated with the Sadducees, while the Pharisees represented the defense of God's providence. The intellectual component in this discussion derives from those roots rather than from a christological heresy or theosophical position like Gnosticism. Behind the question of providence of course is the complex issue of creation and of the relation between God and the world. It is a debate with surprisingly contemporary relevance.

Peter's point, however, is not first of all an abstract one but one about "what sort of persons ought you to be" (3:11). Those who see the world as contingent and dependent on God live in reference to that reality, in "holiness and godliness." So Peter wants them to remain "stable" in the face of the skeptics (3:17) and to grow in the knowledge of "our Lord and Savior Jesus Christ" (3:18). He interprets the apparent delay of God's wrath in traditional Jewish terms, as a sign that the living God is also loving, and has forbearance. God wants humans to repent (3:9). His delay is a gift of freedom enabling them to choose either life or death. In this connection, we find Peter's fascinating reference to "all Paul's letters." The theme of God's forbearance scarcely dominates the letters we know, but Peter's essential point here is found in the letter known to the Roman church, Romans 2:3–6. As Peter puts it, the lack of punishment of the wicked within our experience is not a sign of divine impotence but mercy: "Count the forbearance of the Lord as salvation" (3:15).

Literary Form

Second Peter has been characterized as a farewell discourse in epistolary form. Thus, we see the aged apostle shortly before his death (1:14). He prepares his followers for what will happen "after his departure" (1:15).

The emergence of false teachers (2:1) will alert them to the fact that these are the "last days," when such opponents were prophesied to arise (3:2–3). In the face of opposition, the faithful are to hold to the teaching that comes from him and are not to be seduced by dangerous novelty (1:12, 20–21). The proper understanding of the tradition is therefore critical, including the proper interpretation of Scripture. Scripture is the source of truth—and the basis of Peter's argument—but it must be interpreted in accordance with the Spirit who inspired it, and that Spirit is active in the church's tradition (1:19–21). Since Paul's writings also are regarded as Scripture, the same care must be taken not to misinterpret them (3:16).

Within the testamentary form, the credentials of the writer to speak authoritatively for the tradition are important. Second Peter's use of the transfiguration story (1:16–18) known to us from the Synoptic Gospels (Matt. 17:1–8; Mark 9:2–8; Luke 9:28–36) has precisely this certifying function. Whether the writer is a fictional Peter or not, he asserts a connection to an eyewitness account of the revelation of Jesus as God's beloved son. What is important is the claim to an experience of God's revelation, and its being rooted in the gospel story; this is the authoritative basis for the interpretation of Scripture. In contrast to the "cleverly concocted myths" (1:16) that are the sign of "false prophets" (2:1), this writer claims a share in the very story of God's personal involvement with the world, which he then proceeds to argue in chapters 2 and 3: "We have the prophetic word made more secure" (2:1).

Peter can be read as such a farewell discourse. In terms of its form and function, however, it is more accurately called a parenetic letter, because of its deliberate use of memory, models, and maxims (see above, chap. 19, pp. 391–92). In the author's statement of purpose in 1:12–15, we see that he wishes to *remind* his readers of the truth they already know. He wants to *arouse them* by way of a *reminder.* In 3:1–2, again, he stirs them to *remembrance* in order that they might *remember* the prophetic witness. In contrast, we note, the false teachers *forget* their past experience of forgiveness (1:9). They *forget* (RSV: "ignore") the punishment of the flood (3:5). Peter wants his readers not to *forget* but to remember (3:8). Peter's list of scriptural stories that illustrate God's judgment obviously functions paradigmatically, to provide negative and positive *models*, a point he makes explicit in 2:6: "He made them an example [*hypodeigma*] to those who were to be ungodly." As for maxims, these are succinctly stated in the exhortation with which the author begins (1:5–7):

Supplement your faith with virtue
and virtue with self-control
and self control with steadfastness
and steadfastness with godliness
and godliness with brotherly affection
and brotherly affection with love.

BIBLIOGRAPHICAL NOTE

The rather dismal state of scholarship on these two letters can be indicated briefly by the curt and dismissive treatment of Jude in W. G. Kümmel, *Introduction to the New Testament*, rev. ed., trans. H. C. Kee (Nashville: Abingdon Press, 1975), 425–29. D. J. Rowston, "The Most Neglected Book in the New Testament," *NTS* 21 (1974–75): 554–63, does little to reverse the situation.

For an attempt to place Jude at a specific time and place in second-century Egypt, see J. J. Gunther, "The Alexandrian Epistle of Jude," *NTS* 30 (1984): 549–62; for Jude as antiheretical polemic, see F. Wisse, "The Epistle of Jude in the History of Heresiology," in *Essays in the Nag-Hammadi Texts in Honor of Alexander Böhlig*, ed. M. Krause (Leiden: E. J. Brill, 1972), 133–43.

The use of apocalyptic materials by Jude is examined by C. D. Osburn, "The Christological Use of I Enoch 1:9 in Jude 14–15," *NTS* 23 (1976–77): 334–41; idem, "I Enoch 80:2–8 (67:5–7) and Jude 12–13," *CBQ* 47 (1985): 296–303. Jude's use of the *Assumption/Testament of Moses* is thoroughly analyzed by R. J. Bauckham, *Jude, 2 Peter*, Word Biblical Commentary (Waco, Tex: Word Books, 1983), 65–76.

Individual textual problems are considered by M. Black, "Critical and Exegetical Notes on Three New Testament Texts: Heb. xi, 11, Jude 5, James 1, 27," in *Apophoreta*, ed. W. Eltester, BZNW 30 (Berlin: Töpelmann, 1964), 39–45; E. E. Kellett, "Note on Jude 5," *ExpTim* 15 (1904–5): 381; A Wikgren, "Some Problems in Jude 5," in *Studies in the History and Text of the New Testament in Honor of Kenneth Willis Clark*, ed. B. L. Daniels and J. M. Suggs, SD 29 (Salt Lake City: Univ. of Utah Press., 1967), 147–52; G. H. Boobyer, "The Verbs in Jude 11," *NTS* 5 (1958–59): 45–47; C. D. Osburn, "The Text of Jude 22–23," *ZNW* 63 (1972): 139–44.

The connections of 2 Peter to 1 Peter are considered by G. H. Boobyer, "The Indebtedness of 2 Peter on 1 Peter," in *New Testament Essays in Honor of T. W. Manson*, ed. A. J. B. Higgins (Manchester: Manchester Univ. Press, 1959), 34–53; and W. J. Dalton, "The Interpretation of 1 Pet. 3:19 and 4:6: Light from 2 Peter," *Bib* 60 (1979): 547–55. The link to Jude is vigorously and cleverly argued by J. A. T. Robinson in *Redating the New Testament* (Philadelphia: Westminster Press, 1976), 140–99.

One of the few published monographs on 2 Peter in English is T. Fornberg, *An Early Church in a Pluralistic Society: A Study of 2 Peter*, ConBNT 9 (Lund: C. W. K. Gleerup, 1977). The best studies on this letter are J. H. Neyrey, "The Apologetic Use of the Transfiguration in 2 Pet. 1:16–21," *CBQ* 42 (1980): 504–19; and esp. idem, "The Form and Background of the Polemic in 2 Peter," *JBL* 99 (1980): 407–31, to which my treatment of 2 Peter is indebted.

For other individual points, see G. Vermes, "The Story of Balaam in the Scripture: Origin of Haggadah," in *Scripture and Tradition in Judaism*, SPB 4 (Leiden: E. J. Brill, 1961), 127–77; A. B. Kolenkow, "The Genre Testament and Forecasts of the Future in the Hellenistic Jewish Milieu," *Journal for the Study of Judaism* 6 (1975): 57–71; H. C. C. Cavallin, "The False Teachers of 2 Peter as Pseudo-Prophets," *NovT* 21 (1979): 263–70; and F. W. Danker, "2 Peter 1: A Solemn Decree," *CBQ* 40 (1978): 64–82.

For 2 Peter as the quintessential example of "early Catholicism," see

E. Käsemann, "An Apologia for Primitive Christian Eschatology," in his *Essays on New Testament Themes* (Philadelphia: Fortress Press, 1982; London: SCM Press, 1964), 169–95; and C. H. Talbert, "II Peter and the Delay of the Parousia," *VC* 20 (1966): 137–45.

For a recent scholarly commentary with full bibliography and a close reading of the text, see Bauckham, *Jude, 2 Peter* (see above); as in the case of 1 Peter, the commentary of J. N. D. Kelly, *The Epistles of Peter and Jude*, HNTC (New York: Harper & Row, 1969) is reliable.

23

The Letter of James

THE LETTER OF JAMES STILL SUFFERS FROM THE MARGINAL STATUS GIVEN IT
by the Protestant Reformation. Martin Luther did not include it among
the "chief proper books." In comparison with them, he thought it a "right
strawy epistle." Since it contained "many a good saying," however, it could
be read with profit (*German Bible*, 1522). Luther disliked James because
he thought it contradicted Paul's teaching on faith righteousness (in 2:14–
26) and because it did not have any "gospel character," that is, did not
"show thee Christ."

Luther's view was not that of the early church, which regarded James as
a powerful moral exhortation. Its late formal canonization in some areas
was due not to concern about its content but to doubts about its apostolic
origins. The influential critics of the nineteenth century Tübingen school,
however, adopted Luther's view with a vengeance. They saw this letter as
epitomizing the Judaizing opposition to Paul's gospel of freedom from
Torah, sponsored by James, the "brother of the Lord" (cf. Gal. 2:12; Acts
15:1). Although such an interpretation is rarely advanced today, James
continues to be studied almost entirely in terms of its relationship with
Paul. This is doubly unfortunate. It unfairly makes Paul the sole criterion
of canonical acceptability, and it disastrously reduces the significance of
James to a few misunderstood verses. Those who have managed to read
James on its own terms discover in it a writing of rare vigor and life, which
interprets the "faith of our Lord Jesus Christ of glory" (2:1) in a manner
both distinctive and compelling.

LITERARY FORM AND RELATIONS

We know little about the circumstances of the composition. The author
is a "servant of God and of Jesus Christ" (1:1), sufficiently well known to
be recognizable even by such a modest designation (cf. Jude 1), whether
the "brother of the Lord" (Mark 6:3; Gal. 1:19; 2:9; 1 Cor. 15:7; Acts
12:17; 15:13; 21:18) or another James of the first generation (Mark 15:40;

Luke 6:15–16; Acts 1:13; Matt. 10:3) or someone writing pseudonymously. We simply cannot know which is the case. The Greek is a
generally good Koine, with some Semitisms but also some ambitions
toward artistry. James uses some rather rare vocabulary as well as the
rhetorical techniques of assonance and alliteration. A few small details
suggest a Palestinian (1:1; 5:17–18) or at least Jewish-Christian provenience (2:1–7). But like the varying depictions of the audience as (possibly) both poor and wealthy (1:9–10; 2:5–7), oppressing and oppressed
(5:1–6), persecuted (1:2–4, 12–15; 5:7–11) and belligerent (4:1–2), such
evidence is difficult to weigh, for the author is less likely to be reflecting
local circumstances or crises than employing literary allusions or *topoi* (see,
e.g., 3:13—4:10).

An argument for the pseudonymity of the letter usually depends on the
Hellenistic character of the writing—meaning its good Greek and its
knowledge of Greek literary and philosophical turns—which presumably
would place it late and outside Palestine. A second basis for supposing
pseudonymity is James's presumed knowledge of Paul's teaching, reflected
in the discussion of faith and works in 2:14–26. The first point does not
have merit. A first-generation Christian in Palestine could write good
Greek and know something of the commonplaces of Greek rhetoric and
philosophy. The Pauline connection, furthermore, is less certain than is
sometimes supposed. The combination "faith and works" is otherwise
known to us, it is true, only in Paul. But then we do not know all of the
earliest Christian writings nor all the positions of first-century Judaism.
And it is at least possible that this writing could have stimulated the
Pauline combination rather than the reverse. But these observations still
miss the mark, for they allow the presumption to stand that James and
Paul were addressing the same topic. They were not. In Paul, the contrast
between faith and works was one between the faith in and of Jesus, as a
soteriological principle, and the observance of the commandments of
Torah, with its promise of life. The contrast in James is one that was
common among Hellenistic moral philosophers, between speech and action (cf. Epictetus II.1.31; II.9.21; III.22.9; Dio *Oration* 35.2). James
decries a merely verbal profession of faith that fails to be lived out in
appropriate behavior. The Paul who called for "faith working through
love" (Gal. 5:6) would certainly agree. In James, it is faith itself that
works, not faith that is abandoned in favor of human achievement. The
Pauline connection does not therefore help us place James. This writing
could be the earliest of all the Christian compositions, penned by the
brother of Jesus, or it could be one of the latest of the canonical witnesses,
written pseudonymously by a teacher (see 3:1) concerned about the misuse
of misunderstood Pauline slogans. It is certainly not a monument to a
Judaizing movement. It represents a form of Christian self-understanding

neither Pauline nor anti-Pauline but uniquely its own, with its spiritual heir to be the form of Christian writing usually called apostolic, namely, *1 Clement* and the *Shepherd of Hermas*.

The epistolary character of James is restricted to its greeting, addressed to the "twelve tribes of the Dispersion" (1:1). As in 1 Pet. 1:1–2, the designation seems to refer less to the readers' ethnic background or geographical distribution than to their being heirs to the traditions of Torah. The greeting also suggests that James is not responding to the problems of a specific community but addressing issues pertinent to a general Christian readership. James is not a real piece of correspondence but a composition fitted to the epistolary genre.

Neither does James, like Hebrews, have the appearance of a sustained homily, even though much of it has a definite sermonic quality. It is liberal in its use of the direct address "brethren" and "beloved brethren" (1:2, 16, 19; 2:1, 5, 14; 3:1, 10; 4:11; 5:7, 9, 10, 12, 19). It also contains several essays or discourses that are relatively free-standing, such as those on faith (2:14–26), the use of the tongue (3:1–12), and envy (3:13—4:10). In them, we find stylistic features associated with the diatribe, such as the use of rhetorical questions (2:14, 21; 3:13; 4:1, 5), the presence of an imagined interlocutor (2:18–19; 4:13; 5:1), and apostrophe (4:4). These give James much of its color and life. They also remind us that, as with Paul's use of the diatribal form, we are dealing with a *teaching* instrument.

Apart from the essays, James consists mainly of short sayings and commands, which sometimes alternate with longer exhortations. Those seeking an argument in James will be disappointed, for this writing is closer to the form of Jesus' "discourses" in the Gospel of Matthew, or to the Book of Proverbs. Some of the aphorisms in James are connected by catchwords; this is similar to the arrangement of Jesus' words in the Synoptic Gospels and is particularly the case in chapter 1. The first exhortation, "Count it all joy [*charan*]" (1:2), picks up the "Greeting [*chairein*]" of 1:1. Then, the "steadfastness [*hypomonē*]" of 1:3 is linked to the "steadfastness [*hypomonē*]" of 1:4; the "lacking [*leipomai*]" in 1:4 to the "lacking [*leipomai*]" in 1:5; the "asking [*aiteō*]" in 1:5 to the "asking [*aiteō*]" in 1:6a; the "doubting [*diakrinomai*]" in 1:6a to the "doubting [*diakrinomai*]" in 1:6b.

Such a mechanical arrangement at first appears not only artificial but deficient in providing a context for interpreting specific sayings. But even a purely formal ordering of disparate sayings brings them into a greater whole and a new constellation of meaning. The teaching in James is not reducible to proposition or argument, but it was not meant to be. As in all wisdom literature, its reference is not to logic but to life. Its statements are to be tested not against their internal consistency but against their correspondence to reality.

The "structureless structure," furthermore, holds mainly for the first chapter. Isolated sayings do occur later (see 4:11–12; 5:12) but the essays dominate the rest of the composition. When the sayings of chapter 1 are examined more closely, in fact, they appear as an index to topics treated more expansively in the essays. The theme of enduring trials (1:2–4, 12–15) is developed in 5:7–11; the contrast of rich and poor (1:9–11) is treated more fully in 4:13—5:6; the proper use of the tongue (1:19–21) is greatly expanded by 3:1–12; the command to do the word (1:22–26) is enlarged by 2:14–26; the nature of true wisdom (1:5–8, 16–18) is argued by 3:13—4:10; the prayer of faith (1:6–7) is amplified by 5:12–18.

In the broadest sense, then, James is a form of moral exhortation or parenesis. The dominant mood is the imperative. The readers are reminded of what they already know and urged to act on that knowledge (see 1:3; 3:1; 4:4; 5:20). The "mirror of forgetting" in 1:23–24 at least suggests the motif of memory, so familiar in parenesis. The author presents models for his readers to emulate: Abraham (2:21–23), Rahab (2:25), Job (5:11), Elijah (5:17). These elements are not so tightly structured as in 2 Timothy, and it is more precise to call James parenesis within an epistolary format than to call it a parenetic letter.

James is one of the teachers in the NT canon, and is most fairly compared to other parenetic material—not Romans 3—5 but Romans 12—13, not Ephesians 1—3 but Ephesians 4—6, not Galatians 1—4 but Galatians 5—6. James does not develop theories but he reminds his readers of accepted truths; he does not expound theology but he exhorts to virtue. And as often in such moral teaching, the materials used by James are not necessarily specific to the messianic movement but employ the rich materials made available by the wisdom of Judaism and Hellenism alike. Parallels to the sayings in James are found not only in Torah but in the writings of Philo, the *Testaments of the Twelve Patriarchs*, and the *Sentences of Pseudo-Phocylides*, as well as in moralists like Seneca, Dio Chrysostom, and Epictetus.

But is James so traditional that it fails even to be Christian? Luther, we remember, saw no "gospel character" to it. Some scholars have suggested that James originated as a Jewish writing that was taken over with only minor editing for use by Christians. The name Jesus occurs only twice (1:1; 2:1), each time with sufficient awkwardness to make the suggestion of an interpolation at least possible. James certainly has nothing about the death and resurrection of Jesus, except by a very tortuous interpretation of 5:11. But neither does Romans 12—13. A distinction is important here. The search for what is distinctively Christian—that is, idiosyncratically Christian—should neither be identified totally with a search for Christology nor become the basis for a theological judgment of value. Too often, a subtle form of theological anti-Semitism enters these discussions, as though only what differed from Judaism was valuable in earliest Christianity. But that way lies Marcionism.

In fact, however, James has many features of a messianic sensibility, beginning with the ambiguity of his use of "Lord." The "Lord Jesus Christ" (1:1) and "Lord of glory" (2:1) certainly presume the resurrection. In other cases, James's use of "Lord" wavers tantalizingly between a theological and christological reference (see esp. 5:7–8 and 5:14–15). Other turns of language may not be exclusive to the Christian movement but are certainly comfortable within it (see, e.g., 1:16, 21; 2:7; 5:6). The most striking connection to Paul does not come in the discussion of faith and works (2:14–26) but in those touches where both Paul and James presuppose the attitudes of traditional Jewish piety (cf. Jas. 1:2–4 and Rom. 5:1–5; Jas. 2:5 and Rom. 8:28, 1 Cor. 2:9; Jas. 2:10 and Gal. 5:3). Even more impressive are the multiple points of contact with 1 Peter (Jas. 1:1 = 1 Pet. 1:1; Jas. 1:2 = 1 Pet. 1:6; Jas. 1:3 = 1 Pet. 1:7; Jas. 1:10–11 = 1 Pet. 1:24; Jas. 4:6–10 = 1 Pet. 5:5–9; Jas. 5:20 = 1 Pet. 4:8).

James's most fascinating appropriation of Christian traditions is found in his awareness and use of what we know as the gospel tradition, particularly the sayings of Jesus. The command to pray without doubting (1:5–6) is very similar to that given by Jesus (Matt. 7:7–8; Mark 11:23). The threat that "the judge stands at the door" (5:9) echoes Jesus' words in Matt. 24:33. The prohibition of oaths (5:12) is remarkably close to that spoken by Jesus (Matt. 5:34–37). The threat against rich oppressors (5:1–2) resembles the woe against the rich in Luke 6:24. Above all, James contains in 2:8 the command to love the neighbor as oneself from Lev. 19:18, which is enunciated by Jesus as well (Matt. 22:39; Mark 12:31; Luke 10:27). Many other turns of speech remind the discerning reader of the teachings of Jesus, especially those found in Matthew's Sermon on the Mount (cf. Jas. 1:22 and Matt. 7:26; Jas. 2:13–14 and Matt. 5:7, 7:21; Jas. 3:18 and Matt. 5:9; Jas. 5:17 and Luke 4:25).

In James, the experience of Jesus and the symbolic world shared with Judaism stand in a far less dialectical tension than in Paul. The term "Judaizing," however, is totally inappropriate. That term has significance only where Christ and Torah are opposed as soteriological principles. James knows nothing of that opposition. He can consequently speak naturally of the law of freedom (1:25; 2:12). He does not mean the ritual demands of Torah, but a new understanding of *all* of Torah given by the teachings of Jesus.

James makes available to Christians, first, *the wisdom tradition* of Torah not only because wisdom is thematically important (1:5; 3:13–18) but because its exhortations resemble most the practical ethical instructions found in Proverbs, Qoheleth, and Sirach—not the speculative wisdom of hypostasis and gnosis but that of practical living. James also transmits to

Christians *the prophetic tradition* of Torah. The writing contains many allusions to Hosea, Isaiah and Zechariah (see 1:9–11; 2:23; 3:18; 4:4, 8, 14; 5:2, 4), and in the call to conversion in 3:13—4:10, as well as in the condemnation of oppressors in 5:1–6, the voice is that of Isaiah and Amos. James also reinterprets Torah as law in a way unique among the NT writings and mediates *the halachic tradition* to Christians. The way he does this will be more obvious as we turn to the teaching of James.

THE PRACTICAL FAITH OF CHRISTIANS

James teaches an ethics of faith and love. The term "faith" does not carry the heavy theological weight here that it does in Paul. But neither does it mean merely an intellectual assent to divine revelation. James himself caricatures such a faith. He calls it empty and dead: "You believe that God is one; you do well. Even demons believe—and shudder" (2:19). James's own rich understanding of faith is found in the four OT figures who stand as models at the climax of three thematic developments that begin respectively in 2:1; 5:7; and 5:13. Abraham and Rahab exemplify the *works of faith* (2:23–25). Job is the model for the *endurance of faith* (5:11). Elijah provides the example for the *prayer of faith* (5:17–18).

As a moralist, James's concern is for the way people carry out in action what they profess in speech. The contrast he draws is that not between faith and law but between the empty profession of religion and its living expression. His target is the double-minded person (*dipsychos;* 1:7–8; 3:8) who claims to want one thing, God, but lives by another standard, the world's. James regards such a person as self-deluded (1:26–27):

> If anyone thinks himself religious but does not govern his tongue, he is deceiving himself and his religion is empty. Pure religion pleasing to God and the Father is this: to visit orphans and widows in their affliction, and to keep oneself unstained from the world.

And like all moralists, James asks what the "usefulness" or "profit" of convictions is if they are not put into practice (2:15):

> If a brother or sister is ill clad and in lack of daily food, and one of you says to them, "Go in peace, be warmed and filled," without giving them the things needed for the body, what does it *profit?*

It is in this framework that 2:14 must be understood: "What does it *profit*, my brethren, if a person *says* he has faith, but has not works? Can his faith save him?" For James, a faith that is not articulated in action is "empty" (2:20), as "dead" as a body lacking its spirit (2:17, 26)—no faith at all. Since faith is manifested in a person's way of acting (2:18), James declares boldly of Abraham that he was justified by his works (2:21). It is imperative, however, to read as well the next verse, for the participial phrase that follows shows exactly what sort of work James had in mind. He does not mean the observance of Torah but he means the radical obedience of *faith* itself. Scripture itself makes plain that Abraham's call to sacrifice his son Isaac was a testing of his *faith* (Gen. 22:1–19). The sacrifice of Isaac was faith in action (cf. Heb. 11:17–19). James says therefore that faith was active with Abraham's works (the Greek is clearer: "faith co-worked the works") and it was *faith* that was "perfected" by this "testing" (see 1:2–4). Faith is the subject of both parts of 2:22.

James also offers both Abraham and Rahab (cf. Heb. 11:31) as examples of how faith expresses itself in "works of mercy." The background to this allusion is the "hospitality" shown by both Abraham (Gen. 18:1–15) and Rahab (Josh. 2:1–21) when they gave shelter, food, and protection to those in need. They show how the verse that opens this section is fulfilled: "Judgment is without mercy to him who does not show mercy; but mercy conquers over judgment" (2:13). As we see in 2:16–17, it is the lack of mercy that rejects needy brethren with only an empty and ineffectual word. Such is the counterexample of "dead" and "useless" faith; speech without action. In James, faith is spelled out by endurance, prayer, and acts of mercy. What, then, is the meaning of law?

THE LAW OF LIBERTY

James sees the law of liberty (or, freedom: *eleuthēria*) as the measure of Christian identity (1:25), the norm for life, and the basis for judgment: "So speak and act as ones who will be judged by the law of freedom" (2:12). But what is this law? It includes the Decalogue, the "ten words" revealed through Moses (2:11; cf. Rom. 13:8–10). And it must be kept entire (2:10). But the law that structures the kingdom of God (2:5) is the royal law (*nomos basilikos*, 2:8); this can also be understood as the law of the kingdom and is the law of love for neighbor, which Paul calls the fulfillment of the whole law (Rom. 13:10; Gal. 5:14) and which was announced by Jesus as next to "love of God" (Matt. 19:19; 22:39; Mark 12:31; Luke 10:27). Leviticus 19:18, "You shall love your neighbor as yourself," is pivotal within James. He seems deliberately to have based some of his text on a careful reading of that commandment of Torah in its original context. When he says "If you really keep the royal law *according to the Scripture*, you do well" (2:8), he means it literally: the text of Leviticus gives guidance to the full meaning of love for neighbor. Leviticus 19:15 forbids judging with partiality; James says discrimination in judging is incompatible with faith (2:1–12). Leviticus 19:16 forbids slander and evil talk in the land; Jas. 4:11–12 does not allow evil speech against a brother. Oppression and the withholding of wages from laborers is forbidden by Lev. 19:13 as it is also by Jas. 5:4. Vengeance is interdicted by Lev. 19:18a, as Jas. 5:9 warns against holding grudges against one another. Leviticus 19:12 forbids the taking of oaths, just as Jas. 5:12 does. In Lev. 19:17, one is told to reason with a neighbor rather than hate him; Jas. 5:20 commands turning back an erring brother from his way. We notice as well that each of these negative commands in James is accompanied by an explicit mention of the law or judgment (2:9–13; 4:11; 5:9, 12).

The reading of Leviticus, however, is qualified by an understanding of life given by Jesus the Messiah. Thus the prohibition against partiality is because of its incompatibility with the faith of our Lord Jesus Christ (2:1). The prohibition of slander and judging recalls the command of Jesus in Matt. 7:1. The command not to hold a grudge stands under the imminent coming of Jesus as judge (5:8). The prohibition of oaths is found also in Jesus' mouth (Matt. 5:34–37). The ideal of fraternal correction also reflects a saying of Jesus (Matt. 18:15; Luke 17:3). We find in James, therefore, a messianic halachic midrash. The implications of the law of love are found enunciated in the text of Torah and ratified by the teaching of Jesus.

LIFE IN COMMUNITY AND WORLD

The perfection James seeks from his readers (1:4) is one not of solipsistic virtue but of faith and mercy directed to the neighbor. The neighbor is first of all the brother and sister (see 2:15) who meet together in the "assembly" (2:2). This community is aware of bearing a special name (2:7) and promise (2:5). It is called not to destroy but to build up its common identity (4:11; 5:9). The members pray for others as well as themselves (5:16). They confess sins to each other and engage in mutual correction (5:15–16, 19–20). The elders of the church are to gather at the bed of the sick person for prayer and anointing (5:14–15).

Because it uses more universal traditions, however, James also reaches beyond the enclave of the assembly to the larger world. More than other NT writings, James provides the basis for a social ethic. Religion is to be proved, for example, by the care taken for those perennially dispossessed in a patriarchal society: widows and orphans (1:27). The sick too are to receive care (5:13–16). James denies the compatibility of discrimination on the basis of social status with the identity of this community (2:1–7). He traces war and murder to their roots in envy and the insatiable desire for more pleasure and possessions and power (3:18—4:3). He calls on those doing business in the world to recognize the arrogance implicit in untrammeled entrepreneurship (4:13–17). He condemns those who for profit practice oppression, fraud, and murder (5:1–6). These principles are available, James suggests, not by contemplation of the "natural face" but of the "perfect law of liberty" (1:23–25).

FRIENDSHIP WITH THE WORLD AND GOD

The ethic in James is, moreover, in the strictest sense a theological ethic. All human activity is referred to the God who is creator, sustainer, savior, and judge. "Every good and perfect gift" comes from God (1:17). As humans were created in God's image (3:9), so have Christians been "chosen" as heirs of the kingdom (2:5) and "brought forth by the word of truth, that we should be a kind of first fruits of his creatures" (1:18). Christians have been shaped by the "truth." Therefore, they must put away all wickedness (1:21) and above all any form of deceitful or destructive speech (1:13, 19, 26; 2:16; 4:11, 16; 5:12). James considers the control of speech the hardest of all human skills (3:1–12). They, however, are to "receive the implanted word which is able to save [their] souls" (1:21).

They are not independent moral agents. They are defined by their relationship to God. James does not think in terms of virtue and vice, but he thinks in terms of "sin leading to death" (1:15; 5:20) sponsored by the devil (4:7), and of the "crown of life God has promised to those who love him" (1:12), the God who "gives more grace" (4:6). James has no Christology but is among the richest of NT writings in its theology, which is found above all in the form of warrants for right action (see 1:5, 12, 13, 16, 20, 27; 2:5, 11, 13, 19, 23; 3:9; 4:4, 6, 8, 10, 15; 5:4, 9, 10, 11, 15).

The living God alone saves and destroys (4:12), gives grace to the humble while opposing the proud (4:6), answers the prayer of individuals (1:5) and of the community (5:15), turns testing into the maturity of faith (1:2). James knows that "if we approach God, God will approach us" (4:8), because he is essentially a "Lord rich in mercy and compassion" (5:11). God is also the ultimate judge whose recompense is measured by the way humans treat each other: "Judgment is without mercy to one who has shown no mercy; yet mercy triumphs over judgment" (2:13).

Judgment is most clearly spelled out in James's attack on the oppressors. James shares with the Lukan beatitudes and woes (Luke 6:20–26) the perspective of faith: in the light of the kingdom, the poor are blessed and the rich are filled with woe (1:9–11; 2:6). In the present scheme of things, however, the rich dominate. They oppress the poor and drag them into court (2:6). They defraud their laborers by withholding their wages, and even murder them (5:1–6). James does not call for a revolt but he calls for patience and endurance like Job's (5:7–11). Why? First, because "the anger of man does not work the righteousness of God" (1:20), and second, because a reversal is certain: the oppressor will taste the misery he now brings on the poor, in "the coming of the Lord" (5:8).

James sees human behavior as flowing from a fundamental commitment of the heart. A person can choose to respond to the gift of the word (1:21), the wisdom from above (3:15) and the Spirit God made to dwell in humans (4:5), living according to the measure of the kingdom and the perfect law of freedom. Or one can choose to live by the measure of the "world," which is opposed to that of God. This measure regards the world as a closed system in which only self-seeking wins survival. It is characterized by self-aggrandizement, untrammeled desire, pleasure seeking, and above all, envy (1:14, 21; 3:14, 16; 4:1–3). In his call to conversion in 3:13—4:10, James puts this choice in the evocative language of friendship. The double-minded person who wants to be friends with everyone and live by both measures at once, must choose (4:4):

> Faithless creatures! Do you not know that friendship with the world means enmity with God? Therefore whoever wishes to be a friend of the world makes himself an enemy of God.

If the "friend of the world" lives by the measure of selfishness and envy, the "wisdom that comes from below" (3:14–16), how does the "friend of God" live? He or she imitates Abraham and lives by the perspective given by faith: "Abraham believed God and it was reckoned to him as righteousness; and he was called friend of God" (2:23). This person lives not in arrogance (4:6, 16) but in humility (4:7, 10), knowing that one's life comes not from his or her efforts but from God's gift. Such a one has the simplicity that comes from purity of heart (4:8) and seeks not selfish benefit but the fulfillment of the perfect law of freedom (2:8), love for the neighbor.

BIBLIOGRAPHICAL NOTE

A general overview of James can be found in C. E. B. Cranfield, "The Message of James," *SJT* 18 (1965): 182–93; and W. L. Knox, "The Epistle of James," *JTS* 46 (1945): 10–17.

The Pauline connection is variously pursued by J. Jeremias, "Paul and James," *ExpTim* 66 (1955): 368–71; D. O. Via, " 'The Right Strawy Epistle' Reconsidered: A Study in Biblical Ethics and Hermeneutics," *JR* 49 (1969): 253–67; and J. G. Lodge, "James and Paul at Cross-purposes? James 2:22," *Bib* 62 (1981): 195–213.

Aspects of genre and style are handled by A. Wifstrand, "Stylistic Problems in the Epistle of James and Peter," *Studia Theologica* 1 (1948): 170–82; L. G. Perdue, "Paraenesis and the Letter of James," *ZNW* 72 (1981): 241–56; P. B. R. Forbes, "The Structure of the Epistle of James," *Evangelical Quarterly* 44 (1972): 147–53; F. O. Francis, "The Form and Function of the Opening and Closing Paragraphs in the Letter of James," *ZNW* 61 (1970): 110–26.

For the relation of James to various aspects of the symbolic world, see O. J. F. Seitz, "The Relationship of the Shepherd of Hermas to the Letter of James," *JBL* 63 (1944): 131–40; M. H. Shepherd, "The Epistle of James and the Gospel of Matthew," *JBL* 75 (1956): 40–51; P. Minear, "'Yes and No': The Demand for Honesty in the Early Church," *NovT* 13 (1971): 1–13; B. R. Halson, "The Epistle of James: Christian Wisdom?" *SE* 4 (1968): 308–18; M. Gertner, "Midrashim in the New Testament," *JSS* 7 (1962): 267–92; L. T. Johnson, "The Use of Leviticus 19 in the Letter of James," *JBL* 101 (1982): 391–401; W. Wolverton, "The Double-Minded Man in the Light of Essene Psychology," *ATR* 38 (1956): 166–75; O. J. F. Seitz, "Antecedents and Significance of the Term 'Dipsychos,'" *JBL* 66 (1947): 211–19; idem, "Afterthoughts on the Term 'Dipsychos,'" *NTS* 4 (1957): 327–34; J. Marcus, "The Evil Inclination in the Epistle of James," *CBQ* 44 (1982): 606–21; and L. T. Johnson, "James 3:13—4:10 and the *Topos Peri Phthonou*," *NovT* 25 (1983): 327–47.

Studies of particular themes and passages include L. E. Elliott-Binns, "James 1:18: Creation or Redemption?" *NTS* 3 (1957): 148–61; B. Johanson, "The Definition of 'Pure Religion' in James 1:27," *ExpTim* 84 (1973): 118–19; S. Laws, "'Does Scripture Speak in Vain?': A Reconsideration of James 4:5," *NTS* 20 (1974): 210–15; L. A. Schökel, "James 5:6 and 4:6," *Bib* 54 (1973): 73–76; L. T. Johnson, "Friendship with the World/Friendship with God: A Study of Discipleship in James," in *Discipleship in the New Testament*, ed. F. Segovia (Philadelphia: Fortress Press, 1985), 166–83; M. T. Townsend, "James 4:1–14: Warning Against Zealotry?" *ExpTim* 87 (1975): 211–13; R. B. Ward, "Partiality in the Assembly," *HTR* 62 (1969): 87–97; idem, "The Works of Abraham: James 2:14–26," *HTR* 61 (1968): 283–90; J. Wilkinson, "Healing in the Epistle of James," *SJT* 24 (1971): 236–45; J. A. Kirk, "The Meaning of Wisdom in James: Examination of a Hypothesis," *NTS* 16 (1969): 24–38; and S. Laws, "The Doctrinal Basis for the Ethics of James," *SE* 7 (1973): 299–305.

The older commentaries by J. B. Mayor, *The Epistle of St. James*, 3d ed. (London: Macmillan & Co., 1913), and J. Ropes, *A Critical and Exegetical Commentary on the Epistle of St. James*, ICC (Edinburgh: T. & T. Clark, 1916), still contain much insight and a wealth of comparative material. The magisterial commentary of M. Dibelius, *James: A Commentary on the Epistle of James*, rev. H. Greeven, trans. M. A. Williams, Hermeneia (Philadelphia: Fortress Press, 1976 [1964]), has flaws but has proved enormously influential. A straightforward guide through the text is S. Laws, *A Commentary on the Epistle of James*, HNTC (San Francisco: Harper & Row, 1980).

PART SIX

THE JOHANNINE TRADITIONS

CERTAIN PERSISTENT FEATURES ARE PRESENT IN ALL THE NT WRITINGS. ALL THE writings show the impact of the religious experience and continuing societal struggles of Christian groups. They are written for churches, and they use traditions developed by communities. At the same time, none is simply a community production. The traditions are selected and shaped by creative minds. Neither Gospels nor letters conform to the grid of a collective mentality. All bear the impress of poets and prophets.

In all the NT writings, furthermore, the figure of Jesus Messiah stands in tension with the symbols employed by the community to interpret his significance for their lives. Jesus is the catalyst to reflection and its organizing principle. The symbols drawn from Torah and from the wider cultural milieu are not incidental: they are the medium of community self-understanding and communication. But knowledge of the symbolic world in all its dimensions does not lead directly to the understanding of any NT writing. In them, every symbol is reshaped by the experience of the crucified and raised Messiah and the conviction that he is the living Lord.

The writings of the Johannine tradition reflect these same tensions between community, symbolic world, and the interpretation of Jesus. So fascinating in fact are the puzzles presented by these documents that the focus of our discussion must be resolutely set from the beginning. The Johannine documents can be read for the reconstruction of the believing community that was their setting—an interesting subject but not ours. They can be studied to determine which symbols from which part of Hellenistic culture most affected these believers—a more plausible project but still not ours. They can, finally, be read as witnesses to the life of God in Jesus. This is the real subject of the writings and is our subject as well. Our way to that task will be cleared, however, by a few remarks about the other two projects I have mentioned, both of which concern the complex relationship of these writings to a possible history of Johannine Christianity.

The Johannine traditions are found in a narrative in the gospel genre: the Gospel of John, or the Fourth Gospel (FG); three letters, 1, 2, and 3 John; and an apocalyptic writing, the Apocalypse, or Book of Revelation. The ways these writings relate to each other, to the rest of the NT witnesses, and to the community for which they were written have been variously described.

Most scholars consider the FG and the three letters to have the same provenience if not authorship. Many also conclude on the basis of genre, style, and theology that Revelation must belong elsewhere. Yet Revelation provides the only firm connection between these writings, the tradition's eponym (John), and communities in a specific location (Asia Minor). Without Revelation, the Johannine community floats entirely free of any historical constraints. The Book of Revelation, furthermore, despite the transmutations effected by the apocalyptic form, shares far more points of fundamental outlook and symbolism with the Johannine writings than with other parts of the canon.

Nevertheless, much of the contemporary discussion of Johannine Christianity tends to leave Revelation to one side, concentrating instead almost entirely on the FG and the three letters. The implications of this omission for any reconstruction of a Johannine history are obvious. Apart from the random patristic references to

John and the Ephesian church, all evidence for Johannine Christianity comes from these writings. The excision or inclusion of a single document, as well as assumptions about the order of the writings' composition, dramatically affects any history based exclusively on them. Circularity in such circumstances cannot be avoided even if it is not vicious. Hence the intrinsic fragility of such reconstructions, which a short example can illustrate.

It is plausible to regard some version of the FG as the oldest Johannine writing, bearing within itself intimations of tensions that later, as the letters would indicate, divided the community. But nothing prevents us from reversing this order of composition, in which case the FG would appear in quite a different light. The progression would become even more uncertain if Revelation were included. Indeed, it is questionable whether the writings ought to be seen as necessarily representing sequential stages in a community's existence. History based purely on a few literary sources is a hazardous enterprise.

The meaning of talk about the Johannine community is also uncertain. Is something more meant than the Johannine readership? If so, what form of social organization is implied? Some have taken the FG as suggesting in its communal preoccupations and language the setting of an intentional group like a school. Others have observed that the letters appear to presuppose a cluster of local churches organized along the lines of households. Still others have remarked that all these writings share fundamentally sectarian attitudes: they define themselves as much by what they oppose as by what they affirm. Are these characterizations compatible? Do they fit with the impression given by Revelation of many communities in diverse cities, some of which are in competition with other groups? Not only the social organization of the Johannine community or communities is unclear, but also the ethnic background of the believers. Once more, the writings tell us various things: that there was at some point conflict and separation from some form of Judaism (John 9); that there was a Samaritan connection (4:4–42); that Greek-speaking Gentiles or Diaspora Jews were brought into the fold (7:35; 12:20), so that even common Hebrew terms required translation (1:38, 41, 42; 9:7); that some of the believers referred to outsiders as heathen (3 John 7). What this information amounts to, however, is less than clear.

If the documents do not provide a history or sociology of Johannine Christianity, they do reveal something of the great tensions within which the Christians for whom they were written lived and suffered and read these extraordinary books. More than any other part of the NT, the Johannine writings bear the signs of the stress and conflict that so deeply influenced the interpretation of the "good news" in Jesus.

In no other NT writings do we find the ideal of peace and unity and love so clearly expressed—and so clearly at odds with the community's own experience. All of these writings make a sharp distinction between insider and outsider. In the Gospel, the historical conflict between the Jews and Jesus stands for the continuing conflict between the world and Jesus' "friends." In the letters, the issue of who is an insider and who is not tragically spells out the division *within* the community, as different parties claim exclusive rights to the truth. And in Revelation, the battlefront is double: there are both hostility and persecution from the world outside, together with division and corruption within.

The symbolism of all these Johannine writings is therefore bold and clear. The conflicts derive from and necessitate choice. Symbols therefore are clearly drawn and unambiguous. There is good and evil, darkness and light, truth and falsehood, death and life, them and us. In each of these writings, furthermore, it is the figure of Jesus that stands at the center of the conflict. In the Gospel, allegiance to him demands separation from synagogue but also invites identity as his friend. In Revelation, true witness to Jesus against falsehood and idolatry continues his witness to the truth even to death. In the letters, the community divides precisely over the proper understanding of Jesus. The dialectic between experience and interpretation, present in all the NT writings, is manifestly and indelibly impressed into the very symbols of the Johannine writings.

24

The Gospel of John

THE CENTERPIECE OF THE JOHANNINE WRITINGS IS THE FOURTH GOSPEL (FG), a witness to Jesus so simple and powerful that its influence on Christian consciousness is unsurpassed. Like the Synoptic Gospels, the FG tells the story of Jesus' life, death, and resurrection. Matthew, Mark, and Luke gave distinctive shape to the same basic story line by editing and altering their shared traditions. John more fundamentally transmutes the story as a whole, giving the term "Gospel" still another dimension.

The FG has always been attributed to a John, whom Irenaeus says was the disciple of the Lord who wrote at Ephesus (*Against Heresies* III.1.2). The narrative itself invites speculation concerning an anonymous disciple (John 1:35–42; 18:15–18) identified only as one "whom Jesus loved" (13:23; 19:26; 20:2–9). He is identified as the authoritative witness behind this writing (19:35; 21:20–24). Since nothing is ever said in this Gospel about a John, and the Synoptic sons of Zebedee are mentioned only incidentally (21:2), it is not unreasonable to identify the beloved disciple with John the son of Zebedee (cf. Matt. 10:2; Mark 3:17; Luke 6:14; Acts 1:13), who was a "pillar" of the first Jerusalem church (Acts 3:1; 4:13; 8:14; Gal. 2:9). The beloved disciple is important because he roots this version of Jesus' story in an eyewitness. The readers of this Gospel regarded him as their "founder" (19:26), and his death was sufficiently unexpected to create the need for interpretation (21:20–23).

The claim to such firsthand traditions was once regarded as entirely fictitious, but the FG shows as good a knowledge of first-century Palestinian terrain, customs, and ideology, as the Synoptics (see, e.g., 3:23; 4:5, 9, 20, 25; 5:16–18; 6:1, 59; 9:11; 11:54; 12:20; 18:13). Archaeology in fact has verified some specific facts that earlier critical scholars had dismissed as spurious (see 5:2; 19:13).

The FG does not, however, appear as the undeveloped account of an eyewitness. It reveals several stages of composition. The most obvious is the addition to the story in John 21, after the solemn conclusion of 20:30–31. The scribal uncertainty about the placement of the passage about the adulterous woman (7:53—8:11) also testifies to a certain fluctuation in the text. Not surprisingly, the nature and number of redactional stages have been vigorously debated by scholars. One of the simplest theories is that an originally radical version was thoroughly and disastrously reworked by a later "ecclesiastical redactor," who modified the spiritualizing tendencies of the original along more orthodox lines. As a consequence, the "real" FG can be reached only by excerption and rearrangement. Other hypotheses are considerably more complex if no less fragmenting, positing as many as five stages of composition. Many contemporary scholars are convinced that one stage in the process saw an original "signs source" (whose ending was 20:30–31) joined to a "sayings source." The putative discovery of seams and sources is sometimes also connected to "stages in the community's life." The text is thereby treated as an archaeological site whose layers reveal buried history. The reconstructions are, however, sufficiently numerous and unconvincing to diminish confidence in the method itself.

The FG we now read does not have the look of a composition by committee or of a haphazard outcome of heavy-handed editing. Only to minds obsessively concerned with a certain level of consistency are seams always indicators of sources. To other readers, they appear as literary signals. The FG does not require reconstruction. It stands today as it has for two thousand years as a coherent, profound, and challenging witness, itself sufficient evidence that the Johannine community had within it at least one great theologian and writer.

The FG has always been considered the latest of the Gospels. Some nineteenth-century critics made it a late-second-century production. Their dating was based on the assumption that its symbols came from Hellenistic philosophy, which would necessitate its composition outside Palestine, and that its high Christology demanded a long period of development. The archaeological discovery of Greek manuscripts of John's Gospel in Egypt dating from the late (P^{75}, P^{66}) or even early second century (P^{52}) makes a late-second-century date impossible, and one closer to the turn of the first century more likely. Neither redactional nor doctrinal elements require a long period of development. John's Christology is certainly different from that of Paul or Hebrews, but it is no "higher." The compositional complexity of John is no greater than that of Matthew or even Mark. And in the light of better historical knowledge it is no longer necessary to postulate a long sojourn in the Hellenistic world to account for John's symbols.

The symbols we encounter in the FG are certainly different from those in the Synoptic Gospels. In this case, the term "symbolic world" is accurate, for moving from the Synoptics to John is truly like entering another universe. Jesus does not speak in neat aphorisms or in parables of the kingdom. He does not meet Pharisees and Sadducees in short bursts of controversy. Instead we find a language heavy with abstract substantives like "light" and "truth" and "life" combined in complex patterns with verbs like "believing" and "seeing" and "knowing." Jesus speaks more in allegories than parables, and his speech points inexorably to himself rather than to a kingdom. All metaphors meet in him. His self-referential speech describes an ethical and possibly even a metaphysical dualism: humans are faced with a choice that is also a judgment on themselves, between what is from above and what is from below, what is light and what is dark, what is true and what is false, leading to death or to life (see 3:5–21; 5:30–47; 12:44–50). The realms are intersected by the "man from heaven" (3:31), who enters the world to reveal himself and the one who sent him (14:9–11) before returning to his previous place (16:28). The path of descent and ascent defined by the revealer provides the way for his chosen ones to follow (14:6–7).

Small wonder scholars have tried to find in one tradition or another the key to unlock the Johannine symbolic system. Older studies saw a Platonic dualism and traces of Stoicism's *logos* theology. The history of religions school found the symbols in John closest to those of gnostic writings, whether Hermetic or Mandean. Recent scholarship has reaffirmed the native Jewish elements, not only the obvious resemblances to Philo Judaeus but also Pharisaic preoccupations. The perceptions of the Samaritans, particularly their "prophet like Moses" messianism can be traced in the FG. Virtually all of John's dualistic elements can be found even more sharply present in the sectarian writings from Qumran.

Although such investigations have not isolated a single dominant influence on the symbols of the FG, they have made three things clear. First, all elements of John's symbolic structure are present and important in the Judaism of first century Palestine. Second, no less than in other NT writings, the symbols of Torah play a critical role. Third, the symbols are given their coherence by the figure of Jesus.

Why was the FG written? Suggestions on its purpose have not been lacking, but they have tended to exaggerate one thematic element to the neglect of others. Some have thought the Gospel to have primarily an apologetic function, asserting the superiority of Jesus over John (1:6–8, 15, 19–28; 3:22–30; 5:35; 10:41) or demonstrating Jesus' messianic credentials to Jewish unbelievers (5:39–47; 7:21–52; 10:31–38; 12:37–50). Others have emphasized John's persuasive functions, suggesting that it was written to persuade Diaspora Jews, or those not yet severed from the synagogue, or even Gentiles, to convert to the messianic movement (see 1:9, 38, 41, 42; 4:21–26; 7:35; 9:22; 10:16; 11:52; 12:20–22, 32, 42). It is doubtful that a composition as rich as this can be reduced to a single function. Indeed, even the Gospel's own stated intention (20:30–31) has a certain ambiguity:

> Now Jesus did many other signs in the presence of his disciples, which are
> not written in this book; but these are written that you may believe that Jesus
> is the Christ, and that believing you may have life in his name.

That signs should lead to belief and belief to life is clear enough. The
ambiguity comes in the precise construction given to the phrase "that you
may believe." We are not certain whether the tense of the verb should be
present or aorist. If it is aorist, then the phrase would read, "that you
might believe," and the purpose would be conversion. But if it is present
tense, then the phrase would read, "that you might go on believing," and
the purpose would be reinforcement. The present tense seems the more
likely reading, and the whole tenor of the Gospel suggests less a document
for proselytism than one of propaganda for the converted. One of the most
perceptive observations on the literary structuring of John suggests that
the very movement of the story corresponds to the perceptions of a
community that defined itself by opposition to unbelievers, and that the
complex coding of the narrative prohibits understanding by those who are
not already within the symbolic system of the community.

JOHN AND THE SYNOPTIC TRADITION

The special character of John's Gospel can be seen immediately if it is
systematically compared to the Synoptic Gospels. So many and great are
the points of divergence that one might at first wonder whether they really
tell the same story.

Both chronology and geography have a decidedly different character.
Matthew and Luke provide an account of Jesus' infancy; John's prologue
(1:1–18) begins and ends in God. In all the Synoptics, Jesus' ministry
begins in Galilee, and then moves dramatically toward Jerusalem for his
one fatal visit to that city. In the FG, Jesus moves back and forth between
Galilee and Judea. He appears first in Judea, then goes to Galilee (1:28,
43). He makes a brief trip to Jerusalem for a Passover (2:13). While there,
he purifies the temple (2:13–22), an event the Synoptics make the climax
of his ministry. Jesus then goes from Jerusalem to Judea (3:22) and from
Judea back to Galilee through Samaria (4:3, 45). He returns to Jerusalem
for another feast (5:1). For his second Passover (6:4), however, he is back in
Galilee (6:1). He goes to Jerusalem again for the Feast of Booths (7:1–10),
and is still there for the feast of the rededication of the temple (10:22). He
goes from Jerusalem to Judea (10:40), where he sojourns until returning
for his final Passover (12:12). This very mechanical review indicates three
ways in which the Johannine presentation of Jesus' ministry differs from
the Synoptic version. First, his ministry centers in Judea, not in Galilee.
Second, his ministry lasts three years, not one. Third, his ministry is

intimately connected to the observance of the great pilgrimage feasts of Judaism.

The time of Jesus' death is different. Jesus is crucified on the day of preparation for the Passover (19:31); the last supper is not a Passover meal in the FG. In contrast to the Synoptics, here Jesus is already anointed before his burial (19:39–42). Mary Magdalene comes to the tomb alone and discovers Jesus missing (20:1) before she tells Peter and John (20:2–10). Jesus appears once to Mary alone (20:11–18) and twice to his disciples in Jerusalem (20:19–29). His sole Galilean appearance is at the seaside rather than a mountaintop (21:1–14). It is impossible, in short, to reconcile fully the account of Jesus' life and death in the FG and that in the Synoptics.

A more important difference in the FG is the character of Jesus' deeds and words. These will demand closer attention. For now, I simply note that the exorcisms, so important in the Synoptics, are here altogether missing. Jesus does three healings and one resuscitation. His actions are called signs *(semeia)* and have an obvious symbolic importance. In the mouth of Jesus we find none of the Synoptic parables, although Jesus does use some "figures" (10:6; 16:25). Most of all, Jesus is a monologist. Confrontations with his opponents become disputations in which not Jesus' deeds so much as the claims implicit in them become the issue (see esp. 5:10–47; 6:41–65; 9:35—10:39).

The FG also contains definite points of contact with the Synoptic tradition. Specific miracles in John show a greater or lesser resemblance to miracles in the Synoptics: the healing of the official's son (4:46–53; cf. Matt. 8:5–10 and Luke 7:1–10); the healing of the paralytic (5:2–9; cf. Mark 2:1–12; pars.); the multiplication of the loaves (6:1–13; cf. Mark 6:34–44; pars.); the walking on the water (6:16–21; cf. Mark 6:45–51; Matt. 14:22–27). Other events are found both in John and the Synoptics: John's baptism (1:25; 3:23; cf. Mark 1:4; pars.) and arrest (3:24; cf. Mark 1:14; pars.); Peter's confession (6:68–69; cf. Mark 8:29; pars.); the purification of the temple (2:14–16; cf. Mark 11:15–18; pars.); the anointing at Bethany (12:1–8; cf. Mark 14:3–9; Matt. 26:6–13; and possibly Luke 7:36–50); the entry into Jerusalem (12:12–15; cf. Mark 11:9–10; pars.); and above all, the Passion narrative (18:1—19:42), which despite its distinctive elements such as the amplified role of Pilate (18:29—19:22) is recognizably the same as in the Synoptics, having a particularly large number of contacts with Luke's version.

Other thematic elements that the Synoptic Gospels present as single events can be discerned in the FG in a more diffused way. Thus, the Synoptic temptation account (Mark 1:12–13; pars.) finds its equivalent in John 6:14–15 and 7:3–4, and the agony in the garden (Mark 14:32–42;

pars.) in 12:27–29 and 18:11. It is even possible to detect the reworking of Synoptic sayings material in places such as John 1:42; 12:24–26; 13:12–20; 21:22. But most of what is in John is not in the Synoptics, and most of what is in the Synoptics is not in John!

What, then, is the relationship of the FG to the Synoptic Gospels? Some patristic writers considered John as the *supplement* to the synoptic tradition (see, e.g., Eusebius *Ecclesiastical History* III.24.7–13 and Augustine *On the Harmony of the Evangelists* IV.7, V.8). If the term is understood only quantitatively, it is inaccurate. But in a deeper sense, the FG does perform just such a supplemental function to the rest of the gospel tradition. It does this by being explicitly a *theological reflection in the form of a story.* Several distinctive features of the FG will make this clear.

First, John is an ecclesiastical Gospel. The word "church" never occurs, and there is nothing in the Gospel about church organization. But no other Gospel so consciously states its relationship to the community of its readers and its narrator's point of view. The self-consciousness is shown by the narrator's stating the reason for writing (20:30–31), by the way the future presence of Jesus among his followers is promised before his death (14:25–31; 15:1–11), and above all by the way there is repeated acknowledgment of the greater insight that came about because of the resurrection (2:17–22; 12:16; 14:25; 20:9). Because of these warnings to the reader, John is free to collapse the distance between the story of Jesus and the story of the believers. There is the distinct awareness of the difference between that time and this time (14:15–30; 16:7–15, 19–28, 31–33), yet the reality of the *now* is allowed to permeate the narration of the *then.* The signs worked by Jesus are recognizable as the church's own signs; the conflicts faced by Jesus are those faced by the community (9:22; 12:42): "If the world hates you, it hated me first" (15:18).

Second, John is a sacramental Gospel. It contains no institution accounts except that of the foot washing (13:1–14). But the Gospel is pervaded by a consciousness of liturgical traditions, both of the Jews, shown by its fascination with Jewish feasts, and of the Christian community. The FG shows how the sacraments of the church are rooted in the signs of Jesus, and at a deeper level in the sign that *is* Jesus. The sacramental character of the FG has been disputed. But whether original or due to a later redactor, the present text bears language unmistakably suggestive of Baptism (3:5; 7:37–39; 19:34) and the Eucharist (6:35–58).

Third, John's eschatology is predominantly a realized eschatology. As with the sacramental character of the Gospel, this feature is really another aspect of the ecclesiastical focus of the FG. There are important statements that maintain the future expectation of resurrection and judgment (5:28–29; 11:24). But the major emphasis of the Gospel is that the end time is a present reality. For the community of believers, "the time is coming and *now is"* (4:23; 5:25). This point, however, requires qualification. The FG does not suggest that the believers themselves are living the heavenly life. The point, rather, is that the offer of life and the critical judgment of the world have definitively taken place in the coming of Jesus. He is "the resurrection and the life" (11:25), and human judgment takes place in response to him (5:25–27). And, at least in the sense that those who believe in him can be called children of God (1:12), they too share in eternal life (3:18–21): "This is eternal life, that they know thee the only true God and Jesus Christ whom thou hast sent" (17:3).

Fourth, John's presentation of Jesus is more symbolic than literal. The previous three points find their summation in this one, which requires an even more careful qualification. A fuller presentation of the Johannine Christology will follow. John's portrayal of Jesus is sometimes called that of a "naive docetism." That is, Jesus is *said* to be human but he does not really appear so. Some have suggested that the FG so emphasizes Jesus as revealer that his humanity is diminished if not lost. In contrast, for instance, to Mark's Jesus, who obviously suffers, this Jesus is an unearthly figure.

The contrast, however, can be overdrawn. Jesus is scarcely just another human being in Mark's Gospel. Within a different symbolization, he is just as alien as the Jesus of the FG! Traditional Christian piety, in fact, sees in John what scholars sometimes miss. Jesus is "God's Word" but he is also and emphatically "made flesh" (1:14). John's is in many ways the most human portrayal of Jesus. Jesus experiences fatigue (4:6) and anguish (12:27; 13:21). His whole being is convulsed at the death of Lazarus, and he weeps (11:33–35). Jesus changes his mind (7:1–10). Jesus converses with real people in real places: with Nicodemus (3:1–13), the Samaritan woman (4:7–26), the cripple (5:2–9), the blind man (9:35–38), his friends (11:17–37), the disciples (1:38–51; 4:31–38; 6:66–71; 9:1–5; 11:1–16; 13:31—14:31). His controversies with opponents are not quickly finished with a polished one-liner, but are passionately extended (6:41–65; 7:14–36; 8:12–58; 10:22–39). This Jesus performs a miracle simply for human pleasure (2:1–11), shows irritation (2:4; 6:26; 7:6–8; 8:25) and suspicion (2:24–25), and asks for a positive human response (6:66–71). Only this Jesus is portrayed as having friends (11:1—12:9). He has a disciple he prefers to others (13:23; 19:26; 20:2; 21:20); he asks Simon three times, "Do you love me more than these?" (21:15–17), and he calls all his followers friends (15:13–15).

Then how do we account for the other side of John's Christology, which shows Jesus as more than human, speaking "as no man has ever spoken" (7:46)? This side is a function above all of the theological nature of John's narrative, and its literary expression. That which is left implicit in the Synoptic Gospels is made explicit in the FG. The whole drama of God's relationship with humanity is played out in the Gospel, with Jesus as the central character. This is the most consistently christocentric of the Gospels, and for that reason, Jesus is a more symbolic than literal figure.

He is the one who "exegetes" the Father to the world (1:18). The way God always is toward the world implicitly, the FG shows him to be explicitly, in a specific time and place, in the figure of Jesus. Therefore, the human response to Jesus represents as well the universal human response to God. The FG makes fully clear that the claims of Jesus represent God, and it spells out the consequences for human decision: commitment to Jesus is a choice for life, light, and truth; for, in a word, God. Hostility toward Jesus is a choice against light for darkness, against truth for falsehood, against life for death; in short, against God for self.

Because of this explicative function, Jesus always points beyond himself to the one he represents. All Christian theology makes explicit what is implicit in the story of Jesus. The FG is certainly theology, but it is a narrative theology. John retells the story of Jesus so that it bears within itself all the deeper resonances of reflection on the story.

STYLE AND STRUCTURE IN JOHN

The FG is stylistically simple and symbolically dense. Its generally clear and correct "schoolchild" Greek is so apparently artless that the subtlety of the Gospel's literary technique can easily be missed. The following points are meant to illustrate something of the Gospel's art.

Irony is a favorite and multifaceted literary technique in the FG. The readers always know more than the characters in the narrative and can appreciate their words and actions at quite another level. Characters are given lines that state the truth far beyond their own intentions, as when Caiaphas declares that Jesus should die for the whole people (11:50), or when the people respond to Pilate's "enthronement" of Jesus (19:12–14) by shouting, "We have no king but Caesar" (19:15). Apparently prosaic expressions turn out to have deeper significance. When the disciples first meet Jesus, they ask him, "Where do you stay [or "remain": *meno*]?" and Jesus tells them, "Come and see" (1:38–39). Only later do we discover the implications of "remaining with Jesus" (15:4–11). So also the expression "lifted up," *hypsoō*, evokes both the crucifixion of Jesus and his glorious exaltation (3:14; 8:28; 12:32–34). Even single words like "sign" and "hour" and "glory" and "truth" carry several levels of meaning within the narrative, as when Pilate asks the one standing before him (whom the reader has known from the beginning to be "full of grace and truth," 1:14, and who has just told Pilate that he has come to "witness to the truth"), "What is truth?" (18:37–38).

The dialogues of the FG are structured ironically. A statement or deed of Jesus perfectly plain to the readers is misunderstood by the character who is Jesus' dialogue partner. Jesus explains. But the more he explains, the deeper grows the misunderstanding. The reader, of course, enjoys the whole process. The community's "inside" knowledge makes the words of Jesus transparent. Only outsiders do not understand. Thus, Jesus is approached by Nicodemus, a Jewish teacher superficially attracted to this "man from God" (3:2). Jesus tells him a person cannot enter God's kingdom unless born *anōthen*. The adverb can—depending on context—mean either "again" or "from above," or both. Nicodemus naturally takes it in its crudest form: "How can a person enter a second time *(deuteron)* his mother's womb and be born?" (3:4). He shows thereby that he is not "from above" but from below (3:6–8). The community, however, knows (3:11). The dialogue with Nicodemus imperceptibly becomes a monologue, first a monologue by Jesus (3:10–15), then one by the narrator (3:16–21), explicating this more accurate knowledge of the community.

Likewise, Jesus tells the Samaritan woman that if she knew his identity she would ask him for living water (4:10). She dithers on about the depth of the well and his lack of a bucket (4:11–12). She cannot grasp that he means quite another kind of water (4:13–14), but the readers do. Again, Jesus tells his opponents that where he is going they cannot come (7:33; 8:21). They think he is going to the Diaspora (7:35) or planning suicide (8:22). But the reader knows Jesus is going to the Father, and that if people don't believe in him they cannot follow (14:28). The dialogues invite the reader into the process by which the community defines itself against a hostile environment. Jesus spoke "from above" and was misunderstood by all except those "who received him, who believed in his name" (1:12). So does the community that now faces hostility from the outside find in the coded speech of this Gospel reinforcement for its convictions.

Almost everything in the FG has a symbolic value, including names (1:42, 47; 9:7) and numbers (2:1, 6; 6:13, 70; 21:11). Individual persons represent others: Nicodemus stands for all teachers of the Jews, Martha for all believers, Thomas for all doubters. This representative function accounts for the stock character of the Johannine drama, just as Jesus' representative function gives his figure a certain artificiality. The symbolic role of individuals is most important to recognize in the case of the "Jews" in the FG. John does not altogether collapse the distinctions between first-century Jewish sects; the term "Pharisee" occurs only seven fewer times than in Luke. But the Gospel's tendency is to group all Jews together. The distancing term "Jew," *ioudaios*, is used some seventy times, compared to five in Luke. The impression given, therefore, is that all Jews opposed Jesus without distinction. As a result, despite its clear statement that "salvation is from the Jews" (4:22), and despite the fact that Jesus is portrayed as arguing as a Jew with his fellow Jews (8:12–58), the FG is often regarded as anti-Semitic. But the Jews of this narrative have as *symbolic* a function as has the Jesus of the narrative. As Jesus shows how God is toward the world, the narrative's Jews represent the tendency of *all humans* to reject the truth of God in favor of their own. John does not intend to evaporate either Jesus or the Jews from history altogether; but their narrative portrayal results from the Gospel's attempt to make of history something more than merely a chronicle of the past.

The symbiotic relationship of the Johannine symbols to Judaism is exemplified by the Gospel's use of the Jewish feasts. We have seen that the narrative places Jesus in the context of the great feasts of Passover (2:13; 6:4; 12:12), Booths (7:1–10), and rededication of the temple (10:22). The Gospel also appropriates the symbols traditionally associated with these feasts and applies them to Jesus, so that he personifies all the holy times and places of Judaism (see 1:51): he is the slain lamb (1:29, 36; 19:36) and living bread (6:32–51) of the Passover; the living water (7:37–39) and light (8:12; 9:4–5) of Booths; he is the tent where God's glory dwells (1:14), his body the new temple (2:21).

Structurally the FG has four major parts. The prologue (1:1–18) both announces major themes of the story and sketches the story's pattern. The Book of Signs (1:19—12:50)—whose original ending is sometimes considered 20:30–31—dramatizes the proposition of the prologue: "The light shines in the darkness and the darkness cannot accept [or, overcome] it" (1:5). The Book of Glory (13:1—20:31) shows how "those who believe in him become children of God" (1:12). It has two subdivisions: the revelation of Jesus' glory to his disciples through his teaching (13:1—17:26) and the revelation of Jesus' glory through his death and resurrection (18:1—20:31). An appendix (21:1–25) shows the readers how Peter was restored after his betrayal and how Jesus interpreted the death of the beloved disciple.

From another standpoint, the structure of the Gospel is itself christocentric. That is, it circles about the figure of Jesus. Linear plot development is less important here than in the other Gospels. There is neither suspense nor surprise but only irony. Patristic writers compared John to the figure of an eagle. Like birds of prey who circle their target, this evangelist describes outer and inner circles around the figure of Jesus. In this discussion, therefore, the reader should look only for the measurement of a series of radii that point to an identical center. I will observe how John can say the same thing in many ways.

THE BOOK OF SIGNS: THE DEEDS
OF THE MESSIAH

The Prologue (1:1–18)

Characters in Torah are introduced by genealogies *(toledoth)*. Matthew and Luke begin Gospels with infancy accounts that trace Jesus' origins to

Abraham (Matt.) on even to Adam (Luke). John begins with a prologue that makes the story of Jesus begin in the very bosom of God (1:1). Jesus represents in the world the absolute beginning or origin (*archē*) who is God. The prologue consists in a series of rhythmic strophes, some of them chiastic in form. The poetry is twice interrupted by prose interjections dealing with John the Baptist (1:6–8, 15). The prologue's cyclic pattern (the Word comes from God, dwells with humanity, returns to God) defines the dominant spatial movement of the whole Gospel: descent and ascent. The literary antecedents of the prologue are less likely gnostic hymns than the biblical traditions associated with Wisdom (Prov. 8:22–31; Sir. 24:3–34; Wis. 7:22—8:1), which are also used elsewhere in the NT to express the conviction that meeting Jesus meant encountering God (Col. 1:15–20; Heb. 1:1–3).

The prologue anticipates many of the Gospel's themes. We find (1:3–4) that the Word (*Logos*) bears both light (*phōs;* cf. 3:19–21; 8:12; 9:5; 11:9–10; 12:35, 36, 46) and life (*zōē;* cf. 3:15–16, 36; 4:14, 36; 5:24, 26, 29, 39, 40; 6:27; 8:12; 10:10, 28; 11:25; 12:25, 50; 14:6; 17:2–3; 20:31). Light and life are primal metaphors for the very being of God. We see as well that the light is locked in conflict (1:5) with darkness that can neither "accept" nor "overcome" the light (the verb *katalambano* can mean either; cf. 3:19; 6:17; 8:12; 12:35, 46). In the "testimony" of John (1:7) is anticipated as well the mission of Jesus in the world (cf. 2:25; 3:11; 4:44; 5:31; 18:37). Jesus' testimony, however, is that of a light "coming into the world" (1:9; cf. 1:15, 30; 3:8, 19, 31; 4:25; 5:43; 8:14; 14:3). He personifies the truth (*alētheia;* 1:14; cf. 3:21; 4:23–24; 5:33; 8:32; 14:6, 17; 15:26; 16:7, 13; 17:17, 19; 18:37). Against every form of counterfeit claim based on human pretension, he offers the "genuine" life based on the gift of God (cf. 3:33; 4:18; 5:31–32; 6:55; 7:18; 8:13–14, 17, 26; 10:41; 19:35; 21:24). In the prologue as well we find already the contrast between those in the world who refused to know him as he was (1:10; cf. 1:50; 2:24–25; 5:42; 6:15, 70; 8:28, 32, 55; 10:14, 38; 14:7; 16:3; 17:3) and those who beheld and accepted him as he was (1:14; cf. 2:23; 4:19; 6:2, 40, 62; 7:3; 12:45; 14:17, 19; 16:10; 17:24). Their true insight was that Jesus was the only begotten Son of God (1:14; 18; cf. 3:16–18). A second contrast in the prologue is between, on the one hand, what was found only partially in Torah (*nomos;* 1:17; cf. 1:45; 7:19, 23, 49; 8:17; 10:34; 12:34; 15:25; 18:31; 19:7) and in the figure of Moses (1:17; cf. 1:45; 3:14; 5:45–46; 6:32; 7:19, 22–23; 8:5; 9:28–29) and, on the other, what was realized in its fullness (*plērōma;* 1:16) in Jesus: the "grace and truth" (1:14, 16, 17) that are both the gift and the attributes (*chesed we emeth*) of the Father (over 100 times in the Gospel), whom Jesus reveals and represents in the flesh that is the tenting place of God's glory (1:14; cf. 6:51–63).

An element of the prologue not found in the Gospel narrative is the term "Word," *Logos*, used of Jesus. The prologue in this case gives explicit expression to the constant assumption behind the deeds and words of Jesus. He acts and speaks as the incarnate expression of God's speech. As word gives body to thought, so does Jesus give visible expression in the world to the invisible power and presence of God.

The prologue's final words perfectly summarize the literary and theological function of Jesus in the narrative of the FG. "No one has ever seen God; the only begotten Son [or, in another reading, God], who is in the bosom of the Father, he has made him known" (1:18). The Greek phrase, "has made him known," *exegēsato*, contains the sense both of revealing and of interpreting. In its literal sense of leading out, it may also be an allusion to the exodus. Jesus is the tent of God's presence (1:14). Moses could reveal law, but not the very grace and truth of God. Moses could lead the people to the land, but only Jesus can lead them to the bosom of the Father, for only he came from that place. Everything in the FG presupposes this highly explicit framework. In contrast to the Gospel of Mark, there is no "secret" in John's narrative except for outsiders. There is little surprise except perhaps at the way mystery can recede even behind its clearest expressions.

Jesus and John the Baptist

The touch of the evangelist is masterly in the portrayal of John the Baptist. We can guess from this account that the Baptist was an independent and important prophet with a great following, one that for a time rivaled Jesus' own (1:19; 3:22–26; 4:1). The FG had to acknowledge that he was "a man sent from God" (1:6), while simultaneously showing his subordinate position to Jesus.

The prose interpolations in the prologue brilliantly accomplish both ends. John the Baptist is a witness to the light but is not the light (1:6–8); his entire testimony is that a greater than himself comes after him (1:15). The relativization is all the more convincing since it is placed in the Baptist's own mouth. He himself then walks out of the numinous haze of the prologue into the lucid foreground of the Jordan river in 1:19, making a narrative bridge between the eternal Word and the earthly Jesus. Is there a problem having Jesus baptized by John? Not here, for there is no baptism scene; there is only John bearing testimony to the descent of the Spirit so that he can attest, "This is the Son of God" (1:31–34).

John the Baptist twice denies that he is the Christ, each time concluding with a statement reminiscent of the synoptic tradition (1:19–23, 24–27). A third time he reminds the crowds that he never claimed to be the Messiah (3:28). John plays perfectly the role of witness. He points away from himself toward Jesus, "the Lamb of God" (1:29, 36). He frees his disciples to follow another (1:37), and with noble poignancy defines himself as "the bridegroom's friend" who is thrilled to hear the bridegroom's voice (3:29) but knows as well that his role is to decrease, while that of Jesus is to increase (3:30).

There is nothing accidental in this portrayal. Jesus later refers to the Baptist: "He was a burning and shining lamp, and you were willing for awhile to rejoice in his light. But the testimony I have is greater than that of John ... (5:35–36). No other evangelist could manage such a comparison of flickering lamp to eternal light. But then no other evangelist had a Nicodemus creeping in from the night (3:2) or a Judas departing into the night (13:30) or a Peter holding out his hands to a charcoal fire, "standing and warming himself" while his master was on trial (18:18; but see also Mark 14:54, 67).

Naming Jesus (1:29–51)

As in the Synoptics, Jesus' ministry begins with the gathering of his followers, two of whom are first disciples of the Baptist (1:35–40). The process in the FG is considerably more complex than in the Synoptics. First, it is greatly concentrated, with the action carried by a series of questions and answers. The technique is used again in the dialogue between Jesus and these same figures at the last supper (13:36—14:22). Second, the calling of disciples involves a process of assigning names. We already heard the crowds seek a name for John the Baptist. Was he Messiah, Elijah, Prophet? No, said John, just a voice (1:19–23). Those who now encounter Jesus give him the whole range of titles found in the Synoptics, even those which were "secret." John the Baptist begins the process by calling Jesus the "Lamb of God who takes away the sins of the world" (1:29, 36). This is the first epithet given Jesus in the narrative, and its imagery is repeated at his death (19:31–37). John also calls Jesus the Son of God (or, in a variant reading, God's elect; 1:34).

John's two disciples, who play a significant role in this Gospel (6:5–8; 12:21–22; 14:8–9), first call Jesus, Rabbi (1:38). Then Andrew calls him the Messiah (1:41), and Philip, "the one spoken of by Moses and all the prophets, Jesus, son of Joseph, from Nazareth" (1:45; cf. 6:42). Finally, Nathaniel calls Jesus "Rabbi, Son of God, King of Israel" (1:49). In the biblical tradition, the act of naming is an exercise of power; it shows knowledge of an authority over another. In the Johannine progression, however, as the disciples attempt to name Jesus, they come under *his* power: they become disciples. Jesus, in fact, reverses the process of naming. He tells Simon son of John that he is Cephas (which means Peter) (1:42; cf. Matt. 16:18). And Nathaniel, he calls "an Israelite without guile" (1:47).

It is typical for John's narrative that the identifications of Jesus made by others are not inaccurate, only inadequate. Jesus alone can adequately name himself. He responds to Nathaniel with a self-designation: "You will see the heaven opened and the angels of God ascending and descending upon the Son of man" (1:51). Here is the synoptic title, once more in the mouth of Jesus himself. And it is placed within a deliberate allusion to the dream of Jacob in Gen. 28:12–17. Jacob saw the angels ascending and descending and concluded, "This is the house of God, this is the gate of heaven" (Gen. 28:17). In a single deft allusion, John has Jesus identify himself as the Holy Place where humans encounter God, the one who has descended from God and returns to him, and the "gate" through whom others can go to God (see 10:7).

The New Creation

The FG makes another allusion to Genesis and another point about Jesus in the narrative sequence reaching from the prologue through the wedding at Cana. The first words of the prologue, "In the beginning," deliberately recall the opening of Gen. 1:1. The Word is present and active in creation on "the first day." The succeeding incidents are marked by an apparently casual dating: "the next day" (1:29), "the next day" (1:35), "the next day" (1:43). This brings us through four days. The wedding feast at Cana is "on the third day" (2:1). At that feast, as we know, Jesus transforms a natural substance (water) into a new creation (wine). What is at work here is not simple life (*bios*), but Life (*zōē*), the power of God.

The symbolism of John is rarely one-layered. The phrase "on the third day" could but remind Christian readers of the resurrection "on the third day" and enable them to recognize at work in Jesus the power of the resurrection life: "I am the resurrection and the life" (11:25). They could not easily avoid noticing that the water was transformed into wine, a symbol at once of the blood of the lamb and their new Pasch in memory of Jesus. The most alert readers would also notice that this third day also brought to fullness a week of seven days. In Jesus the power of a new creation is at work, which does not deny but transforms the world he himself, as Word, helped shape. And lest any reader miss the significance of the miracle, the evangelist concludes at 2:11:

> This, the first of his signs, Jesus did at Cana in Galilee, and manifested his glory; and his disciples believed in him.

In the deeds and words of Jesus, the reader of the Gospel (like the disciples at Cana) will recognize the "Word made flesh" who makes present the "glory," that is, the effective power of God (1:14). All Jesus' deeds are verbal, signs that point beyond themselves and even beyond him, to the presence of God in the world.

The Signs of the Messiah

Jesus' signs were to reveal the presence of God in him and lead to faith (2:11; 20:30–31). The FG has Jesus perform seven such signs, corresponding to the seven days of the new creation: the wedding at Cana (2:1–11), the healing of the official's son (the "second sign"; 4:46–53), the healing of the paralytic (5:2–9), the multiplication of the loaves (6:1–13; "When the people saw the sign . . . ," 6:14), the walking on water (6:16–21), the healing of the man born blind (9:1–12), and the raising of Lazarus from the dead (11:17–44).

To borrow from Aristotelian categories used in later sacramental theology, all the signs have both matter and form. Their matter is water (Cana, the pool, the walking), bread (the multiplication), light (the blind man), and life (the official's son, Lazarus). Their form is given by Jesus' words that explicate the meaning of the actions. He is the "living water" (4:10), the "bread of life" (6:35), the "light of the world" (8:12), the "resurrection and the life" (11:25). The signs point to Jesus and he points to the presence of God in the world.

But despite the confident assurance of 20:30–31 that the signs lead to belief, they are in fact an ambiguous dimension of the Johannine narrative. For believers, the signs can confirm belief (2:11; 20:30). At other times not the signs but the words of Jesus lead to commitment: "You have the words of eternal life" (6:68; cf. 11:27, and see the contrast in 4:48). For those who did not believe, however, the gestures of Jesus were neither convincing nor self-validating. After he prophetically cleaned the temple, his opponents asked, "What sign have you?" (2:18). After he multiplied the loaves, the crowd cried, "What sign do you do that we may see and believe you?" (6:30). For Nicodemus (3:2) and the crowds who flocked to Bethany after the raising of Lazarus (12:18), the signs were spectacular evidences of a holy man or magician. For the crowd in the desert, the multiplication of food was important not as a sign but as a means of gratification: "You seek me not because you saw signs but because you ate your fill of the loaves" (6:26).

The signs by themselves may fascinate and even lead to superficial assent (see 2:23) but not to the full commitment of faith. This is made plain at the close of Jesus' public ministry (12:37–43). The evangelist tells the reader that all of Jesus' signs did not lead to belief in him (12:37). Like Mark explaining the lack of perception regarding Jesus' parables, John makes use of two citations from Isaiah to interpret this rejection. Isaiah 53:1 identifies Jesus as the suffering servant who has not been believed (12:38; cf. Rom. 10:16). In Isa. 6:10 we find the motif of blindness and hardening that is so extensively employed by the Synoptics (cf. Mark 4:12; Matt. 13:14–15; Luke 8:10; Acts 28:26–27). They saw but did not really see, heard but did not really hear. Here we have an open secret that still cannot be solved except by faith. The Isaiah passage recounts the prophet's vision of the glory of God in the temple and his prophetic call (Isa. 6:1–13). John tells the reader, "Isaiah said this because he saw *his* glory and spoke of *him*" (12:41; cf. 8:56–58). The presence and power of

God are one. As they were at work in the past, so are they now in Jesus with the "fullness of grace and truth" (1:14). Then why could God's power and presence not be grasped? Here John plays on two meanings of *doxa:* "reputation/opinion" over against "presence/glory." Faced with the choice in Jesus, "they loved more the glory that comes from humans than the glory that comes from God" (12:40). The explanation only deepens the mystery. But it enables the evangelist to close Jesus' open ministry with a final prophetic call (12:44–50) before turning to the private instruction of his disciples (13:1—17:26) and his death (18:1—19:42). The mystery in John seems to be this: the more clearly the claim of God is made, the more violent is the world's rejection.

THE BOOK OF SIGNS: THE
CLAIMS OF JESUS

The FG shows us a constant attempt to identify Jesus. And with the exception of the charge that he had a demon and was a Samaritan (7:20; 8:48) virtually everything said of him has some element of truth. There are, however, circles within circles. What is revealed in disputation within the Book of Signs is discovered to be still parabolic, compared to what is revealed to believers in the Book of Glory. Even within the context of the public ministry there are inner and outer circles of identification. I will touch here on what is said about Jesus by outsiders, then by believers, and then by Jesus himself. No level is utterly wrong, yet none is completely adequate for naming Jesus.

Identification by Outsiders

The titles of Messiah (Christ), Prophet, and King are all applied to Jesus by outsiders. Only the Christian reader understands the way in which Jesus both fulfills and exceeds the expectations associated with such designations. John the Baptist aroused messianic expectations because of his preaching and baptizing (1:25) although he did no signs (10:40) and had to reject the titles of Messiah (1:20, 25; 3:28) and prophet (1:21). The populace then shifts its speculation to Jesus, wondering whether he might be the Messiah (4:29) or whether the leaders might secretly know that he is the Messiah (7:26). John tells us in the process a considerable amount about popular messianic expectation. The crowd knows that the Messiah is to come from Bethlehem (7:42), although it is also said that the Messiah's origin is to be unknown (7:27). The Messiah is to reveal all things (4:25), perform great signs (7:31), and remain forever (12:34). In the eyes of Jesus' opponents, of course, Jesus meets none of these requirements. But the narrator and the reader know how Jesus does reveal all things, does perform great signs, does have his ultimate origin hidden from them, and does "remain forever."

The titles of Prophet and King appear to be associated particularly with the expectation of a messiah who was a "prophet like Moses." Jesus is termed a prophet because he can read hearts (4:19) and perform signs (6:14; 9:17). It is when he multiplies loaves in the wilderness like Moses that the people cry out that he is the Prophet, and seek to make him king (6:15). In the Passion narrative, the theme of Jesus' kingship is dominant (see 18:33–39; 19:12–22).

Identification by Believers

The traditional titles are not wrong when used by believers but require supplement by a deeper insight into Jesus' identity. Jesus is called Messiah by those coming to belief in him (1:41; 11:27). The appropriateness of this title is certified by its use by Jesus himself (17:3) and by the narrator (1:17), who is writing so that his readers may continue to believe that Jesus is "the Christ, the Son of God" (20:31). The title Son as we shall see, is Jesus' own, so it provides the "inner" understanding of the traditional role of Messiah. Nathaniel also calls Jesus "Son of God, king of Israel" (1:49), and the Baptist calls Jesus, Son of God (1:34). Martha surely represents all believers when she confesses, "I believe that you are the Christ, the Son of God, he who is coming into the world" (11:27), in a cluster of designations fully in agreement with the prologue (1:9, 14, 17).

Jesus is called "Savior of the world" by Samaritans who were coming to belief in him (4:42), and he could also be called Lord by believers (9:38), though this title is also used indiscriminately in the sense of "master." Peter calls Jesus, in his confession, "the Holy One of God" (6:69). The FG also uses the title God (*theos*) of Jesus, albeit sparingly. We find it first in the prologue, "the Word was God" (1:1), and possibly, "the only God who is in the bosom of the Father, he has made him known" (variant reading, 1:18). Thomas therefore is not out of sympathy with the view of the narrator when he confesses after the resurrection, "My Lord and my God" (20:28).

Self-Identification by Jesus

The most distinctive identifications of Jesus are found in his own mouth. This style of self-referential speech most sets the Jesus of the FG apart from that of the Synoptics. No less than the understanding of Jesus' deeds as signs, of course, do such self-designations reflect the continuing thinking of believers on Jesus' identity. I will consider here in turn his use of the title "Son of man," the language of "I am," and the language of sonship.

Son of Man

This title is found very often in the Synoptics, once more in the speech of Jesus as a self-designation. In the Synoptics, the title had a threefold reference: to Jesus' present ministry, to his suffering, and to his eventual role as judge when he "came on the clouds." In the FG it occurs once as a simple self-designation that calls for a response of belief: "Do you believe in the Son of man?" (9:35). But as in its first occurrence (1:51), the title's predominant use in the FG is within a pattern of descent and ascent. Jesus is the one who will be "lifted up" in his crucifixion (3:14; 8:28), which will also be his exaltation (13:31). When he is lifted up, the Son of man will draw all people to himself (12:32–34) so that they may have eternal life (3:15). But this Son of man is also one who has already "descended"; here is an example of Johannine "realized eschatology." The traditional expectation was for the "descent" to come in the future. In the FG, however, Jesus has already descended from heaven. He is the man from heaven who is uniquely capable of revealing the things "from above" (3:12, 31; cf. 8:23). So when the Son of man is lifted up, he returns to where he was before (6:62). Since for John "no one has seen the Father except him who is from God, he has seen the Father" (6:46), the Son-of-man language establishes a pattern of descent and ascent that validates Jesus' role as revealer and judge: "No one has ascended into heaven but he who descended from heaven, the Son of man" (3:13; cf. 5:27).

"I Am"

Distinctive to the FG are statements made by Jesus using "I am," *ego eimi,* in several different forms. The first is in the form "I am *X*," by which Jesus identifies himself with something supposedly already known to the hearers. There are seven of these statements, corresponding to the seven signs and days of the new creation. In each of them, there is at least an implied contrast between the accepted and sometimes counterfeit versions of *X*, and the "genuine" realization of it in Jesus. In all of them as well, *beneath the metaphor* is a claim to be the source of that life (*zōē*) which comes from God.

After multiplying the loaves, Jesus declares, "I am the bread of life" (6:35, 48). The contrast is to the bread Moses gave in the desert; the manna was not really "bread from heaven" (6:32). Only Jesus is the genuine bread (6:55), because he descends from God and offers the life that comes from God, "for the bread of God is that which comes from heaven and gives *life* to the world" (6:33).

At the Feast of Booths, Jesus claims, "I am the light of the world" (8:12; 9:5). Before his coming, people have lived in darkness (3:19–21; 11:10). He brings the revelation of both world and God for what they really are (1:9; 12:46). The person who sees this light also sees the one who sent it, God (12:45). The light brings with it judgment (3:19). Before its coming, there was neither light nor darkness, only reality; but when the light shines, then for the first time there is a choice—people can tell light from darkness. The choice they make between them is also the judgment they bring on themselves. Those who claim to see without this light are proved blind (9:39–41). But those who see by this light (9:35–38) also live by the *life* it brings: "In him was life and the life was the light of men" (1:4).

Three of the statements emphasize the relationship between Jesus and his followers. In contrast to thieves and robbers who destroy the sheep (10:8), Jesus declares, "I am the door of the sheep" (10:7). Those who enter by him will be saved (10:9) and be given life: "The thief comes only to steal and kill and destroy. I come that they may have *life* and have it abundantly" (10:10). In a second, closely related contrast, Jesus says, "I am the good shepherd" (10:11). He is not like the hireling who has no care for the sheep. He shows his care for them by *laying down his life for them* (10:17). The third statement particularly stresses Jesus as source of life for his followers: "I am the true vine" (15:1). Those who are cut off from him will wither and die (15:6), but those who stay joined to him will live and bear fruit (15:2).

All the previous statements were clearly metaphorical. The final two in the form of "I am *X*" are more straightforward claims to *be* what the metaphors suggest: the source of life. In response to the crisis of Lazarus's death, and to Martha's belief in a future resurrection (11:24), Jesus says, "I am the resurrection and the life" (11:25). Those who believe in him will never "die" utterly, but will live with God's life (11:26). Finally, Jesus tells his disciples at the last supper, "I am the way and the truth and the life; no one comes to the Father but by me" (14:6). This last statement makes clear what all the rest have suggested: in contrast to every form of human self-aggrandizement and pursuit of life, Jesus brings the genuine life that can come only from God. He is revealer and life-giver.

A second kind of "I am" statement is more mysterious. In some cases, it appears to be a rather straightforward response of identification, "I am he." So Jesus tells the Samaritan woman who says the Messiah will reveal everything, "*Ego eimi* speaking to you" (4:26), which simply means: "The one speaking to you, I, is the Messiah." Likewise, when the disciples are frightened at seeing Jesus walking on the water, he says to them, "*Ego eimi*, do not be afraid" (6:20), which probably means, "It is I." But the numinous impact of the phrase is suggested in the arrest scene, when Jesus asks twice, "Whom do you seek?" When he is told, "Jesus," he responds, "*Ego eimi*" (18:5, 6). This would appear to mean simply, "I am Jesus," except that, when they hear this, the men fall back on the ground (18:6); the narrator is telling us something.

The expression is particularly ambiguous in the disputation of John 8:12–58, where it occurs three times. Jesus tells the Jews, "You will die in your sins unless you believe that *ego eimi*." They, understandably, ask, "Who are you?" (8:24–25). A second time he says to them, "When you have lifted up the Son of man then you will know that *ego eimi*" (8:28). Does this mean they will know that he is the Son of man or simply that he *is* in some unspecified sense? The reason this question is pertinent is seen in the final use of the expression. Jesus tells his opponents that Abraham has seen him; they mock him. He replies, "Truly, truly, I say to you, before Abraham was, *ego eimi*" (8:58). That his opponents recognize the deeper implications of the statement is indicated by their picking up stones to hurl at him for blasphemy (8:59). Later, they will say that they wanted to stone him because, "being a human being, he makes himself God" (10:33). This, of course, is exactly what the absolute use of *ego eimi* would suggest. His opponents, and the Gospel's percipient readers, would recognize in all this talk of *ego eimi* the self-identification of the Lord God to Moses in the burning bush, "I am who I am" (Exod. 3:14; cf. Isa. 41:4; 43:10).

Son of the Father

We have seen that the title Son of God supplies the appropriate content for the frame of messianic belief. And in Jesus' language about himself as Son, we find the deepest and most intimate level of his self-revelation in the Book of Glory. Jesus was sent into the world as an only begotten son (1:18; 3:16–17). Like human sons who observe their fathers working, Jesus confesses that he can do nothing of himself, but only what he observes his Father doing; he works as his Father works (5:19). This means that he carries out the same functions as the Father in the world. As the Father is the source of life, so does the Son have this life in him (5:21), which he can also give to others (5:26; 6:40, 57). The Son is a judge as the Father is a judge (5:22) and should receive honor just like the Father (5:23). It is as the Father's son that he bears witness (5:30); he hears the words spoken by the Father and speaks them to the world. He is therefore, obedient Son (8:26, 28). The Father, in return, loves the Son (3:35; 5:20) and gives him glory (8:54; 12:28). The blindness of his opponents can be summarized this way: "They did not know he spoke the Father to them" (8:27). And the gift to the disciples as: "He who has seen me has seen the Father" (14:9). In the language of filial relationship that is expressed by obedience and love, Jesus himself provides the inner meaning of the title "only Son of God" (1:14, 18).

A Christological Controversy
(chaps. 7—8)

The distinctive way in which the Christology of the FG unfolds in the Book of Signs can perhaps best be illustrated by looking at a single section in somewhat greater detail.

Chapters 7 and 8 form a single long controversy between Jesus and his opponents. It is interrupted, however, by the pericope of the adulterous woman (7:53—8:11). Should it be read as part of the evangelist's literary composition? Although the pericope appears here in all printed editions, it is very doubtful that it is in its right place or even comes from the same writer. The vocabulary bears much more of a synoptic than Johannine stamp, and the character of the confrontation is closer to the pericope style of the Synoptics. It also sits uneasily between the two parts of the christological argument. Finally, the passage has an unusual textual history. Many of the manuscripts that have it in this part of the FG are late and of a common tradition. Many other manuscripts also have it here, but they include critical signs indicating doubts as to its proper placement. Other manuscripts put the passage after 7:36, or 21:25. Still others put the passage in the Gospel of Luke, after either 21:38 or 24:53! Most significant, the best and most ancient manuscripts omit the passage. The weight of the textual evidence suggests, then, that this story, which has deservedly enjoyed great popularity, is, like the longer ending of Mark, part of the canonical collection but so mechanically placed in its present location that a literary consideration of the Gospel can safely work around it. In its present setting, the story does serve to emphasize the distance between Jesus and his opponents, providing a dramatic punctuation in the middle of this great debate.

After some initial indecision (7:1–9), Jesus decides to come to Jerusalem for the Feast of Booths (7:2, 10). While in the city, he engages in a running disputation with the Jews, who are full of speculation concerning his identity (7:11–13). John typically uses symbols associated with this feast in reference to Jesus. The Mishnah (*Sukkah* 5.2–4 and 4.9) indicates that a ceremonial libation with water and a procession carrying torches of light were traditional elements of this celebration. The FG therefore has Jesus cry out (7:37) on "the last day of the feast, the great day":

> If anyone thirst, let him come to me and drink, who believes in me. As the Scripture has said, "Out of his heart shall flow rivers of living water."

And shortly thereafter, Jesus also announces, "I am the *light* of the world" (8:12).

The controversy in chapters 7 and 8 is in reality part of the longer running battle between Jesus and the opposition, in which the same points are touched on repeatedly. There is a marked resemblance, for example, between 7:27–28 and 8:14c, d; 7:24 and 8:15; 7:28 and 8:19; 7:30 and 8:20; 7:33–36 and 8:21–22. These chapters also pick up elements of the earlier disputation caused by Jesus' healing of a paralytic (cf. 8:16 and 5:30; 8:14 and 5:31; 8:18 and 5:37). Throughout this fugue-like series of controversies we also hear themes first suggested in 3:19–21. And the points of the present battle build toward the further confrontations in 10:31–38 and 12:27–50.

In the present section of the dispute, there is an ever-greater explication of issues, leading to a greater alienation between Jesus and his interlocutors. Jesus and the Jews talk past each other, as though they really were on different planes (7:23). The pattern of the passage is dialogical, but in fact the questions and answers more resemble a judicial cross-examination. Only the reader knows that the ones doing the examining are the ones being judged. Many of Jesus' answers could not have been intelligible to his opponents but are so to the reader. Characteristic of the deep lack of understanding is Jesus' repeated statement, "Where I am going you cannot come" (7:34; 8:21). Jesus himself indicates that this is because "I go to him who sent me" and the reader understands this to be God. But the Jews think, first, that he is going to the Diaspora (7:35) and then that he is going to commit suicide (8:22). Each conclusion is mistaken. Yet such is the density of the Johannine irony that each conclusion is true at another level. The Gospel *will* go to the Greeks, or the Greeks will come to it (12:20), and Jesus *will* "lay down his life himself" for the sake of others (10:17–18). Another example: At the very beginning of the controversy, Jesus asks his interlocutors, "Why do you seek to kill me?" (7:19), and they vigorously reject the charge. But by the end of the dispute, they are indeed trying to kill him (8:59).

The fundamental problem of the adversaries, the evangelist suggests, is their unwillingness to accept the claims to which Jesus' deeds themselves testify. They avoid the simple equation that Jesus—and the narrator—insist is the only correct one. When they ask, "Where is your father?" Jesus can only answer them, "You know neither me nor my father; if you knew me you would know my father also" (8:19). The circularity and frustration of the controversy is suggested by their exasperated question, "Who are you?" and Jesus' response, which in Greek can mean either "Even what I told you from the beginning" or "Why do I talk to you at all?" (8:25). Both answers fit this maddening exchange, whose function is to demonstrate how the darkness cannot grasp or overcome the light.

Throughout the dispute, of course, Jesus is speaking less to his opponents than to the evangelist's Christian readers. And they learn a great deal about the nature of Jesus' claim to be God's Son. They see that the Jews claim Abraham as their father (8:33) and charge Jesus with having a demon (8:48). But Jesus says that they have proved false to their descent from Abraham. The principle, we have seen, is that children act like their parents (5:19). Since they seek to kill Jesus, they show that their real father is the devil, "who was a murderer from the beginning" (8:44); Abraham would never act like that (8:40). As for their claim to be free children (8:33), it is an illusion since they are slaves of sin (8:34). Only the truth can make them free (8:31–32); that is to say, only the free Son can make them free (8:36). If God were their Father, they would love Jesus (8:42).

Jesus is the free Son because he is the obedient Son: "I declare to the world what I have heard from him" (8:26). He speaks from his Father's authority not his own (8:28). And since Jesus always does what is pleasing to the Father, he is not left alone (8:29). His Father is with him (8:16). As he represents the Father in the world, then (8:19), he is both true revealer and fair judge (8:16).

Indeed, since the Father is always "with" Jesus, he is a second witness to Jesus' words. And this fulfills the requirement of "their law" that the witness of two men is required (8:17–18; cf. Deut. 19:15). Here we meet the Johannine theme that the law revealed by Moses only finds its "fullness" in the "grace and truth" revealed in Jesus (1:16–17). If Torah is not read in the light of that fulfillment it is misread. In the controversy of chapter 5, Jesus told the Jews, "You search the Scriptures because you think in them you have eternal life; and it is they who witness to me" (5:39). His opponents not only cannot hear the Word incarnate; they even fail to understand the import of the texts they prefer to him: "It is Moses who accuses you, on whom you hope; If you believed Moses, you would believe me, for he wrote of me" (5:46). This is similar to Jesus' midrashic reading of Ps. 82:6, which shows that he is scripturally justified in calling himself Son of God: if even those to whom Torah was revealed were called God's sons, how much more the one whom God sanctified and sent into the world (10:34–36). If they were really faithful to Torah, they would also have faith in Jesus: "He who is of God hears the words of God; the reason you do not hear them is that you are not of God" (8:47).

In this controversy, the revelation made through Jesus is seen as continuous with that made through Moses. Openness to one would mean understanding the other. Jesus speaks God's truth. If some have chosen falsehood instead, they have forsworn their own heritage. They have also chosen slavery, sin, and death, whereas "if anyone keeps my word he will never see death" (8:51). The functions of Torah are totally subsumed by Jesus: he reveals God's will, he judges, he offers the spirit, he gives light, he sets free, he gives life. What Torah was as text, Jesus is as living Son: God's Word.

THE BOOK OF GLORY: JESUS
TEACHES HIS DISCIPLES

The great and dramatic turning in the FG is from the open ministry to an inner revelation, from those in the world who, "though he had done so many signs before them, yet did not believe in him" (12:37), to "his own," for "having loved his own in the world he loved them to the end" (13:1). The FG has no direct teaching of disciples except in the Book of Glory, first by Jesus' words and then by his death and resurrection.

Jesus' teaching is set at a supper "before the feast of Passover" (13:1–2). The meal is not emphasized, and there is no "institution" of the Eucharist; John's "eucharistic discourse" in 6:48–58 serves that function. The only ritual action is the foot washing (13:4–12), which is given as an example to be imitated (13:15). This opening scene has elements that resemble those in the Synoptics, although thoroughly reworked (13:16 = Matt. 10:24, Luke 6:40; 13:17 = Matt. 7:24, Luke 11:28; 13:20 = Matt. 10:40, Luke 10:16; 13:21–26 = Matt. 26:21–25, Mark 14:17–21, Luke 22:21–23). In a mirror image of the pattern established by the Book of Signs, Jesus' symbolic actions give rise to a dialogue, made up largely of questions and answers. When first called, the disciples "named" Jesus; now they question him in turn (Simon Peter, 13:36; Thomas, 14:5; Philip, 14:8; Judas, 14:22). The dialogue then becomes a monologue interrupted only by a final common question (16:17–18) and exclamation (16:29–30), culminating in the solemn prayer of 17:1–26.

Jesus' last-supper discourse (13:1—17:26) interprets his ministry as well as the future of the disciples. We find in it therefore the confluence of themes that began earlier in the narrative. We have repeatedly been told that Jesus' "hour" had not arrived, without being told what it was (2:4; 7:30; 8:20). In the climactic scene of the open ministry, that theme intensified: "The hour has come for the Son of man to be glorified" (12:23), and "Save me from this hour" (12:27). Now we are told, "Jesus knew his hour had come to depart" (13:1), and Jesus himself says, "Father, the hour has come; glorify thy Son that the Son may glorify thee" (17:1). At the crucifixion, in turn, the narrator tells us that "from that hour" the beloved disciple took care of Jesus' mother (19:27).

The hour of Jesus is therefore at once his death and his glorification. When we remember the very precise way John uses "glory," we see that Jesus' death is the moment when God's presence is, paradoxically, most powerful. The notion of Jesus' glory (1:14; 2:11; 11:4, 40; 12:41) and of his "being glorified" (7:39; 8:54; 11:4; 12:16, 23, 28), which was associated with his signs, is now intensified by association with the great sign that is his death and resurrection: "Now is the Son of man glorified and in him God is glorified; if God is glorified in him, God will also glorify him in himself and glorify him at once" (13:1; cf. 14:13; 15:8; 16:14; 17:1, 4, 10, 22, 24). It is the hour as well of Jesus' "going away," to use the expression that so tantalized and frustrated his opponents (7:33; 8:21). Now the reader is told plainly that Jesus is going away to the Father from whom he came (13:1, 3, 33, 36; 14:3, 12, 19, 28, 30; 16:5–7, 16, 28; 17:11, 13).

The Johannine theme of conflict and judgment has three aspects in the Book of Glory. First, the conflict between light and darkness is clearly identified as one between God and Satan. We have seen in the earlier controversies that Jesus was called a demoniac (8:48) and that he charged the Jews with having the devil for a father (8:44). Now we see that the "devil" put it in Judas's heart to betray Jesus (13:2), and when he received the morsel from Jesus, "Satan entered into him" (13:27). When Jesus is arrested, it is the coming of "the ruler of this age" (14:30), and when the comforter comes, the "ruler of this age is judged" (16:10).

Second, there is judgment within the group of the disciples. Peter is tested in the foot washing (13:6–10), but it is not of him Jesus speaks when he says, "You are not all clean" (13:11). Judas breaks fellowship by his betrayal, and the portrayal in the FG is chilling indeed. Already in 6:70 we find Jesus say, "Did I not choose you the Twelve, and one of you is a devil," whom the evangelist identifies as Judas. We have seen that Satan was at work in him (13:2). The actual scene of betrayal is powerfully depicted. Jesus has withdrawn from the world of darkness with his disciples. We can almost see the lighted room, illumined by his presence. As in the Synoptics, the disciples ask who will betray him. But in John, Jesus tells the beloved disciple that it is the one to whom he gives the dipped morsel. Given the dense symbolism of bread in his Gospel, the body language here is almost horrifying. Jesus takes the bread, gives it to Judas. As he takes the morsel, Satan enters into him (13:27). And with unmatched simplicity and strength, the narrator says, "So, after receiving the morsel, he immediately went out; and it was night" (13:30).

The third kind of conflict and judgment is that which the disciples will face after the departure of Jesus. The alienation between the world and them, between the insiders and the outsiders, will continue. As the world hated him so it will hate them (14:22; 15:18–27; 16:2–4, 8, 20, 33; 17:13–19).

The farewell discourse makes utterly clear to the disciples and the readers what was hidden from unbelievers, namely, Jesus' ultimate origin and destination: "I came from the Father and have come into the world; again, I am leaving the world and going to the Father" (16:28; cf. 13:1, 3; 14:2, 12, 28; 16:16; 17:5, 8, 13). Jesus is also the way by which others can go to the Father (14:4–7). The relationship between Jesus and the Father is expressed in terms of the greatest intimacy; he and the Father are one (14:8–11; 16:15; 17:21). But Jesus is not the Father. He remains united to God through obedience and love (14:10, 31; 15:9, 15; 17:4, 12, 13).

Jesus leaves only one commandment for his followers. They are to love one another (13:34; 15:12, 17). By so doing, they will "abide" in the love of Jesus (15:9–10, 14). Such a spiritual abiding reveals the deeper implications of the hints dropped in the earlier narrative about abiding or remaining (*meno;* cf. 1:38–39; 5:38; 6:27, 56; 8:31, 35; 12:34; 14:10, 17, 25). The allegory of the vine and the branches establishes a relationship of mutual life and love between Jesus, his disciples, and the Father. They are to remain in Jesus (15:4), just as Jesus remains in the Father (15:10). They do this by obeying the commandment of mutual love.

The earlier narrative suggested that Jesus would be the source of a loving spirit for those who believed in him (4:13–14; 7:37–39). Jesus now makes clear that his departure will lead to a new mode of God's presence (and of his own presence) among his friends, through the Holy Spirit, who is called Paraclete or Comforter (*paraklētos*). This is the Spirit of truth (14:17) that will lead them into all truth (16:13). Specifically, the Spirit will "bring to remembrance all that I have said to you" (14:26). So the Spirit continues the witness of Jesus (15:26) through the disciples. This witness will "convict" the world in exactly the way Jesus does, concerning sin and righteousness and judgment (16:7–11). And since the disciples continue to represent Jesus in the world, they can expect a fate like his. They too will be hated by the world (15:18—16:4) and experience great sorrow (16:20). But since they have the love of God within them (15:10), even this sorrow will be reversed into joy (15:11; 16:22). The final prayer of Jesus states that the disciples too have been given eternal life (17:3) and glory (17:22) and have been sanctified (17:19), all because the love of God is in them as it was in Jesus (17:26).

In the FG, as we have seen, both ecclesiology and soteriology are rooted in Jesus. This is a community of "friends" bound together by their love for each other, which comes from the love Jesus first showed them, the very love of God. It is present among them in the Holy Spirit, sent from both Father and Son, to draw them into unity. No better expression can be found for the life of the Spirit than, "that they may be one even as we are one" (17:22). We are forewarned that this is a community for which disputes over true and false spirits, or any disunity, would create the most severe sort of identity crisis (cf. below, on 1, 2, 3 John).

THE BOOK OF GLORY: THE SON
OF MAN IS LIFTED UP

Passion and Death

John's Passion narrative includes a considerable amount of material also found in the Synoptics, such as the arrest in the garden (18:1–11), including Peter's excision of an ear (18:10); Peter's betrayal (18:15–27); the trial before Pilate (18:29—19:16), including the offer of Barabbas (18:39–40); the place of crucifixion (19:17); the title on the cross (19:19); the execution of two others (19:18); and the dividing of the garments (19:23–24). Even the shared elements, however, are given a special Johannine shading. Thus Judas appears as the leader of the mob (18:2), and when Jesus identifies himself, "I am he," the crowd falls back (18:4–6). And Jesus' response to

Peter's violence amounts to a version of the synoptic temptation account: "Put your sword in its sheath; shall I not drink the cup the Father has given me?" (18:11; cf. 12:27–29). As in the Synoptics, Peter's betrayal is juxtaposed to Jesus' witnessing. In John, the contrast is sharper because the two accounts are interwoven (18:15–27). And only a dull reader misses the point of Peter's reaching to a fire for warmth while the light of the world is captured by the powers of darkness (18:18).

The distinctive thematic element in the FG's Passion concerns the kingship of Jesus. John has no trial before the Sanhedrin, only private hearings before Annas and Caiaphas (18:19–23, 24, 28). Jesus is quickly shunted to Pilate. His trial before the Roman procurator becomes an extended dialogue on the reality and nature of his kingship. Pilate plays the role the Jews played in the earlier controversies. In response to Pilate's dull questions (18:33, 35, 37, 38; 19:10), Jesus makes clear that his kingship is not of this world (18:33), that earthly political power is a sham (19:11). His kingship consists in his witnessing to the truth (18:36–37). But when Pilate asks the critical question of the FG, "Where are you from?" Jesus says nothing at all (19:9).

The climax of the trial comes in 19:12–16, when the narrator pulls Pilate's gestures into the ironic framework of the entire narrative. Pilate had already dressed Jesus in royal robe and mock crown (19:5); now he deliberately places him (the Greek text demands this transitive form of *kathizo*) on his own judgment seat, symbol of his authority (19:13). The narrator signals the event's importance by telling us the time and place (19:14). Pilate cries out, "Here is your king!" And the response of the people? "We have no king but Caesar!" (19:15). The reader knows that they have in fact chosen to be ruled only by human powers and have rejected the kingship of God. The deliberateness of this imagery is made clear by the exchange between Pilate and the Jews on the appropriateness of the title, King of the Jews (19:21), and by Pilate's response, "What I have written, I have written" (19:22). The figure of Pilate is important for our understanding of the FG, for it shows that the Johannine treatment of the Jews is not truly a form of anti-Semitism. Pilate also represents the world that refuses the truth about God and itself. Faced with one who came only to bear witness to the truth and who said, "Everyone who is of the truth hears my voice" (18:37), Pilate can only answer, "What is truth?" (18:38).

The crucifixion scene in the FG looks very different from in the Synoptics. Jesus is not abandoned by his disciples; rather he has released them (18:8). At the cross, he is still surrounded by his mother, Mary the wife of Cleopas, Mary Magdalene, and the beloved disciple (19:25). As Jesus had loved his friends to the end (13:1), so do they love him till the end. This is the second appearance of Jesus' mother. The first was when Jesus showed his glory in a sign of resurrection life (2:1–11). The second is for his glorification in death. We see that for the Johannine as for the Lukan community, the figure of Mary has an important symbolic value. Jesus gives her and the beloved disciple into each other's care (19:26–27).

Consistent with the whole Johannine presentation, Jesus shows himself fully conscious on the cross and aware. He knows that now "all has been brought to completion" (19:28) and declares, "It is finished" (see 13:1; 17:4). As he had said he would "hand over his life" (10:18), the evangelist shows us that to be the case: he bows his head and "hands over" his spirit (19:30). No less than in the Synoptics, but with different texts, this scene is interpreted by the symbols of Torah. Thus, Jesus' words "I thirst" are said to fulfill Ps. 22:15. And the image of Jesus as the lamb whose bones are not broken (19:36; cf. 1:36), recalls Exod. 12:46.

The strangest element of the Johannine crucifixion scene is also the most revealing of the author's intentions. The narrator alerts us by stressing the presence of the eyewitness (19:35). But what is so important to note? When the soldiers came they broke the legs of the others, but not Jesus'; so Jesus is the Paschal Lamb. But then Jesus is pierced in the side, and water and blood flow from his side (19:34). This happens, we see, immediately after Jesus says, "It is finished," and "hands over" his spirit (19:30). We only grasp the meaning of this sequence when we consult the full context of Zech. 12:10 to which the narrator points in 19:37: "They shall look on him whom they have pierced." The passage in Zechariah (12:10; 13:1) reads:

> And I will *pour out* on the house of David and the inhabitants of Jerusalem a *spirit* of compassion and supplication, so that, when they *look on one whom they have pierced*, they shall mourn for him as one weeps for an *only child*, and weep over him as one weeps for a firstborn. . . . *On that day*, there shall be a *fountain opened* for the house of David and the inhabitants of Jerusalem to cleanse them of sin and uncleanness.

Just such a fountain does the eyewitness see in the side of Jesus. The water and blood signal the outpouring of the Spirit. The reader remembers the "water bubbling up to eternal life" (4:14), and that "out of his heart shall flow rivers of living water," which, we were told, was "the Spirit which those who believed in him were to receive; for as yet the Spirit had not been given, because Jesus had not yet been glorified" (7:37–39). Now, he is glorified and the Spirit is given. Nor does John lack his own version of the *kenosis*, or emptying, of God's Son. It is from the side of one who cries, "I thirst," that the living waters flow.

The Resurrection

The powerful grip of the resurrection traditions on Christian communities is indicated by their inclusion in the FG, which could so well have done without them. We can once more in these accounts find traces of shared gospel traditions thoroughly reworked according to Johannine perspectives. His empty-tomb account (cf. Mark 16:1–8; pars.) focuses on the single woman (20:1) and the footrace between Peter and the beloved disciple (20:2–9), but above all on the fact that the beloved disciple was the first to believe. His mistaken-identity account (cf. Luke 24:13–35) also involves Mary Magdalene, who thinks Jesus is the gardener (20:11–18). John includes a double appearance to the gathered disciples (cf. Luke 24:36–49), the second to accommodate the doubting Thomas (20:19–29). Finally, in a story reminiscent of Peter's call to discipleship in Luke 5:3–7, Jesus appears to all the disciples in Galilee (21:1–14), to restore Peter (21:15–19) and clarify the fate of the beloved disciple (21:20–24).

The stories have, overall, the same functions as in the Synoptic Gospels. The empty tomb certifies that Jesus is not among the dead, even though he has already been extravagantly anointed and buried (19:39–42). His linens are left lying, but his napkin is folded, off by itself (20:6–7). The failure to recognize Jesus shows that he now lives in a new way, and can appear anywhere. He will be recognized by those who know his voice when he calls them by name (20:16; cf. 10:3). He enters rooms locked by fear, because the power of his life drives away fear and brings peace (20:19). He shows his wounds so that his friends may know that the one who lives is also the one who was slain, and that he bears forever on his body the marks of wounded humanity (20:20). He is mysteriously present to the disciples as they work and as they eat together (21:1–14).

But as always in this Gospel, the words of Jesus himself provide the transition from the gospel narrative to the story being lived out by the community. The members of the community live with the assurance that he was ascended to the Father as he told them he would (20:17). They know that they possess the Spirit that comes directly from him so that they can be for the world as he was (20:21–23). They are those who now not seeing yet are believing and are blessed (20:29). They are those who are to show their love for Jesus by their care for the "sheep," the Messiah's community. They live by the last words from the risen one, which tell them what all the Gospels say, "Follow me . . . you follow me" (21:19, 22).

BIBLIOGRAPHICAL NOTE

Because literature on the Fourth Gospel is vast and ever growing, this bibliography must be even more selective than the others in mentioning only works that represent significant contributions or that may be especially helpful to the reader on specific points.

A helpful review of recent Johannine scholarship as a whole is R. Kysar, *The Fourth Evangelist and His Gospel* (Minneapolis: Augsburg Pub. House, 1975). For a thematic overview, see R. E. Brown, "The Kerygma of the Gospel According to John," *Int* 21 (1967): 387–400. Useful collections of essays are C. K. Barrett, *Essays on John* (Philadelphia: Westminster Press, 1982); idem, ed. *Studies in John,* NovTSup 24 (Leiden: E. J. Brill, 1970); D. M. Smith, *Johannine Christianity: Essays on Its Setting, Sources, and Theology* (Columbia: Univ. of S. C. Press, 1984).

For various aspects of the Johannine community and literature, see J. A. T. Robinson, "The Destination and Purpose of St. John's Gospel," *NTS* 6 (1960): 117–31; P. Minear, "The Audience of the Fourth Evangelist," *Int* 31 (1977): 339–54; D. M. Smith, "Johannine Christianity: Some Reflections on Its Character and Delineation," *NTS* 21 (1975): 222–48; R. A. Culpepper, *The Johannine School,* SBLDS 26 (Missoula, Mont.: Scholars Press, 1975); R. E. Brown, "Johannine Ecclesiology: The Community's Origins," *Int* 31 (1977): 379–93; E. Schüssler Fiorenza, "The Quest for the Johannine School: The Apocalypse and the Fourth Gospel," *NTS* 23 (1976–77): 402–27.

Studies that seek the history of the community in the FG include J. C. Martyn, *History and Theology in the Fourth Gospel,* rev. ed. (Nashville: Abingdon Press, 1979); R. E. Brown, *The Community of the Beloved Disciple* (New York: Paulist Press, 1979); J. D. Purvis, "The Fourth Gospel and the Samaritans," *NovT* 17 (1975): 161–98; J. Bassler, "The Galileans: A Neglected Factor in Johannine Community Research," *CBQ* 43 (1981): 243–57; J. L. Martyn, *The Gospel of John in Christian History* (New York: Paulist Press, 1978); J. Painter, "The Farewell Discourses and the History of Johannine Christianity," *NTS* 27 (1980–81): 525–43; F. F. Segovia, "The Theology and Provenance of John 15:1–17," *JBL* 101 (1982): 115–28; idem, "John 15:18—16:4: A First Addition to the Original Farewell Discourse?" *CBQ* 45 (1983): 210–30.

The perennial problem of the relationship between John and the Synoptic Gospels is examined by C. H. Dodd, *Historical Tradition in the Fourth Gospel* (Cambridge: At the Univ. Press, 1965); F. Neirynck, "John and the Synoptics: The Empty Tomb Stories," *NTS* 30 (1984): 161–87; W. O. Walker, "The Lord's Prayer in Matthew and John," *NTS* 28 (1982): 237–56; and D. M. Smith, "John and the Synoptics: Some Dimensions of the Problem," *NTS* 26 (1979–80): 425–44.

The following studies build on the great commentary by Rudolph Bultmann (see below) in seeking multiple sources for the Fourth Gospel: R. T. Fortna, *The Gospel of Signs: A Reevaluation of the Narrative Source Underlying the Fourth Gospel* (Cambridge: At the Univ. Press, 1970); D. M. Smith, *The Composition and Order of the Fourth Gospel* (New Haven: Yale Univ. Press, 1965); H. M. Teeple, *The Literary Origin of the Gospel of John* (Evanston, Ill.: Religion and Ethics Inst., 1974); and D. A. Carsen, "Current Source Criticism of the Fourth Gospel: Some Methodological Questions," *JBL* 97 (1978): 411–29.

Various aspects of the FG's symbolic world are investigated by C. K. Barrett, "The Old Testament in the Fourth Gospel," *JTS* 48 (1947): 155–69; H. Odeberg, *The Fourth Gospel Interpreted in Its Relation to Contemporaneous Religious Currents in Palestine and the Hellenistic-Oriental World* (Chicago: Argonaut, 1968 [1929]); W. A. Meeks, *The Prophet-King: Moses Traditions and the Johannine Christology,* NovTSup 14 (Leiden: E. J. Brill, 1967); W. A. Meeks, " 'Am I a Jew?' Johannine Christianity and Judaism," in *Christianity, Judaism, and Other Greco-Roman Cults: I. New*

Testament, ed. J. Neusner, Studies in Judaism in Late Antiquity 12 (Leiden: E. J. Brill, 1975), 163–86; N. A. Dahl, "The Johannine Church and History," in his *Jesus in the Memory of the Early Church* (Minneapolis: Augsburg Pub. House, 1976), 99–119; C. H. Dodd, *The Interpretation of the Fourth Gospel* (Cambridge: At the Univ. Press, 1968); and P. Borgen, *Bread from Heaven*, NovTSup 10 (Leiden: E. J. Brill, 1965).

Some of the theological dimensions of John are considered by D. M. Smith, "The Presentation of Jesus in the Fourth Gospel," *Int* 31 (1977): 367–78; E. Käsemann, *The Testament of Jesus*, trans. G. Krodel (Philadelphia: Fortress Press, 1968); R. Fortna, "From Christology to Soteriology," *Int* 27 (1973): 31–47; R. Bultmann, "The Theology of the Gospel of John and the Johannine Epistles," in his *Theology of the New Testament* (New York: Charles Scribner's Sons, 1953), 2:3–92; H. Schlier, "The World and Man According to St. John's Gospel," in his *The Relevance of the New Testament* (New York: Herder & Herder, 1968), 156–71; and C. K. Barrett, "The Dialectical Theology of St. John," in his *New Testament Essays* (London: SPCK, 1972), 49–69.

Helpful exegetical and thematic studies include E. Käsemann, "The Structure and Purpose of the Prologue to John's Gospel," in *New Testament Questions of Today*, trans. J. Montague (Philadelphia: Fortress Press, 1969), 138–67; C. K. Barrett, "The Prologue of St. John's Gospel," in his *New Testament Essays* (London: SPCK, 1972), 27–48; P. Minear, "The Original Functions of John 21," *JBL* 102 (1983): 85–98; J. H. Neyrey, "The Jacob Allusions in John 1:51," *CBQ* 44 (1982): 586–605; P. B. Harner, *The "I Am" of the Fourth Gospel* (Philadelphia: Fortress Press, 1970); M. E. Boismard, *St. John's Prologue* (Westminster, Md.: Newman Press, 1957); L. J. Kuyper, "Grace and Truth: An Old Testament Description of God and Its Use in the Johannine Gospel," *Int* 18 (1964): 3–19; B. Vawter, "The Johannine Sacramentary," *TS* 17 (1956): 151–66; R. E. Brown, "Incidents That Are Units in the Synoptic Gospels but Dispersed in St. John," *CBQ* 23 (1961): 143–60; J. A. T. Robinson, "The Relationship of the Prologue to the Gospel of St. John," *NTS* 9 (1962–63): 120–29; D. Rensberger, "The Politics of John: The Trial of Jesus in the Fourth Gospel," *JBL* 103 (1984): 395–411; and F. F. Segovia, "Peace I Leave with You; My Peace I Give to You: Discipleship in the Fourth Gospel," in *Discipleship in the New Testament*, ed. F. F. Segovia (Philadelphia: Fortress Press, 1985), 76–102.

An influential article that brought together the social world of Johannine Christianity and literary analysis is W. A. Meeks's "The Man from Heaven in Johannine Sectarianism," *JBL* 91 (1972): 44–72. Other studies that reflect an increasingly self-conscious use of literary methods are R. A. Culpepper, *Anatomy of the Fourth Gospel: A Study in Literary Design* (Philadelphia: Fortress Press, 1983); X. Leon-Dufour, "Towards a Symbolic Reading of the Fourth Gospel," *NTS* 27 (1980–81): 439–56; and S. M. Schneiders, "The Footwashing (John 13:1–20): An Experiment in Hermeneutics," *CBQ* 43 (1981): 76–92.

The commentary tradition for the FG is a rich one. In recent scholarship, the most brilliant example, however flawed by its redactional hypotheses, is R. Bultmann, *The Gospel of John: A Commentary*, trans. G. Beasley-Murray et al. (Philadelphia: Westminster Press, 1971 [1966]). Three commentaries are marked by exegetical thoroughness and a full consideration of scholarly debates: R. E. Brown, *The Gospel According to John*, 2 vols. Anchor Bible (Garden City, N.Y.: Doubleday & Co., 1966–70); R. Schnackenburg, *The Gospel According to John*, 3 vols., vol. 1: *Introduction and Commentary on Chs. 1—4*, trans. K. Smythe (New York: Seabury Press, 1980 [1965]); vol. 2: *Commentary on Chs. 5—12*, trans. C. Hastings et al. (New York: Seabury Press, 1980 [1971]); vol. 3: *Commentary on Chs. 13—21*, trans. D. Smith and G. A. Kron (New York: Crossroad, 1982 [1975]); E. Haenchen, *John 1: A Commentary on the Gospel of John 1—6*, trans. and ed. R. W. Funk with U. Busse, Hermeneia (Philadelphia: Fortress Press, 1984 [1980]); and idem, *John 2: A Commentary on the Gospel of John 7—21*, trans. and ed. R. W. Funk with U. Busse, Hermeneia (Philadelphia: Fortress Press, 1984 [1980]). As always, an accessible and reliable guide to the text is provided by C. K. Barrett, *The Gospel According to John* (London: SPCK, 1956).

25

1, 2, and 3 John

THE THREE LETTERS ATTRIBUTED TO JOHN EMERGE FROM A CONTEXT OF conflict and appear to provide a window onto the history of Johannine Christianity. Close examination of the letters, however, leads to the conclusion that they provide less a basis for a precise historical reconstruction of a community's history than one for an appreciation of the distinctive Johannine understanding of Christian existence.

Since our knowledge of a Johannine church is at best vague, it is impossible to assign these three very short writings to precise places in the church's putative history. A complete lack of external controls prohibits any history in the full sense. The best we could hope for would be traces of an internal development within the group. And even this depends entirely on reading between the lines of the writings themselves. Although it is likely that these documents had a common authorship, we cannot be utterly certain that they did; indeed, a common style and symbolic structure would be expected from both sides of a divided community. Nor can we be totally confident that the letters were written in a particular sequence. They could have been written at intervals and could represent stages in a conflict. But it is far more likely that they were all sent at once, so that we cannot even trace a development but can describe only a single moment.

Even the attempt to describe the situation to which these letters were addressed, therefore, must to some extent consist of a recital of the difficulties confronting any such description.

THE SETTING: CONFLICT AND DIVISION

Each of the letters indicates in its own way that there is conflict among the readers. In 3 John, the dispute appears at first reading to be purely a political one between rival leaders. In 2 John, that conflict is connected to the issue of proper teaching. And in 1 John, doctrinal and moral conflicts dominate. The conflict appears to be one generated from within rather

than from without. Not hostility from the world or persecution but
internal disputes and rivalries are causing the division. And at least the
manifest issue concerns the proper understanding of Jesus.

The dimensions or even the precise nature of the conflict, however, are
not easy to determine. First and Second John clearly indicate that convictions concerning Jesus have become—if not the cause of the divisions—
the banners of respective parties. In the most explicit fashion, the content
of belief, rather than simply the assent of faith, becomes here a criterion
for membership. The terms "orthodoxy," "heterodoxy," and "heresy" are
appropriate ones in these letters. Thus, we find the use of the verb "to
confess," *homologeō, exhomologeō* (1 John 2:23; 4:2, 3, 15; 2 John 7) and
"to deny," *arneomai* (1 John 2:22–23). The opponents are not unbelievers
but fellow Christians; they are not purely outsiders but ones who had at
first belonged to the author's own group. They are those "who went out
from us" (1 John 2:19). Now, they are given traditional titles of op-
probrium; they are "false prophets" (1 John 4:1) and "antichrists" (1 John
2:18, 22; 4:3). In the description of 2 John 7, they are above all "deceivers
who have gone out into the world," people who are at once "deceivers and
antichrists."

These designations do not, however, make clear what doctrinal points
separate the Johannine groups. How literally does the author understand
"antichrist"? There are a number of creedal statements in 1 and 2 John
that are pertinent. In 1 John we find the phrases "he who denies that Jesus
is the Christ" and "he who denies the Father and the Son"; together, these
phrases designate a liar and an antichrist (2:22). In contrast, the readers
are to "believe in the name of his Son Jesus Christ" (3:23). There is a
similar opposition later between "every spirit which confesses that Jesus
Christ has come in the flesh" and "every spirit which does not confess
Jesus" (4:2–3). In the same chapter, the orthodox group testifies "that the
Father has sent his Son as Savior of the world," and this is placed next to
"whoever confesses that Jesus is Son of God" (4:14–15). A series of
confessional phrases follows in chapter 5: "whoever believes that Jesus is
the Christ" (5:1); "he who believes that Jesus is the Son of God" (5:5); "he
who believes in the Son of God" (5:10); "believe in the name of the Son of
God" (5:13); and "we know that the son of God has come" (5:20). Finally,
2 John 7 gives us, "who will not acknowledge the coming of Jesus Christ in
the flesh."

These phrases make fairly obvious what this orthodox group confesses.
But it is not at all clear what the content of the "heterodox" belief is. It is
not certain that everything the author's group affirms is being denied by
their opponents. Nor does it appear that the denials add up to a coherent
confession. A pure antichrist position would be the denial that "Jesus is
the Christ" (1 John 2:22). But do the denials of Jesus (1 John 4:3) and

"that Jesus Christ has come in the flesh" (2 John 7) represent expansions, refinements, or equivalents to that first denial? Do the opponents challenge the confession that Jesus is Messiah? Or that he is Son of God? Or that he is truly human? Or that he "came" as God's son rather than was "adopted" as God's son in his resurrection? We cannot be sure; nor is it certain that the author himself knew exactly the position of those who had separated themselves. But he is convinced that they are deficient in their understanding and appreciation of *Jesus*. The figure who was, according to the Fourth Gospel, the abiding center of their life and unity, is here the focal point of dissension and division.

Any attempt to reconstruct a coherent position for the "opponents" must deal with two methodological difficulties. First, we cannot assume from every positive statement or exhortation of our author that the opposition held a different view. Not every plus implies a minus. The author's insistence on love, and particularly on the practical expression of love, may reflect a lack of care among the opposition party; on the other hand, it need not. Second, we cannot assume that the ideological framing of the division was either more or less important than the social dimensions of the conflict. These were at least twofold: the mutual withholding of hospitality, and rival claims to leadership (see 2 John and 3 John). We do not have sufficient information to decide whether the political and social conflicts preceded, accompanied, or followed the ideological disagreement.

Whatever the precise nature of the disputes, any sort of division would be a severe crisis for a church that lived within the symbolic framework we have seen in the Fourth Gospel. The farewell discourse of Jesus (John 15:1—17:26) had portrayed a community of friends. They shared in one Spirit. They were joined to Jesus as Jesus was to the Father, in a fellowship of unity and love. For a community with such a self-understanding, any dissension and deviance would be difficult to understand or assimilate. But a clash over the right understanding of Jesus, and a division leading to mutual excommunication, would challenge this community's very identity and existence.

A THREE-LETTER PACKET FROM THE ELDER

The three letters were probably sent at the same time to the same destination, for it would be difficult otherwise to account for the preservation of letters as unprepossessing as 2 and 3 John were they not the companions of a more significant writing. The function of each writing will be considered more in detail as we examine them in turn, but it is most likely that 3 John was a letter of recommendation from the elder to Gaius, certifying that the carrier of the other two letters, Demetrius, was to be

received. Second John was to be read to the entire assembly as an introduction and cover letter for 1 John, which is not really a letter at all but a word
of exhortation, closer in nature to a sermon. As in the case of the correspondence carried by Tychichus from Paul to the Lycus valley (Philemon,
Colossians, Ephesians), the Johannine letters make most sense when seen
as parts of the same epistolary package. As for the identity of the elder who
wrote the letters or the location of the recipients, there have been many
theories but few widely acknowledged solutions.

3 JOHN: LETTER OF COMMENDATION
FROM THE ELDER

Third John is a genuine personal letter and provides us with the only
specific names in this dispute: Gaius, Demetrius, and Diotrephes are all
good Greco-Roman names. We cannot draw conclusions concerning the
letter's provenience on that basis, but the names indicate a very probable
gentile component in the Johannine communities. The short farewell
indicates that these churches call themselves friends (v. 15), as Jesus
taught them (John 15:12–15). The elder who writes aligns himself with the
"true witness" of the Fourth Gospel: "You know that our testimony is
true" (v. 12; cf. John 19:35; 21:24). The author calls Gaius beloved (vv. 1,
2, 5, 11), but he is otherwise unknown to us. He appears to be the head of
a household, since the elder praises him for his hospitality to traveling
Christians (vv. 5–6).

The elder is pleased that Gaius is prospering—there is little religious
coloration in this stock phrase (v. 2)—and above all that his emissaries
have testified to the fact that Gaius "walks in the truth" (v. 3). There is
considerable communication between these local churches. Those who
provide hospitality for the messengers and missionaries become "fellow
workers for the truth" (v. 8).

The hospitality of Gaius and his household is all the more important for
the elder, since neither his letters nor his emissaries are being accepted by
another church leader, Diotrephes. Diotrephes here appears as a rival to
the elder, one who seeks primacy of place among the Johannine churches
(v. 9). His bid for power is exemplified by his refusal to accept those sent
by the elder. What is more, he expels from the assembly those who do
accept them (v. 10). At the very least, then, 3 John shows us a power
struggle between two church leaders. We receive only hints of a deeper
doctrinal division in 3 John (as in the emphasis on "walking in the truth").
But Diotrephes could well be a leader among those "who went out from
us" (1 John 2:19; 2 John 7).

Gaius is a local leader still in communion with the elder and willing to
receive his delegates and teaching. Without such hospitality, the elder's

branch of the church would face extinction, for those who traveled "for the name" would or could take no support from the "heathen" (v. 7). This small aside reminds us of the separatist tendencies of all Johannine Christians. Now, however, those outside may even include dissident Christians. Those who provided refreshment and new outfitting ("sending them on," v. 6) for these messengers became their "fellow workers" and "friends" because the sharing of their possessions symbolized as well a share in their spiritual ideals.

The pertinence of all the talk about hospitality is revealed by the specific purpose of this short note. The elder has "written something for the church" (v. 9). This epistolary aorist refers not to a previous communication but to the exhortation that he now wants read to the assembly (1 John). The present note serves as a letter of recommendation for the messenger who carries these letters. Demetrius is well attested by everyone and "by the truth itself" (v. 12). Gaius can therefore safely accept him and his messages. The "many things" the elder does not want to commit to paper but is postponing for a face-to-face meeting (v. 13) concern practical matters, such as dealing with the Diotrephes situation. The elder hopes to come soon himself (v. 14); then he will discuss Diotrephes with Gaius (v. 10). In the meantime, with a classic parenetic flourish, the elder reminds Gaius not to follow the example of Diotrephes: "Do not imitate the wicked but the good" (v. 11). Nothing could sound more Greek. But the motivation given for such behavior places us once again within the distinctively Johannine symbolic world: the one who does good is "from God," whereas the one who does evil "has not seen God" (v. 11).

2 JOHN: COVER LETTER TO THE CHURCH

The second of the short letters carried by Demetrius is a note from the elder to Gaius's community. The "elect lady with her children" (v. 1) is a feminine honorific for the community as such, as the closing also suggests: "the children of your elect sister greet you [singular]" (v. 13). The letter supposes a collective audience (vv. 2, 3, 6, 8, 10, 12). The greeting is more extended than in 3 John but with the same emphasis on "truth." "All who have come to know the truth" love this community, on the basis of "the truth dwelling within us" (vv. 1–2). The elder prays that his reader receive grace and mercy and peace "in truth and love" (v. 3), and he rejoices to see them "walking in the truth" (v. 4). The closing suggests again that the elder defers personal matters for a later face-to-face conference, when he hopes "their joy might be made full" (v. 12; cf. 1 John 1:4).

The issue of false teaching emerges explicitly in this letter. The elder warns his readers of the "many deceivers who have gone out into the world" (v. 7). We are reminded by this of the deep ambivalence of the

Johannine writings toward that entity called the world. As the Fourth Gospel narrative shows, the world is at once the arena for the revelation of Jesus and the object of God's love and salvation (John 1:9; 3:16–17; 4:42; 6:14, 33, 51; 8:12; 9:5; 10:36; 11:27; 12:46–47; 17:21–24) and, because of its rejection of God in Jesus, a place defined by the absence of God and hostility toward believers (John 1:10; 7:4–7; 8:23; 11:9; 12:25, 31; 14:17–31; 15:18–19; 16:8, 11, 33; 17:6, 9, 11, 14, 16, 18, 25). The same tension is carried over with equal intensity in 1 John: "the world" was the recipient of God's love and salvation through Jesus (1 John 2:2; 4:9, 14, 17) but exists now as a place dominated by a power other than God's (5:19); this is reflected in its perverted values and hatred for the "children of God" (1 John 2:15–17; 3:1, 13; 4:1–5; 5:4–5).

Those who have left the elder's community and "gone out into the world" therefore partake of its values. They are collectively "the deceiver and the antichrist" (2 John 7). Whether by their explicit teaching or their actions, their deception amounts to this: "They deny Christ's coming in the flesh" (v. 7). The elder portrays them as progressives who do not hold to the community traditions: "Whoever goes forward [*proagei*] and does not remain in the teaching of Christ does not have God" (v. 9). The ambiguity of the expression "teaching of Christ" may be deliberate. It includes teaching "about Christ," that is, a proper understanding of the Christ, for that is required to "have both Father and Son" (v. 9). But it may also include the teaching "from Christ," meaning the commandment that Jesus himself taught them "from the beginning" (v. 5).

Concern for false teaching is here combined with practical directives on hospitality. What the elder complained of in the practice of Diotrephes he now recommends to this church! Its members are not to receive into their houses anyone not carrying the proper teaching. They are not even to greet such people (v. 10). We see here the survival techniques of intentional communities faced with deviance: shunning and excommunication. The stakes are stated succinctly: "Whoever greets them makes fellowship [*koinōnei*] with their evil deeds" (v. 11). This compact observation contains a complex of interconnected concepts. First, as we have seen often in the NT writings, hospitality means more than the sharing of space and food; it implies a spiritual communion. Second, as we saw in the Pastorals and 2 Peter, evil behavior is thought to follow directly from wrong thinking. Even wrong teaching about Jesus is here thought to lead to evil deeds. The refusal of hospitality in this case is not an act of hostility toward individual persons but a defensive measure against error and evil by a community fighting to maintain its own identity.

The elder alerts his readers to the message they would also hear read to them in the assembly (i.e., 1 John). They are to hold to the commandment they learned from the beginning. They are not to wander off but to stay put (vv. 5–6). The commandment is simply that they love one another (v. 5). So, if they love one another, they also keep his commandment (v. 6). That single all-inclusive commandment that came to them from Jesus (John 15:12, 17) is, the elder insists, still the necessary and sufficient way for this community to define itself.

1 JOHN: EXHORTATION TO
A REMNANT COMMUNITY

We would not expect a writing so beautiful or compelling as 1 John to emerge from the hard circumstances suggested by 2 and 3 John. This is the "something written for the church" that Demetrius carried to the household of Gaius. Although clearly a written composition (see 2:1, 7, 8, 12, 14, 21, 26; 5:13), it has no epistolary character at all, retaining instead a distinctive sermonic style of exhortation. The author "announces" or "proclaims" (1:2, 3, 5) to his audience a message (1:5) that really has no new content (2:7) but is a reminder and exhortation to live by that commandment which was "from the beginning" (1:1; 2:7, 13, 14, 24; 3:11).

The style of 1 John is much like that of the Fourth Gospel. Its Greek is, if anything, even simpler and its vocabulary more abstract. The combination makes it a difficult composition to read sequentially; the same points appear to be made repeatedly with only slight variations. The style can be deceptive, for it sometimes contains the form of argument, while lacking its logic. Thus from 1:6 to 2:5 we read eight conditional sentences. Each of them has an internal coherence. But when read in sequence, not only the connection between them but also their individual points are easily forgotten. The most striking stylistic element in 1 John is the apparent self-contradiction found sometimes sentence by sentence. What is granted by way of proposition is taken away by way of exhortation! One sentence affirms something that the next sentence appears to deny. Not surprisingly, various source theories have been invoked to account for this phenomenon. They are not necessary. The vacillation between affirmation and exhortation in 1 John derives not from a multiplicity of sources and editors but from the internal tension created by the author's task.

This composition certainly shares the same symbolic world as the Fourth Gospel. We find in it many of the Gospel's major themes: the distinctions between light and darkness (1:5; 2:8–9, 10), truth and falsehood (1:6; 2:4, 21, 27; 3:19; 4:6, 20; 5:7), the community and "the world" (2:15; 3:1, 13; 4:3, 4, 5; 5:19), and life and death (1:2; 3:14–15; 5:11, 13). Here is the same conviction of being in touch with the "beginning" in both a chronological and ontological sense (1:1; 2:12, 14, 24; 3:11) and being in communion with the Holy Spirit (2:20, 27; 3:24; 4:2, 6,

13; 5:7). The believers are those who are "born of God" (3:1, 2, 10; 4:4, 7; 5:1, 4, 18, 19). They "bear testimony" (4:14; 5:7, 10) to what they "see and hear" (1:3; 2:24; 3:2, 6; 4:13) even as they "abide" (2:6, 10, 17, 24–25; 3:6, 24; 4:12, 13, 15) both in the commandment (2:3; 3:22; 5:2) and in the love (3:11, 14, 18; 4:7, 11–12, 21) revealed to them in the Son of God (4:7–10).

What distinguishes the shaping of these symbols in 1 John, however, is that none of them can be affirmed as straightforwardly as before. This is a community divided: some have "gone out from us" (2:19). And although the author insists that if they "had really been of us" they would not have left, the identity of this community that defines itself in terms of its share in the Spirit, its unity and its love, is severely shaken. At least two groups now lay claim to being the community of the beloved disciple, and their claims appear to be mutually exclusive. The task before the author is therefore to assert the traditional claims for his readers but at the same time to take into account this new circumstance.

The remarkable thing about 1 John is that it does not consist of a bitter polemic against those who departed or a sustained refutation of their claims. The focus of this writing is not on the outsiders but on those who remain. But they are not simply congratulated for holding on to the truth. They are rather challenged to a renewed affirmation of their identity, which cannot be simply a matter of correct doctrine. This is a practical exhortation: "I am writing to you so that you may not sin" (2:1). Its final command is grim indeed: "Little children, keep yourselves from idols" (5:21).

In 1 John we find the rare phenomenon of a perfectionistic and separatist community dealing with failure and division not by blaming those who left but by engaging in a form of self-criticism. The faithful remnant is encouraged not to smugness but to a new alertness, not to possible attacks from the outside but to their own failures. And these failures, it becomes clear, are those of smugness, of an unheeding and comfortable confidence in the sufficiency simply of being an insider. Now it is not enough to claim the Spirit; now everyone must "test every spirit to see whether they are of God" (4:1). Now it is not enough to claim distinction from "the world," for the departure of some has shown that "the world" is not simply out there but also in here.

The community of the elder is therefore required to examine its symbols to discover elements of a shared tradition that may have been only latent before. So, for example, it is imperative for the community to acknowledge its own sinfulness (1:9), in the confidence that Jesus will be their expiation and advocate with the Father (1:7; 2:2; 4:10). No longer can they be content with the simple affirmation that the one born of God does not sin (3:9); that conviction is true but must be understood in a new way.

Now, it is clear that the denial of sin is not only self-deception (1:8) but may be itself the "sin unto death" (5:16–17), for in it one places one's confidence in one's own perfection, not in the mercy of God; and that is a closure to God. This is a community that confesses its sin and prays for its members who sin (5:14). Its confidence is not in its own perfection but in the gift of life that came from the side of the crucified (5:6–8; cf. John 19:34).

For the remnant community, the truth cannot remain simply the abstract confession of Jesus as Son of God come in the flesh, as important as that is (2:22–23; 3:23; 4:2–3, 14; 5:1, 10–11, 20). The truth must be translated into appropriate behavior. This means a real and effectual love, which is in contrast to the hatred characteristic of the world (2:15; 3:1, 13; 4:3, 4, 5; 5:13, 19) and those false brethren who have joined its pattern (2:9–10; 3:14–15; 4:20). The sad fraternal relationship between this community and those who have departed is suggested by the example of Cain. He murdered his brother simply because "his own deeds were evil and his brother's righteous" (3:12–13; cf. Gen. 4:8–16).

The members of this community must "perfect" their love (that is, bring it to its term), by removing the defensiveness that comes from fear and opening their hearts to each other in care (2:5; 4:12, 17–18). They cannot any longer remain isolated as though the identity of the community would be maintained no matter what they did. They are to pray for each other and correct each other (5:14–17). They are to care for each other in as practical and direct a fashion as that in which God's love in Christ operates (1 John 3:16–18):

> By this we know love, that he laid down his life for us; and we ought to lay down our lives for the brethren. If anyone has the world's goods and sees his brother in need, yet closes his heart against him, how does God's love abide in him? Little children, let us love not in word or speech but in deed and in truth.

This is a community, therefore, that must now face up to the task of renewing its integrity in action and understanding. This accounts for the apparent inconsistency in the composition, between assertion and exhortation. There is a sense in which this community can continue to assert that it has the message of life (1:1–4) and has experienced victory over the evil one (2:12–14). Its members can state with truth that their sins have been forgiven (2:12), that they have knowledge of truth (2:20–21) and are God's children (3:2). They can even declare that no one born of God sins (3:9–10; 5:18) and that their own hearts do not condemn them (3:21). They are sure that they do abide in God (3:24) and have overcome the antichrist (4:4). They have the Spirit (4:13) and love is perfected among them (4:17). Their faith overcomes the world (5:4). They bear a testimony within themselves (5:10) and have confidence (5:14) that they are within the God who is true (5:20).

But even while they assert these convictions, which form the very structure of their symbolic world, they must assert as well the imperatives that arise from the failure of the community to live by the convictions. If they should now walk in darkness they would be liars (1:6). If they say they have no sin, they deceive themselves (1:8) and make God a liar since he sent Jesus as expiation for their sins (1:10). If they hate their brethren they are still in the dark (2:9). They must hate the world and refuse to live by its standards (2:15). They are to abide in God (2:27). They must cleanse themselves (3:3) and are commanded to love one another (3:11) not just in word but in deed (3:18).

In short, the elder indicates to this remnant community that its symbols of self-understanding are true and correspond to reality. But the reason for their failure is that they did not appreciate that the gift carried with it an imperative. They had grown satisfied with being "the perfect" and hence had lost their integrity. They needed to realize once more that it was not *their* perfection that made them "children of God," but the gift of God. They needed to look once again at the source of their identity, to learn the pattern for their lives together (1 John 4:7–12):

> Beloved, let us love one another; for love is of God, and he who loves is born of God and knows God. He who does not love does not know God, for God is love. In this the love of God was made manifest among us, that God sent his only Son into the world, so that we might live through him. In this is love, not that we loved God, but that he loved us and sent his Son to be the expiation for our sins. Beloved, if God so loved us, we also ought to love one another. No man has ever seen God; if we love one another, God abides in us and his love is perfected in us.

BIBLIOGRAPHICAL NOTE

The English-language literature on the Johannine letters is not vast. For an overview, see the introduction by F. F. Bruce, "Johannine Studies Since Westcott's Day," in B. F. Westcott's *The Epistles of St. John* (Grand Rapids: Wm. B. Eerdmans, 1966 [1892]), lix–lxxvi. For theories of destination and purpose, see J. A. T. Robinson, "The Destination and Purpose of the Johannine Epistles," *NTS* 7 (1960): 56–65; and J. J. Gunther, "The Alexandrian Gospel and the Letters of John," *CBQ* 41 (1979): 581–603.

Literary aspects, particularly, of 1 John are treated by W. F. Howard, in "The Common Authorship of the Johannine Gospel and Epistles," *JTS* 48 (1947): 12–25; A. P. Salom, "Some Aspects of the Grammatical Style of I John," *JBL* 74 (1955): 96–102; O. Piper, "I John and the Didache of the Primitive Church," *JBL* 66 (1947): 437–51; J. C. O'Neill, *The Puzzle of I John* (London: SPCK, 1966); and

F. O. Francis, "The Form and Function of the Opening and Closing Paragraphs of James and I John," *ZNW* 61 (1970): 110–26. Helpful guidance through the symbolism of the letters is offered by R. E. Brown, "The Qumran Scrolls and the Johannine Gospel and Epistles," *New Testament Essays* (Milwaukee: Bruce Pub. Co., 1965), 138–173.

For the reconstruction of the historical setting of the letters, see R. E. Brown, *The Community of the Beloved Disciple* (New York: Paulist Press, 1979), 93–144; idem, " 'Other Sheep Not of This Fold': The Johannine Perspective on Christian Diversity in the Late First Century," *JBL* 97 (1978): 5–22; and P. Perkins, "*Koinōnia* in I Jn 1:3–7: The Social Context of Division in the Johannine Letters," *CBQ* 45 (1983): 631–41. A shift away from historical reconstruction to the exhortatory function of the letter is found in J. M. Lieu, "Authority to Become Children of God: A Study of I John," *NovT* 23 (1981): 210–28.

Specifically on 2 and 3 John, see R. W. Funk, "The Form and Structure of II and III John," *JBL* 86 (1967): 424–30; and A. J. Malherbe, "Hospitality and Inhospitality in the Church," in *Social Aspects of Early Christianity,* 2d ed., enl. (Philadelphia: Fortress Press, 1983 [1977]), 92–112. See also C. H. Kim, *Form and Function of the Familiar Greek Letter of Recommendation* (Missoula, Mont.: Scholars Press, 1972).

Individual themes or passages are considered by E. Malatesta, *Interiority and Covenant* (Rome: Biblical Inst. Press, 1978); T. Barosse, "The Relationship of Love to Faith in St. John," *TS* 18 (1957): 538–59; P. S. Minear, "The Idea of Incarnation in I John," *Int* 24 (1970): 291–302; N. H. Cassen, "A Grammatical and Contextual Inventory of the Use of *Kosmos* in the Johannine Corpus with Some Implications for a Johannine Cosmic Theology," *NTS* 19 (1972): 81–91; B. Noack, "On 1 Jn 2:12–14," *NTS* 19 (1972): 236–241; J. Townsend, "The Sin Unto Death: 1 Jn 5:16f.," *Restoration Quarterly* 6 (1962): 147–50; J. E. Weir, "The Identity of the *Logos* in the First Epistle of John," *ExpTim* 86 (1974–75): 118–19; P. Trudinger, "Concerning Mortal Sins and Otherwise: A Note on I Jn 5:16–17," *Bib* 52 (1971): 541–42; and M. DeJonge, "The Use of the Word *Christos* in the Johannine Epistles," in *Studies in John,* ed. C. K. Barrett, NovTSup 24 (Leiden: E. J. Brill, 1970), 66–74.

Although obviously dated in many respects, B. F. Westcott, *The Epistles of Saint John,* with a new intro. by F. F. Bruce (Grand Rapids: Wm. B. Eerdmans, 1966 [1892]), still provides a useful guide through the Greek text and Johannine theology. R. Bultmann, *A Commentary on the Johannine Epistles,* trans. R. P. O'Hara et al., Hermeneia (Philadelphia: Fortress Press, 1973 [1967]), does not have the stature of his Gospel commentary but has some virtues. R. E. Brown, *The Epistles of John,* Anchor Bible (Garden City, N.Y.: Doubleday & Co., 1982), is characteristically thorough and well balanced, with fine bibliographies. See also J. L. Houlden, *A Commentary on the Johannine Epistles,* HNTC (New York: Harper & Row, 1973).

26

The Book of Revelation

Few writings in all of literature have been so obsessively read with such generally disastrous results as the Book of Revelation (= the Apocalypse). Its history of interpretation is largely a story of tragic misinterpretation, resulting from a fundamental misapprehension of the work's literary form and purpose. Insofar as its arcane symbols have fed the treasury of poets, its influence has been benign. More often, these same symbols have nurtured delusionary systems, both private and public, to the destruction of their fashioners and to the discredit of the writing.

Misunderstandings appear to be invited by the text itself, for it claims to offer a "revelation from Jesus Christ" which makes known to the readers "what is going to happen shortly" (1:1). No wonder it has often been taken to be a divinely certified blueprint for the future. Already in the second century, Papias found in passages like Rev. 20:4–6 a literal promise of an earthly thousand-year reign of the saints before the end:

> They came to life and reigned with Christ a thousand years. The rest of the dead did not come to life until the thousand years were ended. This is the first resurrection. Over such the second death has no power, but they shall be priests of God and of Christ, and they shall reign with him a thousand years. (20:4–6; cf. Eusebius *Ecclesiastical History* III.39.12)

Papias was among the first of many "millenarians"—including Irenaeus, the Montanists, Joachim of Fiore, and radical reformers—who found in Revelation a guide to the restored heaven and earth (21:1–2). The oppressed and unsettled in every age could also find in these pages—with their whispered injunctions to read between the lines (13:18; 17:9)—the identity of *their* "beast" (13:18) at whom their otherwise random hostility might legitimately be directed. Rulers and usurpers from Nero to Hitler have unwittingly borne the sobriquet "666." For the dispossessed and resentful, Revelation (in passages such as 21:1–8) offered, with the idealized picture of the primitive church in Acts 4:32–37, the basis for utopian, egalitarian projects that sought by human effort to bring about the vision of a heavenly Jerusalem. No matter that such movements invariably led to the destruction of their sponsors. The ideal is born again in every age, including our own, when many Christians find in Revelation the most helpful handbook for the determination of the inevitable Armageddon (16:16). In short, the Book of Revelation is one of those rare compositions that speak to something deep and disturbed in the human spirit with a potency never diminished by fact or disconfirmation.

This history of interpretation has several constant elements. Most important, the book is considered a literal prophecy of future events. Two aspects of this definition are significant: first, "prophecy" is taken in its narrowest sense, to mean "prediction"; the text's frame of reference is not the author's age but that contemporary with the reader. The reading of contemporary events is therefore an essential part of reading this text: how does the pattern of world affairs indicate signs of the approaching end time? The symbolism of the writing is, furthermore, treated as though it were a cryptogram; the reader is concerned not with intertextual connections or allusions to the religious heritage of the writing but only with the ways in which textual symbols can be aligned, point by point, with aspects of the present situation. This process of interpretation has shown itself to be incapable of disconfirmation by experience. If the reading of contemporary events turns out to be erroneous—if in fact the end does not come—it is never the nature of the text or of the interpretive process that is blamed; only the calculations were off.

Something more than historical curiosity or even moral and religious fervor is involved in such a process. Among some of its readers, this text is capable of eliciting an obsessive and sometimes paranoid *need to know*. To a remarkable extent, such readings leave aside completely what Revelation might have to say about *how* Christian existence should be lived. The point of the text is reduced to certainty about what is going to happen. The text is thereby given the status of a train schedule, and the motivation for the interpretive process is at the level of biorhythms and astrology.

The problem here is that exegesis is swallowed up in hermeneutics. The conviction that God's Word speaks directly to every age has not been accompanied by the appreciation that it does so as mediated through its first historical expression. The contemporary significance of an NT writing does not derive from the fact that it was written expressly for this age but derives from the conviction that a truth spoken to the first age of Christians can and does remain a truth for every age of believers. Failure to appreciate the historical fashioning and function of Revelation has bred great mischief. The remembrance of things past in this case means freedom from a literalist prison and openness to the fresh message the text can speak, out of its historical contingency.

Above all for the Book of Revelation, therefore, the perspective given by historical-critical analysis can provide an antidote to spiritual sickness. It enables us to grasp the literary conventions within which the book's meaning is expressed and which must be grasped if that meaning is to be found. From it, we learn to read the Book of Revelation as a writing in the apocalyptic genre and discover how the frame of that genre is itself reshaped by the experience of a crucified and raised Messiah who is confessed in the church as Lord.

REVELATION AND APOCALYPTIC

Since there was a fairly extensive discussion of apocalyptic in an earlier section of this book (chap. 2), I will here review only some salient points of that outlook and literature. It arose as a form of literary prophecy within Judaism in response to an erosion of values from within and an attack on those values from the outside. It found classic expression in the Book of Daniel in the Maccabean period. It proliferated in a large number of pseudonymous writings both Jewish and Christian. To those wavering in their convictions it counseled fidelity; to those losing confidence it encouraged endurance. Apocalyptic offered the oppressed and persecuted comfort by providing an interpretation of history. Writing in the name of a prophet or sage of the past, a contemporary writer assumed the mantle of prophecy and with it the authority of antiquity in his analysis of the contemporary situation.

Apocalyptic is essentially a revelational literature. In the spirit, the prophet ascends to heaven, or has portentous dreams, or is transported to nether regions, so that he can see both the present transcendental reality and its future empirical realization. Such visions of the future and the predictions they breed always have a fictive quality. We have seen as well that apocalyptic uses a standard range of symbols, with a heavy emphasis on numerology, cosmic catastrophes, and fabulous beasts.

The Book of Revelation obviously shares many of the same characteristics. It is, first, a self-consciously *written* composition: "Blessed is he who reads . . . hears . . . what is written" (1:3; cf. 2:1, 8, 12, 18; 3:1, 7, 14; 22:9); and, "Blessed is he who keeps the words of prophecy of *this book*" (22:7). The writing is *visionary* in nature. But because of the literary self-consciousness displayed by the author, we are less likely to find the raw experience of mystical states than their literary distillation. The whole work can be called an *apocalypsis Iēsou Christou* (1:1), with the phrase "of Jesus Christ" understood both in the sense that the revelation comes from him, and in the sense that it is about him. John is told, "Come up hither and I will show you what must take place after this" (4:1), and as he passes through the open door of heaven, he "sees" and "hears" both what now is happening "there" and what will happen on earth. The most charac-

teristically apocalyptic expression in this writing is "I saw" (1:2, 12, 17;
4:1; 5:1–2, 6, 11; 6:1–12; 7:1–2, 9; 8:2, 13; 9:1, 17; 10:1, 5; 13:1–2, 11;
14:1, 6, 14; 15:1, 2, 5; 16:13; 17:3–18; 18:1; 19:11, 17, 19; 20:1, 4, 11–12;
21:1, 2, 22). John is told, "Write what you see in a book" (1:10).

Revelation shares with other apocalyptic writings a standard set of
symbolic structures. Numbers are important, for they combine an aura of
precision with mystery. Above all, we find the number 7: lampstands and
stars standing for angels and churches (1:20), spirits of God (1:4; 3:1; 4:5),
seals (5:1), horns and eyes of the lamb (5:6), trumpets (8:2), thunders
(10:3), heads of the dragon (12:3) and of the beast (13:1), bowls (15:7),
plagues (15:1), kings (17:10), and thousands killed (11:13). The number 4
occurs with the living creatures (4:6–8) and horsemen (6:1–8) and the
angels at the corners of the earth (7:1). In the biblical tradition, multiples
of the number 12 have a certain obvious significance. So we find that the
heavenly Jerusalem has twelve gates and foundation stones, corresponding
to twelve apostles and angels (21:11–14); that the tree of life gives twelve
fruits (22:2); that the woman clothed with the sun has a crown with twelve
stars (12:1); that there are in heaven twenty-four elders and twenty-four
thrones (4:4); and that the number of the elect is one hundred forty-four
thousand, which comes out to be twelve thousand from each of Israel's
twelve tribes (7:4; 14:1–5). The point of all these numbers, of course, is
that there is no point to them; numbers are simply numinous, and that is
enough.

Revelation also has a well-stocked apocalyptic menagerie: the "four
living creatures" (4:6–8), the "Lamb who was slain yet lives" (5:6), the
four horses (6:1–8), the eagle (8:13; 12:14), locusts like cavalry (9:3–11),
and the white horse (19:11–16). On the opposite side, there is the red
dragon (12:3), also known as the ancient serpent (12:9); a "beast out of the
sea" who combines the qualities of leopard, bear, and lion (13:1–2);
another "beast out of the earth" (13:11); and the scarlet beast (17:3, 7–12).
Nor is there a lack of cosmic phenomena. Heavens open (4:1); there are
earthquakes, eclipses, and dissolutions (6:12–17), angelic guards who hold
the four corners of the earth like a carpet and prevent the winds (7:1),
thunder, earthquake, and lightning (8:5), a series of plagues (8:7–12), and
a woman clothed with the sun and with a crown of stars (12:1). The feel of
this imagery can perhaps best be communicated by Rev. 10:1–3:

> Then I saw another mighty angel coming down from heaven, wrapped in a
> cloud, with a rainbow over his head, and his face was like the sun, and his legs
> like pillars of fire. He had a little scroll open in his hand. And he set his right
> foot on the sea, and his left foot on the land, and called out with a loud voice,
> like a lion roaring; when he called out the seven thunders sounded.

These fantastic images can, possibly, be teased into some coherent picture, but that would be quite beside the point. No particular number or beast or star is significant; it is the cumulative effect that creates the sense of mystery and transcendence essential for the revelation.

Revelation is like other apocalyptic works in this respect as well: despite its elaborate symbolism, it presents a rather straightforward interpretation of history. Appearances to the contrary, God is in charge of the world. Even though his people suffer tribulations and evil appears to be triumphant (12:7—13:8), God will decisively intervene in behalf of the oppressed (14:14—20:15), bringing history to its goal with the presence of God among humans (21:1—22:5). The climax to this history is to come "quickly" (1:1; 2:16; 3:11; 11:14; 22:6, 7, 12, 20). The point of this historical interpretation is exhortatory. Since the outcome is certain and soon, those suffering are given the strength to hold on till the end. The text tells the reader at critical moments, "Here is a call to the endurance and faith of the saints" (13:10), and, "Here is a call for the endurance of the saints, those who keep the commandments of God and the faith of Jesus" (14:12). The final vision of the heavenly Jerusalem descending to earth is accompanied by this assurance: "He who conquers shall have this heritage" (21:7). Those who remain steadfast are "victorious" (see 2:7, 11, 17, 26; 3:5, 12, 21). By their suffering they share in a victory over evil and death (15:2) that was first won by the Lamb who was slain yet now still lives (5:6; 17:14).

In three important ways, however, Revelation also breaks the mold of the "ordinary" apocalypse and secures its unique place among such writings. First, it is a work of great artistry. One need only read patches of *1 Enoch* to appreciate this point. There is nothing accidental or haphazard in the composition of Revelation; however obscure it appears to the reader, one of the continually fascinating qualities of the book is the sense of an active and subtle intelligence at work. Even its almost barbarous Greek seems to be deliberate, an evocation of the "sacred and biblical" world. Although Revelation contains no direct citation from the OT, it is an elaborate reworking of scriptural texts so seamless and creative that the reworking genuinely seems to be "its own" language. Revelation makes particularly heavy use of the classical prophetic texts, like Amos and Isaiah, and even more of its antecedents in apocalyptic, Zechariah, Daniel, and most of all, Ezechiel. From Ezechiel we recognize the heavenly throne chariot, the living creatures, the sea of glass, the sealing of the thousands, the eating of the scroll, the living waters through Jerusalem, the measuring of the temple. All of this Revelation brings alive in a new and powerful synthesis.

Second, Revelation has elements that resemble the writings coming from Jewish Merkabah mysticism. Such Hekhaloth literature (descriptions of the heavenly halls) itself derived from the esoteric interpretation of

Ezechiel, so the connections are not altogether surprising. The ascent of the adept into the heavenly places (4:1) is, of course, standard. But the furnishings of the heavenly court are particularly interesting: the throne with one seated on it (4:2), the rainbow of gems (4:3), the living creatures (4:6), the sea of glass (4:6), the torches of fire (4:5), the attendant and praising angels (4:6–9), the fiery glassy sea (15:2), the lake of fire (19:20), the courts of the heavenly city paved with gems (21:15–21). Above all, Revelation resembles the Hekhaloth writings because of the numinous hymns interspersed throughout the visions. They are sung by the angels (4:11), the elders (11:16), and the saints (15:2–4). They give the visions a quality of liturgy and prayer (see 4:9–11; 5:9–12; 7:10–12; 11:15b, 17–18; 16:5b–7b; 19:1–4). The hymns also function, in the style of Greek drama, to give an authorized commentary on the proceedings.

Third, Revelation transcends the apocalyptic genre because of the Christians' experience of Jesus. Like all the writings of the NT, its expectations concerning the future are shaped by its acute awareness of God's present power demonstrated by the resurrection of Jesus and the gift of the Spirit. So we find not an anonymous or pseudonymous writing but one written by a contemporary well known to his readers, who tells them of his experience of the risen Lord at a specific time and place in the present (1:9–10). Nor does John engage simply in the fictional predictive prophecy of apocalyptic. In the letters to the seven churches of Asia Minor, he addresses what is happening among them now. The voice of prophecy is alive in the land (2:1—3:22).

Most of all, the conviction that Jesus has risen from the dead as Lord transforms the symbols of apocalyptic. We read not only a revelation about Jesus but one that comes *from* him (1:1). His is the voice that speaks through the prophet in the letters. The Son of man is not simply one who will come as judge (14:14) but one who lives now (1:13): "I am the living one; I died and I am alive forevermore" (1:18). Jesus stands before the throne of God as the Lamb who was slain but is now alive (5:6; 7:10). He sits on the white horse bearing the title Faithful and True (19:11); his garments are, like the servant's, dipped in blood (Isa. 63:3), and he is called the Word of God (19:13). He is King of kings and Lord of lords (19:16). He is the husband of the new Jerusalem (21:9) as well as her temple (21:22) and her lamp (21:23).

For revelation, therefore, the triumph of God over evil and death is not only a future expectation; it has already been realized *in heaven*. Jesus' resurrection is the pledge of God's cosmic victory over evil. The hope of the saints is not based simply on the promise of God in the distant past but it is based on the present power of God manifest in the resurrection of Jesus, *and* of the saints who have joined him in heaven. Already the church shares in the resurrection victory through those who have gone ahead. As the visions reveal to the readers, then, the essential victory has already been won. The issue is no longer in doubt. The visions of the future only spell out the inevitable consequences of the triumph already accomplished by Jesus. In the Book of Revelation, too, the characteristic Christian experience of the "already" and the "not yet" transforms the symbols of apocalyptic itself.

REVELATION AND THE JOHANNINE LITERATURE

For a writing preoccupied with the heavenly places, Revelation is firmly rooted in the world of human passions. The seven churches of Asia to which John writes (1:4) are located in well-known cities: Ephesus, Smyrna, Pergamum, Thyatira, Sardis, Philadelphia, and Laodicea. The letters contain small touches that may reflect knowledge of local conditions and traditions. The churches in Philadelphia and Smyrna also received letters from Ignatius of Antioch early in the second century, and Ephesus was written to by both Paul and Ignatius. Laodicea was mentioned in Paul's Colossian letter (Col. 4:13–16).

In the seven "spirit letters" that follow his opening vision (1:9–19), John addresses the conditions of these churches. He names allies (like Antipas, the faithful witness, 2:13) and opponents (like Jezebel, the prophetess, 2:20–23). Some opponents are called false apostles (2:2). A group of opponents are named Nicolaitans (2:6, 15), a name possibly derived from the Nicholas who was one of the Hellenists of Acts 6:5. These advocated a liberal policy regarding eating idol meat (2:6, 14, 20), a practice reprehensible to John (cf. 1 Cor. 8:1–13; 1 John 5:21!). John refers to "false Jews" (3:9) and to the "synagogue of Satan" (2:9), as well as to "Satan's throne" (2:13) and "the deep things of Satan" (2:24). The allusiveness of these identifications suggests that the opponents were already well known to the readers. The opposition is more elaborately disguised in the visions, but the "great harlot" Babylon who brings destruction on the saints clearly is meant to represent the Roman Empire (see 17:9–14).

Do these concrete references suffice to place Revelation within the Johannine world? Tradition associated the seer either with the beloved disciple or with the elder who wrote the Johannine letters. Papias thought him to be the elder (see Eusebius *Ecclesiastical History* III.39.5–14). The late second-century bishop of Ephesus, Polycrates, in dispute with Victor I of Rome (189–199) over the date of Easter (the so-called quartodeciman controversy), appealed to the ancient tradition of the Asian churches, which he traced to Philip and John, the beloved disciple (Eusebius *Ecclesiastical History* V.24.2–5). In either case, some scholars have great difficulty imagining this writing's outlook as existing side by side with that of the letters and Gospel. They can find a place for it only by thinking of it very early or very late in the scale of chronological development. Others think of Revelation as another production of the circle or school of Johannine Christianity. They attribute its differences less to the passage of time than to the transformations required by the apocalyptic, as opposed to the epistolary or narrative genre. This explanation is reasonable. As for the dating of the work, the clear evidence it presents of active and organized persecution unto death makes a date toward the end of the first century the most likely.

Once it is granted that the apocalyptic genre drastically reshapes the view of the world, the deep harmony in outlook and symbolization between Revelation and the other Johannine writings is all the more impressive. Only a few points can be touched on here, beginning with the designations for Jesus. In the Fourth Gospel, the title of Lamb of God was applied to him (1:29, 36). In Revelation, the title becomes the central image for the crucified and raised Messiah. He is the Lamb who was slain but now lives (5:6–8, 12–13; 6:1, 16; 7:9, 10, 14, 17; 12:11; 13:8, 11; 14:1, 4, 10; 15:3; 17:14; 19:7–9; 21:9, 14, 22, 23, 27; 22:1–3). He is also Son of man (1:13; 14:14; cf. John 1:51) and Son of God (2:18; cf. John 11:27; 20:31; 1 John 3:8). He is the Word of God (*logos tou theou*; 1:2, 9; 6:9; and above all, 19:13; cf. John 1:1–14). He is king and even King of kings (1:5; 15:3; 19:16; cf. John 18:29—19:22). As in the other Johannine writings, Jesus is the faithful witness (1:5; 3:14; 19:11; cf. John 5:32; 8:14; 1 John 5:9), the one who "loved us and freed us from our sins by his blood" (1:5; cf. 1 John 1:7; 5:6–8; John 19:34). He is "the one who comes" (1:4, 8; 2:5; 3:11; cf. John 1:9; 11:27; 1 John 4:2; 5:6; 2 John 7).

Even more striking are some designations identified with the Johannine writings alone. Jesus, for example, identifies himself with "I am" sayings (1:8, 17; 2:23; 21:6; 22:13, 16; cf. John 6:35; 8:12). He is called "the beginning [*archē*] of God's creation" (3:14) as well as the "beginning and the end" (21:6; 22:13; cf. John 1:1–2; 1 John 1:1). Picking up Jesus' characteristic speech in the Fourth Gospel, Revelation calls him simply the Amen (3:14; cf. John 1:51; 5:19). He refers to "my Father" (2:28; 3:5, 21; cf. John 5:17, 43; 14:2) and "my God" (3:2, 12; cf. John 20:17). He says that even as he received authority from the Father, so does he give it (2:26–28; cf. John 1:12; 17:2). And the fundamental metaphors of water, light, and life are (each in its way) attached to Jesus. He is the one who will give to the thirsty to drink from the fountain of the water of life (7:17; 21:6; 22:1, 17; cf. John 4:14; 7:37–39). From him comes life (2:10; 3:5; 11:11; 22:2, 14, 19; cf. John 1:4; 3:15). He is the light of the new Jerusalem (21:24; 22:5; cf. John 8:12; 1 John 2:8).

The conflicts and loyalties of this community are also symbolized in a fashion close to that of the other Johannine writings. The community's members are in opposition to those they call false Jews (2:9; 3:9), members of the "synagogue of Satan" (2:9; 3:9). We remember how the Fourth Gospel placed Jesus in conflict with the Jews (see esp. John 8:12–58), and believers in conflict with the synagogue (John 9:22). As in the Johannine letters (1 John 3:7; 4:6; 2 John 7), the opponents are deceivers (Rev. 2:20; 12:9; 13:14; 18:23; 19:20; 20:3, 8, 10) who speak with a spirit not from God (1 John 4:1–3; cf. Rev. 13:15; 16:13–14; 18:2). Ultimately, the community's conflict is with Satan, as was that of Jesus (Rev. 2:9, 13, 24; 3:9; 12:9, 12; 20:2, 7, 10; cf. John 6:70; 8:44; 13:2, 27). And like the beloved disciple and the believers of the letters, the community in the Book of Revelation is one of witnesses (1:2; 2:13; 6:9; 11:3, 10; 19:10; cf. John 19:35; 21:24; 1 John 1:2; 4:14; 5:9–12; 3 John 3, 12) who have by their faith and love become "conquerers" over evil and falsehood (Rev. 2:7, 11, 17, 26; 3:5, 12, 21; 21:7; cf. 1 John 2:13–14; 4:4; 5:4–5) just as Jesus had already conquered (Rev. 5:5; 17:14; cf. John 16:33). Finally, as we shall see in greater detail, this is a community defined by its prophetic role in the world.

A PROPHETIC COMMUNITY

In each of the NT writings, we are given some sense of the self-understanding of the community in its social structure and its relationship to Israel and the world. This self-understanding is conveyed in various ways, including images and titles for community leaders. Among the images, we have already seen the church designated as temple (1 Cor. 3:16; Eph. 2:21) and house of God (Heb. 3:2; 10:21; 1 Pet. 2:5; 4:17) and the saints (1 Cor. 1:2; Eph. 1:1; Heb. 13:24; 1 Pet. 1:15; Jude 3). Among the titles for leaders, we have met apostles and prophets (1 Cor. 12:28–30; Eph. 4:11–12; Rom. 12:6), teachers (Acts 13:1; 1 Cor. 12:28; Eph. 4:11; Jas. 3:1); bishops (Acts 20:28; Phil. 1:1; 1 Tim. 3:2; Titus 1:7), elders (Acts 11:30; 15:2; 20:17; 1 Tim. 5:1–19; Titus 1:5; Jas. 5:19; 1 Pet. 5:1), and deacons (Rom. 16:1; Phil. 1:1; 1 Tim. 3:8, 12).

When we look at the Johannine writings apart from Revelation, we are struck by the relative paucity of such designations. The term "apostle" occurs only once, in a nontechnical sense (John 13:16). The only "prophet" is Jesus (John 4:19; 6:14; 9:17), just as the only "teacher" is Jesus (John 1:38; 3:2; 11:28; 13:13–14; 20:16). There are no "bishops" or "deacons," and the only "elder" is the author of 2 and 3 John.

A similar reticence can be observed in Revelation. The term "apostle" is used three times. Twice it refers to contemporaries. The first time, it is used with reference to "men who call themselves apostles but are not" (2:2), a characterization that reminds us of *Didache* 11.3. The second use comes in the vision of Babylon's fall, when the "saints, apostles, and prophets" rejoice together over it (18:20). Finally, the walls of the new

Jerusalem have twelve foundations, "and on them the twelve names of the twelve apostles of the Lamb" (21:14). These few passages remind us that the symbolism of the Twelve is by no means confined to Luke-Acts, and that the apostles were regarded as playing a foundational role (cf. Eph. 2:20). Except for pretenders, however, that role appears to be one of the past.

The term "elder" is used by Revelation in a very restricted way. The seer is not identified by that title, nor is any other human figure on earth. The term "elder" is reserved for the twenty-four elders in heaven (4:4, 10; 5:5, 6, 8, 11, 14; 7:11, 13; 11:16; 14:3; 19:4). As for the designations "teacher" and "bishop" and "deacon," they do not occur at all.

In contrast, Revelation prefers the language of *prophecy* when speaking of the community. The title "prophet" is used eight times (10:7; 11:10, 18; 16:6; 18:20, 24; 22:6, 9), the verb "prophesy" twice (10:11; 11:3), and the noun "prophecy" seven times (1:3; 11:6; 19:10; 22:7, 10, 18, 19). More important than the number of uses is the pattern. First, the language is used not only of specific leaders or holders of office but of the community as a whole. Second, the language intersects repeatedly with other favorite terms of self-designation. Some of these connections deserve attention.

The author uses the term "servant," *doulos*, for believers some thirteen times (1:1; 2:20; 7:3; 13:16; 15:3; 19:2, 5, 18; 22:3, 6), and several times it is found in combination with prophet language: " . . . as he announced to his *servants* the *prophets*, should be fulfilled" (10:7), and " . . . for reward-ing thy *servants*, the *prophets* and *saints*" (11:18; cf. 19:9–10). The language of witness or testimony is also heavily used of this community. The verb form "to bear witness" or "to testify," *martureō*, is used four times (1:2; 22:16, 18, 20), most interestingly in the combination "I *testify* to everyone who hears these words of *prophecy*" (22:18). The noun form "testimony" or "witness," *marturia*, is used some eight times, and when it appears as *marturia Iēsou*, it means both witness *by* Jesus and *to* Jesus (see 1:2, 9; 6:9; 11:7; 12:11, 17; 19:10; 20:4). The most fascinating occurrence is one to which we shall return: "The witness [*marturia*] of Jesus is the spirit of prophecy [*prophēteias*]" (19:10). Finally, the substantive "witness" or "tes-tifier," *martus*, is used, twice of Jesus (1:5; 3:14), once of Antipas (2:13), once of the mysterious "two witnesses" (11:3), and once in the plural of those who died and "witnessed in their blood" (17:6).

The term "saints" or "holy ones," *hagioi*, is employed frequently. It is used three times in the singular to refer to God (4:8; 6:10) or Jesus (3:7) as the Holy One, but more often (some twelve times) it refers to believers on earth and the elect in heaven who have triumphed over death (see 5:8; 8:3, 4; 13:7, 10; 14:12; 17:6; 18:20; 19:8; 20:6, 9; 22:21). The author again brings this term into combination with the language of prophecy; he can speak of "thy servants, the *prophets* and *saints*" (11:18) and say, "Men have shed the blood of *saints* and *prophets*" (16:6), and, "In her was found the blood of *prophets* and of *saints* and of all who have been slain on earth" (18:24).

These combinations suggest that the author of Revelation regards the church as a *prophetic community*. It is a community of saints and of servants, whose prophetic office is carried out by their bearing witness. We notice as well that these terms are applied alike to those still struggling on earth, to those triumphant in heaven, and to Jesus. The prophetic self-image is further enhanced by the way language about the Spirit *(pneuma)* is used. As we have already seen, this simple equation can be drawn: "The witness of Jesus is the spirit of prophecy" (19:10). And God can be called "the Lord, the God of the spirits of the prophets" (22:6). It is both the Spirit and the Bride who call out to the Bridegroom, "Come" (22:17).

The description of the representative figures of the church also employs the language of prophecy. First, there is the seer himself. He has written a "book of prophecy" (1:3; 22:18–19). When he addresses the seven churches, it is the "Spirit" who speaks (2:7, 11, 17, 29; 3:6, 13, 22; cf. 14:13). In his visions, he is "caught up" by the Spirit (1:10; 4:2; 17:3). After eating the scroll, he is told, "You must again prophesy about many peoples and nations and tongues and kings" (10:11). When he bows to worship the angel who has shown him the visions, the angel says to him (22:9):

> You must not do that; I am a fellow *servant* with you and *your brothers the prophets*, and with those who keep the words of this book. Worship God.

The other representative figures of the community are the "two witnesses" (11:3–13). They appear during an interlude following on the command of the angel to "prophesy again" (10:11). They are not named but are sufficiently known to the readers to be recognizable by the sobriquets "olive trees" and "lampstands" (11:4). Of them, the terms "witnessing" and "prophesying" are used interchangeably. We read, "I will grant my two witnesses power to prophesy" (11:3), and find that "the days of their prophesying" (11:6) are the same as "the days of their witnessing" (11:7). Their works, furthermore, recall those of the prophets Elijah and Moses (11:6). Their end is like that of the witness and prophet Jesus. They are killed as he was "in the city where their Lord was crucified" (11:8). The one responsible for their death is the "beast that ascends from the bottomless pit and makes war on them" (11:7). This beast anticipates the "beast from the sea" in 13:1, who also "makes war on the saints to conquer them" (13:7). Like Jesus also, the two witnesses/prophets rose from the dead, and "went up to heaven in a cloud" (11:12). Commentators debate whether they are real individual persons within the community or are representative personalities of the community as a whole. That there should be such a debate indicates how the community is conceived of in prophetic terms. We can thus trace the succession: Jesus, the community, and its representatives—all are prophets who bear witness.

The prophetic imagery affects the picture of the community's opponents as well. In the letter to Thyatira, the rival leader Jezebel is termed a prophetess (2:20) whose encouragement to her followers to eating idol meat amounts to teaching "the deep things of Satan" (2:20, 24). In the visions, the demonic opponents of the saints bear caricatured prophetic features. Just as Jesus is a "faithful witness" who is seen as a slain lamb, so is the second beast (the one from the earth, the second representative of the dragon Satan, 12:13—13:2) pictured as having "two horns like a lamb"; but his voice is "like a dragon" (13:11–18). The beast is later referred to as a false prophet (16:13):

> I saw issuing from the mouth of the dragon and from the mouth of the beast and from the mouth of the false prophet, three foul spirits like frogs, for they are demonic spirits, performing signs.

We also read, "The beast was captured, and with it the false prophet who in its presence had worked the signs by which it deceived those who had received the mark of the beast" (19:20). And the final victory is achieved when "the devil who had deceived them was thrown into the lake of fire and sulphur where the beast and the false prophet were" (20:10).

The Book of Revelation regards the church as a community of prophets who by the spirit of Jesus bear witness in the world. They are opposed by demonic powers who sponsor false prophecy. The servants and saints on earth are bound together with their Lord and with those who have gone before them in a fellowship of prophecy. Once again we see the seer fall to worship the one who reveals visions to him; now he receives this response (19:10):

> You must not do that. I am a fellow servant with you and your brethren who hold the testimony [witness] of Jesus. Worship God. For the testimony [witness] of Jesus is the spirit of prophecy.

THE WITNESS OF JESUS IS THE
SPIRIT OF PROPHECY

Christians continue in the world the witness first given by Jesus. He was the faithful and true witness (1:5; 3:14) who came into the world to "bear witness to the truth" (John 18:37). Because of his testimony, he was killed by a hostile world, and his witness was therefore sealed with his blood (1:5; 5:9; 7:14; 19:13). As in the other Johannine writings, Revelation sees the Spirit's function as one of continuing in the lives of Christians the witness of Jesus in the world (see John 16:7–11). Insofar as Jesus continues to "speak" through the Spirit, of course, his prophetic role continues even in this book, which is a "revelation from Jesus Christ" (1:1) and a "witness of Jesus" (19:10). But as Christians continue to keep his commandments and live by his faith, they also "witness to Jesus" in the world.

Witness in Tribulation and
Ambiguity: The Letters
(2:1—3:22)

Just as in the Book of Daniel the esoteric message of the visions (chaps. 7—12) was preceded by a series of folk tales that contained the same basic message in exoteric "wisdom" (chaps. 1—6), so are the great visions of the Book of Revelation preceded by seven letters to the churches of Asia Minor, which prepare for the visions by confronting similar issues in straightforward and nonecstatic ways.

In the letters, the voice of prophecy is open and direct. The prophet speaks in the name of Jesus and with his Spirit. Jesus is revealed in the opening vision as "standing in the midst of the lampstands" (1:13), which, we are told, "are the seven churches" (1:20). Here is the resurrected Lord present to the church through the Spirit. Such prophetic speech as we find here may reflect the liturgical practice of the primitive community (cf. 1 Cor. 12—14). We find in the prophetic utterances sayings that also appear in the epistolary and Gospel writings (cf. Rev. 3:3 and 1 Thess. 5:2, Matt. 24:43; and cf. Rev. 3:20 and Matt. 24:33, Jas. 5:9).

The letters follow a strict formal pattern. (1) Each begins with the command to write to a specific church, as, "to the angel of the church at Ephesus, write" (2:1; cf. 2:8, 12, 18; 3:1, 7, 14). (2) Then Jesus is identified by one of a series of epithets. He is the one who holds the seven stars in his right hand (2:1, connecting the letters to the opening vision; cf. 1:20). He is "the first, the last, who died and came to life" (2:8; cf. 1:17; 22:13); the one "who has the sharp, two-edged sword" (2:12; cf. 1:16); and "the Son of God" (2:18). He has the spirits of God and the seven stars (3:1; cf. 1:4; 5:6; 22:6); he is the Holy One, the true, who has the key of David (3:7; cf. 5:5; 22:16); he is the Amen, the faithful and true witness, the beginning of God's creation (3:14). This assemblage of names and titles reminds us of nothing so much as the process of "naming Jesus" in the opening sequence of the Fourth Gospel (John 1:29–51). The epithets also provide literary signals that connect the letters not only to the opening vision but to the later visions of the book. (3) There follows the statement "I know," which leads to the description of the churches' respective situations (2:2, 9, 13, 19; 3:2, 8, 15). (4) For some of the communities, there is praise: they have patiently endured (2:2, 3); they have come through tribulation and poverty (2:9); they have held fast to the name

(2:13); they have kept love, faith, service, and patient endurance (2:19; 3:10). Other communities receive mostly blame: for having abandoned love (2:4), for falling into idolatry (2:13–15, 20–22), for immorality (3:10), for tepidity (3:15). (5) Every one of the communities receives an exhortation (2:5, 7, 10–11, 16–17, 25, 29; 3:3–4, 11, 18–19). (6) Each is given a *promise* (2:7, 11, 17, 26–28; 3:5, 12, 20–21).

Beneath the various symbols, the letters contain only one message: Hold fast. Despite their tribulation and poverty, the communities are to continue their witness. And in the face of the subtler testing that is the temptation to idolatry and immorality, they are to show patient endurance. There is nothing complicated in this exhortation, just as there was not in the stories of Daniel. Jesus as the resurrected Lord is present with them in their experience; he knows what they suffer; he will reward them if they endure and punish them if they fall away. By maintaining their fidelity to Jesus, they continue to bear prophetic testimony in the world.

Witness in Persecution and Death: The Visions

Once the seer passes through the open door of heaven (4:1), he and the readers are swept into a phantasmagorical world quite unlike any other. The visions of Revelation are dazzling in their imagery, even if not altogether coherent. I will not add here to the endless store of studies devoted to the structure, sequence, and symbolism of these visions. Beneath the complex sequences of seals and trumpets and bowls and beasts, several fundamental convictions are expressed. These deep beliefs are of more religious significance than the play of plot and poetry. The first conviction is that "in heaven" the victory over evil and death has already been won by God and his Messiah. The idolatrous powers strutting the earth are illusory; there is but one power controlling history. Second, the apparent dominance of evil in human affairs is itself part of God's triumphant plan; those who come through suffering and persecution faithfully receive the reward of eternal life with God. Third, the history of humans has a goal even on earth: the time of the suffering of the saints will come to an end, in the visible and effective rule of God among humans. Fourth, the point of all the visions is to encourage and exhort those undergoing such sufferings with these convictions: if they share the witness of Christ on earth in the face of death, they will share as well in heaven his victory over death.

In the visions, we see that the witness of believers *to* Jesus can lead to the shedding of their blood and to their death (6:10; 7:14; 12:11; 16:6; 17:6; 18:24). More than the avoidance of idolatry and immorality may be demanded of the Christian. Life itself may be asked. And if it is, there is the knowledge that those who so die share in the witness of the one "who was slain but now lives" (5:9) and who ransomed humans by his blood (1:5). His garments were sprinkled with blood as were those of the servant (19:13; cf. Isa. 63:1–6), just as the garments of the saints are "washed in the blood of the Lamb" and made pure (7:14). Now we understand the logic of being a witness (*martus*), as it is spelled out in "martyrdom."

That the Christians addressed by the visions faced real death cannot be doubted. The seer observes in heaven "under the altar the souls of those who had been slain for the word of God, and for the witness they had borne" (6:9); and, in the battle against the dragon, "they have conquered him by the blood of the Lamb and by the word of their testimony, for they loved not their own lives even unto death." (12:11). The beast from the earth, the false prophet, makes war on the saints to conquer them (13:7); he marks everyone with his seal and makes them slaves (13:16).

The persecution suffered by the saints is one sponsored by the Roman Empire. The great harlot Babylon, who represents the Roman Empire, makes her first appearance in 14:8, and 18:2—19:8 is devoted to a proleptic paean to God for her great fall. But for those whose lives are still within her grasp, she remains powerful and fearful: "In her was found the blood of the prophets and saints and of all who have been slain on the earth" (18:24).

Here there can be no positive evaluation of the governing powers such as we saw in Rom. 13:1–7 or 1 Pet. 2:13–17, for the simple reason that here the state has usurped powers never intended for it, becoming a "beast" that demands ultimate allegiance; such idolatrous claims cannot be recognized by Christians. At the same time, Revelation does not advocate a violent or armed rebellion against the iniquitous power of the state. It essentially advocates a passive resistance. If Christians do not organize a revolt against Rome, neither can they obey its idolatrous commands. They must keep the commandments of God and the faith of Jesus, even if it means their death. The message underlying all the visions comes down, therefore, to precisely the same exhortation as in the letters: "Here is a call for the endurance and faith of the saints" (13:10), and "Here is a call for the endurance of the saints, those who keep the commandments of God and the faith of Jesus" (14:12).

This prophetic church can bear such witness because of its conviction, rooted in the experience of the resurrection of Jesus, that this earthly life is not all there is, that there remains a heavenly reward for a life now given in prophetic witness to the truth of God's claim over the world. Indeed, such Christians are convinced that their suffering and death itself helps speed the victory of God (12:10–11):

Now the salvation and the power and the kingdom of our God and the authority of his Christ have come, for the accuser of our brethren has been thrown down, who accuses them day and night before our God. And they have conquered him by the blood of the Lamb and by the word of their testimony, for they loved not their lives even unto death.

The final and glorious vision in Revelation is, of course, that of the heavenly Jerusalem, coming down from heaven, together with the ringing affirmation from the throne (21:3):

> Behold, the dwelling of God is with men. He will dwell with them, and they shall be his people, and God himself will be with them.

Here is the final reconciliation of earth and heaven, of God's life and creation, by which Revelation draws full circle back to Genesis 1—2. It cannot be accomplished by human effort, but can only come from the source of all reality, who declares, "Behold, I make all things new" (21:5). Only with this final restoration will evil truly be banished from the earth (21:8, 27). And despite the threat of eternal punishment for those who reject this gift, there is still the hope for a universal extension of this life. By the light of the Lamb even the nations shall walk (21:24), and "the leaves of the tree were for the healing of the nations" (22:2):

> There shall no more be anything accursed, but the throne of God and of the Lamb shall be in it and his servants shall worship him. They shall see his face and his name shall be on their foreheads. And night shall be no more; they need no light of lamp or sun, for the Lord God will be their light, and they shall reign for ever and ever. (22:3–5)

The reign of the saints, we see, is in actuality an eternal act of worship. They have been called to be a "kingdom of priests" (1:6; 5:10; 20:6); their final and best witness is to join the heavenly creatures in praising God.

BIBLIOGRAPHICAL NOTE

The impact of the Book of Revelation on historical movements in the West has been traced by N. Cohn, *The Pursuit of the Millennium* (New York: Harper & Row, 1961). Some of the social and psychological dynamisms set off by apocalyptic are examined by L. Festinger et al., *When Prophecy Fails* (New York: Harper & Row, 1964), and F. Kermode, *The Sense of an Ending* (New York and London: Oxford Univ. Press, 1966), 3–31. Christianity as a millennial movement also served as the main analytic tool for J. G. Gager, *Kingdom and Community: The Social World of Early Christianity* (Englewood Cliffs, N.J.: Prentice-Hall, 1975).

Some sense of the history of scholarship on Revelation can be gained from J. Court, *Myth and History in the Book of Revelation* (Atlanta: John Knox Press, 1979), esp. 1–19; and E. Schüssler Fiorenza, "Composition and Structure of Revelation," in her *The Book of Revelation: Justice and Judgment* (Philadelphia: Fortress Press, 1985), 159–80. A useful overview of the writing is provided by J. Bowman, "The Revelation of John: Its Dramatic Structure and Message," *Int* 9

(1955): 436–53; and less idiosyncratically, by M. Rissi, "The Kerygma of the Revelation of John," *Int* 22 (1968): 3–17.

For the symbolism and outlook of apocalyptic generally, see first the bibliography for chap. 2, p. 65. The relationship of the Book of Revelation to apocalyptic is variously examined by D. S. Russell, *Method and Message of Jewish Apocalyptic* (Philadelphia: Westminster Press, 1964), 205–34; J. Kallas, "The Apocalypse—An Apocalyptic Book?" *JBL* 86 (1967): 69–80; B. W. Jones, "More about the Apocalypse as Apocalyptic," *JBL* 87 (1968): 325–27; P. Vielhauer, "Apocalyptic, Introduction," in *New Testament Apocrypha*, ed. L. Hennecke and W. Schneemelcher (Philadelphia: Westminster Press, 1959), 2:581–642; and J. J. Collins, "Pseudonymity, Historical Reviews, and the Genre of the Revelation of John," *CBQ* 39 (1977): 329–43.

The background of Merkabah mysticism is provided by G. Scholem, *Major Trends in Jewish Mysticism* (New York: Schocken Books, 1941), 1–79; idem, *Jewish Gnosticism, Merkabah Mysticism, and the Talmudic Tradition* (New York: Jewish Theological Seminary Press, 1960); M. Smith, "Observations on Hekhalot Rabbati," in *Biblical and Other Studies*, ed. A. Altmann (Cambridge: Harvard Univ. Press, 1963), 142–60, esp. 142–43; and A. J. Saldarini, "Apocalypses and 'Apocalyptic' in Rabbinic Literature and Mysticism," *Semeia* 14 (1979): 187–205.

For a discussion of Revelation's connections to history, see E. Schüssler Fiorenza, "The Quest for the Johannine School: The Book of Revelation and the Fourth Gospel," in *The Book of Revelation: Justice and Judgment*, 85–113; idem, "Apocalyptic and Gnosis in Revelation and Paul," in *The Book*, 114–32; W. M. Ramsay, *The Letters to the Seven Churches of Asia* (London: Stoughton & Hodder, 1904); W. H. C. Frend, *Martyrdom and Persecution in the Early Church* (New York: Doubleday & Co., 1967), 58–67; J. N. Sanders, "St. John on Patmos," *NTS* 9 (1962–63): 75–85; B. Newman, "The Fallacy of the Domitian Hypothesis," *NTS* 10 (1963–64): 133–39; A. A. Bell, "The Date of John's Apocalypse: The Evidence of Some Roman Historians Reconsidered," *NTS* 25 (1978–79): 93–102; C. K. Barrett, "Things Sacrificed to Idols," *NTS* 11 (1964–65): 138–53; L. Mowrey, "Revelation 4—5 and Early Christian Liturgical Usage," *JBL* 71 (1952): 75–84; and L. Thompson, "Cult and Eschatology in the Apocalypse of John," *JR* 49 (1969): 330–50.

Studies that deal with the visions include A. Farrer, *A Re-Birth of Images: The Making of St. John's Apocalypse* (London: Dacre Press, 1949); A. Feuillet, *The Apocalypse* (New York: Alba House, 1965); P. Minear, *I Saw a New Earth: An Introduction to the Visions of the Apocalypse* (Washington, D.C.: Corpus Pub., 1968); M. D. Goulder, "The Apocalypse as an Annual Cycle of Prophecies," *NTS* 27 (1980–81): 342–67; M. Rissi, *The Future of the World: An Exegetical Study of Rev 19:11—22:15* (London: SCM Press, 1966); idem, "The Rider on the White Horse: A Study of Revelation 6:1–8," *Int* 18 (1964): 403–18; A. Yarbro Collins, *The Combat Myth in the Book of Revelation*, HDR 9 (Missoula, Mont.: Scholars Press, 1976); idem, "The History of Religions Approach to Apocalypticism and 'The Angel of the Waters' Rev 16:4–7," *CBQ* 39 (1977): 367–81; P. Minear, "The Wounded Beast," *JBL* 72 (1953): 93–101; and M. Black, "The 'Two Witnesses' of Rev. 11:3f in Jewish and Christian Apocalyptic Tradition," in *Donum Gentilicum*, ed. E. Bammel, C. K. Barrett, and W. D. Davies (Oxford: At the Clarendon Press, 1978), 226–38.

Other thematic aspects are treated by A. Trites, "*Martus* and Martyrdom in the Apocalypse," *NovT* 15 (1973): 72–80; R. Bauckham, "The Worship of Jesus in Christian Apocalyptic," *NTS* 27 (1980–81): 322–41; A. Feuillet, *Johannine Studies* (New York: Alba House, 1965); A. Yarbro Collins, "The Political Perspective of the Revelation to John," *JBL* 96 (1977): 241–56; D. Hill, "Prophecy and Prophets in the Revelation of St. John," *NTS* 18 (1971–72): 401–18; P. Minear, "Ontology and Ecclesiology in the Apocalypse," *NTS* 12 (1955–56): 89–105; W. Klassen, "Vengeance in the Apocalypse of John," *CBQ* 28 (1966): 300–311; D. L. Barr, "The Apocalypse as a Symbolic Transformation of the World," *Int* 38 (1984): 39–50.

Among English language commentaries, the old standard is R. H. Charles, *A Critical and Exegetical Commentary on the Revelation of St. John*, ICC (Edinburgh: T. & T. Clark, 1920), 2 vols., and it is still helpful on specific points. More helpful to the general reader is C. B. Caird, *A Commentary on the Revelation of St. John the Divine*, HNTC (New York: Harper & Row, 1966).

Epilogue
The New Testament
as the Church's Book

I HAVE SPOKEN THROUGHOUT THIS BOOK OF THE NEW TESTAMENT AS though it were of self-evident reality. As a historical fact of the Christian religion, it is. But as a religious issue within contemporary Christianity, it is much disputed. We have examined the individual writings that make up this collection, in the process of their creation and in their respective reshaping of the symbolic world of Torah. It is therefore appropriate to consider the collection as a collection. Our subject is the NT canon and its implications for the community that takes the canon seriously.

FRAMING THE DISCUSSION

The subject draws us immediately into a well-trodden battleground of divided Christianity: the relationship between Scripture and tradition, or to use other language, the Bible and the church. The clearest and in some ways the most tragic result of the Reformation debates on the subject was that terms that made sense only in relationship were distorted by their separation. Martin Luther's cry of *sola scriptura*, "Scripture alone," in response to ecclesiastical abuses was countered by the slogan, *scriptura et traditio*, "Scripture and tradition." The distinction, however, spelled disaster for both sides.

In Protestantism, an emphasis on Scripture as sole and self-validating norm for Christian life led not only to a diminished appreciation of the community as the bearer of the book but also, paradoxically, to the breaking up of the book itself. Already in Luther we find the application of content criticism *(sachkritik)* of the writings from the standpoint of the "pure gospel" found in Paul. Already in Luther we find the germ that will later grow into the notion of a "canon within the canon," the conviction that within the historically transmitted canon there must be located a pristine and essential core. The result of this process was an effectively narrowed collection. On the Catholic side the distortion was no less grievous. The shibboleth "tradition," which had been intended to stress the *context* for the reading of Scripture, quickly became regarded as an independent source of authority, another norm for Christian life. And increasingly, tradition became identified with the magisterium of the church with its draconian legal system, so that in effect, the canon of Scripture was swallowed by canon law.

The distortions and diminutions resulted from the separation and isolation of realities that had meaning only in their marriage. Far from being opposing principles or independent norms, Scripture and tradition represent two moments of the same dialectical process by which the church in every age rediscovers and reaffirms its identity as one that is continuous with the church in previous generations. It is a process that was there from the beginning. The very birth of the church is its first exemplification. The coming into being of the canon is its most visible and enduring symbol.

THE PROCESS OF CANONIZATION

For the historical process of canonization properly to be understood, it is necessary to distinguish five distinct but interrelated stages. Only the last stage is really visible to us now, and it is therefore taken to be the most important, which it is not. This last stage is ratification, when in response to challenges of various kinds, the church began to draw up definitive lists and began to offer reasons that these books were its own and none others. Naturally enough, the reasons given have a certain artificiality, since they represent rationalizations of a process far more organic and uncalculated.

Long before ratification and the crises that called it forth, there was a gradual growth of a Christian collection of writings that derived primarily from customary use, and it was this that provided the substantial basis for the later official decisions. Those first stages of the process are now mostly hidden from us, but from the few glimpses the remaining evidence offers us, we are able to make a reasonable surmise on its progress. It is most important to maintain the reality of this previous progress, for otherwise what was largely a natural and organic development over a period of many years would appear to be a late, arbitrary, and artificial imposition. Although it is only strictly proper to speak of the canon of the New Testament at the stage of ratification, when such language came into play, it would be overly cautious to deny the existence of substantially the same collection of writings long before that time in the customary usage of the churches. Indeed, we are only able to appreciate the nature of the Christian canon when we follow through as best we can those earlier stages in the process of canon formation.

Composition

It is obvious that the church came into being before the NT. The writings themselves arose as crystallizations of community traditions. Form and redaction analysis of the letters and Gospels alike show how earlier oral and written traditions were taken over and given new settings within these writings that addressed the changing circumstances of specific Christian communities. The community contexts of preaching, worship, and teaching are reflected in the sayings and stories of the Gospels. The letters bear fragments of and make allusion to liturgical formulas, hymns, ritual practices, and prophecies. Above all, as we have repeatedly observed, the NT writings give new symbolic shape to the Scripture the first Christians shared with Judaism, the writings of Torah. In the most proper sense, the NT remains always a commentary on the Torah. What Christians eventually came to call the Old Testament remains an essential component of the Christian Bible.

Use

The first Christian writings were not composed for private devotion or edification. They were public writings, meant to be read in the assembly. Increasingly, they were read in the liturgy together with the readings from the Law and the Prophets. Not surprisingly, such liturgical use hastened the perception of the NT writings themselves as Scripture and the Word of God. Because of this public and liturgical use, these writings also came to be employed in the preaching and teaching activities of the church. Thus they increasingly helped shape—as writings—the continuing tradition of the community as they were quoted as authorities alongside passages from Torah.

From the very beginning as well, writings were exchanged between churches for the purpose of being read aloud in the assembly. The apostolic letter of Acts was sent to gentile believers in Antioch, Syria, and Cilicia (Acts 15:23). Second Corinthians is for "all the saints who are in the whole of Achaia" (2 Cor. 1:1). Galatians is written for all the churches of that province (Gal. 1:2). The Colossians and Laodiceans are to exchange the letters Paul wrote to each church (Col. 4:16). Ephesians and 1 Peter are circular letters. Already in the first Christian generation, news and admonition from an apostle or teacher to one community became a source of encouragement and news for other communities as well.

Collection

As writings were exchanged, local churches began to build collections of writings more extensive than those written specifically for them. This is the critical step toward the writings' becoming a canon. By collecting writings originally composed for others and by reading these in its own assembly, a community asserts the relevance to itself in the present of what was written for others in the past. The particular begins to bear the possibility of becoming general.

The evidence suggests that Paul's letters were the first Christian writings gathered into a collection. We have previously examined hypotheses connecting the composition of Acts or Ephesians to this process. Whatever the validity of such theories, it is clear that within thirty years of his death, Paul's letters were being used by churches other than the ones for whom they were originally written, and were regarded as having a special authority. Only a few traces of this process can still be detected in the Christian writings of the late first and early second century.

Clement of Rome wrote a letter of exhortation to the Corinthian congregation (ca. 95 C.E.). In it, he explicitly refers to Paul's First Letter to the Corinthians (*1 Clem.* 47.2–4). In addition, he makes extensive and unmistakable use of the Letter to the Hebrews (*1 Clem.* 17.1–6; 36.1–6; cf. Eusebius *Ecclesiastical History* III.38.1). This means simply that both documents had by that time not only reached the Roman church but had attained significant authority there. Some twenty years later (ca. 115 C.E.), Ignatius, the bishop of Antioch in Syria, writes to the Ephesian church as he makes his way to Rome and martyrdom. He tells its members that Paul "in all his letters mentions your union with Christ Jesus" (Ign. *Eph.* 12.2). We do not know how many of Paul's letters were known by Ignatius. Certainly he knew 1 Corinthians (cf. *Eph.* 16.1; 18.1; *Magn.* 10.2; *Trall.* 2.3), quite probably Romans (cf. *Eph.* 8.2; 18.2) and Ephesians (cf. *Smyrn.* 1.2; *Pol.* 5.1; 6.2). Shortly after, Polycarp, the bishop of Smyrna, writes to the Philippians. He is sending them the letters of Ignatius he has collected (*Letter of Polycarp* 13.2). He not only recalls Paul's personal presence in that community, but refers to letters Paul wrote to them (3.2). The style of his letter makes definite attribution difficult, but it is obvious that he knows and uses a large number of Pauline letters, including—in my judgment—the Pastorals (4:1). We have also seen that the author of 2 Peter speaks of "all" Paul's letters, and regards them as being "like other Scriptures" (2 Pet. 3:16). These references suggest that collections of some or many of Paul's letters were extant by the end of the second century's first decade in such major centers of Christianity as Rome, Corinth, Antioch, Smyrna, Ephesus, and Philippi, and that for such churches Paul was already well on the way toward—if he had not already arrived at—the status of Scripture.

Progress toward a Gospel collection is harder to trace. If the two-source solution to the Synoptic problem is correct, then we know that by the year 85 at the latest the Matthean scribal group had both Mark and Matthew available to them. Luke likewise makes reference to earlier attempts at gospel narratives, and he certainly used Mark (Luke 1:1). In his Letter to the Corinthians, Clement of Rome tells them to "recall the words of our Lord Jesus" (*1 Clem.* 13.2; 46.8–9) and follows with what appear to be mixed citations or reminiscences, most resembling passages from Matthew. Ignatius of Antioch shows the probable use of the Fourth Gospel (cf. *Eph.* 5.2; *Magn.* 7.1; *Rom.* 7.2–3; *Phld.* 7.1; 9:1) and of Matthew (cf. *Eph.* 14.2; *Smyrn.* 1:2; 6:1). Polycarp's *Letter to the Philippians* may show some use of Matthew (7.2; 12.3) and of the Johannine letters (2.1; 7:1). The *Didache* (ca. 90–100 C.E.) has many allusions to Gospel sayings and what appears to be an extended citation from Matthew 6:9–11 in its version of the Lord's Prayer (*Did.* 8:2).

This pattern of use continues into the middle of the second century. In his *First Apology* (ca. 155 C.E.), Justin Martyr describes the Christian worship service as including both reading and preaching from the apostles and prophets (67). He refers to the "memoirs" of the apostles in the plural, and cites them (66). Likewise in his *Dialogue with Trypho*—an extended disputation with a Jew involving debates over messianic texts of Torah—Justin again makes frequent allusion to the "memoirs of the apostles" (101, 105, 106, 107), and makes many explicit citations of the Gospels (12, 18, 32, 49, 76, 78, 112, 125, 133).

In addition to the testimony of Justin that the NT writings were the subject of preaching, we have the direct evidence from the homily called *2 Clement* (ca. 150), which quotes Mark 2:17 as Scripture: "... and another Scripture says, 'I did not come to call the righteous but sinners' " (2:4; cf. 3:2; 6:1–2; 11:5–7). And in the apologetic literature of the middle and late second century, we find some explicit citations of the NT, as in Theophilus of Antioch's *To Autolycus* II.27 and III.14, Athenagoras's *Supplication for the Christians* 12, 32, 33, and the *Epistle to Diognetus* 12.5.

Three points should be made to summarize this collection of evidence. There are not many citations, and they are obviously not made from a New Testament. On the other hand, the citations are frequent enough to be noticed, and more important, are cited as authoritative, even at times as the equivalent of Torah. Finally, it is even more striking that we do not find other Christian writings cited in preference to these that later are to be called the NT. In other words, as few as these citations are, they show a primacy of place and authority from the start.

The process of exchange and collection was a critical factor in the process of many churches' becoming one church, a development begun by Paul's gentile collection and circular letter. By reading the same texts, communities would inevitably be shaped according to a shared identity and would grow increasingly aware of the catholicity of their faith. Three statements were made by the communities that assembled such collections. By placing the writings of "apostles and prophets" as foundational documents to be read in the liturgy together with Torah, they asserted at once the continuity of their identity with that expressed in those writings, as well as the authority of these writings as God's Word, meant to shape the worshipping community. Second, they affirmed their communion with the other local churches throughout the inhabited world (*oikoumene*) who were reading the same writings. Third, they stated that these writings had a universal pertinence: what Paul said to the Corinthians in past generations applies as well to the Smyrneans in this generation, and therefore, to every generation of the church in every place.

Selection

The Christian movement produced many more writings than found their way into the canon. Some of them were written later than those now in the canon. This is the case with most if not all of the "gnostic gospels." But others, such as the *Didache* or *1 Clement* were probably written earlier than some that were canonized (e.g., 2 Peter). The second century in particular produced many gospels, apocalypses, and acts of various apostles. Communities therefore had to choose which of these they wanted read in the worship and to serve as the basis of proclamation and teaching.

Not all churches agreed from the beginning on every choice. Some churches had local favorites they regarded as Scripture, while they rejected one or the other choices favored elsewhere. We have no evidence of anyone in the West's regarding James as Scripture, for example, until the late fourth century (although there was no active rejection of it either). In the East, in contrast, James was regarded as Scripture already by the time of Origen (184–254). On the other hand, the *Shepherd of Hermas* enjoyed strong local popularity for a period in the West, and the *Apocalypse of Peter* the same sort of favor in the East. Because of the enthusiastic excesses of the prophetic movement called Montanism in the late second century, the Book of Revelation was regarded with deep suspicion by some, as was also the Fourth Gospel, and both had to struggle for full inclusion in the canon.

For the most part, however, our earliest evidence shows that there was a rather remarkable degree of unanimity from the start concerning the great majority of the writings. Even so eclectic a thinker as Clement of Alexandria, who was capable of drawing inspiration anywhere, made some distinctions on the basis of the church's tradition: "We do not find this saying in the *four gospels that have been handed down to us*, but in that according to the Egyptians" (*Stromata* III.13, emphasis added). By the end of the second century, writers as diverse as Irenaeus, Tertullian, and Origen are using a canon substantially the same as that used today.

One of the earliest canonical lists available to us is a fragmentary and fractured Latin text called the Muratorian canon. It is generally thought to represent the canon of the Roman church in the late second century, though some scholars argue for a later date. The precise date or provenience of the document is of less importance to us than its witness to the process and principles of canonization.

The document is both fascinating and difficult. In it, we find most of the writings of the present canon: the four Gospels and Acts; the letters of Paul, including the Pastorals; two letters of John and one of Jude; the Apocalypse of John—twenty-two writings that are also in today's canon. More interesting are the variations. There is no mention of a third letter of John, nor of Hebrews, nor of James, nor—and this seems strange for Rome—of any letters of Peter! None of these documents is rejected; they are simply not mentioned at all. On the other hand, the Muratorian list includes the Wisdom of Solomon. It also includes an *Apocalypse of Peter* although it acknowledges that not everyone agrees that it should be "read in church." A middle ground is held by the *Shepherd of Hermas*. It can be read by the faithful, (its popularity attested in fact by the need to discuss it in this list), but it should not be read publicly in the church nor included among the apostles and prophets. We notice how the key factor for canonization is not whether documents can be read or used by individuals but whether they are to be read publicly in worship. Finally, the Muratorian list vehemently excludes the fictitious letters that claim to come from Paul but are in reality forgeries of Marcion; these "cannot be accepted in the catholic church." Equally vigorous is the rejection of writings by gnostic teachers such as Valentinus and Basilides.

The process of selection inevitably involved the rejection of some writings. This aspect of canonization was accelerated by the challenge of Marcionism in the middle of the second century. Marcion broke from the great church and established a dissident brand of Christianity, complete with a "canon" that was made up solely of Paul's letters—with the exception of the Pastorals (see Tertullian *Against Marcion* V.21)—and an expurgated version of Luke's Gospel, which Marcion thought Paul meant when he referred to "my gospel."

The same obsessive dualism that led Marcion to identify the visible world as the work of an evil demiurge from which the good news of Jesus was to free humans led him to reject the OT as the work of that demiurge, and all other NT writings except Paul's as the "corruptions" of a Judaizing spirit. Some scholars have thought that Marcion's abbreviated canon made up of a gospel (*to euangelion*) and apostle (*to apostolikon*) provided both the impetus and structural principle for the creation of an orthodox canon. This is probably to overstate the case. But Marcion's truncated version of the church's shared if inchoate canon certainly forced the orthodox leaders to look more closely at their communities' lists and their reasons for holding them.

Another second-century challenge to the canon was posed by the composition of the *Diatesseron* by Tatian (ca. 170). This cleverly woven version of the gospel story used all four Gospels and sought to replace their messy multiplicity with its single harmonized rendition. The *Diatesseron* was enormously popular in Syria. Indeed, it *was* the canonical version there for several centuries, since it was read in worship and served as the basis for preaching. It was not displaced until the fifth century. The *Diatesseron* did not enjoy the same favor elsewhere. The rest of the churches did not accept this harmony as a replacement of the four Gospels. They thereby showed that they did not regard them as historical sources but as separate and valuable witnesses, precisely in their literary diversity. For that matter, even Tatian's attempt paid tribute to the priority and place of the four Gospels in the life of the church.

Ratification

The threats posed respectively by expansionism and contraction were neither mild nor only temporary. The *Diatesseron* flourished in Syria, and Marcionism was the dominant form of Christianity in parts of the empire. If orthodoxy was to survive, or to put it another way, if Christian identity was to avoid being fragmented in diverse directions, there would need to be some limits set. So we begin to see the process of definition becoming increasingly precise.

Early in the fourth century Eusebius, Bishop of Caesarea, states that "the writings of the New Testament" consist of the four Gospels (the "Holy tetrad"), the Acts of the Apostles, the letters of Paul, 1 John, 1 Peter, and—with some hesitancy—the Book of Revelation. If we include Hebrews as one of Paul's letters, this makes Eusebius' firm canon to be twenty-two writings that are shared today. These he calls the recognized books (*homologoumenoi*), about which there is unanimity. He then adds five writings that he calls disputed (*antilegomenoi*): James, Jude, 2 Peter, and 2 and 3 John. Thus, we have the present canon of twenty-seven writings. Eusebius goes on to list works he calls not genuine, by which he means works that may have at some times and places enjoyed canonical status but that should not enjoy it—writings such as the *Shepherd of Hermas* and the *Apocalypse of Peter*. Finally, he rejects altogether the gospels and acts that go by names of apostles but that have been "put forward by heretics." These are not only spurious but "wicked and impious." Eusebius shows us a firm but still somewhat flexible canon. He is not certain about Revelation, and knows that others are not as well. But he is clear about the majority of writings that belong and those that do not. It is also instructive to note the critical spirit Eusebius brings to the discussion. The reasons for rejecting the gospels and acts of the heretics? They have not appeared in the writings of orthodox writers as Scripture; their phraseology is not consonant with that associated with the apostolic age; and, their contents and perspective differ greatly from orthodoxy. Three criteria—use in the

church, apostolic derivation, and theological consistency—are here operative (see Eusebius *Ecclesiastical History* III.25.1–7).

The defensive character of the ratification process is shown by the
Paschal Letter of Athanasius, bishop of Alexandria, written in 367. He lists
the twenty-seven writings of our present canon and calls them the springs
of salvation (10). He also approves of other writings to be used for
instruction, such as Wisdom, Esther, Judith, and the Shepherd. And he is
even more vehement than Eusebius in rejecting other writings: "There is
nowhere mention of the secret writings, but they are a device of heretics,
who write them when they will, furnishing them with dates, and adding
them, that bringing them forth as ancient, they might thus have an excuse
for deceiving the undefiled" (12).

Finally, we can note the list put out by the North African Council of
Carthage (397), which corresponds precisely to the canon of the present
church (in its canon 39):

> . . . apart from the canonical Scriptures
> nothing is read in church under the name of
> the divine Scriptures. The canonical writings
> are . . . [there follows a list of the OT
> writings] . . . of the New Testament,
> four books of the Gospels,
> of the Acts of the Apostles, one book,
> of Paul's letters, thirteen,
> of the same to the Hebrews, one
> of the apostle Peter, two,
> of John, three,
> of James, one,
> of Jude, one,
> of the Apocalypse of John, one book.
> Let the church across the sea be consulted
> for the confirmation of this canon.

We observe that for this North African church, communication with Rome
on the matter was important. We also notice the canonical principle: these
are the writings that "are to be read in the church as divine Scripture."

By the end of the fourth century, then, not only had the organic process
of canonization been for some time accomplished but that of ratification
was complete. This was the canon of all Christians, apart from the remaining dissidents of a gnostic stripe, for the next millennium. In response to
Luther's reopening of the question by his demotion of Hebrews, James,
Jude, and Revelation from "the proper books," and to Ulrich Zwingli's
rejection of Revelation, the Council of Trent in 1546 reaffirmed a canon of
twenty-seven writings, as did also the Articles of the Church of England
(1562/1571) and the Westminster Confession (1647).

PRINCIPLES OF CANONIZATION

What can we learn about the nature of the canon from this process? Two things immediately become apparent. First, the rejection of Marcionism shows that the canon is *in principle pluralistic*. Whatever the dissonances between OT and NT, between Paul and James, the canon is not the isolation of a single "correct" theology, even one so important as Paul's. With the rejection of Marcionism with its truncated canon, there can be read as well an implied rejection of any sort of "canon within the canon," for Marcion simply proposed a bold version of that concept.

Second, the ultimate rejection of Tatian's *Diatesseron* also tells us that the canon is made up of a plurality of witnesses rather than a single version. Equally important, however, the maintenance of four Gospels affirmed that the canon is a collection of writings. For the life of the church, not the life of Jesus or the history of the church is normative but this set of literary compositions in all their particularity. This is a "fourform gospel" (Irenaeus *Against Heretics* III.11.8). It is a good news "according to" these witnesses. Neither biography nor history was ever the point of them. Matthew does not supplant Mark because it is fuller; John is not rendered invalid because of its disagreements with the Synoptics. They are not competing histories but convergent witnesses.

So much seems to me to be clear. What is less obvious are the criteria used for the canonization of some writings and the rejection of others. Certainly custom played a role and should not be neglected as a factor. The opinion of learned people in the churches also counted, as we are told by Eusebius and also Augustine (cf. *Ecclesiastical History* III.25.6; Augustine *Against Faustus* XXII.79). They were able to make reasoned judgments on such matters as previous citation by Christian writers as Scripture, apostolic style, and theological coherence. But was something more at work than a scholarly examination? Surely, yet it is difficult to pin it down.

A criterion for canonization we might expect to play a great role does not. "Inspiration" does not seem to figure as a reason for inclusion in the canon. The *Shepherd of Hermas* and many other writings either claimed inspiration or had it claimed for them, yet were neither universally nor finally accepted into the canon. In contrast, no NT writing claims inspiration for itself. The statement of 2 Tim. 3:16 that all Scripture is inspired by God (*theopneustos*) refers to Torah. Second Peter 3:16 refers to Paul's letters as though they were Scripture but does not say they were inspired. No doubt there was an increasingly widespread conviction that the NT writings were divinely inspired, but that notion did not appear to play a role as a criterion for canonization.

The criterion of apostolicity, on the other hand, does find explicit expression. A writing should somehow derive from an apostle. The influence of Paul was undoubtedly important in this regard, but equally so was the fight against gnostic teachers who claimed a secret succession (*diadochē*) for the secret transmission of their esoteric books. The orthodox claim of apostolicity stated that the NT writings did not emerge from nowhere or only recently. They could be traced along the public and universally recognized line of ecclesial tradition. We see therefore the concern to connect all the writings to an apostle, as in Papias. Mark's Gospel comes from Peter's companion and translator; Luke's from a companion of Paul; Matthew and John from apostles. Besides the letters of Paul, also those of John, James, Jude, and Peter came from apostles. The Council of Trent only made this tendency explicit when it attributed the Letter of James to an apostle.

Two important claims were made against the Gnostics by this principle of apostolicity. The first was the claim of historical priority: these were the writings that first gave expression to the Christian identity. The second is the claim to historical continuity: the church of today reads and understands—as though written to itself—the writings of Jesus' first followers. It requires no esoteric code for understanding their plain meaning. The context was given with the text, in the church's public life. The criterion of apostolicity was important, but it was also somewhat artificial and it was certainly not decisive (see Augustine *On the Harmony of the Evangelists* I.2). Writings that were attributed to apostles were not accepted, such as the *Gospels of Thomas* and *Peter*, or the *Apocalypse of Peter*. The Gospels of Luke and Mark were, on the other hand, clearly accepted for reasons transcending their apostolic pedigree.

Canonization clearly involved the recognition on the part of a community of a writing's authority, but once more, this was scarcely an absolute norm. There were authoritative writings in the early church that were not taken into the canon or that enjoyed only local acceptance. The *Didache* and the "church orders" that followed it (such as the *Didascalia Apostolorum* and the *Apostolic Constitutions*) illustrate the point. So do the letters of Ignatius of Antioch, which were regarded as important enough to be collected and distributed by Polycarp. An important distinction here is between a local or temporary authority and a general and permanent authority. The writings finally accepted into the canon were seen to have transcended simply local or temporary authority, having the capacity to address the church in every place and time.

If we search for the intrinsic qualities in the writings that were perceived as giving them authority, we are told little by the ancient sources and must rely on guesswork. Certainly, some judgment on the content of the writings was involved. It is apparent in the writings of many patristic authors that there is a *regula fidei* (rule of faith) that provides the proper frame for Christian understanding. The *regula* (which is simply the Latin version of "canon") is not spelled out definitively but appears as a transition point between the NT kerygma and the fully developed creeds of the councils. We find explicit reference to such a *regula* in writers as diverse as Clement of Alexandria (*Stromata* I), Irenaeus (*Against Heretics* I.8.1; I.22.1) and Tertullian (*On the Prescription of Heretics* XIII; XXXVI.1–5; *Against Praxeas* II.1–2; *Against Marcion* I.21). Even so adventuresome a theologian as Origen pays explicit and sincere tribute to the *regula* as the essential framework for his investigations (*On First Principles* I. pref., 3–4).

The significance of this *regula* is that it helps provide a frame as well for the determination of orthodox writings. Some circularity is involved, since the *regula* itself claims to be derived from the same orthodox writings. But the circle is not entirely vicious. It is clear, for example, that the orthodox teaching in both its kerygmatic and its creedal forms places great emphasis on the incarnation of the word and on the crucifixion and death of Jesus. It is no accident that gospels with a docetic Christology, whatever their apostolic attribution, are not found in the canon, nor are gospels that treat the death of Jesus as either unimportant or only an embarrassing episode on the way to apotheosis.

Such a doctrinal norm is not inconsistent with the outlook of the NT writings themselves, for we have often observed how, each in its fashion, they fought against deviance in teaching as much as in behavior. As important as the *regula fidei* was, however, it did not stand alone. Irenaeus must combine it with both the canon of Scripture and the apostolic succession in order to combat the heretics. And even this combination would be convincing only to those who already shared his convictions. The *regula* also focused mainly on doctrinal elements. It provided a negative measure but not a positive one. Perfectly orthodox writings such as the *Shepherd of Hermas* and the *Didache* still did not find their way into the canon. Can we find a more positive criterion?

THE SENSE OF THE CHURCH

There was in all likelihood not a single criterion for canonization. The best historical account of the process may be to attribute it to what is in fact a theological category, the sense of the church *(sensus ecclesiae)*. This is an expression that denotes both a process and a perception. The process is the way in which the church as a whole makes its decisions. The perception is the church's way of seeing itself. This "sense of itself" is what ultimately, I would suggest, determined canonicity and the final shape of the NT.

For those inside the community, the process is one guided by the Holy Spirit that inspired the writings. But the process is not for all that a mystic one. It is rather the communal awareness of many communities sharpened and tested by intercommunication, disputation, and debate. It is not made all at once but over the course of time. It is not a decision made by a special authority or office; the discernment of all in the church is involved.

What is the perception involved in the *sensus ecclesiae*? The communities perceive in these writings a deep cogency, or a congruence with its own best identity: not only what the church is now but also what it ought to be, is called to be. It is the sense that these writings, taken in concert, accurately and authentically represent what the church is and ought to be, though none of the writings alone states that exhaustively. More important still, these writings are seen to have the ability to reshape that identity and regenerate that life for succeeding generations of the church.

The *sensus ecclesiae* perceives that these writings possess catholicity of authority. They not only address the past or even the present but have the power to address as well future situations, and to create capacities for Christian existence in those who read them, capacities that are authentic and continuous with the experience of the first Christians. This potency, we note, is one aimed not primarily at individuals but at communities. This collection of writings can bring the church into being and shape it according to the pattern of its first best realizations.

It is not by accident, I suggest, that the canon of the NT does not include writings that dissolve the difference between the Christ and Christians in mystical unity, or writings that cut the bonds of this people with the Jewish people, or writings that systematically distinguish between the elite and the herd, or writings that make the denial of creation the mark of authentic holiness. For such tendencies work precisely to destroy community. The present writings of the NT have as their almost exclusive focus the shaping of communities into a communal identity. That is why they were chosen in preference to others that had no such interest.

Such a *sensus ecclesiae* is difficult to defend on strictly historical grounds. It has been asserted in the past, and more urgently in the present, that the process of canonization was one that was inherently corrupt. According to this view, entirely worthy writings of diverse forms of Christian life were ruthlessly suppressed by orthodox leaders out of unworthy motives. Because of this, the whole issue of the canon ought to be opened again, with all the writings produced by earliest Christianity given an equal weighting as this generation decides what its Bible ought to be.

According to this argument, the important stage of canonization was that of ratification by bishops. These bishops were politically motivated, and conditioned as well by the cultural attitudes of their day. In every decision, they chose that which was conservative over that which was radical; chose institution rather than charism; fought for hierarchy rather than egalitarianism; preferred doctrine to mysticism; suppressed women in favor of men. The canon we now have, therefore, is not the canon of the whole church, but only of a victorious segment of the church. In effect, all Christians have been shaped by a sectarian canon no less tendentious than that of Marcion.

This is not the place to engage that position in detail. Only a few points need to be made here by way of response. First, a realistic appreciation of history and historical processes is important. All human decision making involves politics and power. The church has never been the new Jerusalem; its grasp on the truth is always fragile and sometimes faithless. These things need not be disputed. The story of the early church councils is sometimes horrific. But that said, we must not romanticize the opposition any more than we romanticize the orthodox. There were dirty tricks enough to go around for all parties to those ancient disputes. Despite that, it is also clear that higher motivations than the simple drive for power or control were at work.

Second, although the process of canonization is a historical process, the canon itself is a theological fact. It results from the decision of the church in every age to reaffirm and ratify those earlier decisions. This the church does by reading these and only these writings in its public worship and by using these writings alone in its debate over the nature of the kingdom. The decision for or against the canon never has been, nor should it have been, based on the purity of the process by which the writings were selected or ratified in the first place.

Third, the critical contemporary question with regard to the canon is not the motivation or means of the first ratifiers. The question, rather, is whether those factors betrayed the *sensus ecclesiae* in a fundamental way. Did those bishops, in other words, still make the right decision, even if for the wrong reasons (if indeed their reasons were wrong)? This is the appropriate subject for the debate and discernment and decision of the church in this age and the next age, for it concerns not the past process but the present prophetic voice of these writings. In this connection, when the credentials of other ancient or modern candidates for canonization are presented, or when canonical writings are considered for rejection, critical questions need to be asked: What sort of Christian identity will these writings generate in the succeeding generations? Do these writings enable the church to maintain not only its connection to the identifiable past but also its capacity to embrace humans in every circumstance of place and time?

CANON AND THE CHURCH

Canonicity, in sum, is a statement of relevance. By it the church affirms that the particular and historically conditioned meaning of these writings is not their only meaning. They are not utterly defined by their first circumstances but possess enduring worth and normative force. They can bring the church into being and shape it according to the "mind of Christ" (see 1 Cor. 2:16).

The term "relevance," however, needs qualification. Relevance is not the same in every time and place. For this reason, the whole *collection* of writings must be kept alive if the church in every time and place is to live. In times of reform, it may be the voice of Paul that is most pertinent; in times of moral lassitude, that of James or Matthew. In periods of persecution, the Book of Revelation is read in ways quite different than in periods of calm. In times of alienation, 1 Peter reveals new and rich significance to its readers. In the face of moral corruption, Jude suddenly seems pertinent. Before rationalistic skepticism, 2 Peter becomes surprisingly contemporary. Nor is this only a matter of different times. The church is universal and exists in very different circumstances throughout the world. Here, the church may enjoy prosperity and position; there, it is persecuted and poor. In this place, it may require the voice of prophecy; there, the comfort of promise. The canon must be able to address every time and place where the church exists.

Nor is the relevance of these writings to be found in them individually; rather, it is found in them as parts of a collection related dialectically to all the other parts of the collection. The church holds in a creative tension the very human Jesus of Luke's Gospel, and the transcendent Jesus of the Fourth Gospel. It walks delicately between the gift of freedom from Paul and the law of freedom from James. It is precisely the way in which these writings work *together* to shape Christian identity that makes the canon such an important and delicate organism and that reveals the "canon within the canon" as a fundamentally arrogant proposition, for it claims to know for every age and time which documents possess relevance, and is willing to close the possibility of other canonical witnesses' testifying to new ages and realizations of the church.

SOME CANONICAL THESES

I want to close this book with ten theses on the canon as the book of the church, and a concluding proposal. I intend this to be provocative. Some of the points restate or elaborate statements made earlier but I would not want them to go unrepeated. By now the reader surely knows that all these statements make sense only within the context of a commitment to the reality we call the church. My main point is that the entity called the New Testament only makes full sense within that commitment.

1. The canon is simply the church's working bibliography. Whatever else is read or studied by individual Christians, these are the writings to which the church as such turns for debating and defining its identity.

These are the public documents of the church, the framework for its discussions. They are public in the sense that their first use is to be read aloud in worship. They are also public because they offer themselves to the whole community's debate and discernment.

2. The canon is more than the residuum of a historical process. It is a faith decision for the church to make in every age and place. The acceptance of these specific writings by a community, not in council but in liturgical use, is the most fundamental identity decision the community makes. The selection excludes any contemporary writings that may attempt to win such complete allegiance, and it asserts the church's continuity with the historical realizations of the church in the past. By this selection, the church assumes as well the responsibility for transmitting entire the same measure for the church in ages to come.

3. The canon and the church are correlative concepts. The canon establishes discrete writings from the past as Scripture. Without the church there is no canon; without canon there is no Scripture in the proper sense. As the church stands under the norm of Scripture in every age, finding life and meaning in the reading of it, so do these writings find their realization as Scripture by being so read by a community, age after age, as the measure of its life and meaning.

4. It is the nature of a canon to be closed. An unlimited canon is no canon, any more than a foot ruler can gain inches and still be a foot ruler. Because it is closed, the canon is able to perform its function of mediating a certain identity through the successive ages of the church. Because the church today reads the very same writings as were read by Polycarp and Augustine and Thomas and Luther and Bonhoeffer, it remains identifiably the same community. Only such a steady measure can provide such continuity. If a lost letter of Paul's should be discovered, there would undoubtedly be great excitement, but there should be no expansion of the canon, for that letter never, from the time of its composition to now, shaped the identity of the catholic church.

5. It is because the canon is closed and exclusive that it can be catholic, have universal and enduring pertinence. This is only an apparent paradox. A measure that can be altered by addition or subtraction at any time and place cannot have the capacity to address every time and place.

6. What distinguishes the Scripture scholar and theologian from the historian of ideas and student of literature is the effective acceptance of the canon. For history and literature as such, the concept of canon is meaningless, except as a convenient categorization or the recognition that a certain group of writings achieved classical status for a certain period of history. But such recognition does not affirm the distinctive interrelationship between texts and a living community over an extended period of time, which is essential to the notion of canon.

7. The ecclesial decision to regard these writings as Scripture bears with it the recognition that they have a peculiar and powerful claim on the lives of individuals and the community as a whole. The community asserts that it does not control these writings but that they in a very real sense control it, by providing the definitive frame for its self-understanding. Within this community, the critical questions posed to the texts by a reader are far less significant than the critical questions the texts pose to the reader.

8. Implicit in the recognition of the canonical writings as Scripture is the acknowledgment that they not only speak in the voice of their human authors but also speak for another. These texts speak prophetically to every age, and analytic to the concept of prophecy is the speaking of God's Word. These texts play a role in the process of God's revelation. Within their time-conditioned words and symbols, which come from many persons in the past, there speaks as well the single Word of God, which endures through all ages. This conviction can be expressed by the statement that the texts are "divinely inspired," for to speak of the Word of God is to speak as well by implication of the work of God's Spirit. Divine inspiration is one of the ways of expressing the unique authority of the writings in the canonical collection. Explanations and interpretations of inspiration, however, vary widely. They range from psychological theories that virtually equate it with literary inspiration, through metaphysical distinctions between primary and secondary causality, to the attribution of the whole creative process of composition within the social context of earliest Christianity to the real but subtle working of the Holy Spirit as part of the constitutive act of founding a church.

9. Since the canon consists of a disparate collection of writings, with both the OT and NT to form the Christian Bible, it resists reduction to any single unifying principle imposed from the outside. If it excludes by its nature any "canon within the canon," it certainly also resists any conceptual mold that either relativizes or removes the texts themselves in all their hard particularity. This resistance applies as well to any "New Testament theology." In all its forms, NT theology is simply another attempt to reduce the many to the one by the discovery of some abstract and unifying principle, whether it is called salvation history, or justification, or liberation, or kerygma, or *regula fidei*, or narrativity, or existential decision. All such principles demand the selection of some texts as more central and governing than others. All fit the writings themselves to frames of greater or lesser abstraction. The canon resists such attempts precisely because it is made up of multiple and irreducible writings. They cannot without distortion be shaped into a static symbolic system.

On the other hand, the canon opens itself to the doing of theology in the church, which is quite another sort of enterprise. In it, the articulation of the experience of God in the lives of contemporary persons and events is brought into a faithful dialogue with all the writings of the OT and NT, not in an attempt to fix their meaning but in a living conversation that ranges freely and leads to surprising results.

10. Since the canon has meaning first of all as the public documents of a community that are meant to be read in the assembly, the church requires a hermeneutic appropriate to the nature of the canon. Such a hermeneutic would not be concerned primarily with the reading of texts by individuals for their pleasure or transformation. There have been no end of interpretive models for this sort of reading, from allegory to existential interpretation, to reader-response theories. None of them need be rejected. Freedom and fantasy open the minds and hearts of individuals. But such models of interpretation scarcely reach to the neighbor and certainly do not provide a way of reading these texts for their primary function, which is to mediate the identity of the church as church.

What is needed is a properly *ecclesial hermeneutic*, one that places the writings in their proper canonical context and that involves the entire faith community in the interpretive process. For such a hermeneutic to work, there must be the active discernment of the work of God in the lives of contemporary believers, raised to the level of a narrative of faith; there must be at the same time, the active discernment of the canonical texts in the light of these experiences and narratives. And this discernment must occur in a public context that enables discussion, debate, disagreement, and decision. In this creative if tension-filled context, the canonical witnesses can again shape the identity of the Christian community in this age.

A MODEST PROPOSAL

I began this book with the search for a model. I close it with a modest suggestion.

The formation of an ecclesial hermeneutic can follow the example of the process by which the writings themselves came into existence, and allow the dialectic of experience and interpretation to take place again.

The experience of God continues, however darkly. But now, not only the texts of Torah but those of the NT canon form the symbolic world that will be reshaped and renewed by that experience, and come to new clarity in the life of the church.

In describing a model for grasping the nature of these writings and their appearance, I suggested the notion of midrash was a useful one to employ. Here, I renew that suggestion with regard to a hermeneutical model.

The Christian church can again learn something from Judaism and regard the NT canon as analogous to the Talmud.

As the Talmud was a crystallization of a long history of interpretation of

Torah mediated by new experiences, which became authoritative for the
Jewish tradition not as the replacement of Torah but as the inescapable
prism through which Torah would be read and understood, so can the NT
writings be regarded as crystallizations of reflection on Torah in light of the
experience of Jesus the Lord. The NT writings remain authoritative and
normative for the Christian tradition not as the replacement of Torah, but
as the indispensable prism through which Torah is to be read and
understood.

There is this difference: in the Talmud there are not separate writings,
but voices, whereas in the NT there are diverse literary forms.

But there is this even more important similarity: In the study of Talmud
one never listens to only one voice or authority. One never follows the
views of Rabbi Judah through every tractate. Nor is there ever any single
abstractable answer that need not be reinterpreted in the light of new
circumstances. Indeed, the whole point of midrash is to hear the various
voices in all their conflicts and disagreements, for it is precisely in those
elements of plurality and even disharmony that the texts open to new
meanings, so that they are allowed to speak to the disharmonies and
disjunctions of contemporary life.

In exactly this fashion, I suggest, Christians should learn to read the
canon of the NT not in search of an essential core or purified canon within
the canon, not within the frame of a single abstract principle, but in a
living conversation with all the writings in all their diversity and divergence. Only so can they continue to speak.

BIBLIOGRAPHICAL NOTE

This epilogue has covered much material without the space to support adequately the many positions that have been advanced. This note is therefore
unusually long. Please bear in mind that even these references provide only some
starting points on subjects extensively studied and vigorously debated.

For the historical process of canonization, the older survey of A. Souter, *The Text
and Canon of the New Testament*, rev. C. S. C. Williams (London: Duckworth,
1954) is still useful, particularly for its primary documents. Original language texts
of the pertinent primary sources are found together with English translations in
D. J. Theron, *Evidence of Tradition* (Grand Rapids: Baker Book House, 1958). For
short treatments of canon, see R. E. Brown, "The Canon of the New Testament,"
in *Jerome Biblical Commentary*, ed. R. E. Brown et al. (Englewood Cliffs, N.J.:
Prentice-Hall, 1969), 2:525–34; W. Schneemelcher, "The History of the New
Testament Canon," in *New Testament Apocrypha*, ed. E. Hennecke and
W. Schneemelcher (Philadelphia: Westminster Press, 1963), 1:28–60; C. F. D.
Moule, *The Birth of the New Testament* (New York: Harper & Row, 1966), 178–209.
A full and very influential historical analysis is that of H. von Campenhausen, *The
Formation of the Christian Bible* (Philadelphia: Fortress Press, 1972), esp. 147–209.

Two short studies separated by many years but both offering a succinct historical survey together with remarks concerning pertinence are A. Harnack, *The Origin of the New Testament and the Most Important Results of the New Creation*, trans. J. R. Wilkinson (New York: Macmillan Co., 1925 [1914]); and H. Y. Gamble, *The New Testament Canon: Its Making and Meaning*, GBS (Philadelphia: Fortress Press, 1985).

I have referred to many extra-canonical writings in this chapter. A sense of their placement can be gained from E. J. Goodspeed, *A History of Early Christian Literature*, rev. and enl. R. M. Grant (Chicago: Univ. of Chicago Press, 1966 [1942]).

A consideration of specific historical problems connected with canonization is found in O. Cullmann, "The Plurality of the Gospels as a Theological Problem in Antiquity," in *The Early Church*, ed. A. J. B. Higgins (Philadelphia: Westminster Press, 1956), 39–58; N. A. Dahl, "The Particularity of the Pauline Epistles as a Problem in the Ancient Church," in *NeoTestamentica et Patristica*, NovTSup 6 (Leiden: E. J. Brill, 1962), 261–71; and K. Stendahl, "The Apocalypse of John and the Epistles of Paul in the Muratorian Fragment," in *Current Issues in New Testament Study*, ed. W. Klassen and G. F. Snyder (New York: Harper & Row, 1962), 239–45. In a series of articles, A. C. Sundberg has challenged an early date of canon formation, although to this reader he seems to confuse the stage of ratification with the whole process; see "Canon Muratori: A Fourth Century List," *HTR* 66 (1973): 1–41; idem, "Towards a Revised History of the New Testament Canon," *SE* 4 (1968): 452–61. He argues further for the reopening of the canon, in "The Bible Canon and the Christian Doctrine of Inspiration," *Int* 29 (1975): 352–371.

A sense of the contemporary debate over the reopening of the canon can be gained from D. L. Dungan, "The New Testament Canon in Recent Study," *Int* 29 (1975): 339–51. Part of the stimulus for this discussion has been the development of an articulate feminist critique of Christian origins together with the discovery of the gnostic documents that appear to sponsor a more egalitarian vision of community. The points are adumbrated in E. Pagels, *The Gnostic Gospels* (New York: Random House, 1979), and more fully developed in E. Schüssler Fiorenza, *In Memory of Her: A Feminist Reconstruction of Christian Origins* (New York: Crossroad, 1983); see also M. A. Tolbert, "Defining the Problem: The Bible and Feminist Hermeneutics," *Semeia* 28 (1983): 113–26. Other representative statements on the normative relation of canon to church can be found in R. E. Brown, *The Critical Meaning of the Bible* (New York: Paulist Press, 1981), and W. Marxsen, *The New Testament as the Church's Book*, trans. J. Mignard (Philadelphia: Fortress Press, 1972).

Recent critical scholarship has taken up the challenge of several scholars to trace the interpretive consequences of a serious acceptance of the canon. The fullest attempt to push this beyond the programmatic stage has been the work of B. Childs, *The New Testament as Canon: An Introduction* (Philadelphia: Fortress Press, 1985), esp. 3–33; see also the useful comments of A. C. Outler, "The 'Logic' of Canon-Making and the Tasks of Canon-Criticism," in *Texts and Testaments*, ed. W. E. March (San Antonio: Trinity Univ. Press, 1980), 263–76.

Representative statements on the history and nature of biblical theology are
K. Stendahl, s.v. "biblical theology: contemporary," *Interpreter's Dictionary of the
Bible* 1:418–32; W. J. Harrington, *The Path of Biblical Theology* (Dublin: Gill and
Macmillan, 1973); and B. Childs, *Biblical Theology in Crisis* (Philadelphia: West-
minster Press, 1973). Specifically on NT theology, see esp. R. Bultmann, *Theology
of the New Testament* (New York: Charles Scribner's Sons, 1955), 2:237–81; and
N. A. Dahl, "The Neglected Factor in New Testament Theology," *Reflection* 73
(1975): 5–8.

More theoretical statements on the failure or future or possibility of such a
discipline are found in E. Käsemann, "The Problem of a New Testament Theology," *NTS* 19 (1973): 235–45; G. Ladd, "The Search for Perspective," *Int* 25
(1971): 41–62; C. Peter, "The Role of the Bible in Roman Catholic Theology," *Int*
25 (1971): 78–94; and L. Keck, "The Problem of a New Testament Theology,"
NovT 7 (1964): 217–41.

Diametrically opposed views as to the "implicit" unity sought by NT theology
in the writings are offered by H. Braun, "The Problem of a New Testament
Theology," *JTC* 1 (1965): 169–83; and H. Schlier, "The Meaning and Function of
a Theology of the New Testament," in his *The Relevance of the New Testament*
(New York: Herder & Herder, 1968), 1–25. For an illuminating example of the
divergent uses of the concept of canon in NT theology, see E. Käsemann, "Unity
and Diversity in New Testament Ecclesiology," *NovT* 6 (1963): 290–97; and R. E.
Brown, "The Unity and Diversity in New Testament Ecclesiology," *NovT* 6
(1963): 298–308.

For a short statement on inspiration, see G. W. H. Lampe, s.v. "inspiration and
revelation," *Interpreter's Dictionary of the Bible*. A classic two-causes analysis of
personal inspiration is developed by B. Warfield, *Biblical Foundations* (Grand
Rapids: Wm. B. Eerdmans, 1958). The theories of Thomas Aquinas are developed
in the light of contemporary scholarship by P. Benoit, *Inspiration and the Bible*
(New York: Sheed & Ward, 1965). A more sophisticated treatment along the lines
of literary inspiration is found in A. Shökel, *The Inspired Word* (New York: Herder
& Herder, 1965). Discussions of inspiration that take fuller account of contemporary redactional studies and the social processes of earliest Christianity are
K. Rahner, *Inspiration in the Bible* (New York: Herder & Herder, 1961);
J. L. McKenzie, "The Social Character of Inspiration," *CBQ* 24 (1962): 115–124;
and P. J. Achtemeier, *The Inspiration of Scripture: Problems and Proposals* (Philadelphia: Westminster Press, 1980).

A helpful survey of hermeneutics through the history of Christianity is provided
by R. M. Grant with D. Tracy, *A Short History of the Interpretation of the Bible*, 2d
ed. rev. and enl. (Philadelphia: Fortress Press, 1984). A more extensive survey is
The Cambridge History of the Bible, 3 vols., vol. 1: *From the Beginnings to Jerome*,
ed. P. R. Ackroyd and C. F. Evans; vol 2: *The West from the Fathers to the
Reformation*, ed. G. W. H. Lampe; vol. 3: *The West from the Reformation to the
Present Day*, ed. S. L. Greenslade (Cambridge: At the Univ. Press, 1963–70).
Specialized studies of respective periods are J. Danielou, *From Shadows to Reality:
Studies in the Biblical Typology of the Fathers*, trans. W. Hibberd (London: Burns &
Oates, 1960); B. Smalley, *The Study of the Bible in the Middle Ages* (Notre Dame,

Ind.: Univ. of Notre Dame Press, 1964); J. S. Preus, *From Shadow to Promise: Old Testament Interpretation from Augustine to the Young Luther* (Cambridge: Harvard Univ. Press, 1969); H. Frei, *The Eclipse of Biblical Narrative: A Study of Eighteenth and Nineteenth Century Hermeneutics* (New Haven: Yale Univ. Press, 1974); A. Wilder, "New Testament Hermeneutics Today," in *Current Issues in New Testament Study*, ed. W. Klassen and G. F. Snyder (New York: Harper & Row, 1962), 38–52; and D. Kelsey, *The Uses of Scripture in Recent Theology* (Philadelphia: Fortress Press, 1975). The impact of philosophical hermeneutics and literary criticism is shown by E. McKnight, *Meaning in Texts: The Historical Shaping of a Narrative Hermeneutics* (Philadelphia: Fortress Press, 1978), and the influence of liberation ideologies in N. K. Gottwald, ed., *The Bible and Liberation: Political and Social Hermeneutics* (New York: Orbis Books, 1983).

Further background for the constructive proposals offered in this chapter can be found in D. Kelsey, "The Bible and Christian Theology," *JAAR* 48 (1980): 385–402; and esp., L. T. Johnson, *Decision-Making in the Church: A Biblical Model* (Philadelphia: Fortress Press, 1983). In light of my final comparison to the Talmud and midrash, it is instructive to see the approach taken to precisely these issues within the Jewish tradition by J. Neusner, *Midrash in Context: Exegesis in Formative Judaism*, The Foundations of Judaism: Method, Teleology, Doctrine; part 1: Method (Philadelphia: Fortress Press, 1983). For him, the difference between canon and interpretation is dissolved by the process of midrash. After the completion of this manuscript, I was delighted, on the other hand, to find a similar constructive suggestion made from another angle by H. Frei, "The 'Literal Reading' of Biblical Narrative in the Christian Tradition: Does It Stretch or Will It Break?" in *The Bible and the Narrative Tradition*, ed. F. McConnell (New York and London: Oxford Univ. Press, forthcoming).

Index of
Scriptural Passages

OLD TESTAMENT

NEW TESTAMENT

Index of
Ancient Authors

GRECO-ROMAN

JEWISH

CHRISTIAN